International Political Economy

International Political Economy

Edited by Greg Anderson
Christopher J. Kukucha

OXFORD
UNIVERSITY PRESS

OXFORD

UNIVERSITY PRESS

Oxford University Press is a department of the University of Oxford.
It furthers the University's objective of excellence in research, scholarship,
and education by publishing worldwide. Oxford is a registered trade mark of
Oxford University Press in the UK and in certain other countries.

Published in Canada by
Oxford University Press
8 Sampson Mews, Suite 204,
Don Mills, Ontario M3C 0H5 Canada

www.oupcanada.com

Library and Archives Canada Cataloguing in Publication

International political economy / edited by Greg Anderson
and Christopher Kukucha.

Includes bibliographical references and index.
ISBN 978–0–19–900968–8 (paperback)

1. International economic relations. I. Kukucha, Christopher
John, author, editor II. Anderson, Greg, 1969–, author, editor

HF1359.I58 2015   337   C2015-904236-4

Cover image: Mina De La O/Getty Images
Photo, page 48 from Keppler, Udo J. *The Greatest Juggling Act on Earth*. J. Ottmann
Lithography Collection, Puck Building, 1907 February 6. Library of Congress,
LC-DIG-ppmsca-26138, http://www.loc.gov/item/2011645982/.
Accessed 18 June 2015.

Oxford University Press is committed to our environment.
Wherever possible, our books are printed on paper which comes from
responsible sources.

Printed and bound in the United States of America
1 2 3 4 5 — 20 19 18 17 16

Contents

Preface

The idea for this volume originated at the 2012 meeting of the Canadian Political Science Association at the University of Alberta. Through an odd set of circumstances we began considering the possibility of an edited collection of readings for an upper level undergraduate International Political Economy (IPE) course. We had no history of working together but it quickly became apparent that both of us had a similar vision of what the volume should include.

First, we knew there were several IPE readers and texts in the marketplace, many of which had strong theoretical components, but our goal was to build upon these (and be different from them) by also making the influences of economists on IPE more explicitly part of the thematic and analytical frame. As an extension we wanted to ensure that contributions would be theoretically pluralist, including positivist and post-positivist perspectives, so we could engage in debates across disciplines. Second, we made the decision to place an emphasis on Canada, to address the need to move beyond IPE's tendency to focus on major powers and study smaller, open economies. The vast majority of our junior and senior contributors are also Canadian, or teaching at universities in Canada, which is also unique for a text in this market. In addition, we decided to commit a specific section to levels of analysis in IPE, clarifying the relevance of international, regional, state, sub-federal, municipal, and societal aspects of the global political economy. Fourth, we made an attempt to ensure that a number of contributions would emphasize a practical knowledge of basic economic principles related to trade and finance. Finally, we wanted to ensure the volume had an up-to-date analysis of current topics in IPE across a wide range of issue areas.

Part I, our theoretical section, is designed to give students a strong working knowledge of the diverse range of theoretical perspectives and debates in IPE. Our first chapter provides the background for this evolving theoretical discussion as well as an outline of the key issues in the volume. Axel Hülsemeyer follows with a chapter focusing on "traditional" theories in IPE while Rob Aitken and Siobhan Byrne follow with an analysis of post-positivist and gender-based perspectives in chapters 3 and 4. Part II shifts attention to economic fundamentals. Eric Helleiner's chapter examines history and ideological change in the global political economy and Mark Brawley focuses on an overview of motivations and impediments related to international trade. Chapter 7 is a reprint of a speech by David Dodge, the former governor of the Bank of Canada, which provides an excellent, and accessible, analysis of monetary policy, with an emphasis on Canada.

Part III shifts attention to rules, norms, and governance, and the challenges of managing economic anarchy. Stephen Clarkson, Isabel Duchesne, and Amy Tieu begin with a discussion of the role of transnational corporations and the difficulty they present in the pursuit of regulation. In chapter 9, however, Jacqueline Best raises the important normative question of international development in the context of international institutions, in this case the World Bank. Finally, chapters 10 and 11 direct attention to international trade, with

Robert Wolfe discussing options for the global trading system, given the stalled Doha Round negotiations, and Gilbert Gagné evaluating dispute settlement in the context of liberalized trade and stability. Part IV then shifts the focus away from institutions to regions, with a specific emphasis on the European Union (Lori Thorlakson), North America (Geoffrey Hale), Japan and China (Jennifer Hsu), and Africa (Adam Sneyd).

Parts V and VI conclude the volume with a wide range of chapters not often included in IPE collections. As noted, levels of analysis is dealt with specifically in Part V and begins with Hans Michelmann examining the role of sub-federal governments in the global economy. Trevor Harrison then looks at the "global cities" of London and New York and the significant impact they have on finance capital, and Laura Macdonald and Jeffrey Ayres focus on the important, and often neglected, relevance of civil society. Anil Hira concludes Part V with an excellent review of industrial policy as a tool for economic development in chapter 19. The last section of the text, Part VI, introduces students to numerous contemporary issues in IPE. It includes Patrick Leblond's discussion of the global financial crisis, Michael Howlett and Jeremy Rayner's analysis of global natural resource and environmental regimes, and Monica Gattinger and Rafael Aguirre's detailed review of the shale revolution and its impact on Canada–United States energy relations. The last three chapters offer very interesting contributions on the negative impact of "mega-events" on development (David Black and Katelynn Northam), corruption (Ellen Gutterman), and identity and migration (Yasmeen Abu-Laban).

Contributors

Yasmeen Abu-Laban is a professor in the Department of Political Science at the University of Alberta.

Rob Aitken is an associate professor in the Department of Political Science at the University of Alberta.

Rafael Aguirre is a PhD Candidate in the School of Political Studies at the University of Ottawa.

Greg Anderson is an associate professor in the Department of Political Science at the University of Alberta.

Jeffrey Ayres is a professor in the Department of Political Science at Saint Michael's College, Colchester, Vermont.

Jacqueline Best is a professor in the School of Political Studies at the University of Ottawa.

David Black is the Director of the Centre for Foreign Policy Studies and Lester B. Pearson Professor of International Development Studies in the Department of Political Science at Dalhousie University.

Mark R. Brawley is a professor in the Department of Political Science at McGill University.

Siobhan Byrne is an assistant professor in the Department of Political Science at the University of Alberta.

Stephen Clarkson is a Member of the Order of Canada, Fellow of the Royal Society of Canada, and professor emeritus in the Department of Political Science at the University of Toronto.

David Dodge is a senior advisor at Bennett Jones LLP and former Governor of the Bank of Canada, 2001–2008.

Isabel Duchesne is a graduate student at the University of Toronto.

Gilbert Gagné is a professor in the Department of Politics and International Studies at Bishop's University.

Monica Gattinger is an associate professor in the School of Political Studies at the University of Ottawa.

Ellen Gutterman is an associate professor in the Department of Political Science at Glendon Campus, York University.

Geoffrey Hale is a professor in the Department of Political Science at the University of Lethbridge.

Trevor W. Harrison is a professor in the Department of Sociology at the University of Lethbridge.

Eric Helleiner is a professor and Faculty of Arts Chair in International Political Economy in the Department of Political Science at the University of Waterloo.

Anil Hira is a professor in the Department of Political Science at Simon Fraser University.

Michael Howlett is a professor and Burnaby Mountain Chair in the Department of Political Science at Simon Fraser University and Yong Pung How Chair in the Lee Kuan Yew School of Public Policy at the National University of Singapore.

Jennifer Y.J. Hsu is an assistant professor in the Department of Political Science at the University of Alberta.

Axel Hülsemeyer is an associate professor in the Department of Political Science at Concordia University.

Christopher J. Kukucha is a professor in the Department of Political Science at the University of Lethbridge.

Patrick Leblond is an associate professor in the Graduate School of Public and International Affairs at the University of Ottawa.

Laura Macdonald is a professor and Director of the Institute of Political Economy in the Department of Political Science at Carleton University.

Hans J. Michelmann is a professor emeritus in the College of Arts and Science at the University of Saskatchewan.

Katelynn Northam is a political organizer in Halifax, Nova Scotia, and an MA graduate from the Department of Political Science at Dalhousie University.

Jeremy Rayner is a professor and Centennial Research Chair in the Johnson-Shoyama Graduate School of Public Policy at the University of Saskatchewan.

Adam Sneyd is an assistant professor of political science at the University of Guelph.

Lori Thorlakson is an associate professor, Jean Monnet Chair in European Politics, and Director of the European Centre of Excellence in the Department of Political Science at the University of Alberta.

Amy Tieu is a graduate student at the University of Toronto.

Robert Wolfe is a professor in the School of Policy Studies at Queen's University.

Acknowledgements

Edited volumes are not completed without the assistance of a large number of people. We are especially indebted to our impressive list of contributors. We were amazed at the generosity and selflessness of everyone who participated in this project. There is an impressive IPE community in Canada, ranging across numerous disciplines. We hope the volume highlights this quality of scholarship and helps strengthen ties within this excellent group of scholars.

We also want to thank the numerous people at Oxford University Press who helped facilitate the completion of the text. In addition, we are also indebted to the anonymous reviewers who provided excellent input on how to improve earlier drafts.

PART I

IPE Perspectives

1

Back to the Future

IPE and the Evolution of Global Politics

Greg Anderson and Christopher J. Kukucha

As US Secretary of Defense between 2000–06, Donald Rumsfeld seemed to take special pleasure in verbal jousting with journalists. In February 2002, in perhaps his most infamous engagement, Rumsfeld defended the Bush Administration's interest in Iraq with an oral exploration of the distinctions he saw between knowns and unknowns, saying:

> There are known knowns; there are things we know we know. We also know there are known unknowns; that is to say, we know there are some things we do not know. But there are also unknown unknowns—the ones we don't know we don't know. (Rumsfeld 2011)

Linking Rumsfeld's knowns and unknowns to any discussion of IPE might seem a stretch of the imagination. Yet the emergence of international political economy in the past several decades is the reflection of a whole series of knowns and unknowns arising out of the complexities of postwar global politics.

As the name of the discipline implies, international political economy is some mixture of the international with politics and economics. In its relatively short life as a distinct academic discipline, IPE has become the quintessential interdisciplinary field and has contributed to important debates both in and, perhaps more significantly, outside the ivory tower.

The introduction to this volume is intended both as a broad overview of the emergent importance of IPE in the last several decades, some of the discipline's ontological and epistemological concerns, and an articulation of some of the many content areas in which IPE scholars can be found. The chapter is organized into three parts.

Part I will outline the emergence of IPE as a discipline alongside changes in global politics that necessitated a return to an older style of integrated social science enquiry. Part II will build upon this by exploring some of the early ontological and epistemological divisions within IPE, many of which are also found throughout the social sciences, but whose manifestation in IPE results in profound contrasts of approach, purpose, and outcome. Finally, Part III will attempt to outline some of the many areas in IPE where scholars are turning the field's interdisciplinary lens toward appreciating more of the world's "known unknowns, and unknown unknowns."

Broadly, the introduction concludes that while IPE is beset with the standard disciplinary divisions and debates endemic to all social science, its interdisciplinary approach to enquiry is well-situated to appreciate the growing complexity of global politics.

Part I: Old Wine in New Bottles?

"It's called political economy because it has nothing to do with either politics or economy."

Stephen Leacock

Many people forget that Canadian humorist Stephen Leacock was an academic, who completed his PhD at the University of Chicago and spent his career in the Department of Economics and Political Science at McGill University. Although Leacock died in 1944 his observations about political economy would prove to be prescient. At its most basic, international political economy amalgamates ideas and observations related to the global interaction amongst factors of production and their historical, social, and political ramifications. As such, it is often difficult to categorize or label, with contributors coming from many intellectual backgrounds and training.

Interdisciplinary Origins, International Relations Theory, and the "Three Debates"

The origins of international political economy arguably go back to a period when the social sciences and humanities were more unified, with fewer of the familiar divisions between disciplines and sub-disciplines. In recent years, however, scholars have become highly interdisciplinary in their research, breaking down many of the disciplinary silos that have segmented the social sciences and humanities into ever more narrow niches. These disciplinary silos are problematic for a variety of reasons, not the least of which is that scarce academic positions are too frequently driven by the purity of one's training: departments of history, economics, or political science tend to seek new colleagues who have immersed themselves narrowly in those disciplines. Such research programs can leave one focused on, and with less depth in, any particular disciplinary canon or broader research tradition.

As a result, it is crucial to first clarify broader debates in the philosophy of social science. At the core of all theory in the social sciences are assumptions about ontology, epistemology, and methodology. **Ontology** is the study of the nature of being, centred on questions such as, what is important about the objects we study? What things exist, or can be said to exist? What elements are fundamental to our object of study? If the state, for example, is our subject matter, what are the base elements comprising the state? **Epistemology** is the study of the nature of knowledge, how it is acquired and to what extent a given subject or phenomenon can be known. Once the base objects of study are identified, questions arise as to the manner in which our knowledge about them is acquired and the extent to which the nature of those objects can be known. In contrast, **methodology** is how one goes about the business of knowing; the procedures and principles we use to investigate a particular subject or issue.

All three of these considerations shape the nature of inquiry in the social sciences. The choices that researchers make, and the assumptions they hold, directly affect the outcome and conclusions of a particular study. Before IPE, questions of ontology and epistemology were more generally applied to the study of international relations (IR). The tension surrounding the application of these concepts was almost always focused on the question of whether IR was a "science."

At the core of this debate was *positivism*. Positivism is a philosophy of science that relies on observable data, which is analyzed for relationships and patterns, tested and re-tested over time, in an attempt to identify definitive conclusions or laws. Positivism in the social sciences is less rigorous but maintains an emphasis on observation and measurement. The goal is to avoid "speculative" analysis and instead adopt a science-based approach to identifying patterns and causal relationships in social, economic, and political settings. As a result, positivists in the social sciences emphasize systematic observation over time using clearly defined methodological frameworks. For a positivist, all conclusions must be based on observable events and data demonstrating causal relationships and patterns. At no point will a positivist give ontological significance to something that is not observable, thereby avoiding the need to explain the underlying causes of events. "What is" drives the ontology, epistemology, and methodology of a positivist.

There are three, and arguably four, "great debates" in the twentieth century that have shaped the evolution and relevance of positivism in the study of IR and, ultimately, IPE. At the bottom of all the debates are disagreements about what the most important units of analysis are, how we describe those units, and the methods applied in trying to uncover how they relate to one another. In the first half of the century, the study of international relations was directly influenced by the carnage of both world wars and questions of conflict and peace. Scholars of all stripes argued about power, anarchy, and the utility of international law and institutions but none were truly positivist in a scientific sense. In fact, this "first debate" is largely understood as one between idealism and realism and the pursuit of international stability, what Ole Waever has characterized as "politics." The first debate was also more concerned with ontology (the nature of IR) as opposed to epistemology and

methodology. According to Waever, these deeper "philosophical" discussions focused on the nature of inquiry in IR around polarizing questions of war and peace and morality versus relativism (Waever 1996, 157).

The behaviouralist revolution throughout the social sciences in the 1960s, however, would dramatically alter the relevance of positivism and reshape the debate about how social science evaluates competing truth claims about the world around us. In this period, the goal was to adopt a comprehensive form of inquiry driven by the ontology, epistemology, and methodology of the natural sciences. Like their scientist colleagues, social scientists hoped to bring a common set of terms and methodologies to the study of human interaction that would facilitate the comparison and evaluation of social phenomena. Positivism became the dominant form of accepted social science enquiry so quickly that realists, liberals, and Marxists in the 1970s and 1980s even in their intense debates seldom questioned the basic orientation toward positivism. This was especially clear in North America, with the emergence of "interdependence" theories in the 1970s and neoliberal institutionalist and neorealist frameworks (what would become known as the "neo-neo" debate) in the decade that followed. Interestingly, however, many British scholars distanced themselves from this fixation on positivism, focusing instead on broader questions of an international society and the mitigation of anarchy, in what was known as the "English School."

Yet, by the mid-1980s, a growing number of scholars were pointing to the possibility that scientific inquiry was highly contingent on history and culture, that is, it was socially constructed. This was a direct challenge to the accepted definition and utility of "science" and, therefore, the positivist legacy of the behaviouralist revolution. It was a Canadian, Robert Cox (1981), who helped spark this initial shift by noting that theory "is always for someone and for some purpose." In doing so, he was drawing attention away from positivist understandings of IR and IPE and toward an existing international order in which most knowledge is politicized and tied to specific interests. These ideas were not entirely new. Antonio Gramsci highlighted oppression and marginalization in his *Prison Notebooks*, written in the 1920s and 1930s and published in English in the 1970s. What is important is that Cox was part of a new wave of "critical" theorists, many of whom were adopting a neo-Gramscian framework, during this period. These new "critical" theories, however, were not a complete departure from previous positivist contributions. As Rob Aitken makes clear in chapter 3 they were based on common **materialist** assumptions that highlight "material" inequality arising from the use of social, political, and economic power in a sovereign state system. As much as Cox was questioning traditional understandings of the international system, and the need to move toward "critical" analysis and away from "problem-solving" theory, he was essentially focusing on economic power and how dominant social forces exercise control, as did Karl Marx before him. Cox may have driven a wedge in the dominant realist and liberal theoretical traditions of the era, but due

to its materialist foundations it was not a complete departure from positivism.

However, "critical" theory was part of an upsurge of theoretical challengers that would soon be known as the "third debate" in IR and IPE. For the most part, this debate is associated with the emergence of post-positivism, which draws from a wide range of philosophical traditions, but especially the philosophy of science. Notably, post-positivism questions the capacity of "science" to reveal truths about both the observable and unobservable world around us. Influencing post-positivism is **phenomenology**, which questions the possibility of any "objective" reality. **Hermeneutics** also shapes post-positivism with the assumption that all ideas are defined by meanings associated with specific periods of history, language, and culture. Both phenomenology and hermeneutics are interpretive methods of analysis that inspire post-positivists to search for deeper and potentially hidden meanings behind observed realities. As Aitken suggests, post-positivism includes materialist-based approaches, influenced by Cox and Gramsci, but it is also important for its emphasis on the concept of discourse. Unlike materialist perspectives, **discursive** approaches focus on the role of language, categories, ideas, and concepts, and how they shape our understanding of IR and IPE.

Table 1.1 Themes of the Three Debates

	Discursive	Materialist	Politics	Philosophy	Ontology	Epistemology	Methodology
First Debate		XX	XXX	XXX	XX		
Second Debate		XX			XX	XX	XXX
Third Debate	XXX	X	X	XXX	X	XXX	

XXX – Main focus of debate
XX – Secondary focus of debate
X – Tertiary level of debate
Source: This table is adapted from an original by Waever (1996: 157).

Three commonly cited post-positivist approaches are Critical Theory (as opposed to "critical" theory), standpoint feminism, and postmodernism. At the core of Critical Theory is the concept of emancipation. This can be traced to the Enlightenment and scholars such as Georg Wilhelm Friedrich Hegel and Immanuel Kant. For Kant, emancipation meant the transformation of a competitive power-based sovereign state system into a cosmopolitan order of "perpetual peace." In the twentieth century these themes were advanced by the Frankfurt School, founded in 1923, which focused on freedom from authoritarianism and ideology, as opposed to economic oppression. In a contemporary context the work of the Frankfurt School continues with the influence of Jürgen Habermas who made a distinction between three types of knowledge in his famous work, *Knowledge and Human Interests*. Habermas said that knowledge could be categorized as: (1) empirical-analytical (natural sciences), (2) historical-hermeneutic (meaning and understanding), and (3) critical sciences (emancipation). In doing so, he argued that those seeking to maintain control of knowledge dominated each form. In his later work Habermas shifted to an emphasis on "discourse ethics" and an "ideal speech situation" where power, control, and the manipulation of knowledge would be removed from discourse, leading to an unbiased consensus on the validity of specific arguments. To highlight this discursive emphasis, theorists from the Habermas/Frankfurt tradition typically capitalize "Critical theory" to clearly differentiate their work from other "critical" approaches (Smith 1996, 27–8).

Feminist perspectives in IR and IPE are diverse and consist of both positivist and post-positivist contributions. In chapter 4 of this volume Siobhan Byrne highlights the renewed focus of feminist perspectives in the 1980s and 1990s as part of the post-positivist wave and singles out the important work of J. Ann Tickner and Marysia Zalewski.

Although Byrne intentionally avoids the "categorization" of emerging feminist scholarship, this discussion will focus on feminist standpoint theory as another example of post-positivism in the third debate. This framework, most commonly associated with Nancy Hartsock (1983), is based on the understanding that most knowledge and science is produced and controlled by males, especially western, white males. According to feminist standpoint theory however, women have an advantage in this scenario as they understood both the "fact" of contemporary knowledge (at least as provided by male-dominated society) and also what is needed to challenge this dominance. Crucially, standpoint feminists argued there can be no detached, disinterested observation. For standpoint feminists, knowledge is socially based and thereby constructed by individuals with the capacity to frame these debates. Positivism, therefore, is impossible due to its assumption that individual identity is irrelevant in the pursuit of rationalist and empirical conclusions (Smith 1996, 28–9). Other feminist scholars, such as Cynthia Enloe (2004), have also emphasized the discursive nature of feminism by calling for an inclusive discussion of IR with a "feminist consciousness." This will not exclude masculine perspectives but will include the actions, ideas, experiences, and priorities of women.

Post-modern approaches, feminist, and otherwise, also defy easy categorization. In simplistic terms, post-modernists reject all existing understandings of epistemology and knowledge. Generally, these arguments can be traced to the works of Michel Foucault and Jacques Derrida which emphasized that knowledge was not a natural extension of intellectual inquiry but rather an exercise of power, leading to the conclusion there is no "truth" but rather multiple "truths." In the third debate, however, this argument became dominated by "post-structuralists" in the 1980s, such as

Richard Ashley and Rob Walker, who questioned the materialist focus of existing IR theory, and its claim that this reality was the "natural order" of the international system. As Ashley succinctly noted, this "limits rather than expands political discourse, negates or trivializes the significance of variety across time and place, subordinates all practice to an interest in control, bows to the ideal of a social power beyond responsibility, and thereby deprives political interaction of those practical capacities which make social learning and creative change possible" (Ashley 1986, 258). In chapter 3, Marieke de Goede's analysis of the shifting perception of the stock market as an instrument of gambling toward an institution of risk management and financial analysis is cited as an example of power shaping knowledge to serve specific interests.

Not surprisingly, the post-positivist focus of the third debate was not well received by many IR scholars. As a means of challenging this "invasion," some participants attempted to shift the nature of the discussion away from positivists and post-positivists, toward new *rationalist* and *reflectivist* distinctions. One of the first to make this argument was Robert Keohane in his famous speech to the International Studies Association in 1988. In his address Keohane stressed the importance of rational choice theory, which adopts a highly positivist methodology, focusing on the assumption that all actors, including states, act in their own self-interest. Keohane was not defending the rationalist model but believed it allowed for predictions about likely behaviour. Keohane also drew a sharp line between the rationalists and reflectivists, who, in his view, rejected positivist assumptions and did little more than criticize the existing order. In what many observers viewed as an attempt to co-opt the reflectivists, Keohane challenged these scholars to adopt a research program and provide evidence that supported critical conclusions. Ultimately, the goal was not theoretical pluralism, but rather clear

choices for both young and experienced scholars, between traditional theory and new post-positivist reflectivist discourses.

The increasingly muddled positivist/post-positivist struggle, summarized in Figure 1.1, led many, but not all, to conclude that IR had entered a "fourth debate" in the 1990s. Waever (1996), for example, suggested categorizing reflectivists as those who fully embraced post-positivism, namely post-structuralists, Critical theorists, post-modernists, and some constructivists. The rationalists, for Waever, were "traditional" theories such as neoliberalism and neo-realism. Others argue there is no fourth debate and that Keohane and Waever's rationalist and reflectivist characterizations are simply an ongoing part of the third debate. Those who accept the reality of a fourth debate are also divided on what it looks like. Some stress an extension of positivist/post-positivist distinctions. Others focus on rationalist/reflectivist differences. And still others, such as Martin Hollis and Steve Smith (1990), reflect on differences between *explaining* and *understanding*, where there are two "stories" to tell in IR, that can never be combined, because of irreconcilable differences related to agency, structure, internal understanding, and external explanation. What a stew of ideas! But this is the nature of intellectual inquiry, where scholars struggle for dominance in the hope of shaping knowledge for subsequent generations.

So What Did this Mean for IPE?

The "messiness" of contemporary IPE is a direct byproduct of these confusing interdisciplinary debates in the social sciences and international relations theory. While most scholars place the origins of contemporary IPE somewhere in the mid- to late-twentieth century, a strong case could be made that some of the earliest explorations of the relationship between the factors of production and their relationship to politics are to be found in

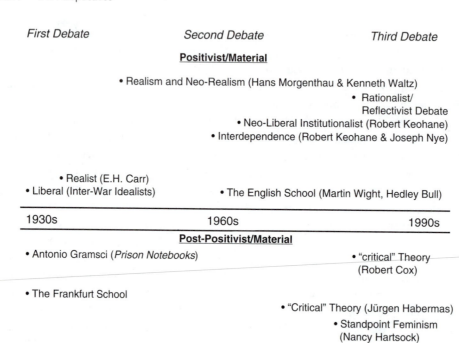

First Debate   *Second Debate*   *Third Debate*

Positivist/Material

• Realism and Neo-Realism (Hans Morgenthau & Kenneth Waltz)

• Rationalist/
Reflectivist Debate

• Neo-Liberal Institutionalist (Robert Keohane)

• Interdependence (Robert Keohane & Joseph Nye)

• Realist (E.H. Carr)
• Liberal (Inter-War Idealists)

• The English School (Martin Wight, Hedley Bull)

1930s   1960s   1990s

Post-Positivist/Material

• Antonio Gramsci (*Prison Notebooks*)

• "critical" Theory
(Robert Cox)

• The Frankfurt School

• "Critical" Theory (Jürgen Habermas)

• Standpoint Feminism
(Nancy Hartsock)

• Post-Structuralists
(Marieke de Goede
& Richard Ashley)

Post-Positivist/Discursive

Figure 1.1 Summary of the Three Debates

Plato's *Republic*, written around 380 BCE, where Plato explores elements of the division of labour (Irwin 1996, 13). However, the most prominent early political economy treatments of the nexus of economics and politics emerged from the eighteenth-century intellectual transformation from mercantilism to free trade typified by Adam Smith's 1776 classic, *The Wealth of Nations* (See Irwin 1996, 26–74, 75–86). In that work, Smith engaged in a detailed analysis of the relations between the state and the factors of production, most famously describing the domestic efficiency gains to be had from specialization and the division of labour. However, Smith went further and argued that these same principles could augment those gains internationally by sourcing some products abroad rather than wasting resources producing them at home. While

David Ricardo (1817) later built upon this in articulating the case for free trade rooted in comparative advantage, Smith's was undoubtedly one of the most famous analyses of the political and social relationships between domestic and international stakeholders in the conduct of economic policy—the principal subject matter of modern IPE scholars (see Cohen 2008, 16–19).

However, as an identifiable discipline, the origins of IPE might reasonably be traced to Susan Strange and 1970. That year, Strange, sounding much like Leacock and reflecting broader debates in the social sciences, published a pivotal piece in which she complained that the study of global politics had not kept up with some of the rapid changes taking place in international economic relations (Strange 1970). While there were many who both preceded and antedated Strange, and are now considered giants in the field (Keynes 1937; Polanyi 1944), it was Strange who really crystalized the problem; scholars of international politics and of macroeconomics had carved out separate intellectual worlds that were, in fact, increasingly impossible to separate:

> The economists do not even try to deal with the political aspects of international economic relations and international economic problems; and few political scientists even try to explore the economic dimension of international politics or diplomacy. (Strange, 313)

Strange's call to interdisciplinary arms was driven, in part, by the perceived weaknesses of individual disciplines within the social sciences to fully appreciate the profound changes taking place in the global postwar order. The institutionalization of large swaths of international affairs after the Second World War as typified by the United Nations, the Bretton Woods institutions (IMF and World Bank), and the management of trade relations through the General Agreement on Tariffs and Trade (GATT), seemed to harken a new form of international relations wherein the Westphalian state was increasingly sharing the global political stage with other actors. Moreover, many of those actors were private or transnational in character (the multinational firm), and had economic interests as their prime function, the consequences of which were often deeply political.

Then, in 1977, Robert Keohane and Joseph Nye published *Power and Interdependence*. As Keohane and Nye wrote in the preface to the second edition, by the beginning of the 1970s:

> The Vietnam War had become highly unpopular in the United States, and detente seemed to have reduced the importance of the U.S.–Soviet nuclear competition. At the same time,

international trade was growing more rapidly than world product: transnational corporations were playing dramatic political roles; and from 1971 on the international monetary system was in flux. Meanwhile, the relative economic predominance of the United States was declining as the European and Japanese economies grew at more rapid rates. (Keohane and Nye 2001, xi)

The state was not about to disappear. Nor was the United States, as the dominant example, about to fade away. Yet, there were clearly other actors vying for influence alongside the state (see also Keohane and Nye 1974). The oil shocks of the 1970s, the end of the Bretton Woods system, and the persistent stagflation of the era, with roots at home and abroad, all suggested the need for a more complex analytical lens to help understand this evolving world.

Keohane and Nye gave impetus to the research programs of countless scholars, arguably spawned at least one subdiscipline of its own (globalization studies in the 1990s), and, as noted earlier, permanently inserted "interdependence" as a core concept throughout much of the social sciences. The complex mix of global forces, and the analytical mix needed to understand them, drew scholars of all stripes—but especially international relations theorists and macro-economists—into what has become a heavily interdisciplinary enterprise.

The growth of IPE since the 1970s, first as a subdiscipline of international relations, and increasingly as a social science discipline in its own right, has been dramatic. Initially, this growth was also driven by positivist and rationalist assumptions. Why? One problem was that disciplinary silos that walled off the social sciences from each other remained stubbornly intact. Few formal programs in IPE actually existed and, as a result, few IPE scholars were actually formally trained in this interdisciplinary approach. Most received their formal academic training in political science, economics, or perhaps international affairs, later immersing themselves in the traditions of a second discipline.

Regrettably, the consequences of disciplinary rigidity continue to be felt in everything from the hiring decisions of departments to the choices of majors and minors by undergraduates. In spite of lip service to interdisciplinary research, departments still tend to hire those trained in traditions with which they themselves are familiar. Young scholars pursue genuinely interdisciplinary research programs at some peril to their prospects for landing a tenure-track job since they may be perceived to lack the necessary depth of training in any one discipline: jack of all trades, master of none. This in turn cascades down the pedagogical ladder all the way to majors and minors offered to undergraduates, most of which remain anchored in tradition.

For all the work that remains, IPE scholars can also be proud of the progress that has been made. The discipline has important flagship journals, including *International Organization*, *World Politics*, *International Studies Quarterly*, the *Review of International Political Economy*, and the *New Political Economy* (Cohen 2010). Professional associations, some of them offshoots of larger social science organizations, have also emerged, becoming quite influential in a short period of time, including the International Political Economy Group (IPEG) in the United Kingdom or the International Political Economy Society (IPES) in the United States (Cohen, 2008, 47–8).

Perhaps most important, however, there is increasing evidence that IPE scholars are now studying an increasingly complex world through a number of interdisciplinary perspectives. In turn, the slow nexus of disciplinary traditions has fostered deeper epistemological and ontological debates, consistent with those found throughout the social sciences. Interestingly, the emerging scholarship of IPE soon became divided geographically, as well as intellectually.

It is to that divide and the unique questions that IPE brings to the study of world politics that this chapter now turns.

Part II: The Transatlantic Divide

"We have really everything in common with America nowadays except, of course, language."

Oscar Wilde, *The Canterville Ghost* (1887)

If one reads the key journals noted above or attends the meetings of their related associations, one could be forgiven for coming away dazed and confused. While there is now broad agreement among IPE scholars about the need for a blend of disciplinary influences in the study of world politics, there is much less when it comes to the kinds of questions that ought to be asked and the methods by which they should be explored. In the broadest of terms, IPE now occupies two very different camps, categorized by Benjamin Cohen in 2007 as the "British" and "American" schools of IPE (Cohen 2007).

Catherine Weaver usefully compared this split in IPE to the differing functions of the left and right sides of the brain identified by cognitive psychologists (Weaver 2009, 338–9):

Left Brain	Right Brain
Uses logic	Uses feeling
Detail-oriented	"Big Picture"-oriented
Fact-ruled	Imagination-ruled
Words and language	Symbols and images
Math and science	Philosophy and religion
Knowing	Believing
Reality-based	Fantasy-based
Practical	Impetuous
Safe	Risk-taking

According to Weaver, the transatlantic divide within IPE is much the same, pitting causal explanations against interpretive or reflective approaches to assessing global politics. American IPE tends to be highly positivist and reductionist in its epistemological approach whereas the British school tends to reject reductionism in favour of pursuing much broader, normative questions (Weaver 2009, 339). American IPE has increasingly looked to the methodologies of economics and mathematics, the use of large-N data sets, formal modelling, and a focus on quasi-experimental approaches to social science enquiry that build incrementally by focusing on narrow sets of questions. The British variant of IPE, by contrast, doubts the utility of positivist social science and is instead drawn toward post-positivist or C/critical approaches that focus on broad normative questions of social justice, equality, morality, and ethical matters (Cohen 2007, 199–202). American IPE is oriented around solving specific problems, and purports to be value neutral in seeking descriptions and explanations for how things work. The British variant rejects the notion that social science investigation is value neutral and has at its core a more overtly normative political project aimed at transformation. In effect, the American school is preoccupied with "what is" while the British school is focused on "what ought to be" (Cohen 2007, 199).

The bipolar nature of IPE has spilled over into the pages of the aforementioned academic journals and professional meetings. The pages of *International Organization* and *World Politics*, for example, have become increasingly quantitative and oriented around analyses of specific policy-oriented puzzles whereas the *Review of International Political Economy* and the *New Political Economy* tend to be more pluralist in content and outlook (See Cohen 2010).

Classifying the entirety of IPE into two simple categories would make appreciating the field much easier if it actually reflected reality. In fact, categorizing IPE into American and British camps offers little more than a starting point. The debate over the American and British schools has been the focus of at least one book (Cohen 2008), one special issue of *New Political Economy* (2009), and several review articles in the pages of *Review of International Political Economy* (Keohane 2009; Maliniak and Tierney 2009; McNamara 2009). An obvious critique of the simplistic characterization of IPE as being in two camps is that many IPE scholars straddle the territory between the two. Mark Blyth of Brown University is a prime example. A British citizen trained as an undergraduate in the UK, Blyth then went to the United States for graduate training in political science, where he remains. He writes:

> I have lived "over there" for nearly two decades. Despite being both an admirer and consumer of a great deal of the work that British IPE scholars produce and being Scottish by birth, I am by training and temperament an American scholar. (Blyth 2009)

Hence, although IPE may be riven by significant differences over some of the most basic questions of epistemology and ontology (Cohen 2007, 215–16), these questions are in fact complementary. Whereas the American school is the more dominant, some would say hegemonic, branch of IPE, the British school is more critical, with an emancipatory agenda of social change. Whereas the American school might be oriented around the resolution of narrow problems, the British school pursues grand systemic questions. Epistemologically and ontologically, the two schools (or mixtures thereof) have their strengths and weaknesses.

Yet the reader of this section might reasonably ask "So what, who cares?" Are these not the same kinds of ivory tower debates found in other disciplines? Historians, economists, sociologists, and traditional political scientists all have their epistemological, ontological, and ideological differences, don't they? Moreover, some of these debates seem at odds with both Susan Strange's plea for interdisciplinary collaboration and many of the problems of the 1970s that drove the emergence of the discipline. Efforts to delineate some of the divisions within IPE are probably a natural product of the discipline's growing prominence as a stand-alone part of social science. Regrettably, some have even begun defining the split between British and American IPE as constituting two completely different disciplines (McNamara 2009; Weaver 2009). However, these same efforts are problematic for a young discipline still trying to distinguish itself as something more than a collection of international relations scholars conversant in economics. Moreover, since so many IPE scholars reside in the "interdisciplinary middle" between several traditions, such divisions can also be seen as artificial constructions that replicate some of the inadequacies of traditional disciplinary boundaries that frustrated IPE scholars in the first place.

Nevertheless, debates over which of two or more boxes to toss IPE scholars into are important for what they reveal about IPE's contribution to the study of global politics. As this volume suggests, it is also important for understanding the evolution of IPE scholarship in Canada.

Students of international relations are likely familiar with the basic tenets of realism and liberalism, two of the dominant paradigms. Although nuanced differences between them are many, a central point of contention revolves around the role of the state in international affairs. Is the state a purely sovereign entity with maximum latitude to pursue its "interests" relative to measures of power that might constrain its behaviour? Is international cooperation merely the product of a coincidence of self-interest by two or more states? Or, are there international bodies, agreements, or conventions that, by enlightened design, incentivize the subjugation of self-interest to some collective? Debates over the proper units of analysis (ontology) are seldom far from fights over how to actually measure and evaluate any of it (epistemology).

IPE has contributed to the study of world politics by, perhaps regrettably, making it more complicated. International relations scholarship has certainly expanded the range of actors deemed worthy of examination. A near-bottomless pit of non-state actors (institutions, private sector actors, social movements, interest groups, individuals) is now vying for attention alongside states as key actors in international affairs. IPE has complicated this picture by explicitly adding economics to politics in the study of this complex mix of actors. British school, American school, or somewhere in between, IPE scholars of all stripes are interested in teasing apart the complex mix of problems at the heart of global politics. IPE is more than the simple addition of economics to the study of politics, or vice versa and hence is about more than the economic incentives for actors within international politics or how politics augments or undermines economic efficiency. Instead, the totality of IPE scholarship represents an integrated whole of economic and political relationships at all levels (state and non-state) that connect, transform, and propel our global politics.

Although IPE's diversity makes the boundaries of enquiry difficult to define, most IPE scholars would allow that there are at least six broad areas of investigation that are quintessentially IPE topics: international trade, international monetary relations, the multinational corporation, development, globalization, and, increasingly, climate change. The balance of this introduction is devoted to a brief examination of the merits of IPE in sorting through each of these. The chapters that follow will engage all of these issues, either individually or as part of broader studies of IPE.

Part III: Some Central Passions of IPE

"Send me a one-armed economist"

President Harry S. Truman

Harry Truman's famous quip about having his advisors send him a one-armed economist because they kept sitting on the fence by saying "on the one hand this, on the other hand that" signals the clash between the ambiguity of social science research and the need for certainty on the part of policy-makers. It was this same need for additional degrees of certainty in understanding our global politics that drove Strange to call for greater dialogue between economists and political scientists. The need to blend politics with economics in international affairs has not always been obvious. As this volume suggests, however, it is crucial when examining the five basic areas of focus for most IPE scholars.

International Trade

International trade connects the factors of production and the stakeholders behind them as they cross borders, transform, and enter increasingly global production chains. Hence, trade is also about the poisonous mix of politics and economics that is at the heart of IPE. As Douglas Irwin's (1996) fantastic history of the evolution of free trade thought depicts throughout, trade is among the most controversial areas of public policy. It is also evident throughout Irwin's history that the liberalized trading regime that has been in place for most of the postwar period, the one most of us are familiar with, and the source of some of the anxiety among some critics, has been the historical exception rather than the rule.

International trade has always pitted domestic interests against their foreign counterparts, often infused with the language of economic nationalism, forms of xenophobia, periodically, and always complicated trade-offs for political leadership. In fact, the roots of these conflicts are inherent parts of the case in favour of trade liberalization put forward by Adam Smith and David Ricardo. Smith and Ricardo reasoned that there was a heavy price (inflation) to be paid for mercantilism's emphasis on exports while limiting imports. They argued that through specialization and exchange, the market for exports could be dramatically expanded to foreign countries and domestic productive capacities could be enlarged to service them. By allowing other countries to do the same, and accepting some of their surplus production in exchange for domestic manufactures, there would be broad consumer benefits in the form of lower prices and product differentiation, as well as a more efficient use of domestic productive capacities that only economies of scale could bring.

At the same time, Smith and Ricardo both implicitly acknowledged that there were bound to be adjustment costs with this specialization and trade. As trade between countries expanded, some industries would increasingly specialize and expand at home, while others would shrink and give way to more efficient production abroad. Smith and Ricardo's arguments were elegant, but were entirely about efficiency. Why not, they reasoned, allocate more scarce resources into the production of those products that we can produce most efficiently, earn income from foreigners by exporting them, while ceding the production of those manufactures in which we lack natural advantage (efficiency) to foreigners and then import them to the benefit of our consumers?

For IPE scholars who are economists, the elegance of Smith's theory of absolute advantage and Ricardo's of comparative advantage are compelling.

Moreover, the two theories still form the basic intellectual rationale for liberalized trade. However, the politics of this liberalization is messy and, therefore, of recurring interest to IPE scholars. As nearly every student of international trade knows, liberalization generates "winners" and "losers" at home and abroad. The "winners" are those consumers who reap the benefits of lower prices and greater varieties of consumables, and the employees in sectors of comparative advantage whose firms expand, hire more workers, and add more shifts to supply products for export markets. In specific instances, the benefits are only narrowly felt, but overall, they are spread broadly throughout the economy.

By contrast, the "losers" in trade liberalization are displaced workers and non-competitive land and factory owners. As Ricardo argued in 1817, the process of adjusting to a more efficient form of trading relations involved shifting workers out of sectors of comparative disadvantage and into those of comparative advantage. However, as workers are "released" from one sector to the next, the politics of trade liberalization become complicated by the inevitable transition period. Agricultural workers "released" as a result of liberalization are unlikely to find employment in high-tech computer chip design, thus creating a problem for a nation's political leaders in advocating for liberalization in the first place. Whereas the consumer groups enjoying the benefits of liberalization are spread throughout the country and unlikely to write to their elected leadership praising their trade liberalization initiatives, unhappy factory workers who have seen their jobs move to a country that enjoys a comparative advantage are concentrated and often powerful stakeholders that only the bravest politicians are often willing to take on by pointing to Smith and Ricardo.

Yet, it is these domestic stakeholders, the sectors they represent, the politics they pursue, and their direct connection to their equivalents abroad, all filtered through an economic model premised on efficiency, that makes the study of international trade so inherently a part of IPE.

However, IPE analyses of international trade also examine the implications of global and regional patterns of trade for what they say about everything from patterns of production (Feinberg and Keane 2006; Humphrey 2003; Soloaga and Wintersb 2001) to the relative distribution of political power in the global economy (Narlikar and Tussie 2004). A related focus of IPE scholars involves an analysis of the rules of international trade and the institutional structures that have formed around them. The distributional consequences of trade liberalization have already been noted. However, the rules that enshrine this liberalization between states involve forms of governance between them that are also the subject of intense scrutiny by IPE scholars.

IPE scholars are also interested in shifting patterns of regional trading relationships, many of which have devolved into significant "trading blocks" anchored by one or more large countries: the United States in North America, Brazil in South America, and Germany in Europe. It is important to understand not only how these regional preferences are distorting trading patterns and complicating multilateral processes, but also how the politics of these regional blocks as anchor countries conclude new arrangements with partners where the economic benefits are slight but the political benefits may be large. This particular set of dynamics has been popular with a variety of Marxist approaches, including world systems theorists like Immanuel Wallerstein (1974). For these scholars, large "core" states draw smaller, "peripheral" states into their economic and political orbit, perpetuating dependency on market access to the large state while the large state uses the terms of preferences agreements to "lock in" economic and political reforms favourable to itself.

The dimensions of international trade of interest to scholars of IPE continue to proliferate. They include, among other things, the effects of outsourcing (Bhagwati et al. 2004; Drezner 2004), the environment (Audley 1995; Bhagwati, 2000; Droege 2012), civil society (Ayres 1999), and security (Anderson 2012; Goldfarb and Robson 2003).

International Monetary Relations

Unlike trade relations, the IPE of international monetary relations is, for some, much more abstract and less accessible to non-economists. Yet, for anyone that has followed the rapid growth of the Chinese economy and its relationship to the United States, trade relations and monetary relations between the two have become a key political lightning rod that increasingly begs for additional understanding. IPE scholars have been happy to provide it.

An important difference between the IPE analyses of trade relative to monetary relations revolves around the issue of sovereignty. Students of the neoclassical stages of economic integration will be familiar with the fact that engaging in trade relations entails a relatively small loss of sovereign policy power on the part of the state. The reduction of tariff barriers through multilateral or regional agreement entails some restriction of policy latitude, but really only over the imposition of tariffs and other border measures on imports.

Monetary policy, by contrast, involves the sovereign control over interest rates and the money supply. In only a select few jurisdictions has the state ceded control over its own money supply and capacity to set interest rates and thereby given up a significant degree of policy latitude. In some instances, sovereignty is pooled and delegated to a multilateral body such as, in the case of the European Union, a common central bank (The European Central Bank). Such an institution manages a common currency and interest rates for all. In other cases, such as Ecuador, the state may simply elect to adopt the currency of another country (the US dollar), again ceding its sovereignty over monetary affairs.

These analyses are inherently about the state and its relationship to some international body. As we have seen in the debt crisis roiling the European Union in recent years, the state's relationship to the European Central Bank and the other members of the European Union has been the focus of intense scrutiny. As Ireland, Greece, Spain, Portugal, and Italy have experienced varying degrees of financial turmoil, bailouts, and structural adjustment imposed by other member states, the citizenry of those states have had occasion to question the merits of euro area membership.

Analyses of monetary relations elsewhere are equally statist in orientation, but tend to focus on domestic policy institutions such as central banks whose prime function and purpose have important international spillover effects. Students of monetary economics will appreciate the trade-offs associated with the choice of exchange rate regime (Caramazza and Aziz 1998). In Europe, the members of the euro area have essentially adopted a fixed exchange rate, severely restricting their monetary policy latitude, and restricting their freedom of movement in the midst of the current debt crisis. China has nominally done the same by committing to a fixed exchange rate tied to the value of the US dollar.

Yet, currency manipulation is also one of those political allegations that exists mainly in the eyes of the beholder. Central banks around the world are constantly intervening in global currency markets, even those whose currencies float and are ostensibly responsive to supply and demand signals in the market place. Central banks around the world, notably the US Federal Reserve and the European Central Bank, have been engaging in "quantitative easing" by purchasing private bank assets, greatly expanding the potential money supply, and, in theory, depreciating the value of the dollar and the euro relative to other currencies.

The point is that one of the main functions of IPE as an interdisciplinary approach is to tease out the unique mix of politics and economics that drives so much of global politics. Trade and monetary relations are not just about trade or monetary issues, nor are they just about economics. In fact, the analysis of monetary relations between countries necessarily involves capital flows and foreign direct investment, which in turn frequently spills over into matters of international development.

Since 1991, the United Nations Conference on Trade and Development (UNCTAD) has published an annual report on global capital flows, the *World Investment Report*. Economic theory suggests that capital ought to flow "downhill" in the sense that returns on capital in areas of the world in which capital is scarce (and therefore expensive) ought to attract it from areas in which capital is abundant (and therefore cheap). Until very recently, UNCTAD's reports repeatedly demonstrated that most capital flows occur between rich, capital-abundant, developed economies. Very little of it flowed to the global south, where it was seemingly needed most. The potential benefits of foreign direct investment (FDI) for developing countries, including direct employment, infrastructure development, technology transfer, increased local product quality, and higher wages (Graham 2000) are well known to economists. However, the search for rules to govern the relationship between private multinational firms and their sovereign hosts under international law complicates FDI and spills over into the realm of politics (Salacuse 1990; 2007). One significant impediment of FDI flows from capital-abundant regions to those where it is scarce is the ever-present threat of expropriation by the sovereign host. Over the years, thousands of bilateral

investment treaties and investment provisions within trade agreements between nations have sought to govern those relations by setting terms under which greenfield investment enters a host country (ibid.). Prominent recent examples of expropriation, notably in the Venezuelan oil and gas sector, suggest that such treaties are not sacrosanct and that host countries are not always happy with the terms of those arrangements.

Recent financial crises have also focused attention on flows of portfolio capital in and out of countries, sometimes with remarkably destabilizing velocity. Some have actively promoted the use of limited capital controls, such as the so-called Tobin Tax (McCulloch and Pacillo 2011; Raffer 1998) that would impose a transaction cost on large currency exchanges. Some have pointed to the fact that capital flight out of Asian economies during the financial crisis there in the late 1990s has strongly informed contemporary policy measures, such as the holding of large reserves, which contributed greatly to the large macro imbalances that fueled the financial crisis in the United States (Diamond and Rajan 2009). The accumulation of large reserves in Asian central banks has, in turn, transformed patterns of FDI flows reported by UNCTAD such that developing countries such as China remain significant targets, but increasingly also sources of FDI flows.

Finally, no discussion of IPE's contribution to the analysis of international monetary relations can ignore the ongoing debate about the role of the US dollar in global finance. While the dollar's prominence as the globe's key currency is arguably just a byproduct of a postwar history that saw the United States as the world's only economy not ravaged by war and the dollar as the only widely accepted currency, the dollar has had remarkable longevity as the key currency, conferring unique advantages on the United States as a global power (Kunz 1995, 29–56). With so many of the world's most important commodities, notably oil, priced in dollars, the United States has been relatively immune to fluctuations in the dollar's value relative to other currencies. The US simply buys commodities in dollars that it actually prints. However, this privilege has been most important at moments of financial crisis that would have left other nations in much more serious trouble. Unlike most other nations, the United States finances much of its overconsumption by issuing debt denominated in its own currency. Hence, while America finances its deficit spending by effectively issuing IOUs, increasingly to foreigners, it is debt that will only ever have to be repaid in dollars the US prints in the first place. Hence, the United States does not have to worry about the decline in value of the US dollar ballooning America's deficit in the midst of crisis. In fact, it is the holder of US debt abroad that might worry about declines in the value of their US dollar holdings if the dollar were to fall relative to other currencies (See Setser et al. 2005).

America's dollar diplomacy would be significantly weakened were there a serious alternative to the dollar. The Japanese yen or German deutschmark have periodically attracted scholarly attention as possible rivals to the dollar, but it wasn't until 1999 and the introduction of the euro that a serious key currency rival seemed to emerge. However, the ongoing European debt crisis has called into question the future of the euro (*The Economist*, 13 June 2009) and, in effect, reaffirmed the dollar as the globe's key currency.

Whatever lies ahead for the dollar, there is little doubt that IPE scholars will continue dissecting the complex interplay of politics and economics that undergirds monetary relations. These complexities are a never-ending source of interest for scholars because of the difficult trade-offs so often associated with the choice of exchange rate regime, the consequences of debt financing for currencies,

or the power that comes simply from printing the world's key currency.

The Rest

Trade and monetary relations form a sort of core subject matter common to all stripes of IPE. However, as even this brief description makes abundantly clear, IPE has extended its investigatory reach into other areas and has the potential to do so in many more.

The multinational corporation has been the subject of intense scholarship for a very long time, dating back to the formation of the British East India Company in 1600. However, the modern multinational corporation has attracted the attention of scholars because of its role in several other areas of interest to IPE scholars. Multinationals as sources of foreign direct investment have already been noted, but the implications of private activities for international development in this regard is obvious. For developing countries, the prospect of FDI brings with it the promise of jobs, skills, and technology transfers, productivity-enhancing competition, greater local product quality, and wage rates higher than those prevailing locally (Bhagwati 2004; Wolf 2004). However, critics of multinationals argue that many of these benefits fail to materialize as promised. Worse, a range of human rights activists, corporate watchdog groups, and anti-corporate crusaders have periodically exposed apparent negligence on the part of firms in maintaining core labour standards throughout their entire production chain. Corporations have been major drivers of efficiency in global supply chain management that has frequently entailed extensive offshoring and outsourcing of both materials procurement and manufacturing, but they have also been burned by poor oversight of far-flung operations that have too often resulted in embarrassing public relations fiascos (Blinder 2006; Wolf 2004, 220–48).

Yet, for some analysts, the same globalization that generated the conditions that created embarrassing situations for multinationals also facilitated their exposure and resolution (Bhagwati 2004, 162–98). An interesting consequence of all of this has been the growing focus on the accountability and social responsibility of firms in a number of areas, including labour rights and environmental protection. Whereas a decade ago corporate social responsibility was a relatively new concept to which firms largely paid lip-service, it is now a booming and vitally important component of most corporate structures. Moreover, for many firms, appealing to socially conscious consumer tastes is proving to be big business (*The Economist*, 19 January 2008; Mohan 2009). Fair trade coffee can be found in virtually all coffee shops (Arnot et al. 2006; de Pelsmacker et al. 2005; Le Mare 2008). Products manufactured in environmentally sustainable ways are a growing component of consumer purchasing behaviour.

Although FDI has implications for evolving economies, as noted above, international development has also become a substantial subdiscipline of its own in IPE (Collier 2007; Dollar and Kraay 2002; Sachs 2005; Sen 1999), especially in the context of relations between the developed global north and the comparatively underdeveloped global south. Much of this attention has also focused on the institutions charged with development as well as the management of elements of the global economy, namely, the Bretton Woods institutions, the World Bank, the International Monetary Fund, and the World Trade Organization. IPE scholars have been interested in both the internal governance of these institutions (Einhorn 2001), their effectiveness (Easterly and Pfutze 2008), and possible avenues for reform (Kenen 2001; Schott 2001). In recent years, IPE scholars have examined the relationship between development and GDP growth, international trade and monetary flows, as well as regional and global

politics. Other areas of interest include indebtedness levels, governance reforms (Radelet 2003; Reuter and Truman 2004; Toke 2009), components of a so-called post-Washington Consensus on economic policy (Kuczynski and Williamson 2003; Rodrik 2006), appropriate levels of official development assistance (Birdsall and Williamson 2002), and even the role of private philanthropy (Werker and Ahmed 2008). Even more recently, some of the rapidly changing dynamics of development flowing from the nation-building exercises of the 1990s (Somalia, Kosovo, Haiti), as well as the conflict zones of the early 2000s (Iraq and Afghanistan) have turned the attention of IPE scholars toward the shifting mixture of civilian and military components of development (Kinsey 2005; Spearin 2008).

Finally, one of the most interesting and complex emergent areas of IPE study is climate change, mainly due to the intersection of so many different subdisciplines of the social sciences and, in this case, sciences. In fact, the growing body of hard science demonstrating that climate change is caused largely by human activity (i.e., productive economic activity), is beginning to bounce up against the politics and economics of IPE (Esty 1994). Early work in the GATT and WTO focused on the links between productive activity and individual species protection, such as dolphins or turtles (ibid.). Interestingly, much of that work concluded that the rules of global trade and conservation were not in competition with each other. However, global climate change and its mitigation efforts are on a different scale of importance entirely and renewed work into the compatibility of current trading rules and mitigation has only just begun (Hufbauer et. al. 2009). The early evidence suggests that political clashes are on the horizon. Apart from whether developed and developing countries can decide who bears the largest burden for mitigation—rich versus poor—and whether generations of productive activity merit paying a heavier burden, the actual mechanisms for mitigation may come into direct conflict with existing trading rules (ibid.). For instance, as carbon life-cycle tracing for individual products becomes more fine-tuned, a tax on the carbon footprint of many products as they cross borders might be a way to initiate the mitigation process. However, such a tax would conflict with the process–product distinctions currently governing the non-discrimination principle within the WTO system (Esty 1994; Hufbauer et. al. 2009).

Themes and Organization of the Book

Obviously, attempts to integrate all relevant aspects of the contemporary global political economy in one volume are daunting, if not impossible. There will, thus, be notable omissions in some chapters. Having said that, this project set out to accomplish several goals and objectives. This volume has a number of new and unique features not usually found in an international political economy undergraduate reader:

1. In Part I, a pluralist theoretical orientation, including positivist, critical, and post-positivist perspectives, engaging debates across disciplines (political science, economics, history, sociology, etc.). It also emphasizes the influence of economists on IPE theory.
2. In Part II, contributions that emphasize a practical knowledge of basic economic principles related to trade and finance.
3. In Part III, a focus on rules and norms in the international system from an institutional viewpoint from a range of theoretical perspectives, including an examination of poverty and the impact of transnational corporations.

4. In Part IV, chapters on the regional dynamics of North America, Africa, Asia, and the EU.
5. In Part V, a focus on the "level of analysis" question in IPE, clarifying the relevance of international, regional, state, sub-federal, municipal, and societal considerations, including industrial policy. Particularly important here is the role of a range of sub-state, local, and private civil society actors whose impact on national politics has been well-documented, but are increasingly important in shaping the contours of the global economy.
6. An emphasis on up-to-date discussion of current issues in the global political economy in Part VI, including chapters on the global financial crisis, the environment, corruption, civil society, energy, international sports and development, and identity and migration.
7. Finally, wherever possible, this volume has attempted to place an emphasis on Canada, addressing the need to move beyond IPE's tendency to focus on major powers and study smaller, open economies. It also provides relevant examples and insight for Canadian students.

Conclusions

The contribution of international political economy to global politics since its emergence as a coherent discipline in the 1970s can be read as a social science response to fundamental changes in global politics itself. As the unified sovereign state appeared to be giving way to a much more nuanced, complex, and linked global politics in the 1970s, social science groped for an equally nuanced and complex set of tools with which to approach it all. Susan Strange's plea for more dialogue between economics and political science was a clarion call for just such an approach.

It was an approach that has been answered by a growing number of scholars, so many in fact, that IPE is less a subdiscipline of international relations than a fully fledged discipline of its own, complete with internecine debates about ontology and epistemology typical of academic debate. However, as IPE has become a discipline of its own, it has also spread its reach into a near-bottomless pit of areas that reflect the complexity around us. Whereas the 1970s was a period in which economics seemed to be as pivotal to understanding global political phenomena, and vice versa, as the high politics of military strategy, IPE has increasingly been expanding its investigatory tentacles into newish areas of contemporary global politics rooted in far more than just the mix of economics and political science. As an inherently interdisciplinary approach, IPE is well positioned to continue adapting alongside global politics itself.

Acknowledgement

The authors would like to thank Rob Aitken, Jacqueline Best, Trevor Harrison, and Hans Michelmann for their helpful comments on earlier drafts of the introduction.

Key Terms

discursive
epistemology
hermeneutics
materialist

methodology
ontology
phenomenology

Questions for Review

1. How can we account for the divisions within the social sciences on epistemological and ontological terms?
2. Are the core elements of IPE described in this chapter likely to remain the same set of core elements for the next 20 years?
3. Do the origins of IPE as a discipline suggest changes to both the discipline and its subject matter are inevitable?
4. What are the advantages of inter-disciplinarity that cannot be had within the bounds of a single discipline alone?
5. Why are British and American IPE so different? Is there a "Canadian" IPE?

Further Resources

Bhagwati, J. (2004). *In defense of globalization.*
Easterly, W. (2006). *The white man's burden.* New York: Penguin Press.
Freidman, T. (1999). *The lexus and the olive tree.* New York: Farrar, Strauss & Giroux.

Rodrik, D. (1997). *Has globalization gone too far?* Washington, DC: Institute for International Economics.
Wolf, M. (2004). *Why globalization works.*

References

Anderson, G. (2012). "Securitization and sovereignty in post-9/11 North America." *Review of International Political Economy* 19(5), 711–41.

Arnot, C., Boxall, P. C., and Cash, S. (2006). "Do ethical consumers care about price? A revealed preference analysis of fair trade coffee purchases." *Canadian Journal of Agricultural Economics* 54(4), 555–65.

Ashley, Richard K. (1986). "The poverty of neo-realism." In Robert O. Keohane, ed. *Neo-realism and its critics*. New York: Columbia University Press, 255–301.

Audley, J. (1995). "Environmental interests in trade policy: Institutional reform and the North American Free Trade Agreement." *The Social Science Journal* 32(4), 327–60.

Ayres, J. (1999). "From the streets to the internet: The cyber-diffusion of contention." *The Annals of The American Academy of Political and Social Science* 566(1), 132–43.

Bhagwati, J., Panagariya, A., and Srinivasan, T. N. (Fall 2004). "The muddles over out sourcing." *Journal of Economic Perspectives* 18(4), 93–114.

———. (2004). *In defense of globalization*. Oxford: Oxford University Press.

———. (2000). "On thinking clearly about the linkage between trade and the environment." *Environment and Development Economics* 5(4), 483–529.

Birdsall, N. and Williamson, J. (2002). *Delivering on Debt Relief: From IMF gold to a new aid architecture*. Washington, DC: Institute for International Economics.

Blinder, A. (March/April 2006). "Offshoring: The next industrial revolution?" *Foreign Affairs* 85(2), 113–28.

Blythe, M. (2009). "Torn between two lovers? Caught in the middle of British and American IPE." *New Political Economy* 14(3), 329–36.

Caramazza, F. and Aziz, J. (1998). "Fixed or flexible?: Getting the exchange rate right in the 1990s." *Economic Issues 13*. Washington, DC: International Monetary Fund.

Cohen, B. (2010). "Are IPE journals becoming boring?" *International Studies Quarterly* 54(3), 887–91.

———. (2008). *International political economy: An intellectual history*. Princeton: Princeton University Press.

———. (2007). "The transatlantic divide: Why Are American and British IPE so different?" *Review of International Political Economy* 14(2), 197–219.

Collier, P. (2007). *The Bottom Billion: Why the poorest countries are failing and what can be done about it*. New York: Oxford University Press, 2007.

Cox, R. (1981). "Social Forces, States and World Orders: Beyond international relations theory." *Millennium: Journal of International Studies* 10(2), 126–55.

de Goede, M. (2005). *Virtue, fortune and faith: A genealogy of finance*. Minneapolis: University of Minnesota Press.

de Pelsmacker, P., Driesen, L., and Rayp, G. (2005). "Do consumers care about ethics? Willingness to pay for fair-trade coffee." *Journal of Consumer Affairs* 39(2), 363–85.

Diamond, D. and Rajan, R. (2009). "The credit crisis: Conjectures about causes and remedies." *American Economic Review* 99(2), 606–10.

Dollar, D. and Kraay, A. (2002). "Spreading the wealth." *Foreign Affairs* 81(1) (January/February), 120–33.

Drezner, D. (2004). "The outsourcing bogeyman" *Foreign Affairs* 83(3) (May/June), 22–34.

Droege, S. (2012). "The Challenge of reconciliation: Climate change, development, and international trade." *Climate Policy* 12(4), 524–6.

Easterly, W. and Pfutze, T. (2008). "Where does the money go? Best and worst practices in foreign aid." *Journal of Economic Perspectives* 22(2) (Spring), 29–52.

The Economist. 2009. "Holding together: A special report on the euro area," 13 June.

The Economist. 2008. "Just good business: A special report on corporate social responsibility," 19 January.

Einhorn, J. (2001). "The World Bank's mission creep." *Foreign Affairs* 80(5) (September/October), 22–35.

Enloe, C. (2004). "'Gender' is not enough: The need for a feminist consciousness." *International Affairs* 80(1), 95–7.

Esty, D. (1994). *Greening the GATT*. Washington, DC: Institute for International Economics.

Feinberg, S. and Keane, M. (2006). "U.S.-Canada trade liberalization and MNC production location." *The Review of Economics and Statistics 83*(1), 118–32.

Goldfarb, D. and Robson, W. (2003). "Risky business: US border security and the threat to Canadian exports." *C.D. Howe Institute Commentary* No. 177. Toronto: C.D. Howe Institute.

Graham, E. (2000). *Fighting the wrong enemy: Antiglobal activists and multinational enterprises*. Washington, DC: Institute for International Economics.

Habermas, J. (1987). *Knowledge and human interests* (first published 1968). Cambridge: Polity.

Hartsock, N. (1983). "Feminist standpoint: Developing the ground for a specifically feminist historical materialism." In S. Harding and M. Hintikka (Eds). *Discovering reality: Feminist perspectives on epistemology, metaphysics, methodology and philosophy of science*. Dordrecht, Holland: Reidel, 283–310.

Hollis, M. and Smith, S. (1990). *Explaining and understanding international relations*. Oxford: Clarendon Press.

Hufbauer, G., Charnovitz, S., and Kim, J. (2009) *Global warming and the world trading system*. Washington, DC: Peterson Institute for International Economics.

Humphrey, J. (2003). "Globalization and supply chain networks: The auto industry in Brazil and India." *Global Networks 3*(2), 121–41.

Irwin, D. (1996). *Against the tide: An intellectual history of free trade*. Princeton: Princeton University Press.

Kenen, P. (2001). *The international financial architecture: What's new, what's missing?* Washington, DC: Institute for International Economics.

Keohane, R. O. (2009). "The old IPE and the new." *Review of International Political Economy 16*(1), 34–46.

———, and J. Nye Jr. (2001). *Power and interdependence*, 3rd ed. New York: Longman Press.

———. (1974). "Introduction: The complex politics of Canadian-American interdependence." *International Organization 28*(4), 595–607.

Keynes, J. M. (1937). "The general theory of employment." *Quarterly Journal of Economics 51*(2), 209–23.

Kinsey, C. (2005). "Challenging International law: A dilemma of private security companies" *Conflict, Security and Development 5*(3), 269–93.

Kuczynski, P-P. and Williamson, J. (2003). *After the Washington Consensus: Restarting growth and reform in Latin America*. Washington, DC: Institute for International Economics.

Kunz, D. (1995). "The fall of the dollar order: The world the United States is losing," *Foreign Affairs 74*(4) (July/August), 22–6.

Le Mare, A. (2008). "The impact of fair trade on social and economic development: A review of the literature." *Geography Compass 2*(6), 1922–42.

Maliniak, D. and Tierney, M. (2009). "The American school of IPE." *Review of International Political Economy 16*(1), 6–33.

McCulloch, N. and Pacillo, G. (2011). "The Tobin tax: A review of the evidence." *IDS Research Reports 2011*(68), 1–77.

McNamara, K. (2009). "Of intellectual monocultures and the study of IPE." *Review of International Political Economy 16*(1), 72–84.

Mohan, S. (2009). "Fair trade and corporate social responsibility." *Economic Affairs* (December 2009), 22–8.

Narlikar, A. and Tussie, D. (2004). "The G20 and the Cancun Ministerial: Developing countries and their evolving coalitions in the WTO." *The World Economy 27*(7), 947–66.

Polanyi, K. (1944). *The great transformation: The political and economic origins of our time*. Boston: Beacon Press.

Radelet, S. (2003). *Challenging Foreign aid: A policy maker's guide to the millennium challenge account*. Washington, DC: Institute for International Economics.

Raffer, K. (1998). "The Tobin tax: Reviving a discussion." *World Development 26*(3), 529–38.

Reuter, P. and Truman, E. (2004). *Chasing dirty money: The fight against money laundering*. Washington, DC: Institute for International Economics.

Ricardo, D. (1817). *On the principles of political economy and taxation*. In *The works and correspondence of David Ricardo*. 11 vols. Piero Sraffa (Ed.), with the collaboration of M.H. Dobb. Cambridge: Cambridge University Press, 1951–73.

Rodrik, Dani. (2006). "Goodbye Washington Consensus, hello Washington confusion? A review of the World Bank's 'Economic growth in the 1990s: Learning from a decade of reform'" *Journal of Economic Literature 44*(4), 973–87.

Rumsfeld, D. (2011). *Known and unknown*. New York: Penguin.

Sachs, J. (March/April 2005). "The development challenge" *Foreign Affairs 84*(2), 78–90.

Salacuse, J. (1990). "BIT by BIT: The growth of bilateral investment treaties and their impact on foreign direct investment in developing countries" *International Lawyer 24*(3), 655–75.

Schott, J. (2001). *The WTO after Seattle*. Washington, DC: Institute for International Economics.

Sen, A. (1999). *Development as freedom*. New York: Knopf.

Setser, B., Roubini, N., Levey, D., and Brown, S. (2005). "Our money, our debt, our problem." *Foreign Affairs 84*(4) (July/August), 194–200.

Smith, A. (1776). *An inquiry into the nature and causes of the wealth of nations*. London: Methuen & Co.

Smith, S. (1996). "Positivism and beyond." In Steve Smith, Ken Booth, and Marysia Zalewski (Eds), *International theory: Positivism and beyond*. Cambridge: Cambridge University Press, 11–44.

Soloaga, I. and Wintersb, A. (2001). "Regionalism in the nineties: What effect on trade?" *North American Journal of Economics and Finance 12*(1), 1–29.

Spearin, C. (2008). "Private, armed and humanitarian? States, NGOs, international private security companies and shifting humanitarianism." *Security Dialogue 39*(4), 363–82.

Strange, S. (1970). "International Economics and International Relations: A case of mutual neglect." *International Affairs 46*(2), 304–15.

Toke, A. (2009). "Corruption, institutions, and economic development." *Oxford Review of Economic Policy 25*(2), 271–91.

Waever, O. (1996). "The rise and fall of the inter-paradigm debate." In Steve Smith, Ken Booth, and Marysia Zalewski (Eds), *International theory: Positivism and beyond*. Cambridge: Cambridge University Press, 149–85.

Wallerstein, I. (1974). *The modern world system, Vol. I: Capitalist agriculture and the origins of the European world-economy in the sixteenth century*. New York/London: Academic Press.

Weaver, C. (2009). "IPE's split brain." *New Political Economy 14*(3), 337–46.

Werker, E. and Ahmed, F. (2008). "What do non-governmental organizations do?" *Journal of Economic Perspectives 22*(2) (Spring), 73–92.

Wolf, M. (2004). *Why globalization works*. New Haven: Yale University Press.

2 Traditional Theories[1]

Axel Hülsemeyer

Introduction

What qualifies as a "traditional" theory in international political economy (IPE)? One place to begin is by looking at the origin of the discipline in the eighteenth and nineteenth centuries. Political science and economics, as separate fields of inquiry, did not exist then. Instead, scholars agreed that economic problems could not profitably be analyzed without close attention being paid to the political environment, and vice versa. Consequently, political economy spawned research across all theoretical convictions, from Adam Smith (1723–1790) and David Ricardo (1772–1823) as the forefathers of liberal thought, to the mercantilist response to them by Friedrich List (1789–1846) and Alexander Hamilton (1755–1804), to Karl Marx (1818–1883) and Friedrich Engels (1820–1895). Regardless of the fundamental differences between these early thinkers, none of them would have conceived of economic and political phenomena as distinct modes of inquiry. Because they are inextricably linked, they necessarily had to be analyzed as one.

However, this view was challenged at the beginning of the twentieth century. Economics gradually became a distinct subject, as it embraced mathematics, which itself had become more accessible to scholars outside the natural sciences. Simultaneously, the developing field of political science included legal studies, focusing in its early days on the comparative examination of different constitutions (e.g., between federal and unitary ones), and how political outcomes are affected by them.[2] Even so, political economy did not somehow stop at the end of the nineteenth century; it has continued to develop despite having been separated into two disciplines. Indeed, there is a lineage from the "older" to the "newer" theoretical approaches. Since the 1980s, the term "globalization" has entered the public and academic debate, leading to a resurgence of interest in political economy. To capture the international dimension that globalization implied, the discipline became known as *international* political economy. Since then, IPE has become a subfield of international relations, which in turn is part of political science.

While typically meaning different things to different people, globalization has given rise to some theoretical novelties, often related to the economic meaning of the term.

In this chapter, we first cover each of the three traditional theories (i.e., **liberalism**, **mercantilism**, and **Marxism**) from their origins to their latest versions at the cusp of the twentieth and twenty-first centuries. Later forms often use the suffix "neo" (the Latin term for "new") to indicate that a theoretical departure supposedly has occurred from the original; for instance, the twentieth-century version of Marxism is neo-Marxism. After becoming familiar with these three theoretical approaches, three sets of questions arise: (1) Do they follow a scientific approach to gathering their knowledge? How do we know they do? Is this concern different from the social sciences more generally? (2) What are the systematic similarities and differences between these theories? (3) Are these "traditional" theories just that, effectively confined to the dustbin of history? Or do they have any analytical purchase for current events?[3]

Given that they exist simultaneously, how, logically, could they *all* be correct? We discuss (1) and (2) in the second and third sections of this chapter, and (3) throughout. In the fourth section, I conclude with some review questions and a few recommendations for further reading.

This chapter can, undeniably, only be an overview of these exceptionally large schools of thought. Naturally, it cannot provide a deep foundation for traditional IPE theories. In my view, such an introduction is appropriate for novices to the field. I hope that some students may indeed be inspired to dig deeper into any or all of these traditional approaches in further studies.

The Three Classical IPE Theories

Given that the three sets of theoretical approaches were conceived in the eighteenth and nineteenth centuries to address the potent political and economic problems of the time, we need to be mindful that theories always reflect a particular period in history. Put differently, if Karl Marx and Friedrich Engels were alive today, and not in the context of the factory system during the middle of the nineteenth century, they would not have written in the same way.

Liberalism

We start our analysis with liberalism, since mercantilism and Marxism are largely responding to liberal arguments.

The roots of liberalism are found in the work of the Scotsman Adam Smith (1723–1790), who wrote at a time when it was quite common for craftsmen to manufacture their products (whether shoes, furniture, or pottery) from start to finish. In his treatise, *The Wealth of Nations*, Smith developed two related concepts: the *division of labour* and the *invisible hand*. For the first concept, using the example of nail production, he showed that daily output would increase considerably if the employees divided their labour into several steps (e.g., one only cuts copper; one straightens it; one hammers, and so forth), rather than each of them making complete nails. Think of an assembly line for cars. The process is also broken down into many small steps, and none of the workers who, for example, screw in the dashboards or apply the paint, see the finished car. For the second concept, as each individual specializes in what s/he is best at, society as a whole benefits invisibly. There is no need for altruism, only the sole pursuit of one's professional self-interest.[4] For instance, by attending university, you also follow this logic of self-interest. You assume that you will earn a higher salary than someone who graduates from high school, but does not go to university. Through your self-interested action, you ultimately contribute to an increase in the public money available for, say, repairing potholes or hiring nurses.

The second giant of liberal thought is David Ricardo (1772–1823). He opposed the so-called Corn Laws that were in place between 1815 and 1846 to protect British agriculture against cheaper foreign competition. Ricardo showed that specialization is mutually beneficial in the trade between different countries, and that this is the case under conditions that were previously thought to make little sense; he took Smith's division of labour to the international level. To demonstrate this, Ricardo developed the concept of *comparative advantage*.[5] Although most textbooks try to cover this in a fairly abstract manner in a paragraph, the example Ricardo himself used might help us to better understand the argument. Assume two countries, both producing the same two goods, with labour as the only cost factor. One country is Great Britain (GB), the other one is Portugal (P). Both make wine and cloth. The labour costs are measured as the number of workers it takes to produce one bottle of wine and one bolt of cloth per day. The argument proceeds in three steps. In a matrix, this would look as follows in Table 2.1:

Table 2.1   Step 1 (Production Costs)

	Wine (bottles)	Cloth (bolts)
GB	3	7
P	1	5

In this example, in Great Britain it takes three workers to make one bottle of wine per day and seven workers to produce a bolt of cloth in one day. In Portugal, only one worker is needed to produce one bottle of wine per day and five workers for a bolt of cloth. This means that Portugal manufactures both goods more cheaply; it has the *absolute advantage*. Given these differences in labour costs, why should both countries trade in the first place? Ricardo held that a comparison of the different

ratios between the costs in each country is the rationale for exchanging goods. In this example, cloth (7 workers) is about twice as expensive to produce in Great Britain compared to wine (3 workers); or, making wine costs half (3 workers) of what it costs to produce cloth (7 workers). Hence, the ratio between wine and cloth production in Great Britain is about 1/2. By contrast, in Portugal, making cloth is five times more expensive (5 workers) than producing wine (1 worker). Juxtaposing these two ratios (i.e., 1/2 and 1/5) determines the comparative advantage. Making wine is cheaper in Portugal than in Great Britain, whereas producing cloth is comparatively cheaper in Great Britain than in Portugal. Thus, Great Britain has the comparative advantage in cloth production, while Portugal's advantage is in making wine. Note that the idea of comparative advantage is frequently conceptualized, not only by economists, as *opportunity costs* (i.e., how many units of one thing [e.g., wine] do you have to give up in order to produce one more unit of something else [e.g., cloth]?).

In the second step (see Table 2.2), a country specializes in the product in which it has the comparative advantage. Since we abstracted from all costs (e.g., transportation, retraining) other than labour, specialization can only occur by shifting workers between products. In this example, 21 workers in Great Britain are taken out of wine making and added to cloth manufacture. In Portugal, workers move in the opposite direction: ten workers are added to wine production, after being removed from cloth making.[6]

Table 2.2   Step 2 (Specialization)

	Wine (bottles)	Cloth (bolts)
GB	3 (–21)	7 (+21)
P	1 (+10)	5 (–10)

Table 2.3 Step 3 (Output)

	Wine (bottles)	Cloth (bolts)
GB	−7	+3
P	+10	−2
Aggregate	+3	+1

David Ricardo's overall purpose is to show that trade on the basis of comparative advantage will increase the aggregate output (akin to Adam Smith's division of labour). The third step (see Table 2.3) is a reflection of the movement of workers in Step 2. In Great Britain, 21 workers would have made 7 bottles of wine. However, since these workers are now manufacturing cloth, those 7 bottles are no longer being produced. Instead, these 21 workers manufacture three additional bolts of cloth. By contrast, in Portugal the additional workers in wine making will turn out 10 more bottles of wine, whereas these 10 people used to produce 2 bolts of cloth prior to specialization. Thus, in sum, 3 additional bottles of wine and 1 bolt of cloth resulted from this three–step operation. Today, of course more than a hundred countries each produces thousands of products and services. It is impossible to analyze such an environment without sophisticated computer models to determine who, if anyone, has the advantage for a particular product or service compared with someone else. Yet, these models are essentially just Ricardo writ large.[7]

With the British scholar John Maynard Keynes (1883–1946), we enter twentieth-century economics (as opposed to political economy). Keynes witnessed the Great Depression between the two world wars and was determined to find a way to prevent a recurrence. He therefore advocated state intervention as necessary to curb the adverse effects of recessions (of which the Great Depression was the epitome). The hallmarks of Keynesian economics are the interconnected terms *demand management* and *deficit spending*.[8] The premise is that a recession happens when private demand for products is too low because most consumers only purchase absolute necessities but refrain from purchasing consumer goods, like cars or washing machines. Consequently, the state itself by virtue of its size can best stimulate demand (e.g., it could "purchase" weaponry for its armed forces; and/or pay for the construction of technical infrastructure).[9] This demand management must be financed by money the state does not have, since in a recession a larger portion of the workforce is unemployed and thus collects welfare payments, while at the same time the state revenue falls due to less corporate and individual taxes being paid by the failing companies and the unemployed. Hence, the state has to borrow the funds on the financial market, thus spending beyond its means, creating a deficit (similar to what people often do with their credit cards). Since this increased state demand has to be met by private supply (i.e., companies that produce the arms or build/repair the roads), more people will be working again and collecting fewer welfare payments. (Like state demand, we also only pay for a TV set that is being built by a company.) Instead, a growing individual and corporate tax base will enable the state to repay its debt and achieve a balanced budget once the economy is on track again.[10] Keynes wanted to boost employment through these means. Beyond the Great Depression, one can see how this policy could be attractive in countries like Spain or Greece that currently (in mid-2014) have unemployment rates well above 20 per cent.

However, the critics of Keynesianism have charged that it does not work that well in practice because the population gets used to a variety of services being provided by the "state"—whether at the federal, provincial, or municipal level. (Think, for instance, of child care benefits or additional assistance to single parents.) It is hard to simply roll back all these policies, which means that the state cannot reduce its expenses as much as Keynesianism wants to.[11] These critics therefore hold an opposite view on how to get out of a recession; they are another group of liberals known as monetarists; their chief advocate was Milton Friedman (1912–2006). Being generally pessimistic about the state's ability to manage the economy with fiscal policy (as opposed to Keynes), Friedman argued that the problem of why people are not spending in a recession is that money is too expensive for individuals (because taxes and interest rates are too high); if both were lowered, citizens would have more disposable income available, and they would have access to cheaper loans through lower interest rates.[12] With this larger amount of money, individual demand would grow *directly*, i.e., increased spending would thereby stimulate supply (companies producing again). The state's active involvement thus lies not in stimulating demand but in lowering taxes.[13]

Not surprisingly, the Keynesian critics pointed out why monetarism does not work in practice either. Individuals will either not spend their higher disposable income, but instead save it for an uncertain future—recall that we are in a recession where workers fear losing their jobs. In addition, a government can only return part of the taxes to citizens (i.e., thereby lowering state revenue) if it rolls back some welfare state payments (e.g., by reducing the number of high school teachers or by increasing daycare costs). Hence, to the extent that individuals spend at all, they do so in order to make up for the services the state no longer provides (e.g., by now paying tuition for private school instead.)

Keynes and Friedman employ very different strategies for the same problem, namely an economy that is not doing so well at that moment. Criticisms for either approach are about its practicality, not about the theory behind it. Keynesianism and monetarism tend to be tied up politically. Conservative parties favour supply-side policies, while political parties left of centre support a demand-side approach. This dichotomy works in any democracy, but watch for this phenomenon during the next federal election: the NDP is clearly Keynesianist; so is the left flank of the Liberal party. The right flank of the Liberal party is a bit more agnostic, but the Conservative party is decidedly monetarist.

Hence, each approach has a theoretical basis and concrete policies to pursue. This means they are so different that they cannot be applied simultaneously without disastrous results. An illustration of this took place during the reign of former US President Ronald Reagan (1911–2004), who governed from 1981–89. As a conservative, he pursued monetarism, actually with Milton Friedman as his personal advisor at the time; hence, both income and corporate taxes were lowered. However, at the same time the ideological disagreement with the Soviet Union during the Cold War reached new heights, and Reagan's Secretary of Defense, Caspar Weinberger (1917–2006), resolved to outspend Moscow on armaments. The result was that the US government pursued monetarism (thus reducing state revenue) and Keynesianism (increased state spending on defense) simultaneously. It is not difficult to see that applying both concepts, dubbed "Reaganomics," quickly amplified the disparity between revenue and expenditure and became untenable.[14]

Mercantilism

Mercantilism is the oldest of the theoretical approaches, so it may appear contradictory that we only deal with it second. The reason is that although it dates back to the French King Louis XIV (1638–1715), France's practice of mercantilism only lasted a short time in the history of Mercantilism. At the time, it simply amounted to making other countries dependent on France while retaining its own autarky (economic independence). This was to be achieved by quantitatively exporting more than importing, and qualitatively exporting goods crucial for the trading "partner" but importing only goods of minor significance to France.

Mercantilism only gained theoretical prominence in the nineteenth century in the form of so-called economic nationalism, which itself was a direct response to early liberalism. Its main proponents were the German Friedrich List (1789–1846) and his American contemporary Alexander Hamilton (1755–1804). Germany did not exist yet as a country, and the United States was in its very early stages. Both territories were the less developed countries of the time, with Great Britain the only industrialized power.[15] Given this, the quest of economic nationalism was what Germany and the United States had to do to become as industrialized as Great Britain. The predicament of this economic disparity becomes clear through terms of trade. This concept is always viewed from the perspective of the lesser developed country (LDC) in exchange with an industrialized country (i.e., exchanging agricultural products for manufactured goods). By way of illustration, how many tonnes of grain does an LDC have to export in order to import one tractor? The price of unprocessed grain does not increase in value, whereas industrial products do. (The next generation of tractors is always both better and more expensive.) The result is that an LDC has to export ever-increasing amounts of grain in order to import one tractor. The terms of trade are continually declining over time for the lesser developed country.

If *both* countries were exchanging manufactured goods, this problem would not exist. List criticized Adam Smith for analyzing wealth itself but not its *cause*—namely, industrialization. He coined the concept of national productive powers, meaning that it was a state imperative for a lesser developed country to invest in the education of its populace. (In keeping with this view, Germany, as a country with no natural resources, effectively has no tuition to this day.) Only through this would it be able to ultimately develop an infant industry (i.e., any manufacture in which a dominantly agrarian society did not yet have any expertise). To stay with our previous example, its first tractors would not work as well as those manufactured with longstanding proficiency in Great Britain. Germany would hence immediately be flooded with British tractors and never get its own industry up and running. It is therefore necessary, argued List, to shelter the infant industry behind temporary customs duties to achieve a level of international competitiveness. In other words, economic nationals were ultimately free traders, but only once the industrial playing field had been levelled. To be clear, levelling the industrial playing field takes several decades. From elementary school to completing a doctorate takes up to 25 years of education, provided a country even has the academic infrastructure in place. Even thereafter, one does not immediately create a first industry from scratch.

Twentieth-century neomercantilism differs fundamentally from the earlier approaches in that it now deals exclusively with industrialized countries. It can be categorized by two strands: first, economic statecraft[16] identifies the commercial means that can be used to advance the state's political power vis-à-vis other developed countries.[17] Second, strategic trade theory[18] targets only selected industries;[19] this typically happens because domestic producers are under some danger from international competition (e.g., with a geographically concentrated large labour force, like the steel industry; or with significant electoral power, like farmers in rurally overrepresented areas of industrialized countries). Note that the so-called industrial policy also falls into this strand.

It is an active strategy of influencing the national economy vis-à-vis foreign competition. It can take the form of picking a national champion industry, earmarked for particular state subsidies. France is among the countries that routinely employs such a strategy (e.g., in car manufacturing). Canada used a different version of industrial policy under Prime Minister Pierre Elliott Trudeau. The controversial National Energy Program (mostly known by its acronym NEP) was introduced by Trudeau in 1980, sparked by the second worldwide oil crisis within a decade in 1979. The NEP lasted until 1985. It was intended to promote energy self-sufficiency by redistributing the oil wealth of Alberta to benefit the country as a whole, by enforcing both a price ceiling and export duties thus giving the federal government practical control over petroleum prices.

The selected measures that neo-mercantilist governments employ in coming to the aid of these industries are known as *non-tariff barriers* (NTBs); unlike the transparent tariffs, the incidence and precise value of NTBs to third parties (i.e., to the target country) are often hard to detect. Four kinds of non-tariff barriers are routinely used by industrialized countries: (1) *subsidies*, which effectively lower the cost of uncompetitive domestic production down to the world market price—thus artificially making that good competitive; (2) *quotas*, which prohibit the import of a particular commodity beyond a pre-defined quantity—in order to protect domestic production; (3) *voluntary export restraints* (VERs), whereby an exporter (e.g., a Japanese car company) "voluntarily" restricts its shipment to the destination market (e.g., the United States);[20] and (4) technical *or health standards*—as in the refusal of the European Union to let North American genetically modified food be sold without specific labelling.

The political underpinning for all strands of (neo-) mercantilism is *realism*, itself one of the main theories in the field of international relations. Realism focuses on *anarchy* (i.e., the absence of a world government) as the most important condition of international politics. Having no enforceable rules requires nation states to secure their own physical survival.[21] This entails a willingness to forego economic gain *if* another state were perceived to be attaining comparatively more from an economic exchange on a *continuous* basis—the concept of *relative gain*—and thus potentially threatening one's own well-being.

Marxism

In contrast to economic nationalism, Marxism attempted to show that liberal economies would ultimately cease to exist out of logical necessity. What we call classical Marxism today refers to Karl Marx (1818–1883) and Friedrich Engels (1820–1895) together, as they were lifelong friends and collaborators. Witnessing the factory system of the mid-nineteenth century in which women as well as children reportedly worked up to 14 hours a day 7 days a week (called "Manchester capitalism" after the English city in which the cotton industry became notorious), classical Marxism was the last attempt in the social sciences to establish deterministic laws that govern all human behaviour throughout history.[22]

To understand this, we need to acquaint ourselves with some Marxist terminology: the philosophical basis of Marxism is *historical materialism*. It means that all of our economic thinking is predetermined by our material condition in our formative years, i.e., whether we come from an affluent background or were less fortunate. Based upon this principle, two materially defined *classes* (the factory owners, or bourgeoisie, and the workers) exist that are in a *dialectical* (i.e., opposing) relationship.[23] The classes will ultimately clash in a violent revolution, bringing about the next stage of history. By way of illustration, in feudalism (the previous historical period), the materially opposing classes were the nobility (termed by classical Marxism *the thesis*) and the serfs (the *anti-thesis*). When the lower class overthrew the higher one, the next stage became our current capitalism (the *synthesis*).

Capitalism itself is defined by two features: private property and *wage* labour. The former is a legal entitlement to ownership of the means of production for the bourgeoisie, whereas the latter notion signifies that labour becomes a commodity itself, i.e., the working class "sells" its labour in the factories and receives a salary.[24] Note that the sole purpose of Marx and Engels' writing was to demonstrate how capitalism would *inevitably* "dig its own grave." This would lead to a revolution in which the workers, as the materially lower, but numerous class, overthrow the factory owners. At the end stands the next historical stage, namely socialism (the first historical period without materially opposing classes).

The beginning of this inevitability is the labour theory of value, according to which every product is ultimately reducible to the amount of labour involved in its production. Thus, a car is more expensive than a table because of the vast differences in the work hours that have gone into their manufacture.[25] This thought stresses the importance of wage labour; rather than the material itself (e.g., the steel in the car production or the wood for a table), it is the work of melting steel or cutting trees that matters for Marxism. These workers are paid a *subsistence wage*; it is more than is needed for mere physical survival, but enough to keep them in the production process.[26] What surpasses the subsistence wage constitutes the *surplus value* (equivalent to what we today call "profit") of the factory owner. As an example, think of a working day of 10 hours. The labourer needs six hours to earn the subsistence wage; the remaining four hours s/he works "for free," creating the surplus value for the factory owner.

The bourgeois can now enlarge the surplus value in two possible ways: first, by making the working day longer (called *absolute* increase), e.g., to 15 hours. The subsistence wage will increase slightly, for instance to seven hours; so the surplus value would still grow by four hours. Clearly, there is a physical limit to this approach. The second way to raise the surplus value is by replacing some of the workers with machinery—nowadays we use the term "rationalization" for the same idea. Starting from this *relative* growth, Marx and Engels, in their quintessential three-volume *Capital*,[27] developed the three laws that were intended to show how capitalism would ultimately, out of logical necessity, lead to its own demise; they begin with the ideal liberal economy (in which there are so many sellers and buyers that no one can influence the price without risking an immediate loss), which Marx had read extensively. The three laws reinforce each other; therefore it is not important which comes first. They are as follows:

(1) The *Law of Disproportionality*: According to all liberal authors, supply and demand always meet at some equilibrium point, even in a recession. Yet, Marx and Engels held that this could not happen, other than by accident. As all factory owners replace workers with machinery, the now laid-off workers can no longer consume the ever-increasing output. Supply and demand are in disproportion to each other, creating a *problem of under-consumption* and leading to a recession. Marx and Engels maintained that these recessions would get worse over time as the disproportion increases.[28]

(2) The *Law of the Concentration of Capital*: As the rationalization of workers and capital advances, some factory owners are faster and better able to do so than others. The former will purchase the latter, and over time the capital will thus become concentrated in ever fewer hands. (Today we call this either a "hostile takeover" or a "merger".) The consequence of this law is that the ideal liberal market will

disappear over time. Moreover, this concentration of capital will lead to further layoffs (as it does today), further worsening the disproportionate supply and demand. We have also witnessed this in modern times. For example, in 1987, Chrysler bought Jeep; both companies now only needed one joint distribution network; so, many Jeep employees became redundant and lost their jobs. Then, in 1996, Daimler-Benz (the makers of Mercedes) bought Chrysler, renaming the new company Daimler-Chrysler.

(3) The *Law of the (Tendency of) Falling Rate of Profit*: Although the absolute amount of profit grows, the overall costs (for labour and machinery) will grow faster. Therefore, the rate of profit (i.e., profit relative to costs) tends to decline over time, making it less enticing to invest more in one's own factory, but instead taking this excess capital elsewhere. As this occurs, more workers will lose their jobs due to factory owners abandoning their production and employing the funds elsewhere, thus further exacerbating the law of disproportionality.[29]

Note that Marx and Engels did not view "capitalists" (i.e., the factory owners) as inherently "bad" people—they simply do what all capitalists have to do; that is their historical function. If the roles were reversed and a member of the working class became a bourgeois, in exactly the same way, s/he would try to increase their relative surplus value. Therefore, Marx and Engels were *not* revolutionaries (despite what one may infer from their early pamphlet "Communist Manifesto")—indeed, this would otherwise run counter to the notion that the end of capitalism would historically occur with logical inevitability. They nonetheless expected the revolution (although they did not predict it as such) in the most industrialized society at the time (i.e., the one with the starkest material differences), namely Great Britain.

With hindsight, we know that this did not occur, but why? Vladimir Lenin (1870–1924) identified a fourth law, effectively explaining away why the revolution had not materialized in Britain. The law of *uneven development* posits that, due to the Marxist law of the falling rate of profit, the bourgeoisie will shift its excess money (because it now no longer profitably invests it in its own factories) to the colonies for investment. By definition, colonies did not yet have any infrastructure (i.e., the rate of profit could not fall), and the government as the colonial power was paying companies to create precisely this infrastructure. Therefore, having more colonies would enable governments and companies to perpetuate this process. Lenin thus regarded the First World War as a struggle not over Europe but over control of the colonies.[30] Hence, the uneven development between industrialized countries and the less developed colonies—or, put differently, *imperialism* (i.e., the acquisition of colonies)—was the highest stage of capitalism (Lenin 1938). Workers were the soldiers fighting the wars on behalf of governments that enabled the bourgeoisie to divest in their own companies, thereby, again, exacerbating the law of disproportionality. These workers will ultimately refuse to fight these wars; in other words, Lenin took the Marxist laws to the international level. Until the globe is carved up between colonial powers, the revolution would not occur.[31]

Perhaps best known is Lenin as the revolutionary who successfully staged the overthrow of the most agrarian society in Europe to create the Union of Soviet Socialist Republics (USSR).[32] Note that the demise of the Soviet Union in 1991 is not a concern for classical Marxist scholars. On the contrary, according to Marx and Engels, it could have never worked. It was a feudal society that was transformed into a socialist political system, with capitalist industrialization put in place *afterward* (i.e., without bourgeoisie and workers as materially dialectical classes). In other words, a necessary historical stage of human development (namely capitalism *before* socialism) had been skipped.

Similar to the theoretical departure of neomercantilism from its nineteenth century versions, neo-Marxist authors also deviate from classical Marxism in one important point. Marx and Engels presumed a technological trickle-down effect to less developed countries due to the Law of the Falling Rate of Profit, i.e., as their economies were being developed by their colonial powers. In contrast, Immanuel Wallerstein, one of the foremost neo–Marxist scholars from the early 1970s onward, emphasizes the existence of the *core* (the industrialized countries) and the *periphery* (the LDCs); the core's wealth is dependent upon exploitation of the periphery, i.e., the former has every interest in keeping the latter underdeveloped. Wallerstein coined the term *World System Theory* (WST) for this idea, positing that it is not analytically fruitful to investigate at the level of the nation state because the world system as a whole is capitalist (Wallerstein, 1979).[33] Between core and periphery are now several countries (chiefly the so-called Asian tigers) in the *semi-periphery*. They were originally in the periphery and now function as a buffer; they are exploited by the core and they themselves exploit the periphery. Although Wallerstein details how the world system came about and how it will eventually end, this was little comfort for any head of state in an LDC. Should the president's message of, say, Senegal be that the population should throw up their hands in despair because the country will be stuck in underdevelopment with no reprieve? This void between Wallerstein's general assessment and a more activist agenda was filled by a second group of neo-Marxist scholars, known as *Dependency Theory*. André Gunder Frank, its chief proponent, coined the phrase "development of underdevelopment." Since core countries simply exploit LDCs, the prescription is to cut economic ties with industrialized economies and instead pursue development on their own, labeled *Import Substitution Industrialization* (ISI), i.e. substituting imports from industrialized countries with one's own industrialization.[34] This notion is familiar as *infant industry* from economic nationalism, above; however, since many Latin American countries (where ISI was developed) are very small, the requisite market size for viable industrialization led to the first attempts at regional integration. Since the developmental aspirations by LDCs associated with neo–Marxism were disappointed by the mid-1980s, both strands of Neo-Marxist scholarship have subsided.[35] Instead, many LDCs attach themselves today to their respective region's so-called BRICS country (Brazil; Russia; India; China; South Africa) to gain a voice through this in international fora like the World Trade Organization.

Traditional Theories as Science

Central not only to IPE but to the social sciences in general is the problem of "how do we know what we know?" All three sets of traditional theories, despite their differences, subscribe to the purpose of research as explaining particular events, as generalizing from them across a larger group of phenomena, and as using the latter for potentially predicting the likely outcome of similar occurrences. To regard this endeavour not only as desirable but also as possible is the hallmark of what is known as **positivism**.[36] As such, scholars working within this framework believe that the social scientific advancement is not fundamentally different from the "hard" sciences.[37] Although IPE is not a science like physics or chemistry—e.g., we do not have an equivalent to water always boiling at a constant temperature—there are five pairs of scientific vocabulary that the traditional theories share with the natural sciences:

(1) *Law vs. Theory*: A *law* denotes a repeatedly observed relationship between two or more

phenomena. Consider the laws of gravity in physics as an example. In this case, laws are *deterministic* ("if A then always B"); Marx and Engels' three laws fall into this realm. However, nearly all laws in the social sciences generally are *probabilistic* ("if A then sometimes B with probability *X*"). Hence, laws are descriptive, i.e., they tell us *that* a relationship between two or more phenomena holds, whereas a "good" *theory* seeks to explain *why* the said relationship occurs. We therefore should always evaluate the explanatory contribution of traditional theories according to this yardstick. Hence, as you read about IPE theories in this chapter and in the following ones, ask yourself: what exactly do any of these theories explain? And what (hidden) assumptions do they make?

(2) *Hypothesis vs. Null–Hypothesis*: In order to determine whether or not a law or theory holds, one uses a *hypothesis*. It has to be formulated in such a way that a "test" gives a result that could be replicated by other researchers. Therefore, it takes either the form of an "if ... then" statement or of "the higher/lower/stronger/weaker, etc. ... the higher/lower/stronger/weaker, etc." We know at the outset what we expect to find *if* any particular traditional theory were correct. The *null–hypothesis* is the opposite; it would only be confirmed *if* the expected relationship of the hypothesis could *not* be shown. However, a hypothesis requires that we have a theory to test in the first place, but this may not be the case. One can instead also build a research question (e.g., "Why do liberal democracies never fight wars against each other?").

(3) *Independent vs. Dependent Variables*: In testing a hypothesis or in answering a research question, the *dependent variable* (DV) identifies what exactly we want to explain. The *independent variable* (IV) is the one doing the explanation. There can be—and often is—more than one IV; however, they then need to be ranked according to their extent of explanatory power on the DV. There

sometimes also is an *intervening variable* (IVV) between IV and DV. If present, it would strengthen the connection between IV and DV. However, if the IVV were weak or missing, the IV/DV relationship would not be as strong, but it would nonetheless hold. To actually measure these variables, we need to determine the *indicators* we use to do so; these have to be clearly *quantifiable*, not necessarily quantitative. For instance, to research how often neomercantilist language has been used by the Canadian government during the global financial crisis, one could use the two national newspapers in Canada and speeches by the prime minister as sources for a specific period. We could count how often the terminology of non-tariff–barriers has been featured. This would make qualitative sources quantifiable, but we would need to pay close attention. If a sentence reads: "The government is opposed to using subsidies or other non-tariff measures," the indicators we decided to count are in this sentence, but the meaning is actually the opposite of our study. Thus, positivist research would have to decide beforehand how to count such instances.

(4) *Causation vs. Correlation*: The connection between independent and dependent variables is one of *causation*; whether or not it would hold in a particular investigation is not important, but showing causation is the purpose of positivist research. The opposite is a *correlation*, which means that two phenomena occur simultaneously only by chance.[38]

(5) *Deduction vs. Induction*: If an established theory already exists, a hypothesis can be built around it that can then be tested for a particular empirical situation. Does the theory explain this case as well? Such work is *deductive*; we begin with a general theory and apply it empirically to particular cases. All three sets of traditional theories lend themselves to deduction. However, such tests may reveal that a number of empirical cases could not be explained by this theory. If so, more

deductive inquiries may reveal the limitations of the original theory and lead to a reformulation of the theory in light of the findings. This is *inductive* research, i.e., building/reformulating a theory based upon a wealth of empirical data. Positivism thus iterates between deduction and induction continuously; otherwise, no theoretical advancements are possible. We could see this oscillation in operation in the way the early versions of the traditional theories (being clearly deductive) turned into the more inductive twentieth-century forms.

Systematic Similarities and Differences

IPE scholars tend to agree that the state has two roles in the economy: the first is to regulate the market to enable it to even function; an example is common weights and measures, which we take for granted today, but which did not exist in the Middle Ages. Since their absence inhibited economic exchange across larger distances, market actors depended upon political decision-making. Another example is the guarantee of private property by the state. A DVD bought at an electronics store changes ownership once the requisite price is paid. If the product turns out to be defective, the owner has the right to exchange it for free at the store. Without this legal assurance, most business interactions would not take place—and the remaining ones would be in an environment akin to the Wild West.

The second role of the state is to provide so-called public goods that the market would not produce in sufficient quantities. An example of such a good is a public park. For both, the "seller" (who builds the park) cannot recoup the cost directly from the "buyer" (the citizens strolling through it), nor can any "buyer" exclude others (i.e., here: other citizens) from its use. If these two conditions are fulfilled, the good in question is "public" and could

only be provided (i.e., financed) by the state. Goods where these aspects are *not* present are "private," which means they are produced and purchased by market actors. For instance, a TV set will only change hands if the store receives the money from the buyer, and the purchaser could subsequently limit the number and kind of persons allowed to watch TV with him/her.

Whether or not a specific good is regarded as "public" is not predetermined; rather, it depends upon societal consensus. A particular level of environmental standards can be controversial, as the intended ecological protection might be juxtaposed against the costs of installing new filters borne by companies or motorists. What policy is acceptable to the general public will then have to be determined. As another illustration, Health Care is widely demanded in Canada to be a public good (i.e., to be provided by "the state"), whereas this is not the case in the United States. Thus, scholars and the general public alike may have different, ideologically motivated, views on the *degree* to which the state should intervene in the market, but the state's general function in the economy is beyond doubt.

How can three different theories exist simultaneously and still claim to explain the same reality? There are four sets of differences: first, an analytical variance exists according to the *unit of analysis*, i.e., the entity most fundamental to the respective understanding of the world. Liberals focus on the individual and the possibility of wealth creation with limited resources. (Indeed, this is the main preoccupation of Economics and International Business.) Mercantilists concentrate on the state, its position vis-à-vis other countries, and thereby the very physical and economic survival of this unit. Finally, Marxists emphasize class, with the dominant one in any historical period effectively running the state, i.e., there is no "national interest" independent of the dominant class. In other words, the theories focus on different things; they do not deny the existence of the other entities. Yet, when the crunch comes, these alternative units are not as important.

Second, the unit of analysis distinction is related to a bigger issue, namely the primacy of *structure vs. agency*, the perennial problem in the social sciences. Liberals emphasize individual choice, i.e., everyone has the ability to act according to their desires and is thus also responsible for the consequences of their independent agency. Mercantilists point to the agency of states to act prudently in security and economic matters but this agency is dictated by the anarchical (i.e., structural) imperative of the international system (i.e., all states are alike, whether the United States or Senegal). At last, Marxists are often structuralists, i.e., individual and state choices are so significantly constrained by the logic of capitalist accumulation that any notion of independent agency (e.g., "it is your choice") is mere fiction.

The third difference is that all three theories make claims to explain empirical regularities, but they also espouse ideological commitments. This is the distinction between the descriptive "how the world *is*" and the prescriptive "how the world *should be*." Fourth, the three theories vary between *nature* and *nurture*, i.e., whether it is natural for humans "to truck and barter" (as Adam Smith posited) or whether private property is a concept that is merely learned (as Marx and Engels surmised). The consequence of the former is to limit the role of the state in the market, whereas the latter would enable the state to reeducate citizens to embrace common property instead.

These similarities and differences beg the question of whether or not the diverse theories can be combined. Two of the chief IPE scholars since the 1980s, Robert Gilpin and Susan Strange (1923–1998) have opposing views on this. Gilpin asserts that the differences according to the unit of analysis mean that the theories effectively talk about varied things. Each theory will employ *ad hoc–hypotheses* to fit supposedly deviant empirical observations within its realm. By contrast, Susan Strange asserted that the three theories differ according to four values: security, wealth, equality, and justice. Each theory favours one or two clearly over the others, but they also incorporate some measure of all values. Consequently, they indeed can be combined and become a *menu for choice*.[39]

Notes

1   I wish to thank Greg Anderson for his continued support throughout and the two anonymous reviewers for improving this chapter. Of course, all remaining errors are solely my own responsibility.

2   Among learned journals in Canada, the formal separation only took place in 1967, when the Canadian Journal of Economics and Political Science split into the Canadian Journal of Economics and the Canadian Journal of Political Science. Note, however, that the separate disciplines were already contained in the title of the joint journal, rather than "political economy."

3   See also Chapter 5 in this book by Eric Helleiner.

4   Smith, A. (1976). *An Inquiry into the Nature and the Causes of the Wealth of Nations*, R. H. Campbell and A. S. Skinner (Eds). Oxford: Clarendon Press.

5   Ricardo, D. (1965 [1821]). *The Principles of Political Economy and Taxation*, 3rd ed. London: Dent.

6   Note that the numbers 21 and 10 are random. I only selected them to make the computing simple. It only matters that the amount of workers shifted has to be the same *within* each country, but *not* across them.

7   The "comparative" advantage of Ricardo's time was based upon the initial natural endowment of a country (e.g., for wine production). Today, the concept is one of "competitive" advantage, i.e., one that needs to be artificially created. Consider semi-conductors; they had to be conceived of first. Hence, they had nothing to do with natural endowment, but with educational levels and entrepreneurial spirit.

8   Keynes, J. M. (1947 [1936]). *The general theory of employment, interest, and money*. London: Macmillan.

9   The "state" can, but need not, be national/federal. A number of tasks are the prerogative of subnational units like the provinces in Canada, the individual states in the US, the *Länder* in Germany, or even the *departements* in unitary France.

10   Internationally, John Maynard Keynes continued his concern for economic stability, as he became one of the main architects of the so-called Bretton Woods institutions (named after the village in New Hampshire in which they were established in 1944), the International Monetary Fund (IMF) and the International Bank for

Reconstruction and Development (IBRD), better known as the World Bank.

11 The second criticism is called "crowding out." Because the state(s) has/have to borrow so much money in order to stimulate the economy that the price for money, the interest rate, will increase. But the small construction company that needs a loan to buy new machinery and employ more people in order to pave the road the state just paid for, may not be able to shoulder this higher interest for its loan. Then, state demand for money ultimately "crowds out" private demand for loans.

12 The government itself can reduce the tax rate, but cannot lower the interest rate; this is a matter only for the banking sector. Since Canadian commercial banks tend to get most of their own money from the Bank of Canada, if the latter lowers the interest rate, e.g., RBC would give some of that reduction back to consumers for cheaper loans.

13 Friedman, M. (1982 [1962]). *Capitalism and freedom*. Chicago: University of Chicago Press.

14 The second effort to institute the recommendations of the academe in practice took place almost simultaneously to Reagonomics, this time known as "Thatcherism." The then British Prime Minister Margaret Thatcher (who governed from 1979–1990) deregulated the economy (among others, the railway) and effectively demolished the influence of the powerful coal miner's union. The political economist that affected her thinking most fundamentally was not Milton Friedman, but the Austrian Friedrich von Hayek (1899–1992) whose 1944 book *Road to Serfdom* was the template for "Thatcherism."

15 List, F. (1966 [1885]). *The National System of Political Economy*. New York: Augustus M. Kelley; Hamilton, A. (1957). *Papers on Public Credit, Commerce and Finance*, S. McKee, Jr. (Ed.). New York: Liberal Arts Press.

16 Knorr, K. (1975). *The Power of Nations: The Political Economy of International Relations*. New York: Basic Books; Baldwin, David A. (1985). *Economic Statecraft*. Princeton, NJ: Princeton University Press.

17 Note that economic power lies in the *threat* to interrupt trade. If this threat is perceived to be credible, a country invested with this power would not actually have to act upon it.

18 Stegemann, K. (1989). "Policy Rivalry Among Industrial States: What Can We Learn from Models of Strategic Trade Policy?" *International Organization 43*(1): 73–100.

19 Hence, it no longer exhibits the blanket approach for the entire economy taken by early mercantilism.

20 An exporter is usually "convinced" to do so through issue linkage. The U.S. government made it known that it may not be able to maintain its naval bases in Japan (upon which the country relies for its security) if Japanese car manufacturers would not voluntarily restrict its exports to the American market.

21 Waltz, K. N. (1979). *Theory of International Politics*. Boston, MA: McGraw–Hill.

22 Engels, F. (1975 [1844]). "Outlines of a Critique of Political Economy," in *Karl Marx, Frederick Engels: Collected Works*, Volume 3. New York: International Publishers, 418–443.

23 *Dialecticism* denotes that one term has no meaning without an understanding of its opposite. For instance, we cannot appreciate what "hot" feels like without knowing "cold."

24 Compare this to Feudalism: the nobility's land claims were simply hereditary, but not entitlements in the legal sense. The serfs had to work the land, but did not receive a formal salary for their efforts.

25 Recall that the illustration we used for David Ricardo's comparative advantage was similarly based on a labour theory of value.

26 This idea exists also today in what we call a "basket of basic needs." It defines the threshold for social assistance and thereby also the material belongings that cannot be forcibly removed in case of personal bankruptcy.

27 The first volume was published in 1869, the second and third ones only after Marx's death and edited by Engels in 1886 and 1895, respectively.

28 The Great Depression in 1929 would have proven their point, but neither one lived to witness it.

29 Most liberals agree with all three laws, but they devised responses to ensure capitalism's continued existence. They maintain that the Law of Disproportionality can be mitigated by artificially increasing the demand through Keynesian economics. Their response to the Law of the Falling Rate of Profit is state funding for research and development to create marketable technological advance. Finally, the Law of the Concentration of Capital can be alleviated through anti-trust legislation at the corporate level and through the welfare state for individual income disparities. Marx and Engels, in whose time active state policies did not exist, would reply that these liberal policies will delay the demise of capitalism, but they do not challenge the very logic of the three laws; thus, liberal policies are equivalent to curing symptoms instead of a disease.

30 Critics have suggested that this would have meant a war between the two chief colonial powers at the time, France and Great Britain—yet, they were allies. The "Leninist" response would be that Germany and Italy had started to obtain colonies themselves at the turn of the century. France and Great Britain wanted to dislodge them.

31 While the Soviet Union and its satellite states still existed, the discipline of Political Economy was taught as Marxism–Leninism. Until 1989, the official view prevailed that nothing fundamental had been written since Lenin's extension of the Marxist Laws (i.e., not even by neo-Marxist authors).

32 At the outbreak of the war in 1914, Lenin was in Swiss exile. Since Germany was fighting a two-front war, the German High Command wanted to end the war on the eastern front (the Russian czar was even the cousin of the German emperor). It secretly brought Lenin by train to St Petersburg (later Leningrad) with the understanding that if the revolution were successful, he would immediately end Russia's war against Germany—which he did. While Germany did not win the war in the West, the point here is the historical context that led to the Russian Revolution in the first place.

33 Wallerstein, I. (1979). *The Capitalist World-Economy: Essays*. Cambridge: Cambridge University Press.

34 Frank, A. G. (1969). *Capitalism and Underdevelopment in Latin America: Historical Studies of Chile and Brazil*. New York: Monthly Review Press.

35 A third neo-Marxist school is connected with the work of Antonio Gramsci (1891–1937). I encourage those wishing to expand their knowledge in this tradition to begin with an article by Robert Cox on Gramsci's relevance. See: Cox, Robert W. (1983), "Gramsci, Hegemony and International Relations: An Essay in Method," *Millennium: Journal of International Studies 12*(2), 162–75.

36 The French philosopher and mathematician René Descartes (1596–1650) is typically considered to be the father of this line of reasoning, labeled the scientific method. However, *post-positivist* scholars are skeptical about the ability to conduct research in this

manner about social events. Chapter 3 of this book by Rob Aitken will deal with post-positivism in detail.

37 Van Evera, S. (1997). *Guide to methods for students of political science*. Ithaca, NY: Cornell University Press; King, G., Keohane, R. O., and Verba, S. (1994). *Designing social inquiry: Scientific inference in qualitative research*. Princeton, NJ: Princeton University Press.

38 Some scholars hold the view that correlations *can* indicate the *potential* existence of causal relations. Rather, the causes underlying the correlation *may* be indirect and *unknown*. It is difficult to detect an argument in such language.

39 Gilpin, R. (1987). *The political economy of international relations*. Princeton, NJ: Princeton University Press; Strange, S. (1988). *States and markets*. London: Pinter.

Key Terms

liberalism

Marxism

mercantilism

positivism

Questions for Review

1. What are the respective units of analysis for mercantilism, liberalism, and Marxism?
2. Describe the difference between Keynesianism and monetarism. How does so-called *Reagonomics* relate to both concepts?
3. What does the term "infant industry" stand for? Can you identify examples that would fit the definition today?
4. Describe the relationship between the concept of "historical materialism" and the three Marxist laws. The latter were developed to explain human behaviour throughout history. If so, we should be able to see them working in the present. Do you agree with this? Why or why not?
5. What would the arguments and counter-arguments be between a constructivist and a Realist?
6. Explain the difference between a private and a public good for both sellers and buyers.
7. What are the positions of the various traditional theories in the agency/structure dichotomy?
8. What distinguishes a law from a theory?
9. Some social scientists assert that the physical sciences got all the easy problems based on the distinction between probabilistic vs. deterministic arguments. Do you agree? Why or why not?
10. Are inductive and deductive approaches mutually exclusive or rather complementary?

Further Resources

Caporaso, J. A. and D. P. Levine (1992). *Theories of political economy*. New York: Cambridge University Press.

(Carporaso and Levine cover the various theories available in IPE one by one—rather than giving an author-driven historical account as Heilbroner does.)

Heilbroner, R. L. (1999). *The worldly philosophers: The lives, times, and ideas of the great economic thinkers*, 7th ed. New York: Touchstone.

(Heilbroner's book is likely the best introduction to the history of thought in political economy. The scholars become understandable in the particular context in which their ideas formed.)

Lakatos, I. and Musgrave, A. (Eds). (1970). *Criticism and the growth of knowledge.*

(How do we know that we know what we know? When, if at all, is a theory considered to be refuted? Should this actually occur, what happens then? These are the questions with which the philosophy

of science grapples. The giants of this field, Karl Popper, Thomas Kuhn, and Imre Lakatos, among others, met for a conference in the late 1960s. This volume contains the proceedings of this meeting— fascinating but demanding reading.)

References

Baldwin, D. A. (1985). *Economic statecraft.* Princeton, NJ: Princeton University Press.

Cox, R. W. (1983). "Gramsci, hegemony and international relations: An essay in method." *Millennium: Journal of International Studies 12*(2), 162–75.

Engels, F. (1975 [1844]). "Outlines of a critique of political economy." in *Karl Marx, Frederick Engels: Collected works*, Volume 3. New York: International Publishers, 418–43.

Frank, A. G. (1969). *Capitalism and underdevelopment in Latin America: Historical studies of Chile and Brazil.* New York: Monthly Review Press.

Friedman, M. (1982 [1962]). *Capitalism and freedom.* Chicago: University of Chicago Press.

Gilpin, R. (1987). *The political economy of international relations.* Princeton, NJ: Princeton University Press.

Hamilton, A. (1957). *Papers on public credit, commerce and finance.* (Samuel McKee, Jr., Ed.). New York: Liberal Arts Press.

Hayek, F. (1991 [1944]). *The road to serfdom.* London: Routledge.

Keynes, J. M. (1947 [1936]). *The general theory of employment, interest, and money.* London: Macmillan.

King, G., Keohane, R. O., and Verba, S. (1994). *Designing social inquiry: Scientific inference in qualitative research.* Princeton, NJ: Princeton University Press.

Knorr, K. (1975). *The Power of Nations: The political economy of international relations.* New York: Basic Books.

Lakatos, I. and Musgrave, A. (Eds). (1970). *Criticism and the growth of knowledge.* Cambridge: Cambridge University Press.

Lenin, V. I. (1938). *Imperialism, the highest stage of capitalism.* Moscow: Foreign Languages Publishing House.

List, F. (1966 [1885]). *The national system of political economy.* New York: Augustus M. Kelley.

Ricardo, D. (1965 [1821]). *The principles of political economy and taxation*, 3rd ed. London: Dent.

Smith, A. (1976). *An inquiry into the nature and the causes of the wealth of nations.* R. H. Campbell and A. S. Skinner, (Eds). Oxford: Clarendon Press.

Smith A. (1976 [1759]). *The theory of moral sentiments.* D. D. Raphael and A. L. MacFie, (Eds). Oxford: Clarendon Press.

Stegemann, K. (1989). "Policy rivalry among industrial states: What can we learn from models of strategic trade policy?" *International Organization 43*(1), 73–100.

Strange, S. (1988). *States and markets.* London: Pinter.

Van Evera, S. (1997). *Guide to methods for students of political Science.* Ithaca, NY: Cornell University Press.

Wallerstein, I. (1979). *The capitalist world-economy: Essays.* Cambridge: Cambridge University Press.

Waltz, K. N. (1979). *Theory of international politics.* Boston, MA: McGraw–Hill.

3 Theoretical Challengers
Post-Positivist Methods in IPE

Rob Aitken

Introduction

In 1981, Robert W. Cox famously noted that "theory is always for someone and for some purpose" (Cox 1981). In doing so, he initiated a period of theoretical innovation in IPE, a field that had been insulated from broader currents in critical, cultural, and social theory. Cox also issued a radical challenge to approaches in IPE committed to science and detached inquiry. Cox's claim signalled the coming of age of a new kind of theoretical orientation that would be self-conscious about its own political and normative commitments. Not only was theory situated in time and space—that is, a product of the social and political preoccupations of particular moments and particular places—theory was also an explicit intervention into those moments. What distinguished critical theory was not some sense of objective or scientific knowledge, but an attempt, as Cox noted, to "stand apart from the world" and inquire into the possibilities of change in the existing political and economic order. In short, the goal of theory was to contribute to practices of social and political change (See, for example, Neufeld 1995).

Much theoretical innovation has occurred in the now 30-plus years that have passed since Cox's immensely influential formulation. Although Cox's formulation pits "critical theory" against "problem-solving" or mainstream, approaches, the theme I develop in this chapter implies that it is now time to take stock of the differences that permeate *within* the variety of approaches that challenge the mainstream rather than simply contrasting theoretical challengers with mainstream approaches. The purpose of this chapter is to chart the theoretical innovation of the past 30 years by reviewing two related but distinctive methods of **post-positivism** that have posed challenges to mainstream or positivist approaches in IPE. Although both of these approaches—what I am calling "materialist" and "discursive" approaches—share a skepticism about the claims of objective or scientific knowledge in IPE, and acknowledge the importance of Cox's suggestion that theory is always for "some purpose," they differ in important ways. Materialist approaches are keen to understand the powerful forces that lie at the heart of how the global economy is organized. In doing so, these approaches shed light on the inequalities in the global political economy and the ways in which those inequalities might be contested. In some important ways, "who" questions ultimately lie behind the work of many important contributors to this approach to post-positivism in IPE: who benefits from the ways in which the global economy is organized? Which social forces have helped write the rules at the very core of the global political economy? By contrast, discursive approaches are interested in the ways in which "economic" categories, and the language of the global political economy more broadly, are created in the first place. Although discursive approaches are also interested in the question of history, their focus is more immediately on the very language, categories, ideas, and concepts that shape our understanding of the global political economy. In this sense, discursive approaches organize analysis of the global political economy by offering "how" questions: how have the basic categories of analysis we use to understand the global political economy been created? How has knowledge of the global economy been built up and how does that knowledge shape how we think and act? This chapter reviews both of these approaches and argues that this diversity is indicative of theoretical maturity in the field—a field that is more willing to entertain a much wider range of theoretical questions than it did in 1981 when Cox first wrote about IPE as a critical venture.

In thinking about your own relationship to post-positivist approaches in the field, it will be important to determine, in your own view, which of these inflections provides the most useful way of understanding and diagnosing issues in the global political economy. This is not to suggest, however, that these two approaches present students of IPE with an "either/or" choice. Rather, it might be more productive to conceive of critical theory as a diverse set of "tools" that can be experimented with, used in different ways and adapted to

particular contexts. In contrast to approaches that often assume a pure way in which theories are to be "applied," post-positivist theories should be seen in a more open-ended manner: as flexible devices that, depending on the object of analysis, might prove useful. In using post-positivist approaches, therefore, there is less an emphasis on perfect application than on a spirit of experimentation. As you approach a particular research topic, this experimental approach is guided by unique questions: in what ways can concepts be used in relation to particular issues or to generate new ways of looking at issues, actors, or practices in the global political economy?

This chapter is organized into four main sections. The first section reviews the introduction of post-positivism in IPE by focusing on the body of theoretical challengers most associated with Cox and his work: neo-Marxism, Gramsci, and materialist approaches. A second section demonstrates the recent widening of post-positivist work in IPE by examining approaches that have moved beyond this initial focus. This newer set of approaches, what I loosely label "discursive" approaches, have paid particular attention to questions of language and to the ways in which the very categories central to IPE have been constituted in the first place. This focus on discourse and language, however, should not imply a lack of interest in the "real" or "material" world. As this section notes, discursive approaches are deeply interested in concrete practices. To dramatize this more fully, a third section offers something of a brief "case study" of one recent example of discursive work in IPE—work relating to the "social studies of finance." As this section demonstrates, this work examines the ways in which the language, concepts, models, practices, and rules associated with global financial markets have been constituted in the first place. Indeed, as this section notes, the "sciences" associated with financial markets (like accounting, financial economics, auditing, etc.) are not conceived as objective forms of knowledge but as powerful political and historical practices often insulated from meaningful forms of accountability. A fourth and concluding section reminds us that these approaches should be understood not so much as grand or general theories of IPE as "tools" that we can use as we develop our own analysis of the global political economy.

Neo-Marxism, Gramsci, and Emancipation: Introducing Post-Positivism

When Cox issued his famous declaration about the purposefulness of theory, he was making a distinction between what he described as "critical" and "problem-solving" theory (Cox 1981). Problem-solving theory, according to Cox, "took the world as it is" and largely addressed questions relating to the stability or maintenance of the existing global economic system. This kind of managerial approach accepts the political and economic order as given and beyond question. Critical theory, by contrast, attempts to "stand back from the existing order" and ask important questions about the very nature of existing political and economic institutions: what were the historical conditions that gave rise to particular forms of "world order"? What interests ("social forces") were important in shaping those conditions? This contrast is riddled with explicitly political and normative implications. By inviting us to stand back from the existing order and inquire into the ways in which it was shaped, Cox is asking us not to accept political and economic arrangements as neutral but as political projects authored by particular constellations of social groups in their own interest. By extension, this approach also suggests that the current arrangement of things is not given or unchangeable but

politically malleable. Writing from a perspective explicitly concerned with the possibilities of social transformation, Cox argues for an approach that would take an explicit stance on how the existing global political economy might be changed to better meet the needs of those who have been excluded or victimized under current arrangements. Some critical voices have described this as a commitment to "emancipatory" social change (See Linklater 2007; Neufeld 1995). As Cox himself notes:

> Action is purposive. Social action can be broadly divided into that which tends to conserve the existing order and that which tends to change it. At the outset, I indicated my purpose was a critical one—to search for the most useful way of understanding the social and political world in order to change it. (Cox 1987, 393)

In making this kind of claim, Cox effectively pried opened space for a critique of positivism in IPE. Positivism entails an abiding respect for science and the possibility of technical objectivity. In general terms positivism refers to a very particular way of "doing" science—including social science—that holds out the possibility of detached and objective analysis. There are three basic assumptions that mark positivism and its enormous influence in IPE. The first assumption is often referred to as the "correspondence theory of truth," which grounds all knowledge (and the truth or falsity of that knowledge) in direct sensory experience. In this view, truth is rooted in direct empirical observation and testing. Perhaps more important for our purposes, the second key assumption of positivism emphasizes the radical separation of object and subject or, put differently, the separation of "knower" from the object of analysis. This assumption implies that scientists, and the experiences, values, norms, politics and "subject positions" they embody, are separate from the scientific process. This assumes both the possibility of objective knowledge and the contention that we, and our political-normative commitments, have no bearing on the kind of knowledge we produce. A third, and final, assumption associated with positivism is the "unity of science" claim. This claim, broadly speaking, implies that all forms of "science", including physical, natural, biological and, crucially, social sciences can essentially pursue the same scientific method. The "social" world (of politics and economics) can be studied in the same ways as phenomena belonging to the natural and physical world (Neufeld 1995; see also Hacking 2000; Thaddeus-Jackson 2010).

Many approaches in IPE remain committed implicitly or explicitly to some form of positivism. This is particularly true of Economics, one of the "founding" disciplines of IPE, which has often sought to offer itself as a "pure" science modelled on the practices of biology, or more recently, physics (Mirowski 1989; Mitchell 2002). Cox's intervention in the early 1980s, however, made a bold call for a different kind of knowledge in IPE; one that was committed less to scientific rigour and more to the clarification of possibilities for social change in a global political economy increasingly subject to upheaval and instability. Cox's timing is important here, coming at a historical juncture after a decade of intense change in the global political economy— the dissolution of the postwar Bretton Woods institutions, the emergence of fiscal imbalances, the crushing impact of the OPEC "oil shocks" in the 1970s, the persistence of inflationary pressures, a slow-down in economic growth and productivity in the United States, and, in general, a weakening of faith in the American dollar and in global American economic leadership. In the wake of these pressures, and in an attempt to diagnose the prospects for a more egalitarian set of international economic arrangements, Cox turned his attention

to a set of concepts developed in the 1920s and 1930s by Italian socialist Antonio Gramsci. For Gramsci, dominant political–economic institutions are the work of a *hegemonic bloc*, the coalition of leading social forces who rule by both coercion (the legal and judicial institutions) but also by consent, by which he meant the institutions (popular culture, media, education) that organize dominant ideas and which often depict the dominant political economic order as "inevitable," "desirable" or in the general interest. **Hegemony** implies the importance of both material power and ideas. For Cox, the period of international economic upheaval unleashed in the 1970s could be understood as a transformation in both the dominant social forces that governed the global economy and the ideas that animated those forces. The shifts of the 1970s witnessed a collapse in a hegemonic political coalition, and set of ideas, that emerged in the period after the Second World War. In contrast to a coalition built around ideas of (moderate) state intervention and gradual openness to the global economy, new political forces of the 1970s began to articulate a vision centred around neoliberalism. This entailed a renewed commitment to open markets and the deregulation of controls on the movements of goods and capital across borders. All of this was underpinned by ideas of a new kind of ideal citizen—a citizen not protected from risk by the welfare state but one that embraces risk as a key part of individual responsibility (Blyth 2002; Brodie 2009; du Gay 1996; Foucault 2008).

This approach to post-positivism embodied in Cox's particular diagnosis of the crises of the 1970s and 1980s can be broadly described as materialist. By materialist I mean to emphasize the ways in which these approaches link power, in some ultimate form, to the economic conditions—the material conditions—of capitalist development. Although materialist perspectives often place a great deal of emphasis on ideas (as in Cox's emphasis on shifts at the level of dominant economic discourse), ideas are fundamentally related to economic power and the dominant social forces that exercise that power. Although ideas are key to political-economic power, this type of analysis places ultimate emphasis on what Cox referred to as the "realm of production," or the material power derived from the control over economic resources. Ideas are ultimately shaped by (and in turn help shape) powerful interests with leading authority over processes of production, broadly defined. This type of materialist approach has now been incorporated into a wide range of attempts to investigate the ways in which power is exercised in the global political economy, including studies of: the decisive influence that loosely formed transnational class formations exercise over key global economic institutions (Van Der Pijl 1998); the work of elite global-oriented institutions like the Trilateral Commission in forging a neoliberal policy consensus (Gill 1992); the impact of neoliberal practices at an everyday level (Harmes 2001); the historical production of a capitalist "common sense" among working class actors (Rupert 1995); issues of state restructuring along neoliberal lines (Morton 2011); the organization of labour in the context of economic globalization (Bieler 2012); as well as the various forms of resistance to these dominant groups in the global political economy (Robinson 2008; Gills and Gray 2012; Gill 2003). Importantly, this work has also intersected with feminist analysis keen to explore the particularly gendered ways in which power in the global political economy has been structured and experienced (Peterson 2013).

Materialist approaches influenced by Cox and Gramsci are, of course, not the only style of post-positivist reasoning in IPE. There is now a wide range of work that challenges the assumptions of mainstream theories and the ways in which those theories approach the field of IPE. Nonetheless, materialist approaches were among the earliest, and most impactful of post-positivist theories in IPE. Given their success, and acknowledging that there are now several important genres of post-positivism relevant to IPE, it is now important to lay materialist approaches alongside other "theoretical challengers," including those associated with a very different notion of *discursive* power.

From Materialism to Ideas and Back Again: Discourse in IPE

If materialist approaches in IPE were influenced by the legacy of neo-Marxist analysis, recent experimentation in IPE uses other languages or styles of post-positivism. Among the most important and innovative of these experiments is work influenced by **discourse** and discursive conceptions of power. Discourse, in common usage, refers to language and to systematically organized sets of statements. A discourse, in this general sense, is not a disconnected group of words but a systematic set of statements built up around a particular topic, object, or category. In several strands of critical theory, however, discourse has a related but slightly more specific meaning implying a set of statements that give meaning to any object or category of the social world. For these approaches, including those that would come to be associated with the label "poststructuralism," language and discourse are not simple matters. Language does not, for instance, simply "reflect" some pre-existing object with an obvious or stable meaning. Rather, the language we use to describe a certain object or practice deeply shapes the ways in which we understand that object. This is not to suggest that there is no such thing as a "reality" apart from us, but, rather, that there is no way to access that reality without recourse to the language, concepts, and *discourses* we have invented ourselves. Because that language is a human invention, it is as partial, arbitrary, and riddled with ambiguity as we are. Perhaps more important, these discourses, the systems of language available for understanding a certain object in a certain way, can be said to *constitute* or shape the object they discuss. Put a bit differently, although we often think of language as a neutral vehicle for transmitting knowledge, it is, according to this view, a deeply powerful way of representing, and by extension, determining what we mean when we refer to particular objects. Language does not simply reflect the world but is a key place where we create meaning about the world. Creating and investing meaning is a powerful act. For example, language limits *and* enables action in relation to the objects it describes. Before we can intervene in a particular object or practice, we must first constitute a language and a knowledge of that object that makes intervention possible. Language constitutes objects not in the physical sense (not in bringing their very physical being into existence) but by inventing the very way in which we relate to, understand, and, ultimately, act on objects. Discourses, then, are systematically organized sets of statements that invest meaning in the object that they discuss and target. In the words of Michel Foucault, a French philosopher closely associated with this approach, "discourses are practices which simultaneously form the objects of which they speak" (Foucault 1974).

This focus on discourse offers a very particular, and particularly unique, understanding of power. Power is not grounded in the material forces of production or in the control over economic resources, but is fundamentally related to knowledge and language. Power cannot be exercised without knowledge and knowledge is always fraught with power relations. Foucault emphasized this relationship by denoting "power/knowledge" where the slash indicates an inseparability of, a deep mutual implication, between the two. There are many ways in which scholars have approached and explored this conception of power/knowledge. One particularly important example is the debate about the national economy. One major recent preoccupation in IPE has been a debate about the future of the national economy in the context of the increasing pressures of economic globalization. As global flows of capital and trade intensify, many states increasingly struggle to manage their own national economy, or to preserve forms of national economic autonomy in the face of globalizing pressures. This has sparked something of a debate in IPE about the relative importance of the national economy in an era of globalization. Both sides in this debate often speak of the national economy as if it exists outside of historical or social relations. Although we might debate the relative importance of the national economy in a moment of globalization, we often speak of it as if we nonetheless know with certainty what the national economy actually is—that it is simply a given in our usual discourse in IPE.

The "national economy" however, is actually a relatively recent and constantly changing object. Some references to national economic space abound in the nineteenth century, for example, during a period when economic nationalism emerged as an important feature of the global political economy (List 1856). Nonetheless, as recently as the 1920s, references to the "national economy" (and its "performance") were not to be found in the financial pages of newspapers or in the reports of economists (Mitchell 2002). Moreover, there was no language available for describing the national economy or measuring its progress over time. Before the national economy could be managed—or even before its performance could be tracked on the financial pages—there needed to be a knowledge or language that could render it understandable, measurable, and comparable in the first place.

Before this language, there was no codified way of actually understanding or representing the economy as a cohesive national system, or, for that matter, depicting its movement.

The knowledge and language that would eventually constitute the national economy as an identifiable category has an important political history. The language of national economy was made partly possible, for example, by the rise of econometrics and other strands of economic reasoning, which began to conceptualize the economy as a self-contained and integrated system (partly borrowed from physics) in the early part of the twentieth century. Most important, however, was the work of British economist John Maynard Keynes and his unique innovations of the 1930s, which opened a novel way of understanding the space of the national economy (at a macro-level) and the ways in which the moving parts of that national economic system related to each other (Aitken 2006; Keynes 1933, 1936; Mirowski 1989; Mitchell 2002). This language, so important to the way in which we have understood economic relationships over the past eighty years, constituted a strikingly novel way of *knowing* the economy—a new way of actually representing the economy in terms of the calculations that macroeconomics facilitated. Macroeconomics allowed us to understand the national economy in terms of levels and measures of effective demand, rates of un/employment, calculable rates of interest or investment, and so on. Perhaps even more important, this knowledge of the national economy—eventually codified by the 1950s in standardized techniques of national accounting—facilitated a new way of intervening into and governing the economy. What seems so evidently a part of our world—the techniques of national accounting such as Gross Domestic Product—was actually only enabled once a language of the national economy was developed and measures were invented to make that space calculable. This language, and the tools of macroeconomics it facilitated, allowed the widespread adoption of new policy mechanisms: forms of national macroeconomic planning; new approaches to economic management; and novel ways of managing taxation, fiscal balances, spending, and budgeting.

As this quick summary suggests, before the national economy could be governed in a certain way—as an object that could be managed through programs of macroeconomic intervention—a *discourse* was first required that could make visible, that could measure, and that could render knowable the national economy as an identifiable category.[1] As this account should imply, however, discourse is not detached from the *materiality* of power. To be sure, some distance separates the notion of discursive power from the emphasis of materialist approaches outlined in Section 1. The focus on discourse and the constitution of objects in knowledge is quite different from the concerns of scholars influenced by Marx and Gramsci and the complex forms of power they analyzed rooted in the material conditions of production. In contrast to materialist approaches, discursive conceptions of power often invite quite different kinds of questions: How are the basic categories and knowledge in IPE constituted? How does that knowledge constitute areas of intervention and ways of acting on economic practices, spaces or identities? This focus however is not simply a focus on knowledge or language in any abstract sense, but precisely on the ways in which those forms of knowledge and language are inscribed in tangible practices: in institutional contexts and systems; in all variety of technologies; in forms of statistical knowledge that mobilize or enable action; and in the practice of experts operating across a wide range of settings. The discourse of the national economy reviewed above, for example, is not simply an abstract language but an entire ensemble of ideas, technologies (national accounting), and modes of intervention (macroeconomic planning). In making these kinds of claims, scholars interested in questions of discourse have not connected their analyses to the "big" forces of capitalist production, or the social forces and interests that underpin those forces. Rather, they have been interested in the ways in which knowledge about the global economy is built up and the ways in which that knowledge comes to enable (and foreclose) certain areas of intervention. Put succinctly, a focus on discourse trains less attention on *who* manages the global political economy (and whose interest is served by it) than on *how* knowledge about the global political economy is constituted and to what effect. This entails treating knowledge in the global political economy not as given or objective but as partial and political. This includes knowledge about the most seemingly prosaic or technical parts of the global political economy, including the spaces of finance and financial markets.

The Social Studies of Finance: Science as Object of Analysis

Both materialist and discursive accounts of power are post-positivist in that they reject any easy claim to scientific certainty or objective knowledge in IPE. One of the unique ways in which discursive approaches have accomplished this is by turning their gaze directly onto science itself. Although we often conceive of science as objective and universal, Foucault understood it in a very different way; as a historicized, contingent, and partial form of knowledge. What counts as science, indeed what counts as "truth," both change over time and vary across different contexts. Foucault's research often entailed questions about the very ways in which certain forms of knowledge come to claim status as

science or how they circulate as "truth" in particular contexts. This provoked a whole series of novel questions about science as a particularly powerful form of knowledge in the modern world: What makes a body of knowledge "scientific"? How does what counts as "scientific knowledge" change over time? These questions are of particular importance to post-positivists because they focus critical and analytical attention onto science itself not as an objective or "given" form of knowledge but as a residue of particular historical, political, and social contexts. Given the authority and power associated with scientific expertise in political, economic, and social settings, it is often politically useful to disrupt the authority that science exerts on the ways in which we understand (and intervene into) the social world.[2]

Much of the knowledge associated with our global political economy precisely circulates as highly scientific, technical, or expert knowledge; knowledge that is often conceived as both objective but also inaccessible to average populations. As a result, the work of many experts who shape the global political economy are often insulated from critical scrutiny or meaningful forms of accountability (Sinclair 2010). In Cox's terms, these experts often practise a kind of "problem-solving" approach, focusing on technical questions that are separated from any broader political or social issues. Key sectors of the global economy are now dominated by the authority and technical acumen of all varieties of problem-solving expertise: accountants, lawyers, auditors, financial economists, patent specialists, and other technical experts. This is perhaps nowhere more evident than in financial markets, a domain seemingly dominated by technical experts operating in narrow fields of operation (Riles 2011). Often shrouded in the language of accountants and economists, financial markets are reserved as a topic of discussion only among highly technical specialists who claim to "understand" those markets in ways that average citizens may not, even though those markets often exert a staggering influence over the shape of political-economic life. This framing of finance as a rational and legitimate pursuit is actually quite a recent achievement. Up until the Second World War, and certainly for the two centuries preceding it, the activities of the financial sector were deeply contested. Throughout the nineteenth century, for example, finance was seen less as a rational and scientific domain, and more often depicted as an irrational, politically dubious, even immoral set of practices. Associated with gambling, with the intense wealth of "stock operators" and with the irrationalities of

THE GREATEST JUGGLING ACT ON EARTH.

Figure 3.1 The Greatest Juggling Act on Earth: An Early Caricature of Market Manipulation

financial panic, "Wall Street" was often subjected to serious political attacks that effectively undermined its own credibility and legitimacy (de Goede 2005).

Part of the story of finance and its slow and uneven move from dubious to legitimate practice is the gradual association over the twentieth century of finance with various forms of science. In a complex set of ways, financial markets and institutions began to reframe themselves as scientific practices, expanding the realms of financial science and the claims those sciences made to understand and render predictable financial behaviours and trends. Partly, this required that financial exchanges and institutions began to separate themselves—in law and in culture—from those practices that tainted their claims to scientific legitimacy. Most important, financial interests throughout the late nineteenth and twentieth centuries worked hard to distinguish themselves from gambling (See de Goede 2003, 2005). This "rationalization" of finance also entailed its deepening connection with "objective" forms of expertise; not only the rise of accountants and auditors but a whole range of specialized experts who would study the financial world (including a whole new field of financial economics) and develop complex techniques to manage that world (financial analysis, portfolio assessment). By the middle of the twentieth century the world of finance was no longer associated with the corruption or irrationality of Wall Street and its "operators" and "panics" but with the rather buttoned-down world of financial analysis, risk assessment, and asset management.

Reframing finance as a science, as opposed to a dubious and uncertain pursuit, has greatly enhanced the power and prestige of the financial world. This is not to suggest that the financial world is immune to political questions. The very serious political fallout from the 2008 financial crisis attests to the ways in which financial institutions and markets remain the target of serious political pressures. This is to suggest, however, that those political pressures have to now contend with a widespread way of thinking about finance as a scientific endeavour: insulated within its own highly technical language and ostensibly governed by objective scientific laws. As critics have noted, this association with science has been powerful because it has largely inoculated the financial sector from forms of critical scrutiny or forms of accountability (Porter 2005; Sinclair 2009). In some important ways the power associated with finance as a science is very potent, shaping the behaviour of financial markets, and the ways in which we relate to them (Riles 2011). Donald Mackenzie, for example, has examined the role of financial economics in powerfully shaping derivatives markets—a special set of financial markets increasingly central to the global trade in foreign exchange—and the broader impact those markets have. For Mackenzie, the pricing models economists have developed for these markets do not merely explain behaviour in these markets but, because they have become important for all actors in the markets, actually shape that behaviour directly. Over time, the behaviour of markets has actually come into alignment with the "predictions" the market generated in the first place (Mackenzie 2006).

To address this move to finance as a "normal science," a range of critical scholars over the past ten years have developed a new field of analysis designed to assess and disrupt the scientific discourse of finance—the social studies of finance. The social studies of finance draw heavily on a longer tradition of social studies of science and technology that situate all varieties of scientific knowledge in their social and historical conditions of existence. Among many other things, this has entailed focused attention to the very technologies with which financial markets operate and the knowledges that shape those technologies, including the networks of information and communication devices that actually link financial markets; mechanisms, like the price ticker, that display and standardize financial information; accounting devices that format financial knowledge; the basic infrastructure of global payments processes; as well as the "conceptual technologies"—the models, the pricing formulae, asset management approaches—with which actors orient themselves to financial markets (Knorr-Cetina and Bruegger 2002). In focusing on the very concrete technologies associated with finance, this approach offers a certain kind of *materiality*, not focused on the social forces that govern economic relations, but on the actual concrete practices that make financial markets work. As Mackenzie has noted, for the social studies of finance the "properties of artefacts, technological systems, conceptual tools, and so on are not 'details' that sociological analyses should set aside" (Mackenzie 2009, 2–3) but paying attention to the ways in which finance is treated as a science, and the technologies that make that treatment possible in all of its details, is critical to understanding, and potentially disturbing, the power invested in technical experts. This approach, a kind of ultimate expression of post-positivism, of a skepticism toward the universal claims of objective knowledge, turns the critical gaze on science itself and to the practices that render science such an important place in the ways in which our economic lives are governed.

Conclusion and Summary

"I would like my books to be a kind of tool-box which others can rummage through to find a tool which they can use however they wish in their own area . . . I write for users, not readers."

Michel Foucault (1974, 523–4)

In this chapter, I have delineated some of what is at stake in recent challenges to the mainstream of IPE. Although many theoretical challengers are united around a commitment to post-positivism (a rejection of certain and objective scientific knowledge), they are divided around what that commitment might mean. Two broad but distinctive approaches to post-positivism now characterize much of the work done at the margins of IPE. One of these is directly indebted to the work of Robert Cox, his particular way of understanding Gramsci, and his emphasis on a materialist conception of power. For Cox, power is directly related to those who exercise decisive authority over economic resources and the interests of dominant economic actors. This contrasts with discursive approaches to power that focus not on the relationship between power and material interests but on the relationship between power and knowledge. Whereas Cox's materialism asks questions about which social forces exercise power in the global political economy, discursive approaches open questions related to the knowledge that frames how we understand the global political economy in the first place— less about "who" exercises power than "how" knowledge about the global economy is assembled and how that knowledge opens up or closes down political possibilities. Although both are deeply skeptical about the possibility of objective knowledge, they remain wedded to quite distinct views about what power is, and about what our role as critics might be.

Despite these important distinctions, I do not want to imply that we are necessarily presented with an "either/or" choice between either materialist or discursive notions of power. Although it will be important for you to think carefully about which of these approaches appeals more to you, and for what reasons, you might also want to consider the merit of these approaches in a more situational manner, that is, the ways in which the commitments of each theory might be useful in particular contexts to help you address or understand particular processes or issues in the global political economy. This might mean, for example, treating these theories not as completed or general theories, but as clusters of concepts or "devices" that can be useful to gain analytical purchase in particular contexts. Each theory has developed a rich set of concepts. Although it is important to know the broader theoretical framework from which these concepts come, there is also some use in thinking about the concepts in a more discrete manner, as devices that might help advance our understanding of particular kinds of issues in particular kinds of contexts; not as generalized answers, but as devices that might provoke novel lines of analysis. This invites questions about the particular intersection between the topics that interest you and the concepts that various traditions of post-positivism help make clear: is there a particular concept that helps you make sense of some particular issue in the global political economy? How do specific concepts open new "lines of sight", new ways of seeing the ways in which power operates in the global political economy? What concept gives you the most useful way of understanding the particular issues in the global political economy that interest you? Foucault famously implored that his concepts not be treated as finished products that only needed to be "applied" in some pristine way, but rather, as "tools" from a broader tool box that might help address particular problems or assist, in whatever minor or significant manner, in unlocking unique and useful ways of understanding particular analytical problems. In this way, you might develop your relationship to the kinds of post-positivist theories outlined in this chapter not by accepting or rejecting the broad outlines of each theory (or by making some pure choice between the two), but by "working with" the concepts each theory provides and assessing the kinds of insights they make possible for you in relation to particular topics or issues.

In some ways this is an invitation to adopt a certain sense of experimentation. Foucault's insistence that we treat his work as "tools" is an invitation to pick them up, see how they work, and experiment with them in all kinds of settings. Unlike the kind of parsimonious science pursued by positivist approaches, post-positivism does not demand experiments marked by laboratory perfection or an immaculate application of existing methods. Rather, it invites us to critically work with theories in the ways that make sense to us in relation to particular contexts and to adjust those concepts in terms of the "real world" problems we are addressing. This entails a slightly different meaning of "experiment" not as rigorously applying scientific method but as an attitude of open creativity—a willingness to "play" with concepts in an innovative fashion. After all, post-positivist approaches have always been more of a *practice* than merely a way of thinking about the world. As you assess the usefulness of post-positivism, and of the challenges it poses to mainstream theories in IPE, you should understand it as a body of ideas best evaluated "in practice." This requires, as Foucault puts it, to think of yourself not merely as a "reader" but also as a "user" of theories designed to assess—and ultimately challenge—the politics of the global economy.

Notes

1 Neo-Marxist scholars have often subsumed this history of the Keynesian national economy within a broader shift in the social forces that governed the global political economy of the interwar and postwar period. Deeply marked by global economic and geopolitical crisis, this period witnessed a basic transformation of the hegemonic bloc that exercised decisive control over the global political economy. What emerged was an American-centred bloc organized around an emerging consensus of "embedded liberalism"—a coalition of productive capital, some elements of organized labour and state planners committed to both limited forms of domestic intervention, and cautious global economic openness. (Cox 1997; Ruggie 1982)

2 One key concept Foucault used to turn critical gaze onto science itself is the notion of "subjugated knowledges." In order for any body of knowledge to make the transition to science, it must first purge itself of any association that might taint its claims to objectivity, parsimony, or scientific rationality. This entails purging what Foucault referred to as "subjugated knowledges," the parts of any practice or body of knowledge that do not conform to the model of science and instrumental knowledge. Subjugated knowledges, he notes, are "the historical contents that have been long buried and disguised in . . . formal systemisation . . . blocs of historical knowledge which were present but disguised" (Foucault 1980, 81). In order for any practice—psychiatry, medicine, economics—to achieve the status of science, its associations with those "blocs of knowledge" that are non-scientific, politically illegitimate, or "irrational" must first be buried.

Key Terms

discourse
hegemony

post-positivism

Questions for Review

1. What are the basic claims of "post-positivism"? How does it challenge mainstream or "scientific" views of IPE?

2. What are the two main types of post-positivist approaches in IPE? What commitments do they share? In what important ways do they differ?

3.   What do we mean by discourse? What kinds of issues are raised by an attention to discourse in IPE?

4.   How do politics and "theory" interact? Is it possible or desirable to be "objective" when thinking about or understanding the global political economy?

Further Resources

Cox, R. W. (1983). "Gramsci, hegemony and international relations: An essay in method." *Millennium 12*(2): 162–75.

Goede, M. de. (2003). "Beyond economism in international political economy." *Review of International Studies 29*: 79–97.

Mackenzie, D. (2009). *Material markets: How economic agents are constructed*. Oxford: Oxford University Press.

Miliken, J. (1999). "The study of discourse in international relations: a critique of research and methods." *European Journal of International Relations 5*(2): 225–54.

Mitchell, T. (1998). "Fixing the economy." *Cultural Studies 12*(1): 82–101.

References

Aitken, R. (2006). "'The vital force': Visuality and the national economy." *Journal for Cultural Research 10*(2): 87–112.

Best, J. (2005). *The limits of transparency: Ambiguity and the history of international finance*. Ithaca: Cornell University Press.

Bieler, A. (2012). "Workers of the world unite?: Globalization and the quest for transnational solidarity." *Globalizations 9*(3): 365–78.

Blyth, M. (2002). *Great transformations: Economic ideas and institutional change in the twentieth century*. Cambridge: Cambridge University Press.

Brodie, J. (2009). "From social security to public safety: Security discourses and Canadian citizenship." *University of Toronto Quarterly 78*(3): 687–708

Cox, R. W. (1981). "Social forces, states and world orders: Beyond international relations theory." *Millennium: Journal of International Studies 10*(2): 126–55.

———. (1987). *Production, power and world Order: social forces in the making of history*. New York: Columbia University Press.

de Goede, M. (2005). *Virtue, fortune and faith: A Genealogy of finance*. Minneapolis: University of Minnesota Press.

———. (2003). "Beyond economism in international political economy." *Review of International Studies 29*(2): 79–97.

du Gay, P. (1996). *Consumption and identity at work*. London: Sage.

Foucault, M. (1974). *Dits et ecrits*. Vol. II. Paris: Gallimard.

———. (2008). *The birth of biopolitics: Lectures at the College De France, 1978–79*. Michel Senellart (Ed.). London: Palgrave Macmillan.

Gill, S. (1992). *American hegemony and the trilateral commission*. Cambridge: Cambridge University Press.

———. (2003). *Power and resistance in the new world order*. New York: Palgrave Macmillan.

Gills, B. And K. Gray. (2012). "People power in the era of global crisis: Rebellion, resistance and liberation." *Third World Quarterly 33*(2): 205–24.

Hacking, I. (2000). *The social construction of what?* Cambridge: Cambridge University Press.

Harmes, A. (2001). "Mass investment culture." *New Left Review 9*: 103–24.

Keynes, J.M. (1933). "National Self-sufficiency." *Yale Review*.

———. (1936). *The general theory of employment, interest and money*. London: Palgrave Macmillan.

Knorr-Cetina, K. and U. Bruegger. (2002). "Global Microstructures: The Virtual Societies of Financial Markets," *American Journal of Sociology 107*(4): 905–50.

Linklater, A. (2007). *Critical theory and world politics: Citizenship, sovereignty and humanity*. London: Routledge.

List F. (1856). *National system of political economy*, translated from the German text by G.A. Matile. Philadelphia: J.B. Lippincott.

Mackenzie, D. (2006). *An Engine, not a camera: How financial models shape markets*. Cambridge: MIT Press.

Mackenzie. D. (2009). *Material markets: How economic agents are constructed*. Oxford: Oxford University Press.

Mirowski, P. (1989). *More heat than light: Economics as social physics, physics as nature's economics*. Cambridge: Cambridge University Press.

Mitchell, T. (2002). *Rule of experts*. Berkeley: University of California Press.

Morton, A. D. (2011). *Revolution and state in modern Mexico: The political economy of uneven development*. Boulder: Rowman and Littlefield.

Neufeld, M. (1995). *The restructuring of international relations theory*. Cambridge: Cambridge University Press.

Peterson, V. S. (2013). "How is the world organized economically?" *Global Politics: A New Introduction*. Eds J. Edkins and M. Zehfuss. London: Routledge.

Porter, T. (2005). *Globalization and finance*. Cambridge: Polity Press.

Riles A. (2011). *Collateral knowledge: Legal reasoning in the global financial markets*. Chicago: University of Chicago Press.

Robinson, W. (2008). *A theory of global capitalism: Production, class and state in a transnational world*. Baltimore: Hopkins Fulfillment Service.

Rupert, M. (1995). *Producing Hegemony: The Politics of Mass Production and American global power*. Cambridge: Cambridge University Press.

Sinclair, T. (2009). "Let's Get it Right this Time: Why regulation will not solve or prevent global financial crises." *International Political Sociology 3*(4): 450–3.

Thaddeus-Jackson, P. (2010). *The conduct of inquiry in international relations: Philosophy of science and its implications for the study of world Politics*. London: Routledge.

Van der Pijl, K. (1998). *Transnational classes and international relations*. London: Routledge.

4 Gender, Feminism, and the Global Political Economy

Siobhan Byrne

Introduction

From the 2007–08 global financial crisis to the politics of big bank bailouts by governments; from the collapse of local housing markets and rising unemployment to mass protest camps in New York, Toronto, Madrid, London, and beyond; from the eruption of the 2010 Arab Spring revolutions in the Middle East and contagious local uprisings against corruption and abuses of power to the ouster of a handful of despots. These are the kinds of local, national, and global political events that animate research and practice in the International Political Economy/International Relations (IPE/IR) field of study.

The field is characterized by new academic journals and a growing number of research specializations, with an appetite for integrating literatures and theoretical frameworks that reflect diverse perspectives and disciplines, including feminist theory, critical literary theory, and international law.[1] As the story is conventionally told in textbooks and classrooms, IPE/IR has transformed over the last two decades, moving away from a preoccupation with theories like neorealism and neoliberal institutionalism and a core interest in inter-state relations.

Of course, IPE/IR was never really such a narrow field where, once upon a time, scholars agreed on a limited range of theories and issues.[2] Nevertheless, common accounts of the field date a radical opening up of scholarship to the mid to late 1980s. It is during this period that a critical turn in theory and practice emerges, including a uniquely feminist perspective on global politics.

The focus of this chapter is on the conceptual and analytical contributions of feminist and gendered approaches to the study of global politics. It identifies how scholars, activists, and practitioners *take women and gender seriously* in research and practice. Key concepts, including **gender** and "intersectionality" are introduced, as well as feminist methodologies for research and feminist insights on traditional research concerns, including power and transformation in the global political economy. The chapter concludes by applying feminist and gendered insights to the case of the 2007–08 global financial crisis and the popular anti-austerity Occupy demonstrations that swept across North America.

A few notes about the content and organization of the chapter: the intent is not to rehearse the story of feminism as an approach that sits on the margins of mainstream theorizing; this is a story of exclusion that textbooks and scholars have covered well in other places. And while it is true that feminist and gender approaches are inconsistently incorporated into the field, it is also the case that scholars have developed a rich body of political thought and analysis that has had important impacts on theory and practice in the field. Thus, this chapter does not construct feminist thinking as a critique of mainstream theory only, but emphasizes the contribution of feminist scholarship to our understanding of global politics. Further, this chapter is not organized around a list of archetypal feminist theoretical frameworks, commonly grouped under radical, liberal, and socialist perspectives or other similar typologies. Again, this is well-covered terrain that does not always capture shared feminist insights. Where appropriate, however, the chapter identifies the influence of theoretical traditions on key concepts or analyses.

The purpose of this chapter is not to fix a single feminist theory or to map a single way to study gender. Rather, it is to define and demonstrate the value of alternative categories of analysis and different methods of research used by feminist and gender theorists for understanding the global political economy.

Engendering The Field: The Emergence Of Feminist Thinking In IPE/IR

A Note on Terminology

Before outlining the development of feminist and gender thinking in the field, it is important to say a few words about just what to call this amorphous field of study. Scholars sometimes refer to the *International Political Economy (IPE)* or *Global Political Economy* (GPE) subfields of international relations (IR). This characterization serves to highlight the trajectory of economic analyses as an offshoot of IR scholarship. Some feminist scholars prefer the term "global political economy" to "international political economy," thereby highlighting a preference for including non-state actors that operate within, as part of, or beyond the state and a commitment to working at all levels of analysis.[3] This preference for the term "global" over "international" is not unique to feminist scholarship—some mainstream scholars similarly argue that "global" more accurately describes the kinds of actors central to this field of study.[4]

Still other scholars blur the distinction between IPE and IR. A "slash" punctuation mark between the two terms— IPE/IR (or IR/IPE)—commonly signifies an intrinsic relationship between political and economic forces. This is true for feminist theorists who do not describe their work as either political economy or international relations; rather, such theorists understand the global political economy and global politics as inextricably linked.

This chapter uses IPE/IR to refer to the academic field of study, following a conventional way to emphasize the relationship between the study of global economics and politics, but uses "global political economy" to refer to the subject of study to emphasize the diversity of actors and localities studied in the scholarship.

The Emergence of Feminist and Gender Analysis in the Field

Feminist IPE/IR approaches entered the field in the 1980s alongside other critical post-positivist theories such as neo-Gramscianism/historical materialism, post-structuralism, versions of critical constructivism, and post-colonialism. Feminist IPE/IR theorists reject an artificial separation of politics and eco-nomics. They also call into question the "who" of IPE/IR—bringing in *new actors* beyond states, like individuals, grassroots groups, regional bodies, and transnational movements. They refuse a strict separation of the "*high politics*" of the state and global finance, which is characterized as part of the public sphere, from the "*low politics*" of people's everyday lives, which tends to be relegated to the private sphere and therefore invisible in orthodox political analyses. Further, they challenge concepts central to the field like power, security, and violence.[5]

Conventionally, scholars link the introduction of feminist thinking to the publication of a special edition of the academic journal *Millennium: Jour-nal of International Studies* in 1988. In this issue contributors consider the role of women in inter-national politics, offer feminist critiques of core IR/IPE theories, analyze the war/peace problema-tique, and work through feminism and women in development themes. This issue developed out of a symposium held at the London School of Econom-ics and was later produced as an edited book.[6]

There was a sense among some critical schol-ars that IPE, sometimes characterized as a distinct critical branch of a conservative IR discipline, could be a more hospitable home for feminist theorizing and gender analysis than IR.[7] They link the emergence of political economy approaches in the 1970s to the adoption of interdisciplinary thinking in the field, a concern with issues of global economic inequality and class relations and there-fore an openness to critical theoretical approaches and a commitment to transform unequal power relations. Feminist theorizing in IPE/IR is viewed as part of an overall theoretical pluralizing of the field. Today, however, some scholars are concerned that such pluralism is in decline due to a field seem-ingly preoccupied with the issues and concerns of industrialized states and capitalism and focused on quantitative research methods.[8]

Commentators point out that there is still a clear dominance of orthodox approaches in IPE, including neoliberalism and neorealism, which can marginalize feminist questions.[9] Attempts to engage mainstream theory in IPE/IR have been a central aim of feminist scholarship from the outset. Consider, for example, the now canonical exchange between feminist theorist J. Ann Tickner and mainstream neoliberal institutional theorist Robert O. Keohane. In a 1997 article titled "You Just Don't Understand: Troubled Engagements between Feminists and IR Theorists," Tickner chal-lenges orthodox approaches to consider the value of alternative feminist epistemologies and method-ologies. Here, she outlines the value of understand-ing global politics from a bottom-up perspective, which begins with disempowered individuals and communities, as opposed to a top-down perspec-tive, which begins with a focus on the state and the structure of the international system.[10]

Central to her argument is the view that con-ventional theories in the field depend on research methods borrowed from the natural sciences, like statistical data testing, that value "objectivity" or impartiality. For feminist scholars, such an under-standing of objectivity is impossible to achieve in the social world; researchers' own perspectives, social locations and identities necessarily affect their research. Accounting for this in one's own research—known as "strong objectivity"—can pro-duce better knowledge about the social world.[11] Keohane responded in his 1998 article *Beyond Dichotomy: Conversations between International Relations and Feminist Theory*, arguing that the "scientific method, in the broadest sense, is the best path toward convincing current nonbelievers of the validity of the message that feminist are seek-ing to deliver."[12] For feminists, such a view of research rarely captures the richness of people's lived experiences.

Feminist theorists followed up Tickner's "You Just Don't Understand" article with responses like Georgina Waylen's 2006 article "You Still Don't Understand," Marysia Zalewski's 2007 article "Do We Understand Each Other Yet?," and Tickner's 2010 article, which seems to offer the final word on the problem: "You May Never Understand."[13] The project to encourage theoretical engagement between mainstream and feminist theories continues, albeit with a tone of exasperation rather than optimism that anyone is listening.

Other scholars point out how critical approaches also exclude feminist insights and gender analyses. Such work tends to focus on categories like class to explain inequality, ignoring other identities and social locations like gender and race, and failing to account for politics in the private sphere.[14]

While women and gender analysis may still be marginal in the field—both in terms of mainstream and critical theory—feminist IPE/IR thinking has also expanded since its emergence in the field, with the introduction of critical texts, new research, special conferences, influential journals like *International Feminist Journal of Politics* and *Politics & Gender*, and edited volumes that enrich the field and our understanding of the global political economy.[15] The next section reviews some of the core concepts that are important to feminist and gender analyses.

Taking Women and Gender Seriously in Theory and Practice: Key Concepts

Feminist and gender IPE/IR scholars sometimes speak in terms of "taking women seriously" or "taking gender seriously" in global politics.[16] What does this entail, both in theory and practice? Certainly, feminist scholars agree that gender matters to the study of the global political economy, sometimes empirically, in terms of studying the lives of men and women, and sometimes analytically, in terms of studying masculinities and femininities. They do not agree, however, on just *how* gender should be studied.[17] This section considers some fundamental concepts and approaches for integrating a feminist and gender perspective.

What is Sex, What is Gender?

Sex and gender are conventionally differentiated along biological/physiological and socially constructed lines. The term **sex** typically refers to anatomical, hormonal, and/or chromosomal differences between male and female bodies. The term **gender** typically refers to socially constructed differences between boys and girls, men and women, which are acquired after birth. Gender differences might include cultural preferences and expectations that emphasize stereotypically masculine or feminine traits.

It is important to note that gender differences do not simply catalogue equal but different preferences and expectations; they also refer to a hierarchical *gender order* where masculinity is valued over femininity.[18] The valuing of masculinity over femininity has implications for women and men, and boys and girls, but also for gender discourses in IPE/IR. In the first sense of the term, a hierarchical gender order is sometimes understood as a patriarchal social order, which literally means rule by the father or rule by men. In such an order, men and boys who are thought to embody ideals of manhood, which in some societies might include traits like heterosexuality, rationality, objectivity, and physical strength, receive social and political privileges and power. R.W. Connell refers to such impossible ideals of manhood as "hegemonic masculinity" or the "most honoured way of being a man." While most people fail to live up to such an exceptional ideal of manhood, it nevertheless produces particular expectations of men, while also legitimating the subordination of women.[19]

A gender order also produces particular expectations of women. Whereas men are expected to be rational and physically strong, women are expected to be irrational or emotional and weak or delicate. These traits are not, however, similarly valued in society or in global politics. Rather, they are considered to be the stuff of low politics and relegated to the private spheres of family and community. When boys or men, girls or women fail to live up to or otherwise challenge orthodox masculine and feminine conventions, they may be thought to be transgressive and anomalous and cast as outsiders.

This hierarchical gender order also has implications for gender discourses and gender ideologies in global politics, beyond sexed bodies. For example, Carol Cohn conducted an early study of language used by US defence intellectuals in the 1980s during the Cold War. Cohn found that the use of sexual imagery such as "vertical erector launchers," "thrust-to-weight ratios," and "deep penetration" in everyday discussions about military capability among defence specialists served to minimize the violence and destructiveness of war—viewed as nothing more than "an act of boyish mischief"—while at the same time suggesting that military ventures are about manhood and masculine competition.[20] Such discourses and ideologies make some geopolitical actions, like military arms races or economic exploitation of foreign states, permissible.

Feminist scholars talk about "taking gender seriously," which entails studying not just women and femininities but also men and masculinities.[21] Understanding—and dismantling—the hierarchical gender order requires that we study the construction of both sides of the dyad in global politics.

Gender: Empirical vs. Analytical Category

Feminist scholars further distinguish between the use of gender as an **empirical category** and gender as an **analytical category**. Gender analysts that enumerate or otherwise aggregate data based on *quantitative* differences between women and men understand gender as an empirical category. Researchers may measure gender differences in areas like political representation, education, or the labour force. Global development agencies like the World Bank also gather data in the global South related to female mortality, literacy, and participation in the workforce with an eye to closing gender gaps and improving development outcomes.[22] Understanding gender as an empirical category is really about asking the question famously posed by Cynthia Enloe over 20 years ago: "Where are the women in international relations?"[23]

Locating women in global politics, however, is only one form of feminist theorizing.[24] Other scholars critique quantitative research as an "add women and stir" approach to analysis.[25] According to V. Spike Peterson, gender is more than just an empirical category that refers to male and female bodies; it is an analytical category that references hierarchical constructions of valorized masculinity and devalorized femininity.[26] Accordingly, some critical feminist scholars prefer *qualitative research* practices, which use research methods such as interviewing women and other marginalized actors who operate below the state level of analysis, participant observation methods, and in-depth case studies. Such methods allow feminist researchers to build the kind of knowledge that can be used to transform unequal social relations.[27]

The debate between quantitative and qualitative research in feminist IPE/IR continues to play out in key IPE/IR texts. This is perhaps a false dichotomy as scholars routinely choose research methods along one or both of these methodologies to respond to a particular research question or problem. One form of research is no more or less feminist as both methodologies are employed to further basic feminist research and goals.

Feminist vs. Gender Analyses

This discussion of gender as an empirical category and gender as an analytical category is closely related to debates about the differences between a **feminist analysis** and a **gender analysis** in IPE/IR. All feminist theorists take gender differences seriously in their analysis of global politics. However, not all theorists who study gender identify their research as *feminist*.

Charli Carpenter, for example, argues that gender can operate as an explanatory framework in the field, divorced from particular feminist commitments, such as women's empowerment. Separating gender from a feminist commitment to transform unequal gender hierarchies could make "gender analysis" more palatable to mainstream theorists who are resistant to "feminism." Further, understanding gender can help us better explain important research topics in IPE/IR, such as armed conflict. Such research does not have to take the second step to push to transform gender hierarchies or advocate for women's empowerment in conflict zones.[28]

While some scholars define studies that investigate gender from a quantitative methodological perspective as non-feminist,[29] others find the very idea of "non-feminist gender studies" to be an oxymoron.[30] And certainly scholars like Mary Caprioli use quantitative research methods to study gender but nevertheless insist that such research is "feminist" because the results can transform inequalities between men and women.[31]

For feminist scholars, the purpose of inquiry is not just to *explain* the world but to *change* unequal relations of power in theory and practice.[32] Value-free research, where scholars attempt to separate the fact of how global politics *are* from the value of how they *ought to be*, is undesirable and perhaps impossible. In this sense, whether gender or feminist, or whether realist, neo-Gramscian, neoliberal institutionalist, or the like—all theory is normative. As Zalewski explains: "[T]he notion that feminism is political and IR is not is unsustainable and, therefore, cannot act as a basis on which to bestow favor on one (that is, IR) at the expense of the other (that is, feminism)."[33]

Accordingly, "non-feminist," quantitative, or orthodox theories of IPE/IR, in an attempt to explain the world, do in fact serve to rationalize existing power relations. In this way, they are also *normative* and *political* theories.

Intersectional Thinking in IPE/IR

Feminists have also pointed out the limits of using "gender" as a single analytical category of analysis, embracing instead what is commonly termed "intersectional thinking" or *intersectionality*. The term intersectionality was coined by Kimberle Crenshaw in the late 1980s as a way to signal the "intersecting" oppression of not just gender, but other social categories of difference such as race, sexuality, and class.

Feminist IPE/IR scholars recognize that the impacts of larger global processes, such as the opening up of state borders, the increasing movement of people and goods, and other patterns of globalization and global restructuring, are not equally shared among all people. Economic austerity and high unemployment push some people across borders in search of employment and skills upgrading opportunities. Such migration patterns are deeply gendered and raced, opening up differential opportunities and imposing unequal constraints on some men and some women. An intersectional framework can help us understand such global processes.

Consider the particular experiences of migrant workers. In Canada, thousands of temporary foreign workers arrive from overseas in search of jobs through government programs like the Canadian Seasonal Agricultural Workers Program and the Live-in Caregiver Program. The Canadian government estimates that by the end of 2013, 386,406 temporary foreign workers would be working in Canada, more than double the number of temporary foreign workers in 2006;[34] a majority of these workers are men.[35] Often these workers send financial "remittances" or deductions from their pay home to help their families and children. In fact, no country sends more remittances home per capita than Canada's immigrant population—an estimated $23.4 billion a year.[36]

Workers' rights organizations like *Justicia for Migrant Workers* (J4MW) and the *Migrant Workers Alliance for Change* point out that temporary foreign workers, such as labourers who come to Canada from Mexico and selected Caribbean states as part of the Canada Seasonal Agricultural Workers Program, are particularly vulnerable because they are typically ineligible to collect the Employment Insurance benefits they pay into due to unfair qualifying work hour requirements; they face governmental hurdles that prevent them from applying for citizenship in Canada, regardless of the number of years they may have travelled to Canada to work; and sometimes they live in hazardous, dirty, and overcrowded housing conditions.[37] In the summer of 2014, the federal government began overhauling the program; it is not yet clear what impact new and proposed policy changes will have on workers and the program.

The effects of the international division of labour are apparent in the global South too. The tragic death of over 1,100 garment workers in the collapse of Rana Plaza textile factory in Bangladesh in April 2013 brought global economic inequality into stark relief. Making clothes for companies like Canadian grocer-retailer Loblaw's Joe Fresh brand,

survivors reported working 12-hour shifts, seven days a week.[38] According to the International Labour Organization, women make up 80 per cent of workers in the garment industry, versus just 36 per cent of the entire labour force in Bangladesh.[39]

In these examples, we see how the global political economy differentially affects people. Thinking intersectionally, feminist scholars tell us to pay attention to the international gendered division of labour in our evaluation of global markets and international politics.

Feminist and Gender Reflections on Power

No concept is more central to the study of global politics than "power." The IPE/IR field tends to focus on the rise and decline of hegemons and other great powers in the global realm. For mainstream theories like neorealism and neoliberal institutionalism, power is a measure of the absolute economic wealth and military capabilities of an individual state and, in particular, the relative distribution of wealth and capabilities among states. Some versions of neorealism, but especially constructivist theories, also include a state's perceived prestige or legitimacy to act in the international realm to such definitions of power.[40]

Critical neo-Gramscian accounts of power look beyond the material capabilities of states and consider the role of ideas and institutions in constituting power.[41] In today's global political economy, ideas—such as free trade, open borders, and the deregulation of financial markets, and institutions like the World Trade Organization and the World Bank—work in concert with American economic and military interests to help consolidate a US hegemonic world order. Power also refers to counterhegemonic forces, which today might include participants in mass movements like the Occupy Wall Street protests discussed below, to challenge such ideas and institutions.[42]

Critical feminist scholars are similarly interested in challenging inequality and argue that power is also gendered and hierarchically organized, typically wielded by male leaders and defined in masculine terms as the expression of the rational self-interest of states that pursue dominance in global politics. Post-colonial feminist scholars Geeta Chowdhry and Sheila Nair note that focusing exclusively on powerful states leaves out the experiences of non-western and non-white peoples, thereby reproducing the power hierarchies in the international system that keeps the global South out of view.[43]

Feminist scholars also consider relations of power beyond the state. As Enloe explains: "in most formal analyses of international politics, what strikes me is how far their authors are willing to go in *under*estimating the amounts and varieties of power it takes to form and sustain any given set of relationships between states."[44] Feminists are curious about the complex ways in which hierarchies of "power"—from the international, national, and local levels of analysis—keep some people at the margins of global politics and invisible in our analyses.[45]

Like the neo-Gramscians described above, feminist scholars understand power as the *empowerment* of individuals, communities, and transnational actors. This is distinct from the neorealist/neoliberal understanding of power as domination.[46] Thinking about power *as empowerment*, however, can be tricky. A feminist analysis also asks who is empowered to speak for women and other groups and how empowerment discourses can be co-opted to serve the interests of hegemonic powers.[47]

Feminist thinking and gender analyses take social locations and identities like race and class seriously. Such thinking helps us understand how some political and economic events and crises happen, how they are experienced by people within and across state borders, and how they may be challenged or transformed in the global political realm.

Gender and the Global Financial Crisis

The 2007–08 global financial crisis (GFC) was precipitated by the collapse of the US subprime mortgage market and the subsequent bankruptcy of Lehman Brothers investment bank in the US alongside the collapse of other major financial institutions in 2008. Rocking financial markets and institutions around the world due to the global integration of markets and trade, the crisis was described by economists as second only to the Great Depression.[48] It provides an excellent backdrop to illustrate how we can take women and gender seriously in IPE/IR.

Perhaps surprisingly, IPE/IR scholars have been slow to analyze the GFC, despite the importance and impact of the crisis.[49] Those mainstream scholars who have studied or commented on it have tended to do so by reflecting on macro political-economic processes, actors, and consequences. Neoliberal institutionalists have, for example, considered how multilateral institutions like the World Bank, IMF, and WTO, are able to help maintain cooperation and order in the face of a relative decline in US global leadership.[50] Constructivists have focused on actors like the World Bank and IMF too, but also financial fund managers, creditors, economists, and major investors. They are interested in the role "ideas" and practices play, for example, in constructing the global economy.[51]

A feminist and gender lens can help to discern the gendered impacts of the GFC. Further, the gendered stories of mass protest movements can help show the difference a feminist and gender analysis can make to our understanding of such an important global crisis.

Gendered/Intersectional Impact of GFC

In the spirit of Enloe, a feminist IPE/IR scholar might begin by asking: where are the women in the GFC? Save for a few reports,[52] most of the people we hear from in the press, economic analyses, and scholarly treatments since 2007 have been men—those who are in charge of the banks, the financial policies of the states grappling with the crisis, and the most visible members of protest camps. This is characteristic of a gender order where men hold positions of authority at the levels of global affairs, the state, and local communities, including activist circles.

While we are only beginning to learn about the impacts of the GFC on ordinary people, we know from new research and past studies that women and men, girls and boys, experience economic recessions differently. These experiences are further affected by whether one lives in the so-called global North, where the major financial houses and wealthy states are located, or the global South, where inexpensive labour and emerging markets for manufacturing goods are.

For example, in the global North, men dominate the high finance jobs that were hit first with lay-offs as banks and other financial institutions began to fail. This meant that in places with a concentration of financial institutions, like the US, the economic recession left many more men unemployed than women.[53] The converse has been true in those European states that are still reeling from the crisis. For example, in Greece, the country with the highest unemployment rate in the European Union, female unemployment stood at 31.1 per cent as of July 2013, compared with 25 per cent male unemployment.[54]

Temporary foreign workers, like the people working in Canada's agricultural sector described earlier in the chapter and those workers in the hard-hit construction industry, also find that the economic crisis impacts employment opportunities. People have less money to spend and construction on new houses and infrastructure slows down. Without employment, the ability of workers to send financial remittances home to their families in some instances is affected. According to the UNDP (United Nations Development Programme), for example, remittances in Latin American and Caribbean countries declined by 12 percent between 2008–09.[55]

In the global South, economic crises can create job opportunities for women in informal employment sectors like the garment industry but also reduce opportunities in industries like manufacturing. For example, a World Bank study finds that in low-income households, women entered the labour force in higher numbers during financial crises like the Latin American debt crises of the 1980s and late 1990s and the 1997 East Asian crisis. However, women tend to have lower levels of education and therefore earn less money.[56] Post-crisis job growth for women will likely be in the unskilled and informal employment sector.[57]

A feminist and intersectional framework helps us to see the gendered and racialized impacts of the GFC. In the example above, such an analysis considers the GFC from the perspective of women and men working in the financial sector in the countries like the US, manufacturing and garment sector workers in countries like Bangladesh, temporary migrant workers in construction and other industries across Canada, and large numbers of unemployed workers in Greece and other European states. From each of these vantage points we learn about the unequal global and local distribution of wealth and the differential burdens people and communities shoulder. A "gender-neutral" lens that focuses only on the most powerful states misses such differential impacts, offering an incomplete analysis of events like the GFC.

Occupy Movement

Beyond the gendered impacts of the GFC on the global political economy and on the everyday lives of women and men is the question of how people have responded to the crisis in sometimes gendered ways. Through local, national, and transnationally organized public demonstrations, activist networks and protest movements, individuals and communities have worked to challenge the economic impacts and articulate an alternative and democratic vision for national and global economic policies. While also overlooked in the mainstream IPE/IR literature, these movements demonstrate how global issues get taken up at local levels and how local political engagement works to transform global inequalities. Paying attention to politics at the local level of analysis is an approach to which feminist IPE/IR scholars are well attuned.

In response to the GFC, protestors across Europe banded together to demand economic equality and social justice for those people hardest hit by the crisis. Notably, hundreds of thousands of protestors marched under the banner "Geração à Rasca," or "Precious Generation," in Portugal in 2011, inspiring activists in Spain, who organized mass protest camps in city squares like Madrid's Puerto Del Sol. When a small group of activists attempted to "occupy Wall Street," taking over New York City's Zuccotti Park on 17 September 2011, the North American-based "Occupy Wall Street Movement" was born.

Broadly, the movement was critical of global capitalism and the concentration of wealth in the hands of 1 per cent of the population. Critical scholars celebrated the democratic vision of the movement. For example, Immanuel Wallerstein describes Occupy as "the most important political happening in the United States since the uprisings in 1968."[58] S.A. Hamed Hosseini notes that while there were some divisions along race and gender lines among participants, Occupy participants nonetheless worked to negotiate these differences through consciously organized democratic deliberations.[59]

In the encampments at Occupy, but also Spain and other places, Michael Hardt and Antonio Negri similarly applaud the participatory assemblies participants created. They refer to such participation as a "multitude form."[60] Writing about both Occupy and the Arab Spring public protests in Tahrir Square, Egypt, Judith Butler points out how these movements challenge distinctions between the public and private spheres:

> And when crowds move outside the square, to the side street or the back alley, to the neighborhoods where streets are not yet paved, then something more happens. At such a moment, politics is no longer defined as the exclusive business of public sphere distinct from a private one.[61]

Despite the participatory assemblies and occupation of public spaces, however, these were also deeply gendered spaces; women found themselves, in some instances, excluded, targeted, and threatened.

CodePink, a US-based women-led peace group, took an early role in Occupy protests in New York City in the summer and fall of 2011, drawing a connection between their anti-war activism and the economic crisis. Blogging from the protest camps, CodePink organizer Melanie Butler outlined the importance of women's voice at Occupy, noting the disproportionate impact of the financial crisis on women.[62] While women were active participants in Occupy, it was largely men who were interviewed by the media, who spoke up at general assembly meetings, and who represented the movement.[63]

CodePink cofounder Medea Benjamin explains in an interview that she sought to remedy women's exclusion and ran workshops to teach women how to speak up at activist meetings and to the media. Of the workshops Benjamin recalls:

> It was very hard for women to hear themselves echoed in a mic check. Women tend to think that what they have to say is not so important . . . And so we do our own mic check and make people feel like "alright your voice is important, you are saying something important."[64]

Women formed separate spaces in the Occupy camps, which became particularly important as reports of sexual assaults surfaced.[65] Violence against women was making headlines not just in Occupy, but also in Arab Spring demonstrations, such as the mass protests in Tahrir Square. Like Zuccotti Park, people built a mass movement in this public square to demand political change; it was also a space similarly marked by old gender hierarchies and violence against women.

Tens of thousands of protesters made their way to Tahrir Square during the 2011 Egyptian revolution and again in 2013. Demonstrators were successful in their demand for the ouster of Egyptian president Hosni Mubarak and his replacement Mohamed Morsi. In the press, we learned of the sexual assaults of western journalists in Cairo like the 2011 rape of CBC News reporter Lara Logan, the 2012 mob attack of French journalist Sonia Dridi by a group of men, and the 2013 gang rape of a Dutch journalist.[66] According to reports from Human Rights Watch and local Egyptian sources, dozens of Egyptian women, whom we do not tend to hear about in press reports, were also violently assaulted by mobs.[67]

For critical IPE/IR scholars, movements like Occupy represent an important challenge to an unjust global political and economic order. However,

a feminist analysis that takes the experiences of women in Occupy camps and public demonstrations seriously shows just how masculinist, undemocratic, and sometimes dangerous such movements can be. These are important considerations for those scholars and activists who are interested in building a diverse and radical alternative politics, capable of resisting an unjust global order. The dismantlement of gendered hierarchies requires conscious and sustained attention, both within the high politics of global finance and the grassroots politics of activism.

Conclusion

In the late 1980s, new theoretical pluralism brought into view new issues, actors, and locales that were once dismissed as irrelevant to the IPE/IR field. It is within this context of interdisciplinary research that "gender" and feminist IPE/IR perspectives emerged, influencing our understanding of a dynamic and multifaceted geopolitical landscape.

This chapter introduced key feminist analytical concepts and perspectives, highlighting the importance of gender and intersectionality in research. It considered the differences between gender as an empirical category and an analytical category of analysis; what it means to understand gender as hierarchically ordered, privileging men and masculinities over women and femininities in our analyses; it brought other social locations and identities into view, such as race and the repercussions of an unequal global economic order—all with the goal of demonstrating what it means to take gender seriously.

The chapter also addressed "power" in global politics—a central preoccupation of the field. Feminist IPE/IR understandings of power bring into view the political resistance and new possibilities for collective action that develops on the margins of the global political economy.

Throughout this chapter, these concepts and insights were applied to contemporary problems and crises in global politics. In a variety of areas of concern in the global political economy, feminist scholars are demonstrating:

- the differential impacts of political economic forces on men and women, boys and girls;
- the everyday workings of gendered hierarchies in theory and politics, which value men and (some) masculinities and devalue women and femininities;
- the many varieties of power, beyond raw state resources, that it takes to maintain unequal global relations of power; and
- the relationship between campaigns and movements for economic and political equality and the goals of gender equality.

Considering the 2007–08 global financial crisis from the perspective of the people hardest hit by the crisis and by paying attention to public resistance, we come to see how the crisis affected men and women differently in the global North and the global South. Like other critical scholars, feminist scholars take social movements like the Occupy protests against punishing national austerity programs as important articulations of political resistance. As the experiences at Occupy, but also Tahrir Square too, demonstrate, public spaces are deeply gendered. As such, communities must work deliberately and consciously to transform resistant gendered hierarchies.

There is not one kind of feminist or gender IPE/IR approach—differences in categories of analysis, theoretical orientation, research methodology and design, and areas of political concern are evident in the growing body of literature, which has been contributing to the field for more than 25 years. Such diversity and endurance is a sign of the vitality and utility of feminist and gender approaches for understanding—and perhaps transforming—key features of the global political economy.

Notes

1 See: C. Sylvester, "Experiencing the end and afterlives of international relations/theory," 611.

2 See: B. C. Schmidt, "On the history and historiography of international relations."

3 For example, see: V. S. Peterson and A. S. Runyan, *Global gender issues in the new millennium*, 208, note 1.

4 For example, see: R. O. Keohane, "The old IPE and the new," 42.

5 See: G. Youngs, "Feminist international relations: A contradiction in terms?"

6 Grant and Newland (Eds), *Gender and international relations*. Also see the ten-year anniversary special issue and book: Odysseos and Seckinelgin (Eds), *Gendering the international*; "Anniversary special issue: Gendering the international," *Millennium—Journal of International Studies* 27(4) (1998).

7 For example, see: S. Whitworth, "Theory as exclusion: Gender and international political economy," 116–17.

8 See: N. Phillips, "The slow death of pluralism"; K. R. McNamara, "Of intellectual monocultures and the study of IPE."

9 G. Waylen, "You still don't understand: Why troubled engagements continue between feminists and (critical) IPE," 145; P. Griffin, "Refashioning IPE: What and how gender analysis teaches international (global) political economy."

10 J. A. Tickner, "You just don't understand: Troubled engagements between feminists and IR theorists," 628–9.

11 S. G. Harding, *Whose science? Whose knowledge?: Thinking from women's lives*, 142.

12 R. O. Keohane, "Beyond dichotomy: Conversations between international relations and feminist theory," 197.

13 Waylen, "You still don't understand"; M. Zalewski, (2007), "Do we understand each other yet? Troubling feminist encounters with(in) international relations," *The British Journal of Politics & International Relations* 9(2); J. A. Tickner, "You may never understand: Prospects for feminist futures in international relations."

14 S. M. Rai, "Gender and (international) political economy"; Waylen, "You still don't understand."

15 S. V. Peterson, "How (the meaning of) gender matters in political economy," 499.

16 H. Charlesworth, "Are women peaceful? Reflections on the role of women in peace-building," 360; Cynthia Enloe, *Seriously!: Investigating crashes and crises as if women mattered*; V. S. Peterson, "Security and sovereign states: What is at stake in taking feminism seriously."

17 Peterson, "How (the meaning of) gender matters in political economy," 499.

18 See V. S. Peterson's excellent discussion of the effects of a hierarchical gender dichotomy: Peterson, V. S. "Feminist theories within, invisible to, and beyond IR," 35–46.

19 R. W. Connell and J. W. Messerschmidt, "Hegemonic masculinity—Rethinking the concept," 832.

20 C. Cohn, "Sex and death in the rational world of defense intellectuals," 693, 696.

21 Also see: J. Parpart and M. Zalewski, eds, *Rethinking the man question*.

22 "World Bank. World development report 2012: Gender equality and development."

23 C. Enloe, *Bananas, beaches & bases: making feminist sense of international politics*. Also see: V. S. Peterson, "Feminist theories within, invisible to, and beyond IR," 38.

24 Peterson, 39.

25 For example, see: Waylen, "You still don't understand: Why troubled engagements continue between feminists and (critical) IPE," 148. Peterson, "Feminist theories within, invisible to, and beyond IR."

26 Peterson, "Feminist theories within, invisible to, and beyond IR," 39.

27 J. A. Tickner, "Feminism meets international relations: Some methodological issues," 24–30.

28 R. C. Carpenter, "Gender theory in world politics: Contributions of a nonfeminist standpoint?"

29 For example, contributors to the following volume take the view that qualitative research practices are better able to advance feminist IPE/IR goals as opposed to quantitative methods that focus on measuring gender only: B. A. Ackerly, M. Stern and J. True (Eds), *Feminist methodologies for international relations*.

30 T. Carver, "The forum: Gender and international relations. Gender/feminism/IR," 290.

31 M. Caprioli, "Feminist IR theory and quantitative methodology: A critical analysis."

32 Tickner, "Feminism meets international relations: Some methodological issues," 21–2.

33 M. Zalewski, "'Women's troubles' again in IR," 292.

34 Citizenship and Immigration Canada, "Facts and figures 2012—Immigration overview."

35 Ibid.

36 R. Westwood, "Should Canada make it easier for immigrants to send money home?"

37 "Decent housing," Migrant workers alliance for change; "About us," Justicia for Migrant Workers: J4MW. Also see: N. Keung, "Abuse of migrant workers 'endemic' in Canada, new study says"; F. Faraday, "Made in Canada: How the law constructs migrant workers' insecurity."

38 "Bangladesh garment workers' lives still at risk, the Fifth Estate finds," *CBC.ca*.

39 "Bangladesh: Decent work country programme 2012–15."

40 On constructivism, see: C. Reus-Smit, "Constructivism," in *Theories of international relations*. On realism, see: R. Gilpin, *War and change in world politics*.

41 See R. W. Cox, "Social forces, states and world orders: Beyond international relations theory."

42 For example, see: M. Rupert, "Globalising common sense: A Marxian-Gramscian (re)vision of the politics of governance/resistance."

43 G. Chowdhry and S. Nair, "Power in a postcolonial world: Race, gender, and class in international relations," 1.

44 C. Enloe, *The curious feminist: Searching for women in a new age of empire*, 19.

45 Ibid., 23.

46 For example, see: J. B. Elshtain, "Reflections on war and political discourse: Realism, just war, and feminism in a nuclear age," 51.

47 See: Peterson, "Feminist theories within, invisible to, and beyond IR," 36; J. Bricmont *Humanitarian imperialism: Using human rights to sell war*. See M. T. Nguyen, "The biopower of beauty: Humanitarian imperialisms and global feminisms in an age of terror," *Signs: Journal of Women in Culture and Society* 36(2) (2011).

48 See: "The financial crisis inquiry report"; J. Bradford DeLong, "The second great depression"; H. Stewart, "We are in the worst financial crisis since depression, says IMF."

49 P. J. Katzenstein and S. C. Nelson, "Reading the right signals and reading the signals right: IPE and the financial crisis of 2008," 2.

50 R. O. Keohane, "The future of multilateralism and American global leadership," 30 October 2012.

51 See C. Weaver, "The meaning of development: Constructing the World Bank's good governance agenda," 67.

52 J. Weiner, "Five women of the financial crisis: Who they are and why they mattered."

53 A. Şahin, J. Song, and B. Hobijn, "The unemployment gender gap during the 2007 recession."

54 "Euro area unemployment rate at 12.2%."

55 "Towards human resilience: Sustaining MDG progress in an age of economic uncertainty."

56 "Discussion paper: Impact of the global economic crisis on women, girls and gender equality."

57 K. Chandararot, S. Sina, and L. Dannet, "Rapid assessment of the impact of the financial crisis in Cambodia."

58 Immanuel Wallerstein, "The fantastic success of Occupy Wall Street."

59 S. A. Hamed Hosseini, "Occupy cosmopolitanism: Ideological transversalization in the age of global economic uncertainties," 431.

60 M. Hardt and A. Negri, "The fight for 'real democracy' at the heart of Occupy Wall Street."

61 J. Butler, "Bodies in alliance and the politics of the street."

62 See: M. Butler, "Occupy Wall Street: The other 99% is not 90% men"; also see S. Knafo and A. Kaufman, "Occupy Wall Street, faces of Zuccotti Park: The woman in pink."

63 Knafo and Kaufman, "Occupy Wall Street," 2011.

64 M. Benjamin. "Interview with author."

65 See: T. A. Lomax, "Occupy rape culture"; Melissa Gira Grant, "Making safer spaces: Occupy Wall Street addresses questions of security at Zuccotti Park."

66 See: B. Stelter, "CBS reporter recounts a 'merciless' assault; A-R. Hussein, "France 24 journalist Sonia Dridi attacked in Tahrir Square"; R. Kais, "Foreign reporter raped in Tahrir Square."

67 "Egypt: Epidemic of sexual violence." Also see: P. Kingsley, "80 sexual assaults in one day—the other story of Tahrir Square"; "Mob rapes in Tahrir Square worry rights groups"; "Women sexually assaulted in Egypt protests."

Key Terms

gender
gender analysis vs. feminist analysis
gender, analytical category

gender, empirical category
sex

Questions for Review

1. According to the story of the IPE/IR field described in the chapter, why did feminist approaches emerge in the 1980s?

2. According to feminist IPE/IR scholars, what does it mean to "take gender seriously" in our analyses of global politics? Please provide an example of how you might take gender seriously in a contemporary event or problem in the global political economy.

3. What are the key differences between using gender as an empirical category and gender as an analytical category to understand the global political economy?

4. In your view, what aspects of the global political economy might a feminist and gender perspective bring into view that we might not see with another IPE/IR perspective? Please provide at least two examples in your response.

Further Resources

Ackerly, B. A., Stern, M., and True, J. (2006). *Feminist methodologies for international relations*. Cambridge: Cambridge University Press.

Enloe, C. (2000) [1990]. *Bananas, beaches & bases: Making feminist sense of international politics*. Berkeley: University of California Press.

Parpart, J. and Zalewski, M. (Eds). (2008). *Rethinking the man question*. London, New York: Zed Books.

Peterson, V. S. (2003). *A critical rewriting of global political economy: Integrating reproductive, productive and virtual economies*. London: Routledge.

Peterson, V. S. and Runyan, A. S. (2010). *Global gender issues in the new millennium*. 3rd ed. Boulder, Colo.: Westview Press.

Rai, S. M. (2013). "Gender and (international) political economy." In *The Oxford Handbook of Gender and Politics*, edited by Georgina Waylen, Karen Celis, Johanna Kantola and S. Laurel Weldon, 263–88. Oxford: Oxford University Press, 2013.

Steans, J. (2013). *Gender & international relations*, 3rd ed. Cambridge and Malden, MA: Polity Press.

Waylen, G., Celis, K., Kantola, J., and Weldon, S. l. (Eds). (2013). *The Oxford handbook of gender and politics*. Oxford: Oxford University Press.

References

"About us," Justicia for Migrant Workers: J4MW. (2013). http://www.justicia4migrantworkers.org/justicia_new.htm (16 October).

"Mob rapes in Tahrir Square worry rights groups," *CBC. ca*. (2013). http://www.cbc.ca/news/world/story/2013/07/03/egypt-tahrir-square-women-sex-assaults.html (1 September).

"Women sexually assaulted in Egypt protests," Aljazeera. com. (2013). http://www.aljazeera.com/news/africa/2013/07/20137312315973608.html (1 September).

"Bangladesh garment workers' lives still at risk, the Fifth Estate finds." *CBC.ca* (11 October 2013). http://www .cbc.ca/news/world/bangladesh-garment-workers-lives-still-at-risk-the-fifth-estate-finds-1.1959518 [accessed 15 October 2013].

"Euro area unemployment rate at 12.2%," Eurostate Press Office http://epp.eurostat.ec.europa.eu/cache/ ITY_PUBLIC/3-31102013-BP/EN/3-31102013-BP-EN.PDF (1 November 2013).

"Special issue: Women and international relations." (1988). *Millennium—Journal of International Studies 3*(17).

"Anniversary special issue: Gendering the international." (1998). *Millennium—Journal of International Studies 27*(4).

"World Bank. World Development Report (2012): Gender equality and development." 2013. The International Bank for Reconstruction and Development/The World Bank. http://siteresources .worldbank.org/INTWDR2012/Resources/ 7778105-1299699968583/7786210-1315936222006/ Complete-Report.pdf (1 August).

"Decent housing," Migrant workers alliance for change. (2013). http://www.migrantworkersalliance.org/ makeitright/decenthousing/ (17 October).

Discussion paper: Impact of the global economic crisis on women, girls and gender equality. Geneva: UNAIDS: Joint United Nations Programme on HIV/AIDS, August 2012. http://www.unaids.org/en/media/ unaids/contentassets/documents/document/2012/ discussionpapers/JC2368_impact-economic-crisis-women_en.pdf.

The financial crisis inquiry report. (2011). Washington, DC: The Financial Crisis Inquiry Commission, January. http://fcic-static.law.stanford.edu/cdn_ media/fcic-reports/fcic_final_report_full.pdf.

"Egypt: Epidemic of sexual violence." (2013). Human Rights Watch. https://http://www.hrw.org/print/ news/2013/07/03/egypt-epidemic-sexual-violence (accessed 4 July).

"Bangladesh: Decent work country programme 2012–15." (2012). (November). http://www.ilo.org/pub lic/english/bureau/program/dwcp/download/ban gladesh.pdf [accessed 1 September 2013].

Towards human resilience: Sustaining MDG progress in an age of economic uncertainty. (2011). New York: NY: UNDP, September. http://www.undp.org/content/ dam/undp/library/Poverty Reduction/Towards_Sus tainingMDG_Web1005.pdf.

Ackerly, B. A., Stern, M., and True, J. (Eds). (2006). *Feminist methodologies for international relations*. Cambridge: Cambridge University Press.

Benjamin, M. (2013). Interview with author. Digital voice recording, 18 August.

Bricmont, J. (2006). *Humanitarian imperialism: Using human rights to sell war*. D. Johnstone (trans.) New York: Monthly Review Press.

Butler, J. "Bodies in alliance and the politics of the street," European Institute for Progressive Cultural Policies. http://www.eipcp.net/transversal/1011/butler/en.

Butler, M. (2013). "Occupy Wall Street: The other 99% is not 90% men." Alternet.org. http://www.alternet .org/story/152593/occupy_wall_street%3A_the_ other_99_is_not_90_men?paging=off (accessed 1 Aug).

Caprioli, M. (2004). "Feminist IR theory and quantitative methodology: A critical analysis." *International Studies Review 6*(2), 253–69.

Carpenter, R. C. (2002). "Gender theory in world politics: Contributions of a nonfeminist standpoint?" *International Studies Review 3*,153–65.

Carver, T. (2003). "The forum: Gender and international relations. Gender/Feminism/IR." *International Studies Review 5*, 288–90.

Chandararot, K., Sina, S., and Dannet, L. (2009). *Rapid assessment of the impact of the financial crisis in Cambodia* ILO Asia-Pacific Working Paper Series: International Labour Organization, March. http:// www.ilo.org/public/english/support/lib/financial crisis/download/cids_report_final.pdf.

Charlesworth, H. (2008). "Are women peaceful? Reflections on the role of women in peace-building." *Feminist Legal Studies 16*, 347–61.

Chowdhry, G. and Nair, S. (2002). "Power in a postcolonial world: Race, gender, and class in international relations." In *Power, postcolonialism and international relations*, G. Chowdhry and S. Nair (Eds), 1–32. London and New York: Routledge.

Citizenship and Immigration Canada. (2014). "Facts and figures 2012—immigration overview: Permanent and temporary residents." http://www.cic.gc.ca/english/resources/statistics/facts2012/temporary/04.asp (23 October 2014).

Cohn, C. (1987). "Sex and death in the rational world of defense intellectuals." *Signs 12*(4), 687–718.

Connell, R. W. and J. W. Messerschmidt. (2005). "Hegemonic masculinity—Rethinking the concept." *Gender & Society 19*(6): 829–59.

Cox, R. W. (1981). "Social forces, states and world orders: Beyond international relations theory." *Millennium—Journal of International Studies 10*(2), 126–55.

DeLong, J. B. (2013). "The second great depression." *Foreign Affairs*, (11 June).

Elshtain, J. B. (1985). "Reflections on war and political discourse: Realism, just war, and feminism in a nuclear age." *Political Theory 13*(1), 39–57.

Enloe, C. (2000) [1990]. *Bananas, beaches & bases: Making feminist sense of international politics*. Berkeley: University of California Press.

Enloe, C. (2004). *The curious feminist: Searching for women in a new age of empire*. Berkeley: University of California Press.

Enloe, C. (2013). *Seriously! Investigating crashes and crises as if women mattered*. Berkeley: University of California Press.

Faraday, F. (2012). *Made in Canada: How the law constructs migrant workers' insecurity*: Metcalf Foundation, September. http://metcalffoundation.com/publications-resources/view/made-in-canada/-.Unfsp6XvbfM (accessed 15 August 2013).

Fausto-Sterling, A. (2000). *Sexing the body: Gender politics and the construction of sexuality*. New York: Basic Books.

Gilpin, R. (1999 [1981]). *War and change in world politics*. Cambridge: Cambridge University Press.

Grant, M. G. "Making safer spaces: Occupy Wall Street addresses questions of security at Zuccotti Park." (2011). *AlterNet* (6 November). http://www.alternet.org/story/152989/making_safer_spaces%3A_occupy_wall_street_addresses_questions_of_security_at_zuccotti_park/ [accessed 1 September 2013].

Grant, R. and Newland, K. (Eds). (1991). *Gender and international relations*. Bloomington and Indianapolis: Indiana University Press.

Griffin, P. (2007). "Refashioning IPE: What and how gender analysis teaches international (global) political economy." *Review of International Political Economy 14*(4), 719–36.

Hamed Hosseini, S. A. (2013). "Occupy cosmopolitanism: Ideological transversalization in the age of global economic uncertainties." *Globalizations 10*(3), 425–38.

Harding, S. G. (1991). *Whose science? Whose knowledge? Thinking from women's lives*. New York: Cornell University Press.

Hardt, M. and Negri, A. (2011). "The fight for 'real democracy' at the heart of Occupy Wall Street." *Foreign Affairs* (11 October).

Hoffman, J. (2001). *Gender and sovereignty: Feminism, the state and international relations*. New York: Palgrave.

Hussein, A-R. (2013). "France 24 journalist Sonia Dridi attacked in Tahrir Square," Guardian.com http://www.guardian.co.uk/world/2012/oct/21/sonia-dridi-attacked-tahrir-square (1 August).

Kais, R. (2013). "Foreign reporter raped in Tahrir Square," Ynetnews.com http://www.ynetnews.com/articles/0,7340,L-4399041,00.html (1 September).

Katzenstein, P. J. and S. C. Nelson. (2013). "Reading the right signals and reading the signals right: IPE and the financial crisis of 2008." *Review of International Political Economy*, 1–31.

Keohane, R. O. (1998). "Beyond dichotomy: Conversations between international relations and feminist theory." *International Studies Quarterly 42*(1): 193–7.

Keohane, R. O. (1989). "International relations theory: Contributions of a feminist standpoint." *Millennium— Journal of International Studies 18*(2): 245–53.

Keohane, R. O. (2012). "The future of multilateralism and American global leadership, 30 October" http://youtu.be/hfMHcdPo7fk; http://www.iiea.com/events/the-future-of-multilateralism-and-american-global-leadership (accessed 1 July 2013).

Keohane, R. O. (2011). "The old IPE and the new." In *International political economy: Debating the past, present and future,* Nicola Phillips and Catherine E. Weaver (eds). 35–44. New York: Routledge,.

Keung, N. (2013). "Abuse of migrant workers 'endemic' in Canada, new study says," Thestar.com http://www.thestar.com/news/gta/2012/09/17/abuse_of_migrant_workers_endemic_in_canada_new_study_says.html (1 September).

Kingsley, P. (2013). "80 sexual assaults in one day—the other story of Tahrir Square," Guardian.co.uk http://www.guardian.co.uk/world/2013/jul/05/egypt-women-rape-sexual-assault-tahrir-square (1 September).

Knafo, S. and Kaufman, A. (2013). "Occupy Wall Street, faces of Zuccotti Park: The woman in pink," Huffingtonpost.com http://www.huffingtonpost.com/2011/12/01/occupy-wall-street-faces-codepink-melanie-butler_n_1117875.html (1 August).

Lomax, T. A. (2013). "Occupy rape culture," thefeministwire http://thefeministwire.com/2011/11/occupy-rape-culture/ (1 September).

McNamara, K. R. (2009). "Of intellectual monocultures and the study of IPE." *Review of International Political Economy* 16(1): 72–84.

Marchand, M. H. (1998). "Different communities/ different realities/ different encounters: A reply to J. Ann Tickner." *International Studies Quarterly* 42(1): 199–204.

Odysseos, L. and Seckinelgin, H. (Eds). (2002). *Gendering the international.* Hampshire and New York: Millennium and Palgrave Macmillan.

Parpart, J. and Zalewski, M. (Eds). (2008). *Rethinking the man question: Sex, gender and violence in international Relations.* London and New York: Zed Books.

Peterson, S. V. "(2005). How (the meaning of) gender matters in political economy." *New Political Economy* 10(4): 499–521.

Peterson, V. S. (1992). "Security and sovereign states: What is at stake in taking feminism seriously." In *Gendered states: Feminist (re)visions of international relations theory,* V. Spike Peterson (Ed.). Boulder, Colorado: Lynne Rienner.

Peterson, V. S. (2004). "Feminist theories within, invisible to, and beyond IR." *Brown Journal of World Affairs X*(2): 35–46.

Peterson, V. S. and Runyan, A. S. (2010). *Global gender issues in the new millennium: Third edition.* Boulder, CO: Westview Press.

Phillips, N. (2009). "The slow death of pluralism." *Review of International Political Economy* 16(1): 85–94.

Rai, S. M. (2013). "Gender and (international) political economy." In *The Oxford handbook of gender and politics,* G. Waylen, K. Celis, J. Kantola and S. L. Weldon (Eds), 263–88. Oxford: Oxford University Press.

Reus-Smit, C. (2009). "Constructivism." In *Theories of international relations,* 4th ed., Burchill, Scott et al. (eds), 212–36. New York: Palgrave-Macmillan.

Rupert, M. (2003). "Globalising common sense: A Marxian-Gramscian (re-)vision of the politics of governance/resistance." *Review of International Studies,*181.

Şahin, A., Song, J., and Hobijn, B. (2010). "The unemployment gender gap during the 2007 recession." *Current Issues in Economics and Finance* 16(2) http://www.newyorkfed.org/research/current_issues/ci16-2.pdf [accessed 1 September 2013].

Schmidt, B. C. (2008). "On the history and historiography of international relations." In *Handbook of international relations,* Walter Carlsnaes, Thomas Risse and Beth A. Simmons (eds), 3–22. London: Sage.

Stelter, B. (2011). "CBS reporter recounts a 'merciless' assault." *New York Times* 29 April, A.13.

Stewart, H. (2008). "We are in the worst financial crisis since depression, says IMF." *The Guardian* April 10.

Sylvester, C. (2013). "Experiencing the end and afterlives of international relations/theory." *European Journal of International Relations* 19(3): 609–26.

Tickner, J. A. (1997). "You just don't understand: Troubled engagements between feminists and IR theorists." *International Studies Quarterly* 41(4): 611–32.

Tickner, J. A. (2006). "Feminism meets international relations: Some methodological issues." In *Feminist methodologies for international relations,* Maria Stern Brooke A. Ackerly, Jacqui True (eds), 19–41. Cambridge: Cambridge University Press.

Tickner, J. A. (2010). "You may never understand: Prospects for feminist futures in international relations." *The Australian Feminist Law Journal* 32: 9–20.

Wallerstein, I. (2013). "The fantastic success of Occupy Wall Street" http://www.iwallerstein.com/fantastic-success-occupy-wall-street/ (accessed 15 July).

Waylen, G. (2006). You still don't understand: Why troubled engagements continue between feminists and (critical) IPE." *Review of International Studies* 32(1), 145–64.

Weaver, C. (2010). "The meaning of development: Constructing the World Bank's good governance agenda." In *Constructing the international economy*, Rawi Abdelal, Mark Blyth and Craig Parsons (Eds), 47–67. Ithaca, NY: Cornell University Press.

Weber, C. (1994). "Good girls, little girls, and bad girls: Male paranoia in Robert Keohane's critique of feminist international relations." *Millennium—Journal of International Studies* 23(2), 337–49.

Weiner, J. (2013). "Five women of the financial crisis: Who they are and why they mattered," Washington Post.com http://www.washingtonpost.com/blogs/she-the-people/wp/2013/09/17/five-women-of-the-financial-crisis-who-they-are-and-why-they-mattered/ (2 October).

Westwood, R. (2013). "Should Canada make it easier for immigrants to send money home?" *Maclean's* (19 February). http://www2.macleans.ca/2013/02/19/homeward-bound-2/ [accessed 1 September 2013].

Whitworth, S. (1994). "Theory as exclusion: Gender and international political economy." In *Political economy and the changing global order*, Richard Stubbs and Geoffrey R.D.Underhill (Eds), 116–29. Toronto: McClelland & Stewart.

Youngs, G. (2004). "Feminist international relations: A contradiction in terms? Or "Why women and gender are essential to understanding the world 'we' live in." *International Affairs* 80(1), 75–87.

Zalewski, M. (2003). The forum: Gender and international relations. "'Women's troubles' again in IR." *International Studies Review* 5(2), 291–4.

PART II

Economic Fundamentals

The global financial crisis that emerged out of the US housing market and exploded in dramatic fashion in the fall of 2008 was a fascinating, and, in many cases, painful, lesson in Wall Street finance for a large number of people. For those with little formal training in economics, there was an entirely new vocabulary required to understand even the basics of what was happening; credit default swaps, collateralized debt obligations, derivatives, mortgage backed securities, financial instruments: all were bewildering to the uninitiated.

Yet, as the crisis unfolded, it became clear that many who actually studied finance or worked on Wall Street often had the same problem. As mortgages were created and offered to would-be home-owners, they were then sliced, repackaged, and repackaged again into complex financial instruments by banks who seldom knew anything about the underlying mortgages they were based upon. Wall Street banks would then put these instruments in front of ratings agencies for an evaluation of their underlying value as investment vehicles. Much like the banks that repackaged the mortgages, the ratings agencies too often failed to understand what they were evaluating, often blindly giving favourable ratings (See Sinclair 1994; 2005). Investors themselves compounded this problem by assuming these instruments had been properly vetted, relying too heavily on the flawed assessments of ratings agencies for their own investment decisions. Finally, all of these financial instruments were "insured" via an entirely different set of tradable financial instruments, called credit default swaps, that few even knew existed (See Lewis 2010; McDonald 2009; see also Mallaby 2010).

It all became a house of cards that crashed spectacularly in the fall of 2008, wiping out nearly two decades of accumulated household wealth (Federal Reserve 2012). Villains could be found everywhere: Wall Street banks, fund managers, unscrupulous loan officers, greedy home-owners and, of course, regulators and policy-makers who were asleep at the wheel.

In the wake of the crisis, there has been considerable hand-wringing over what had happened and how to prevent it from happening again (See Reinhart and Rogoff 2011; Sorkin, 2009). As the crisis unfolded, "contagion," a term more people were familiar with, was increasingly heard as deteriorating economic conditions in the United States seemed to spread elsewhere. Paralleling the rising fear of contagion were analyses of what had gone wrong and how it might have been avoided (Diamond and Rajan 2009). Carmen Reinhart and Kenneth Rogoff's (2011) masterful analysis of centuries' worth of financial crises, and their findings that financial bubbles were more similar than different, and that it would take nearly a decade to unwind, was particularly sobering. Among the more important areas of policy in which the dust has still not settled is monetary policy. Central banks, notably the US Federal Reserve, have since late 2008 been engaged in the massive purchase of bank assets (quantitative easing) as an innovative (some argue desperate) way of keeping interest rates low and credit accessible. The longer-term implications of this stimulus remain unclear. Some have likened the impact and consequence of quantitative easing to patterns of euphoria and withdrawal experienced by addicts.

An important commonality flowing from each of the world's financial crises has been the political and social reactions they have spawned. As the wreckage from the financial crisis piled up and the search for culprits began, bankers became today's robber barons and modern Wall Street the symbol of a new gilded age. And, much as the political and economic crises of the past, the recent financial crisis has spawned a series of reform movements of its own, notably the Tea Party and Occupy Wall Street movements.

Economic Orthodoxy?

A little later in this volume (chapter 20), Partick LeBlond explores the origins, progression, and aftermath of the 2008 financial crisis in detail. In this section, however, we aim to revisit some of the fundamentals driving the longer-term postwar global economy and remind readers of some of its theoretical foundations. It's an important reminder because of the reconsideration of the proper balance of relationships among public institutions, firms, and individuals in the stewardship of economic activity. The reform movements spawned by the financial crisis are undoubtedly disappointed with the results of that reconsideration, particularly proponents of semi-revolutionary changes to the role of the state (Tea Party) or even to capitalism itself (Occupy).

However, it is hard to escape the vigorous debate within the economics profession about the path forward. In the years immediately following the end of the Cold War, social scientists (and political scientists, in particular) were debating the reasons for having failed to predict the end of the Cold War (Gaddis 1992/3; Gaddis 1997; Lebow 1994). Critics wondered how, after so many years of intense theory building and study, social science could have so badly misread the events of 1989 and the fall of the Berlin Wall? Similarly, the economics profession is in the midst of some self-reflection over its apparent failure to see the onset of the financial crisis or accurately forecast its aftermath (see OECD 2014; Lewis 2010; Wolf 2010, 28–57). Such confusion extends to the policy prescriptions for responding to the crisis.

Europe and the US suffered different forms of financial trauma; in America it was a traditional financial asset bubble, in Europe a fiscal debt crisis fueled by incomplete institutionalization in the Euro area. More interesting are the strongly divergent responses to financial trauma on each side of the Atlantic and the revival of an old intellectual debate about the best route to recovery. In Europe, austerity and structural adjustment have been the dominant policy prescriptions. Interestingly, the structural adjustment programs implemented in Ireland, Portugal, Greece, and Cyprus represent a remarkable reassertion of an approach to economic reform and recovery badly discredited by experiences in Latin America and Asia in the 1990s (Stiglitz 2002; Rodrik 1997; Rodrik 2006). By contrast, the United States has engaged in a large fiscal stimulus accompanied by an unprecedented and extraordinary monetary expansion that has upset conventional wisdom about the role of monetary policy in economic management.

Most interesting of all, the economic policy debates of today are remarkably similar to those from earlier periods in which the ideas of Friedrich Hayek and John Maynard Keynes (Wapshott 2011) or Milton Friedman and Paul Samuelson were vigorously debated (Hammond 2011). The reckoning within the profession has intensified along with each new employment or GDP report depicting an anemic recovery. In the United States, the Federal Reserve's program of quantitative easing has maintained low interest rates and helped improve the balance sheets of major financial institutions. Yet, each time the Fed has hinted at "tapering" its asset purchases alongside signs of economic recovery, jittery financial markets have reacted negatively, some seeing quantitative easing as the best policy prescription, others seeing it as akin to heroin for the economy—take it away and the economy experiences withdrawal symptoms.

Finally, it should be noted that Canada was somewhat unique among developed economies in that neither the financial bubble in the United States nor the debt crisis in Europe seemed to put a significant dent in Canadian economic performance. Several factors contributed to Canada being able to weather the storm, including sound fiscal policies and high commodity prices driven by economic growth in the developing world. Moreover, many American politicians looked north of the border at the structure and regulatory framework of the Canadian banking sector for reforms to be applied in the US. Such was the robustness of Canada's economy that some spoke of a "decoupling" of Canada's economy from its traditional reliance on US consumption for its economic prosperity. Yet, these recent differences in economic performance do not change the fact that Canada has contributed significantly to the evolution of postwar trade and finance through its membership in organizations like the World Trade Organization, International Monetary Fund, G8, or G20, as well as less well-known organizations like the Bank of International Settlements, or the Financial Stability Board, chaired since 2011 by Mark Carney, former governor of the Bank of Canada. In part because of its experience in weathering the financial crisis, Canada may play a significant role going forward in shaping changes to economic orthodoxy.

The three pieces that follow represent a preview for the convulsions in the global economy and the economics profession we have witnessed in recent years, many of which are dealt with in Part 5 of this volume. They are important historical and conceptual reminders of how the postwar global economy has evolved and where many people thought it might be headed. As significant as the new terminology of the global financial crisis has become, these pieces also represent a refresher on the terminology and theory undergirding the spread-open markets.

This section begins with Eric Helleiner and his sweeping account of the dominant intellectual and ideological debates shaping the evolution of the modern global economy.

Of particular note here are the successive crises that have cast doubt upon the stability and merit of openness in global economic relations, and the reactions. While each of these "crisis" moments reveals numerous political and economic fault lines whose impact on the system reverberates long afterward, we also come to appreciate more fully the broad rationale for why openness is pursued in the first place. Yet, as Helleiner notes, concepts such as embedded liberalism have begun mediating the tensions arising between economic openness, the state, and societal interests. Mark Brawley then focuses more narrowly on the debates between openness and protection in trade liberalization. The contemporary global trading regime is popularly depicted as a multilateral system governed by the World Trade Organization. However, as Brawley describes, the path taken by the global trading regime has hardly been a straight line toward greater and greater degrees of liberalization. Indeed, the intellectual case in favour of trade liberalization has been a long time in the making and has periodically been confronted by strong intellectual and, more often, political challengers. He reviews the options from a historical perspective predating, and including, the period of the modern sovereign state. The protection of local interests has often dominated short-term decision-making, yet the longer-term patterns continue to point toward the extension of openness in trade relations to more and more parts of the globe. Finally, David Dodge, former governor of the Bank of Canada, looks back at the postwar history of Canadian monetary policy, and the postwar function of central banking in modern economies. While readers will note that Dodge's piece is actually a reprint of a public speech from February 2008, the timing of that speech and the observations he makes about the important role of the Bank of Canada in crafting Canadian prosperity through the management of monetary policy could not be more important. Later that year, after the fall of Lehman Brothers and the onset of the Global Financial Crisis, governments and central banks in many countries commenced a series of extraordinary stimulus measures, including so-called quantitative easing, that will reverberate for years to come. In the years ahead, we may pinpoint 2008 as the end of a long era of monetary relations and policy practice. To those unfamiliar with how monetary policy is made or implemented, Dodge's piece may be difficult to follow in some places. Yet, in light of what has transpired since, it will not be lost on anyone both how much has changed and how much is still to be settled about the future of monetary policy.

References

Diamond, D. and Rajan, R. (2009). "The credit crisis: Conjectures about causes and remedies." *American Economic Review: Papers & Proceedings 2009* 99(2), 606–10.

Federal Reserve. June 2012. "Changes in U.S. family finances from 2007 to 2010: Evidence from the Survey of Consumer Finances," *Federal Reserve Bulletin* 98(2), 1–80.

Gaddis, J. L. (1997). *We now know: Rethinking cold war history*. Oxford: Oxford University Press.

Gaddis, J. L. (1992/93). "International relations theory and the end of the cold war." *International Security* 17(3) (Winter), 5–58.

Hammond, J. D. Fall (2011). Friedman and Samuelson on the business cycle. *Cato Journal* 31(3), 643–60.

Lebow, R. N. (1994). "The long peace, the end of the cold war, and the failure of realism." *International Organization* 48(2) (March), 249–77.

Lewis, M. (2010). *The big short*. New York: Norton.

Mallaby, S. (2010). *More money than god*. New York: The Penguin Press.

McDonald, L. (2009). *A colossal failure of common sense*. New York: Crown Publishing.

OECD. (2014). *OECD forecasts during and after the financial crisis: A post mortem*. OECD Economics Department Policy Note no. 23. Paris: Organization of Economic Co-operation and Development.

Reinhart, C. and Rogoff, K. (2011). *This time is different: Eight centuries of financial folly*. Princeton: Princeton University Press.

Rodrik, D. (2006). "Goodbye Washington Consensus, hellow Washington Confusion? A review of the World Bank's economic growth in the 1990s: Learning from a decade of reform." *Journal of Economic Literature 94*(December), 973–87.

———. (1997). *Has globalization gone too far?* Washington, D.C.: Institute for International Economics.

Sinclair, T. (2005). *The new masters of capital*. Ithaca: Cornell University Press.

———. (1994). "Passing judgement: Credit rating proceses as regulatory mechanisms of governance in the emerging world order." *Review of International Political Economy 1*(1), 133–59.

Sorkin, A. R. (2009). *Too big to fail*. New York: Viking Press.

Stiglitz, J. (2002). *Globalization and its discontents*. New York: Norton.

Wapshott, N. (2011). *Keynes Hayek: The clash that defined modern economics*. New York: W.W. Norton.

Wolf, M. (2010). *Fixing global capitalism*. Baltimore: Johns Hopkins University Press.

5 History and Ideological Change in the Global Political Economy

Eric Helleiner

Students seeking to analyze the contemporary global political economy (GPE) can benefit enormously from an understanding of its historical evolution. Policy-makers and analysts constantly invoke the past to justify their policies and judgments. Historical analysis also helps us to recognize patterns of human behaviour that are relevant to interpreting the current world. And perhaps most important, knowledge of the evolution of the GPE provides an appreciation of the possibilities for change in the future.

This chapter provides a very schematic overview of the historical trajectory of the GPE since the nineteenth century, with a special focus on the evolution of dominant ideologies that have influenced the politics of the world economy. The nineteenth century has been chosen as the starting point because it witnessed the emergence of the first GPE ideology with worldwide influence: economic liberalism. Other important ideologies—economic nationalism, Marxism and **embedded liberalism**—emerged in reaction to nineteenth century economic liberalism and had a growing impact on the politics of world economy from the nineteenth through the middle decades of the

twentieth century. After outlining this history, this chapter explores briefly the more contemporary history of the birth of **neoliberalism** out of the crisis of 1970s and some of the growing challenges it has faced.

Globalization and the Rise of Economic Liberalism

The nineteenth century was a period of extensive economic globalization that served as an important precedent for post-1945 globalization trends. Of course, a global economy had already begun to emerge between the fifteenth and eighteenth centuries in the context of Europe's commercial and military expansion around the world. But the technologies of that earlier era ensured that trade was largely restricted to high value items that were relatively easy to transport across long distances. Moreover, while there were some famous overland trade routes (e.g., the Silk Road, trans-Saharan trade), most long-distance trade was waterborne, often connecting major port cities across the world more closely to each other economically than to their nearby inland regions.[1]

In the nineteenth century, the industrial revolution overcame these limitations. New technologies—particularly railways, steamships, and telegraphs—enabled people, money, and a much wider range of objects to be transported more quickly and extensively across both land and water. The industrial revolution also generated new demand for faraway resources to serve the factories and urbanizing populations of industrializing regions. For the first time in human history, most regions of the world in this period began to be influenced, to varying degrees, by global economic processes and trends.[2]

Rapidly expanding global commerce was also encouraged and was accompanied by the rise of the ideology of **economic liberalism**. Economic liberals in the nineteenth century drew inspiration from Adam Smith's 1776 book *The Wealth of Nations*, famously attacking the restrictions that most European governments imposed on what Smith considered to be the natural propensity of humans to "truck, barter and exchange."[3] If individuals were freer to pursue their economic interests through markets and trade, Smith argued that they would enhance a country's wealth by encouraging a more efficient and specialized division of labour.

Smith extended his support for freer markets to the international level, critiquing restrictive "mercantilist" trade practices associated with colonization and the protection of local merchant interests. But his support for free trade was inconsistent. Particularly striking was his support for one of Britain's most notorious mercantilist regulations, the Navigation Acts, which restricted trade between Britain and its colonies to British-owned ships. Although this restriction curtailed trade, Smith defended it on national security grounds: "As defence . . . is of much more importance than

opulence, the act of navigation is, perhaps, the wisest of all the commercial regulations of England."[4]

The case for free trade was developed in a more consistent and detailed manner in 1817 by British economist David Ricardo, who famously demonstrated mathematically through his theory of comparative advantage how free trade would raise incomes worldwide.[5] Addressing Adam Smith's security concerns, economic liberals such as the British merchant and politician Richard Cobden also argued forcefully that free trade would promote international peace by increasing countries' interdependence and undermining the power of warmongering aristocratic classes.[6]

The liberal case for free trade became increasingly popular across the world by the middle decades of the nineteenth century, particularly among merchants whose economic activities had an increasingly global reach and whose political influence grew in this period. The idea that free trade would usher in a new world of peace and prosperity was seen by many of its supporters as a scientific truth and they often backed it with almost religious fervour. As Cobden himself put it, "Free trade is a divine law: if it were not, the world would not have been differently created. One country has cotton, another wine, another coal, which is proof that, according to the divine order of things, [people] should . . . exchange their goods and thus further peace and goodwill on earth."[7]

This political trend encouraged trade liberalization in countries across the world. Some of the most important initiatives involved the world's leading industrial power, Britain, which unilaterally abolished its Navigation Acts in 1849 as well as its protectionist Corn Laws in 1846 (which had imposed tariffs on many commodity imports from outside the British Empire). The British government also promoted trade liberalization abroad. Bilateral trade agreements were negotiated with other countries, such as the famous 1860 Cobden-Chevalier Treaty with France (which helped pioneer the most-favoured-nation clause, ensuring that concessions offered to one country would need to be given to all others with the status). Britain also sometimes opened foreign markets by force, as in the case of the 1839–42 Opium Wars in China. The expansion of international trade after 1850 was also encouraged by the fact that leading economic powers increasingly converged on a common monetary standard—the gold standard—whose introduction Britain had also pioneered earlier in the century.[8]

Britain's particular enthusiasm for free trade did not only reflect just the influence of economic liberal ideas and merchant lobbying. British policymakers recognized that their country, as the leading industrial power, would benefit economically from greater access to foreign markets and had less to fear from foreign competition. Indeed, some advocates of the abolition of the Corn Laws argued that free trade would mean "we might supply the whole world with manufactures and have almost a monopoly of trade of the world."[9] These kinds of sentiments—along with the use of force to promote trade liberalization abroad—encouraged growing criticism abroad of the liberal idea that free trade would bring peace and prosperity to all.

List and the Nationalist Critique of Economic Liberalism

One of the most influential critics of the liberal case for free trade was the German thinker Friedrich List. In his 1841 book *The National System of Political Economy*, List argued that free trade, far from ushering in a world of peace and prosperity, was a deliberate tool of British domination. Because it allowed British manufactures to lock in their competitive advantage by wiping out manufacturers abroad, free trade would force the rest of

the world to specialize in commodity production in ways that left them economically weak and militarily subordinate to Britain. To avoid this fate, List and other "economic nationalists" argued that governments needed to use tariffs and other policies to support local manufacturers in ways that fostered the development of the "productive powers" of their nation.[10]

From this perspective, the international division of labour was not a product of a natural "divine law" but rather of active state policy. Indeed, List and his supporters highlighted that Britain itself had previously followed these kinds of activist policies to achieve its economic pre-eminence. As List put it in a memorable passage critiquing Britain's newfound enthusiasm for free trade, "it is a very common clever device that when anyone has attained the summit of greatness, he kicks away the ladder by which he has climbed up, in order to deprive others of the means of climbing up after him." More generally, List also critiqued liberals for seeing "individuals as mere producers and consumers, not as citizens of states or members of nations" and for being concerned only with "the mere exchangeable value of things without taking into consideration the mental and political, the present and the future interests, and the productive powers of the nation."[11]

These ideas found particular support in countries that felt threatened by Britain's growing economic and military dominance in the nineteenth century. The United States was one such country. Although the agricultural exporting southern states of the country favoured free trade, the northeastern states successfully pressed for tariff protection throughout the nineteenth century to support the country's "latecomer" industrialization. After Germany's unification in 1871, Listian economic nationalist ideas also attracted growing support in that country. Arguing that free trade was a "weapon" of the strongest, Chancellor Otto von

Bismarck introduced a tariff in 1879 and backed German industrialization in other ways, such as subsidies and support for railways.[12]

The most fascinating example of successful state-sponsored latecomer industrialization was Japan, a country that had largely sealed itself off from economic contacts with the outside world since the seventeenth century until the US forced open its ports in 1853. After a period of political instability, new rulers came to power in 1868 determined to avoid the fate of nearby China whose sovereignty had been increasingly undermined by western powers. To bolster their country's economic and military power vis-à-vis the West, the new "Meiji" leaders in Japan were influenced by Listian economic nationalism and they promoted industrialization through government subsidies, public ownership, and the building of national infrastructure (but not tariffs, which could not be used until trade treaties with the West were renegotiated in 1900).[13]

These kinds of state interventions in the economy became increasingly popular in many other countries as well, particularly when a long depression in the world economy during the 1870s and 1880s undermined support for the dominant liberal policy paradigm. But state interventions sometimes assumed a distinctive form in countries where local elites benefited from their country's status as a commodity exporter to the industrializing core of the world economy. For example, although the Canadian government introduced a new tariff under its "National Policy" in the same year as Bismarck did, its architects were less concerned with cultivating the growth of a nationally-owned industry than German politicians had been. They wanted to raise tariff revenues to help pay for railway construction aimed at consolidating control over the west of the country and encouraging greater agricultural production. They also hoped US manufacturing firms might jump over the tariff wall to establish branch plants that could provide enough jobs to reduce emigration to the US.[14]

In other contexts, these state interventionist policies were weakened by foreign opposition. For example, in the first half of the nineteenth century, the Ottoman governor of Egypt, Muhammad Ali, sought to fend off European power through extensive economic reforms, including the establishment of state-owned industries. But the initiative was undermined when Britain limited his use of tariffs and eventually helped forced the liquidation of the state enterprises, increasingly leaving Egypt in the position of cotton exporter to Europe.[15] In late-nineteenth century India, economic nationalists such as Mahadev Govind Ranade also lamented how British colonial rule forced his country to remain an agricultural exporter and prevented the use of tariffs and subsidies that would have promoted local industrialization. As he put it, "It is not open to us to adopt certain plans of operation, which . . . have been followed with practical success in many of the most enlightened countries of Europe and America."[16]

The sudden colonization of Africa and much of Asia in the late nineteenth century by European powers (as well as the US and Japan by the end of the century) imposed the same constraints on those regions. Indeed, colonial powers often severely distorted the economies of colonized territories in this period by forcing them to produce commodities for export to serve the colonizing country's interests. Local merchants, landowners, and manufacturers were also often marginalized as colonial authorities granted special privileges to those from the home country. The prospects for economic development were also undermined when profits and economic surpluses were withdrawn from the colony rather than reinvested locally.[17]

In fact, the division of much of the world into rival colonial empires in the late nineteenth century went hand-in-hand with the growing nationalism of that period. Indeed, nationalist thinkers such as List had advocated the colonization of countries in what he called the "torrid zone" (as opposed to "temperate zone") of the world. Nationalists elsewhere also often adopted a similar stance; for example, the Meiji leadership in Japan saw no contradiction between their desire to resist US and European imperialism and their colonization of Taiwan (in 1895) and Korea (in 1905).

For many economic liberals, however, the age of imperialism represented a further challenge to their ideals. Liberals had hoped that free trade would generate worldwide peace and prosperity. But the scramble for colonies in the late nineteenth century signalled a return to restrictive trade practices and conflicting commercial rivalries reminiscent of the mercantilist age critiqued by Adam Smith. To explain this turn of events, liberals such as Joseph Schumpeter blamed the enduring power of pre-capitalist aristocratic classes that he argued favoured, and derived much of their social position from, militarism and war.[18] This liberal explanation of the rise of the age of imperialism, however, was challenged by another school of thought that emerged in the nineteenth century: Marxism.

Marxist Theories of Imperialism

In his writings about the politics of global economy, Marx himself (who died in 1883) had been more informed more by the free trade era of the mid-nineteenth century than the age of imperialism. Indeed, his views on free trade often surprise contemporary analysts. Although he was a strong critic of economic liberalism, he had welcomed the fact that the free trade era accelerated the worldwide spread of capitalism. As he put it, "the Protective System, in *these days*, is conservative, while

the Free-Trade system works destructively. It breaks up old nationalities and carries antagonisms of proletariat and bourgeoisie to the uttermost point. In a word, the Free-Trade System hastens the Social Revolution."[19]

It was Marx's followers who developed the **Marxist theories of imperialism** that became so well-known in the twentieth century. These theories argued that the age of imperialism was a product not of the preferences of aristocratic remnants of the old feudal society but rather of the dynamics of modern capitalism itself. When the global economy entered a depression in the 1870s and 1880s, many Marxists saw this development as a signal of capitalism's imminent demise. But a global economic boom had then followed between the 1890s and the First World War. For Marxists such as Vladimir Lenin, Rosa Luxemburg, and Rudolph Hilferding, writing in the early twentieth century, imperialism offered an explanation for capitalism's unexpected vitality.[20]

From their standpoint, the acquisition of colonies had postponed the collapse of capitalism by providing capitalist powers with new export markets, new investment outlets for surplus capital, and/or new resources and labour to exploit. Most of these Marxist theorists of imperialism predicted that the age of imperialism would be the final phase—or what Lenin in his famous 1916 book called "the highest stage"—of capitalism.[21] As the geographical limits of imperial expansion were reached, declining profits would set in and capitalist powers would engage in increasingly violent conflicts with each other for scarce resources, markets, and investment outlets. In a context of worsening economic conditions and unpopular inter-imperialist wars, revolution by the proletariat would become increasingly likely.

Lenin's role in the 1917 Russian revolution in the midst of the First World War encouraged such predictions. Even though that social upheaval had not taken place in a country at the core of world capitalism, he and others hoped the Russian experience would encourage revolutions across Europe. As Lenin put it optimistically in 1916, "imperialism is the eve of the social revolution of the proletariat."[22] Once in power, Lenin also encouraged anti-colonial movements (whether they were Marxist or not) on the grounds that capitalism at the core of the world economy would be weakened by the undermining of imperial expansion.

Anti-capitalist revolutions did not, however, spread across Europe during the First World War in the way many Marxists had hoped. The working classes often showed more enthusiasm in fighting for their country than in joining a revolution against their respective national capitalist classes. Moreover, after the war, the leading capitalist powers declared their new willingness to cooperate economically. At conferences organized under the auspices of the League of Nations in Brussels (1920) and Genoa (1922), resolutions were passed calling for cooperation to restore the international gold standard and other aspects of the pre-1914 international economic order. British policy-makers and financiers then worked closely with their counterparts from the world's new leading creditor, the United States, to realize this goal. By the late 1920s, it appeared that they had been very successful: the international gold standard had been rebuilt, large-scale international capital flows had been restored, and the world capitalist economy was booming.

A few Marxist theorists of imperialism had anticipated this kind of inter-imperialist cooperation. The German thinker Karl Kautsky, in particular, had predicted in 1914 that the age of imperialism would be followed by one more stage of capitalism, "ultra-imperialism," in which capitalists from the leading economic power would work together to collectively exploit the world.[23]

Lenin had dismissed this scenario, arguing that the uneven development of capitalism across countries would prevent long-term cooperation of this kind. But the cooperative initiatives among capitalist powers during the 1920s initially seemed to confirm Kautsky's predictions.

In the end, however, the success of the post-1918 initiative to restore the pre-war international economic order was short-lived. The 1929 stock market crash in New York ushered in the Great Depression of 1929–33, the worst economic crisis experienced by the global economy in modern times. During the crisis, overall national output declined precipitously in most countries and levels of unemployment rose to record heights. International financial markets and world trade collapsed, while debtors defaulted on their external obligations. Governments everywhere—even those of Britain and the US—increased trade barriers and abandoned the gold standard.[24]

The latter policies signalled a turn toward a much more inward-oriented and closed form of economic nationalism than the kind List and his followers had advocated in the nineteenth century. Given the severity of the crisis, governments sought to insulate their citizens from external instability and to prioritize domestic needs over international economic commitments. Even famous British liberal economists such as John Maynard Keynes defended the need for "national self-sufficiency" at the height of the Great Depression. Explicitly turning his back on the liberal idea that free trade brings peace and prosperity, Keynes argued that countries had a greater need at that historical moment for policy autonomy to experiment with policies to generate a recovery.[25]

The causes of the global economic collapse of the early 1930s have been debated ever since. One particularly well-known analysis among IPE scholars is that of Charles Kindleberger who argued that a key cause was a leadership vacuum at the international level. In the pre-1914 period, the stable world economy had been fostered by the leadership of Britain, a country that had maintained open markets, lent long-term capital, and provided emergency short-term finance during crisis. Weakened by the First World War, Britain no longer had the ability to play this leadership role by the late 1920s and early 1930s. Although the US was emerging as the new dominant economic power, it was unwilling to play the same kind of leadership role during the crisis, as evidenced particularly by its pullback of foreign lending after 1929, its protectionist Smoot-Hawley tariff of 1930, and its refusal to write down foreign debts or act as a lender-of-last-resort when the crisis worsened.[26]

Whatever its cause, the collapse of the global economy signalled a dramatic reversal of globalization trends that had accelerated throughout the nineteenth century. Indeed, by the mid-1930s, the world economy had split up into a number of increasingly closed economic blocs centred around each of the world's leading economic powers. While many liberals lamented the complete unravelling of the nineteenth-century world, Marxists celebrated this turn of events as a sign that the final collapse of capitalism was near. How wrong they turned out to be.

Embedded Liberalism and the Postwar Order

If the reticence of US policy-makers to assume international leadership contributed to the Great Depression, their changed attitude during and after the Second World War played a central role in the rebirth of an integrated global capitalist economy. The greater willingness of US policy-makers to play an active global economic leadership role was apparent from the moment their country entered the Second World War in late 1941. Within

weeks of that decision, US officials had begun to develop detailed plans for the rebuilding of a more open and liberal postwar international economic order. These plans formed the basis of the Bretton Woods agreements, signed by 44 governments in 1944, which created a constitution for that postwar order.[27]

US officials were motivated partly by the recognition that the US would be the dominant economic power after the war and its firms could thus benefit enormously—just as British firms had—from such an order. But leading US policy-makers were also driven by a belief that the widespread protectionism and unstable exchange rates of the 1930s had contributed to both the Great Depression and the international political tensions that generated the war. From this perspective, the interwar period had taught an important lesson about the validity of the classic liberal arguments that linked free trade to global peace and prosperity.

US officials also sought to modify international economic liberalism to accommodate a second lesson of the 1930s experience: governments needed to be able to intervene in the economy to a greater degree than in the past. Across the industrialized world (including in the US with Roosevelt's New Deal), the trauma of the Great Depression had prompted politicians to assign greater priority to providing full employment and social security for their citizens. If a liberal international economic order was to be reconstructed, it would need to support, and be more embedded in, this new social purpose. As the author of the first US postwar plans, Harry Dexter White, put it in May 1942, what was needed was a "New Deal in international economics."[28]

The Keynesian revolution in economics only reinforced support for this new kind of "embedded liberal" ideology by legitimizing economic planning.[29] In his 1936 book *The General Theory of Employment, Interest and Income*, Keynes had developed a case for national macroeconomic management to prevent experiences like the Great Depression.[30] Some liberals saw Keynes as a traitor to their cause, but he highlighted that his ideas were designed to reform capitalism in order to save it. Keynes's thinking quickly attracted supporters around the world, including among many US officials involved in postwar planning.

Keynes then found himself working directly with these officials when he was put in charge of British negotiations with the US over the content of the postwar international financial system. Encouraged not just by the progressive views of his US counterparts but also by the prospects of US financial assistance, he abandoned his 1933 support for "national self-sufficiency" and became one of the most prominent supporters of the new embedded liberal ideology that sought to reconcile liberal multilateralism with the new government interventionism in economic life.[31] Indeed, alongside Harry Dexter White, Keynes is widely seen as one of the key architects of the Bretton Woods agreements.

In developing their postwar plans, US postwar planners were initially determined to reconcile liberal multilateralism not just with the new Keynesian and social security goals of industrialized countries but also with new state-led development goals that had become increasingly influential in many less industrialized countries.[32] The Great Depression had starkly revealed the vulnerability of commodity exporters to protectionism abroad and volatile (and declining) commodity prices. The collapse of agricultural exports had also undermined the political power of agricultural elites and opened the door to political groups that backed industrialization and more statist policies. Arising from this context, policy-makers from many poorer—or "Southern"—countries highlighted to US officials during the Bretton Woods negotiations their postwar commitment to state-led

growth and industrialization. This commitment was particularly strong among policy-makers from Latin American countries—which made up nineteen of the forty-four countries represented at the Bretton Woods conference—as well as among officials from China and India (still a British colony but whose Bretton Woods delegation included Indian nationalists).

Although the goals of these Southern officials were similar in some ways to those of nineteenth century Listian economic nationalists, a key difference was their interest in exploring how the international community might assist their national development. Encouraged by broader questioning of liberal orthodoxy at the time, they asked whether international organizations could be created to regulate or even supplant international market actors in ways that supported their development ambitions. They also called for the creation of international trade and financial rules that permitted the economic intervention of governments to support industrialization and development goals. This effort to marry liberal multilateralism with more interventionist practices aimed at supporting state-led development represented a kind of "Southern side" of embedded liberalism, and it appealed to many US officials inspired by the values of the New Deal.

The content of the Bretton Woods agreements reflected these "embedded liberal" values in both the Northern and Southern context. Governments committed to stable exchange rates and the free convertibility of their currencies for trade payments, but they also insisted on being allowed to protect their policy autonomy through controls on financial flows and adjustments of currency pegs. The Bretton Woods conference also established two international economic institutions—the IMF and the IBRD (International Bank for Reconstruction and Development (part of the World Bank))—to foster multilateral cooperation and manage the world economy by extending short-term loans to countries suffering balance of payments problems (the IMF) and long-term loans to foster development in poorer countries and postwar reconstruction (the IBRD).

These provisions created a much more legalized and institutionalized multilateral framework for the international financial order than had existed before the 1930s. The same approach was then applied in 1947 to the governance of international trade when 23 countries signed the General Agreement on Tariffs and Trade (GATT). In keeping with the embedded liberal ideology, the GATT supported freer trade in a multilateral context but subject to provisions that protected policy autonomy in various ways. The GATT was initially designed as a temporary arrangement until the creation of a more ambitious International Trade Organization (ITO) that also addressed the stabilization of commodity markets and the regulation of multinational corporations. But when the US Congress refused to ratify the ITO, the GATT became the permanent trade content of the new "Bretton Woods system."[33]

The onset of the Cold War in the late 1940s quickly changed the political context surrounding the implementation of the Bretton Woods system. The Soviet Union, which had participated in the Bretton Woods negotiations, refused to join the US-dominated order and soon created an alternative socialist economic bloc for its East European allies in 1949 called the Council for Mutual Economic Assistance (Comecon). After Mao Tse-tung came to power in 1949, the People's Republic of China was excluded from the Bretton Woods system and began to participate informally in Comecon, until Mao severed ties with the Soviet Union in the late 1950s and turned to a strategy of self-reliance.[34]

The Cold War also encouraged the US to initially sideline the Bretton Woods institutions.

Through Marshall Plan aid and other initiatives, the US chose to extend most loans directly to its allies rather than working through the IMF and IBRD. These allies were also allowed to delay commitments they had made to allow their currencies to be fully convertible into other currencies for cross-border trade transactions. By the 1960s, however, the Bretton Woods monetary system was more fully operational among the core western industrialized allies. That same decade also saw the completion of GATT trade negotiations that lowered trade barriers in more ambitious ways.

The period from the late 1940s until the late 1960s is often seen in retrospect as a kind of economic "golden age" for western industrialized countries. They experienced rapid growth rates with economic benefits that were widely shared across their populations. Trade and investment among these countries also expanded rapidly, encouraged by advances in communication and transportation technology. Throughout this period, US officials continued to promote embedded liberal norms in their relations with Europe and Japan, supporting domestic interventionist practices that were aimed at promoting social security and full employment.

Southern countries in regions such as Latin America, however, encountered more of a shift in US attitudes after the war.[35] Instead of supporting their state-led development goals, US policy-makers steered financial assistance toward more strategically important countries in Cold War battlegrounds in East Asia and Europe. This change in US priorities generated growing frustrations among Latin American officials, who called throughout the 1950s for the Bretton Woods system to provide more support for their state-led industrialization and development goals. Particularly vocal and influential was the Argentine head of the UN Economic Commission for Latin America, Raúl Prebisch, who became well-known for his argument that countries stuck in commodity exporting would suffer declining terms of trade over time.

In calling for greater international support for development goals, Prebisch and his Latin American supporters were also joined by Indian officials after that country's independence in 1947 and then by many others from elsewhere in Asia and Africa after the wave of decolonization in the late 1950s and 1960s. Taking advantage of their growing numbers in the United Nations system, this coalition of G77 countries pushed for the 1964 creation of the UN Conference on Trade and Development (UNCTAD)—with Prebisch as its first head—as a forum to press their cause. In response to this pressure, the US and other western powers endorsed a generalized system of trade preferences allowing greater access for manufactured exports from poor countries on a non-reciprocal basis. They also agreed to create a soft loan facility within the World Bank for poor countries (1960) and to back the establishment of regional development banks in Latin America (1960), Africa (1964), and Asia (1966). The IMF also created a new loan facility to provide greater support to poorer countries facing sudden declines in export earnings. These various initiatives helped to strengthen the Southern side of embedded liberalism.

Crisis in the 1970s and the Rise of Neoliberalism

The political context surrounding these reforms was transformed by the decision of the Organization of the Petroleum Exporting Countries (OPEC) countries to quadruple the price of oil in 1973. Emboldened by OPEC's display of "commodity power," a wide coalition of Southern governments used a special session of the UN General Assembly in 1974 to demand a comprehensive "New International Economic Order." Supporters of the NIEO proposed to reform the Bretton Woods system to benefit poorer countries through initiatives such as increasing aid, improving terms of trade, strengthening preferential and non-reciprocal trade arrangements, regulating transnational corporations, and providing more influence to the South in international economic decision-making.[36]

Many western analysts saw the NIEO as too radical a challenge to the status quo and the liberal principles of the Bretton Woods system. At the same time, some in the South argued that the NIEO was not radical enough. These neo-Marxist "dependency" theorists argued that the NIEO project was merely a reformist strategy of "the Third World bourgeoisie" to accelerate capitalist industrialization in poorer countries.[37] They urged instead a more radical "de-linking" from the capitalist Bretton Woods system altogether on the grounds that global capitalism was inherently exploitative of poorer countries.

The NIEO proposal and the ideas of dependency theorists were not the only challenges to the existing international economic order. As the US faced growing economic competition from countries such as West Germany and Japan, prominent American policy-makers began to ask whether their country needed to defend its economic interests with more nationalist policies. In August 1971, this position emerged ascendant when President Richard Nixon unilaterally imposed tariffs on a range of imports and ended the dollar's convertibility into gold (a monetary arrangement that had been a key foundation of the Bretton Woods monetary order) as a way of addressing growing US trade deficits and constraints on US policy autonomy.[38] By 1973, the US and other major western countries began to allow their currencies to float vis-à-vis each other, signalling the collapse of the fixed exchange rate system of Bretton Woods.

Compounding the sense of crisis in the early 1970s was the fact that the western-centred international economy had entered into a serious recession, signalling the end of the long postwar economic boom. The economic slowdown was accompanied by rising inflation, provoking widespread criticism in the US and other western countries of Keynesianism and the economic status quo. To address "stagflation," many analysts and business leaders demanded a return to a more limited economic role for the state and freer markets. Inspired by "neoliberal" intellectuals such as Friedrich Hayek, they argued that Keynesian economic policies, the growth of the welfare state, and other interventionist policies had generated growing inefficiencies and was corrosive of individual freedom.[39]

By the end of the decade, it was increasingly clear that the neoliberal position was gaining the upper hand politically in key western countries, particularly after the elections of Margaret Thatcher in Britain in 1979 and Ronald Reagan in the US one year later. Throughout the 1980s and 1990s, policy-makers across the OECD region rolled back government intervention in their own domestic economies through deregulation and privatization initiatives. At the international level, western governments began to liberalize restrictions on cross-border trade and foreign direct investment through unilateral initiatives and various bilateral, regional, and multilateral agreements. In 1995, the multilateral trading system was also strengthened with the creation of the World Trade Organization, a body with more teeth to enforce international trade rules than the GATT.

Even more dramatic was the liberalization of capital controls across all industrialized countries. During the early postwar years, most industrialized countries had employed such controls as tools to protect their policy autonomy from speculative cross-border financial flows. By the early 1990s,

however, all OECD countries had abolished these controls, a move that provided investors greater freedom to operate internationally than they had had since the 1920s. Encouraged by the information technology revolution, they took full advantage of this freedom as cross-border financial flows grew exponentially during the 1980s and 1990s.[40]

The neoliberal revolution in economic policy also spread to many Southern countries in this same period. An important catalyst for this policy shift was the international debt crisis that was triggered by rapidly rising interest rates after 1979 and the accompanying global recession of the early 1980s. After borrowing heavily from abroad in the 1970s (often encouraged by western banks that were trying to recycle the new wealth of oil producing countries), many Southern countries—particularly in Latin America and Africa—could no longer easily service their external debts in this changed economic context. The grand ambitions of global reform through the NIEO quickly collapsed as policy-makers in these countries scrambled to address severe financial crises at home. To avoid defaulting, they accepted emergency funding from the IMF and promised to undergo "structural adjustment programs" involving deregulation, privatization, cuts to government spending, currency devaluations, and external liberalization.

The IMF's role in this process was a far cry from the Bretton Woods vision that its lending would protect a country's policy autonomy. Instead of supporting embedded liberal values, the Fund came to be seen as the lead agent of a creditor cartel that was forcing a dismantling of the postwar statist policies across the South. The introduction of more free market, export-oriented policies encountered much domestic political resistance in these countries, but it was also welcomed by some local elites and domestic groups that were attracted to neoliberal ideas (or what began to be called the "Washington consensus"). Indeed, the political power of these latter groups may help to explain why governments of larger debtor countries did not bargain harder with the IMF and their creditors for debt writedowns or less strict conditions on IMF loans.

The 1980s and 1990s also witnessed one further transformation of the Bretton Woods system: its expansion to include communist and formerly communist countries. In the wake of Mao's death in 1976, the new Chinese leadership under Deng Xiaoping signalled its interest in rejoining the IMF and the World Bank as part of its new more outward-looking and market-oriented development strategy.[41] After being admitted in 1980, China quickly became one of the Bank's largest clients. China's increasingly deep re-incorporation into the global economy was then reinforced by its accession to the WTO in 2001.

Russia joined the Bretton Woods institutions a decade after China in 1992, soon after the dissolution of the Soviet Union. Russian authorities saw IMF and World Bank membership—and access to their loans—as an important part of their broader economic reform strategy at the time and the IMF subsequently became deeply involved in backing Russia's initial efforts to move decisively and quickly toward a market economy. It played a similar role with other former members of the Eastern bloc, some of which had joined the Bretton Woods institutions even earlier in the context of debt crises, such as Hungary (1982) and Poland (1986). The formal dissolution of Comecon in 1991 then signalled the final collapse of a formal alternative bloc to the Bretton Woods system.

After Neoliberalism?

If the 1980s and 1990s were the age of neoliberalism, the millennium closed with several developments that signalled its political fragility. One was the growth of transnational protest movements against global neoliberalism as well as the WTO, IMF, and World Bank. These protest movements garnered considerable political support in the late 1990s, forcing neoliberal advocates onto the defensive. In 1998, an OECD initiative to create a new Multilateral Agreement on Investment was abandoned in the face of widespread popular opposition. The next year, protestors converged on Seattle to help shut down an initiative to launch a new round of WTO trade negotiations (although it was subsequently launched in Doha two years later).[42]

These protest movements included a diverse collection of critics. Well-represented were familiar opponents of economic liberalism such as economic nationalists, neo-Marxists, and supporters of embedded liberal values. But the transnational protests also drew political strength from new lines of criticism. Environmentalists and "green" thinkers argued that free-market policies and economic globalization were undermining ecological sustainability in both local and global settings.[43] Feminists called attention to the ways that neoliberal global economic restructuring often reinforced gender inequalities.[44] Groups representing indigenous peoples also highlighted the dangers that neoliberal globalization posed to local cultures and long-standing ways of living.[45]

Given the diversity of views, the transnational protest movements were often more successful in opposing neoliberal initiatives than in advancing a coherent alternative. Indeed, they often celebrated this diversity, arguing that they represented "the one no and the many yesses."[46] In places such as the World Social Forum (created in 2001), however, important coalitions were formed and alternative worldviews strengthened. While neoliberals such as Thatcher declared that there was "no alternative" to neoliberalism, the World Social Forum highlighted that "a new world is possible."[47]

Another important challenge to supporters of neoliberalism in the late 1990s was the East Asian financial crisis of 1997–98. Neoliberal policy-makers in the dominant G7 powers attributed the crisis to policy mistakes in the afflicted countries. But many others blamed the newly unfettered and lightly regulated global financial markets as well as the IMF which imposed very intrusive and often unhelpful conditions on its emergency lending during the crisis. In the wake of the crisis, many countries in East Asia and Latin America began to reduce their vulnerability to global financial flows and the IMF's neoliberal advice by accumulating large foreign exchange reserves. The accumulation of these reserves represented a new kind of economic nationalism that protected the policy autonomy of governments seeking to pursue more state-led development strategies, while often helping those governments to also maintain undervalued currencies that boosted the competitiveness of their countries' firms in world markets.[48]

The 2007–08 global financial crisis provided further evidence of the political fragility of the neoliberal project. Unlike the 1997–98 crisis, it unfolded in the core of the world economy, highlighting very starkly to US and European citizens the dangers and costs of unregulated finance. Not surprisingly, there were quickly many calls for a return to the tighter control of finance that had existed in the embedded liberal era. Indeed, at the height of the crisis when western governments were engaged in massive public bailouts of private financial institutions, some IPE scholars predicted that the neoliberal era had come to an end. As Benjamin Cohen put it, "like the collapse of the Soviet Union, the crash of the global financial structure has all the earmarks of a genuine systemic transformation—the end of an age of vast, untrammeled market expansion and neoliberal deregulation."[49]

In the wake of the crisis, however, it quickly became apparent that the situation was not that clear. Although the US and European authorities introduced new regulations over financial markets, the content of those regulations was remarkably tame.[50] Growing public fiscal deficits generated by financial bailouts and the economic recession also prompted cutbacks to public spending and austerity measures that often seemed to reinforce neoliberal policy paradigms rather than challenge them.[51]

But neoliberal ideology faces challenges in the wake of the crisis not just from within the core of the world economy. Policy-makers in emerging powers such as China and many southern countries have emerged from the crisis experience with a much more skeptical view of US-backed neoliberal policies as a model to emulate. As one Chinese official put it, "we used to see the US as our teacher but now we realise that our teacher keeps making mistakes and we've decided to quit the class."[52] Alternative development models, often endorsing a larger economic role for the state, are gaining new ground.

This change is being reinforced by the erosion of the G7's dominance of global economic governance, an erosion that the 2007–08 financial crisis highlighted very clearly. At the height of the crisis, the G7 leaders recognized their need for support from emerging powers, particularly China, which had emerged as the world's largest creditor (and holder of an enormous stash of US financial assets). They responded by creating the G20 leaders' forum in November 2008 which quickly replaced the G7 as the premier body for global economic cooperation. At the G20's urging, reforms were launched to give emerging powers more say in the IMF, and international financial regulatory bodies also quickly widened their membership to include all G20 members. The growing influence of emerging powers in international economic policy-making has already been apparent in areas such as the IMF's greater acceptance of capital controls (which Brazil, India, and China all employ).[53]

The crisis also encouraged emerging powers to launch initiatives to begin to reduce their dependence on the US-centred global economic order in the coming years. China, for example, has suddenly begun to promote the internationalization of its currency in an effort to reduce its dependence on the dollar's global role. It has also worked closely with other East Asian countries to strengthen regional financial cooperation, including through the creation of a $240 billion regional fund for crisis lending. Countries in other regions such as Latin America have also been taking steps to reduce their dependence on the US dollar and US markets. In 2014, the BRICS countries (Brazil, Russia, India, China, and South Africa) also announced the creation of two institutions with lending mandates similar to the World Bank and IMF: a New Development Bank (headquartered in Shanghai) and a Contingent Reserve Arrangement to provide liquidity to address short-term balance of payments pressures.

In short, we are living in a period of flux in which the future of neoliberalism and even of the US-centric global economic order is increasingly uncertain. Another major international financial crisis could well serve as a catalyst for further change. It remains very unclear what ideologies will emerge from this period of flux as the most influential in the politics of the world economy. But an historical perspective does make one point very clear: no single ideology has ever remained hegemonic for long. Change is the one constant.

Acknowledgement

Many thanks to Greg Anderson for his helpful comments.

Notes

1   Braudel 1985.
2   See for example Hobsbawn 1975, 64–87.
3   Smith 1976, 25.
4   See Earle 1966, 123.
5   Ricardo 1817.
6   Cain 1979.
7   Quoted in Cain 1979. See also Neff 1990.
8   Gallarotti 1995.
9   Quoted in Semmel 1993, 72.
10 The precise meaning of "economic nationalism" is sometimes contested. I use it here simply to refer to an ideology that prioritizes nationalist values in economic policy. With this definition, it is clear that not all nineteenth century economic nationalists were opposed to free trade policies. As noted above, many British policy-makers backed free trade for nationalist reasons—it would bolster British economic power over other countries—rather than liberal ones. The best known "economic nationalists" of the nineteenth century, however, were List and his followers. See Helleiner 2002.
11 Quotes from Helleiner 2002, 311.
12 Chang 2002.
13 Morris-Suzuki 1989.
14 Granatstein 1985, Henley 1989–90.
15 Waterbury 1999, 325.
16 Quoted in Gopalakrishnan 1959, 106.
17 See for example Rodney 1972.
18 Mommsen 1981.
19 Quoted in Hoselitz 1949, 232.
20 Mommsen 1981, Brewer 1980.
21 Lenin 1916 [1970].
22 Lenin 1916 [1970], 14.
23 Kautsky 1914 [1970].
24 James 2001.
25 Keynes 1933.
26 Kindleberger 1973.
27 Gardner 1980, Van Dormael 1978, Helleiner 2014a.
28 Quoted in Helleiner 2014a, ch. 4.
29 The phrase "embedded liberalism" was developed by Ruggie 1982.
30 Keynes 1936.
31 Skidelsky 2000.
32 For this and next two paragraphs, see Helleiner 2014a.
33 Zeiler 1999.
34 Friedman 1989.
35 For this and the paragraph, see Helleiner 2014a, Conclusion.
36 Murphy 1984.
37 Quote from Amin 1990, 115.
38 Gowa 1983.
39 One of Hayek's most influential works was his 1944 *The road to serfdom* (Hayek 1944). See also Wapshott 2012.
40 Helleiner 1994, Abdelal 2007.
41 Vogel 2011.
42 Seoane and Taddei 2002.
43 Helleiner 1996.
44 Marchand and Sisson 2011.
45 Maiguashca 1994.
46 Klein 2001, 89.
47 Quoted in Houtart and Polet 2001, 122.

48 Chin 2010.
49 Cohen 2009, 437.
50 Helleiner 2014b, ch.4.
51 Blyth 2013.

52 Unnamed official quoted in Beattie, Alan and Dyer, Geoff, "Free-market ideals survive the crunch," *Financial Times*, 27 November 2009.
53 Helleiner 2014b.

Key Terms

economic liberalism
embedded liberalism

Marxist theories of imperialism
neoliberalism

Questions for Review

1. Does free trade generate peace and prosperity?
2. Which of the critiques of classical economic liberalism, if any, do you find the most persuasive?
3. Is the influence of neoliberal ideology waning?

4. What are the most significant challenges to neoliberalism in the contemporary age?
5. What explains the changing political influence of GPE ideologies over time?

Further Resources

Blyth, M. (Ed.) (2009). *Handbook of IPE: IPE as a global conversation*.

Frieden, J. (2006). *Global capitalism: Its fall and rise in the twentieth century* (New York: W.W. Norton.

Heilbroner, R. (1999). *The worldly philosophers*, 7th ed. New York: Touchstone.

Paul, D. and Amawi, A. (2013). *Theoretical evolution of international political economy*, 3rd ed. Oxford: Oxford University Press.

Phillips, N. and Waever, C. (Eds). (2010). *International political economy: Debating the past, present and future*.

Schwartz, H. (2010). *States versus markets: The emergence of a global economy*, 3rd ed. New York: Palgrave MacMillan.

References

Abdelal, R. (2007). *Capital rules: The construction of global finance*. Cambridge: Harvard University Press.

Amin, S. (1990). *Delinking*. London: Zed Books.

Blyth, M. *Austerity: The history of a dangerous idea*. Oxford: Oxford University Press.

Braudel, F. (1985). *Civilization and capitalism*. London: Fontana.

Brewer, A. (1980). *Marxist theories of imperialism*. London: Routledge.

Cain, P. (1979). "Capitalism, war and internationalism in the thought of Richard Cobden." *British Journal of International Studies* 5(3), 229–47

Chang, H-J. (2002). *Kicking away the ladder*. London: Anthem Press.

Chin, G. (2010). Remaking the architecture: The emerging powers, self-insuring and regional insulation. *International Affairs* 86(3), 693–715.

Cohen, B. (2009). "A grave case of myopia." *International Interactions*, 35, 418–44.

Earle, E. (1966). "Adam Smith, Alexander Hamilton, Frederick List: The economic foundations of military power." In E. Earle (Ed.), *The makers of modern strategy*. New York: Atheneum.

Friedman, E. (1989). "Maoist and post-Mao conceptualizations of world capitalism." In S. Kim (Ed.), *China and the world*. Boulder: Westview.

Gallarotti, G. (1995). *The anatomy of an international monetary regime: The classical gold standard, 1880–1914*. New York: Oxford University Press.

Gardner, R. (1980). *Sterling dollar diplomacy in current perspective*. New York: Columbia University Press.

Gopalakrishnan, P. (1959). "Mahadev Govind Ranade." In P. Gopalakrishnan, *Development of economic ideas in India*. New Delhi: People's Publishing House.

Gowa, J. (1983). *Closing the gold window. Domestic politics and the end of Bretton Woods*. Ithaca: Cornell University Press.

Granatstein, J. (1985). "Free trade between Canada and the US: The issue that won't go away" in D. Stairs and G. Winham (Eds), *The politics of Canada's economic relationship with the US*. Toronto: University of Toronto Press.

Hayek, F. (1944). *The road to serfdom*. London: Routledge.

Helleiner, E. (1994). *States and the re-emergence of global finance*. Ithaca: Cornell University Press.

Helleiner, E. (1996). "International political economy and the Greens." *New Political Economy 1*(1), 59–78

Helleiner, E. (2002). "Economic nationalism as a challenge to economic liberalism?" *International Studies Quarterly 46*(3), 307–29.

Helleiner, E. (2014a). *Forgotten foundations of Bretton Woods: International development and the making of the postwar order*. Ithaca: Cornell University Press.

Helleiner, E. (2014b). *The status quo crisis: Global financial governance after the 2008 Meltdown*. Oxford: Oxford University Press.

Henley, K. (1989–90). "The international roots of economic nationalist ideology in Canada 1846–85." *Journal of Canadian Studies 24*, 107–21.

Hobsbawm, E. (1975). *The age of capital: 1848–75*. New York: Scribner.

Hoselitz, B. (1949). "Socialism, Communism, and International Trade" *Journal of Political Economy 57*(3), 227–41.

Houtart, F. and Polet, F. (Eds). (2001). *The other Davos*. London: Zed Books.

James, H. (2001). *The end of globalization: Lessons from the Great Depression*. Cambridge: Harvard University Press.

Kautsky, K. (1914)[1970]. "Ultra-imperialism" *New Left Review 59*, 41–6.

Keynes, J. M. (1933). "National self-sufficiency" in *Collected writings of J.M.Keynes—Activities 1931–39* (1980), 233–46.

Keynes, J. M. (1936). *The general theory of employment, interest, and income*. London: MacMillan.

Kindleberger, C. (1973). *The world in depression*. Berkeley: University of California Press.

Klein, N. (2001). "Reclaiming the commons." *New Left Review 9*(May–June), 81–9.

Lenin, V. (1916) [1970]. *Imperialism: The highest stage of capitalism*. Moscow: Progress.

Maiguashca, B. (1994). "The transnational indigenous movement in a changing world order." In Y. Sakamoto, ed., *Global transformations*. New York: United Nations University Press.

Marchand, M. and Sisson, A. (2011). *Gender and global restructuring*. New York: Routledge.

Mommsen, W. (1981). *Theories of imperialism*. London: Weidenfeld and Nicolson.

Morris-Suzuki, T. (1989). *A history of Japanese economic thought*. London: Routledge.

Murphy, C. (1984). *The emergence of the NIEO ideology*. Boulder: Westview.

Neff, S. (1990). *Friends but no allies: Economic liberalism and the law of nations*. New York: Columbia University Press.

Ricardo, D. (1817) [1948]. *On the principles of political economy and taxation*. London: Dent.

Rodney, W. (1972). *How Europe Underdevelooped Africa*. London: Bogle-L'Ouverture Publications.

Ruggie, J. (1982). "International regimes, transactions and change: Embedded liberalism in the postwar economic order." *International Organization 36*, 379–415.

Semmel, B. (1993). *The liberal ideal and the demons of empire.* Baltimore: John Hopkins University Press.

Seoane, J. and Taddei, E. (2002). From Seattle to Porto Alegre: The anti-neoliberal globalization movement. *Current Sociology 50*(1), 99–122.

Skidelsky, R. (2000). *John Maynard Keynes: Fighting for Britain 1937–46.* Oxford: Macmillan.

Smith, A. (1976). *An inquiry into the nature and causes of the wealth of nations.* New York: Oxford University Press.

Van Dormael, A. (1978). *Bretton Woods: Birth of a monetary system.* London: Macmillan.

Vogel, E. (2011). *Deng Xiaoping and the transformation of China.* Cambridge: Belknap Press of Harvard University Press.

Wapshott, N. (2012). *Keynes Hayek: The clash that defined modern economics.* New York: W.W. Norton.

Waterbury, J. (1999). The long gestation and brief triumph of import-substituting Industrialization. *World Development 27*(2),323–41.

Zeiler, T. (1999). *Free trade, free world: The advent of GATT.* Durham: University of North Carolina Press.

6

To Trade or Not to Trade?

The Political Economy of International Exchange

Mark R. Brawley

Ever since Adam Smith's criticisms of eighteenth-century mercantilism (1776), thinkers have offered potent arguments favouring the liberalization of trade. Smith and others claim that free trade provides an effective route to increase a country's wealth. Smith's arguments gained added support as others elaborated the argument over time. If modern economists agree on one thing, it is the wisdom of opening up trade between countries. Yet, historically, countries rarely adopt free trade. Why this disparity between economists' logic and political practice? Consider the experience of Western Europe as it emerged from the Middle Ages; the volume of trade grew rapidly. Monarchs observed wealth being generated, and reacted by taxing this new activity. Then they attempted to manipulate trade patterns to their state's advantage, through a set of policies—what we call mercantilism. Mercantilist thought dominated European policies covering trade between competing kingdoms, as well as between Europe and the rest of the world (Heckscher 1955). Mercantilist policies persisted from their origin in the fourteenth century until well into the nineteenth. Smith's key criticism of these policies can be boiled down to one central

notion: governments were interfering with markets for political purposes. Smith had more to say than just that, of course, because he also wanted to challenge how people thought about wealth as well as how they understood the functioning of international trade. (Smith also thought that there were a number of circumstances where government needed to interfere in markets.) Yet, at its core, his argument carries on. Modern political economists build on Smith's thinking to explain both why states adopt free trade, but also why they so often veer away from this policy.

The challenge is to understand why trade policy has varied across states, as well as over time. If we were to look at current international political economic practices, goods flow relatively freely over many borders. Trade has become more liberalized over the past few decades. Most states appear to be following relatively open trade policies today, compared to almost any period in the past. To explain these differences, analysts focus on several potential causes. Some arguments emphasize the aggregate effect trade might have on a state, but juxtapose the potential material gains with other values or goals. Other arguments disaggregate the impact of trade, evaluating the way trade redistributes wealth inside a country. Contemporary debates focus on the best way to model the role trade plays in the domestic economy, and the adjustment processes trade triggers. Below, I summarize the development of these ideas, describe recent debates, highlight where research appears to be headed, and then suggest some areas for further consideration. As trade has become more and more important to contemporary societies, its political significance has grown. Our understanding of the politics of trade has likewise progressed, but several important questions remain.

Trade in the Aggregate

Adam Smith contributed two rather important insights into our comprehension of trade and the politics surrounding the choice of policies. First, as the title of his seminal work implies, Smith challenged the mercantilist concept of wealth. Monarchs had sought to tax and control trade, to amass more power than their rivals. Trade could be manipulated via regulations, skewing the balance of payments. Kings and queens developed policies they believed would lead to more money flowing into their own country, rather than their trading partners' lands. It was the balance—the difference owed or owing—monarchs concentrated on. In those days, the generally accepted means of international payment consisted of gold or silver; monarchs needed the precious metals to pay for mercenaries, to maintain their security against internal and external threats. Mercantilist writers preached that there was a finite amount of gold and silver available. Thus, if one state successfully accumulated more of these metals through the payments received from trade, there would be less precious metals available for everyone else. Smith challenged this concept of the nature of wealth. Having a large reserve of gold and silver was a

limited vision, he claimed. Instead, he suggested that money was merely the means of obtaining other items; it was the ability to consume goods and services that measured the wealth of a nation, not its stockpile of precious metals.

Second, Smith attacked the protectionist trade practices mercantilists recommended. Mercantilists designed policies to attain a positive balance of payments. High **tariffs** (as taxes) were intended to add to the government's revenues, but also to discourage imports while promoting exports. Mercantilists' understanding of wealth meant their aim was not to increase economic activity per se, but to ensure a positive flow of payments—they wanted to make sure more gold and silver came into the country than left. When all states tried to do the same thing, however, they effectively discouraged trade. Smith argued that opening up the flow of goods over borders would increase the volume of trade. Items difficult to produce in Britain were naturally relatively expensive when little trade took place; international exchange allowed one to locate these goods more cheaply elsewhere. By selling more to foreigners, and using the earnings to purchase from abroad these goods they had difficulty making at home, Britons would be able to consume more in total—thus adding to the country's wealth. Smith's logic provides not only a new view on wealth, but also a key insight into what we refer to as **comparative advantage**. All producers cannot make the same good with equal efficiency (i.e., at the same cost). For example, eighteenth-century Britain could not meet all its agricultural needs easily, given its climate, soil, and population density. It made more sense for the country to focus production on a range of industrial goods, selling the excess abroad in exchange for the excess foodstuffs foreigners had to sell. Importing food made more sense than trying to get the same agricultural output from local suppliers.

Writing in the early nineteenth century, David Ricardo refined Smith's ideas by popularizing the logic of comparative advantage using basic math and geometry. By using assumptions to simplify the discussion, then concentrating the logic in these forms, Ricardo made a more persuasive case for liberalizing trade. The liberal arguments also found a more receptive audience in Britain in these years. On the one hand, Britain had been industrializing, giving it a clear advantage in manufacturing over other states. On the other hand, the country lost a chunk of its mercantilist empire when the Americans won their War of Independence. British political leaders therefore had good reason to reconsider trade policy. Following the recommendations of Smith and Ricardo, Parliament began stripping away tariffs and other bits of mercantilist legislation in the 1840s. The country's economy responded much as Smith or Ricardo would have predicted. Farmers grew less of the goods that were difficult to produce in Britain (such as wheat), and shifted their emphasis to products more suitable to the skills and inputs British farmers held. With tariffs lower, foreign suppliers served the domestic market. Grain prices fell, but British farmers did well by focusing their production on livestock; urban industrial workers, taking advantage of cheaper bread, could now afford to spend more on meat and dairy products. As agriculture changed, more capital and workers were concentrated in urban areas, producing manufactured goods; Britain's manufactured exports boomed. Britain's adoption of Smith's advice made the country decidedly richer.

For many foreigners who watched Britain's economic rise in the early nineteenth century, the lesson was clear. Freeing up trade—eliminating tariffs—made one's country wealthier. Britain's success prompted governments elsewhere to emulate its trade policy. There were also critics, however.

Some questioned whether an increase in the volume of trade would play out the same way for these other states as it had for Britain. Perhaps best known among these critics is Friedrich List, a German economist who emigrated to the United States in 1825. List understood that if other states adopted free trade, the economic pressures would prompt these countries to pursue their comparative advantage (1966). Trade brings **specialization**. If others engaged in free trade with Britain in the mid-nineteenth century, would not Britain focus on what it was already good at? If Britain continued to pursue industrial manufacturing, Britain's trading partners would concentrate production on other sorts of goods—and thus be discouraged from developing industrial sectors. List pointed out that this would surely suit Britain's desires, for although all the trading partners might grow wealthier, this pattern of exchange would have other consequences. Industrial capacity also serves as a basis for national power, List pointed out. Free trade with Britain actually meant discouraging industrial development in favour of the pursuit of wealth, but it also conceded an advantage in power to Britain.

Despite such criticisms, liberal trade policies were adopted across much of the world by the middle of the nineteenth century (Kindleberger 1975). Britain may have moved to free trade first, but it took a trade deal between Britain and France to trigger broader changes. France maintained a number of trade agreements with other European powers. In these treaties, France agreed to grant these other states access to the French market at the same rate as the "most favoured nation," as long as the other state reciprocated. The thing was, prior to 1860, the "most favoured" tariff rate remained very high. Only when France agreed to lower its tariffs on British imports (in the Cobden–Chevalier Treaty of 1860), did trade treaties offer a chance for other states to make similar offers to France. As they sought to gain equally easy access to the French market, they had to lower their rates for French exports. If these other states had treaties with most favoured nation clauses with their neighbours, then those other states could take advantage of France's actions. Cobden–Chevalier started a chain reaction, so that within a few years, most European states had lowered their tariffs (Pahre 2001). Trade grew rapidly, especially because transportation and communication technologies were improving at the same time. Railroads and steamships allowed for the rapid movement of bulky commodities over great distances, integrating markets around the world. The expanding telegraph network made it possible for merchants to select the best markets to ship goods to, and allowed entrepreneurs to coordinate production internationally.

The following decade brought a sharp economic downturn, however, and the growth of trade was an essential culprit. Excess production of grain, iron, and other goods drove prices down sharply. Producers in a number of places faced intense global competition. With industrial producers on the brink of ruin, farmers unable to turn a profit, and labourers thrown out of work, governments often reintroduced protectionist tariffs. Another wave of protectionist tariffs came in the 1890s. A few states—notably Britain—stuck with free trade. Most raised tariffs in one way or another. When the First World War broke out, even those states that had rigidly adhered to free trade broke with that tradition. Like Britain, they adopted measures to reshape international exchange to support their war efforts. Once the war ended, Britain and others encouraged all states to return to something like free trade. Despite widespread belief in the benefits of liberal trade, it proved difficult to resurrect open international exchange. The new states of eastern and central Europe, created out of the disintegrating Austro-Hungarian and Russian empires, preferred to develop their own domestic industries. They considered manufacturing a key component of national power, which they sought to boost if they were to maintain their sovereign independence. Even among the victors, tariffs proved attractive as a way to help them shift back to peacetime production, as well as for governments to gain revenues needed to pay down debts.

The onset of the Great Depression in 1930 drove states to again erect barriers to trade. Governments saw tariffs as a useful way to defend employment at home; even if they believed they could adopt other policies to stimulate recovery, each government wanted its efforts to translate into jobs and profits within its own borders, so they applied tariffs alongside other responses to the crisis. A series of problems plagued the international economy as a result. The volume of trade (which had never recovered from the First World War) collapsed. Soon, some states were manipulating international economic activity in anticipation of another major war. Several countries—most notably Nazi Germany and Imperial Japan—concluded from the experiences of the First World War that any future contest would be settled by economic might. Leaders in these countries assumed the next war would be another struggle of attrition; resources would determine the victors. Since the other major powers in the system either dominated far-flung empires (e.g., Britain and France) or controlled continental-scale territories (e.g., the US and Soviet Union), politicians in Germany and Japan designed their countries' foreign economic policies to amass the material resources necessary to prosecute a future conflict.

The fascist countries' policies harkened back to mercantilism in some ways, but as Albert O. Hirschman described in 1945, they were quite sophisticated, and intended to achieve political as well as economic ends (1969). One goal was obviously the amassing of specific assets, to directly enhance the country's war-fighting capacity. A second goal, however, was clearly political: to insulate the national economy from external pressure. The fascist states sought economic autonomy, because they knew they could not increase their power without provoking responses from the status-quo powers. In the wake of the high casualties of the First World War, the established states were reluctant to employ military force again. Instead, in the 1920s the great powers, either individually or through the League of Nations, hoped to enforce international order by applying economic sanctions. Autonomy meant that the fascist states could resist such pressures. Finally, Hirschman noted how fascist foreign economic policies were also designed to give these states political influence over others. In that sense, countries such as Nazi Germany sought to establish trade between themselves and nearby states, but with a particular volume and content. The logic was less about markets or the pursuit of wealth, and more about national governments finding leverage vis-à-vis one another. By trading in goods significant to one's partner, but not to itself, the Nazi government generated patterns of trade that granted it influence over others. Hirschman revived the sorts of concerns List and others had raised—while international trade could add to a country's wealth, there could be important non-economic consequences.

These same ideas received an additional boost in prominence in the 1950s and 1960s. An Argentinian economist, Raúl Prebisch, had observed how economic downturns affected the goods exchanged in trade (1950). Prebisch noted that primary products, as commodities, often suffered sharp drops in their price whenever economic activity slowed. Prices for industrial goods would drop too, but not by as much. Moreover, a similar pattern could be seen during economic upswings, where the prices for primary products recovered, but not as quickly as the prices for manufactures. Prebisch also recognized that the primary products

remained roughly similar over time, whereas industrial manufactures became increasingly sophisticated, which meant it took ever larger amounts of the primary products to exchange for manufactured goods (Toye and Toye 2006). Prebisch concluded that liberalized trade concentrated benefits in the hands of the more economically advanced countries, and left the non-industrialized countries falling farther and farther behind. He therefore recommended that economically developing countries employ protectionism as part of an economic development strategy.

Although Prebisch was working within the confines of neoclassical economics when he developed his arguments, his reasoning echoed concerns also voiced by a great number of Marxists. They borrowed Prebisch's thinking, refining and adapting it to argue that international market relations created patterns of dependency (Frank 1966). The economically less developed states remained poor and non-industrialized because they participated in international markets, according to this analysis. The combination of Marxist and non-Marxist thinking helped drive most economically developing countries away from free trade policies from the 1950s until the 1980s. That trend only reversed once the burdens of international debt forced many states to re-engage the international market, whether they liked it or not. The collapse of the Soviet Union in 1991 then signalled the end of the clearest ideological alternative to market-based economic practices. Since the end of the Cold War, almost all states have adopted more liberal trade policies—with some striking results.

The resurgence of liberal thinking [neoliberalism], often referred to in global circles as the "Washington Consensus" (because those beliefs were reflected in policies recommended by the circle of international institutions based in Washington, DC, including the IMF and World Bank), encouraged countries to adopt freer trade. Although economic statistics suggest the basic insights of Smith and Ricardo still attain at the aggregate level, debates over the wisdom of free trade haven't ended. As in the case of critics such as List and Hirschman, the volume and content of the goods in trade matter for non-economic reasons. Increasingly, we find people accepting the claim that freer trade increases a state's total wealth; despite this consensus, people raise different sorts of concerns. They juxtapose the advantage of being able to consume cheaper goods with possible disadvantages that are more difficult to measure, such as cultural change, environmental damage, and so on. Many people express concern that by accepting goods in trade from any and all countries, they are essentially endorsing any and all economic practices—if you buy shoes made in a foreign land by child labour, aren't you accepting that practice? The list of possible concerns is long: use of child workers, prison labour, unsafe working conditions, environmental degradation, and so on. Thus the debate about how to evaluate the costs and benefits associated with trade continues.

These debates largely focus on the overall gains from trade—what does each state get, in the aggregate? There are other considerations as well. As during the great economic downturns of the 1870s or the 1930s, governments introduced tariffs because they saw trade as a source of trouble, rather than an economic solution. Why would they look on trade in that way? The answer lies in how trade (or more specifically the pursuit of comparative advantage) triggers specialization. Increases in trade may mean cheaper goods for consumers, but they also mean reorganizing production, as local production shifts to alternative goods. That process redistributes wealth within society. This provides a different way for us to think about how governments set trade policy.

Disaggregating the Impact of Trade

While economists understood the logic of comparative advantage in the early nineteenth century, they struggled with questions concerning the implementation of theory for a very long time. Producers should focus on the goods they could make more efficiently than others—but what specific goods or services did that mean for any one country? A clear answer only emerged in the 1920s. Eli Heckscher and Bertil Ohlin, two economists studying regional variation in markets and prices in Sweden, observed exchange occurring between parts of the country. As they modelled the microeconomic bases for the patterns of this internal trade, they realized they could translate their findings to the international level. Heckscher and Ohlin observed that any good requires a particular mix of inputs to produce. In some places, the inputs needed to produce a particular good were readily and cheaply available, while in another location those same inputs were rarer (and thus more expensive). The placement of these inputs (or factors of production, as they are also called) made it easier for producers in one locale to make a certain good efficiently, while the absence of other inputs in that same place made producing alternative items too expensive. By breaking down production into combinations of inputs, and then considering the relative cost of these factors of production, Heckscher and Ohlin came to an understanding of the bases of comparative advantage (Heckscher 1919; Ohlin 1933; for an insightful history, see Flam and Flanders 2000). Their thinking remains the foundation for most modern neoclassical economic theories of trade.

The **Heckscher-Ohlin (or H-O) model** provides the essential logic for understanding the gains from trade. In its simplest form, there are two countries, with two possible goods, and two possible factors of production. Usually, we think of capital and labour as the two factors; thus one good requires a higher amount of capital input per unit of labour used, whereas the other good requires a lower amount of capital per unit of labour. We refer to the former good as the capital-intensive good, the latter as the labour-intensive item. Prior to trade taking place, both countries have two industries (or sectors). One makes the capital-intensive good, the other the labour-intensive good. Each country has a certain total of capital and labour; we can compare their endowments of the factors of production, by measuring the *ratio* of one factor to the other. One country will have a greater ratio of capital to labour compared to the other. In that country, capital is relatively abundant compared to labour, meaning capital is comparatively cheaper there than in the other country. The capital-abundant country can make the capital-intensive good relatively cheaply, compared to the second country; in the second country, labour is relatively abundant (and thus cheap) compared to capital. This second country can more efficiently produce the labour-intensive good. The two countries would each be better off if the capital-abundant country focused production on the capital-intensive good, the labour-abundant country concentrated on making the labour-intensive good, and then the two engaged in trade.[1]

From this understanding of the bases of comparative advantage, economists could then address some of the more interesting policy questions. Trade triggers specialization—focusing production on the goods the country can make efficiently, exporting those goods, and using the proceeds to pay for the items the country could not produce efficiently. Specialization therefore requires adjustment in production—the country makes more of the good it has a comparative advantage in (the one

requiring the locally abundant factor), and produces less of the good it has a comparative disadvantage in (the one requiring the locally scarce factor). Wolfgang Stolper and Paul Samuelson (1941) took this information to disaggregate the impact of trade on people inside the country. Individuals draw their income from ownership of one or another of the factors of production. In the simplest version, with two factors of production, some people possess capital, others own their labour. Trade essentially alters the prices each factor of production commands; in the discussion above, each country imports goods it cannot make efficiently—goods are defined by the fact that they require the locally scarce input. Imports undercut the price necessary to produce the good locally; imports thereby reduce local production, and lessen demand for the locally expensive input. Meanwhile, to pay for the imports, the country must export more. That requires increasing production of the abundant-factor intensive good—which also increases demand for the locally abundant factor.

The **Stolper–Samuelson theorem** demonstrated that while a move to free trade could be understood to reward the country as a whole, it would affect the prices of factors of production, driving up the earnings of the locally abundant factor (or factors) while reducing the returns to the locally scarce factor. This could clearly affect political decisions regarding trade policy. Stolper and Samuelson developed their model in 1941, to explain why free trade was not particularly popular in the United States. As an advanced industrial economy, well-endowed with land as well as capital, labour was the scarce factor of production. Free trade meant the US would export capital- and land-intensive goods, and import labour-intensive goods. Those imports would exert downward pressure on wages. Curiously, for many years economists remained the only ones posing questions about the domestic distribution of the gains from trade. Eventually, Ronald Rogowski (1989) took up the Stolper–Samuelson argument to explain how political coalitions might form on the basis of trade policy. Rogowski examined a wide range of countries across history, noting how this picture of the domestic distribution of the gains from trade could explain why some particular groups might align together—especially when the volume and value of goods involved in trade rose (as they had in the 1870s).

The Stolper–Samuelson approach makes some assumptions about how trade influences the domestic economy, however, which sparked criticisms. To keep things simple, Stolper and Samuelson assumed that specialization (trade adjustment) occurred smoothly and instantly. When imports and exports increased, the production of scarce-factor-intensive goods fell, while production of the abundant-factor-intensive goods rose. Land, capital, and labour employed in the production of the former switched over automatically to production of the latter—instantly and at no cost in their model. (Now, models are supposed to be simplifications of reality, which is why we introduce assumptions—to cut away the complexity of the real world. In this case, however, the assumptions may have excluded some important considerations.) In truth, shutting down one form of production throws people out of jobs, and typically leaves land and capital idle, if only temporarily. Finding new work, or transforming machinery for another purpose, often involves expenses. If the costs associated with this friction in factor markets is high, adjustment may not just be slow, it may be blocked altogether.

This sort of problem was recognized some time ago by economists, as well. Observers such as Jacob Viner had interpreted Ricardo's depiction of trade to discuss what might happen if one particular input could only be profitably applied to the production of one good. Formal versions of this logic emerged in the 1970s (Mussa 1974). It isn't hard to imagine an input being specific to one sector—think of a piece of machinery designed to execute one task and one task only. A blast furnace is good for one thing, and can't easily be adapted to any other use. The earnings of this sector-specific factor are clearly tied to the price earned by the good the sector produces. If it is the scarce-factor-intensive good, and thus the good's price would fall if trade takes place, the earnings of any factors specific to that sector would also fall. Owners of the inputs tied to the sector would obviously oppose free trade, and prefer protection, if given the choice.

This sector-specific view of trade differs in its assumptions about the ability for factors of production to flow from one application to another; as a consequence it predicts that the owners of factors of production will align on trade policy based on where their input is employed. Interests align along sectors, rather than by factors. For political scientists this distinction is readily recognizable. Factor ownership relates to the political or social category of class: capitalist, labour, or landowner. Sector-based alignments are set by the industry where one's capital, land, or labour is employed. Does trade evoke a class cleavage, or one based on sectors? Stephen Magee, writing in a book that appeared in the same year as Rogowski's application of the Stolper–Samuelson theorem, observed that most evidence in American politics pointed to a sector-based cleavage on trade (1989). If one scrutinized lobbying in Washington, DC, labour and management from the firms in a single industry often line up together. In an obvious example from the 1980s, American auto manufacturers and the United Auto Workers Union cooperated in their efforts to get protective measures in place, blocking automobile imports.

Which set of assumptions offers the more accurate disaggregation of the domestic interests?

Efforts to establish the accuracy of one over the other have failed to give us much guidance. Historical evidence demonstrates that both types of cleavages appear. One can find cases where the class (or factor-based) split mattered politically, but there are also examples where the sector-based cleavage certainly dominated. This led Michael Hiscox to intuit that both are possible (2002); the economic conditions shaping the mobility of factors of production across industries vary across countries, and from one point in time to another. Thus we should find some countries characterized by class cleavage when trade is an issue, but others experiencing a sector-based cleavage. To identify when and where one cleavage would appear when trade policy arose politically, Hiscox proposed using the range of wages across sectors as an indicator of sector-specificity. If labour can move freely and easily from one sector to another, then wages will be similar across sectors. If sector-specificity dominates, then labour cannot switch employment as freely, and wages will vary from one industry to another.[2] Although this approach may work for some of the cases Hiscox examined, little follow-up work has been done. The argument may also have built-in weaknesses due to its assumptions about political processes.[3]

In each of these instances, economic arguments carry the brunt of the burden in explaining policy outcomes. Economic models identify preferences by describing ways trade may redistribute income and wealth inside a country. Two problems emerge from limiting the analysis to this facet of trade alone. First, as noted at the end of the earlier discussion about the gains from trade in the aggregate, trade policy decisions may be shaped by issues other than material gains. Other values may be at stake. Second, and more important from our perspective, knowing the distribution of preferences within a state does not mean you can accurately describe or predict policy outcomes. Preferences on

trade still have to be translated into government policy.

James Alt and Michael Gilligan broke down this process into several steps, in order to model the factors that might shape how individual preferences influence policy choice (1994). In any situation, individuals must organize into groups to be heard politically. As Alt and Gilligan stress, not all groups can organize with equal ease. In some cases, individuals who share a preference on trade policy might gather on a regular basis for cultural or social reasons, but in other instances individuals sharing a preference might face severe obstacles in organizing for political purposes. A classic example of these issues would be from the nineteenth century, when trade policy often separated urban from rural interests. Urban dwellers were often easier to organize, simply because of geographical proximity; farmers, being dispersed across the countryside, and typically lacking the means to communicate with one another, often had a difficult time forming groups powerful enough to influence policy.

As Alt and Gilligan also stress, effective organization by itself is no guarantee of command over political outcomes. Once groups have formed, they then compete for control over policy. Institutional rules and practices shape the competition. In democracies, we expect groups to join into larger coalitions—political parties—to contest elections. Different sorts of electoral rules empower particular groups, while weakening others. Some electoral rules favour geographically concentrated groups. In parliamentary systems, where a simple plurality wins each seat, sectors that are thinly spread across all seats are less likely to influence outcomes compared to sectors that enjoy regional concentration. The concentrated interests have a better chance of controlling the outcome in the districts where they are located. The same distribution of interests translates into a different set of seats in a legislature following proportional representation (PR). Under

PR, seats are distributed proportionally, based on the percent of votes won in the district; parties don't need to be locally concentrated to win representation. In general, PR allows multiple parties to win seats in a legislature, whereas first-past-the-post (or plurality) rules push for two or three parties to dominate.

We can identify other factors that might influence which domestic interests get heard, and which do not. These include the presence of other social cleavages (based perhaps on linguistic or religious divisions, for example) that interact with the trade-based cleavage. Sometimes these fault lines reinforce trade-based divisions; sometimes they cut across them. We can also imagine cleavages based on other sorts of economic interests. Monetary policy, for instance, generates a different set of splits within society. In practice, it may be easy to observe how other issues fit with trade policy, but in fact the choices are too wide to easily incorporate into a generalizable model.

By employing more detailed analyses that start with the disaggregation of domestic interests (following some sort of economic model), political scientists can then consider how different groups rallied to control trade policy. These works can examine past examples (such as those states adopting protection in the Great Depression), as well as formulate expectations for who would support or oppose trade liberalization in contemporary settings. Debates continue, however, because we cannot agree on the best way to model domestic preferences, nor can we agree on the best means for modelling domestic political competition.

Country's Preferences

The works described in the section above aim to describe or explain the trade policy of a single country (i.e., they execute comparative foreign policy). Their emphasis on domestic politics exemplified a broader trend in the study of international relations that took hold in the 1990s. These arguments stood in contrast to the dominant approach in the field from the previous decades: structural realism. Structural realism had assumed states to be the most important actors in international relations; states found themselves in the ungoverned, anarchic environment of global politics, and therefore sought power in order to secure themselves and their interests (Waltz 1979). Although this approach had been designed primarily to address questions concerning security issues, it generated theories about international trade as well. As its prime author, Kenneth Waltz, points out, structural realism produces theories of systemic outcomes (i.e., it doesn't address comparative foreign policy questions well). The chief structural-realist claim regarding trade came to be known as hegemonic stability theory; it stated that freer trade policies only become widespread when the distribution of power is concentrated in the hands of a single state (Krasner 1976). The logic ran like this: in a system characterized by several major powers, those states would compete for an edge over one another. Their concerns with relative gains would prompt them to view trade in terms of who "won" or "lost" rather than looking for mutual benefits. States' constant concerns over power would stifle trade. In a system where one state held a dominant position politically and economically, however, that single powerful state would desire free trade, and could be expected to be fairly successful in coercing or cajoling the other states into adopting the same stance.

The works emphasizing domestic politics challenged the structural realist thinking on several grounds. First, they began with different assumptions. Instead of assuming states were roughly similar and sought similar aims, these arguments assumed states wanted different things. You could only understand states' varied goals by looking inside each one. Second, states desired goals other than power. If states sought wealth, they would approach their interactions differently. Foreign policy goals arose from individuals who contested for control of the state in domestic politics. Since these assumptions resonated with those of classical liberals such as Adam Smith, Andrew Moravcsik (1997) described this emerging alternative approach as a version of liberalism, though one focused on carrying through the full range of tasks for theoretical scholarship, beginning with analysis and description. This analytical liberalism has become the most prominent approach in international political economy, especially in the study of the politics of trade.

Moravcsik (1997) made an important observation about the relationship between the study of comparative foreign policy and the study of systemic outcomes. Analytical liberal arguments start by emphasizing individuals' preferences on a policy, then trace how those work their way up through domestic politics, to identify which interests define the state's goals as it conducts foreign policy. By conducting similar examinations of several states simultaneously, one could draw a picture of how their interests fit together—what Moravscik labelled a "structure of preferences." If the major states in the system were all dominated by domestic groups favouring free trade, for instance, then they would easily agree on pursuing free trade together. The key causal forces structural realists would emphasize (such as the number of states involved, or the distribution of power) wouldn't matter. Instead, states could easily cooperate in pursuit of mutual benefits.

Analytical liberal arguments also echo arguments made by prominent experts in international political economy focused on the role of international institutions. In the late 1970s and early 1980s, structural realist arguments pointed to the relative decline of the United States to predict disruption in the international political economy.

Structural realists used this argument to explain why the rules of the Bretton Woods monetary regime had collapsed. They fully expected other sets of international regimes to come unravelled, including the free trade being practised by members of GATT (General Agreement on Tariffs and Trade). Robert Keohane (1984) challenged that assessment, arguing instead that free trade would persist. He argued that the monetary regime had been contentious because it distributed costs and benefits in a particular fashion. The distributional effect of the international practices drove some states to contest the rules, or even be willing to abandon them altogether. GATT worked differently. With trade, states were engaged in mutually advantageous exchange, so benefits were distributed more evenly. Institutionalized arrangements such as the trade rules—enhanced further when GATT transformed into the World Trade Organization—helped strengthen the cooperative efforts of the members.

As you can see, a steady theme runs through these different arguments. We can understand the politics of trade from various perspectives, but current arguments agree in their appreciation that trade involves economic gains for those who participate. Analytical liberals reach that conclusion by looking at individuals first, and then work their way up through the domestic political process to explain why states would (or would not) choose to pursue freer trade; institutionalists (such as Keohane 1984) would consider the pursuit of free trade an example where states achieve international cooperation, overcoming the problems posed by the lack of a higher political authority above states. The lure of mutual gains drives action in both cases.

Policy Questions

So far, the discussion has been kept in a simple form, laying out policy as a dichotomous choice: free trade or protection. Often this may be the way options are presented politically, though very few states have ever attempted to pursue either pure free trade or pure protection. States typically adopt a mix of the two—applying protective measures on certain goods and services, while allowing trade for others. This presents both an opportunity for refining the analytical liberal arguments presented above, and a challenge for interpreting just what governments attempt to do. The obvious opportunity lies in pursuing the disaggregation of interests further, and translating that into competing preferences. It would not be surprising to find that states open themselves up to trade in goods and services their citizens produce competitively, yet retain protection for those items and services their constituents cannot make as efficiently. This variation might be better explained by, for instance, starting with a sector-based economic model, then demonstrating which groups successfully get their interests pursued in policy.

A second sort of variation that can be addressed refers to the type or form of protectionist measure employed. WTO (World Trade Organization) rules and regional trade agreements push states to avoid using tariffs, even when domestic groups might be demanding protection about their specific good or service. Governments have long understood that they could wield their regulatory practices in ways that would affect trade (Mansfield and Busch 1995). By expressing concerns over health and safety, states successfully blocked livestock and agricultural imports back in the 1890s. The larger scope for government regulation today creates opportunities for states to raise lots of different barriers to trade that are not tariffs.

The ability to make policy quite distinct—to support the domestic price of a particular good via a tariff, while leaving other similar goods untouched—makes trade policy particularly appealing to politicians. If we were to look at some historical examples, for instance, we would find some incredibly complex tariff schedules. At the beginning of the twentieth century, American, German, and French tariff legislation distinguished hundreds of different categories of goods, and then within the categories elaborated further differences. The particular qualities of the goods in question then determined which rate applied to the import. In this way, politicians were able to serve the interests of very small groups of domestic producers.

Where in all this discussion of disaggregation are consumers?[4] The points above highlight how protectionists are in fact a number of small groups, with narrow specific interests. Consumers, on the other hand, constitute a much larger group, with a single shared interest. Why then do protectionists do well politically? The intensity of the interest differs. Producers are very much affected by a slight change in the price their output earns. For consumers, each particular good is merely one item among many they purchase, so they might not even notice slight changes in the price. Producers are motivated to act—whereas consumers only become aware of the issue when the stakes are raised significantly.

The combination of the ability to make very discrete interventions in the market, without provoking a large reaction, stands in stark contrast to an alternative policy instrument. The exchange rate affects all international transactions. If the local currency depreciates against all others, it acts much like a tariff, by increasing the relative price of all imports. Yet note what a broad policy instrument this is—it affects all goods and services in the same way.

It is perhaps surprising then, given how appealing protectionism is to politicians, that so many states have moved towards freer trade in recent decades. One of the key questions political scientists might still want to answer, for instance, is why protectionism has largely disappeared. If we look back to the nineteenth and early twentieth centuries, protectionism was all too common. Since the end of the Cold War, free trade has become the norm. Increasingly we find states that have adopted free trade, and after several decades the opposition to liberalized trade has shrunk substantially. What processes are at work? How well entrenched has free trade become? Is it equally set in place in countries with less experience with this policy, such as China or India?

Conclusions

The current consensus in international political economy around the analytical liberal perspective on trade reflects a good deal of satisfaction with the results generated by current models. We have reasonably accurate descriptions of many past trade policy decisions, and have a good sense of why some states have cooperated in the pursuit of free trade, while other states refused to act together. There remain many anomalous outcomes, however. Recent research has therefore moved largely toward alternative methods for understanding how domestic preferences form. Some have suggested that citizens don't always understand their material interests well (Hiscox 2006; Ardanaz, Murillo, and Pinto 2013). Others recognize that in contemporary politics, trade issues trigger concerns over employment levels—something difficult to address given that economists' models don't readily link trade with unemployment. Economic globalization is often contested, not on the grounds of economic benefits, but on the potential losses associated with other values. People want both to make economic advances but also to hold onto their culture; Thomas Friedman captured this tension in the title of his well-known book *The Lexus and the Olive Tree*. Taken together, these perspectives suggest that the domestic struggles over trade policy may be better understood via models downplaying the economic approach.

Those who wish to keep the focus on economists' understanding of trade have two paths for further refinement of their models, which we are likely to see develop in the coming years. The first involves an ever-more detailed analysis of the domestic distribution of the gains from trade. Economists have moved beyond the models political scientists have been relying on. The Stolper–Samuelson approach divided domestic actors into classes, and the sector-specific approach split them into industries; the latest economic models look at particular firms within industries (Melitz 2003; Bernard, Jensen, Redding, and Schott 2011). Political scientists will certainly be able to use these newer models of economic interests to break down the preferences of domestic actors into finer detail than they could with previous models.

Another possible refinement would come from an improved understanding of the process of trade adjustment. The firm-level arguments referred to above are one step in that direction, because they examine which businesses in an industry are able to exploit opportunities in trade, and which businesses cannot. That leads to reallocating activity from some firms to others. We have always known that the pursuit of comparative advantage—specialization—is a complex process. As part of that process, people lose jobs, or machinery or land sits idle, if only for as long as it takes to reorganize production. We've largely treated these costs through simplifying assumptions. Greater detail in economic modelling might improve our understanding of how people view the possible risks in trade adjustment. That information would provide a useful bridge between past models of the politics of trade (built on economics) and the newer arguments political scientists have introduced (constructed around framing and other approaches). Either way, these debates will continue, further refining our understanding the politics of trade.

Notes

1   In an important extension, Jaroslav Vanek (1968) demonstrated that the logic works when one goes beyond the simple two-factors, two-goods version.
2   This hinges on a critical assumption—that all factors in a country share a similar level of mobility. While there may be some evidence in contemporary economics providing support for making this assumption, contrary evidence also exists.
3   Hiscox implicitly assumes parties form on the basis of factors—thus parties are expected to fragment on trade policy when sector-based cleavages arise. In countries with institutional factors that drive interests to coalesce into two or three parties, such an assumption may be fair; in many settings, however, we find multiple political parties. In those conditions, parties will form on a number of bases, thus limiting the applicability of Hiscox's measures.
4   Consumers benefit from free trade—which contrasts with the whole discussion so far, which has concentrated on viewing domestic actors as producers only. See Ruffin & Jones 1977.

Key Terms

comparative advantage
GATT
Heckscher-Ohlin model
specialization

Stolper-Samuelson theorem
tariff
WTO

Questions for Review

1.   If trade offers countries economic benefits, why would they ever adopt protectionist tariffs?
2.   How are the gains from trade distributed within countries?
3.   Although trade can deliver economic benefits, what non-material issues might governments also consider when deciding upon a trade policy?
4.   When viewed historically, the international economy has experienced periods when free trade was widespread, but also eras when most countries adopted high barriers to trade. What best explains this variation across time?

Further Resources

Hiscox, M. (2001). "Class versus industry cleavages: Inter-industry factor mobility and the politics of trade." *International Organization* 55(1), 1–46.
Irwin, D. (1997). *Against the tide: An intellectual history of free trade*. Princeton: Princeton University Press.

Krugman, P. (1993). "What do undergrads need to know about trade?" *American Economic Review* 83(2), 23–6.
Rogowski, R. (1987). "Political cleavages and changing exposure to trade." *American Political Science Review* 81(4), 1121–37.

References

Alt, J. and Gilligan, M. (1994). The political economy of trading States. *Journal of Political Philosophy* 2(2), 165–92.

Ardanaz, M., Murillo, V., and Pinto, P. (2013). "Sensitivity to issue framing on trade policy preferences:

Evidence from a survey experiment." *International Organization 67*(2), 411–37.

Bernard, A. B., Jensen, J. B., Redding, S. J., and Schott, P. K. (2011). "The empirics of firm heterogeneity and international trade." *NBER Working Paper 17627*, available at http://www.princeton.edu/~reddings/papers/NBERWP17627.pdf.

Flam, H. and Flanders, M. J. (2000). "The Young Ohlin and the theory of 'interregional and international trade," Institute of International Economic Studies Seminar Paper #684, available at http://www.diva-portal.org/smash/get/diva2:328550/FULLTEXT01.pdf

Frank, A. G. (1966). "The development of underdevelopment." *Monthly Review 41*(2), 17–31.

Friedman, T. (1999). *The lexus and the olive tree*. New York: Anchor Books.

Heckscher, E. (1955). *Mercantilism*. London: Allen & Unwin.

Heckscher, E. (1919). "The effects of foreign trade on the distribution of income." *Ekonomisk Tidskrift 21*, 497–512.

Hirschman, A. O. (1969). *National power and the structure of foreign trade*. Berkeley: University of California Press.

Hiscox, M. (2002). *International trade and political conflict*. Princeton: Princeton University Press.

Hiscox, M. (2006). "Through a glass and darkly: Framing effects and individuals' attitudes towards international trade," *International Organization 60*(3), 755–80.

Keohane, R. O. (1984). *After hegemony*. Princeton: Princeton University Press.

Kindleberger, C. (1975). "The rise of free trade in Western Europe, 1820–1875." *Journal of Economic History 35*(1), 20–55.

Krasner, S. (1976). "State power and the structure of international trade." *World Politics 28*(3), 317–47.

List, F. (1966). *The national system of political economy*. New York: A.M. Kelley.

Magee, S., Brock, W., and Young, L. (1989). *Black hole tariffs and endogenous policy theory*. New York: Cambridge University Press.

Mansfield, E. and Busch, M. (1995). "The political economy of non-tariff barriers: a cross national analysis." *International Organization 49*(4), 723–49.

Melitz, M. (2003). "The impact of trade on intra-industry reallocations and aggregate industry productivity," *Econometrica 71*, 1695–725.

Moravcsik, A. (1997). "Taking preferences seriously: A liberal theory of international relations," *International Organization 51*(4), 513–54.

Mussa, M. (1974). "Tariffs and the Distribution of Income: The importance of factor specificity, substitutability and intensity in the short and long run," *Journal of Political Economy 82*(6), 1191–203.

Ohlin, B. (1933). *Interregional and International trade*. Cambridge: Harvard University Press.

Pahre, R. (2001). "Most-favored-nation clauses, domestic politics, and clustered negotiations." *International Organization 55*(4), 861–92

Prebisch, R. (1950). *The economic development of Latin America and its principal problems*. Lake Success: United Nations Dept. of Economic Affairs.

Ricardo, D. (2001) [1817]. *On the principles of political economy and taxation*. London: Electric Book Co.

Rogowski, R. (1989). *Commerce and coalitions*. Princeton: Princeton University Press.

Ruffin, R. and Jones, R. (1977). "Protection and Real Wages: The neoclassical ambiguity," *Journal of Economic Theory 14*(2), 337–48.

Smith, A. 1776. *An inquiry into the nature and causes of the wealth of nations*.

Stolper, W. and Samuelson, P. (1941). "Protection and real wages," *Review of Economic Studies 9*(1), 58–73.

Toye, J. and Toye, R. (2006). "The origins and interpretation of the Prebisch-Singer hypothesis." *History of Political Economy 35*(3), 437–67.

Vanek, J. (1968). "The factor proportions theory: The n-factor case" *Kyklos 21*(4), 749–56.

Viner, J. (1948). "Power versus plenty as objectives of foreign policy," *World Politics 1*(1), 1–29.

Waltz, K. (1979). *Theory of international politics*. Menlo Park, CA: Addison-Wesley.

7 Monetary Policy Forty Years On[1]

David Dodge

In 1988, Governor John Crow gave a Hanson lecture, in which he discussed in considerable detail "The Work of Monetary Policy," in which he touched on many monetary policy topics that were the subject of active debate in 1988—several of which continue to be debated today. The two most noteworthy elements of his lecture were (1) his clear commitment to the goal of **price stability**, and (2) his clear intention to actively pursue it. Although the identification of price stability as the Bank's primary objective was not necessarily new, Crow's strong affirmation of this goal's importance was noteworthy, and helped lay the groundwork for much of the monetary policy success that followed in later years.

The understanding and practice of **monetary policy** has changed dramatically since I was a university student at Queen's and Princeton in the 1960s. This is not intended as a slight or criticism of what was known in the 1960s—indeed, I am often struck by how much was understood by earlier economists, how well their thoughts were expressed, and how much unnecessary re-learning we occasionally do of things that should never have been forgotten. Nevertheless, despite this important base of knowledge, remarkable progress has continued to be made over the last 40 years in the area of monetary policy, as well as in many other areas of economics. Economic history, in other words, has not been a process of merely recycling and relearning past ideas, but rather a steady progression, punctuated on occasion by a few unfortunate digressions and detours.

When I was a student, Keynesian economics was at its peak, but had started to be challenged by Milton Friedman and the New Quantity Theory of Money. Since then we have witnessed the rational expectations revolution and real business cycle theory, the emergence of neo-classical economists and, most recently, the New Keynesians. My presentation tonight begins with a review of the major goals that monetary policy, and macroeconomic stabilization policy more generally, were expected to pursue in the 1960s, and how these have shifted over time. I then examine changing views on the effectiveness of monetary policy and how it should be implemented. This is followed by a discussion of increased policy transparency, the move to inflation targeting, and the greater emphasis that is now being given to communication and accountability. The speech ends with some thoughts on a few old ideas that may be reappearing in a new guise, and a brief conclusion. In this regard, I will make specific reference to the financial turbulence that has been observed in recent months, the challenges that it has posed for policy-makers, and the new questions that it has raised concerning the appropriate formulation and implementation of monetary policy. Academic advances and real world events have always played a critical role in shaping policy design, and may be changing accepted wisdom even as we speak.

What Should Monetary Policy Try to Do?

The Preamble to the Bank of Canada Act, drafted in 1934, states that the Bank should

> regulate credit and currency in the best interests of the economic life of the nation, . . . control and protect the external value of the national monetary unit and . . . mitigate by its influence fluctuations in the general level of production, trade, prices and employment.[2]

Fortunately, although this legislation predated Tinbergen's seminal work on policy tools and targets, the drafters realized that not all of the goals that they had identified would be mutually compatible nor attainable with a single policy instrument. They therefore added the words

> "so far as may be possible within the scope of monetary action."[3]

Nevertheless, this is a rather long and ambitious list. One objective, however, clearly assumed primary importance in policy circles. Governments in the immediate postwar period were determined to avoid any reoccurrence of the massive unemployment experienced in the Great Depression, and were also committed to creating employment for returning veterans. These sentiments were perhaps expressed most forcefully in the White Paper on Employment and Incomes, issued by the Government of Canada in 1945.

> the Government has stated unequivocally its adoption of a high and stable level of employment and income, and thereby higher standards of living, as a major aim of Government policy. It has been made clear that, if it is to be achieved, the endeavour to achieve it must pervade all government economic policy . . . transcending in importance all sectional and group interests.[4]

This policy guidance presumably included monetary policy as well as other macro-policy levers. Through much of the 1950s, it looked like it might be possible to achieve the ambitious goals laid out in the White Paper without any serious long-run effects on other macro goals such as price stability. Strong output and employment growth were recorded during this period, along with sharply rising real wages and incomes, without putting undue pressure on prices or interest rates, owing to the exceptional growth in productivity.

Little had changed by the mid-1960s, in spite of some temporary bouts of higher inflation in the late 1940s and in the period immediately following the Korean War. Growth and employment were still the primary objectives of macro policy, while price stability occupied an evident secondary position. When the Economic Council of Canada was created in 1964, the five main **macroeconomic** goals for Canada, as specified in the Council's terms of reference, were

– full employment
– a high rate of economic growth

– reasonable stability in prices
– a viable balance of payments, and
– an equitable distribution of rising incomes[5]

Although it is difficult to quibble with these objectives, their order and the wording of the third objective (concerning "reasonable price stability") are both significant, since this was the height of Keynesian economics—a time when it probably exerted its greatest influence over policy-making in Canada and in most other advanced industrial countries.[6]

The downward sloping Phillips curve, and the notion that there could be a permanent trade-off between growth and inflation, had by then gained widespread acceptance in academia, and in many parts of the policy-making community.[7] In addition, pressure to find jobs for returning veterans had been replaced by worries about the wave of baby boomers who were now entering the workforce and needed to find employment. While many central bankers, including James Coyne, voiced concern about price stability, and questioned whether there was any long-run trade-off between inflation and output growth, their warnings were typically ignored, and were seldom followed by disciplined actions either in their own institutions or elsewhere. A little inflation was not necessarily a bad thing, it was argued, and whatever harm it might cause could be easily corrected through indexation. Keynes's famous dictum, "In the long run we are all dead," had become the leit-motif for a generation of economists.

The "Great Inflation" of the 1970s was a consequence of this thinking, although there were other contributing factors. Subsequent experience showed how serious the costs of inflation could be, and how difficult they were to eradicate once an inflationary mindset had replaced an earlier generation's presumption of proximate price-stability. Experience with dramatic price deflation in the

Great Depression had taught older Canadians that prices could go down as well as up, which provided a form of social capital that helped anchor expectations through much of the 1950s and early 1960s. Once an inflationary mindset was firmly embedded, however, the costs of eliminating inflation rose appreciably. Dealing with the symptoms, rather than the disease, was not any easier. Indexation was not the simple panacea that some had assumed, and created a new set of problems, making inflation even more persistent.

During the past 20 years, all this has changed. Much greater prominence is now given to achieving and maintaining low and stable inflation. Moreover, it is generally agreed that this is the best contribution that monetary policy can make to sustainable growth, high employment, and economic welfare. John Crow captured the essence of this in his Hanson lecture, when he stated

> Monetary policy shares the same bottom line as other broad economic policies to contribute to raising our living standards. But how can it best do so? . . . To say that the goal of monetary policy should be price stability is not simply an arbitrary preference. Rather it is a recognition of the plain fact that because inflation creates distortions, output will be higher over time in conditions of price stability than those of inflation.[8]

This goal was made explicit in the inflation reduction targets agreement jointly announced by the government and the Bank of Canada in 1991, and subsequently renewed as inflation control agreements on four separate occasions over the last 17 years. It is not that the earlier policy prescription was fundamentally wrong; price stability is, after all, simply a means to an end. It is just that there is now a greater appreciation of the economy's capacity limits and how a stable price environment contributes to better real economic outcomes. Olivier Blanchard has recently referred to this as the "divine coincidence" of price stability and full employment.

How Effective Is Monetary Policy?

In the early 1960s, an active debate developed in the United States over whether the rising unemployment that had been observed was structural or cyclical. Charles Killingsworth, long-time advisor to multiple state governors on labour and employment in the 1950s and 1960s, suggested that it was caused principally by changing structural forces, such as demographics, and that attempts to reduce it through macroeconomic stimulus would end in failure. Killingsworth argued that the natural rate of unemployment, as it would later be called, helped determine the capacity limits of the economy. Structural reforms and improved institutional arrangements might lower the natural rate, but demand management could do nothing in this regard. Others, like Arthur Okun, argued that the problem was deficient aggregate demand and called for standard "Keynesian" remedies. Because subsequent events in the early 1960s appeared to support Okun's argument, the broader implications and applicability of Killingsworth's message over the long run were largely ignored.

Among those who favoured stimulative measures, there was also a sharp divide. Okun, and most other economists of the day, championed **fiscal policy** (and the Kennedy tax cuts) as the best way to deal with the employment problem. Little attention was given to monetary policy, except by a small and increasingly vocal group of monetarists. Keynesian economists, for the most part, did not regard monetary policy as a very effective or

reliable policy instrument.[9] This was true not only in states of suspected liquidity traps, such as the Great Depression, but during normal periods, especially if there was a need for additional easing. Phrases such as "pushing on a string" were used to characterize the questionable potency of monetary policy in these circumstances. Whatever effectiveness monetary policy might have was believed to come largely through policy directives, credit controls, interest rate ceilings, and moral suasion, as opposed to the more indirect, market-based, channels that are favoured today.

The unfortunate events of the 1930s had left many economists deeply suspicious of financial markets and the ability of price mechanisms to sensibly direct economic activity. Adjustments in the cost of credit as a means of conducting monetary policy were dismissed as impotent and/or possibly destabilizing. The primary focus of central banks, therefore, was controlling the quantity of credit in the financial system and, where appropriate, redirecting it to the most deserving ends. The skepticism about the usefulness of monetary policy action was reinforced by a concern that credit and money were difficult, if not inherently impossible, to control. Indeed, owing to the emergence of near-banks and the fungibility of money, authors like Gurley and Shaw argued that efforts to contain the growth of credit were typically futile. The US Commission on Money and Credit, the Radcliffe Committee in the United Kingdom, and the Porter Commission in Canada, all reached similar conclusions.[10]

The answer to this problem for many central banks was to adopt a "belt and suspenders" approach to conducting monetary policy, in which a variety of instruments and direct controls were relied upon to keep the growth of credit in check. These controls included primary and secondary reserve requirements, additional liquidity provisions, and a host of other interventionist measures.

Although some of them might have been helpful from a regulatory, prudential perspective, their application in the context of macro stabilization was more problematic. One of the most popular and enduring misconceptions of this period concerned the money multiplier and the widespread belief that without legislated reserve requirements the multiplier would be infinite, and the money supply would soon become unbounded. There was no sense that price adjustments in the form of changes to interest rates and the cost of credit would automatically prevent this.

Toward the end of the 1960s, an animated debate developed between "fiscalists" and "monetarists," about which macro instrument had the greatest influence over output growth and inflation. The monetarist camp had been attracting increased attention and support, owing largely to the tireless efforts of Milton Friedman, Allan Melzer, Karl Brunner, Phillip Cagan, and a coterie of other devoted followers based in Chicago and the Federal Reserve Bank of St Louis. The debate was conducted largely in terms of simple reduced-form equations, with output growth as the dependent variable on the left-hand side of the equation, and a string of independent and supposedly exogenous variables on the right. The latter included crude proxies for the stance of fiscal policy and monetary policy. Both sides claimed victory and criticized the work of the opposing camp. Neither group seemed to realize how misleading such exercises could be, until Blinder and Goldfeld (1976) showed how even policies that allowed the dependent variable to be perfectly controlled could appear disconnected and ineffectual in the context of a reduced-form equation. Their simplest example involved a world in which monetary policy could control output with almost perfect precision. Interest rates in this world would be seen to move frequently in anticipation of incipient fluctuations in output. However, by keeping actual output

perfectly stable, interest rates would appear to have no obvious connection to developments in the real economy. Monetary policy, as judged by these equations, would be a victim of its own success.

One important way in which monetary policy was potentially ineffective through much of the postwar period was never fully appreciated until Mundell's path-breaking work in the early 1960s.[11] Drawing on economic developments in Canada, he demonstrated how most countries operating under a fixed (or pegged) exchange rate system, such as Bretton Woods, would have the potency of monetary policy effectively vitiated, while fiscal policy would play a much more dominant role.[12] The reverse would be true for renegade countries, such as Canada, which operated outside the Bretton Woods system under a flexible exchange rate system. Mundell's "impossible trinity," as it came to be known, highlighted the fact that countries could not simultaneously (1) have open capital markets, (2) operate under a fixed exchange rate regime, and (3) conduct an independent monetary policy. Only two of these three conditions could be simultaneously satisfied. In the event, most industrial countries in the immediate postwar period opted for capital and currency controls as a way of preserving some degree of monetary policy independence under a pegged exchange rate system. These controls lasted through much of the 1980s and early 1990s in many cases, with countries like Canada, which had open capital markets, being a clear exception.

Summing up, this was an era in which there was widespread mistrust of the price signalling mechanism, and a failure to fully appreciate the capacity limits of the economy and their implications for macro stabilization. It was also an era of extensive capital controls, fixed exchange rates, and relatively closed economies. Contrasting this earlier era of monetary policy skepticism with the present situation, one is struck by the dramatic change that has taken place. The advocates of monetary policy have won the day. Monetary policy is no longer regarded as fiscal policy's weak sister. While the policy tools recommended by the early monetarists, based on money-aggregate targeting and rules-based reaction functions, have largely been discarded, inflation control via monetary-policy means and the primacy of the goal of low and stable inflation have both gained widespread acceptance. Economists are more aware of structural issues, the natural rate of unemployment, and the capacity limits of the economy, and they have also discarded their earlier skepticism of price signals. In the post-Bretton Woods world, most industrial countries operate with floating exchange rates, thereby avoiding the potential problem of monetary policy impotence that Mundell had diagnosed. Now, in cases of deficient or excessive demand, monetary policy is commonly regarded as almost "everywhere and always effective," and the instrument of choice for short-run stabilization in those countries that are willing to let their exchange rates float.[13,14] Indeed, some observers, including several central bankers, feel this confidence in the ability of monetary policy may have gone too far.[15] They worry that market participants may have become too sanguine about the fine-tuning capabilities of central banks, and in their ability to rescue investors from their own excesses. I believe that the Great Moderation that we have witnessed over the past 15 to 20 years does owe a great deal to improved monetary policy, aided, of course, by substantial growth in productivity and the enhanced competition that has come from the opening of international markets. (Here there are echoes of the 1950s.) However, I certainly recognize that the business cycle is still very much alive, and that financial crises are not necessarily a thing of the past. The financial turbulence that we have recently experienced might have a silver lining in this respect, to the extent it encourages a more appropriate pricing of risk and prevents the emergence of even greater dislocations and imbalances.

Does Monetary Policy Need to Be Complicated and Opaque to Work?

Another stark difference between monetary policy then and now concerns the manner in which it is conducted. In the 1960s and through much of the 1970s and 1980s, to the extent monetary policy was deemed to have any effectiveness, it was seen to rely importantly on the element of surprise or even conscious misdirection on the part of authorities. The transmission process was typically viewed as inherently complicated, and central banks had little interest in explaining exactly how it worked. Some of the opaqueness reflected deficiencies in our understanding of the macro economy, while the rest might be credited to a deliberate desire on the part of some authorities to preserve an air of mystery and uncertainty. Many central bankers felt that too much information sharing would weaken the effectiveness of policy and also erode credibility—akin to Dorothy peeking behind the curtain in the *Wizard of Oz*.[16]

For a significant portion of the postwar period, there was also a deep-seated distrust of financial market forces, and a sense that only direct means of controlling the provision of credit, buttressed by an array of instruments, restrictions, and regulations, could be relied upon to implement policy. As noted earlier, chartered banks in Canada were subject to multiple reserve requirements, supplementary liquidity provisions, and interest rate ceilings.[17] And moral suasion was often used to achieve the desired outcome as opposed to any more transparent and market-oriented way of conducting policy.

What I will call the "modern view" has turned much of the earlier received wisdom on its head. In place of **intervention** and offline "window guidance," central banks now rely on interest rates and market-oriented means of adjusting the stance of policy.[18] Money and credit aggregates, while preserved as one of many financial indicators that we continue to monitor, have a greatly diminished role. Indeed, many modern macro models do not even include them—"monetary policy without money" is how one noted academic has referred to it.[19]

Canada has been in the vanguard of the revolution to reduce the implementation of monetary policy to its essential elements and to eliminate the unnecessary costs and uncertainty that market participants have had to endure in the past. The most dramatic changes have involved the payments system and the reserve requirements that were imposed on banks. Early in the 1990s, Canada began to reduce the required reserve ratios on chartered bank deposits, and by the mid-1990s had reduced them to zero. Reserve ratios are now regarded as an unnecessary burden on banks and have no usefulness in terms of implementing monetary policy. The introduction of a Large Value Transfer System in 1996, and other changes to the payments and settlements system, meant that virtually all uncertainty connected with the clearing process was also eliminated. The principal reasons for chartered banks to hold required reserves had therefore disappeared. In other words, almost every tenet of 1950s- and 1960s-style monetary policy implementation had been overturned, without any evident loss of control. I must admit that over the past couple of years, somewhat greater attention should perhaps have been paid to the effects that changing financial market structures, securitization, and compressed yield spreads were having on the relationship between policy interest rates and "effective monetary conditions." This might have helped prevent some of the excesses that were later observed. Certainly, it is still true that prudent regulators should care about the liquidity position of banks and their capital requirements. It's just that, from a monetary policy and macro-stabilization perspective, required reserves and other direct interventions were found to be unnecessary.

This revolution in policy implementation has also involved a significant improvement in transparency in monetary policy, though not in the transparency of financial instruments. Rather than have market participants guess at what the Bank's target for the overnight rate might be, target interest rates are now publicly announced. Uncertainty about when the target rate of interest might be changed has also been largely eliminated. Changes in the target overnight rate, barring exceptional circumstances, are announced on one of eight Fixed Announcement Dates throughout the year.

Policy-makers in other countries were initially surprised by these developments, and questioned whether such a simple system could actually work. Some referred to it as a system of "virtual control," in which the Bank of Canada simply declared its target interest rate and magically the financial system responded. But appearances can be deceiving. While this is essentially how it works, the Bank's declaration of the target interest rate has more substance and influence than if you or I, as private citizens, tried to do it. It works because the Bank has the ability to back its words with actions. And in more turbulent times, such as this summer and fall (2007), the words were backed by strong actions.[20] However, in normal times, when the structure of financial markets is stable or unchanging, the process is as simple as it sounds.[21]

Expectations and Inflation Targeting

The difference between the 1960s and now goes well beyond debates about the goals of monetary policy, the effectiveness of monetary policy, and the simple process that is currently used to implement it. The philosophical shift toward working with markets rather than against them is also manifest in a more open and transparent approach to the formulation of monetary policy. Central banks, as noted earlier, used to believe that unexpected policy moves were often the most effective. They also believed that the less said about economic conditions and prospective policy moves the better. The rational expectations revolution of the 1980s appeared to provide further support for this "sneak attack" approach, although, along with the introduction of real business cycle theories, it also undermined most of the justification for any sort of consistent counter-cyclical policy.

While not everyone subscribed to this extreme form of rational expectations, greater recognition of the importance of forward-looking expectations and anticipatory behaviour did have an influence on the economics profession. Opinions evolved toward what many would regard as a more balanced and realistic view of the way the world operates. Instead of naive regressive and extrapolative expectations mechanisms, we suddenly had the Lucas critique and the realization that you could not fool all of the people all of the time. By being clear about their objectives, establishing a credible commitment to a specific policy framework, and sharing information more fully with markets, central banks could simplify their task. Policy implementation could be made easier and more efficient, in the sense of requiring smaller interest rate changes to accomplish the job, with the market doing much of the work for us. In addition, unnecessary dislocation and confusion could be eliminated.

Elements of this modus operandi were evident in the 1970s regime of explicit money targeting, but were perhaps not fully appreciated. A clear target for the growth of money aggregates was identified, and central banks were more explicit about how they hoped to achieve it. Enhanced accountability was also an important part of the new policy framework, together with a hope that credibility would be improved and expectations could be conditioned in a way that facilitated the disinflationary process. By establishing a clear, gradual, path for reducing the growth of money, economists hoped that the output and employment costs associated with squeezing inflation out of the system could be minimized. Policy-makers started from an unenviable position, however. Inflation was already very high and policy credibility was very low.

Canada tried to overcome this "credibility deficit" by introducing a program of wage–price controls in 1975. The hope was that by forcing the growth of wages and prices to decline gradually over a three-year period, consistent with the implementation of tighter monetary and fiscal policy, the country might be able to minimize the negative effects of disinflationary policy on output and employment. A critical element in the program was supposed to be a meaningful change in the stance of fiscal and monetary policies over the controls period, in order to validate and then sustain the disinflation once the controls were lifted. While the concept was sound, some significant real world complications intervened to undermine the initiative when the program was launched. An unstable velocity of money, coupled with a lack of fiscal discipline, meant that, in fact, macro policy was far too loose to be consistent with the inflation targets. Various structural changes that had taken place over the 1970s, including the "deform" of the unemployment insurance system, and an unrecognized slowing of productivity growth, also posed a problem. By the start of the 1980s, inflation had returned to a post-war high. Policy-makers were forced to rely on the traditional medicine of sharply higher interest rates and high unemployment to bring inflation down.

However, by the end of the 1980s, inflation was on the rise again, and we all knew that more restrictive macroeconomic policies would be required. John Crow's Hanson lecture could be viewed as an attempt, once again, to condition expectations, and to reduce the costs associated with the tightening of policies we knew had to come. It is not obvious however, that the implications of this renewed commitment to price stability were fully appreciated by governments, or banks, or the public at large. Monetary policy based on **inflation targeting** had never been contemplated as a possible solution to the expectations problem, here or elsewhere, but would prove to be a useful aid in this regard.

When Canada moved to inflation targeting in February 1991, the academic literature provided very little guidance.[22] Essentially, the Department of Finance and the Bank of Canada embarked on an exercise of learning by doing. In the end, it is fair to say that this exercise exceeded even our highest hopes. Inflation expectations adjusted far faster than even we had anticipated. Having experimented with many other monetary policy frameworks, running from fixed exchange rates to unstructured full discretion, the Bank of Canada is convinced that inflation targeting has outperformed all of them. While positive structural reforms, supportive fiscal policies, and perhaps a more competitive external environment certainly account for some of the improved macroeconomic performance that has been seen in recent years, it is clear that the new monetary policy regime has also played a critical role.

Inflation in Canada has remained low and remarkably stable over the past 17 years, averaging close to 2 per cent—our official inflation target—since 1995. Long-run inflation expectations have become firmly anchored at 2 per cent, adding to the efficiency of monetary policy. Output growth has also been steady and displayed much less volatility than over the preceding 16 years. In addition, the employment rate in Canada has reached all-time highs, the unemployment rate has reached 33-year lows, and interest rates are lower than at any point since the 1950s and have often fallen below US levels (something that most people would have thought impossible in the early to mid-1990s).

The inflation targeting framework has made the objective of monetary policy explicit and thereby enhanced accountability. Canada's monetary policy has also been supported, as in every other inflation targeting country, by a more comprehensive and timely communication strategy. This has given businesses and households a clearer understanding about our prospective policy actions and our views on the state of domestic and international economies. It also makes any policy errors that we might make more evident, but this is part of its purpose. Greater discipline leads to better policy outcomes. And the more active debate created by increased transparency leads to better policies and smoother economic adjustment. In retrospect, it is surprising that central banks did not recognize these potential benefits sooner, and move to inflation targeting before the 1990s. Some important players, of course, such as Japan and the United States, have yet to be convinced. But even they seem to be operating on the basis of a very close variant of inflation targets—opting for an implicit target or something that is an explicit inflation target in all but name.[23]

Are Any Further Improvements Possible?

It might seem natural at this point to ask where all of this leaves us. Are any further improvements in the monetary policy framework possible? Is this as good as it gets? Are we at the end of monetary policy history? The present monetary policy framework and the success that we have enjoyed do set a pretty high bar for any future changes. Nevertheless, there is reason to believe that additional substantive changes might be possible. Moreover, it is our obligation as policy-makers to pursue these possibilities if there is any chance that they might improve the economic well-being of Canadian households and businesses. Two classes of issues need to be examined in this regard: the inflation target itself and how it is pursued and the monetary policy transmission mechanism and improving our understanding of the way the macro economy operates.

When the Bank of Canada renewed its inflation targeting agreement with the government for another five-year period in 2006, the 2 per cent target and 1 to 3 per cent control range were left unchanged. However, the Bank—with the support of the Government—committed itself to an ambitious medium-term research program, focusing on two major questions.

(1) What are the costs and benefits of an inflation target lower than 2 per cent? Would an inflation target lower than 2 per cent generate significant net benefits for the economy and for Canadian households?

(2) What are the costs and benefits of replacing the current inflation target with a longer-term, price-level target? Would a price-level target produce significant net benefits for the economy and for Canadian households?[24]

These are not new questions. Bank of Canada researchers and economists elsewhere have thought about them intermittently for many years.[25] The first inflation target agreement in Canada, announced in February 1991, stated that while the medium-term objective for monetary policy would be 2 per cent,

Thereafter, the objective would be further reductions on inflation until price stability is actually achieved.... A target path after 1995 ... remains to be fixed, but again pending new evidence, the aim would be to continue to make steady progress.[26]

At the time of the next renewal, in 2011, Canada will have been operating under an inflation target for slightly more than 20 years. The research plan outlined in the most recent renewal is motivated in part by the sense that it should be possible to provide more definite answers to these questions after such an extended period of experimentation and analysis, provided it is buttressed by a more concerted effort on the research front.

Central banks generally agree that 2 per cent is a reasonable target and is consistent with low, stable, and predictable inflation. However, it is not consistent with what one might call true price stability. Through the magic of compounding, an inflation rate of 2 per cent a year causes prices to double every 35 years. Targeting an inflation rate of zero has considerable intuitive appeal and widespread economic support, if all other things are constant. However, we know that all other things are not constant. Three main arguments have been advanced as to why it might be unwise to aim for such a low rate of inflation. The first is about measurement error and the positive bias that is believed to exist in the present Consumer Price Index. If this is correct, aiming for a measured inflation rate of zero would imply a modest amount of ongoing price deflation. Second, the presence of nominal wage–price rigidities might become more serious close to a zero inflation rate, reducing employment and output by constraining necessary movements in relative prices. This worry was most recently popularized by Akerlof, Dickens, and Perry,[27] but has a long history in economics. Economists in the 1960s, such as George Shultz, often observed that a little inflation might be necessary to "grease the wheels" of the economy.[28]

The third reason for not being more ambitious about lowering the inflation target has only become prominent in recent years: the "zero-interest-bound." James Tobin and Larry Summers were among the first to note that monetary policy might be overly constrained and perhaps ineffective at low rates of inflation, since nominal interest rates cannot go below zero. (If interest rates were, for some reason, able to go below zero, the rates of return they offered would be dominated by zero-interest-earning cash balances. With zero therefore representing an effective barrier to monetary easing, it might be difficult for central banks to stimulate economic activity in times of depressed demand.)

Past research at the Bank of Canada has indicated that the first two arguments described above—measurement error and wage–price rigidities—are not as important as previously thought, and would not, on their own, justify an inflation target as high as 2 per cent. Measurement error in Canada's CPI is estimated to be, at most, 3/4 per cent, but is probably closer to 1/2 per cent.[29] And wage-price rigidities have not been found to have any significant effect on output growth or employment.[30] While future work may overturn these results, wage–price rigidities are not regarded as major obstacles to a lower inflation target. The third argument, in contrast, is taken far more seriously, especially after Japan's experience with ongoing deflation through the 1990s and early 2000s. Although a number of means have been proposed for dealing with the problem and restoring the effectiveness of monetary policy in the presence of the zero-bound, few observers question the challenges that this poses for effective counter-cyclical measures. More research will clearly be needed in this area before any proposal to lower the target inflation rate can be seriously contemplated.[31]

A separate, but complementary, line of research that the Bank is pursuing centres on the possibility of switching from an inflation-targeting framework to a price-level targeting framework. For those not already familiar with the distinction between these two terms, a short explanation might be in order. Price-level targeting is not a new concept, but has admittedly received much less attention than inflation targeting in the academic literature. In fact, only one other country to my knowledge has ever tried it. Sweden experimented with price-level targeting in the 1930s, and by all accounts it was quite successful.[32] The key difference between inflation targeting and price-level targeting is that the former forgives past errors, while the latter does not. For example, if a central bank targets a 2 per cent inflation rate, but fails to achieve it, there is no need to offset the error in subsequent periods. If actual inflation were 3 per cent, there would be no need to target 1 per cent the following year to bring the average back to 2 per cent. Under price-level targeting, in contrast, the economy would have to experience a period of below 2 per cent inflation to bring the price-level back to the desired track over time. The main benefit of this is that households and businesses would have greater confidence in where the price level would be over the long term, and could therefore make economic decisions with greater certainty.

The downside to this prospective benefit is perhaps greater volatility in inflation and output growth as past errors are corrected, even if a suitably long averaging period is used. Not all economists are convinced that this would be true, however. While it is impossible to bring any conclusive empirical evidence to bear, since only Sweden has ever tried price-level targeting, several papers have appeared in recent years demonstrating that it might be possible to lower the volatility of inflation and achieve more stable output growth under price-level targeting, depending on how inflation expectations are formed. An added bonus might be that it would also be possible to overcome, or at least minimize, the problems posed by the zero-interest-bound. I will not go into all of this here, but suffice it to say that price-level targeting and its implications for macroeconomic performance has also been the subject of intensive research at the Bank. Some of the more specific questions that will be addressed in this research agenda are described in the background paper that the Bank published last year at the time of the most recent inflation targeting renewal.[33]

Of course, improving the Bank of Canada's monetary policy framework is not the only monetary policy issue that requires more attention. Our understanding of more basic questions, such as the structure of the macroeconomy, the channels through which monetary policy operates, and how all of this is changing over time, is far from complete. While much has been learned, a great deal more remains to be studied and then applied to policy-making. The development of new financial instruments and the dramatic changes that have occurred in the global financial system over the past few years have exerted an important influence on the transmission of monetary policy and the role of credit in the economy. Productivity growth and the other factors that determine the capacity limits of our economy—indeed, the global economy—are only partially understood. Improving our understanding of these issues is critical to making monetary policy work well.

Most of what we have learned and thought we understood over the years has been incorporated in the econometric models that we have built and used for our projections. The Bank of Canada has a long tradition of being at the forefront of macro modelling, beginning with RDX, developed in the late 1960s and early 1970s and one of the earliest large-scale econometric models in the world. Our latest model, ToTEM, or Terms of Trade Economic Model, is a vast improvement over RDX.[34] It is one of a growing number of Dynamic Stochastic General Equilibrium Models, with multiple sectors and many advances from earlier models in terms of economic rigour and the way it incorporates expectational effects. Nevertheless, we know that even it has important deficiencies.

Macroeconomics textbooks in the 1950s and 1960s often began with a discussion of the various factors that distinguished microeconomics from macroeconomics. One well-known text, by Edward Shapiro, described the differences as follows:

> What microeconomics takes essentially as given—namely, the total output for the economy as a whole—is what macroeconomics takes as the prime variable whose size or value is to be determined. What macroeconomics takes as given—namely, the distribution of output, employment, and total spending among particular goods and services of individual industries and firms—are all variables in microeconomics.[35]

The disaggregated approach used in ToTEM to examine the behaviour of different sectors of the economy, coupled with the more rigorous microeconomic foundation that underlies each of the central relationships in the model, makes this distinction less meaningful today. Macroeconomics, in general, now rests upon a more secure and conceptually appealing microeconomic base. The challenge, at times, has been to incorporate these theoretical refinements without sacrificing the explanatory and predictive capabilities of the models.[36] Work is underway to try to narrow this gap and address other issues, but we know the task is in reality never ending, as new insights emerge along with major changes in the underlying structure of the Canadian economy.

Conclusion

Monetary policy has changed dramatically over the past 40 years. Opinions about the appropriate macroeconomic objective(s) for monetary policy, as well as the effectiveness and usefulness of monetary policy have all shifted, giving more prominence to the need for controlling inflation and more reliance on monetary policy for countering cyclical fluctuations in the macroeconomy. Our monetary policy framework has also improved, along with our understanding of the way the macroeconomy operates. Our knowledge is still very limited, however, and monetary policy-makers must always approach their task with considerable humility and crossed fingers.

New questions are always appearing, and some old questions occasionally reappear, albeit in a new guise. When I was a student, many economists questioned the efficacy of monetary policy, largely in a closed economy setting. This skepticism was gradually overturned by advances in economic theory and real world developments. In the last few years, however, new doubts have been raised about its usefulness in a globalized world. Are monetary authorities in national economies, especially those in small, open economies such as Canada, losing control over domestic economic activity and inflation? I do not think so, for a variety of reasons, but it may well be that additional regulatory tools are at times required to deal with pressures in specific sectors of the economy. Recent problems in New Zealand's housing market associated with Japanese carry trades may be a case in point.

Another topical issue reminiscent of an earlier debate involves the new exotic instruments that have been introduced in financial markets, and the appearance of large, often uncontrolled, financial institutions and investment funds that operate much like banks. Although significant benefits are likely to be realized in the form of more complete financial markets, recent developments do raise serious concerns about the implications of these highly levered firms and complex financial instruments for market stability and the conduct of monetary policy during periods of major structural change in financial markets and institutions. While it is too early to draw firm conclusions about any reforms and institutional changes that might be required to guard against these risks, questions have been raised about some of the views that I presented earlier regarding monetary policy objectives and implementation. William White, senior adviser at the Bank of International Settlements and a former deputy governor of the Bank of Canada, has written a paper entitled "Is Price Stability Enough?"[37] He and other authors suggest that it is not, and have argued that monetary policy should give more explicit attention to asset prices, not simply the Consumer Price Index, and adjust their targets to give greater priority to financial stability as opposed to monetary stability. My view is that, while monetary authorities do indeed need to recognize ongoing changes in financial markets and institutions, it is regulators who have the primary responsibility for oversight of the financial system.

Other researchers and policy-makers have questioned whether the present monetary policy instruments are sufficient to deal with a securitized world in which banks play an increasingly smaller role. There is no time to go into these intriguing issues in any detail. I will simply note that most practitioners and academics believe that the consensus views I described earlier still hold true. While some flexibility might be required in the pursuit of our inflation target from time to time, I want to emphasize that monetary policy must keep its focus on medium-term macroeconomic stabilization issues. First-best solutions involve central banks focusing on their comparative advantage, macro stabilization, and having regulators concentrate on questions of allocative efficiency and the stability of financial markets. It is also very important for bank supervisors, market regulators, and monetary authorities to communicate regularly, and know what one another is doing as well as what is expected of each of them. It has been my experience in this regard that we in Canada are second to none, but there always remains room for improvement. In particular, I would note the need to work together to improve the oversight of the market for residential mortgages and to improve transparency in the so-called exempt market for securities, especially highly structured securities. And in a world where accounting standards require

immediate marking to market of all assets and liabilities, we all need to consider the best ways to deal with the greatly magnified volatility of earnings. While these are issues that relate primarily to the efficiency and stability of financial markets, as we have seen in the past six months, they can certainly affect the ability of monetary policy to act as a macroeconomic stabilizer.

The only other point that I would add relates to the dangers of "fine tuning." Monetary policy, as is often stated, is subject to long and variable lags. It is a blunt but very effective instrument at a medium-term horizon. It should not be expected to deal with every short-term bump or wiggle in the economy, nor should people ask it to do so.

Notes

1   Eric Hanson Memorial Lecture, Department of Economics, University of Alberta, 4 February 2008. © David Dodge. Reprinted with permission.

2   Bank of Canada Act, r.c., C.B.–2, S.1. Preamble.

3   Ibid.

4   Government of Canada, "Employment and Income with Special Reference to the Initial Period of Reconstruction." (Ottawa: King's Printer, 1945).

5   Economic Council of Canada, "Economic Goals for Canada to 1970," First Annual Review, December 1964, 1.

6   Of course, what we now regard as "Keynesian economics" is based on one part of Keynes's contribution to economic thinking, drawn from his "General Theory of Employment, Interest and Money" and popularized by Alvin Hansen (1953).

7   Phillips (1958).

8   Crow (1988).

9   This is somewhat ironic, since Keynes himself regarded monetary policy as an important policy tool except in the presence of a liquidity trap. See, for example, Keynes's famous "Treatise on Money." Indeed, even the General Theory is about "Money, Employment and Interest."

10   See Report of the Commission on Money and Credit (1961), Radcliffe Report (1959), and Porter Commission Report (1964).

11   Mundell (1961, 1962, 1963).

12   This was especially true of small open economies, like Canada. Larger economies, such as the United States, which served as the anchor country or "nth-currency" for the Bretton Woods system, could enjoy a greater degree of monetary policy discretion.

13   China is an example of a country that has tried unsuccessfully to rein in money and credit growth without allowing sufficient exchange rate flexibility.

14   The one possible exception concerns countries, such as Japan in the 1990s, that have to contend with the "zero-interest-bound."

15   See, for example, recent speeches by Mervyn King, Ben Bernanke, Rachel Lomax and myself.

16   Some researchers, such as Acheson and Chant (1973), drew on the emerging theory of bureaucracies, and credited this behaviour to a natural desire on the part of policy-makers to avoid accountability.

17   Some of these tools may have useful application in the context of prudential oversight, but they have proven to be unnecessary for effective macro stabilization.

18   Another important aspect of this renewed faith in market mechanisms was the decision by an increasing number of industrial and emerging market economies to move from the system of pegged exchange rates to a system of flexible exchange rates. The latter are a necessary condition for effective monetary policy independence, and are also valued for the insulation properties they provide in response to economic shocks.

19   Friedman (2003).

20   These actions included carrying out Special Purchase and Resale Agreements (SPRA) at the target overnight rate, sometimes in multiple rounds, and raising the targeted amount of settlement balances.

21   When times are calm, the target for settlement balances is a constant $25 million, SPRAs are not conducted, and the auction of Receiver General deposits during the afternoon ensures that actual amount of settlement balances meets the targeted amount.

22   In an entirely different context, the Reserve Bank of New Zealand had adopted inflation targets one year earlier.

23   The European Central Bank, the Swiss National Bank and the Bank of Japan, for example, all have explicit inflation objectives and clear definitions of what constitutes reasonable price stability, but claim they are not inflation targeters. The US Federal Reserve has no explicit target for inflation, but is known to have a comfort zone of 1 to 2 per cent inflation for the core PCE deflator, and has recently

announced a new communication strategy that implicitly reveals the FOMC's goals for output growth and inflation.

24 Bank of Canada and Government of Canada. "Renewal of the Inflation-Control Target," November 2006.

25 See "Economic behaviour and policy choice under price stability," Bank of Canada (1993).

26 Bank of Canada, "Targets for reducing inflation." *Bank of Canada Review* (March, 1991), 11.

27 Akerlof, Dickens and Perry (1996).

28 See also Fortin, Akerlof, Dickens, and Perry (2002).

29 Crawford (1998) and Rossiter (2005).

30 Crawford and Wright (2001).

31 A minor variant of this, which has been suggested, is to expand the target bands surrounding the 2 per cent target mid-point. The bands are presently 1 to 3 per cent, and could be expanded to 0 to 3 per cent, effectively lowering the target mid-point to 1.5 per cent.

32 Based on this positive, yet admittedly limited experience, it is not obvious why other countries have never followed the Swedish example.

33 Bank of Canada, "Renewal of the Inflation-Control target: background Information—November 2006."

34 Murchison and Rennison (2006).

35 Shapiro (1966).

36 One notable feature that ToTEM shares with most other modern macro models is that it has no role for money. Indeed, money and credit aggregates do not appear in the model, nor is there a banking sector. This is one of the reasons that the Bank of Canada has always supplemented the information drawn from its main econometric models, with results taken from a suite of other satellite models, which are based on different paradigms and offer different points of view.

37 White (2006).

Key Terms

fiscal policy
inflation targeting
intervention

macroeconomic
monetary policy
price stability

Questions for Review

1. What were some of the factors that brought monetary policy level with fiscal policy in its importance to Canada's economy?

2. In what ways is monetary policy different from fiscal policy?

3. How does the Bank of Canada "make" monetary policy? What policy instruments is it manipulating?

4. Why is transparency such an important issue for central bankers?

5. Why is inflation the main worry of central banks? And what is "inflation targeting?"

Further Resources

Bernanke, B. S. (1995). "The macroeconomics of the Great Depression: A comparative approach," *Journal of Money, Credit and Banking* 27(1) (February), 1–28.

Caramazza, F. and Aziz, J. (1998). "Fixed or flexible?: Getting the exchange rate right in the 1990s," *Economic Issues 13* (Washington, DC: International Monetary Fund).

Eichengreen, B. (1996). *Golden fetters: The gold standard and the Great Depression, 1919–1939*. Oxford: Oxford University Press.

Eichengreen, B. and Temin, P. (2000). "The gold standard and the Great Depression," *Contemporary European History* 9(2) (July), 183–207.

Rockoff, H. (1990). "The 'Wizard of Oz' as a monetary allegory," *Journal of Political Economy* 98(4) (August), 739–60.

References

Acheson, K. and J. Chant. (1973). "Bureaucratic theory and the choice of central bank goals: The case of the Bank of Canada." *Journal of Money, Credit, and Banking*, 637–55.

Akerlof, G., Dickens, W., and Perry, G. (1996). "The macroeconomics of low inflation." *Brookings Papers on Economic Activity* 1, 1–59.

Bank of Canada. (1991). "Targets for reducing inflation." *Bank of Canada Review* (March).

——. (1993). Economic behaviour and policy choice under price stability. Proceedings of a conference held at the Bank of Canada, October, 1993. Ottawa: Bank of Canada.

——. (2006). *Renewal of the Inflation-Control Target: Background Information*. Ottawa: Bank of Canada.

Bank of Canada Act. R.C., C.B.–2, S.1. Preamble.

Bank of Canada and Government of Canada. (2006). *Renewal of the inflation-control target*. Ottawa: Bank of Canada.

Blinder, A. and Goldfeld, S. (1976). "New measures of fiscal and monetary policy: 1958–73." *American Economic Review* 66(5), 780–96.

Crawford, A. (1998). "Measurement biases in the Canadian CPI: An update." *Bank of Canada Review* (spring), 31–7.

Crawford, A. and Wright, G. (2001). "Downward nominal-wage rigidity: Micro- evidence from Tobit models." Bank of Canada Working Paper No. 2001-7.

Crow, J. (1988). "The work of Canadian Monetary policy." Eric John Hanson Memorial Lecture Series. University of Alberta, 18 January.

Economic Council of Canada. (1964). "Economic goals for Canada to 1970." *First Annual Review*, December.

Fortin, P., Akerlof, G., Dickens, W., and Perry, G. (2002). "Inflation and unemployment in the U.S. and Canada: A common framework." Département des sciences économiques, Université du Québec à Montréal Working Paper No. 20–16.

Friedman, B. (2003). "The LM curve: A Not-so-fond farewell." In *Macroeconomics, monetary policy, and financial stability*. A festschrift in honour of Charles Freedman. Proceedings of a conference held by the Bank of Canada. Ottawa.

Friedman, M. (1956). "The quantity theory of money—A restatement." in *Studies in the quantity theory of money*; edited by M. Friedman. Chicago: University of Chicago Press.

Government of Canada. (1945). *Employment and income with special reference to the initial period of reconstruction*. Ottawa: King's Printer.

Hansen, Alvin. (1953). *A guide to Keynes*. New York: McGraw-Hill Book Company, Inc.

Keynes, J. M. (1930). *Treatise on money*. King's College Fellow, Cambridge: Cambridge University Press.

——. (1936). *The general theory of employment, interest and money*. Cambridge: Macmillan Cambridge University Press.

Mundell, R. (1961). "Flexible exchange rates and employment policy." *The Canadian Journal of Economics and Political Science* 27(November), 509–17.

——. (1962). "The appropriate use of monetary and fiscal policy for internal and external stability." *IMF Staff Papers* 9 (March).

——. (1963). "Capital mobility and stabilization policy under fixed and flexible exchange rates." *The Canadian Journal of Economics and Political Science* 29(November), 475–85.

Murchison, S. and Rennison, A. (2006). "ToTEM: The Bank of Canada's new quarterly projection model." Bank of Canada Technical Report No. 97.

Phillips, A. (1958). "The relationship between unemployment and the rate of change of money wage rates in the United Kingdom, 1861–1957." *Economica* 25(November), 283–99.

Porter Commission Report. (1964). *Report of the Royal Commission on Banking and Finance*. Ottawa: Queen's Printer.

Radcliffe Report. (1959). *Committee on the Working of the Monetary System* (August). London: Her Majesty's Stationery Office.

Report of the Commission on Money and Credit. (1961). *Money and credit: Their influence on jobs, prices and growth*. New Jersey: Prentice-Hall.

Rossiter, J. (2005). "Measurement bias in the Canadian consumer price index." Bank of Canada Working Paper No. 2005–39.

Shapiro, Edward. (1966). *Macroeconomic analysis*. New York: Harcourt Brace Jovanovich, Inc.

Thiessen, G. (1999). "Then and now: The change in views on the role of monetary policy since the Porter Commission." The Tony Hampson Memorial Lecture, delivered at the C.D. Howe Institute, Toronto, 11 March.

White, W. (2006). "Is price stability enough?" BIS Working Paper No. 206.

PART III

Rules, Norms, and Governance: An International Society?

In a modern context, rules, norms, and governance are understood as the byproducts of Westphalian sovereign states working to achieve consensus on issues to create stability in an anarchical international system. As the sovereign state evolved in Europe, however, cooperation was based on simpler principles, namely non-intervention and the survival and exclusivity of these earliest sovereign states. Cooperation, therefore, would exist amongst this "family of states" but would not extend to "uncivilized" areas of the world, which instead were subject to control and domination, either through the pursuit of unequal treaties or, in many cases, colonization and occupation. Theoretically, this period of history formed the basis of what would become the Society of States approach or the English School of international relations.

As Hedley Bull famously stated, a Society of States "exists when a group of states, conscious of certain common interests and common values, form a society in the sense that they conceive themselves to be bound by a common set of rules in their relations with one another, and share in the working of common institutions" (Bull 1977, 13). Although critics argue that the English School legitimizes a western narrative based on European understandings of sovereignty, often accompanied by oppressive and exploitive relations with other territorial units, Bull's definition does provide a framework for understanding rules, norms, and cooperative frameworks at various times in human history.

Specifically, it is clear that international cooperation predated the European sovereign state. It existed anywhere groups came together for common economic, political, military, or cultural interests, and was evident in ancient Egyptian, Greek, Roman, Indian, Chinese, Christian, and Islamic societies. Cooperation was not always long-term but in many cases these relations were based on a combination of self-interest and normative considerations (Armstrong 2011, 36–41).

The modern Society of States, however, at least from a European perspective, took centuries to unfold. Italian city-states appointed resident ambassadors and accepted principles of diplomatic immunity first adopted by Greek and Roman empires. For several centuries, Europe was also divided by several competing sources of identity (guilds, nobility, clans, and tribes), as well as an asymmetrical array of territorial entities, including principalities, kingdoms, city-states, and larger geographical units formed through conquest and marriage. As these early pre-states engaged in voyages of discovery, colonial claims were codified in treaties and agreements, and international law slowly emerged to clarify issues such as borders, commercial trade, and the potential rights of indigenous peoples.

It was also during this period that the historically unifying influence of the Roman Catholic Church was challenged during the Reformation, leading to a number of religious conflicts. It was the Thirty Years War in 1618 that ultimately ended the supremacy of the papacy in Europe. The Treaty of Westphalia in 1648 established the initial working parameters of the modern European sovereign state. These included the concept of non-intervention in domestic affairs, most notably the power to determine the religious affairs of inhabitants within territorial borders. The concept of sovereignty was further affirmed with the right to conduct diplomatic relations but also with the understanding that new states would only be accepted with the acknowledgement of existing sovereign governments. A balance of power was also affirmed with the Treaty of Utrecht in 1713, in which sovereign states accepted a multipolar system as a means of maintaining peace and stability in Europe.

In reality, however, conflict and war continued, especially as the emerging constructs of liberalism and nationalism challenged the authority of traditional ruling monarchies. This was most evident with the French Revolution in 1789, which marked the growing influence of both liberalism and nationalism as challenges to the imperialism of the entrenched monarchies of the Napoleonic era.

In response, the great powers banded together to form the Concert of Europe, which met regularly in conferences and created new norms and rules on functional issues, such as sanitation, and postal services. The Concert also attempted to ensure peace by prohibiting unilateral attempts to disrupt the balance of power in Europe and to sanction any domestic intervention, as well as the recognition of new sovereign states in Europe. The Concert, however, also continued to endorse colonialism, including the Conference of Berlin in 1885, which finalized outstanding territorial claims in Africa. The emergence of a unified Germany and the First World War effectively ended the Concert but its existence provided a legacy for other attempts to establish rules and norms in the inter-war period, such as the League of Nations.

In contrast, the end of the Second World War marked the emergence of a bipolar international system dominated by the United States and the Soviet Union. Although stark ideological divisions and the threat of nuclear war defined the Cold War, it also ushered in a new period of cooperation and a proliferation of international institutions and regimes. In addition to the United Nations (UN), the North Atlantic Treaty Organization (NATO) became the forum for western security interests and the North American Aerospace Defence Command (NORAD) sought similar objectives for Canada and the US in North America. The Soviet Union countered with the Warsaw Pact but was also active in the International Labour Organization (ILO) and numerous departments and agencies of the UN including the World Health Organization (WHO) and the International Atomic Energy Agency (IAEA), although not the World Bank or the International Monetary Fund (IMF). Other postwar cooperative frameworks included the General Agreement on Tariffs and Trade (GATT), La Francophonie, the Commonwealth, the Organization of American States (OAS), the Arab League, and the Organisation for Economic Cooperation and Development (OECD).

As a result, liberal IPE began to explore the potential impact of institutions and regimes in the global political economy. Early studies focused on Europe from a functionalist and neo-functionalist perspective (Haas 1958; Mitrany 1943). Advancing changes in technology, communication, and transportation, however, helped to coordinate policy across state lines and highlighted ties between global and domestic economies. This was reflected in the "interdependence" literature that emerged in the late 1960s (Cooper 1968). Although interdependence theory adopted realist principles of power, it also placed a greater emphasis on non-state variables, challenged the assumption that states were unitary, rational actors, and focused on economics, and other "non-traditional" issues such as the environment, pollution, immigration, and human rights. Robert Keohane and Joseph Nye would later develop this concept more fully with "complex interdependence," with its characteristics of multiple channels of interaction, diminished utility of military force in interstate relations, and its blurred agenda of both "high" and "low" issue areas (Keohane and Nye 1977).

Interdependence theory also contributed to the neoliberal, neorealist debate that dominated international relations theory in the United States throughout the 1980s. Both approaches accepted that cooperation was possible, although neorealists stressed the importance of state power in this process. In contrast, neoliberals prioritized absolute gains, pursued within international regimes and institutions, as a means of managing anarchy in an anarchic international system (Baldwin 1993; Oye 1986). In a related debate, hegemonic stability theory emphasized the importance of a single dominant or hegemonic state with the resources and political will to pursue policies required to maintain a liberal capitalist global economy. It also acknowledged that the rules and norms established by hegemons could survive following the collapse of a hegemonic power (Keohane 1984).

All of these theoretical contributions helped observers to better understand cooperation in the global political economy in the postwar period. Even though the economic strength of the United States (the hegemon) was in decline, the economic and social purpose of Bretton Woods continued to guide economic relationships in the international community. These foundations, referred to as "embedded liberalism" by John Ruggie, provided the framework for a dramatic increase in international trade and investment, albeit with ongoing protectionism (Ruggie 1982). At the same time, however, the postwar period also saw an increase in other liberal challengers. Friedrich Hayek and Milton Friedman aggressively critiqued state intervention in the economy (Friedman 1962; Hayek 1978). The "neoliberal" theories of Friedman and Hayek eventually became the cornerstones of US and British economic policy in the 1980s. Under the administrations of Ronald Reagan and Margaret Thatcher considerable efforts were made to promote privatization, deregulation, free trade, and increase foreign investment.

This is not to suggest that critical theoretical approaches were dormant in the liberal/realist debate over rules, norms, and governance. In fact, a very rich stream of the IPE literature continued to evolve in the shadow of traditional theory. Historical materialists and feminists focused on structural realities that marginalized many participants in the global political economy on the basis of class and gender. Constructivists, on the other hand, emphasized historical and social contexts in an attempt to understand IPE. In all cases, however, it is difficult to deny the relevance of Bull's observations about a society of states, although critical theory prioritizes important normative considerations in the global economy.

The first chapter in this section, by Stephen Clarkson, Isabel Duchesne, and Amy Tieu, focuses on an emerging form of governance that Canada has included in a number of international agreements: investor-state dispute mechanisms. They present a compelling argument that transnational corporations are the prime beneficiaries of these new rules and norms, by locking weaker states into an ongoing process of subordination to foreign capital. In the second chapter, Jacqueline Best, draws inspiration from the critical post-positivist literature. Specifically, she argues for a reconceptualization of poverty focusing on social risks and vulnerability, as opposed to the liberal market approaches often adopted or endorsed by international institutions. Robert Wolfe, on the other hand, reviews the challenges facing the World Trade Organization (WTO) during the current Doha Round negotiations. For Wolfe, it is not the institutional framework of the WTO that should be blamed but rather the emergence of China and the failure of the United States to engage its trans-Pacific rival on a number of issues that could serve as a catalyst for what the author calls the "malaise in multilateralism." Finally, Gilbert Gagné examines the evolution of international dispute settlement within the GATT and the WTO. Unlike Wolfe, Gagné views ongoing problems in the dispute settlement process, such as delays in proceedings, judicial activism, and pressures to reconcile trade issues with concerns outside its mandate, as an indicator of broader institutional problems in the WTO.

References

Bull, H. (1977). *The anarchical society: A study of order in world politics*. London: Macmillan.

Armstrong, D. (2011). "The evolution of international society," in J. Baylis, S. Smith, and P. Owens (Eds), *The globalization of world politics*, 5th ed. Oxford: Oxford University Press.

Baldwin, D. A. (Ed.) (1993). *Neorealism and neoliberalism: The contemporary debate*. New York: Columbia University Press.

Cooper, R.N. (1968). *The economics of interdependence: Economic policy in the Atlantic community*. New York: McGraw-Hill.

Friedman, M. (1962). *Capitalism and freedom*. Chicago: University of Chicago Press.

Haas, E. (1958). *The uniting of Europe*. Stanford: Stanford University Press.

Hayek, F. A. (1978). *New studies in philosophy, politics, economics, and the history of ideas*. Chicago: University of Chicago Press.

Keohane, R.O. (1984). *After hegemony: Cooperation and discord in the world political economy*. Princeton, New Jersey: Princeton University Press.

Keohane, R.O. and Nye, J. (1977). *Power and interdependence: World politics in transition*. Boston: Little Brown.

Mitrany, D. (1943). *A working peace system.* London: RIIA.

Oye, K. (Ed.). (1986). *Cooperation under anarchy.* Princeton: Princeton University Press.

Ruggie, J.G. (1982). "International regimes, transactions, and change: Embedded liberalism in the postwar economic order." *International Organization 36,* 2 (Spring), 195–231.

8 The Transnational Corporation
Controversial Dynamo of the Global Economy

Stephen Clarkson, Isabel Duchesne, and Amy Tieu

Among globalization's large cast of jostling characters, none is more central or more controversial than the transnational corporation. The TNC is central because it incorporates the **foreign direct investment** (**FDI**) that is one of the salient motors of economic development around the world. At the same time TNCs are politically controversial in countries that host FDI because their harmful side effects are often believed to outweigh their positive impacts.

Their interactions between the political and the economic also make TNCs archetypical for students of political economy. On the one hand, government efforts to control TNCs at home or to attract them from abroad demonstrate how states depend on markets. At the same time, corporate demands for regulating FDI—whether at home through domestic measures or abroad through international agreements—show how markets depend on states. Meanwhile, civil society is the joker card, generally quiescent but occasionally erupting with volcanic political consequences.

Pressed by their competitive business sectors to provide greater protection for their operations abroad or by their uncompetitive business sectors to ensure greater protection for their operations at home, governments sometimes endorse and sometimes resist adopting treaties that enshrine the rights of FDI. At the same time civil-society organizations, which are systematically excluded from intergovernmental economic negotiations, become exercised by evidence that their nation's sovereignty has been diminished or that hard-won health, environmental, or human-rights measures have been disallowed through foreign corporations' legal manoeuvres.

During the first four decades following the Second World War there was an important debate over the role that TNCs played in national economies. Subsequently, the gradual but largely unnoticed construction of new judicial institutions promoting TNCs' expansion has become a leading but nonetheless highly contested innovation in global governance.

The first part of this chapter will review the transnational corporation's historical emergence and examine the academic debate it provoked—including the indecisive empirical data about its economic impact on host markets. To illustrate how national governments respond to this phenomenon, we will turn in Part 2 to the experience of Canada as a leading *site* for incoming FDI. Part 3 will trace Canada's contribution, as a significant *source* of outward-bound FDI, to creating a new international regime that protects transnational corporations' FDI against host-state efforts to control it.

The Unresolved Debate

Most of the world's largest corporations are transnational, some well-known examples being Toyota (based in Japan), Apple (the United States), Nestlé (Switzerland), HSBC (Great Britain), Philips (Holland), and Volkswagen (Germany). TNCs are companies that own, control, and engage in value-added activities, such as manufacturing, sales, distribution, financial services, and information technology in two or more countries (Dunning 1996, 27). They consist of parent enterprises located in the "home" economy and foreign affiliates sited in the "host" economy. The parent enterprise manages the firm's global operations by controlling its foreign affiliates, typically through owning a share of their equity—from all of it to as little as one tenth (United Nations Conference on Trade and Development, 2014). Through this "direct" ownership, the parent enterprise decides the strategy its foreign affiliates must follow.

TNCs are increasingly locating their production and distribution operations wherever the most cost-efficient labour, resources, and technology are available. Many spread a complete production process over several countries, with manufacturing occurring where it makes the most business sense. Some parts may be sourced in one country, refined in another, and assembled in a third one, if that achieves the most cost-efficient process (Fuchs 2007, 12). Roughly a third of global commerce is intra-firm, that is, trade between the subsidiaries of a single TNC, and approximately 80 per cent of global trade occurs within TNCs' international

production networks (Keane 2014, 2). TNCs are chiefly distinguished from a nationally owned firm operating in its domestic market by the business advantage they enjoy thanks to their superior access to the financial, technological, managerial, labour, and marketing resources that are necessary for these competitors' long-term success, a success that is typically marked by the giant TNC taking over its smaller local rival or driving it out of business (Frischtak and Newfarmer 1996, 297).

The TNC's Historical Emergence

Although enterprises have operated in foreign countries since the 1500s, when the Medici family in Florence expanded its banking activities to other city-states, the enterprise we know today as the transnational corporation emerged in the eighteenth century (Bornschier and Stamm 1990, 211) when large trading companies from expanding countries began founding agencies in their colonies. These local operations were usually staffed by family members, but as industrialization accelerated in Europe and North America in the middle decades of the nineteenth century, manufacturing companies investing outside their home economy started to negotiate licensing arrangements with counterpart firms in the host economy in return for a fee or a share in the economic returns (Bornschier and Stamm 1990, 211). By the beginning of the twentieth century, new communications capacities offered by the telegraph, then the telephone, enabled successful corporations to establish plants to serve more distant locations in their own national market more efficiently. When they set up such branch plants to operate in foreign economies under their continued managerial control, the multi-*branch* corporation became multi-*national*, and the modern transnational corporation was born.

Such companies were both *pushed* by factors in their own market and *pulled* by conditions abroad. Reaching their maximum penetration at home led companies to look abroad, not only to capitalize on new markets but also to reduce costs in their production by capturing economies of scale, by moving to cheaper productive locations, or by acquiring needed natural resources at either cheaper prices or of a better quality than could be acquired locally (Frischtak and Newfarmer 1996, 295). This transnationalization was also pulled by the drive to expand established export outlets, by new opportunities to service foreign markets, and by the competitive desire to buy out local competitors and so increase their oligopolistic capacity to raise prices and increase profits (Bornschier and Stamm 1990, 212; Dunning 1996, 33).

TNCs have proliferated significantly during the last half century. Having emerged largely unscathed from the destruction of both global wars, the United States was at the forefront of this rapid corporate expansion. In 1969, there were roughly 7,000 TNCs. By 1992, there were over 37,000 TNCs controlling some 170,000 foreign affiliates (Outreville 2007, 3). By 2009, those numbers had more than doubled to 82,000 TNCs controlling over 810,000 foreign affiliates and, as a result, wielding enormous political clout both within individual host countries and in global governance regimes (United Nations Conference on Trade and Development 2009). Economically speaking, they had become omnipresent.

In the 1990s, 90 per cent of all TNCs were based in the global North, particularly in the triad of the United States, Japan, and Germany which alone accounted for 73 of the top 100 TNCs, ranked by revenue. Although corporations from the global South now represent an increasing portion of TNCs, the triad is still home to 85 per cent of the top TNCs. In 2004, just five of the top 100 TNCs originated from developing countries (Outreville 2007, 4–7) although the figure had risen to eleven by 2013 (WIR Web Table 28, 2014) Since the turn of the millennium, the top 100 largest non-financial

TNCs have consistently accounted for about 4 per cent of world GDP ("WIR 2009", 17).

In lockstep with TNCs' numerical expansion has been the growth of the FDI they have invested, but the massive circulation of both foreign direct investment and portfolio capital is not a new phenomenon (Nayyar 2006, 138). Though accurate data on global FDI flows are limited, their general pattern is clear. The prosperous era from 1870 to the outbreak of the First World War was characterized by the free flow of capital as well as labour (Nayyar 2006, 138, 139). FDI was already playing a significant role in many countries at the beginning of the twentieth century when flows surged, with total world stock reaching $14 billion by 1914 (ibid.). The average stock of FDI as a percentage of GDP in developing economies is estimated to have been 40 per cent in 1913/14 (Velde 2006, 5). After a severe decline caused by the two world wars, global FDI stocks again increased—from $68 billion in 1960 to $636 billion two decades later and to $6,258 billion by the turn of the new millennium (Nayyar 2006, 141). By the early 2000s, international FDI flows, measured as a percentage of global GDP, reached proportions comparable to those seen before the Great War and moved on to new records (Velde 2006, 2, 5).

Having accounted for 20 per cent of the global FDI stock in 1914 and 30 per cent in 1938, US-based foreign direct investment had risen to 56 per cent by 1960 (Bornschier and Stamm1990, 213). As their economies recovered from the Second World War, European and Japanese firms also expanded, ushering in an era of increased global competition for markets and resources (Radice 2014, 23). By 1978, American TNCs' share of the global stock of FDI had declined to 47 per cent, with European TNCs' share (which had fallen drastically from its peak of 77 per cent in 1914) recovering slightly to 41 per cent (Bornschier and Stamm 1990, 213).

Outward FDI flows from the global South climbed slowly throughout the same period, from a mere 3 per cent in the 1978–80 period to 12 per cent by 2003–05 and 16 per cent in 2008 (Sauvant 2008, 5; United Nations Conference on Trade and Development 2009, 16).

Contrary to what may be expected, the portion of global FDI that goes to the South has fallen since the beginning of the twentieth century, from two thirds in 1913 to one quarter in 2006 (Velde 2006, 6). Table 8.1 documents the increased importance of FDI in the world economy in recent decades. In the aftermath of the 2008 global financial crisis, economies in the North have taken a smaller share of incoming FDI, falling to 39 per cent in 2013 (UNCTAD 2014b, 1). Meanwhile, South–South FDI flows have surged (ibid., 7).

The Academic Debate

As foreign corporations were increasingly seen to predominate in such high-profile sectors as automobile production after the Second World War, concerns were voiced in the public domain about their impact both on national economies and on states' autonomy. This interesting issue led scholars to pay more attention to the phenomenon. Economists rooted in classical trade theory argued that FDI necessarily had a positive impact on a host country's level of development. These proponents of investment of all types argued that less industrialized economies could catch up to the more advanced ones by using the capital, technology, managerial expertise, technical know-how, and connections to international markets that foreign-controlled branch plants brought with them (Herkenrath and Bornschier 2003, 108). For example, a foreign affiliate that buys its inputs from local sources creates a "backward linkage" that improves their technological capacities through the transmission of the TNC's knowledge and technology (Chen 1996, 188). If it generates locally owned sales networks for its products, it creates a "forward" linkage bringing with it more up-to-date standards. The presence of TNCs also creates increased competition, forcing domestic firms either to close down or to adopt more efficient production methods and lower their prices (Chudnovsky 1996, 275). This school of analysts consequently advocated that host governments should encourage, not impede, FDI. After all, they maintained, foreign capital is politically neutral: its benefits have nothing to do with its national provenance (Moran 1996, 419).

There was another side to this thesis. Critics argued to the contrary, that foreign capital is both politically biased (in the sense that it favours the interests of the home country) and economically biased (in the sense that it abstracts the host market's balanced development). They explained the underdevelopment suffered by countries in the South as caused by TNCs trapping them in an impoverishing, asymmetrical dependence on the

Table 8.1   FDI Stock as a Percentage of GDP

	1980s	1990s	2000s	2010–2013
World	7	13	27	31
Developing countries	13	16	27	30
Developed countries	6	13	27	32
Transitional economies	0	3	24	31

Source: United Nations Conference on Trade And Development (UNCTAD), World Investment Report (WIR) Tables, 2014. http://unctad.org/en/Pages/DIAE/World%20Investment%20Report/Annex-Tables.aspx. Accessed June 11, 2015. Reprinted with permission.

North. Through TNCs, the most profitable functions in the production processes are retained in the home investors' "core" economies, while resource extraction and less skilled activities remain on the "periphery" (Herkenrath and Bornschier 2003, 110). Exercising their superior market power, TNCs also control the terms of trade, meaning that they can demand higher prices for the finished goods they export while depressing the prices of the raw materials they import.

If TNCs stand to benefit from these countries' low value-added activities, then their interests necessarily diverge from those of their hosts. While host-state governments seek to move their businesses up the production hierarchy, TNCs are motivated by the very factors that host governments want to change: access to unprocessed resources and a cheaper, less sophisticated labour force. Moreover, critics argue that foreign investment's purported benefits of disseminating technology, knowledge, and skills do not often materialize. State-of-the-art technologies tend to be developed in a foreign investor's home economy thanks to its advanced educational system, its larger local market, its massive financial institutions, and its pools of specialized technical skills (Dean 2000).

By displacing domestic production, altering consumer preferences, and influencing the host country's policies, TNCs create distortions not just in a periphery's economy but in its state's politics through coercive lobbying by host managers and elites whose interests are tied to the foreign-owned TNCs for whom they work (Bornschier and Stamm 1990, 206). Often constituting a host economy's largest corporations, the branch plant's domestic heft is amplified by their parent enterprise's political capacity to push the home governments to safeguard these asymmetrical relationships by using its diplomatic muscle (Herkenrath and Bornschier 2003, 109).

Informed by this school of thought, which was articulated most insistently after the Second World War in the research published by the United Nations Economic Commission for Latin America, host countries there introduced, as part of their strategy of import-substitution industrialization, protectionist legislation to shelter domestically owned enterprises from foreign competition and to restrict TNCs' activities by imposing "performance requirements" on FDI such as meeting domestic job-creation, exporting, technology transmission, and input-sourcing quotas (Frischtak and Newfarmer 1996, 295).

With the shift to neoliberal thinking among elites in the 1980s, public opinion swung in favour of foreign direct investment's proponents, with academic interest in the topic mirroring the subsequent decline of public concern (Bornschier and Stamm 1990, 209). At this point, a third school of thought, typified by researchers writing for the United Nations Conference on Trade and Development's *World Investment Reports*, maintained that TNCs' impacts are neither wholly positive nor wholly negative.

TNCs can certainly act in a way that furthers their interests at the cost of the host economy's; for example by evading taxes through artificially lowering the prices they pay for a subsidiary's exports, sourcing their inputs from foreign rather than local suppliers, or not using domestic service institutions (Lall 1996, 63). Yet the presence of TNCs does not necessarily signal the death knell for a developing country's economy. While some countries do indeed suffer from the negative economic effects of TNCs, others thrive. Thanks to Singapore's policies, which actively incentivized TNCs to set up headquarters there, technology transfers stemming from FDI help explain that city-state's stunning economic growth (Chen 1996, 198; Dean 2000). In sum, the effects of TNCs are largely determined by the receiving state's policies (Herkenrath and Bornschier 2003, 111).

The Empirical Evidence

So far, research on FDI's economic impact has not been able to support either the proponents or the critics conclusively. Some studies from the 1960s and 1970s suggested that TNCs had a negative effect on GDP per capita growth. They also concluded that TNCs exacerbated host countries' income inequality. However, they found as well that fresh FDI inflows had a positive impact on per capita growth, particularly in a host economy with a low number of TNCs. At higher levels of TNC presence, FDI can no longer compensate for the "disadvantageous structural impact" of TNC, and the net effect becomes negative (Herkenrath and Bornschier 2003, 118–9).

More recent studies have produced equally conflicting findings. Herkenrath (1999) could not find an effect on economic growth, while Kentor (2001) found that TNCs still demonstrate a negative effect (Herkenrath and Bornschier 2003, 120). The validity of all these studies was affected by such methodological issues as the small samples that were studied. When Herkenrath and Bornschier retested both schools' hypotheses, they found that TNC presence did increase income inequality but did not have a significant impact on economic growth. They surmised that differing state policies might explain the varying results of previous studies. Even amidst heightened political pressures for liberalization and deregulation, some governments, notably Japan, Korea, and Taiwan, have nonetheless counteracted the potentially negative impact of TNCs by regulating foreign firms (Herkenrath and Bornschier 2003, 130).

The Canadian Case: From Site to Source

Canada's long history as a site of transnational corporations' direct investments and its recent growing importance as the source of TNCs investing abroad makes it an excellent case for studying the phenomenon and its associated controversies in a particular country. Compared with other developed economies, Canada has experienced an exceptionally high degree of foreign ownership. In 1983 the United Nations identified it as the country with the highest value of foreign investment in the world (Laxer 1989, 225). Since 1992, Canada has outpaced both the United States and the G8 group of industrial countries as a whole in this measure, and the level of its FDI continues to grow (Bellan 2006; Statistics Canada 2014, Table 376-0052). At 35 per cent in 2014, Canada had more FDI stock as a percentage of its GDP than its North American neighbours, whether the United States' 29 per cent or Mexico's 31 per cent (United Nations Conference on Trade and Development 2014a, WIR Web Table 7).

From Early Colonial Dependence to Later Industrialization

Following their discovery by European sailors, France and Great Britain's fragile colonies in North America developed embryonic economies of their own thanks to the pull of the European market's demand for fish and fur and the push of these two states' capital, which was directly invested in building local infrastructure to enable these natural resources to be harvested and shipped across the Atlantic. As timber and wheat joined the list of staples for export to Europe, the colonial economies developed their own linkages, both backward (building tools and machinery for farming) and forward (founding banks to finance commerce). In this sense, the early transnational corporate enterprise epitomized for British North America by the London-based Hudson's Bay Company facilitated the colonies' economic development while delivering profits to the imperial centre. The "Bay" was more the exception than the rule. While Canadian industry was never entirely self-reliant, it had tended to employ British capital in the form of loans rather than directly owned stocks, a financial relationship that promoted domestic enterprise (Laxer 1989, 12).

By the end of the nineteenth century, Canada was far from being an economic backwater. By the time Great Britain federated its North American colonies in 1867, the new Dominion of Canada was already a vigorous exporter of manufactured products (Laxer, 11). Supported by a high, import-substituting tariff typical of industrializing capitalist economies, Canada's exports had the world's highest ratio—5 to 1—of finished manufactures to such semi-processed goods as pulp and paper (Laxer, 46–7). The leading manufactures exported by Canada in 1899 were agricultural implements such as mechanical reapers (22 per cent of the total), leather products (20 per cent), and wood products (18 per cent) (Laxer, 47).

By the dawn of the twentieth century Canada stood seventh in the world ranking of industrializing economies, its manufacturing success demonstrated by Massey-Harris's innovative farm equipment that was exported to over 40 countries (Laxer, 11). Indeed, much of the initial capital that arrived from the United States was attracted by the dynamism of Canada's protected industry. Later, American FDI transformed Canada from being a competitive player abroad to an inefficient site for massive numbers of TNCs that restricted manufactured exports (Laxer, 12).

The Influx of American FDI and its Shift of Industrial Structure

The flood of American capital into Canada over the course of the twentieth century can hardly be overstated. On the eve of the First World War, there were already about 450 American subsidiaries north of the border. By the 1920s, nearly 40 per cent of Canada's manufacturing and mining and smelting sectors were foreign-owned (Laxer, 207). By the early 1930s, over 40 per cent of machinery and chemical products, 68 per cent of electrical goods, and 83 per cent of automotive products were made in American-owned factories (Laxer, 13–16).

Following the Second World War, active federal government promotion of US investment both to take over the state-led enterprises that had driven Canada's military industrialization and to develop the minerals with which Canada was richly endowed helped American ownership rise to 45 per cent of Canada's manufacturing economy and 51 per cent of its mining and smelting by 1962 (Laxer 13–14). Though Canada's resource and financial sectors have drawn considerable FDI, manufacturing consistently attracted the greatest share of incoming investment throughout the 20th century (see Table 8.2).

Driven by the TNCs' new manufacturing strategies, which prohibited them from competing with

Table 8.2   Sectoral Distribution of FDI in Canada, 1926–1990 (percentages)

	1926	1930	1939	1955	1970	1980	1990
Manufacturing	53	45	51	46	42	41	45
Petroleum	–	6	–	22	24	26	17
Mining and Smelting	9	9	10	11	12	8	4
Utilities	15	19	17	4	2	1	1
Merchandising	8	7	7	7	6	8	7
Financial	12	13	12	9	11	12	21
Other	3	3	2	2	3	4	4

Note: Petroleum was not consistently listed separately until 1953.
Source: Micheal Twomey, "The Canadian Experience with the Investment Development Path", http://www-personal.umd.umich .edu/~mtwomey/fdi/CanadaText.pdf. Reprinted with permission.

branches in other countries, deepening US ownership shifted the structure of the Canadian economy. Canada's share of world manufactured exports declined, while its reliance on imported products from American TNCs' home operations rose. In 1955, Canada's share of all the finished manufactured exports of the ten largest capitalist economies had fallen to 2 per cent. That same year, some 80 per cent of Canada's manufactured exports were unfinished, but its imports accounted for over one quarter of the total imports of the ten largest capitalist economies (Laxer, 48).

Active American participation in the Canadian economy mattered little to a public committed to fully supporting Washington's leadership in the Cold War with the dreaded Soviet Union. The 1957 Royal Commission on Canada's Economic Prospects was the first major study to voice concerns about both the economic and political impacts of foreign direct investment. Economically, US corporations' oligopolistic dominance of the country's most technologically advanced sectors presented near-insuperable barriers to domestic firms entering or re-entering those economic domains with the most promising future. Politically, excessive US ownership could compromise the Canadian government's autonomy (Royal Commission on Canada's Economic Prospects 1957)

Such worries were deemed absurd by Canada's mainstream economists. Harry Eastman coauthored a study suggesting that it was not US ownership but the federal government's protectionist tariff that accounted for the economy's low productivity (Eastman and Stykolt 1967). Following extensive interviewing of American branch plant managers, A. E. Safarian concluded that their business decisions were determined by the economic and political framework within which they operated, not by their home-office's national interests (Safarian 1966).

This anti-alarmist consensus was challenged in the late 1960s by public opinion led by a new wave of nationalist resentment over foreign control that was stimulated by an influx of American draft dodgers decrying the destruction wreaked by the US war in Vietnam and documented by a rash of academic and popular studies, most poignantly expressed in 1971 by the book *Silent Surrender* (Levitt 2002). Voters' concerns ultimately caused the federal government to commission two economic studies to evaluate the economic impact of TNCs.

The 1968 Watkins Report discovered FDI's "miniature replica effect" when US branch plants, which replicate the structure of their US sector, necessarily operated far below the scale levels necessary for efficient production (Task Force on the Structure of Canadian Industry 1973).

The massive 1972 Gray Report documented in exhaustive detail both FDI's macro-economic impacts (raising the Canadian dollar's exchange rate along with the export-reducing and import-increasing impacts of foreign control in major manufacturing sectors) and TNCs' micro-economic effects (lowering firms' innovation capacity and managerial autonomy) (Government of Canada 1972).

Led by a prime minister, Pierre Trudeau, who was himself strongly anti-nationalist, the federal government moved reluctantly to respond to these concerns (Clarkson and McCall 1994). In 1971 the **Canada Development Corporation (CDC)** was established to buy back control of US-owned corporations. In 1974 the publicly owned Petro-Canada was founded to create a Canadian presence in the petroleum exploration, development, and distribution sector (Bellan 2006). In the same year, the Foreign Investment Review Agency (FIRA) was created to review whether proposed takeovers of Canadian companies by foreign TNCs would be of "net benefit" to the Canadian economy (Rotstein 2006). FIRA favoured proposals that would create domestic jobs or increase local inputs, promote R&D, and expand exports. The agency rejected approximately 10 per cent of the applications it received (Bellan 2006)—in effect instituting an informal system of performance requirements for incoming FDI. By the early 1980s, foreign control had been reduced in a number of sectors, including manufacturing, mining, and the oil and gas sector (Bellan).

One of the most popular but shortest-lived products of Canada's flirtation with nationalism was the National Energy Program (NEP), introduced by Trudeau's Liberal government in 1980 with the goal of decreasing US ownership and increasing the Canadian share of the energy industry (Rotstein 2006; Laxer 1989, 5). Through a system of taxation changes and production incentives, the NEP increased domestic ownership in the petroleum industry from 22 to 33 per cent within just two years (Rotstein 2006). However, overwhelming pressures from the US government on behalf of its furious petroleum corporations and resistance by an equally angry Alberta, the province where most oil and gas resources were located and which was determined to maintain its US market free of federal control, ultimately bore fruit with the election of Brian Mulroney in 1984 (Laxer, 5).

Responsive to both levels of pressure, Mulroney's Progressive Conservative party campaigned against the NEP in the 1984 federal election and dismantled it after winning a huge parliamentary majority. Prime Minister Mulroney also replaced FIRA in 1985 with Investment Canada, an agency mandated to promote rather than screen TNCs' investments (Bellan 2006). During the terms of Prime Minister Mulroney and his Liberal successors, Jean Chrétien and Paul Martin, no foreign proposal to take over a Canadian corporation was blocked (ibid.).

The reversal of the Canadian government's approach to FDI was part and parcel of its shift to a neoliberal policy paradigm—and was itself a response to Canada's changing engagement with international investment.

Canada's Neoliberal Reversal and a New Governance Regime

Noticed by neither scholars nor the media, Canadian companies' direct investments abroad actually started to surpass the inflow of FDI into Canada. In 1990, Canada's outflows of direct investment abroad amounted to $5 billion (compared to FDI inflows of $8 billion). By 2013, this number had shot up to $43 billion (compared to FDI inflows of $6 billion) (United Nations Conference on Trade and Development 2014a, WIR Web Tables 8 and 1). FDI inflows to Canada for the same years were $7.582 billion and $62.325 billion, respectively (United Nations Conference on Trade and Development 2014a, WIR Web Table 1). As Canadian companies extended their reach internationally, the country's stock of FDI abroad rose to 20 per cent of Canadian GDP by 1995 (Velde 2006, 5). Since 1997, Canada has consistently had a greater stock of direct investment abroad than of FDI, measured as a percentage of GDP (United Nations Conference on Trade and Development 2014a, WIR Web Tables 7 & 8). Since 1990, the average annual stock of Canadian direct investment abroad has been 30 per cent of GDP, compared to its FDI stock averaging 28 per cent of GDP over the same period (United Nations Conference on Trade and Development 2014a, WIR Web Tables 7 & 8). However, when analyzing Canada's foreign direct investment abroad, it is important to note that statistical data as presented in Table 8.3 is somewhat skewed by the high number of tax havens to which Canada's "FDI" flows.

As its economy became a significant capital exporter, the federal government's approach to FDI changed, first hesitatingly responding to increased US-government pressure on behalf of American TNCs, then, in its economic treaty negotiations, aggressively favouring Canadian TNCs' interests

Table 8.3   Top Ten Targets of Canadian Foreign Direct Investment

Canada's Top Ten OFDI Partners, 1993 and 2013 (billions of dollars)	
Canada FDI Abroad, Stock, 1993	**Canada FDI Abroad, Stock, 2013**
1. United States: 68	1. United States: 318
2. United Kingdom: 13	2. United Kingdom: 86
3. Barbados: 5	3. Barbados: 63
4. Japan: 3	4. Cayman Islands: 31
5. Ireland: 3	5. Luxembourg: 30
6. Australia: 2	6. Australia: 23
7. Bahamas: 2	7. Netherlands: 18
8. Bermuda: 2	8. Chile: 17
9. Singapore: 2	9. Ireland: 16
10. Brazil: 2	10. Mexico: 12

Source: Statistics Canada 2014, Table 376-0052—International investment position, Canadian direct investment abroad and foreign direct investment in Canada, by North American Industry Classification System (NAICS) and region, annual (dollars), CANSIM (database). (Accessed: 2015-06-09). Reproduced and distributed on an "as is" basis with the permission of Statistics Canada.

abroad at the cost of protecting domestic firms' interests at home.

Stage I: Negotiating Continentally: CUSFTA and NAFTA

Debated during the presidency of Jimmy Carter (1976–80) and crystallized under that of Ronald Reagan (1980–88), the United States' global strategy was devoted to expanding the access of foreign markets for such internationally competitive US sectors as pharmaceuticals, information processing, and biotechnology. Given the European and Japanese resistance to Washington's agenda of revolutionizing the rules of the global economic order, the Canada–US economic negotiations of the mid-1980s became the means for Washington to set precedents for the new economic regime it was advocating.

Despite the Canadian economy's already extraordinary openness to foreign direct investment, the federal government had resisted depriving itself of the capacity to promote domestic enterprise through industrial-strategy measures designed to build national champions. But in negotiating the Canada–United States Free Trade Agreement (CUSFTA 1988), Ottawa made a game-changing concession: it would extend "national treatment," which guaranteed equal treatment to imported goods

once they had entered the Canadian market, to include foreign investment. By making this apparently innocuous change, Ottawa gave up its freedom to provide incentives for domestically owned national champions such as the communications-equipment giant Nortel and the information-technology firm Research in Motion, which made the Blackberry cell phone. Further clauses in CUSFTA's text specifically outlawed the federal government from requiring the kind of performance requirements that FIRA had once imposed as a condition for a foreign company wanting to take over a Canadian firm (Muchlinski 2009, 46). Without admitting it, the Canadian government had quietly abandoned its role in fostering domestic industrial development.

While endorsed by Canada's economics profession and its TNC-friendly business elites, CUSFTA was fiercely resisted by Canadian civil-society organizations because of the constraints that the agreement would impose on federal, provincial, and municipal governments' ability to promote the public's interests in health, education, or labour rights through regulating corporate behaviour. So-called free trade[1] became the central issue of the heated 1988 Canadian election in which 57 per cent of voters supported the parties opposing the deal. Given the distortions of the Canadian electoral system, the Progressive Conservative party's 43 per cent of the votes gave it 57 per cent of the seats and thereby the majority it needed to ratify the economic treaty, which came into effect on 1 January 1989 (Campbell 1999, 3).

CUSFTA marked only a first step in the United States' drive to refashion the global economic rulebook. With its goal of rewriting the General Agreement on Tariffs and Trade (GATT 1947), Washington managed to persuade GATT's members in 1986 to launch new negotiations, the game-changing "Uruguay Round." But the prospect of including such deeply invasive new disciplines on signatory governments as disallowing performance requirements on new FDI caused Japan and the European Community (EC) to resist progress in these palavers.

In a successful tactical manoeuvre to force its GATT counterparts to make concessions in the Uruguay Round, Washington presented them with the threat that it would create a protectionist, three-country bloc in North America. To do this, it engaged Mexico in a new bilateral negotiation aimed at extending the precedents achieved with Canada in CUSFTA. Not wanting to lose the advantages it felt it had gained bilaterally, Ottawa requested a seat at the new bargaining table and, on 1 January 1994, the North American Free Trade Agreement (NAFTA) came into force complete with the United States' coveted provisions on intellectual property rights, services, and biotechnology. The prospect of being shut out of a new trinational fortress North America roughly the size of the European Community successfully induced Japan and the EC to make the concessions necessary to bring the World Trade Organization into being one year later (WTO 1995).

Meanwhile, NAFTA had enshrined greater powers for TNCs than the United States' other interlocutors had been willing to accept for the WTO's own investment clauses. Beyond restricting, the capacity of signatory governments to protect and promote their own corporations, the major precedent of NAFTA's Chapter 11 was to make states in the global North—in this case the USA and Canada—subject to the same private international dispute-settlement arbitration under rules established by the World Bank that had previously been imposed by FDI-exporting states in the North on weaker host states in the South.

With this NAFTA step, Canada joined a piece-by-piece trend of negotiating hundreds of international investment agreements that constructed a radically new but little-noticed regime of global governance, giving corporations unprecedented legal powers to discipline the states where they invested.

Stage II: Negotiating International Investment Agreements

In the nineteenth century, heavy-handed action by imperial governments defending their citizens' corporate interests in weak developing countries had the effect of escalating investment disputes into untoward diplomatic pressuring, and often, in the case of European or US governments, the use of military force (Vandevelde 2009, 7). By the 1860s such attacks on their cherished national autonomy had led Latin American countries to adopt the legal doctrine identified with Argentina's leading jurist, Carlos Calvo: foreign corporations should settle any differences they had with a host government in its domestic courts (Hershey 1907, 27).

Before the Second World War, the Canadian government had played no significant role in foreign investment law, though most international economic treaties were in any case signed simply to regulate trade relations. In these agreements, protection for resident foreigners who were investors dealt with their property, but protection for foreign corporations was found elsewhere, in customary international law that committed host countries to treat foreign investments according to an international minimum standard. Protection of their investments was generally weak, because investors did not have any effective legal mechanisms to use against host governments (Vandevelde, 4–5).

Following the Second World War, the Allies agreed to pursue the liberalization of trade, believing that protectionist policies had caused the economic depression of 1929–33 and the resulting political extremism that had triggered the war. The decolonization that took place after the war soon brought European countries and many of their former overseas possessions into conflict. Led by the leaders of their national liberation movements, these now-independent countries tended to view FDI as a form of neo-colonialism because it perpetuated the North's control over their leading economic sectors, so they often tried to constrain foreign capital lest they lose their newly gained independence. Against this backdrop, the governments of developed economies with major investments abroad negotiated investment treaties bilaterally with their counterparts in the developing world to forestall nationalization or other forms of expropriation without their being compensated. In 1959 Germany was the first to conclude such a bilateral investment treaty (BIT), with Pakistan, and, over the next three decades, 386 more were signed (Vandevelde, 11–16).

To impose some order on the growing legal chaos of hundreds of BITs with different provisions for dispute settlements being signed, the World Bank sponsored negotiations to create an International Convention for the Settlement of Investment Disputes (ICSID). Launched in 1966, ICSID provided private investors with a legal model they could use to trigger arbitration processes for resolving investment disputes with host governments. It was hoped that, along with other arbitration procedures such as UNCITRAL (The United Nations Commission on International Trade Law),

TNCs worried about investing in economies with unstable political conditions would be reassured that they could defend their interests in an international court of law rather than having to cope with corrupt local judiciaries (Subedi 2008, 30). In the event of a claimed breach of an investment treaty, investors had the right in these agreements to sue for damages before private tribunals set up under the auspices of such arbitration institutions as ICSIDs (Schneiderman 2010, 911).

Scholars Against TNCs: A New Debate

Unusually, the debate that this new regime of private international dispute settlement provoked was not so much between opposing scholarly schools as between academics in law faculties on the one side and neoliberal business, government, and media elites on the other. For the latter, this system was a historic breakthrough to be defended at all costs, promising stable investment conditions for TNCs in countries with which their home government had an investment agreement.

However, for most legal academics, the ICSID arbitration system represented a massive setback to historically evolved standards of due legal process. There were no conflict of interest rules to prevent arbitrators from having financial interests in the corporations whose cases they were judging. Lacking any professional tenure in their judicial capacity, these pro-tem judges actually had an incentive to establish a reputation for delivering decisions that favoured the corporate plaintiff by imposing large penalties on the defending host state. If they became known as being generous toward TNCs' claims, they stood a better chance of being chosen to arbitrate other disputes. Indeed, the data suggest that these arbitrators are more concerned with whether investment interests had suffered from a host state's measure than with the public's interests that the measure was designed to promote (Schneiderman, 911).

The secrecy under which investor-states dispute arbitration proceeds, the inadequate appeal mechanism, the exclusion of affected civil-society organizations from witnessing the proceedings—let alone expressing their views—during the hearings, and the barriers to affected groups or even subnational governments' submitting *amicus curiae* briefs were just some of the ICSID system's other features that outraged legal scholars. For their part, social scientists were perturbed about the impact of the huge damages awarded by arbitrators against states that are often weak and/or poor developing countries (Gallagher and Shrestha 2011, 2).

Canada as Site and Source of FDI and Investment-state Dispute Settlement

Canada's model for negotiating what Ottawa calls **foreign investment protection agreements (FIPAs)** has gone through three phases. Its first three FIPAs were signed between implementing CUSFTA in 1989 and NAFTA in 1994. The second set of 16 FIPAs that Canada signed between 1994 and 2004 were closely modelled after NAFTA.

Throughout, the contents of Canadian texts were directly influenced by the United States' model investment treaty and thus by congressional politics. For instance, when the US Congress became outraged that NAFTA's Chapter 11 had given a foreign company—specifically, a Canadian funeral home enterprise—legal rights that trumped US domestic courts, it instructed the United States Trade Representative that any new US investment treaties should not give foreign corporations greater legal rights in the United States than those enjoyed there by US firms. Consequently, the third generation of FIPAs was based on a somewhat softer model that followed Washington's example (Brown 2013, 57).

In comparison, after successfully negotiating only one FIPA and one FTA between 2000 and 2006, by 2012 the Stephen Harper government (2006–) had signed over 20 FIPAs and FTAs (Foreign Affairs, Trade and Development 2012). Given that Canada, as the site for thousands of TNCs' investments, is the sixth most cited defendant in investor-state disputes, the Harper government has modified its unquestioning stance vis-à-vis investment liberalization (United Nations Conference on Trade and Development 2014, 29). On the grounds of security concerns, it blocked two proposed foreign takeovers of Canadian corporations: that of the space division of MacDonald, Dettwiler & Associates by the US firm Alliant Techsystems in 2008, and the proposed 2013 sale of Manitoba Telecom's Allstream division to a foreign private equity firm (Bellan 2006). Although Ottawa ultimately approved the Australian firm BHP Billiton's takeover of Saskatchewan's Potash Corporation in 2010, the stringent conditions it imposed caused BHP Billiton to back out.

Adding to these controversial cases was the Harper government's approval of two takeovers of Canadian resource companies, Alberta-based tar sands producer Nexen and natural gas producer Progress Energy Resources, by Chinese and Malaysian state-owned enterprises (SOEs), respectively. Subsequently, Harper announced that, because SOEs do not operate under normal market conditions, Canadian regulations would be revised to prevent, or at least limit, future takeovers by SOEs (Whittington 2012). Expressing his neoliberal nationalism, he stated that "Canadians have not spent years reducing the ownership of sectors of the economy by our own governments, only to see them bought and controlled by foreign governments instead" (Whittington).

With existing investor-estate dispute arbitration under sporadic attack and new agreements being negotiated, Canada's TNC dossier never closes. The Canada–China FIPA signed in 2012 (but still not ratified by 2014) has roused substantial protest not just amongst jurists and the leading nationalist group, the Council for Canadians, but also in the business community. Because Canada is more a site for capital from China (whose investment in Canada already stood at CAD$10.9 billion by 2014) than a source of direct investment in China (valued at CAD$4.5 billion at the end of 2011), it assumes more risk and stands to benefit less (CBC News 2012); (Foreign Affairs, Trade and Development Canada 2014).

Notwithstanding its doubts regarding SOE takeovers, Ottawa has continued to negotiate more FIPAs, including the disputed investment measures in the mammoth Comprehensive Economic and Trade Agreement (CETA) with the European Union. Canada also sought permission from Washington to join the negotiations of a Trans-Pacific Partnership (TPP) that would comprise almost 800 million people and have a combined GDP of US$28 trillion, nearly 40 per cent of the world's economy. Whether the TPP extends or constrains ISDS (investor-state dispute settlement) throughout the Pacific will be determined long after this chapter sees the light of day.

This additional uncertainty should reaffirm our conclusion that the addition of an extraordinary private arbitration system to the existing institutions of global governance has signalled both a significant expansion of transnational corporations' legal rights and extended to the international level a continuing, unresolved debate over the need for and perils of foreign direct investment.

Conclusion: A Destabilizing Governance Regime

The unintended consequence of this global regime's ambition to establish a stable, adjudicatory environment for TNCs has been to generate international legal turmoil, particularly in Latin America. Of the 58 new cases in 2012, 37 were filed by investors from developed countries, of which almost 27 were brought against developing countries (United Nations Conference on Trade and Development 2013, 3). Particularly affected have been Latin American states which, thanks to TNC investments in their plentiful resources of oil, gas, and metals, have been the most common defendants in investor-state disputes (ibid., 29). By 2012, over half (58 per cent) of the 43 ISDS cases of resource rights had Latin American defendants (He and Sappideen 2013, 229). By 2012, Argentina, the most frequent respondent in investor-state disputes, had lost awards amounting to a total of US$400 million (*The Economist* 2012).

Losing defendants in investor-state arbitrations have not just voiced, but have acted upon, their discontent with ISDS. Nicaragua has threatened to withdraw from ICSID. Bolivian president Evo Morales has complained bitterly (if inaccurately) that "transnationals always win" and, in 2007, Bolivia actually withdrew from the Convention, the first country, along with Ecuador, to go so far in its dissent. Quito terminated nine of Ecuador's BITs in 2008 (He and Sappideen, 229). Since then Quito has proposed that South American states establish their own alternative dispute settlement process which would require TNCs to exhaust the legal remedies available in a state's domestic courts before seeking international arbitration (Fiezzoni 2011, 134).

Empowered by Canada's FIPAs, some Canadian TNCs have been the cause of further instability in Latin America. In a case that has dragged on for a decade with the Costa Rica government over its mining permit, the Canadian-based company Infinito Gold's behaviour caused such public outrage that it was a significant factor in the 2014 election that brought the opposition presidential candidate, Luis Guillermo Solís, to power. In an indirect reaction to granting powerful legal rights to foreign TNCs, President Solís subsequently announced a moratorium on Costa Rica joining the Pacific Alliance, a regional Latin American grouping strongly endorsing the foreign investment protections that Canada had helped entrench.

The instability of the investor-states regime is not just a Third-World phenomenon. In the aftermath of becoming the defendant in an investor-state case in which the Swedish energy company Vattenfall claimed damages of $4.5 billion due to Chancellor Angela Merkel shutting down the country's nuclear-generated electricity stations—after Japan's Fukushima nuclear meltdown in 2011—the German government changed its position. (Plecash 2014). In July 2014, it indicated its unwillingness to support the inclusion of an ISDS process in the EU's CETA with Canada (Gammelin 2014). Berlin did not make it known explicitly, but it apparently feared that American TNCs could use their Canadian branches to initiate investor-state arbitrations that would threaten the very government measures that had helped Germany build its successful social-market economy.

It is, however, known that, while the **transnational corporation** and its accompanying foreign direct investment remain major dynamos of continuing globalization, the maze of investor-states dispute mechanisms, which Canada has played a significant role in constructing, provokes continuing controversy and instability in the global political economy.

Note

1 Genuine free trade areas have no barriers to trans-border commerce, but CUSFTA retained the United States' and Canada's capacity to impose anti-dumping tariffs and countervailing duties on imports.

Key Terms

Canada Development Corporation (CDC)

foreign direct investment (FDI)

foreign investment protection agreement (FIPA)

Questions for Review

1. What arguments support TNCs and what arguments criticize them? How has recent empirical evidence contributed to the debate?

2. Summarize the history of foreign ownership in Canada. Describe how the public and different levels of government have assessed and responded to high levels of foreign control of Canadian industry over time.

3. Discuss the evolution of Canada's role as both an importer and exporter of foreign direct investment. Be sure to detail the norms of investment protection that have emerged in this context.

4. Discuss the role of NAFTA in bringing developed economies under investor-state dispute settlement regimes.

5. Why has Latin America had such a stormy relationship with FIPAs?

Further Resources

Fuchs, D. A. (2007). *Business power in global governance.* Boulder: Lynne Rienner Publishers, 1–12.

Herkenrath, M., and Bornschier, V. (2003). "Transnational Corporations in World Development—Still the same harmful effects in an increasingly globalized economy?" *1*(9) *Journal of World Systems Research* (Winter), 105–39.

Haslam, P. A. (2010). "The evolution of the foreign direct investment regime in the Americas." *Third World Quarterly 7*(31), 1181–203.

Laxer, G. (1989). *Open for business: The Roots of foreign ownership in Canada.* Toronto: Oxford University Press.

Muchlinski, P. (2009). "The framework of investment protection: The content of BITs." In Alvarez, José E. et al. (Eds). *The evolving international investment regime: Expectations, realities, options.* New York: Oxford University Press.

References

Bellan, R. C. (2006). Rev. G. McIntosh, "Foreign Investment," *The Canadian Encyclopedia.* <http://www.thecanadianencyclopedia.ca/en/article/foreign-investment/> (accessed 20 July 2014).

Bornschier, V. and Stamm, H. (1990). "Transnational Corporations" 2:38 *Current Sociology* 203–29.

Brown, C. (2013). *Commentaries on Selected Model Investment Treaties.* Oxford: Oxford University Press.

Campbell, B. (1999), "CUFTA/NAFTA and North American Labour Markets: A Comparative Inquiry" *Labour Market Effects Under CUFTA/NAFTA* (Geneva: International Labour Organization), 1–151.

CBC News. "5 Things to Know About the Canada-China Investment Treaty," (27 Oct. 2012). <http://www.cbc.ca/news/politics/5-things-to-know-about-the-canada-china-investment-treaty-1.1183343> (accessed 1 Aug. 2014.).

Chen, E. K. Y. (1996). "Transnational corporations and technology transfer to developing countries" in *Transnational Corporations and World Development* (London: International Thompson Business Press), 181–214.

Chudnovsky, D. (1996). "Transnational corporations and industrialization" *Transnational Corporations and World Development* (London: International Thompson Business Press), 269–93.

Clarkson, S. and McCall, C. (1994). *Trudeau and Our Times. Volume 2: The Heroic Delusion* (Toronto: McClelland and Stewart).

Dean, G. (2000). "The role of FDI in the development of Singapore—A development path?" *Gary Dean Essays* (April). <https://okusiassociates.com/garydean/works/fdising.html#fn9> (accessed 1 Aug., 2014).

Dunning, J. H. (1996). "The nature of transnational corporations and their activities" in *Transnational Corporations and World Development* (London: International Thompson Business Press), 27–43.

Eastman, H. C., and Stykolt, S. (1967). *The Tariff and Competition in Canada.* Toronto: Macmillan of Canada.

The Economist (18 Feb. 2012). "Come and Get Me: Argentina is Putting International Arbitration to the Test."

Fiezzoni, S. (2011). "The challenge of UNASUR member countries to replace ICSID arbitration," *Beijing Law Review*, 2, 134.

Foreign Affairs, Trade and Development Canada (2012). "Foreign Investment Protection Agreements (FIPAS)." Last updated 18 Dec. <http://www.international.gc.ca/trade-agreements-accords-commerciaux/agr-acc/fipa-apie/index.aspx?lang=eng> (accessed 1 Aug. 2014.).

Foreign Affairs, Trade and Development Canada. "Minister Fast Marks Conclusion of Latest Trans-Pacific Partnership Negotiations" Last updated Feb. 25, 2014. <http://www.international.gc.ca/trade-agreements-accords-commerciaux/agr-acc/fipa-apie/index.aspx?lang=eng> (accessed 1 Aug. 2014.).

Foreign Affairs, Trade and Development Canada. (2014). "Canada-China Foreign Investment Promotion and Protection Agreement (FIPA) Negotiations." Last updated 5 Mar. <http://www.international.gc.ca/trade-agreements-accords-commerciaux/agr-acc/fipa-apie/china-chine.aspx?lang=eng> (accessed 1 Aug. 2014.).

Frischtak, C. R., and. Newfarmer, R. S. "Market structure and industrial performance" in *Transnational Corporations and World Development* (London: International Thompson Business Press, 1996), 294–324.

Fuchs, D. A. (2007). *Business Power in Global Governance,* (Boulder: Lynne Rienner Publishers, 1–12.

Gallagher, K. P. and Shrestha, E. (2011). "Investment Treaty Arbitration and Developing Countries: A Re-Appraisal," Global Development and Environment Institute Working Paper, WP No. 11-01, GDEI (May). <http://ase.tufts.edu/gdae/Pubs/wp/11-01TreatyArbitrationReappraisal.pdf> (accessed 24 Aug. 2014.).

Gammelin, C. (2014). "Streit über Investorenschutz: Berlin lehnt Freihandelsabkommen mit Kanada vorerst ab" (Conflict over Investor Protection: For the Moment, Germany Rejects Free Trade Agreement with Canada) *Süddeutsche Zeitung* (26 July).

Government of Canada (1972). *Foreign Direct Investment in Canada.* (The Gray Report) Ottawa: Government of Canada.

He, L. L. and Sappideen, R. (2013). "Investor-State Arbitration under Bilateral Trade and Investment Agreements: Finding Rhythm in Inconsistent Drumbeats." 1:47 *Journal of World Trade*, 215–41.

Herkenrath, M. and Bornschier, V. "Transnational Corporations in World Development - Still the Same Harmful Effects in an Increasingly Globalized Economy?" *Journal of World Systems Research* 1(9) (Winter, 2003), 105–39.

Hershey, A. (1907). "The Calvo and Drago doctrines," *The American Journal of International Law I*(1): 27.

Keane, J. (2014). "Global value chain analysis: What's new, what's different, what's missing?" *International Economic Development Group* (2014), 2. <http://www.odi.org/publications/8561-global-value-chain-analysis-whats-new-whats-different-whats-missing> (accessed 27 Aug.).

Lall, S. (1996). "Transnational corporations and economic development" in *Transnational Corporations and World Development*. London: International Thompson Business Press, 44–72.

Laxer, G. (1989). *Open for business: The roots of foreign ownership in Canada*. Toronto: Oxford University Press.

Levitt, K. (2002). *Silent surrender: The multinational corporation in Canada*. Montreal & Kingston: McGill-Queen's University Press, new ed.

Moran, T. H. (1996). "Governments and transnational corporations" in *Transnational Corporations and World Development*. London: International Thompson Business Press, 418–47.

Mortimore, M. (2003). "Globalization and transnational corporations," presented at UNCTAD Intensive Training Course on International Investment Agreements, 4. <http://www.cepal.org/ddpe/agenda/4/15304/globa-trans-corp.pdf> (accessed 4 Aug. 2014.)

Muchlinski, P. (2009). "The framework of investment protection: The content of BITs" in *The Evolving International Investment Regime: Expectations, Realities, Options*. Eds José E. Alvarez, et al., (New York: Oxford University Press).

Nayyar, D. (2006). "Globalisation, History and Development: A tale of two centuries." *Cambridge Journal of Economics 30*, 137–59.

Outreville, J. F. (2007). *The universe of the largest transnational corporations* (New York: United Nations), 1–52.

Plecash, C. (2014). "EU trade deal ratification process yet to be settled." *Embassy* (27 Aug.).

Radice, H. (2014). "Transnational corporations and global capitalism: reflections on the last 40 years." *Critical Perspectives on International Business 1*(10), 21–34.

Rotstein, A. (2006). "Economic nationalism," *The Canadian encyclopedia* <http://www.thecanadianencyclopedia.ca/en/article/economic-nationalism/> (accessed 20 July 2014.).

Royal Commission on Canada's Economic Prospects (1957). Final Report. Ottawa: Government of Canada.

Safarian, A.E. (1966). *Foreign ownership of Canadian industry*. Toronto: McGraw-Hill.

Sauvant, K. P. (2008). "The rise of TNCs from emerging markets: the issues." In *The rise of transnational corporations from emerging markets: Threat or opportunity?* K. P. Sauvant (Ed.). Cheltenham: Edward Elgar, 3–14.

Schneiderman, D. (2010). "Investing in democracy? Political process and international investment law." 4(60) *University of Toronto Law Journal.*

Statistics Canada. (2014). "Foreign direct investment statistics (Web Tables)," (Apr.). <http://www.international.gc.ca/economist-economiste/statistics-statistiques/investments-investissements.aspx> (accessed 10 July 2014.).

Subedi,. S. P. (2008). *International investment law: Reconciling policy and principle*. Oxford: Hart Publishing.

Task Force on the Structure of Canadian Industry. (1973). *Foreign ownership and the structure of Canadian Industry: Report of the task force on the structure of Canadian industry* (The Watkins Report). Ottawa, Queen's Printer.

Twomey, M. J. "The Canadian experience with the investment development path," [incomplete]

United Nations Conference on Trade and Development. (2009). "World Investment Report (WIR) New York: United Nations, 3–274. <http://unctad.org/en/docs/wir2009_en.pdf> (accessed 1 Aug. 2014.).

United Nations Conference on Trade and Development. (2013). "Recent developments in investor-state dispute settlement (ISDS)" <http://unctad.org/en/PublicationsLibrary/webdiaepcb2014d3_en.pdf> (accessed 1 Aug. 2014.).

United Nations Conference on Trade and Development. (2014). "World investment report (WIR) 2014: Annex (Web) Tables," (25 Jun.). <http://unctad.org/en/pages/DIAE/World%20Investment%20Report/Annex-Tables.aspx> (accessed 10 Jul. 2014.).

United Nations Conference on Trade and Development. (2014). "Transnational corporations (TNC)," <http://unctad.org/en/Pages/DIAE/Transnational-corporations-(TNC).aspx> (accessed 1 Aug. 2014.).

Vandevelde, K. J. (2011). "A brief history of international investment agreements." In *The evolving international investment regime: Expectations, realities, options*, J. Alvarez, K. P. Sauvant, K. G. Ahmed, G. P. Vizcaino (Eds).

Velde, D. W. te. (2006). "Foreign direct investment and development: An historical perspective," Background paper for "World Economic and Social Survey for 2006," *UNCTAD Overseas Development Institute*. (30 Jan.).

Whittington, L. (2012). "Prime Minister Stephen Harper vows Chinese takeover of oil firm Nexen 'the end of a trend,'" *The Toronto Star* (7 Dec.) <http://www.international.gc.ca/economist-economiste/statistics-statistiques/investments-investissements.aspx> (accessed 4 Aug. 2014.).

9 The World Bank and International Development

Redefining Poverty as Social Risk

Jacqueline Best

Poverty poses a dilemma for international political economy. Of course, poverty has always been a part of free market economies. Yet it remains a troubling reality that does not fit comfortably within mainstream economic theory, which, following Adam Smith, assumes that the rising tide of economic growth will lift all boats.[1] Economists, like mainstream (or "American school") IPE scholars, have always tended to be liberal in their theoretical leanings.[2] Where realists have tended to see poverty as an unfortunate reality and Marxist critics have viewed it as evidence of the need for revolutionary transformation, liberal economists are left with the difficult tasks of explaining, justifying, and seeking to remedy the problem of poverty. In *Savage Economics*, David Blaney and Naeem Inayatullah describe this dark side of capitalism as "the wound of wealth"—a wound that continues to haunt economic theory and practice.[3]

Although poverty has always been with us, it only became an explicit object of global economic governance in the mid-twentieth century. As Rob Aitken suggests in chapter 3, a global problem cannot be managed until it can be conceptualized, counted, and labelled. In the case of global poverty,

once statistics on annual income per capita began to be collected in the early 1940s, suddenly two thirds of the world's population was deemed poor.[4] Since then, definitions of poverty have changed, and poverty rates have varied, yet the problem of poverty remains a global preoccupation. Recent United Nations calculations indicate that 22 per cent of the global population is poor, defined as living on less than $1.25 a day.[5] Efforts to reduce poverty have become a veritable industry—particularly on the global level, where measuring, assessing, and addressing poverty have become a central focus of international development efforts. Most industrialized countries, including Canada, have a long history of providing foreign aid to poor countries to help with economic development and poverty reduction. On the international stage, the World Bank, which is the subject of this chapter, has been the chief institution involved not only in allocating aid for development but also in shaping thinking about how to manage development and reduce global poverty.[6]

In tackling the problem of poverty, these institutions have all been constrained by liberal economists' fear, since Adam Smith's days, of an overly activist state—preoccupied with what Michel Foucault describes as the central dilemma of liberal governmental reason: "how not to govern too much."[7] We are all familiar with this dilemma today: just think of how politically difficult it is for governments to raise taxes, and how often politicians promise to reduce government's interference in the economy once they get into office. This fear of an activist state complicates efforts to combat poverty, since poverty reduction has to somehow be reconciled with a free market.

Because the wound of wealth never seems to heal despite continued attempts to treat it, development experts continue to invent new theories about the causes of poverty and new strategies for reducing it. This chapter looks at these debates, and at the changing definitions of poverty that have been used to guide international policy over the past decades, focusing in particular on some of the most recent developments. This chapter can therefore be broadly understood as a "discursive" post-positivist analysis of global economic development, as outlined in the introduction and chapter 3.

Debates about poverty have in fact been particularly heated over the past two decades. Major shocks, such as the Asian financial crisis and the AIDS pandemic in Africa, reversed progress in reducing poverty levels, making it clear that poverty was a more fluid phenomenon than had been imagined. A growing number of mainstream economic studies also began to question the traditional assumption that economic growth automatically leads to poverty reduction after finding cases in which poverty persisted or even grew despite robust economic growth.[8]

It is in the context of these debates that new definitions of poverty have begun to emerge, as well as new strategies for managing it.[9] This chapter focuses on one important recent development—the redefinition of poverty in terms of **social risk** and vulnerability. This new approach was first developed by the World Bank, and focuses on the vulnerability of individuals and communities to shocks and other risks that might force them into further poverty—by selling off their livestock, pulling children out of school, or in some other way reducing their future chances of making a living. Because they now see poverty as more fluid and contingent, development experts interested in the problem of social risk have sought to develop more flexible and proactive techniques for tackling poverty. For example, World Bank staff have adopted a new, more proactive strategy for **social protection** that seeks, in their words, to transform "safety-nets into springboards" in order to make poverty reduction efforts a more central force in economic development.[10]

This chapter tackles three questions related to this shift in the **governance** of global poverty. To understand the particularities of this shift, I ask how the World Bank has historically sought to contend with the wound of wealth. I then consider how the new concept of poverty as risk and vulnerability came to be institutionalized at the Bank. Finally, I ask what the implications of this shift are for how global poverty is managed, and consider whether this trend to redefine poverty is likely to persist.

How has the World Bank historically addressed the problem of poverty? At different times, Bank staff and management have opted for one of three different strategies, treating poverty as *derivative*, *marginal*, or *integral* to achieving growth and development. During the **structural adjustment** era poverty was treated as *derivative* to the real business of development—a problem that would be automatically resolved with economic growth. By the late 1980s there was some recognition of the need for limited safety nets for the *marginal* unfortunates who were hardest hit by the effects of adjustment. The more recent social risk framework, in contrast, treats poverty as *integral* to development.

By drawing on **new institutional economics**, economists have begun to see poor people's vulnerability as examples of **market failure**—not a peripheral issue but a signal that markets are not working as they should.[11] Solving these failures could therefore be seen as essential to the broader goal of achieving sustained economic growth: the problem of poverty has become integrated—domesticated—into the dominant economic rationality.

How did various organizational units at the World Bank come to adopt the social risk and vulnerability framework? To answer that question, I suggest, we need to consider the role of three inter-related processes: key events that made the problem of poverty more visible, effectively reopening the wound of wealth; expert debates on the nature of the problem; and bureaucratic politics about how to respond to it.

What are the implications of this shift in the conception and governance of poverty, and how influential has this approach become? Whereas poverty was conceived before as relatively static, vulnerability, risk, and resilience are concepts that redefine poverty as something dynamic. This reconceptualization of poverty as dynamic changes the kinds of development techniques deemed appropriate, requiring a more proactive and pre-emptive set of practices that seek to constitute more active, self-governing poor people. While this more active intervention does require a more engaged state apparatus than was evident in the structural adjustment era, its role remains constrained by the liberal preoccupation with limiting governmental power. Thus, this more proactive form of governance involves less direct forms of power, reconstituting patterns of inclusion and exclusion in increasingly obscure forms.

The social risk approach to poverty was first developed by the World Bank in the late 1990s and early 2000s, and was later adopted by the Development Assistance Committee of the Organisation for Economic Cooperation and Development (OECD) as well as some national donor agencies.[12] Interestingly, although it has become more globally influential in recent years, this social risk approach to poverty reduction has not taken hold in Canadian development circles, where the recent trend has been back to treating poverty reduction as both derivative of economic growth and secondary to Canadian economic interests.[13] Although the Canadian government's current approach to development is not representative of the international aid community, it does raise interesting questions about the long-term viability of the social risk approach to poverty.

The remainder of the chapter proceeds in five parts: I begin with a brief history of the management of poverty at the World Bank, focusing in particular on the structural adjustment era, and then trace the recent shift in development thinking and practice about poverty, focusing on the role of key events, expert debates, and bureaucratic dynamics. I then examine the emergence of the new strategy for governing poverty through the concepts of social risk and vulnerability. I go on to analyze how this new strategy works in practice, and conclude by considering the implications and sustainability of this way of governing poverty.

Earlier Conceptions of Poverty

Global poverty may have been an object of economic governance since the postwar era, but the way it has been defined and managed has changed significantly over time. In fact, we can find three different logics at work in the relationship between poverty and liberal economic development: approaches that treat the reduction of poverty as *derivative* of growth, those that treat it as a *marginal* (but costly) problem, and those that see it as a central issue that can be *integrated* into broader efforts to achieve growth. At the same time, all three of these strategies are consistent with the basic parameters of liberal economic governance: they seek to respond to the problem of poverty while avoiding excessive government.

The early postwar years were marked by optimism about the possibility of eradicating global poverty through modernization and growth. While there were different theories of how "backward" economies could be modernized, economists shared a common belief that growth would reduce poverty, as its benefits "trickled down" to the poorest.[14] This "trickle-down" approach saw no need to treat poverty directly, as its solution was assumed to be largely *derivative* of efforts to achieve growth.

When Robert McNamara, one of the World Bank's most influential presidents, first took office in 1968, he challenged this "article of faith," insisting that poverty needed to be directly targeted if it was to be reduced.[15] To make poverty a key focus of Bank efforts, McNamara had to find a way of linking it to the Bank's central mandate of lending money.[16] McNamara also had to find a way of making poverty reduction consistent with the Bank's technocratic culture—and with his own love of numbers. His solution was "redistribution with growth," an approach that treated poverty reduction and growth as compatible, while focusing on absolute rather than relative poverty (or inequality).[17]

McNamara's approach sought to treat poverty as a separate, rather than a derivative, problem. Redistribution with growth was a strategy for *integrating* poverty reduction into mainstream economic goals, while simultaneously avoiding more radical proposals that placed more emphasis on inequality and relied more heavily on government intervention. Yet the policy remained contested within the Bank, as some staff argued for more

interventionist state actions to meet the population's "basic needs," while another (larger) group continued to push in the opposite direction, arguing that policies aimed at alleviating poverty would cause growth rates to suffer.[18]

These more orthodox economists within the World Bank ultimately had their way in the 1980s. Under the leadership of A.W. Clausen as president and Anne Krueger as chief economist, many of the critical researchers were replaced with neoclassical economists.[19] The Bank's focus shifted toward growth, which it sought to achieve through liberalization, privatization, and structural adjustment— a triumvirate of policy prescriptions that came to be known as the Washington Consensus.[20] Poverty largely dropped from the agenda. Where it did appear, the assumption was that growth would resolve it. The trickle-down thesis had made a comeback.

Although the specific policies of the structural adjustment era[21] were very different from those of the 1950s and 1960s, the conception of poverty was remarkably similar: poverty was once again seen as a derivative problem. Key figures within the Bank argued that adjustment was good for the poor, but that the effects were not visible.[22] Moreover, it was believed that the more severe aspects of structural adjustment would be temporary, making it unnecessary to address short-term costs directly.

By the late 1980s, however, under Barber Conable's leadership, Bank staff began to refocus on poverty reduction, recognizing that additional measures needed to be taken to protect the poor from some of the dislocations caused by adjustment.[23] In 1987 UNICEF published a critical report, *Adjustment with a Human Face*, detailing the social costs of structural adjustment.[24] The report sparked a broad debate on the World Bank's policies. It was in this context that the 1990–91 World Development Report, *Poverty*, was prepared, outlining the Bank's emerging strategy for tackling poverty. This report provides a useful snapshot of some of the Bank's staff members' thinking about poverty during the structural adjustment era. A caveat is necessary here, however; although its critics tend to represent the World Bank as a monolithic actor, those who study the organization (like those who have worked for it) know that it is in fact a frustratingly complex institution. The tidy picture presented by the annual World Development Reports (WDR) is therefore more than a little misleading. Yet these reports do serve a useful purpose in outlining major thinking at the Bank at a given moment—particularly the decade-defining reports, which are more central to the Bank's self-definition.

In spite of its nod to some of the costs of adjustment for the poor, the 1990–91 WDR remains a product of the structural adjustment era. The report proposes a two-pronged strategy for reducing poverty: enabling the poor to use their principal "asset"—labour—more effectively and increasing the productivity of that asset through education, primary health care, family planning, and nutrition.[25] As the report goes on to point out, these poverty reduction strategies are consistent with the objectives of structural adjustment, as the goal is to use labour more efficiently. Much of the report reads like an apology for the pro-poor benefits of unrefined neoliberalism: it turns out that reducing taxation on agriculture, reducing such "biases" against labour as excessive regulations, social security taxes, and minimum wages, creating a "neutral" (liberal) trading regime and only lightly regulating the informal sector will all free up poor people's labour, and thus reduce poverty. The report includes a chapter on transfers and safety nets, but treats them as a peripheral part of the poverty-reduction strategy designed for those too ill, old, or remote to participate in growth.[26]

The 1990–91 WDR thus treats the resolution of poverty as both *derivative* of growth and as an additional, but *marginal*, cost. In this report the overwhelming goal of development remains the pursuit of growth through orthodox neoliberal policies. Yet its authors also recognized that some individuals at the margins would suffer from structural adjustment; hence some safety nets become necessary, even if they are unproductive and thus a net cost.[27]

Recent Debates on Poverty

In more recent years, the structural adjustment-friendly approach to poverty articulated in the 1990–91 WDR has been contested and replaced by an approach that has once again sought to integrate poverty into mainstream development. In understanding how this shift occurred, three key factors are worth examining: the role of certain events in highlighting the insufficiencies of existing approaches to poverty and thus reopening the wound of wealth; the debates among development experts about how to define and respond to this wound; and the effects of institutional politics in influencing the kinds of policy responses that emerged.

Catalyzing Events

By the mid-1990s scholars and practitioners alike had begun to raise a number of doubts about past development strategies. Part of the reason for this change of heart was a series of events seen as evidence of failure, forcing the development and finance communities to re-examine the problem of poverty. Increased poverty in sub-Saharan Africa in the 1980s—dubbed the "lost decade"—raised questions about the effectiveness of Bank structural adjustment policies.[28] Moreover, financial crises in Mexico in 1994 and then in Asia in 1997–98, as well as the failure of the IMF's response to the Asian crisis, ultimately led to some rethinking of development finance.[29]

The persistence of poverty in regions including sub-Saharan Africa, in some cases despite GDP growth, challenged Bank economists' assumptions about the straightforward link between growth and poverty reduction.[30] The effects of the Asian crisis, including the sudden immiseration of huge swaths of the population that had achieved a reasonable standard of living, revealed the fragility of income security. The devastating impact of AIDS in Africa, as well as the proliferation of civil conflicts, made it clear that poverty was in part a product of community-level or even nationwide shocks. These events forced World Bank staff to recognize the potential for unexpected events to disrupt development plans. If shocks played a significant role in people's lives, then Bank staff needed to pay more attention to the vulnerability of poor people.[31]

Expert Debates

These events did not automatically translate into new poverty-reduction strategies, but instead sparked a series of debates among development practitioners and economists. These were the kinds of debates that might be called "hot" debates, following Michel Callon,[32] as it was not only the question of how to reduce poverty that was up for grabs, but also far more fundamental questions about what counts as poverty, how to measure it, and the nature of the relationship between poverty and growth. Two debates in particular played a crucial role in redefining poverty at the Bank and in the wider development community: one on the relationship between poverty and growth, and another on the social policies needed in response.

By the late 1990s a number of economists at the Bank and elsewhere were challenging assumptions about the benefits of growth-oriented policies for the poor: they included Dani Rodrik, who called the growth versus poverty reduction controversy a "hollow debate," as well as François

Bourguignon, Ravi Kanbur, lead author of the 2000–01 WDR, and Joseph Stiglitz, then chief economist at the Bank.[33] They pointed to the inconsistent relationship between growth and poverty reduction, suggesting that, in Bourguignon's terms, the extent to which poverty could be reduced through growth was highly elastic, and dependent on domestic factors such as inequality.[34]

Yet they faced an uphill battle. Ranged against them was a group of economists committed to the belief that, as the title of one controversial publication put it, "Growth *is* Good for the Poor" (emphasis in the original).[35] Although Dollar and Kraay, the papers' authors, have since argued that they did not intend it to be seen as a manifesto for growth alone, they did set out to make a case for the virtues of neoliberal growth. In this view they were supported by other Bank economists, by a large number of IMF-based economists, and by leading figures in the US Treasury.[36] Over time a partial compromise was achieved around the idea of "pro-poor growth," which focused on the conditions in which growth produced important reductions in poverty.[37]

A second, less publicized, debate was also underway at roughly the same time among economists interested in social protection. Thinking in this area had begun to shift in the 1980s and early 1990s, following Amartya Sen's work on famines, which showed that they are often the result of failures of social entitlements to food, rather than in the supply of food.[38] Sen's work influenced the growing literature on hazards and disasters, which focused on individuals' vulnerability to their effects—a literature that also began to influence social policy thinking.[39] A later Sen article, co-authored with Jean Dreze, also pointed to the large role of the informal economy in many developing countries and argued that, even in the absence of shocks, formal welfare policies are often ineffective in such contexts.[40] These scholars redefined the goals of social protection as not only protecting individuals from poverty—and the shocks that often led to poverty—but also *preventing* their falling into poverty and *promoting* their capacity to respond to risks.[41]

Underlying both pro-poor growth and social protection policies are several concepts linked to new institutional economics—chiefly those of market failure and the centrality of institutions in resolving it. While this branch of economics dates back to the early and mid-twentieth century with the work of Ronald Coase,[42] it gained wider attention with the contributions of Douglass North and has become particularly influential in development circles over the past decade.[43] Although institutionalist economists remain within the neoclassical tradition that dominated thinking at the Bank and the Fund from the late 1980s until the mid-1990s, rather than assuming that market-based solutions are the most efficient, they emphasize the centrality of institutions in reducing transactions costs and making markets work better.

Both advocates of pro-poor growth and of the new approaches to social protection see poverty as a sign of market failure: the fact that poor people do not have access to the benefits of the market, such as credit and jobs, and that they cannot withstand shocks, are indications that the market is not working as it should. Even with increased growth, such distortions in the market may persist, making it unlikely that growth alone will reduce poverty. Viewing poverty in terms of market failure legitimizes poverty-reduction efforts as central to broader economic development: making markets work better for poor people also ensures that markets work. The problem of poverty—and thus the wound of wealth—is brought back into the fold as an *integral* rather than derivative or marginal issue, in which poverty-reduction efforts and "serious" economic activities are mutually consistent.

New institutional insights thus allow development experts to dig deeper into the causes of poverty without challenging the underlying assumption that the market is the ultimate solution.

Institutional Dynamics

The third major factor influencing the evolution of the social risk framework at the World Bank was the influence of internal institutional politics. The efforts of the Social Protection team to increase its influence within the Bank, national stakeholders'[44] ambivalence about social protection, tensions between different units, and conflicts over the 2000–01 WDR all influenced the policy's ultimate form. In the context of these various pressures, social risk became a means of moving the social protection agenda ahead without provoking much opposition from conservative elements within the Bank and without straying from a market-oriented approach to development.

The Social Protection and Labor unit was the key advocate of redefining poverty as social risk within the World Bank. Created in 1996, this unit is one of the newest at the Bank. It brought together various policy areas that had previously been treated separately: pensions, labour market policy, and safety nets. Robert Holzmann was hired as director of this new unit to lead the process of developing a strategy for the sector and became a powerful driving force behind the idea of defining poverty as social risk.[45] The concept of social risk allowed its advocates to redefine social transfers and safety nets as productive investments, thus increasing the importance of social protection within the institution and promoting it from its previously marginal status. As a later report on the social protection strategy notes:

> Social protection (SP) is moving up on the development agenda. Dismissed as ineffective, expensive or even detrimental to development

in developing countries, it is now increasingly understood that assisting individuals, households and communities in dealing with diverse risks is needed for accelerated poverty reduction and sustained economic and human development.[46]

The focus on social risk and vulnerability was also a way of countering certain national stakeholders' ambivalence about social protection. Many executive board members, including those from East Asia, saw pensions and safety nets as expensive luxuries. The focus on social risk and vulnerability, particularly in the aftermath of the Asian crisis, which revealed the potential costs of those risks, reframed these expenses as investments.[47] As Holzmann noted:

> Social protection strategies were usually a headache to have to bring to the Board: everybody has an opinion and it tends to be an uphill battle (for every two countries, there are five opinions). We used risk management as an organizing framework to appeal to those not always supportive of social protection— those who focus more on efficiency. On the other hand, those who supported redistribution were okay with this approach.[48]

The Social Protection team also chose not to emphasize the issue of inequality in its new strategy, as it thought it would get "more ownership going within the Bank" by avoiding this divisive issue.[49]

Social risk advocates hoped to address the problem of poverty without provoking too much opposition within the organization. Yet, despite such efforts, its advocates encountered resistance from within the World Bank's bureaucracy. Social protection was, after all, a new unit in the Bank; moreover, those economists with the most

intellectual capital in the organization were those working for the research department and the Poverty Reduction and Economic Management (PREM) Network, few of whom had any background in social protection.[50] It is therefore not surprising that many economists in the Bank's research department could not see the value added of this new framework. Holzmann notes that, when he first explained the idea of social risk to Martin Ravallion, now the director of research at the Bank, he responded "Robert, this is rubbish."[51] Other staff saw the effort to redefine poverty as vulnerability and social risk as an attempt to take over other units' territory—for example, those in PREM tasked with measuring poverty using other methodologies.[52] Although the social risk framework ultimately gained influence thanks to its inclusion in the social protection strategy and the 2000–01 WDR, it nonetheless faced opposition within the institution.

The increased influence of the social risk framework, within both the Bank and the broader development community, can also be traced to the fact that it became one of the key pillars of the 2000–01 WDR, *Attacking Poverty*. Tensions underpinning this WDR were widely reported at the time and have been well documented since then.[53] The Bank's chief economist, Joseph Stiglitz, was fired in the lead-up to the report for his criticisms of the IMF's handling of the Asian financial crisis, among other things. The lead author of the WDR, Ravi Kanbur, resigned because of the revisions that had been forced on the writing team. At the heart of these conflicts was the debate about the relationship between poverty and growth discussed above: some economists wanted the report to emphasize the potential costs of liberalization and the need for more activist policies to reduce poverty. Those on the other side of the debate, which included not just key economists but also, as Robert Wade points out, key figures in the US Treasury, wanted to focus on the virtues of growth and freer markets for poverty reduction, and to downplay safety nets and other government policies.[54]

The 2000–01 WDR was organized into three pillars: opportunity, empowerment, and security. While the first was the most growth-oriented, and the second received the most criticism by mainstream economists, the third—security—was primarily about social risk and vulnerability. Although earlier drafts of this third section were criticized for excessive emphasis on safety nets,[55] the focus on reducing social risk and vulnerability was less controversial, as it was essentially a more market-friendly way of addressing social protection.[56] As one former Bank staff member noted, "You couldn't have sold the security pillar with a big government approach that was based on major redistribution." The social risk approach, in contrast, "was skeptical of governments doing everything," making it "more intellectually attractive" to a wider range of economists who were either more market-oriented or dubious about the capacity of most developing country governments.[57]

Redefining Poverty as Social Risk

What form did this new conception of poverty as risk and vulnerability take? How different was it from earlier efforts to mend the wound of wealth? Although the fullest statement of the social risk and vulnerability approach is articulated in the Social Protection Strategy (SPS), it is useful to examine it alongside the 2000–01 WDR, because it allows us to compare it with the 1990–91 WDR discussed earlier.

In contrast to the unabashedly neoliberal tone of the 1990–91 WDR, the 2000–01 report is a much subtler and more sophisticated document. As I mentioned above, the three main elements of the report's strategy are opportunity, empowerment, and security. "Opportunity" bears the most resemblance to the preoccupations of the earlier report, as it is focused on the problem of "making markets work better for poor people."[58] Yet much of the analysis in the more recent report, as well as in the SPS, is structured around a discussion of the ways that markets can fail poor people if they are not managed effectively, highlighting the need to correct market failures.[59]

One way of resolving such market failures is by focusing on increasing poor people's "security," which the 2000–01 WDR authors define as reducing their vulnerability and increasing their ability to cope with risks and shocks. The concepts of security, risk, and vulnerability are closely related:

> In the dimensions of income and health, vulnerability is the risk that a household or individual will experience an episode of income or health poverty over time. But vulnerability also means the probability of being exposed to a number of other risks (violence, crime, national disasters, being pulled out of school).[60]

The report spends a significant amount of time elaborating the risks that poor people face. It maps out the different sources of risk—economic, political, environmental, health—as well as the various levels of society that they affect—household, regional, or national. In both the WDR and the SPS, Bank staff identify two kinds of risk: idiosyncratic risks that affect individuals or small groups, such as job loss or illness, and covariant risks that affect a larger group simultaneously, such as environmental and political crises.[61]

Of course, poor people do have their own coping mechanisms. In fact, the second pillar of the 2000–01 WDR, "empowerment," examines ways of engaging poor people more actively in managing their economic situation. The report and the SPS also discuss the different strategies for responding to risk, both informally through individual efforts to build up assets and through community networks, and formally through market and public provision of safety nets.[62] Whereas in industrialized societies most of the population is able to rely primarily on more formal mechanisms (life and health insurance, pension plans, welfare), poor people rely on informal mechanisms.

Although the earlier 1990–91 WDR made a few references to risks, shocks, and vulnerability in the report, these play a minor part in a strategy that is overwhelmingly oriented toward freeing up labour to help the poor attain a minimum standard of living.[63] The 2000–01 report, in contrast, raises doubts about that strategy: large crises tend to undermine informal efforts, since everyone is affected simultaneously. Moreover, markets are often locally based and therefore not always able to insure against widespread risks.[64]

The reconceptualization of poverty as social risk and vulnerability has had a concrete effect on World Bank practices: over time policy in each of the three areas covered by social protection—labour, pensions, and safety nets—has been reframed to take the new focus on risk and vulnerability into account. In the labour market sector, for example, thinking at the Bank has shifted away from the belief that macroeconomic stabilization and liberalization alone are sufficient to ensure labour-market access by the poor.[65] Bank staff now argue that the various informal and private mechanisms that poorer people use to respond to shocks, including taking children out of school to work, can lead them to under-invest in their human capital: "Thus, public intervention is needed."[66] Another new social protection policy initiative with clear affinities with the social risk approach is the conditional cash transfer (CCT) strategy. Although CCTs were not invented by the Bank, they have become a favourite policy and are

seen as one useful way of responding to social risk.[67] CCTs are funds provided to poor households on the basis of certain conditions—usually that they keep their children in school and send them for regular health check-ups. The cash transfers thus provide two ways of managing risk: in the short term they provide funds to help cope with shocks, while in the longer term they attempt to foster a population that is healthier and better educated, and thus better able to manage risks.

In each of these policy areas government is seen as playing a more important role than in the past because of market failures; yet the public sector is seen primarily as a means of "supplementing" existing private and individual risk management strategies rather than replacing them.[68] As is clear in a later report by Holzmann, the re-engagement with the public sector is premised on a desire to compensate for the limits of the market without displacing it as the central force:

> In an ideal world with perfectly symmetrical information and complete markets, all risk management arrangements can and should be market-based (except for the instruments protecting the incapacitated). However, in the real world, all risk management arrangements will play important roles that are likely to change over time.[69]

Bank staff thus defined the solutions to the market's failures in ways that ensured that the state did not take too large a role, respecting the liberal anxiety about an excess of government.

Implications: Changing How Global Poverty is Managed

By redefining poverty as social risk and vulnerability, Bank staff have sought to reintegrate the problem of poverty into the core of development efforts. Poverty, they suggest, is not simply a short-term side effect of structural adjustment, or a cost caused by the most marginal members of society, but a sign that markets are failing a significant segment of the population. Market failures mean that poor people do not have access to resources like credit, insurance, and employment that might allow them to cope with risk. Reintegrating them into the market economy, moreover, by reducing their vulnerability, will help make markets work better and thus contribute to economic growth and stability.

While this integrationist approach to poverty bears some similarities to McNamara's war on poverty in the 1970s, there are also some important novelties in this most recent attempt to mend the wound of wealth: the concepts of risk and vulnerability not only reabsorb poverty into the economic mainstream, they also reconceptualize it. This new strategy for governing poverty involves a more dynamic ontology and a more proactive and pre-emptive set of governance techniques. Reflecting the liberal concern with excessive government, moreover, the social risk approach operates through a loose configuration of public and private actors and relies on increasingly obscure and indirect forms of power to achieve its ends. Yet, while the social risk approach has taken root at the World Bank and elsewhere, it has not been universally adopted. In this respect, I will suggest, the Canadian government's decision to move in a very different direction raises interesting questions about the sustainability of the World Bank's strategy for responding to the wound of wealth.

A More Dynamic Ontology

Redefining poverty as social risk means reconceptualizing it at an ontological level (see the introduction to this volume for a definition of ontology). A passage from the 2000–01 WDR is especially illustrative of this new, more dynamic conception of poverty:

> As traditionally defined and measured, poverty is a static concept—a snapshot in time. But insecurity and vulnerability are dynamic—they describe the response to changes over time.[70]

Conceptualizing the poor as mobile transforms poverty from a state of being into a process. This is a new ontology of poverty: it radically transforms the object of development analysis and policy (to borrow a metaphor from physics, this is like changing our image of the electron from a particle into a wave). This dynamic conception of poverty also involves a different idea of time. An individual or a community's vulnerability is something that develops over a long period of time; efforts to reduce it must also take a long view. Coping with risk is a short-term challenge; mitigating and even preventing risks requires longer-term planning. In some ways this extension of the time-horizon merely deepens an already existing tendency in development thinking toward focusing on human capital in the form of education and health. Yet the emphasis on risk and vulnerability adds a further dimension to the reconceptualization of time, in its emphasis on the profound unpredictability of the future, as it becomes an uncertain territory filled with shocks and risks.

Proactive and Pre-emptive Techniques

Reconceptualizing poverty as a process in time also enables (indeed requires) a new set of proactive management techniques. It becomes necessary not only to identify those most vulnerable, but also to discover the greatest risks that they face, and develop strategies to deal with shocks long before they have occurred. Thus, those seeking to redefine the Bank's social protection strategy in the late 1990s discovered:

> that a new conceptual framework was needed which moves SP [social protection] from a definition by instruments (such as social insurance) to a definition by objectives (that is assisting in risk management); from a traditional focus on ex-post poverty to ex-ante vulnerability reduction; from seeing SP in our client countries largely as safety nets to conceptualizing them as spring boards.[71]

Social protection, which was once viewed as largely about transfers of funds, is now seen as an active investment in the development process. Risk and vulnerability assessments are designed to deliver a comprehensive picture of the complex relationships among various kinds of potential shocks, government, market, and community actors, and their various risk management strategies. In theory at least this four-dimensional map (time is also a necessary factor) can be used to develop more nuanced, targeted interventions to alter the movement of people into and out of poverty.

The examples of social protection policies discussed above all seek to engage more proactively with the target populations, to promote the right kind of practices and to pre-empt undesired outcomes. Hence labour-market policy is no longer only focused on reducing barriers to labour market flexibility (the classic neoliberal strategy), but is also focused on fostering a better trained, more work-ready population.[72] CCTs work to change individuals' behaviour to make them more resilient to future risks: the World Bank's key study on CCTs also notes that, while it may appear that the conditions placed on individuals are paternalistic, there is an effort to treat them as "co-responsibilities" that "treat the recipient more as an adult capable of agency to resolve his or her own problems."[73] This

new way of conceptualizing the poor, together with the whole wealth of new strategies designed to make this measurement, representation, and management possible, provide an excellent example of what Ian Hacking calls "making up people," or creating new categories of identity that make possible new ways of being.[74]

Engaging but Limiting Government

These more proactive techniques of poverty management pose particular challenges for liberal economic governance: how can policy-makers manage the problem of poverty more actively while avoiding excessive state intrusion? The solution provided by the social risk framework is to rely on a network of public and private actors and formal and informal institutions rather than simply bringing the state back in. New institutional economics provides a useful lens for conceptualizing these more fluid public–private relations: the institutions needed to resolve market failures can be public or private, formal or informal.

The social risk framework seeks to manage poverty by reconnecting public and private actors in different ways—linking them up, getting them to act as checks on each other, infusing one with aspects of another—to create new networks and linkages.[75] As one passage from the WDR 2000–01 notes, "This is not an issue of the state versus the market, but of the use of different agents and mechanisms depending on the type of activity."[76] The rearticulation of these relationships is conceptualized using different market-based metaphors, such as competition, supply, and demand:

> Social protection should contribute to a better match between the supply and the demand of risk management instruments. There are many suppliers of social risk management instruments, such as individuals, households, communities, non-governmental organizations,

financial markets, governments at different levels, bilateral donors, and international organizations.[77]

These heterogeneous kinds of social actors are thus represented in very similar terms: they become parts in a larger, more social kind of market mechanism, in which individuals, NGOs, communities, international organizations and others can act as a source of demand for risk management, as well as supplying it.[78] While the market thus gets hedged around by institutions designed to make it work correctly, those institutions and actors in turn come to be defined through their instrumental relationship with the market.

Productive Forms of Power

The kinds of governance techniques required for reducing poverty by managing risk and vulnerability rely on what Michael Barnett and Raymond Duvall, drawing on Michel Foucault, call "**productive power**."[79] This kind of power seeks not simply to constrain but to actively constitute practices and subjectivities.[80] Thus, the goal of this kind of policy is not just to reduce poverty, but to constitute a new kind of low-income individual more capable of managing risk and thus able to attain a better quality of life.[81] Bank staff are themselves very keen on the productive and proactive aspects of this new poverty-reduction framework.[82] In their 2009 review of social protection, staff note, "The productive, as opposed to the redistributive, role of safety nets is becoming more recognized."[83] Moreover, the concept note and the consultations for the new 2012–22 Social Protection Strategy emphasize the importance of promoting more resilient communities and individuals.[84]

Risk is a category rather than a thing—it is a way that we make the world calculable in particular kinds of ways.[85] Risks are beyond our control and yet also very much subject to our understanding: a risk by definition is something that can be understood through a logic of probability (as opposed to uncertainty, ambiguity, and other kinds of indeterminacy).[86] As such, risk-based policies are particularly suited to this kind of productive application of power. This is particularly the case in the context of a market economy, in which risk is never viewed as an entirely bad thing. According to the Bank, risk is an essential tool for understanding poverty, not only because shocks can wreak havoc with efforts to raise incomes (risk as a bad thing), but also because, as poor people find themselves with fewer tools for managing risks, they are less likely to undertake riskier activities—such as borrowing money to invest in new farming equipment—that have the potential to improve their livelihoods (risk as a good thing).[87] Risk is thus understood as a double-edged problem: it is not universally bad, but instead needs to be both mitigated and exploited through particular kinds of interventions.

The more productive forms of power deployed today are also less direct than the more coercive techniques deployed by the Bank and other international financial institutions in the past. There is less emphasis on formal conditionality and more focus on constituting the right kinds of risk-bearing individuals and creating the conditions necessary for them to take on governance tasks themselves. Yet the fact that these forms of power are productive does not make them any less exclusionary.[88] As a number of social policy analysts have pointed out, even as the social risk framework seeks to engage a wider range of poor people more actively in the process of managing risks, it also tends to neglect those less capable of such active forms of self-governance. The framework's emphasis on the dynamic character of poverty leads it to downplay the problems of the chronically poor.[89] Its advocates' emphasis on shocks leads them to de-emphasize subtler sources of vulnerability, such as those associated with gender, class, ethnicity, or other structural fault lines. More fundamentally, the tendency of advocates of the social risk framework to define poverty in absolute rather than relative terms, and to emphasize poverty reduction as a "win-win" policy means that more difficult, structural solutions to poverty tend to get short shrift.[90]

How Widespread is This Shift? The Canadian Exception

Although the World Bank has been the main champion of the social risk approach to poverty reduction, this new conception of poverty has spread to other development organizations over time. The OECD's Development Assistance Committee (DAC), a forum for major donor countries, has been particularly active in promoting this approach to poverty reduction among its members. Among DAC members, the British Department for International Development (DFID) has been the most enthusiastic in its uptake of this policy framework, with the Nordic countries and Germany adopting and modifying different elements of the social risk approach in their policies.[91] Notably absent from this list of donors, however, is the Canadian government.

Until recently, the Canadian approach to fighting global poverty has roughly followed the same trends as the World Bank: the trickle-down approach dominated policy in the 1950s but was discredited in favour of more direct poverty-focused strategies in the 1960s and 1970s, when the Canadian International Development Agency (CIDA) was first created. CIDA followed the World Bank's lead toward structural adjustment and a return to trickle-down economics in the 1980s and, again following the Bank, its staff began to pay more attention to poverty in the 1990s, although it was in the context of a precipitous decline in Canadian foreign aid levels.[92] Although aid levels

increased throughout the early 2000s, in recent years Canada has moved in a rather different direction from most of the international donor community.

In March of 2013, the Conservative government announced that it was shutting down CIDA and rolling its functions into the foreign affairs department, creating a new super-ministry of Foreign Affairs, Trade and Development (FATD). As many commentators feared at the time, this move has only reinforced the government's growing tendency to treat international aid—and poverty reduction in particular—as *derivative* of the Canadian government's other foreign policy goals. As an internal government report obtained by the *Globe and Mail* reveals, the main criterion upon which Canadian aid is being evaluated is its effectiveness in supporting "Canadian commercial interests," a phrase that crops up time and time again in the (heavily redacted) document.[93] Although by law all Canadian aid must be consistent with the goals of poverty reduction, in practice this goal has been largely subordinated to other economic ends. When the FATD website on development priorities states, "Growing the economy is the best way to help people lift themselves out of poverty and stay out," it is echoing the kind of derivative, trickle-down approach to poverty that dominated the 1950s and 1980s.[94]

Yet the concept of risk is not entirely absent from Canadian social policy debates. There has been considerable interest in the concept of social risk among staff in the Policy Research Initiative, a strategic policy unit within the Canadian government that undertook research into the social management of risk between 2008 and 2011.[95] The documents prepared as part of this project drew explicitly on the World Bank's social risk framework. Yet their authors were interested in reflecting on how this framework could be applied within Canada rather than as a part of international development policy. This is not to say that Canadian development policy-makers are unaware of the concept of risk. Recent policy documents regularly refer to the risks posed by development work—but these risks are defined as potential problems for the donor project and agency, not for the recipients.[96] This narrow framing of risk echoes the broader tendency of the Canadian government to emphasize donor over recipient priorities.[97]

Where the World Bank, the OECD, and some donors have adopted a more integrated approach to poverty reduction under the rubric of social risk and vulnerability, the Canadian government has chosen to move back toward a more derivative approach to the problem, focusing on other priorities and assuming that their resolution will ultimately benefit the world's poorest. While the current Canadian approach to global poverty reduction is not shared by many other major donors, it is nonetheless consistent with the principles of a liberal political economy. In fact, in refusing to engage in the kind of micro-level policy work that the social risk framework requires, this trickle-down approach arguably does an even better job of avoiding an interventionist state.[98] As I will discuss further below, the persistence of this old school liberal approach to poverty raises some serious questions about the sustainability of the social risk approach to the problem of the wound of wealth.

Conclusion

Over the past few years, the World Bank's treatment of poverty as a residual or marginal problem has given way to a more active conception of poverty reduction as integral to economic management. I have suggested that in order to understand these changes—what drove them and what they mean—we need to pay attention to both the broad macro-principles of liberal economic governance and to the specific dynamics of expert debates and institutional negotiations. Two key liberal principles can be seen as shaping efforts to manage poverty throughout the World Bank's history: the need to address the wound of wealth; and the need to do so in such a way that the scope of state action is always kept in check. Within these broad parameters, the form that poverty-reduction policies take has historically varied through some combination of three treatments of the relationship between poverty and growth—as a residual, marginal, or integral part of broader development efforts. Each of these approaches has its advantages and disadvantages as governance strategies. Yet successive efforts to find a liberal solution to global poverty have all proven insufficient, as poverty persists, like dirt in the wound.

In the 1990s a series of financial, health, and development crises forced the wound of wealth back into the consciousness of development practitioners and helped to unsettle assumptions about poverty, emphasizing the contingent and risk-prone character of poverty-reduction efforts. In the context of the expert debates that ensued, new institutional economics played an important, if subtle, role in redefining poverty as market failure, and thus treating its reduction as integral to broader development efforts. At the World Bank, internal institutional dynamics, driven by intellectual debates about the relationship between poverty and growth, bureaucratic rivalries, and the need to placate those skeptical of social protection all played a role in influencing the form of the social risk framework.

Like previous World Bank approaches to poverty, the emphasis on risk and vulnerability is both consistent with the principles of liberal economic governance and yet subject to significant tensions. In many ways the efforts by advocates of social risk and pro-poor growth to integrate poverty into mainstream development are consistent with the principles of liberal governance: because poverty is defined through market failure, efforts to manage it can be seen as an attempt to re-establish a more perfect market system. Moreover, by treating poor people as potential participants in their own economic rehabilitation, capable of managing risk effectively if given the right tools, the social risk strategy fulfills the liberal preoccupation with governing through the freedom of its subjects.[99]

Yet tensions remain. As Robert McNamara found in his earlier effort to bring poverty reduction into the fold of economic development, many economists resist such efforts. The Canadian case reminds us that the idea that poverty is merely a residual problem—resolvable by the pursuit of growth and stability—is seductive. Many liberal economists view the kind of integrationist move involved in McNamara's redistribution with growth or the current social risk framework with considerable skepticism—not least because of the tendency to demand a more active form of governance, which always runs the risk of governing too much.

In the aftermath of the recent financial crisis (discussed by Patrick Leblond in chapter 20), the concepts of vulnerability and risk have gained even more momentum within the World Bank and more generally among development organizations. Yet the future of the social risk approach to poverty—like those of previous liberal poverty-reduction strategies—remains far from certain. On the one hand, for the many old-school liberals, like those in the Canadian government, the social risk approach will always involve too much government and will therefore never be liberal enough. On the other, there are many others, myself included, who argue that the social risk approach remains too liberal. Because its advocates are constrained by the liberal fear of too much government intervention, the social risk approach cannot acknowledge the problems posed by narrowly market-based solutions. Blinded by a desire to make poverty fit within the mainstream of economics, the social risk approach cannot recognize the profound challenge that poverty poses to liberal economics. Thus it seems likely that the wound of wealth will continue to fester, a continual irritation to the promises of liberal political economy and a provocation to the institutions that seek to manage the problem of global poverty.

Acknowledgements

This chapter is a revised version of an article that appeared in *Third World Quarterly* in 2013: "Redefining poverty as risk and vulnerability: Shifting strategies of liberal economic governance." *Third World Quarterly* 34(2), 2013, 109–29.

An earlier version of the chapter was presented at the workshop on "Public/Private Interaction and the Transformation of Global Governance," held at the University of Ottawa in May 2009. I would like to thank the participants in that workshop for their feedback on the earlier draft, particularly Alexandra Gheciu. I also benefited from some excellent research assistance from Marie Langevin, Kailey Cannon, and Christopher Leite. The chapter was researched and written with the financial support of the Social Sciences and Humanities Research Council of Canada.

Notes

1 See the introduction to this volume for a brief discussion of Adam Smith's foundational role in IPE.

2 Robert Keohane's highly influential approach to IPE is labeled "neoliberal institutionalist" (quite a mouthful) and combines neoliberal IR theory with institutionalist economics. Keohane, R. 1984. *After hegemony: Cooperation and discord in the world political economy.* Princeton: Princeton University Press.

3 D. L. Blaney and N. Inayatullah, (2010). *Savage economics: Wealth, poverty, and the temporal walls of capitalism*, London: Routledge.

4   A. Escobar, *Encountering development: The making and unmaking of the third world*, Princeton, NJ: Princeton University Press, 1995, 23; and W. Sachs, "The archaeology of the development idea." *Intraculture 23*(4), 1990, 9.

5   United Nations. (2013). *The Millennium Development Goals report 2013*. New York, United Nations, 4.

6   There are two major international financial institutions concerned with managing the financing of international development—the International Monetary Fund (IMF) and the World Bank. While this chapter focuses just on the second of these, I have written elsewhere about the IMF: J. Best, "Legitimacy dilemmas: The IMF's pursuit of country ownership." *Third World Quarterly 28*(3), 2007, 469–88; "Bringing power back in: The IMF's constructivist strategy in critical perspective," *Constructing the international economy*. R. et al. Abdelal, (Eds). Ithaca, Cornell University Press, 2010, 194–210; "Bureaucratic ambiguity." *Economy and Society 41*(1), 84–106.

7   M. Foucault, (1989). *Résumés des cours*, Paris: Collège de France, 111; and Foucault, 2004. *Naissance de la biopolitique: Cours au Collège de France, 1978–79*, Paris: Seuil, 10–14 [author's translation].

8   F. Bourguignon, (2002). *The growth elasticity of poverty reduction: Explaining heterogeneity across countries and time periods*, DELTA Working Paper, 2002–03, Paris; and M. Ravallion, (2004). *Pro-poor growth: A primer*, World Bank Policy Research Working Paper 3242, Washington, DC: World Bank.

9   As I discuss in my book, *Governing failure*, the move to redefine poverty as risk is just one of a number of new governance strategies in global development over the past few decades, alongside the focus on country ownership, results measurement, and standardization: J. Best, 2014. *Governing failure: Provisional expertise and the transformation of global development finance*, Cambridge: Cambridge University Press.

10 World Bank. (2001). *Social protection sector strategy: From safety net to springboard*, Washington, DC: World Bank.

11 Market failures occur when the market does not allocate goods efficiently, often due to the absence of crucial institutions or information.

12 Department for International Development (DFID), Pro-Poor Growth Briefing Note 2, London: DFID 2004; *OECD Promoting pro-poor growth: Policy statement*, Paris: OECD 2006; and R. S. Wheeler & L. Haddad, 2005. *Reconciling different concepts of risk and vulnerability: A review of donor documents*, Brighton: Institute of Development Studies.

13 As I will discuss further below, there has nonetheless been some interest in this approach by other parts of the Canadian government.

14 D. Kapur, J. P. Lewis, & R. Webb, (1997). *The World Bank: Its first half century*, Vol 1, Washington, DC: Brookings Institution Press, 148.

15 M. Finnemore, (1996). *National interests in international society*, Ithaca, NY: Cornell University Press; Kapur et al., *The World Bank*, 148, 217; and R. McNamara, 1975. *The Assault on World Poverty: Problems of rural development, education and health*, Washington, DC: World Bank.

16 Moving funds out the door is the single most important objective at the World Bank, one that can easily distort other goals.

17 R. Ayers, *Banking on the poor: The World Bank and world poverty*, Cambridge, MA: MIT Press.

18 Ibid; Kapur et al., *The World Bank*, 265–7.

19 Kapur et al., *The World Bank*, 23. There nonetheless remained a core group of Bank staff committed to advancing the social policy

agenda, although it did not have the opportunity to exercise much influence again until the late 1990s. See A. Vetterlein, (2007). "Economic growth, poverty reduction, and the role of social policies: the evolution of the World Bank's social development approach," *Global Governance*, 13, 513–33; and C. Weaver, 2008. *Hypocrisy trap: The World Bank and the poverty of reform*. Princeton, NJ: Princeton University Press.

20 J. Williamson, 1990. "What Washington means by policy reform," in Williamson (ed.), *Latin American adjustment: How much has happened?* Washington, DC: Institute for International Economics, 5–20.

21 Structural adjustment policies typically sought to open countries up to international trade and investment, liberalise financial flows, reduce inflation, make labour markets more flexible, reduce the size of the public sector, privatise government-owned companies and remove government subsidies.

22 Kapur et al., *The World Bank*, 356.

23 World Bank, *World Development Report 1990–91: Poverty*, Washington, DC: World Bank, 1990, 3.

24 UNICEF, *Adjustment with a human face*, New York: United Nations, 1987.

25 World Bank, *Poverty*, 3.

26 Ibid., 56–57, 62, 63–64, 90, 100–1.

27 Vetterlein, A. "Economic growth."

28 United Nations Development Programme (UNDP), *Human Development Report*, New York: UNDP, 1999, 99.

29 J. Best, "Legitimacy dilemmas."

30 I discuss the impact of this and other apparent "failures" in development thinking in *Governing failure*, chs. 1, 2 and 9.

31 World Bank, (2003). *Social risk management: The World Bank's approach to social protection in a globalizing World*, Washington, DC: World Bank, 2; and World Bank, 2009. *Social protection and labor at the World Bank, 2000–2008*, Washington, DC: World Bank, 1, 12.

32 M. Callon, 1998. "Introduction: The embeddedness of economic markets in economics." In Callon (Ed.), *The laws of the markets*, Oxford: Blackwell, 1998, 1–57; and A. Barry, 2002. "The anti-politics economy," *Economy and Society 31*(2), 268–84.

33 Phone interview with former senior World Bank staff member, February 2012. See also F. Bourguignon, *The growth elasticity of poverty reduction*; D. Rodrik, "Growth versus poverty reduction: A hollow debate." *Finance and Development 37*(4), 2000; and J. Stiglitz, 1998. "Towards a new paradigm for development: Strategies, policies and processes," Prebisch Lecture, Geneva.

34 F. Bourguignon, *The growth elasticity of poverty reduction*. It is worth noting that, while Bourguignon was well respected within the Bank well before his term as head of the Research Department, his emphasis on equality only came to be widely accepted in the mid- to late 2000s.

35 D. Dollar & A. Kraay, (2001). *Growth is good for the poor*, Working Paper 2587, Washington, DC: World Bank.

36 P. Masson, (2001). *Globalization: Facts and figures*, Policy Discussion Paper 01/04, Washington, DC: IMF; and R. Wade, 2001. "Showdown at the World Bank," *New Left Review*, 7, 124–37.

37 Ravallion, *Pro-poor growth*.

38 A. Sen, (1983). *Poverty and famines: An essay on entitlement and deprivation*, Oxford: Clarendon.

39 M. Prowse, (2003). *Towards a clearer understanding of "vulnerability" in relation to chronic poverty*, Chronic Poverty Research Centre (CPRC) Working Paper 24, Manchester: CPRC.

40 J. Dreze & A. Sen, (1991). *Hunger and public action*, Oxford: Oxford University Press.

41 F. Ellis, P. White, P. Lloyd-Sherlock, V. Chhotray, & J. Seeley. (2008). *Social protection research scoping study*, East Anglia, UK: Governance and Social Development Resource Centre; and N. Kabeer, 2009. *Scoping study on social protection: Evidence on impacts and future research directions*, London: DFID.

42 R. Coase, (1937). "The nature of the firm," *Economica* 4(16), 386–405; and Coase. (1960). "The problem of social cost," *Journal of Law and Economics* 3, 1–44.

43 Classic institutionalist texts include North, D. (1990). Institutions, *Institutional change and economic performance*, Cambridge: Cambridge University Press; and Williamson, O. 1985. *The economic institutions of capitalism*, New York: Free Press. North, in particular, is cited in a number of Bank documents as an inspiration for governance policy, particularly from the 2002 WDR on institutions onwards, in which the first footnote cites North, Williamson, and Coase on institutions. See World Bank, *World Development Report 2002: Building institutions for markets*, Washington, DC: World Bank, 2002, 5. Joseph Stiglitz's Nobel Prize winning work on asymmetric information is also linked to the insights of institutionalist economics. Stiglitz, J. 1977. "Monopoly, nonlinear pricing, and imperfect information: The insurance market," *Review of Economic Studies* 44, 407–30.

44 The term "stakeholder" refers to the countries that are members in the World Bank and influence its policies through their Directors (who meet twice a year) and, more importantly, their Executive Directors (a much smaller group of representatives who meet throughout the year to decide on Bank affairs). Not surprisingly, some stakeholders, particularly the USA and the European countries, are more influential than others.

45 Interviews with senior World Bank staff, June 2010 and May 2011; World Bank, *Social Risk Management*, 4.

46 R. Holzmann, L. Sherburne-Benz, & E. Tesliuc, (2003). *Social risk management: The World Bank's approach to social protection in a globalizing world*, Washington, DC: World Bank, 1.

47 Interviews with senior World Bank staff, June (2010, May 2011, and February 2012).

48 Phone interview with Robert Holzmann, former Director of Social Protection, 15 June 2010.

49 Ibid.; and interview with former senior World Bank staff member, February 2012. As Holzmann himself noted, the attitude to inequality has shifted since then, and "now you can openly talk about equity" at the Bank.

50 Phone interview with former senior World Bank staff member, February 2012.

51 Phone interview with Holzmann, 15 June 2010.

52 The PREM and Research Departments tended to support one another in their skepticism about the social risk framework, in opposition to the Social Protection unit. Interviews with senior World Bank staff members, June 2010 and May 2011.

53 Wade, "Showdown at the World Bank"; and Wade, (2002). "US hegemony and the World Bank: The fight over people and ideas." *Review of International Political Economy* 9(2), 215–43.

54 Wade, "Showdown at the World Bank," 133–4.

55 Ibid., 132.

56 Interview with Holzmann, 15 June 2010; and phone interview with former senior World Bank staff member, February 2012.

57 Interview with Gordon Betcherman, former lead economist in the Social Protection Unit, World Bank, February 2012.

58 World Bank. (2001). *World Development Report 2000/01: Attacking poverty*, Washington, DC; World Bank, ch. 4.

59 World Bank, *Social protection sector strategy*.

60 World Bank, *Attacking Poverty*, 19.

61 Ibid., 136–41, 12, 23.

62 World Bank, *Social protection sector strategy*, ch 2; and World Bank, *Attacking poverty*, 141–59.

63 Ibid., 26.

64 World Bank, *Attacking poverty*, p148–50.

65 World Bank, *Social protection and labor at the World Bank*, 45–6.

66 Ibid., 46.

67 World Bank. (2011). "Building resilience and opportunity: Better livelihoods for the 21st century—Emerging ideas from the World Bank's 2012–22 social protection and labor strategy," powerpoint presentation, Washington, DC; and A. Fiszbein & N. Schady, 2009. *Conditional cash transfers: Reducing present and future poverty*, Washington, DC: World Bank.

68 World Bank, *Attacking poverty*, 142.

69 Holzmann et al., *Social risk management*, 9.

70 World Bank, *Attacking poverty*, 139.

71 Holzmann et al., *Social risk management*, 4.

72 There are clear parallels here with the kinds of processes of active economic citizenship described by Ruth Lister and Nikolas Rose. R. Lister, 2001. "Towards a citizens' welfare state: the 3 + 2 "R"s of welfare," *Theory, Culture & Society* 18(2–3), 91–111; and N. Rose, 1996. "The death of the social? Re-figuring the territory of government." *Economy & Society* 25(3), 327–56.

73 Fiszbein & Schady, *Conditional cash transfers*, 10. For an excellent discussion of the various ways in which CCTs use co-responsibilites and other techniques to construct particular economic subjectivities, see: Cannon, K. "Anti-poverty policy as the construction of market subjects: The case of the conditional cash transfer program *Oportunidades*." MA Thesis, University of Ottawa, 2014.

74 I. Hacking, 2002. *Historical ontology*. Cambridge, MA: Harvard University Press, 99–114.

75 For a discussion of the reconstitution of the public and private in global governance, see: J. Best & A. Gheciu (Eds). 2014. *The return of the public in global governance*, Cambridge: Cambridge University Press.

76 World Bank, *Attacking poverty*, 86.

77 Holzmann et al., *Social risk management*, 9.

78 I have provided a much more thorough analysis of the "demand side" of good governance in J. Best, "The "Demand Side" of Governance: The return of the public in World Bank policy," in J. Best & A. Gheciu (Eds), *The return of the public*.

79 In using the term "productive," I am borrowing Barnett and Duvall's very useful term, while at the same time defining it more broadly than they do, including practices as well as discourse. In many ways this is a return to the richer conception of discourse that Foucault himself used—although with more attention to its concrete manifestations. See M. Barnett & R. Duvall, 2005. "Power in Global Governance," in Barnett & Duvall (Eds). *Power in global governance*, Cambridge: Cambridge University Press; Foucault, M. 1970. *The order of things: An archaeology of the human sciences*, New York: Vintage Books; and Foucault, "Two lectures," in C. Gordon (Ed.). 1980. *Power/knowledge: Selected interviews and other writings, 1972–1977*, Brighton: Harvester Press.

80 This conception of power thus has much in common with the "discursive" approach to power that Aitken outlines in ch. 3.

81 M. Dean, (1999). *Governmentality: Power and rule in modern society*, Thousand Oaks, CA: Sage.

82 Interviews with senior World Bank staff, 10 and 15 June 2010, and 17 May 2011.

83 World Bank, *Social protection and labor*, 138.

84 World Bank. 2011. *Building resilience and opportunity: The World Bank's social protection and labor strategy 2012–2022—concept note*, Washington, DC: World Bank.

85 I thus follow Mitchell Dean's conception of risk here, rather than the somewhat more realist conception that one finds in Ulrich Beck's work. See U. Beck, 1992. *Risk society: Towards a new modernity*, London: Sage; and M. Dean, 1999. "Risk, calculable and incalculable." In D. Lupton (Ed.), *Risk and socioculture theory: New directions and perspectives*, Cambridge: Cambridge University Press.

86 For a discussion of the differences among these kinds of indeterminacy, see J. Best, 2008. "Ambiguity, uncertainty and risk: Rethinking indeterminacy," *International Political Sociology* 2(4), 355–74.

87 This is, of course, a particular financial conception of risk and reward, in which greater risks can be accurately measured, priced, and rewarded with greater returns. This kind of conception of risk was at the heart of the current financial crisis. See J. Best, 2010. "The limits of financial risk management: Or, What we didn't learn from the Asian financial crisis," *New Political Economy* 15(1), 29–49.

88 I have provided a much more comprehensive discussion of the complex relationship between productive or bio-power and exclusionary or exceptionalist power in Best, "Why the Economy is Often an Exception to Politics As Usual."

89 A. Shepherd, (2004). *General review of current social protection policies and programmes*, London: DFID.

90 J. Farrington, (2005). *Social Protection and livelihood promotion in agriculture: Towards operational guidelines*, Paris: OECD–Povnet; and N. Kabeer, K. Mumtaz, & A. Sayeed, (2010). "Beyond Risk management: Vulnerability, social protection and citizenship," *Journal of International Development*, 22, 1–19.

91 For a useful overview of different countries' approach to social risk, see: Wheeler & Haddad, *Reconciling different concepts*.

92 D. Morrison, (1998). *Aid and ebb tide: A history of CIDA and Canadian Development assistance*. Waterloo, Wilfred Laurier University Press, 35, 59, 20, 356. On the changing trajectory of Canadian aid levels, see: S. Brown, "Aid Effectiveness and the Framing of New Canadian Aid Initiatives," in S. Brown (Ed.). 2012. *Struggling for effectiveness: CIDA and Canadian foreign aid*. McGill-Queen's University Press, 79–107.

93 CIDA. 2012. *Reviewing CIDA's Bilateral engagement: Countries of focus and modest presence partners—Qualitative Assessment*. Ottawa, Canadian International Development Agency, 6, 7, 9, 10, 13, 21. I thank Stephen Brown for bringing this document to my attention.

94 Government of Canada, "Stimulating sustainable economic growth." Retrieved 10 February 2014, from http://www.acdi-cida.gc.ca/acdi-cida/acdi-cida.nsf/en/FRA-101515146-QKD.

95 The Policy Research Initiative has since been renamed Policy Horizons. Government of Canada, "The social management of risk." Retrieved 10 February 2014, from http://www.horizons.gc.ca/eng/content/social-management-risk. The most comprehensive study included in this project is: Government of Canada. 2010. *Addressing lifecourse risks through social innovation: Opportunities and challenges for the community sector*, Policy Research Initiative, March.

96 For example, CIDA. (2013). *Canadian International Development Agency 2013–14: Report on Plans and Priorities*, Canadian International Development Agency, Government of Canada, 10–12.

97 As Brown points out, this trend also extends to the Canadian government's use of the term "aid effectiveness": Brown, "Aid Effectiveness."

98 Although the Canadian government's explicit intention of making foreign policy interests one of the major determinants of aid policy does bring the state back in—through its security agenda.

99 M. Foucault, (1991). "Governmentality." In G. Burchell, C. Gordon, & P. Miller (Eds), *The Foucault effect: Studies in governmentality*. London, Harvester Wheatsheaf, 87–104. For a particularly thoughtful examination of this element in Foucault's conception of liberal governance, see: B. Hindess, 1996. *Discourses of power: From Hobbes to Foucault*. Oxford: Blackwell, ch. 5.

Key Terms

governance	social protection
market failure	social risk
new institutional economics	structural adjustment
productive power	

Questions for Review

1. Why is poverty a problem for liberal political economy?

2. How has the World Bank defined and dealt with the problem of poverty throughout its history?

3. What were the different forces that led to the adoption of the social risk approach at the World Bank?

4. What are the similarities and differences between the social risk and structural adjustment approaches to poverty?

5. Why is risk a relevant concept for understanding poverty? How does it change our conception of poverty? How does it affect policy responses?

6. What is the role of the state in the social risk approach to poverty?

7. Do you think that the social risk approach is a better strategy than earlier ones?

Further Resources

On the World Bank's approach to poverty

Best, J. (2014). *Governing failure: Provisional expertise and the transformation of global finance for development*. Cambridge: Cambridge University Press.

Holzmann, R. L. et al. (2003). *Social risk management: The World Bank's approach to social protection in a globalizing world*. Washington, World Bank.

Wade, R. (2001). "Showdown at the World Bank." *New Left Review* 7 (January–February), 124–37.

Weaver, C. (2008). *Hypocrisy trap: The World Bank and the poverty of reform*. Princeton: Princeton University Press.

World Bank. (2001). *World development report 2000/01: Attacking poverty*. Washington, DC.

On risk, power, and governance

Best, J. (2008). "Ambiguity, uncertainty and risk: Rethinking indeterminacy." *International Political Sociology 2*(4), 355–74.

Dean, M. (2010). "Risk and reflexive government." In Dean, M. *Governmentality: Power and rule in modern society*, 2nd ed. Thousand Oaks, CA: Sage, 205–27.

Rose, N. and Miller, P. (1992). "Political power beyond the state: Problematics of government." *British Journal of Sociology 43*(2), 172–205.

10 Reshaping the Trading System after the Doha Round

Robert Wolfe

After staggering along for six years, the Doha Round of multilateral trade negotiations in the World Trade Organization (WTO) hit an impasse in July 2008 and has been stalled ever since. The WTO itself is not sick. World trade is still growing, if slowly; protectionism did not accelerate during the Great Recession (Wolfe 2012); the dispute settlement system works well; and the transparency and surveillance mechanisms are used more than ever, with substantial improvements since 2008 (Wolfe 2013). But something is manifestly wrong with the Doha Round.

Trade negotiations take place in so-called "rounds" that have been getting longer and longer; recalling the rise and decline of the Doha Round will help to provide context for the analysis that follows.[1] The round arguably started at the first WTO Ministerial Conference at Singapore in 1996 when ministers agreed to a work program including new issues and leftovers from the Uruguay Round. The round was launched, and China joined the WTO at the Doha Ministerial Conference in 2001 after a failed attempt at Seattle in 1999. The mandate for the negotiations was clarified in July 2004 after the collapse of the Cancún Ministerial Conference in 2003, and was refined again at the Hong Kong Ministerial Conference in 2005. By July 2008, serious texts were on the table, if full of square brackets, and many areas were at least stable, if not closed, but that meeting ended in breakdown. The conventional story about the July 2008 informal ministerial is that the proposed "special safeguard mechanism" (SSM) for developing countries in agriculture (Wolfe 2009b), and sectoral negotiations in trade in goods, known as non-agricultural market access (NAMA), were the main obstacles to overall agreement, and that the split on both was essentially between the United States and India. Neither country stood alone, however, and these two issues were not the only obstacles to agreement. While the trade in services signalling conference showed promise, intellectual property (TRIPS) also failed, and other issues were hardly discussed (Wolfe 2010b). The last attempt to salvage the core of the round fizzled in April 2011 when the G5 (US, EU, China, Brazil, and India) essentially gave up. The Doha Round collapsed on a small number of issues among a handful of members.

I am not trying to build a determinant causal model: explaining why 160+ countries did NOT do something is harder than explaining why they did.[2] But in a probabilistic model we can at least identify the major factors. Scholars place the factors that might explain these lengthy delays and frequent setbacks in negotiations in two groups. Each understands negotiations differently.

In the first set of models are approaches that stress the salience of power or material interests. If multilateral economic negotiations are worthy of any attention, such analysts will look outside the process for an explanation of deadlock or agreement.[3] Negotiations are then explained by such exogenous *structural* factors as the identifiable economic interests of participants or their domestic industries, or by the general political, security, or economic context. If institutions enter at all, they are simply the equilibrium outcome of competing sets of domestic preferences acting as constraints on the possibility of agreement. If the institutions of the trade regime have any role, it would be to allow power to overcome the reality that the WTO has 150+ veto points and two or three times that many veto players. These *exogenous* factors are things the WTO cannot change, and that might not have been anticipated, but that might lead you to give up on the WTO if you think some other forum might be better.

The second set of models attributes negotiation delay to *institutional* factors inside or endogenous to the negotiations. In these bargaining models, something about the process is significant to the outcome. Perhaps the agenda is more complex, allowing trade-offs between issues. Perhaps participants acquire information about each other at the table that was not available in some other way; for example, through voting that reveals their partners' preferences. Perhaps a mediator is able to help them see the possibility of agreement. Other endogenous models assume that something happens at the multilateral negotiation table in addition to bargaining, something that alters the

understanding of themselves and their interests that participants brought to the table, allowing them to see their preferences in a new way (Wolfe 2010a). *Endogenous* factors are things that in principle the WTO can do something about, and perhaps ought to have anticipated, though trying to change is then only worth doing if these factors can be shown to have contributed to the ailment.

Following the logic above, in the first part of the chapter I discuss the possibility that the Doha Round failed for exogenous *structural* reasons, while the second part considers the *endogenous* institutional factors where *agency* by members might have been possible. In both cases my analysis uses examples from trade in goods, the issues on which the round broke down, but in neither case do I attempt a negotiating history of key events in the round. A third part brings both sets of factors together in a reflection on how the WTO, in common with most multilateral organizations, has not caught up with the shifting centre of gravity in global governance. The trading system is no longer a transatlantic bargain. The regulatory issues on the twenty-first-century trade policy agenda will inevitably be negotiated in Geneva, but only after a new trans-Pacific accommodation recognizes China's central role.

Structural Factors (exogenous)

Diagnosing what ails Doha begins by analyzing the exogenous factors that doomed the round. International relations scholars often start by considering the systemic or political/security factors that promote or constrain international collective action. Nobody doubts that the 9/11 attacks provided a powerful impetus for a successful ministerial conference at Doha in November 2001, barely two months later. That impetus dissipated quickly, however, in part due to the 2003 invasion of Iraq, to which the world was not so sympathetic. In retrospect, the more salient exogenous factor affecting everybody's political calculus in the WTO has been the changing role of China (Mattoo and Subramanian 2011). We can see that challenge more clearly by considering how ongoing structural change in the world economy undermined the Doha Round. Regardless of how the round was managed, the focus of part 2 of this paper, what the round was designed to do in 2011, no longer made sense by July 2008.

How the Markets Changed During The Round, Undermining The Basis for Agriculture and NAMA

It might be imagined that the financial crisis hurt the Doha Round, but the trade collapse from the third quarter of 2008 to the first quarter of 2009 happened *after* the July 2008 informal ministerial, and so cannot explain the impasse. While the Great Recession with its associated decline in GDP and rise in unemployment might have made it difficult to resume negotiations,[4] more significant were other factors that undermined the logic of the round. The importance of addressing unresolved issues in agriculture was part of the motivation for Doha: Developed countries achieve little on agriculture in their bilateral or regional negotiations, and developing countries have huge numbers of people dependent on farming. Paragraph 13 of the Doha declaration covered the mandate for agriculture negotiations on market access, export competition, and domestic support (WTO 2001). Market access was perceived to be a North–South issue, despite the reality that the most significant remaining barriers affected South–South trade. Export competition mattered politically to the EU, but the relative volumes of export subsidies in 2001 were already insignificant compared to domestic

support in OECD countries, which itself fell anyway during the round. The agenda, in brief, was influenced by assumptions about the trade flows of the 1980s and 1990s, assumptions that, in the event, proved wrong.

The standard picture of the long-run decline in real terms of commodity prices in Figure 10.1 is familiar, and it held until 2001. But then a decade-long boom fueled by Chinese demand caused prices to skyrocket to levels not seen since the mid-1970s. Change in commodity prices alters all sorts of pressures in the WTO, but especially in agriculture, because subsidies move inversely to prices. At 2000 prices, and 2000 subsidy levels, the agriculture deal on the table would look interesting, but it had lost its appeal in the circumstances of 2008 and 2013. The percentage of farmers' incomes coming from subsidies in OECD countries has been declining, from 40 per cent at the peak of the farm wars in the 1980s to 18 per cent in 2010 (OECD 2011, Figure 1.3). In contrast, Chinese farm subsidies seem to have been trending up, which is not surprising in any country when the relative size and wealth of the urban population is increasing. Indeed, domestic support levels have been rising to levels not seen before in developing countries, and may soon rival some large developed countries (Brink 2013). The new disciplines proposed in the last draft agriculture modalities (WTO 2008a) will not have much effect on OECD subsidies that have fallen anyway, and were not designed to cut China's subsidies (Brink, Orden, and Datz 2013). In consequence, much of what had been arduously negotiated will not change most trade flows much because the new provisions will not reduce current *applied* subsidies and *applied* tariffs. And yet farmers are strongly attached to current policies, so developed country governments would face political pain for changing things that could not be changed in the Uruguay Round, for no gain.

The other big issue was trade in goods (NAMA), where paragraph 24 of the Hong Kong Ministerial

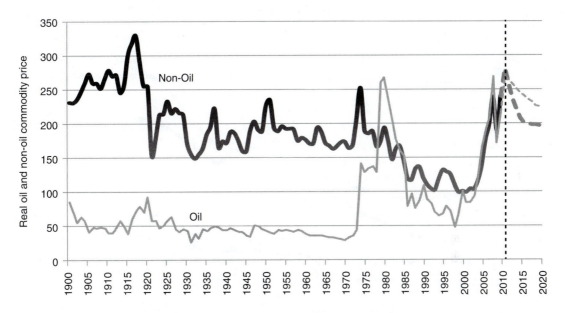

Figure 10.1 How the Markets Changed during the Uruguay Round

Source: World Bank

Conference declaration explicitly required a level of ambition comparable to agriculture (WTO 2005). Here too the mandate was based on assumptions about a world that is gone. China only joined the WTO in 2001, at Doha. Two years later, China still represented only 12.5 per cent of US trade, but by 2010 that share was 19.5 per cent. China is now the world's dominant trader, passing the US in 2007, as shown in Figure 10.2, and may soon pass the EU, which changes everybody's perceptions of what is at stake. The accession obligations were onerous, but China has obviously done well as a member of the WTO. The US public, and certainly many politicians, fear China, as manifested in the chorus of demands to address supposed currency manipulation.[5] Canadians also fear China, judging by the controversy aroused by an investment agreement concluded in 2012. Developing countries worry even more about further trade liberalization if the

consequence is that China is better able to compete in their markets. One experienced ambassador said that if you want to understand any member's position on any Doha issue, just assess how the issue would affect the member's trade relationship with China. The only thing that unites all WTO members is fear of China.

These structural factors provided the context in which the big players could not agree on a level of ambition for market access in agriculture and NAMA, notably on whether cuts in the rates formally bound in a member's tariff "schedules" should go below the rates actually applied—that gap is significant for some developing countries. In the end, the central confrontation was between the US and China, the one thinking that the round was the last time OECD countries would have market access leverage because their tariffs would be too low after the cut envisaged in the round to provide

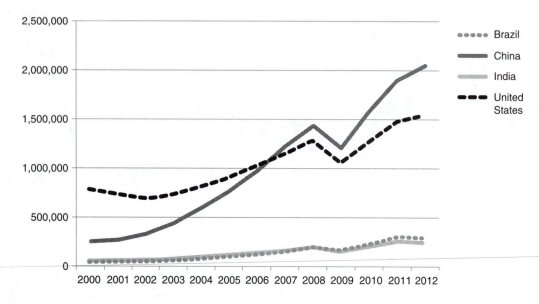

Figure 10.2 World Merchandise Exports 2000–12 (million dollars)

Source: (WTO, 2012) Table A6.

negotiation coin; the other thinking that as a still-poor developing country it had given enough in the lengthy accession negotiations. The other emerging economies were privately relieved by the standoff: had China struck a deal with the US, India and Brazil would have faced intense pressure.

Institutional Factors (endogenous)

The familiar endogenous story is that as multilateral trade rounds in the GATT/WTO have grown in topics and numbers of participants, they have taken longer to conclude. I do not share the conventional wisdom about the implications of this correlation: the supposedly urgent need for WTO reform is not evident to me. Did too many members have a seat at the table? Hardly. Most negotiating took place among small groups, and most meetings had nothing like 150+ members in the

room, so that is not the problem. Was the size and/or complexity of the Doha Round agenda a problem? Sometimes agreement or deadlock can be explained by the presence or absence of shared (consensual) understanding of an issue, whether or not members agree on the implications (Wolfe 2010a). My analysis of one issue showed that the proposed special safeguard (SSM) in agriculture was so poorly understood that bargaining was and remains impossible. (Wolfe 2009a). But if a lack of understanding on some issues had been the only problem, the deal concluded at the 2013 Bali Ministerial Conference would have been somewhat larger. The complexity was a challenge for all negotiators, especially those supported by small numbers of professional staff, but delegations received considerable support from other international organizations, from NGOs, from other members, and from the WTO Secretariat. Many issues appeared stable in July 2008, and as could be seen during 2013 with the negotiations for the Bali package, even a simple well-understood agenda can be hard to advance.

The possibly more relevant endogenous factors can be grouped as those affecting the conduct of the negotiations, or process; and design errors in how the negotiations were structured, principally the modalities. I have previously discussed many process factors that contributed to the July 2008 failure (Wolfe 2010b), as have other scholars (Hoekman 2012b). I will isolate only two that cannot be blamed for the impasse, the **Single Undertaking** and clubs, before discussing the design errors that did contribute.

Is the Single Undertaking a Problem?

A great many observers think that the Single Undertaking has had its day. I disagree (Wolfe 2009c). They think that achieving consensus on all parts of a big deal with 150+ members was part of the Doha Round problem. Others think that rounds are no longer necessary for liberalization, making a device to hold a round together obsolete.

We can see three meanings of "single undertaking" in the Doha Declaration: "the (1) conduct, (2) conclusion and (3) entry into force of the outcome of the negotiations shall be treated as parts of a single undertaking." The Doha mandate (1) is the paragraphs in the declaration calling for negotiations on a specified set of issues with agreed objectives. This mandate as a single undertaking in itself is obviously dead—were it alive nobody would have discussed a mini-package for Bali. And yet it remains difficult to unpick the mandate bargains of 2001, 2004, and 2005. More flexibility might have helped, but the principle (2) that the result must be a package applies to most negotiations, including the mini-package that was agreed at Bali in December 2013, or in the Trans-Pacific Partnership negotiations underway outside the WTO. This principle can neither be changed nor avoided. The WTO

acquis (3) is also a reality, and it was not part of the problem in the round.[6]

Putting a package together is a challenge in any negotiation. The big players have asymmetric interests in the WTO, as they will in any other negotiation involving some combination of them. Countries tend to have asymmetric interests with respect to any one trading partner; and countries tend to have asymmetric interests on any one issue. For example, in the Doha Round,

- The US wants NAMA sectorals, but not "duty free/quota free" access for LDCs or cotton.
- Brazil is keen on agriculture, not NAMA.
- India is keen on what others can offer in services, but pursued defensive interests in agriculture.
- China is keen on Rules (subsidies and anti-dumping issues), but thinks it has done enough on NAMA.
- EU needs geographic indications (an intellectual property issue) and export competition in agriculture.
- Nobody wants fish subsidies on its own.

Given asymmetrical interests among them, can the five reach a deal on one issue in isolation? IF the five have to be part of any deal to get a worthwhile level of participation (critical mass, in the current jargon), and IF they have asymmetrical interests THEN they have to have a package of critical mass deals to reach agreement on any one of the deals. In order to assemble any package, the major players will need the diffuse reciprocity that is enabled by the Single Undertaking mechanism.

The American problem is acute. Given the heterogeneity of Congress, any significant deal must generally have something in it for multiple diverse constituencies. This logic will tend to favour deals with a critical mass of issues and participants. Consider the difficulties getting small preferential trade agreements through Congress—it was easier to mobilize concentrated opponents of the Panama agreement, for example, than diffuse beneficiaries.

If one thinks that the reason China, India, Brazil, the United States, and the EU did not agree with each other is because Bangladesh did not agree with them, then the devil is the Single Undertaking. I think that the evidence does not support the diagnosis. At the end of a round, if a package is big enough, small members are unlikely to deny consensus, especially if the clubs have been working properly. Unfortunately, WTO clubland was dysfunctional for much of the Doha Round, but here too the problem was with the whales, not the minnows.

Problems in WTO Clubland

Every member of the WTO naturally insists on *participation* in making decisions that affect the country directly, while having *influence* on decisions that affect the evolving structure of rules, but plenary meetings of 150+ members in any WTO body are held only for transparency. The real work is done in smaller groups, of which the (in)famous Green Room is only one manifestation. The largest players are in virtually all such meetings, however constructed, but most members are represented by the coordinator of their club, or by a member who holds a similar position on the key issue in question.

Three sorts of clubs are relevant in the Doha Round.[7] Clubs based on a broad *common characteristic* (e.g., region, or level of development, like the Africa Group or the LDCs) can influence many issues, including the round as a whole, but weakly. Clubs based on a *common objective* can have a great deal of influence, but on a limited range of issues. To take just agriculture, the G33 (led by Indonesia) was formed to advance the interests of import-sensitive poor farmers because the Cairns

Group (led by Australia) and the G20 (led by Brazil) were dominated by export interests, while the G10 (led by Switzerland) defends exceptions for "sensitive" products. (Canada as an exporter of grains and red meat belonged to the Cairns Group. Canada as a defender of supply management, especially in dairy, was aligned with the G10.) These clubs, found in all areas of the negotiations, are single-issue lobby groups, not broad alliances. The Doha Round collapse exposed the weaknesses of vertical clubs, as anticipated in the negotiation analysis literature. They work well when they make distributive demands, especially in initial negotiating proposals, but work badly when they make integrative decisions; they are better for blocking than for building consensus. The many South–South clubs that have emerged in the WTO and elsewhere this century are striking, as many scholars have commented, but such clubs exist to make demands of developed countries, not to make mutual concessions among developing countries. And no club had a balanced view of the overall Single Undertaking.

A third sort of horizontal club exists to *bridge* the gaps between opposed positions. The first "bridge club" was created in the Kennedy Round. After also being important in the Tokyo Round, the group was formalized as the Quadrilateral Group of Trade Ministers (US, EU, Japan, and Canada) at the 1981 Ottawa G7 summit, and later played a central role in the Uruguay Round. The old Quad has not met at ministerial level since 1999, though officials still meet in Geneva. Part of the effort to re-start the Doha Round after the failed Cancún ministerial in 2003 was a process involving the principal antagonists on agriculture: the US and the EU, who are opposed to each other; and Brazil and India who are opposed both to each other and to the US and the EU. These four repeatedly tried, and failed, to sort things out as a "new

Quad," especially in 2006 and 2007, sometimes including Japan and Australia in a G6. In July 2008, the Director-General convoked a new G7 by inviting China, evidently catching the minister by surprise. During the last big push to complete the round in the first part of 2011, the core bridge club was called the G5, but a larger group, the G11 (which included Canada), also played a role. Despite trying many configurations, involving ministers away from Geneva and ambassadors at the WTO, nothing stable emerged in the Doha Round. None were effective in building an integrative consensus. The absence of a functional equivalent to the old Quad, despite valiant efforts by Pascal Lamy to bring one into being, hurt the Doha Round.

Design Errors

The conclusion of the first part of this chapter could be summarized simply: given exogenous structural change, Doha *as designed* could not succeed.

If the core of any trade agreement is market access for goods, or bargaining on the terms of trade (Bagwell and Staiger 2011) then economists suggest that there was no deal to be done, not (merely) because of changes in the world but because of how the potential bargain was constructed (Evenett 2013). Elsewhere I discuss the issues at stake in the Doha debates about "modalities," the blueprint for negotiations on market opening agreements. In brief, negotiators failed to reconcile the possible incommensurable objectives of paragraph 16 of the Doha Declaration, to cut high tariffs (mostly in developing countries) more aggressively than low tariffs while expecting "less than full reciprocity" from developing countries, including the large emerging economies of Brazil, China and India.

The other design error was that the Doha Round agenda did not match the twenty-first century trading system following fragmentation in the industrial organization of production. This new reality was not well-addressed in the Doha Round agenda, not least because of its origins in the Uruguay Round "built-in agenda," the residue of the trade policy of the 1980s, based on older theoretical models. Trade theory of the twenty-first century is based on **heterogeneous firm models** (Melitz 2003) and global value chains (Van Assche 2012). The insight from modern trade theory is that the largest productivity gains come from *new* firms entering export and import markets and from incumbent exporters' introduction of *new* products into existing markets and diversification of their exports into *new* markets. This emerging theory provides an explanation for why relatively few firms export their output and why exports represent only a small portion of sales for firms that do trade. The theory also helps us better understand why the firms that participate in international markets tend to be larger and more productive, and pay higher wages than firms that do not. The new trade *policy* is about reducing the barriers that keep potential trading firms from committing to international markets, such as the often cumbersome and expensive procedures that firms face for getting products across borders, or compliance with non-tariff requirements for market access. Trade policy now includes both measures imposed at the border, such as tariffs and import quotas; *and* regulatory policies, such as standards, competition policy, innovation and investment policies, intellectual property rights, and banking and business licenses (Ciuriak et al. 2015).

The positive signals exchanged in July 2008 notwithstanding (WTO 2008b), real negotiations were never engaged on trade in services while negotiators waited for a level of ambition to be set between agriculture and NAMA, consistent with paragraph 24 of the Hong Kong declaration. Was that a design error, an exogenous structural problem, or an endogenous failure of negotiators to adjust their thinking to a changing world?

The Shifting Centre of Gravity in the Trading System

However we describe twenty-first century global governance, something has changed even from the immediate post-Cold War system, let alone the post-Second World War system centred on the North Atlantic. The endogenous and exogenous factors described above can be brought together by considering how the centre of gravity of the trading system has shifted along three dimensions. First, we can argue that a key driver of previous rounds was a need for transatlantic accommodation, as shown in Table 10.1. Not this time—the EU was inside the zone of possible agreement on most issues. And it is now clear that the US cannot supply the systemic public good of an open liberal multilateral trading system either alone or with European help.

Second, in the 1990s, a belief that the world had been dominated by the North Atlantic area for too long combined with a desire to "rebalance" all Uruguay Round bargains led to the "implementation" debates, which led to the Seattle breakdown when developing countries learned to exercise their collective institutional power, which led in turn both to calling the round the "**Doha Development Agenda**" and to paragraph 12 of the Doha Declaration on "implementation-related issues and concerns" (Ndirangu 2011). Members (and scholars) were not all convinced in 2001 that the **special and differential treatment** demanded, notably in paragraphs 16 and 50 of the Doha Declaration, would actually be good for development.

The original claims for rebalancing assumed that all problems in the trading system line up on North–South divides, thereby evading the big South–South barriers in goods, and agriculture, not to mention the many errors of omission and commission in services and other regulatory domains that may limit developing country participation in global value chains. Reducing the impasse to a North–South divide inherently assumes that all issues are equal for all players, and that all players are reducible to north and south, without accounting for tensions among emerging economies (China supported the G20 on agriculture, for example, but did not support the subset who met as NAMA-11), or tensions among OECD countries, or the evident willingness to give the majority of developing countries the round for free by not requiring tariff reductions to be made by various categories of smaller economies. The real problem with asking for "less than full reciprocity" (LTFR) might be that big developing countries now hide behind a principle that made (some) sense when their weight in trade was smaller. India led the rebalancing movement of the 1990s, which

Table 10.1   The Political Motivations of Trade Rounds

Round	Dates	Motivation
First 5 rounds	1947–56	Rebuilding Europe; making the world safe for the New Deal
Dillon Round	1960–1	Treaty of Rome
Kennedy Round	1964–67	Common market begins
Tokyo Round	1973–79	UK joins EEC
Uruguay Round	1986–94	EEC expansion, in part
Doha Round	2001–11	China

certainly led to unhelpful aspects of the Doha Declaration, but how much of that agenda could be conceded to small countries with no harm to the system, if the large developing country markets were not included? LTFR is in effect a redistributive principle, a new way to articulate special and differential treatment, but redistribution always raises questions about who pays, who benefits, and whether the balance is worth it.

The question for negotiations is not merely what the new rules should be, but who the rules should constrain. Since constraints have costs, the related question is who should pay? The US says that the emerging economies have to pay more, but these countries reply, not yet. This understated observation from the 2011 Ministerial Conference may be the heart of the matter: "There was a shared sense that a key question to unlock the current impasse is the balance in contributions and responsibilities between emerging and advanced economies, although there were different views as to what the appropriate shares in this balance should be" (WTO 2011a). The emerging economies insist on equality with the established major players, see international organization rules as a way to constrain the EU and the US rather than themselves, and tend to support the status quo. Conscious of domestic poverty and underestimating their own growing impact on other countries and the world economy, they are unwilling to pay the costs of leadership (Kahler 2013, 718, 22). India and Brazil see themselves as a voice for developing countries, which would be fine if they can help to find compromises in bridge clubs instead of expecting to benefit from the LFTR principle. The indispensable country, however, is China.

Finally, the analysis was that the Atlantic era had come to an end, which was right, but nobody anticipated in 2001 that the real dynamic would be provided by China. The Doha Declaration was not prepared with China in mind, with the exception of one paragraph about "recently acceded Members" (RAMs). Most observers of the Doha Round, me included, hardly mentioned China in commentaries on the round for the first 5 to 7 years. Participants thought that China had changed in July 2008, becoming more assertive and learning to play a broader role in support of the multilateral system. China had never before participated in anything like the G7 in the WTO. They know they benefit from the system. They are now forced to be a major player but do not want to be out in front any more than they wish to be seen as standing in the way. Participants believe that China's ultimate goal is to be like everyone else. China therefore resents some of the terms imposed as part of their WTO accession, apparently, some think, as much as they resented the nineteenth-century unequal treaties, which may have limited their willingness to accept demands for even more liberalization.

Before China joined the WTO, analysts worried that it would be unable to meet transparency requirements due to domestic politics, institutional capacity, and the nature of the legal system (Ostry 1998; Wu 2002). Although reform did occur in the years since accession, issues with regulatory transparency, notification of subsidies, and implementation of reforms at sub-central government levels persist. Notifications under WTO agreements do not cover all years or the magnitude of support provided, and the application of reform is inconsistent at different levels of government. Analysts cannot determine if reform is consciously resisted, or is impeded by limited technical and institutional capacity (Biukovic 2008; OECD 2009; United States 2012). And yet since it joined in 2001, China has submitted over 850 notifications under the Agreement on Technical Barriers to Trade (TBT), many of which are environmental notifications, in some years exceeding the more established members. Of course it has been said that China emphasizes codification rather than implementation—the government may find it easier to file WTO notifica-tions than to make real changes in how things work. Nevertheless, in the final "transitional review" by the TBT Committee, other members praised China for making many of its regulations and policies more transparent and predictable (WTO 2011b). Chinese governance is not as trans-parent as more established members might like, let alone what western firms might like, but WTO documents are a mine of information about the domestic administration of standards and con-formity assessment. Members would like to know more, and would like the administrative proced-ures to be more open and accessible to foreign firms, but much of what members know that they find problematic about China's practices they know because of that country's commitment to WTO transparency. To take a different example, China has learned through participation in the Trade Policy Review process, willingly responding to questions in most areas of policy. They still react conservatively to requests for transparency in areas they think are sensitive such as subsidies or gov-ernment procurement—their cultural predispos-ition to secrecy is the obverse of the American obsession with sunshine. But socialization of Chinese officials through WTO participation does seem to be happening (Johnston 2008). The gov-ernment evidently adjusts its regulatory practices in light of WTO obligations (Wong 2013), but it is still far from the liberal model of the administra-tive state.

Generations of Atlanticism, that is of shared elite perceptions, helped underpin the post-Second World War order. Nothing comparable exists for the new order. Trade policy is still foreign policy, but unlike the US interest in using trade to pro-mote European integration during the Cold War, further integration of China into the world econ-omy presents foreign policy problems as much as opportunities. Every previous round has only

crystallized when the US and the Europeans had reached a basic accommodation. Now everyone can see that this time the blockage is across the Pacific. The WTO is the only place for a trade accommodation between the US and China, but until fundamental problems in the relationship are solved, something that is unlikely to happen in Geneva, the WTO will be blocked. And not just the WTO. Problems exist in every area of global gov-ernance, and one of the reasons is that trans-Pacific relationship. The Americans had learned how to dance with the Russians during the Cold War, as they have with the EU, but they are still trying to figure it out with the Chinese, and vice versa. In a world marked by unprecedented levels of eco-nomic, security, and environmental interdepend-ence, to argue for the necessity of partnership is not wooly liberal idealism, but "the highest form of realism" (Cox 2012, 381).

Conclusion: What Ails Doha?

The WTO is fine, even if the Doha Round is dead. We should avoid the misplaced concreteness of thinking that nothing is happening unless a large multilateral conference is able to promulgate new written rules, and if we cannot see those commitments explicitly implemented. Big conferences or negotiated texts are not the source of order. Codification follows social interaction; it does not lead (Wolfe 2005). Policy changes before it gets written down. The influence on the global trading system of the normative frame-work established by the WTO is undiminished. Members make active use of the transparency mech-anisms and the dispute settlement system. The prem-ise of this chapter, therefore, is that we need a parsimonious diagnosis of the Doha impasse before choosing to prescribe anything from the pharmaco-peia of remedies for what ails the round. We also need such a diagnosis if we are to understand the fac-tors reshaping the trading system.

First Diagnose . . .

Taking *exogenous* structural factors first, the world changed out from under the round, although the ability to perceive that change varied among negotiators. The trends shown in Figures 10.1 and 10.2 above are clear in retrospect, but the way they altered everyone's perceptions of the outside options (the alternatives to negotiated agreement) may have happened too slowly to be obvious. Negotiators can be trapped by misconceptions, holding out for the wrong things, or things no longer attainable. The deal imagined in 2001 was no longer interesting in 2008, and it is not interesting now, even if everyone may come to regret not agreeing to bindings on current applied rates of tariffs and subsidies. The problems with the modalities for the negotiations mentioned above no doubt exacerbated the impact of structural change, contributing to the greater appeal of the outside options for many members. In short, the deal on offer was not rich enough for the major players to be worth the bother, especially when members have other tools to deal with the increasing role of China (Hoekman 2012a).

Turning to *endogenous* institutional factors, the number of participants and the complexity of the agenda did not create the deadlock. The asymmetry of interests among the leading players alone would be enough to ensure that an outcome would only be possible with a package treated as a Single Undertaking. Members want different things from the WTO, all of which are in the Doha mandate, but the breakdown was on core issues. It is the leads that were the problem in this play, not the chorus, even if the leads sometimes played to the gallery. Some think that developing countries hold the trading system hostage for irrelevant issues, but we have no idea what smaller players would do if the largest agreed among themselves, and showed commitment to a stronger and more open trading system. Most small members are represented in clubs, so it was never hard to configure a representative Green Room. The fundamental puzzle remains that the leading members did not and do not agree, and that is not a process issue. IF the G5 had agreed among themselves as late as April 2011, AND IF the other six in the G11 had also agreed, would it have been possible to get the rest of the membership to agree on a Doha Round outcome? We cannot know, but I would give a positive estimate.

Reshaping the Trading System

Analysts often prescribe institutional reform as a solution to the WTO's negotiating difficulties, but given my diagnosis, treatment implies accepting that some factors are beyond the reach of the WTO, while others were not significant to the outcome. And treatment begins by accepting that outcome: the Doha Round is dead. Nobody wants to preside over this first failure by signing the death certificate, but the grieving relatives should send Doha to the Old Rounds Home until members can start fresh on devising an agenda and modalities to harvest the important work that was done during the round, notably on agriculture and NAMA. The full package as it stood in July 2008 or April 2011 will never be agreed on, but the issues have not gone away, even if this round as constructed cannot be concluded. No new package can be crafted by pretending that all the delicate compromises during the Doha Round never took place.

The WTO need not worry overmuch about the noodle soup of bilateral and regional trade negotiations. In the improbable event that all the negotiations succeed, and that strong obligations are actually implemented, firms in global value chains might have trouble learning how to navigate the thicket of rules without some kind of multilateral rectification. One thing is clear: with the exception of vital trade facilitation negotiations, the Doha Round never came to grips with the regulatory issues affecting both goods and services which can be hugely disruptive to global value chains. I am skeptical that the majors can successfully conclude ambitious deals on such domestic issues outside Geneva, not least because China, India, and Brazil are not participating in the so-called mega-regional negotiations (the Trans-Pacific Partnership and the new EU–US negotiations), and probably will not. If their acceptance of any new twenty-first century disciplines is thought important, it seems likely that those disciplines will eventually have to be negotiated at WTO.

While institutional reform in preparation for a new round of WTO negotiations is mostly not necessary, one problem deserves attention: the time has come for developing-country differentiation before resuming negotiations on agriculture and NAMA. While LDCs in the WTO are recognized as such based on the UN definition, members were allowed to designate themselves as "developing countries" when they joined the WTO. Whether or not the LTFR principle makes sense at all, it complicates negotiations among developing countries and makes negotiations between developed countries and emerging economies impossible.

The WTO managed to launch new negotiations at Doha in 2001, but then failed to conclude the round. What has changed during the course of the Doha Round that undermined the possibility of success? China. The temptation is to think that the problem is concluding a new agreement, and that something is wrong with WTO if it cannot do that. But failure to conclude an agreement may not signal a negotiation failure, any more than all the frenetic regional negotiations promise success.

Many of the Doha Round problems were due to a general malaise in multilateralism and to structural changes in the world economy that undermined the premises of the round. The weakness of global governance is a bigger question than this chapter can address, but salient. Power matters, it has changed, and the system has not caught up. The new Leaders G20 talks a lot but does very little. Until the US and China learn how to develop a trans-Pacific accommodation comparable to the one painstakingly established across the Atlantic, new negotiations will be stymied. That accommodation will require both of them to recognize that China now has a leadership role in global governance, and it will probably have to be a discussion that includes money, the environment, and security, not just trade. Improvements in how the WTO negotiates are possible, but the Doha Round did not fail for institutional reasons.

Acknowledgements

This chapter benefits from unattributed confidential interviews with WTO delegates and officials in Geneva at all stages of the Doha Round and from the discussions at the workshop on "The Multilateral Trading System in the 21st Century" hosted by George Washington University on 18 and 19 April 2013. I am grateful for the research assistance of Alina Kwan and Alison Breitman, and for the support of the ENTWINED research consortium, a project funded by the MISTRA Foundation of Sweden.

Notes

1   For background on what the WTO is and what it does, see the first chapter of Annual Report 2013 (WTO 2013).

2   It is more straightforward, for example, to explain a ministerial that succeeds—it can be compared to a ministerial that was deadlocked, with the differential outcome attributed to variation on factors that theory suggests ought to be explanatory (Odell 2009). For a survey of the literature on deadlocks, see Narlikar 2010.

3   For an excellent survey of the themes in these approaches to negotiations, see Hampson 1995.

4   On the difficulties of proving that macroeconomic variables are related to micro policy outcomes see Wolfe 2012, 781.

5   Space does not permit citation of the growing literature on currency movements as a trade issue.

6   The *acquis* is formalized in paragraph 4 of the Uruguay Round Final Act specifying that "the WTO Agreement shall be open for acceptance as a whole." In practice it means that the accumulated rules and practices must be accepted by new Members; and all Members apply all agreements simultaneously with respect to all

other Members. Clear differentiation in practice does not under-mine the principle.

7 I define a "club" as a group of countries united or associated for a particular purpose, a definition that intentionally evokes a looser form of association than the common tendency to see informal groups of states working within international organizations as "coalitions" (Wolfe 2007; Wolfe 2008; On coalitions as an important aspect of actor strategy in negotiations, see Odell 2006).

Key Terms

Single Undertaking
special and differential treatment

Doha Development Agenda
heterogeneous firm models

Questions for Review

1. What are the exogenous and endogenous factors that impeded the Doha Round?
2. Explain the difference between applied and bound tariff rates.
3. How has the role of China in world trade changed since it joined the WTO?
4. Is differentiation among developing countries necessary?
5. Must WTO negotiations be a Single Undertaking?

Further Resources

Bagwell and Staiger (2011); Hampson (1995); Kahler (2013); Narlikar (2010); Wolfe (2013).

References

Bagwell, K. and Staiger, R. W. (2011). "What do trade negotiators negotiate about? Empirical evidence from the World Trade Organization," *American Economic Review* 101,4 1238–73.

Biukovic, L. (2008). "Selective Adaptation of WTO Transparency norms and local practices in China and Japan," *J Int Economic Law 11*(4) (1 December), 803–25.

Brink, L. (2013). "Trends in agricultural domestic support worldwide and sustainable development implications," (paper delivered to the ICTSD workshop on Agricultural Trade Policy and Sustainable Development: Experience from India and Other Countries, New Delhi, India, 17 April 2013, http://ictsd.org/downloads/2013/04/ds-trends-ictsd-delhi-17-april-2013.pdf)

Brink, L., Orden, D., and Datz, G. (2013). "BRIC agricultural policies through a WTO lens," *Journal of Agricultural Economics 64*(1), 197–216.

Ciuriak, D. et al. (2015). "Firms in International trade: Trade policy implications of the new new trade theory," *Global Policy* 6:2 (May 2015), 130–40.

Cox, M. (2012). "Power shifts, economic change and the decline of the West?," *International Relations 26*(4) 1 December, 369–88.

Evenett, S. J. (2013). "The Doha Round impasse: A graphical account," draft ms 18 April 2013.

Hampson, F. O. (1995). *Multilateral negotiations: Lessons from arms control, trade and the Environment*. Baltimore: Johns Hopkins University Press.

Hoekman, B. (2012a). "Emerging economies and the WTO," (paper delivered to the conference on The Future of the WTO, Stanford University, 26–27 April).

Hoekman, B. (2012b). "Proposals for reform: A synthesis and assessment," in A. Narlikar, M. J. Daunton, and R. M. Stern (Eds), *The Oxford handbook on the world trade Organization*. Oxford, New York: Oxford University Press.

Johnston, A. I. (2008). *Social states: China in international institutions, 1980–2000*. Princeton, NJ: Princeton University Press.

Kahler, M. (2013). "Rising powers and global governance: Negotiating change in a resilient status quo," *International Affairs 89*(3), 711–29.

Mattoo, A. and Subramanian, A. (2011). "A China round of multilateral trade negotiations." Peterson Institute for International Economics, Working Paper WP11-22, December 2011.

Melitz, M. J. (2003). "The impact of trade on intra-industry reallocations and aggregate industry productivity," *Econometrica 71*(6) (November), 1695–725.

Narlikar, A., ed. (2010). *Deadlocks in Multilateral negotiations: Causes and solutions*. Cambridge: Cambridge University Press.

Ndirangu, N. (2011). "Special and differential treatment—Continuing saga of stalled negotiations," in P. S. Mehta, A. Kaushik, and R. S. Kaukab (Eds), *Reflections from the frontline: Developing country negotiators in the WTO*. Delhi: Academic Foundation, 177–94.

Odell, J. S. (2006). "Introduction," in Odell, John S., ed. *Negotiating trade: Developing countries in the WTO and NAFTA*. Cambridge: Cambridge University Press, 1–38.

Odell, J. S. (2009). "Breaking Deadlocks in international institutional negotiations: The WTO, Seattle and Doha," *International Studies Quarterly 53*(2), 273–99.

OECD. (2009). *China: Defining the boundary between the market and the state* (Paris: Organisation for Economic Co-operation and Development).

OECD. (2011). *Agricultural Policy Monitoring and Evaluation 2011: OECD countries and emerging economies* (Paris: Organisation for Economic Co-operation and Development).

Ostry, S. (1998). "China and the WTO: The transparency issue," *UCLA Journal of International Law and Foreign Affairs 3*(1) (1998), 1–22.

United States (2012). "U.S. Statement on the trade policy review of China delivered by Ambassador Michael Punke," Office of the United States Trade Representative, 12 June 2012.

Van Assche, A. (2012). "Global value chains and Canada's trade policy: Business as usual or paradigm shift?," Institute for Research on Public Policy, IRPP Study No. 32, June 2012.

Wolfe, R. (2005). "See you in Geneva? Legal (mis)representations of the trading system," *European Journal of International Relations 11*(3) (September 2005), 339–65.

Wolfe, R. (2007). "Adventures in WTO clubland," *Bridges 11*(4) (June–July), 21–2.

Wolfe, R. (2008). "Canada's adventures in clubland: Trade clubs and political influence." In J. Daudelin and D. Schwanen (Eds), *Canada among nations 2007: Room for manoeuvre* (Montreal & Kingston: McGill-Queen's University Press), 181–97.

Wolfe, R. (2009a). "The special safeguard fiasco in the WTO: The perils of inadequate analysis and negotiation." Groupe d'Economie Mondiale, SciencesPo, February.

Wolfe, R. (2009b). "The special safeguard fiasco in the WTO: The perils of inadequate analysis and negotiation." *World Trade Review 8*(4) (October), 517–44.

Wolfe, R. (2009c). "The WTO single undertaking as negotiating technique and constitutive metaphor," *Journal of International Economic Law 12*(4) (December 2009), 835–58.

Wolfe, R. (2010a). "Endogenous learning and consensual understanding in multilateral negotiations: Arguing and bargaining in the WTO," Canadian Agricultural Trade Policy and Competitiveness Research Network CATRPN Working Paper 2010-02 May 2010.

Wolfe, R. (2010b). "Sprinting during a marathon: Why the WTO ministerial failed in July 2008," *Journal of World Trade* 44(1) (February 2010), 81–126.

Wolfe, R. (2012). "Protectionism and multilateral accountability during the great recession: Drawing inferences from dogs not barking," *Journal of World Trade* 46(4) (August 2012), 777–814.

Wolfe, R. (2013). "Letting the sun shine in at the WTO: How transparency brings the trading system to life," World Trade Organization, Staff Working Paper ERSD-2013-03, March 2013.

Wong, S. (2013). "Varieties of the regulatory state and global companies: The case of China," *Global Policy* 4(2), 173–83.

WTO. (2001). "Ministerial declaration," World Trade Organization, Ministerial Conference, Fourth Session, Doha, 9–14 November, WT/MIN(01)/DEC/W/1, 14 November 2001.

WTO. (2005). "Doha work programme: Ministerial declaration," World Trade Organization, Ministerial Conference, Sixth Session Hong Kong, 13–18 December 2005 WT/MIN(05)/DEC, 22 December 2005.

WTO. (2008a). "Revised draft modalities for agriculture," World Trade Organization, Committee on Agriculture, Special Session, TN/AG/W/4/Rev.4, 6 December 2008.

WTO. (2008b). "Services Signalling conference: Report by the chairman of the TNC," World Trade Organization, JOB(08)/93, 30 July 2008.

WTO. (2011a). "Eighth ministerial conference, chairman's concluding statement," World Trade Organization, Ministerial Conference, Eighth Session Geneva, 15–17 December 2011, WT/MIN(11)/11, 17 December 2011.

WTO. (2011b). "Ninth annual transitional review mandated in paragraph 18 of the protocol of accession of the People's Republic of China," World Trade Organization, Committee on Technical Barriers to Trade, G/TBT/30, 23 November 2011.

WTO. (2012). *International trade statistics, 2012* (Geneva: World Trade Organization).

WTO. (2013). *Annual Report 2013* (Geneva: World Trade Organization).

Wu, E. Y. (2002). "China today: Why its accession to the world trade organization is inevitable and good for the international community," *Journal of International Economic Law* 5(3) (Aug), 689–718.

11 The World Trading Regime and Dispute Settlement

Gilbert Gagné

This chapter provides an overview of the evolution and main elements of the international trading system, with an emphasis on dispute settlement. In the first part, "From GATT to the WTO," I briefly consider the particular origins of the **General Agreement on Tariffs and Trade (GATT)**; the main principles of the world trading regime; the GATT rounds of multilateral trade negotiations; the structures, membership, and functioning of the **World Trade Organization** (WTO); the Doha Development Round; the issues raised for the GATT/WTO by the proliferation of **preferential trade agreements** (PTAs); and, finally, some key issues pertaining to the mandate and institutional reform of the WTO, as well as its role during the recent global economic crisis. Part 2 is dedicated to "GATT/WTO Dispute Settlement" and begins with some preliminary considerations, followed by the evolution of the GATT dispute settlement. I then discuss the main provisions of the Dispute Settlement Understanding (DSU) that resulted from the Uruguay Round, before turning to the essential aspects of its implementation, notably through statistics and dispute cases revealing of some

problems in the WTO dispute settlement. Concluding remarks follow.

From GATT to the WTO

The Origins of the GATT

The Great Depression of the 1930s, following the Wall Street Crash of 1929, was accompanied by strong protectionist or "beggar-thy-neighbour" measures on the part of states. In turn, such protectionism was blamed for adding to the severity of the economic crisis and contributing to the onset of the Second World War. Hence, one of the first tasks of the planners of the postwar era was to establish a system of norms, rules, procedures, and institutions to regulate the international economic order, based on the notion of open markets.

The Bretton Woods Conference, held in July 1944, led not only to the creation of the International Monetary Fund (IMF) and the World Bank (WB), but also proposed an International Trade Organization (ITO). The latter was agreed to by over 50 countries at the Havana Conference in March 1948. Beyond provisions to regulate international trade, the Havana Charter for an ITO also included provisions relating to economic development, employment, fair labour standards, investment, restrictive business practices, and commodity agreements. In this regard, it could be considered an ambitious and forward-looking document in that it addressed topics that were to be subject to multilateral rules, in some cases decades later. The Havana Charter exemplifies this period in the first decades after the war marked by the compromise of "embedded liberalism," i.e., the attempt to reconcile free trade at the international level with economic stability and full employment at the domestic level.[1] It is also known by the formula "Keynes at home and Smith abroad."

The ITO never came into being, however, because the United States Congress failed to ratify the Charter, since it satisfied neither American free traders nor protectionists.[2] In the meantime, the GATT[3] was concluded in Geneva in October 1947, whereby tariff concessions between 23 countries were made effective from June 1948. More limited in scope and only dealing with trade in goods, the GATT incorporated some of the provisions of the Charter through a "Protocol of Provisional Application." Devised as an "executive agreement" in US law, it also did not require ratification by Congress. The ITO Charter never having been in force, it was this "provisional" protocol that until 1995 presided over international trade. Thus, GATT referred to both a multilateral agreement and the institution that oversaw that agreement. Despite its informal origins, the GATT gradually evolved into an international organization in all but name.

The GATT, superseded in 1995 by the WTO, has been the main international institution established to promote order and cooperation in world trade relations. It is the only organization that provides a worldwide set of rules—rights and obligations voluntarily accepted by its states' parties—governing international trade. More than 97 per cent of world trade today takes place within the GATT/WTO regime.

The Main Principles of the World Trading Regime

The world trading regime is based on some key principles. One of the most important, and indeed the raison d'être of the GATT/WTO, is certainly **trade liberalization**. This is to be achieved by the gradual elimination of quantitative restrictions and other non-tariff measures, as well as the reduction and "binding" (fixing of maximum levels) of tariffs, which alone are recognized as a legitimate means of protection. Successive rounds of multilateral trade negotiations, until now all held under GATT auspices, led notably to a very substantial lowering of tariffs between states, now at negligible levels on industrial goods between developed countries.

Another central principle is *non-discrimination*, which has both external and internal dimensions. The external one consists of the **most-favoured-nation treatment**, whereby any trade advantage a WTO member gives to any country must be extended, immediately and unconditionally, to all other members (GATT Article I). A major exception is provided for customs unions and free trade areas, now generally referred to as PTAs, whose parties may give more favourable treatment to one another as long as they satisfy certain criteria intended to ensure, above all, that they do not raise new trade barriers vis-à-vis third countries, and that substantially all trade within the grouping is free (GATT Article XXIV). As for the internal dimension of non-discrimination, it revolves around *national treatment*, which requires WTO members to treat imported products no less favourably than domestic products with respect to internal taxes and regulations (GATT Article III).

The principle of *reciprocity* prescribes that a WTO member benefiting from another member's trade concessions must provide roughly equal advantages in return. This general requirement has been subject to exceptions in the case of developing states, which, in negotiations with developed countries, are not expected to fully reciprocate if this implies concessions inconsistent with their development needs (GATT Part IV). A further principle relates to *safeguards* and *fair trade*. Under the former, states may raise duties in response to "import surges" of products that, although fairly traded, cause or threaten serious injury to competing domestic producers. Under the latter, in response to unfair trade practices that cause or threaten material injury to a domestic industry, states may adopt anti-dumping and/or countervailing duties (CVDs) to offset dumping (the sale of a product at a lower price than in the home market or below its production cost) and subsidies (a government financial contribution that confers a benefit and that is specific to certain enterprises). See Table 11.1 for a summary of the main articles of the GATT.

GATT Rounds of Multilateral Trade Negotiations

Negotiation is the driving force of the world trade system. The GATT/WTO is to a great extent a negotiating forum in which trade policy commitments are agreed upon between states, against the background of the provisions of the various agreements already concluded. The multilateral trading regime has been expanded since the late 1940s, principally as a result of eight completed rounds of multilateral negotiations. The two most important and recent ones were the Tokyo Round from 1973 to 1979 and the Uruguay Round from

Table 11.1   Key GATT Articles

Article	Summary
I	General most-favoured-nation requirement
II	Tariff commitments (schedules of bindings)
III	National treatment
VI	Allows anti-dumping and CVDs in case dumping and subsidies cause or threaten material injury to a domestic industry
XI	Requires elimination of quantitative restrictions
XII	Allows trade restrictions if necessary to safeguard the balance of payments
XIX	Allows for emergency action to restrict imports of particular products if these cause or threaten serious injury to a domestic industry
XX	General exceptions— permits trade restrictions if necessary to attain non-economic objectives (health, environment)
XXII	Requires consultations between parties involved in trade disputes
XXIII	Main dispute settlement provision
XXIV	Sets out conditions under which free trade areas or customs unions may be formed
XXVIII bis	Calls for periodic multilateral trade negotiations to reduce tariffs
Part IV	Calls for more favourable and differential treatment of developing countries

Source: Adapted from Bernard M. Hoekman and Michel M. Kostecki, *The Political Economy of the World Trading System*, 3rd ed. Oxford: Oxford University Press, 2009, 186. By Permission of Oxford University Press.

1986 to 1994. Apart from a further reduction of tariffs and quotas, the Tokyo Round addressed trade obstacles known as non-tariff barriers, namely states' policies and measures, such as domestic subsidies and government procurement. As for the Uruguay Round, it included detailed schedules of tariff reductions and topics as diverse as dumping, subsidies, technical standards, customs valuation, as well as agriculture and textiles, the latter two until then having remained largely outside of GATT disciplines. The results of the Round also brought new areas, namely services, trade-related investments, and intellectual property, into the ambit of world trade rules. Comprised in the Uruguay Round agreements were three main institutional features: the charter for a WTO, a Trade Policy Review Mechanism (TPRM), and a new DSU, all meant to assist in the effective implementation of the substantive rules agreed to at the end of the Round.[4]

If successive GATT negotiations had significantly extended the scope of international trade provisions, the Uruguay Round formally transformed the GATT into a permanent institution, the WTO, in charge of overseeing trade relations among its members. The text of the WTO Agreement establishes a legal framework that ties together the various trade pacts negotiated under the GATT and includes institutional and procedural rules governing the activities of the organization.[5] Such a framework was intended to ensure a *single undertaking* approach to the results of the Uruguay Round. In contrast to previous GATT practice, WTO members had to accept all the results of the Round, although two plurilateral agreements remain, whose membership is optional, relating to government procurement and civil aircraft. As for the TPRM, it seeks to achieve "greater transparency in, and understanding of, the trade policies and practices of members," through notification and peer review/pressure, which may induce a change in states' policies toward greater conformity with WTO rules and principles.[6]

The Structures, Membership, and Functioning of the WTO

The WTO is headed by a Ministerial Conference that usually convenes every two years, while a General Council oversees the operations of the organization and its ministerial decisions, and acts as a Trade Policy Review as well as Dispute Settlement Body. The General Council counts three subsidiary bodies: a Council for Trade in Goods, a Council for Trade in Services, and a Council for Trade-Related Aspects of Intellectual Property Rights (TRIPS). Numerous specialized committees, working groups, and working parties deal with specific WTO agreements, such as the Agreement on Subsidies and Countervailing Measures (SCM),[7] and topics such as the environment, development, membership applications, and regional trade agreements (RTAs).[8] Finally, a Secretariat in Geneva, composed of little more than 600 people under the responsibility of a director-general, serves the WTO bodies and ensures the day-to-day functioning of the organization.

As of September 2014, the WTO had 160 members, which makes it ever closer to universal membership. Since its inception, 32 states have acceded to the WTO, including China in 2001, Saudi Arabia in 2005, and Russia in 2012. For new countries to join the WTO, not only should members consent, but the terms of accession must be agreed between the applicant and the WTO members. Each WTO member state may submit specific demands to the applicant country, both with regard to tariff and non-tariff issues, even beyond existing WTO disciplines. When it joins, a country's Protocol Of Accession is legally binding.[9]

Despite specific provisions for certain decisions to be taken, under the formula of one-state-one-vote, either by simple two-thirds or three-quarters major-ity, the WTO, like the GATT before it, has shied away from formal voting. As in the case of most inter-governmental institutions, decisions are usually made by consensus, i.e., when no member present at a meeting formally objects to a proposed deci-sion, as stipulated in Article IX of the WTO Agree-ment. Nevertheless, WTO members have been able to adopt some key decisions by consensus.[10] Even though the WTO Agreement contemplated that new provisions, amendments, and even new agree-ments could be negotiated and adopted at any time, members have also continued the GATT practice of negotiating new rules in the framework of broad, multilateral trade rounds, so that, since 1995, there has only been one amendment.[11]

The Doha Development Round

The ninth round of multilateral trade negotiations, known as the Doha Development Round, was launched in November 2001, with a view to better accommodating the needs of developing countries. Together with further negotiations on topics cov-ered by the WTO, such as geographical indications and the "built-in" agenda on agriculture, it has dealt with "new" issues such as trade facilitation. In December 2013, at the Ninth Ministerial Confer-ence in Bali, Indonesia, a first ever global trade agreement, approved by all WTO members, known as the Bali Package, was concluded. Covering four areas, notably trade facilitation measures, it repre-sents, however, a small part of the agenda of the Doha Round, whose future remains uncertain.[12] In fact, almost all of the Doha negotiations have stalled for the past few years. Among other initia-tives taken in response to this situation, a group of now 23 WTO members (involving most industrial states, with the European Union (EU) counted as one member) began in 2013 to negotiate a Pluri-lateral Trade in Services Agreement.[13]

The main stumbling blocks in the negotiation have again pertained to agriculture, as well as spe-cial and differential treatment for developing coun-tries.[14] The growing number of member states is a factor in explaining such stalemates. So are the emerging powers, mainly Brazil, China, and India, now more in a position to assert their views and interests vis-à-vis the developed countries. Smaller and poorer states have also been better prepared and organized. Unlike the preceding Uruguay Round, the single undertaking, whereby nothing is agreed until everything is agreed, seems to have made a successful outcome less likely.[15] Another factor relates to the fact that all the main powers (US, EU, Japan, China) now conclude their own PTAs, thereby giving them another venue for achiev-ing some of their trade objectives.[16] In such a con-text, no major power, and here the United States comes to mind, is willing to assume leadership to bring the Doha Round to a successful conclusion.[17] See Table 11.2 for a summary of the topics and out-comes of the main rounds of multilateral trade negotiations in the history of the GATT/WTO.

The GATT/WTO and Preferential Trade Agreements

The number of PTAs has been steadily increasing. With the exception of Mongolia, all WTO members are part of one or more of these, with some states belonging to as many as 30 PTAs, creating what has been described as a tangled "spaghetti bowl" of overlapping trade regulations. At the end of 2013, the WTO had received notification of 434 PTAs, 22 in the course of 2013, with 252 of these currently in force. Most of them are bilateral, cross-regional, and take the form of free trade areas. The trend toward PTAs between developed and developing countries continued in 2013, while the number of agreements between developing partners rose slightly compared with previous years. Although

Table 11.2   Main Rounds of Multilateral Trade Negotiations

Name	Period and Number of Parties	Topics	Outcomes
Geneva	1947 23 countries	Tariffs	Concessions on 45,000 tariff lines
Tokyo	1973–79 99 countries	Tariffs; Non-tariff measures	Average tariffs reduced by 33% to 6% on average for OECD manufacture imports; Voluntary codes of conduct agreed for all non-tariff issues except safeguards
Uruguay	1986–94 From 103 to 117 countries	Tariffs; Non-tariff measures; Services; Intellectual property; Trade-related investment measures; Dispute settlement; Transparency and surveillance of trade policies	Average tariffs reduced by 38% on average; Agriculture and textiles subjected to rules; Creation of WTO; New agreements on services and TRIPS; Majority of Tokyo Round codes extended to all WTO members
Doha	2001–150+ countries	Agricultural and industrial tariffs; Services; Geographical indications; Disciplines on competition, investment, government procurement and trade facilitation; WTO rules; Trade and environment	Transparency mechanism for PTAs; "Aid for Trade" initiative; Bali Package (trade facilitation); Market access and rule-making outcomes still undecided

Source: Adapted from Bernard M. Hoekman and Michel M. Kostecki, *The Political Economy of the World Trading System*, 3rd ed. Oxford: Oxford University Press, 2009, 133–4. By Permission of Oxford University Press.

some PTAs only apply to trade in goods, they are increasingly broader and, in many cases, deeper in their coverage, with provisions on services, investment, competition policy, trade facilitation, government procurement, intellectual property, electronic commerce, and, in some cases, labour and the environment.[18] As a result, PTAs often go beyond the rules contained in the multilateral agreements under the aegis of the WTO.[19] Most PTAs also include their own provisions for dispute settlement.[20]

The stalemate in the Doha Round and the proliferation of PTAs raise key issues for the world trading system. One concerns the enduring relevance of the WTO. Many states are now making PTAs the centrepiece of their commercial policy. For some WTO members, preferential trade accounts for more than 90 per cent of their trade exchanges. Another issue is whether PTAs are

"stepping stones" or "obstacles" to global free trade. There are two different views on this question. On the one hand, as some states further liberalize their trade, the overall outcome of PTAs is freer trade, as long as these do not raise new barriers to trade with third countries and trade creation (consumption shifts from high cost producers to low cost producers within the union, leading to an increase in efficiency) outweighs trade diversion (consumption shifts from low cost producers outside the trading bloc to high cost ones within it, leading to a decrease in efficiency). Also, to the extent that the trade principles and provisions at the basis of such PTAs are similar and consistent with WTO rules, and PTAs now involve nearly all countries, this would result in de facto multilateral liberalization. PTAs would then act as a vanguard of trade liberalization, which could later be more easily emulated and formally multilateralized.[21] On the other hand, to the extent that PTAs necessarily involve discrimination vis-à-vis third countries and result in trade diversion, they hinder world trade. Moreover, as various PTAs have their own particular scope and content, usually reflecting the objectives and interests of their most important states' parties, thus allowing these states' preferences to be more easily pursued, this would complicate, if not prevent, the likelihood of such differences later being harmonized at the multilateral level.[22]

To better address the concerns raised by growing economic regionalism/bilateralism, the WTO General Council decided in December 2006 to create a Transparency Mechanism for RTAs. It sets specific guidelines for PTAs, mainly the new ones, but also those concluded prior to 2006 or under negotiation, to be notified to the WTO Secretariat, with the related information and data to be provided. It also requires the Secretariat to prepare a factual presentation on each PTA and for each of them to be reviewed by WTO members.[23]

The WTO: Issues and Context

Within the past few years, attempts to have the WTO deal with issues like investment and competition law or the growing overlap between trade regulations and those in such areas as labour standards and the environment have been strongly resisted by many members, mainly from the developing world. This refers to the trade linkage or "trade and" debate, relating to the boundaries of the WTO, toward which there are two main contending perspectives. For one, issues such as labour market or environmental regulations should remain under the sole responsibility of the international regimes and organizations specifically mandated to deal with them. For the other, the centrality of the WTO should bring it to help resolve the conflicts that may arise between regulations coming under different institutions. Indeed, because

of the key features of its Dispute Settlement Mechanism (DSM), the WTO has seen many voices calling for the broadening of its purview.[24] In early 2001, three former directors-general issued a public statement to the effect that "[t]he WTO cannot be used as a Christmas tree on which to hang any and every good cause that might be secured by exercising trade power."[25]

It might be worth mentioning that this issue arose in the 1980s when tougher international standards were sought for intellectual property rights. After the United States and the EU failed to secure such strengthening within the World Intellectual Property Organization, they moved the issue to the GATT, which was at first reluctant to assume such responsibility arguably outside of its jurisdiction. On the other hand, during the Uruguay Round the US and the EU pushed for TRIPS to be handled by the WTO, especially in view of the stronger DSM that was simultaneously under negotiation.

Much attention was dedicated to the institutional reform of the WTO in the first decade of the twenty-first century, notably the Sutherland Report and the Warwick Report.[26] Both identified key institutional problems in the WTO and made recommendations for reform. Their proposals were crafted so that they could be implemented without new rules or agreements having to be negotiated. For Debra Steger, former director of the WTO Appellate Body (AB) Secretariat, it is not the final phase of decision-making based on consensus that causes a problem, but rather the lack of formal structures at the initial and intermediate stages, as well as the absence of a management or executive body, similar to the executive boards of the IMF and the WB, which leads to a lack of direction and drift in the WTO. The roles of the director-general and the Secretariat should also be enhanced, while developing a parliamentary dimension to the WTO would go a long way to remedy its alleged lack of transparency, accountability, and legitimacy.[27] The mandate of the WTO also needs to be clarified, while the "WTO should be recognized for what it is—an international organization that regulates trade as well as international economic relations generally."[28]

Unlike the Great Depression, the recent global economic crisis has not been followed by broad protectionist measures, and those that were adopted have tended to comply with international trade obligations. This testifies to the importance of the rules-based system of the WTO and its trade monitoring reports. Even the resort to trade remedies, allowed under WTO rules as a means of protection in specific conditions, has not risen to have any significant adverse impact on world trade.[29]

GATT/WTO Dispute Settlement

Some Considerations on Dispute Settlement

The key implementing or enforcement mechanism in the GATT/WTO regime has revolved around dispute settlement procedures, which seek to solve conflicts that may arise between states. This means that apart from state governments notifying the WTO of trade measures and reviews of their trade policies through the TPRM, WTO interventions are limited to cases of complaints brought to its attention. Obviously, a rarity of disputes may not necessarily reflect widespread rule observance,[30] but rather states' reluctance to object to others' measures, either because they use similar ones or fear stimulating counterclaims or detrimental consequences in non-trade areas (e.g., defence cooperation or continued aid flows). Using the same logic, a great number of conflicts may not be attributable to a large disregard for international trade provisions, but rather a desire of members to ensure strict compliance with WTO rules.

A DSM, especially a strengthened one under the WTO, can also act as a deterrent against litigation and play a crucial role in pressing states to solve their differences, sometimes in the course of the dispute settlement process, through a mutually agreed solution (MAS). Yet disputes could still be addressed outside WTO auspices. Trade conflicts between major powers sometimes escalated regardless of the GATT and were resolved bilaterally. In cases of bilateral solutions, disputes may be settled without due regard to international trade provisions.[31] The WTO DSU, then, must not be confused with a "real" enforcement mechanism as, for the most part, "enforcement" of GATT/WTO rules has taken the form of self-discipline or retaliation.[32]

I first review the evolution of the procedures and provisions pertaining to GATT dispute settlement to better grasp the key elements of the stronger DSM under the WTO, before analyzing its implementation.

The Evolution of the GATT Dispute Settlement

An important element of the GATT/WTO framework consists of its provisions for consultation, conciliation, and dispute settlement, as contained in Articles XXII and XXIII of the GATT. States are required to consult with other member countries, particularly when one member feels that benefits due to it are "nullified or impaired" by the conduct of another.[33] In case bilateral consultations fail to settle the problem, GATT/WTO may offer its good offices and act as conciliator. Should the dispute still not be resolved, an ad hoc panel of three neutral experts would examine the factual and legal aspects of the conflict, help the parties find a solution acceptable to both sides, and if no such solution could be attained, make findings and recommendations for the GATT/WTO Council to adopt. Panel reports, as for virtually all decisions in GATT, were adopted by consensus, i.e., when they did not raise objections from any state. When the reports were adopted, in case the recommendations were not carried out, the GATT Council could, as a last resort, authorize retaliation by allowing the impaired party to withdraw trade concessions to the offending member.

If the GATT dispute settlement process were initially a relatively informal one, it became more formal with the use of objective panels from the 1950s. Before that, disputes were considered in broader working parties composed of government representatives. Increasingly, panel reports focused on precise and concrete issues of "violations" of treaty obligations. At the end of the Tokyo Round in 1979, an understanding on dispute settlement was adopted,[34] which embodied these developments.[35]

There was some resistance, including within the Secretariat, to make dispute settlement evolve toward a "rules-based" system from those who saw GATT primarily as a forum for negotiation. Such views echoed the contrast between the perception and treatment of the GATT in the United States and Europe, the former viewing it as largely a legal regime, the latter dealing with GATT as a diplomatic and political system. Over time, these differences lessened in favour of a legal treatment of the GATT/WTO.

The Uruguay Round negotiations sought to remedy the main problems in the DSM that plagued the GATT regime: delays in establishing panels and in concluding dispute proceedings, the ability of disputants to block the consensus needed to approve panel recommendations and authorize retaliation, and the difficulty in securing compliance with GATT rulings. Reforms adopted at the mid-term review of the Uruguay Round, which became effective in 1989, included an optional arbitration procedure whereby disputing parties could agree to abide by the arbitral award, and confirmed the authority of the director-general to form a panel in case disputants disagreed. Hence,

there was greater automaticity in decisions on the establishment, terms of reference, and composition of panels, so that such decisions no longer depended on the consent of the parties to a dispute. There was also a provision to complete panel reviews within nine months. Yet, as to the question of Council adopting panel reports, it was still possible for a losing party to prevent consensus.[36]

The WTO Dispute Settlement Understanding

In the course of the Uruguay Round, states agreed on a strengthened DSU.[37] Mindful of the need for "security," "predictability," and "the effective functioning of the WTO," member states established a DSM characterized as "essential" for achieving a "prompt," "satisfactory," and "positive" settlement of disputes, by providing recommendations and rulings in a way that "serves to preserve the rights and obligations of Members under [all trade agreements covered by the WTO], and to clarify the existing provisions of those agreements in accordance with customary rules of interpretation of public international law" (DSU Article 3).

The DSU provides for an integrated mechanism to settle disputes under all covered agreements (DSU, Article 1 and Appendix 1) with the WTO Council, acting as the Dispute Settlement Body (DSB), exercising authority. The DSU extended the greater automaticity agreed to at the 1988 mid-term review to the whole process, including the adoption of panel reports, and strict time limits were set. It also instituted an AB, to review panel rulings, as well as procedures to ensure the proper observance of WTO decisions, including monitoring compliance actions and retaliation in case of non-compliance.

Of utmost significance are provisions whereby a panel report and, in case of appeal, an AB report, are automatically adopted unless the DSB decides by unanimous consensus against adoption (DSU

Articles 16.4 and 17.14). Also applying to the establishment of panels (DSU Article 6.1), this is known as the *reverse or negative consensus* rule. It represented a complete shift from previous practice when a single state, often the losing party in a dispute, could block the adoption of a panel report and, thus, any possibility of action for GATT. Unlike dispute panels, whose three members continue to be selected on an ad hoc basis, the AB is a standing entity whose essential role is to review, at the request of parties to a dispute, the legal aspects of panel findings to ensure that WTO provisions are interpreted consistently. It is composed of seven persons, three of whom serve on any one case, all of whom are from different member countries, who may serve two consecutive terms of four years.

Panel recommendations, which may be approved or modified as a result of an appeal, are to be fully implemented. If it is impracticable to comply immediately, it should be done within a reasonable period of time, either proposed by the member concerned, mutually agreed by the disputants, or determined by an arbitrator (in the latter case, not exceeding 15 months) (DSU Article 21.3). In case disputants disagree as to the existence or consistency of measures taken to comply, the original panel is reconvened (then referred to as a "compliance panel") and submits a report, which could be appealed (DSU Article 21.5). If the member concerned is found not to be in full compliance with WTO recommendations, and if subsequently no satisfactory compensation has been agreed to, the complaining party may be authorized by the DSB to retaliate by suspending the application of WTO obligations to the offending state (DSU Article 22.2).

Although retaliation should normally entail suspension of concessions or other obligations in the sector subject to a dispute (DSU Article 22.3), when that is not practicable or effective, concessions may be suspended in other sectors under the same agreement. Ultimately, in serious enough circumstances, concessions under another covered agreement may be suspended, i.e., cross-retaliation. Retaliation is authorized unless the DSB decides by consensus against such action. However, at the request of the member concerned, the proposed level of retaliation may be referred to arbitration, normally conducted by the original panel or else by an arbitrator appointed by the director-general. The DSB can then authorize retaliation consistent with the arbitrator's decision (DSU Article 22.6). As under GATT, retaliatory measures should be equivalent to the level of nullification or impairment of benefits accruing to the complaining party(ies) under the relevant WTO agreement(s) (DSU Article 22.4).

Litigation, often over complex legal matters, is not an easy and quick process. Formal and detailed procedures have to be followed. From the time consultations are requested to authorizing countermeasures in case of non-compliance, the whole dispute process may take about 48 months, or four years, less when panel decisions are not appealed. The time allotted for the conclusion of a panel review, as a general rule, is six months and cannot exceed nine months (DSU Article 12.9). Particular consideration is given to developing-country members and special procedures apply in the case of least-developed countries.

Presumably in view of its novelty, a ministerial declaration adopted at the end of the Uruguay Round provided for a full review of the DSU four years after the entry into force of the WTO Agreement. The Ministerial Conference would have to decide whether the DSM should be continued, modified, or terminated.[38] During the review that took place in 1998–99, WTO members expressed their general satisfaction with the DSM, agreed that the system only needed to be fine-tuned, were reluctant to make major changes, and preferred to wait for clearer evidence over a longer period of time.[39] As the legal mandate for the review expired in July 1999 without any conclusion, negotiations on dispute settlement have been included in the Doha Round, where much attention has been devoted to compliance, retaliation, and modifying the remedies available as part of the enforcement stage.[40]

The Implementation of the WTO Dispute Settlement Mechanism

The "contracting parties" during GATT history came to resort more and more to its DSM. Panels were established well over 100 times and, by the end of the Uruguay Round, more frequently than ever before. Many countries, including the United States, which had been the largest single applicant for dispute settlement procedures in GATT, found it useful to bring issues to panels as part of their broader approach to trade diplomacy. Yet, recourse to dispute settlement under GATT remained relatively uncommon.[41]

As anticipated, the number of dispute cases increased with the advent of the WTO in 1995. As of 1 January 2014, 474 requests for consultations had been notified. Nearly 95 per cent of the matters subject to disputes have involved trade in goods. The agreements most often invoked, together with the more general provisions of the GATT (in 379 instances), are those relating to anti-dumping measures (102), subsidies and CVDs (99), and agriculture (71). With respect to "new" areas of regulation, such as services, intellectual property, and sanitary and phytosanitary measures (SPS), the number of disputes has been limited but fairly steady since the WTO's inception.[42]

Even though developing states have more often resorted to the WTO DSM, increasing their use in recent years, developed countries have remained its primary users. The US and the EU have proved its heaviest users, with 196 complaints involving either one or the other as plaintiff. This represents 41.3 per cent of all dispute cases. Either the US or the EU has been the respondent in 199 cases, or 42.2 per cent of the total complaints. Furthermore, 51 of these disputes have been directly between the US and the EU.[43]

Of all complaints, nearly two thirds have ended before the adoption of a panel report, either through MAS or after the disputed measure(s) ceased to exist or the commercial interest changed. The total number of panel reports being circulated is 153, with 66.7 per cent of these having been reviewed by the AB.[44] When different panel requests involved similar issues, these were often consolidated and a single panel was set up. In between 80 and 90 per cent of the disputes, the views of the complainants have prevailed.[45]

There have been 47 disputes over compliance with WTO recommendations and rulings, 60 per cent of these leading to a panel report. To date, the percentage of compliance panel reports subject to appeal is 67.9 per cent.[46] Of all AB reports adopted between 1995 and 2010, 81 per cent modified the panels' findings, four per cent reversed them, and only 15 per cent upheld them.[47] Twelve of these disputes over compliance led to a request for authorization to retaliate and the DSB authorized suspension of concessions in eight cases, with six of these involving two of the WTO's most powerful members, the US (four cases) and the EU (two cases). This makes one conclude that the WTO DSM has an admirable compliance record.[48]

While the DSM under the GATT was often paralyzed, the DSM under the WTO constitutes a significant improvement. Overall, the strengthening of the rule of law has led to a greater respect for international trade rules. States have usually abided by WTO rulings, even when their views did not prevail. As a result, the vast majority of dispute cases have been resolved with due regard to existing WTO provisions. The WTO DSM is widely perceived as an example of the primacy of law and international institutions over *realpolitik*. Yet, the

DSM since the WTO's inception has raised criticism, notably over the level of scrutiny of states' measures, particularly trade remedy decisions,[49] and has experienced some problems, with significant delays at almost all stages of the process.

An analysis of WTO jurisprudence reveals that panels and the AB have in general applied intrusive standards of review, not only for the interpretation of WTO law, but also of factual findings.[50] In some cases the WTO adjudicating bodies have been accused of exceeding their authority by adding to member states' obligations or limiting their rights, instead of merely clarifying the scope of the existing rules of the world trading regime. The main problems with delays pertain to panel reviews, which, from the establishment of a panel until the circulation of its report, have taken on average 14.7 months. The panel process has been completed within the statutory time limits in only 10 instances, while for 42 disputes it took more than 16 months and, in five cases, even more than two years. Yet the prompt settlement of disputes is essential to the effective functioning of the WTO, especially in view of the fact that the DSU lacks interlocutory and retrospective relief.[51]

Besides, the outcomes from the pursuit of the WTO dispute settlement process are not always conclusive, due to respondents' stances, as in the long conflict between four Latin American countries and the United States over the EU regime for the importation, sale, and distribution of bananas (*EC–Bananas* (DS27)) or the Canadian and US complaints against the EU ban on meat and meat products treated with certain growth hormones (*EC–Hormones* (DS26) (DS48)). This is also the case owing to the equivocal provisions, judicial economy,[52] incomplete analysis, and application of the interpretative rules of public international law, as in the dispute over Canada's exports of softwood lumber to the United States (*US–Softwood Lumber IV* (DS257)).

EC–Bananas figured periodically on the WTO dispute settlement agenda for 16 years, from 1996 to 2012, and presented a most difficult implementation problem resulting from divergent US and EU interpretations of the DSU. While the US insisted that it be authorized to suspend concessions following the EU's failure to put in place a WTO-consistent regime, the latter argued for its new regime to be reviewed by the WTO before any retaliatory action could be taken. The resolution of this conflict took so long because the EU was torn between its respect for WTO obligations and its preferential treatment, for development purposes, of African, Caribbean, and Pacific (ACP) countries.[53] As for *EC–Hormones*, under the SPS Agreement,[54] any trade limitation must be scientifically based, whereas the EU insisted on potential health risks posed by growth hormones.[55] In July 1999 the DSB authorized the United States and Canada to suspend concessions to the EU.[56] Interestingly, the absence of a review mechanism for retaliatory action in the DSU gave rise to a dispute when, in 2003, the EU estimated that it had implemented the WTO rulings (DS320) (DS321).[57] The EU later reached an agreement with the US in May 2009 and with Canada in March 2011.[58]

In *US–Softwood Lumber IV*, the panel found one issue to be dispositive of the case, following judicial economy, so did not investigate further. When the AB reversed this key finding, there weren't enough facts for it to rule on the consistency with WTO law of the US CVDs on Canadian lumber.[59] Based on the criteria for the interpretation of treaties under the Vienna Convention on the Law of Treaties (VCLT),[60] the first of which is "the ordinary meaning [of] the terms of the treaty in their context and in the light of its object and purpose" (Article 31), the AB focused on the exact words of the relevant provisions of the SCM Agreement to reverse the panel's finding. Since ordinary meaning can be determined in a number of ways,

WTO tribunals have been particularly keen to establish it by referring to dictionary definitions.[61] Such very extensive use of dictionary meanings has led some to ironize that the *New Oxford Shorter English Dictionary*—the AB's favourite dictionary—has become a "covered agreement"![62] Such "semantic" analysis in this case led to odd results, which arguably were contrary to states' intentions when the relevant provisions were agreed upon.[63] For Gary Horlick, first chair of the WTO Permanent Group of Experts on Subsidies, the AB's conclusions were undoubtedly wrong.[64]

On the trade linkage debate, some argue that the WTO DSM has proved flexible enough, through the general exceptions under GATT Article XX, for balancing trade concerns with others such as public health, as in *EC–Asbestos* (DS135), or environmental protection, as in *US–Shrimp* (DS58).[65] In any case, this is a daunting task as the "[r]ecommendations and rulings of the DSB cannot add to or diminish the rights and obligations [of WTO members] provided in the covered agreements" (DSU Article 3.2). If the applicable law for WTO adjudication is the one referred to in WTO agreements, academic opinion is divided as to whether non-WTO rules could be relevant for WTO adjudication purposes and, if so, under what conditions.[66] Table 11.3 provides a summary of the important WTO dispute cases referred to in this section.

Table 11.3   Important WTO Dispute Cases

Case	Period	Complainant(s) vs. Defendant	Outcome*
Hormones (DS26, DS48, DS320, DS321)	January 1996–July 1999; November 2004–March 2011	United States, Canada vs. EU	EU import ban on hormones-treated beef meat overruled. Cases unsolved after appeals, re-examinations, arbitrations, and retaliations (US: US$116.8 million; Canada: C$11.3 million). After appeals, DS320 and DS321 cases solved through MASs.
Bananas (DS27)	February 1996–May 2000; November 2005–November 2012	Ecuador, Guatemala, Honduras, Mexico, United States vs. EU	EU banana import regime overruled. Case solved through MASs after appeals, re-examinations, arbitrations, and retaliations (US: US$191.4 million; Ecuador US$201.6 million) After re-examinations, appeals and delays, case solved through MASs.
Shrimp (DS58)	October 1996–November 2001	India, Malaysia, Pakistan, Thailand vs. US	US import ban on uncertified turtle-unsafe shrimp imports overruled. Case solved after appeal and re-examination.
Asbestos (DS135)	May 1998–April 2001	Canada vs. EU	French import ban on asbestos permitted. Case solved after appeal.
Softwood Lumber IV (DS257)	May 2002–October 2006	Canada vs. US	Ruling inconclusive on whether Canada provides subsidies to lumber producers. Case solved through MAS after appeals, re-examinations, and arbitration.

* Figures in parentheses refer to the amount of retaliation authorized.
Source: Adapted from Richard Stubbs and Geoffrey R.D. Underhill, eds, *Political Economy and the Changing Global Order*, 3rd ed. Oxford: Oxford University Press, 2006, 178 and Author. By permission of Oxford University Press.

The WTO and Its DSM: Concluding Remarks

There is an imbalance between the strong, legalistic, binding DSM, on the one hand, and the comparatively weak, cumbersome, political rule-making and negotiating machinery, on the other.[67] As a result, WTO members might have come to think that progress can be made through enforcement and that litigation is a faster, more convenient way to resolve difficult issues. This stands in contrast with the WTO as a forum for genuine international trade cooperation and rule-making and prevents a more broad-based participation of all stakeholders in formulating international trade rules.[68] But, more important, all of the WTO's three main functions—negotiation and rule-making; monitoring and surveillance of the implementation of its rules; and dispute settlement—are now in a state of decline, albeit at differing speeds and to varying degrees. As the Doha negotiations

unfolded, there would have been a serious underestimation of the importance of the monitoring, surveillance, and implementation functions, while dispute settlement is at risk of seeing its standing eroded.[69]

With regard to the latter, the DSM has faced some issues, notably over the standard of review and delays, the AB's judicial activism, and its peculiar application of the VCLT's interpretation rules, leading to arbitrary results and its behaving more as a lawmaker than a judge,[70] and the DSM having to reconcile trade with other concerns beyond the WTO's mandate. These problems with the DSM are made more salient in view of the predicaments faced by the other main functions of the WTO. A finer balance between its negotiating, rule-making, monitoring, and dispute settlement functions, combined with a renewed commitment on the part of the international community, and particularly from the big and emerging powers, are indispensable to ensuring the continuing relevance of the WTO.

Notes

1   See J. G. Ruggie, "International Regimes, Transactions, and Change: Embedded Liberalism in the Postwar Economic Order," 379–415.

2   W. Diebold Jr, "The End of the I.T.O."

3   *General Agreement on Tariffs and Trade.*

4   On the Tokyo Round, see G. R. Winham, *International Trade and the Tokyo Round Negotiation*. On the Uruguay Round, see J. Croome, *Reshaping the World Trading System: A History of the Uruguay Round*.

5   "Agreement Establishing the World Trade Organization." The GATT of 1947 as amended until then was terminated and reconducted as the "GATT 1994," the latter encompassing the amendments resulting from the Uruguay Round. On the WTO Agreement, which became effective on 1 January 1995, see: J. H. Jackson, "The World Trade Organisation: Watershed Innovation or Cautious Small Step Forward?," 11–31; Winham, "The World Trade Organisation, 349–68.

6   "Trade Policy Review Mechanism."

7   "Agreement on Subsidies and Countervailing Measures."

8   The GATT/WTO terminology continues to refer to "RTAs," even though most PTAs are now bilateral and no longer between neighbouring countries. The reason might be that the term "preferential" is used to refer to other types of trade arrangements between developed and developing countries.

9   For more on accession, see Olivier Cattaneo and Carlos A. Primo Braga, *Everything You Always Wanted to Know about WTO Accession.*

10   These include: the 1996 Ministerial Declaration on Trade in Information Technology Products; the 2001 Ministerial Declaration on the TRIPS Agreement and Public Health; and the 2003 Waiver Concerning Kimberley Process Certification Scheme for Rough Diamonds.

11   Except for negotiations that were mandated as part of the "built-in" agenda of some WTO agreements, including those on agriculture, dispute settlement, and services. Yet, aside from some decisions relating to information technology, telecommunications and financial services, those negotiations have been subsumed within the Doha Round. The first ever amendment to the WTO was adopted by the General Council in 2005; it pertains to the TRIPS Agreement and formalized a 2003 Decision on Compulsory Licensing.

12   World Trade Organization, Ministerial Conference, Ninth Session. *Ministerial Declaration and Decisions.*

13   "Plurilateral services negotiations set to begin as early as March 2013."

14   On decision-making and negotiations in the GATT/WTO, see Richard H. Steinberg, "In the Shadow of Law or Power? Consensus-Based Bargaining and Outcomes in the GATT/WTO," 339–74. For an enlightening history of the positions and strategies of developing countries within the GATT/WTO, see Amrita Narlikar, "Fairness in International Trade Negotiations: Developing Countries in the GATT and WTO," 1005–29.

15 For a discussion and criticism of, as well as alternatives to, the single undertaking, see S. E. Rolland, "Redesigning the Negotiating Process at the WTO," 65–110.

16 See: L. Bartels and F. Ortino, *Regional trade agreements and the WTO legal system*; R. Buckley, V. I. Loo, and L. Boulle, *Challenges to multilateral trade: The impact of bilateral, preferential and regional agreements*; K. Heydon and S. Woolcock, *The rise of bilateralism: Comparing American, European and Asian approaches to preferential trade Agreements*; World Trade Organization, *World Trade Report 2011. The WTO and preferential trade agreements: From Co-existence to coherence.*

17 In accordance with the theory of hegemonic stability (Kindleberger), such a world leader with a dominant economy is necessary to develop and enforce the rules of the system. For the neorealist version of hegemony (Meirsheimer), the decline of a hegemon, such as the United States in the postwar period, necessarily leads to instability. Yet, for the neoliberal interpretation of hegemony, as advanced by Keohane, despite the decline of the hegemon, as was the case with the US from the 1970s, institutions like the GATT/WTO do not automatically die but take on a life of their own.

18 World Trade Organization, *Annual Report 2014.*

19 See, among others, H. Horn, P. C. Mavroidis, and A. Sapir, "Beyond the WTO: An Anatomy of the EU and US Preferential Trade Agreements," 1565–88.

20 On the relationship between dispute settlement under the WTO and PTAs, see Armand de Mestral, "Dispute settlement under the WTO and RTAs: An uneasy relationship," 777–825.

21 See R. E. Baldwin, "Multilateralising regionalism: Spaghetti bowls as building blocs on the path to global free trade," 1451–518.

22 See J. Bhagwati, *Termites in the trading system: How preferential agreements undermine free trade.*

23 World Trade Organization, General Council, *Transparency mechanism for regional trade agreements*; World Trade Organization, *Annual Report 2014*, 67–8. See P. C. Mavroidis, "Always look at the bright side of non-delivery: WTO and preferential trade agreements, yesterday and today," 375–87.

24 See the symposium: "The boundaries of the WTO" in the *American Journal of International Law* 96, 1 (January 2002): 1–158, in particular S. Charnovitz, "Triangulating the World Trade Organization," 28–55; and J. H. Jackson, "Afterword: The linkage problem—Comments on five texts," 118–25. See also A. T. F. Lang, "Reflecting on 'linkage': Cognitive and institutional change in the international trading system," 523–49.

25 *Joint statement on the multilateral trading system.*

26 World Trade Organization, *The future of the WTO: Addressing institutional challenges in the new millennium*; Warwick Commission, *The multilateral trade regime: Which way forward?*

27 D. Steger, "The future of the WTO: The case for institutional reform," 803–33.

28 *Sutherland Report*, 494.

29 See: B. Ruddy, "The critical success of the WTO: Trade policies of the current economic crisis," 475–95; R. Wolfe, *Did the protectionist dog bark? Transparency, accountability, and the WTO during the global financial crisis.*

30 See, e.g., C. P. Brown and B. M. Hoekman, "Developing countries and enforcement of trade agreements: Why dispute settlement is not enough, 177–203.

31 On MASs, see W. Alschner, "Amicable settlements of WTO disputes: Bilateral solutions in a multipolar system," 65–102. For a proposal to make litigation under MASs reviewable under the WTO DSU, see A. Alvarez-Jiménez, "Mutually agreed solutions under the WTO dispute settlement understanding: An analytical framework after the *Softwood Lumber* arbitration," 343–73.

32 On the limits of the TPRM and the DSU and proposed reforms, see B. M. Hoekman and P. C. Mavroidis, "WTO dispute settlement, transparency and surveillance," 527–42. On the creation of an independent prosecution department within the Secretariat, with an exclusive right to initiate dispute settlement proceedings, so as to secure overall observance of WTO obligations, see C. D. Zimmermann, "Rethinking the right to initiate WTO dispute settlement proceedings," 1057–70.

33 More precisely, as was the case under GATT and now the WTO, members may bring two types of complaints: *violations complaints*, alleging the failure of another member to carry out its obligations under a covered agreement; and *non-violation complaints*, alleging that a measure applied by a member, although not necessarily conflicting with a WTO provision, nullifies or impairs a benefit accruing directly or indirectly under a covered agreement or impedes the attainment of an objective of a covered agreement.

34 "Understanding regarding notification, consultation, dispute settlement and surveillance," in General Agreement on Tariffs and Trade, 210–16.

35 Jackson, "The World Trade Organisation," 19.

36 General Agreement on Tariffs and Trade, *Basic instruments and selected documents*, 61–7.

37 "Understanding on rules and procedures governing the settlement of disputes."

38 *Decision on the application and review of the understanding on rules and procedures governing the settlement of disputes*, Ministerial Declaration, Uruguay Round.

39 G. Gagné, "International trade rules and states: Enhanced authority for the WTO?," 233.

40 On the DSU review, both before and during the Doha Round, see T. A. Zimmermann, *Negotiating the review of the WTO Dispute Settlement Understanding.*

41 Jackson, "The World Trade Organisation," 19–20. For a history of GATT dispute settlement, see Hudec, *The GATT legal system and world trade diplomacy.*

42 K. Leitner and S. Lester, "WTO dispute settlement 1995–2013—A statistical analysis," 192–6. See also H. Horn, L. Johannesson, and P. C. Mavroidis, "The WTO Dispute settlement system 1995–2010: Some descriptive statistics," 1107–38.

43 Leitner and Lester, "WTO Dispute settlement 1995–2013," 193–4.

44 Ibid., 196–8.

45 J. F. Colares, "The limits of WTO adjudication: Is compliance the problem?," 404.

46 Leitner and Lester, "WTO Dispute settlement 1995–2013," 199–200.

47 M. Cartland, G. Depayre, and J. Woznowski, "Is something going wrong in the WTO dispute settlement?," 989.

48 Colares, "The limits of WTO adjudication," 422, 426–7; WTO, *Current status of disputes.*

49 C-D. Ehlermann and N. Lockhart, "Standard of review in WTO law," 493–4.

50 M. Oesch, "Standards of review in WTO dispute resolution," 635.

51 Horn, Johannesson, and Mavroidis, "The WTO dispute settlement system 1995–2010," 1133, 1136; M. Kennedy, "Why Are WTO panels taking longer? And what can be done about it?," 231, 234, 252.

52 Under the principle of judicial economy, panels do not need to rule on every single claim made by disputing parties, but only on those required to resolve a matter.

53 Summaries of the dispute cases adjudicated under the WTO DSM, with the corresponding panel, AB and arbitral reports, are available on the WTO website under "Dispute Settlement." On the Bananas dispute, go to http://www.wto.org/english/tratop_e/dispu_e/cases_e/ds27_e.htm.

54 "Agreement on the Application of Sanitary and Phytosanitary Measures."

55 *European communities—Measures concerning meat and meat products (hormones)*, adopted 13 February 1998.

56 *European communities—Measures concerning meat and meat products (hormones)*, authorized 26 July 1999.

57 *United States—Continued suspension of obligations in the EC-hormones dispute*, adopted 14 November 2008; *Canada—Continued suspension of obligations in the EC-hormones dispute*, adopted 14 November 2008.

58 http://www.wto.org/english/tratop_e/dispu_e/cases_e/ds26_e.htm; http://www.wto.org/english/tratop_e/dispu_e/cases_e/ds48_e.htm.

59 On incomplete analysis and ensuing unsettled disputes in WTO adjudication, see A. Yanovich and T. Voon, "Completing the analysis in WTO appeals: The practice and its limitations," 933–50.

60 *Vienna Convention on the Law of Treaties.*

61 A. D. Mitchell, "The legal basis for using principles in WTO disputes," 812. See also D. Pavot, "The use of dictionary by the WTO appellate body: Beyond the search of ordinary meaning," 29–46.

62 W. J. Davey, "The WTO dispute settlement system: The first ten years," 22.

63 http://www.wto.org/english/tratop_e/dispu_e/cases_e/ds257_e.htm. See also G. Gagné and F. Roch, "The US-Canada softwood lumber dispute and the WTO definition of subsidy," 555–7.

64 Interview with the author, Washington DC, 12 March 2008.

65 For more on the trade and environment debate, see R. Quick, "Do we need trade and environment negotiations or has the appellate body done the job?," 957–83.

66 P. Delimatsis, "The fragmentation of international trade law," 100–3. For an argument to the effect that non- WTO law may be applied in WTO adjudication in the absence of an express prohibition in the DSU and as long as panels and the AB do not apply international law incompatible with WTO law, see notably J. Pauwelyn, *Conflict of Norms in Public International Law: How WTO law relates to other rules of international law.* Among scholars for whom only WTO law can be applied under the DSU, see Joel Trachtman, "Jurisdiction in WTO dispute settlement," 132–43.

67 Steger, "The future of the WTO," 806. See also: C-D. Ehlermann and L. Ehring, "Decision-Making in the World Trade Organization: Is the consensus practice of the World Trade Organization Adequate for making, revising and implementing rules on international trade?," 51; *Joint Statement on the Multilateral Trading System.*

68 Bronckers, M. C. E. J., "Better rules for a new millennium: A warning against undemocratic developments in the WTO," 550.

69 Cartland, Depayre, and Woznowski, "Is something going wrong in the WTO dispute settlement?," 980–1.

70 Ibid., 985–8. See this article for a critical view of the AB's activism and adjudication. See also J. F. Colares, "A theory of WTO Adjudication: From empirical analysis to biased rule development," 383–439. For a thorough discussion of the WTO DSM, see T. N. Srinivasan, "The dispute settlement mechanism of the WTO: A brief history and an evaluation from economic, contractarian and legal perspectives," 1033–68.

Key Terms

General Agreement on Tariffs and Trade
most-favoured-nation treatment
preferential trade agreements

trade liberalization
World Trade Organization

Questions for Review

1. What are the main principles and institutional features of the world trading regime?

2. Are preferential trade agreements stepping stones or obstacles to global free trade?

3. What does the trade linkage debate involve?

4. Which essential provisions and practices of the Dispute Settlement Mechanism under the World Trade Organization differ from the previous Dispute Settlement Mechanism under the General Agreement on Tariffs and Trade?

5. What are the main challenges faced by the World Trade Organization?

Further Resources

Hoekman, B. M. and Kostecki, M. M. *The political economy of the world trading system: The WTO and beyond.*

Hudec, R. E. *The GATT legal system and world trade diplomacy.*

Jackson, J. H. (1997). *The world trading system: Law and policy of international economic relations*, 2nd ed. Cambridge, MA and London: The MIT Press.

Lanoszka, A. (2009). *The World Trade Organization: Changing dynamics in the global political economy.* Boulder, CO: Lynne Rienner.

Narlikar, A. (2003). *International trade and developing countries: Bargaining coalitions in the GATT & WTO.* London: Routledge.

Trebilcock, M. J., Howse, R., and Eliason, A. (2012). *The regulation of international trade*, 4th ed. London: Routledge.

References

"Agreement establishing the World Trade Organization." (1994). In *Final Act embodying the results of the Uruguay Round of multilateral trade negotiations*, 15 April.

"Agreement on Subsidies and Countervailing Measures." (1994). In *Final Act embodying the results of the Uruguay Round of multilateral trade negotiations*, 15 April.

"Agreement on the application of Sanitary and Phytosanitary Measures." (1994). In *Final act embodying the results of the Uruguay Round of multilateral trade negotiations*, 15 April.

"Agreement on Trade-Related Aspects of Intellectual Property Rights." (1994). In *Final Act embodying the results of the Uruguay Round of multilateral trade negotiations*, 15 April.

Alschner, W. (2014). "Amicable Settlements of WTO Disputes: Bilateral solutions in a multipolar system," *World Trade Review 13*(1) (January), 65–102.

Alvarez-Jiménez, A. (2011). "Mutually agreed solutions under the WTO Dispute Settlement Understanding: An analytical framework after the *Softwood Lumber* arbitration," *World Trade Review 10*(3) (July), 343–73.

Baldwin, R. E. (2006). "Multilateralising Regionalism: Spaghetti Bowls as Building Blocs on the Path to Global Free Trade," *The World Economy 29*(11) (November), 1451–518.

Bartels, L. and Ortino, F. (Eds). (2006). *Regional Trade Agreements and the WTO legal system.* Oxford: Oxford University Press.

Bhagwati, J. (2008). *Termites in the trading system: How preferential agreements undermine free trade.* New York: Oxford University Press.

Bown, C.P. and Hoekman, B. M. (2008). "Developing countries and enforcement of trade agreements: Why dispute settlement is not enough," *Journal of World Trade 42*(1) (February), 177–203.

Bronckers, M.C.E.J. (1999). "Better rules for a new millennium: A warning against undemocratic developments in the WTO." *Journal of International Economic Law 2*(4) (December), 547–66.

Buckley, R., Loo, V. I., and Boulle, L. (Eds). (2008). *Challenges to multilateral trade: The impact of bilateral, preferential and regional agreements.* The Hague: Kluwer.

Canada—Continued suspension of obligations in the EC-hormones dispute. (2008). WT/DS321/R, WT/DS321/AB/R, adopted 14 November.

Cartland, M., Depayre, G., and Woznowski, J. (2012). "Is something going wrong in the WTO dispute settlement?," *Journal of World Trade 46*(5) (October), 979–1016.

Cattaneo, O. and Primo Braga. C.A. (2009). *Everything you always wanted to know about WTO Accession.* World Bank, Policy Research Working Paper 5116 (November), http://elibrary.worldbank.org/doi/pdf/10.1596/1813-9450-5116.

Charnovitz, S. (2002). "Triangulating the World Trade Organization," *American Journal of International Law 96*(1) (January), 28–55.

Colares, J.F. (2009). "A theory of WTO adjudication: From empirical analysis to biased rule development," *Vanderbilt Journal of Transnational Law* 42(2) (March), 383–439.

———. (2011). "The limits of WTO adjudication: Is compliance the problem?," *Journal of International Economic Law 14*(2) (June), 403–36.

Croome, J. (1995). *Reshaping the world trading system: A history of the Uruguay Round*. Geneva: WTO.

Davey, W. J. (2005). "The WTO dispute settlement system: The first ten years," *Journal of International Economic Law 8*(1) (March), 17–50.

Decision on the application and review of the understanding on rules and procedures governing the settlement of disputes, Ministerial Declaration, Uruguay Round. (1994). 15 April.

Delimatsis, P. (2011). "The fragmentation of international trade law," *Journal of World Trade 45*(1) (February), 87–116.

Diebold Jr, W. (1952). "The end of the I.T.O.," *Essays in International Finance No. 16*. Princeton University (October).

Ehlermann, C-D. and Ehring, L. (2005). "Decision-making in the World Trade Organization: Is the consensus practice of the World Trade Organization adequate for making, revising and implementing rules on international trade?," *Journal of International Economic Law 8*(1) (March), 51–75.

———, and Nicolas Lockhart. (2004). "Standard of review in WTO law," *Journal of International Economic Law 7*(3) (September), 491–521.

European communities—Measures concerning meat and meat products (hormones). (1998). WT/DS26/R/USA, WT/DS48/R/CAN, WT/DS26/AB/R, WT/DS48/AB/R, adopted 13 February.

European communities—Measures concerning meat and meat products (hormones). (1999). WT/DS26/ARB, WT/DS48/ARB, authorized 26 July.

Gagné, G. (2000). "International trade rules and states: Enhanced authority for the WTO?." In R. A. Higgott, G. R. D. Underhill, and A. Bieler (Eds). *Non-state actors and authority in the global system*. London and New York: Routledge, 226–40.

———, and F. Roch. (2008). "The US-Canada softwood lumber dispute and the WTO definition of subsidy," *World Trade Review 7*(3) (July), 547–72.

General Agreement on Tariffs and Trade, adopted 20 October 1947, effective 1 January 1948.

General Agreement on Tariffs and Trade. (1989). *Basic instruments and selected documents*, 36th Supplement. Geneva: GATT.

Heydon, K. and Woolcock, S. (2009). *The rise of bilateralism: Comparing American, European and Asian approaches to preferential trade agreements*. Tokyo: United Nations University Press.

Hoekman, B. M. and Kostecki, M. M. (2009). *The political economy of the world trading system*, 3rd ed. Oxford: Oxford University Press.

———, and Mavroidis, P. C. (2000). "WTO dispute settlement, transparency and surveillance," *The World Economy 23*(4) (April), 527–42.

Horn, H., Johannesson, L., and Mavroidis, P. C. (2011). "The WTO dispute settlement system 1995–2010: Some descriptive statistics," *Journal of World Trade 45*(6) (December), 1107–38.

———, Mavroidis, P. C., and Sapir, A. (2010). "Beyond the WTO: An anatomy of the EU and US preferential trade agreements," *The World Economy 33*(11) (November), 1565–88.

Hudec, R.E. (1990). *The GATT legal system and world trade diplomacy*, 2nd ed. London: Butterworth.

Jackson, J.H. (1995). "The World Trade Organisation: Watershed innovation or cautious small step forward?," *The World Economy 18*(5) (Autumn), 11–31.

———, (2002). "Afterword: The linkage problem—Comments on five texts," *American Journal of International Law 96*(1) (January), 118–25.

Joint Statement on the multilateral trading system. (2001). (1 February), http://www.wto.org/english/news_e/news01_e/jointstatdavos_jan01_e.htm.

Kennedy, M. (2011). "Why are WTO panels taking longer? And what can be done about it?," *Journal of World Trade 45*(1) (February), 221–53.

Keohane, R. O. (1984). *After hegemony: Cooperation and discord in the world political economy*. Princeton, NJ: Princeton University Press.

Kindleberger, C.P. (1973). *The world in depression: 1929–1939*. Berkeley, CA: University of California Press.

Lang, A.T.F. (2007). "Reflecting on "linkage": Cognitive and institutional change in the international trading system," *Modern Law Review 70*(4) (July), 523–49.

Leitner, K. and Lester, S. (2014). "WTO dispute settlement 1995–2013—A statistical analysis," *Journal of International Economic Law 17*(1) (March), 191–201.

Mavroidis, P. C. (2011). "Always look at the bright side of non-delivery: WTO and preferential trade agreements, yesterday and today," *World Trade Review 10*(3) (July), 375–87.

Meirsheimer, J. J. (2001). *The tragedy of great power politics*. New York: W.W. Norton.

Mestral, A. de. (2013). "Dispute settlement under the WTO and RTAs: An uneasy relationship," *Journal of International Economic Law 16*(4) (December), 777–825.

Mitchell, A. D. (2007). "The legal basis for using principles in WTO disputes," *Journal of International Economic Law 10*(4) (December), 795–835.

Narlikar, A. (2006). "Fairness in international trade negotiations: Developing countries in the GATT and WTO," *The World Economy 29*(8) (August), 1005–29.

Oesch, M. (2003). "Standards of review in WTO dispute resolution," *Journal of International Economic Law 6*(3) (September), 635–59.

Pauwelyn, J. (2003). *Conflict of norms in public international law: How WTO law relates to other rules of international law*. Cambridge: Cambridge University Press.

Pavot, D. (2013). "The use of dictionary by the WTO appellate body: Beyond the search of ordinary meaning," *Journal of International Dispute Settlement 4*(1) (March), 29–46.

"Plurilateral services negotiations set to begin as early as March 2013." (2012). *Inside US Trade* (14 December).

Quick, R. (2013). "Do we need trade and environment negotiations or has the appellate body done the job?," *Journal of World Trade 47*(5) (October), 957–83.

Rolland, S. E. (2010). "Redesigning the negotiating process at the WTO," *Journal of International Economic Law 13*(1) (March), 65–110.

Ruddy, B. (2010). "The critical success of the WTO: Trade policies of the current economic crisis," *Journal of International Economic Law 13*(2) (June), 475–95.

Ruggie, J. G. (1982). "International regimes, transactions, and change: Embedded liberalism in the postwar economic order," *International Organization 36*(2) (Spring), 379–415.

Srinivasan, T. N. (2007). "The dispute settlement mechanism of the WTO: A brief history and an evaluation from economic, contractarian and legal perspectives," *The World Economy 30*(7) (July), 1033–68.

Steger, D. (2009). "The future of the WTO: The case for institutional reform," *Journal of International Economic Law 12*(4) (December), 803–33.

Steinberg, R. H. (2002). "In the shadow of law or power? Consensus-based bargaining and outcomes in the GATT/WTO," *International Organization 56*(2) (Spring), 339–74.

Stubbs, R. and Underhill, G. R. D. (Eds). (2006). *Political economy and the changing global order*, 3rd ed. Oxford: Oxford University Press.

"Symposium: The boundaries of the WTO." (2002). *American Journal of International Law 96*(1) (January), 1–158.

Trachtman, J. (2005). "Jurisdiction in WTO dispute settlement." In R. Yerxa and B. Wilson (Eds). *Key issues in WTO dispute settlement—The first ten years*. Cambridge: Cambridge University Press, 132–43.

"Trade Policy Review Mechanism." (1994). In *Final Act embodying the results of the Uruguay Round of multilateral trade negotiations*, 15 April.

"Understanding on rules and procedures governing the settlement of disputes." (1994). In *Final Act embodying the results of the Uruguay Round of multilateral trade negotiations*, 15 April.

"Understanding regarding notification, consultation, dispute settlement and surveillance." (1979). In General Agreement on Tariffs and Trade, *Basic instruments and selected documents*, 26th Supplement. Geneva: GATT, 210–16.

United States—Continued suspension of obligations in the EC-hormones dispute. (2008). WT/DS320/R, WT/DS320/AB/R, adopted 14 November.

Vienna Convention on the law of treaties, adopted 22 May 1969, effective 27 January 1980.

Warwick Commission. (2007). *The multilateral trade regime: Which way forward?* Report of the First Warwick Commission (Warwick Report). University of Warwick, United Kingdom.

Winham, G. R. (1986). *International trade and the Tokyo Round negotiation*. Princeton, NJ: Princeton University Press.

———, (1998). "The World Trade Organisation: Institution-building in the multilateral trade system," *The World Economy 21*(3) (May), 349–68.

Wolfe, Robert. (2011). *Did the protectionist dog bark? Transparency, accountability, and the WTO During the global financial crisis*, Policy Report 01. Stockholm: Entwined (March), http://www.iisd.org/pdf/2011/protectionist_dog_bark.pdf.

World Trade Organization. (2004). *The future of the WTO: Addressing institutional challenges in the new millennium*. Report of the Consultative Board to the Director-General Supachai Panitchpakdi (Sutherland Report). Geneva: WTO.

———, General Council. (2006). *Transparency mechanism for regional trade agreements*, WT/L/671, Decision of 14 December.

———, *World Trade Report 2011.* (2011). *The WTO and preferential trade agreements: From co-existence to coherence.* Geneva: WTO, http://www.wto.org/english/res_e/booksp_e/anrep_e/world_trade_report11_e.pdf.

———, Ministerial Conference, Ninth Session. (2013). *Ministerial Declaration and Decisions.* Bali, 3–6 December, http://www.wto.org/english/thewto_e/minist_e/mc9_e/bali_texts_combined_e.pdf.

———, *Annual Report 2014.* Geneva: WTO, (2014), http://www.wto.org/english/res_e/booksp_e/anrep_e/anrep14_e.pdf.

———, *Current Status of Disputes.* (2006), http://www.wto.org/english/tratop_e/dispu_e/dispu_current_status_e.htm.

Yanovich, A. and Voon, T. (2006). "Completing the analysis in WTO appeals: The practice and its limitations," *Journal of International Economic Law 9*(4) (December), 933–50.

Zimmermann, C. D. (2011). "Rethinking the right to initiate WTO dispute settlement proceedings," *Journal of World Trade 45*(5) (October), 1057–70.

Zimmermann, T. A. (2006). *Negotiating the review of the WTO dispute settlement understanding.* London: Cameron May.

PART IV

Regionalism

At the international level, there are three forces, not mutually exclusive, that push states together in various forms of regional arrangements. In the first, states share common historical experiences and problems within a particular geographic area. The need to rebuild Western Europe's post-Second World War infrastructure and economy would be one example, as would the Common Market of the Southern Cone's (MERCOSUR) pursuit of liberalized trade in South America. A second factor is the existence of long-term functional relationships across boundaries that contribute to the development of formal and informal linkages to manage these affairs. Obviously the degree of institutionalization will vary from region to region, with the European Union representing a highly developed supranational framework. Finally, states in a particular geographic area also have social, cultural, political, or economic similarities that are unique compared with other regions of the world, such as the Association of Southeast Asian Nations (ASEAN), or the Canada–US and Mexico–US relationships contributing to the North American Free Trade Agreement (NAFTA) (Stubbs and Reed 2006, 290–1).

If pressures exist that push states toward regional integration, there are five generally accepted "stages." The first, and most common, is a *Free Trade Area* (FTA), where member states attempt to limit tariff and non-tariff barriers but still maintain a highly independent and autonomous foreign economic policy. Again, the NAFTA is a good example of an FTA. The next phase in regional integration is a *Customs Union* (CU), which shares many FTA attributes, but also has the added dimension of applying common economic policies and/or tariffs to non-member states. CUs are also typically more highly institutionalized to administer tariffs and/or coordinate foreign economic policy. The number of CUs, however, is significantly lower than the number of FTAs. The EU, which was preceded by the European Economic Community (EC) between 1957–92, provides the best case in point.

The final three phases of regional integration require a higher commitment of sovereignty and coordination. A *Common Market*, for example, has most of the elements of a CU but also has a high degree of labour and capital mobility amongst members. Regulatory rules, such as safety, educational, and health standards, also tend to be similar to promote liberalization and the freer movement of workers across borders. Once again, the EU has the characteristics of a common market. The final two stages, however, are the most difficult to achieve. An economic union goes further and attempts to unify the fiscal, monetary, transportation, and industrial policies for members, as is evident with the European Economic and Monetary Union (EMU) that established the euro as the key currency of the EU. Finally, a *Political Union* will coordinate foreign, defence, and some domestic policies, creating a group of sovereign territorial units operating together in a manner similar to a federal state, such as the Commonwealth of Independent States (CIS) following the collapse of the Soviet Union (Hülsemeyer 2010, 349–52).

Although regionalism is largely considered a twentieth-century phenomenon, regional precedents, usually in the form of trade agreements, date back to the nineteenth century. These include a customs union negotiated between England and Ireland in 1826, the 1854 Canada–US Reciprocity Treaty, and the South African Customs Union of 1910. For the most part, however, regional agreements only became increasingly common following the Second World War. One early effort included the 1949 Council for Mutual Economic Assistance (CMEA) created by the Soviet Union, Bulgaria, Hungary, Poland, Romania, and Czechoslovakia, although strong state-planned socialist economic policies prevented any significant regional integration. Others include the EC in 1957, as noted above, as well as some attempts in Africa and Latin America in the 1960s. This "first wave" of postwar regional integration did not take hold outside of Europe for the most part, although most shared the common characteristics of being multilateral, as opposed to bilateral, and only included states from specific geographic regions.

A "second wave" of regionalism followed by the 1980s, consisting of dozens of regional trade agreements (often bilateral "North–North" and "South–South" treaties), deeper institutional integration in Europe, as well as the Canada–US Free Trade Agreement (CUSFTA) and the first "North–South" trade agreement (NAFTA). These trends have carried over to the twentieth century, although the proposed Trans-Pacific Partnership (TPP) would be the first regional agreement involving a wide range of signatories from northern developed and southern developing economies (Cohn 2010, 213–14).

It is also important to note that regionalism is grounded in well-established IPE theoretical traditions. Liberals, for example, view multilateral agreements as the best means of achieving liberalization but are also willing to embrace regional frameworks as a stepping-stone to wider economic liberalization. Liberals are quick to caution, however, that regional agreements must be non-discriminatory to other nation-states in the region and seek to avoid overlapping or inconsistent measures with already existing multilateral commitments. Liberals also view regional agreements on the basis of absolute gains, where even small states benefit from cooperative linkages, and negative developments, such as unemployment and labour displacement, are temporary problems subject to market readjustments. Realists and mercantilists, on the other hand, view regional agreements as frameworks that benefit the individual self-interest of the most powerful states in a region, which view state interaction on the basis of relative gains and increased competition between governments. In contrast, historical materialist, and other critical theoretical perspectives, focus on the gains made by multinational corporations and possessors of transnational capital, as well as existing class disparities in all states, and the differing nature of poverty in northern developed, as opposed to southern developing, states (Cohn 2010, 211–12).

Regionalism, however, does not guarantee increased economic liberalization. In fact, there is considerable debate about whether or not regionalism enhances or obstructs market integration in the global political economy. Of specific concern is the role of hegemons within regional frameworks, and the attempt to control the economic relations of specific economies, or seek a balance of economic power with hegemons in other regions. However, it is difficult to measure the scope of integration due to the wide range of factors that contribute to economic relations within regions, such as cross-border trade, investment, multinational corporations, supply chains, and labour mobility. For some observers, all of these considerations are secondary to historical and cultural linkages and political, economic, and social institutions that exist within various regions. Obviously, where these exist, so too will the potential for deeper integration (Stubbs and Reed 2006, 291–2).

The chapters in this section of the volume all reflect some of these realities, but they also challenge and expand on the focus of existing studies. Lori Thorlakson begins by questioning common misperceptions of the integrated regionalism of Europe and the European Union (EU), arguing instead that its institutionalism is incomplete and asymmetrical, having a distinct impact on the regions' ability to respond to the 2008 global economic crisis. In the context of North America, Geoffrey Hale proposes a similar argument, noting that the trilateral intentions of the NAFTA have instead evolved into a "dual bilateralism" resulting in greater continental integration and ultimately three distinct economic and political systems in North America. Jennifer Hsu argues further that this pattern exists in the political economies of China and Japan due to historically strong state intervention, as well as historic tensions between both states in the Asian region. Africa, on the other hand, offers a distinctly different regional case study. Adam Sneyd focuses on the increasing scope and diversity of foreign partnerships and engagements, which represent African "revolutions" in finance, agriculture, and information and communication technologies, leading to an increasingly complex and varied African political economy.

References

Cohn, Theodore H. 2010. *Global political economy: Theory and practice*. Longman: New York.

Hülsemeyer, Axel. 2010. "Regional integration: Europe and beyond," in Axel Hülsemeyer, ed., *International political economy: A reader*. Don Mills: Oxford University Press.

Stubbs, Richard and Austina J. Reed. 2006. "Introduction: Regionalization and globalization," in Richard Stubbs and Geoffrey R. D. Underhill (Eds), *Political economy and the changing global order*, 3rd ed. Don Mills: Oxford University Press.

12 European Union

Lori Thorlakson

The European Union (EU), an economic and political union of 28 member states, represents the largest single market in the world, with over a quarter of world GDP. It is a *sui generis* political system—not quite a state, but certainly more than an international organization, with the power to shape policies in areas ranging from the environment, the internal market, agriculture, migration and visas, and foreign policy and defence. The centrepiece of European integration has been the creation of the single market and monetary union. However, the rapid development of the single market since the late 1980s and the subsequent emergence of monetary union from the 1990s can be contrasted with the incomplete and limited integration that we find in areas of economic governance related to fiscal policies and growth. The consequences of this came to light after the 2008 global financial crisis. Europe's sovereign debt crisis revealed fundamental problems with its economic governance and threw the eurozone's very survival into question.

From an international political economy (IPE) perspective, economic governance in the European Union provides an interesting case of a relatively rapid process of development of a supranational regime to govern the economy. It also provides an example of how pressures to develop rules can vary across policy areas, and how this shapes both the reach and rule type of these regimes, ultimately explaining the potential for success for different aspects of the economic governance regime.

The incompleteness and unevenness of integration of the EU's economic governance have been key factors contributing to Europe's economic governance crisis. Rule types and their enforceability vary across areas of economic governance policy. While a supranational regime with strong, treaty-based rules and strong enforceability norms developed to govern monetary policy, it has been much more difficult for the Union to develop an effective framework for economic policy coordination. In this area, the EU relies upon an intergovernmental framework with variable and weak enforceability norms. Finally, EU rules governing structural reforms—such as labour market reforms or growth strategies—are weakest because member states retain control over these policy areas, limiting the EU's actions to employing coordination tools of soft law and benchmarking.

The reach of the EU's economic governance framework is limited. The EU has created a monetary union without a fiscal federalism capable of transferring income from richer to poorer member states. Whereas the **European Central Bank (ECB)** controls monetary policy in the eurozone, national governments control budgets and taxation. Although the budget of the EU includes money earmarked for structural funds whose aim is to reduce economic disparities across regions in Europe, it has too little money to serve as an economic stabilizer. In comparison, in federal states like Canada, the federal government can help to cushion weak economic performance and boost demand through the use of transfer payments from more prosperous provinces to less prosperous provinces.

The consequence of having a monetary union without a full economic union is that it limits the available adjustment mechanisms that can be used when economic conditions differ drastically across regions. According to the theory of optimal currency areas (Mundell 1961), one of the greatest risks to a single currency regime occurs when different regions are exposed to demand and supply shocks. Without the ability to adjust the exchange rate or monetary policy, countries with a single currency can only adjust to maintain competitiveness through labour mobility or downward wage adjustments. When the provinces or states in a federation experience asymmetric shocks, taxation policy and intergovernmental transfers can cushion the blow. The European Union does not have this tool, and there is little evidence that the political will exists to move to full fiscal federalism.

Moreover, until recently the Union's economic governance framework has overlooked a broader range of indicators of macroeconomic imbalance and banking union. The economic governance of the European Union provides an interesting example of how these rules have developed, and

brings into focus debates between neorealists and neoliberals in IPE about how international institutional orders emerge, the degree of control that member states exercise over them, and the inherent stability of these supranational regimes.

Economic governance in the EU is deeply linked with questions of democracy and sovereignty, and the eurozone financial crisis has brought this into sharp focus. While the project of European integration has required member states to accept trade-offs of pooling—and limiting—their sovereignty in exchange for the benefits brought by common **supranational policies**, the sovereign debt crises have also demonstrated that for eurozone countries in crisis, sovereignty is also sharply constrained by international financial markets. As the EU and its member states have struggled to reform the EU's economic governance regime, it has also highlighted inequalities in power between member states, and given rise to debates about fairness, redistribution, and the sharing of risk.

This chapter takes up some of these issues. Why did European integration—and specifically the creation of supranational rules for economic governance—proceed unevenly, and what were the economic and political consequences? How do differences in types of rules affect the relative power between states and supranational institutions, and how have these differences affected the effectiveness of policy? Why has it been such a difficult task for the European Union to develop a comprehensive set of economic governance rules when the single market was developed relatively quickly? Finally, why has Canada, a federation using a single currency, avoided these difficulties that the EU has faced as a union of states using a single currency? Why has economic governance concerning fiscal policy been less problematic in Canada than in the EU?

The policies that create monetary union in the EU are highly supranational: power over monetary policy is delegated to the ECB, which operates with autonomy from political interference and whose mandate is entrenched in the treaties. The economic governance aspects of **Economic and Monetary Union** (EMU), by contrast, are less supranational. Instead we see the imprint of strong member state control through **intergovernmental rule frameworks** and discretion in rule enforcement. This contrast lies at the heart of the problems with the architecture of EU economic governance: integration in the form of monetary union requires a degree of political integration in economic policy that has not caught up. It is questionable whether the political will exists for this integration.

Development of Economic Governance Structures

Economic governance in the European Union covers a range of policy areas, with EMU as a centrepiece, and all operating in the context of an open market economy with free competition, a policy goal enshrined in the treaties, in Article 119, Treaty on the Functioning of the European Union (TFEU). While integration in the single market has been remarkably swift and extensive, integration in other aspects of economic governance has been uneven and incomplete. We find strong integration in monetary policy, but political obstacles have meant that integration lags behind in macroeconomic and fiscal coordination and financial markets. The European Union's policy of EMU pairs highly supranational monetary union with more limited measures for economic policy coordination. The EU has a single currency (the euro), a single monetary policy, and an independent central bank, but it does not have a single finance minister, sole control over national budgets, or the power to raise taxes across the EU.

I consider economic governance policies in the EU here in terms of three types of policies: monetary policy, macroeconomic and fiscal policy coordination, and, finally, the coordination of a broader set of structural policies affecting labour markets, competitiveness, and economic growth. This chapter will contrast rule development and the drivers of integration in these three areas of economic governance.

Economic and Monetary Union

Monetary policy in the eurozone is a highly centralized policy area in EU policy-making, and the area of economic governance policy that has seen the strongest degree of integration. The Treaty on European Union (TEU) established an economic and monetary union with a single currency, and with a monetary policy delegated to an independent central bank. Today, it is one of only five policy areas that is recognized by the treaties as being an exclusive competence of the European Union (Article 3c, TFEU).

The launch of the single currency followed a process of closer economic policy and central bank coordination. Before being invited to join the single currency, member states had to demonstrate that they met macroeconomic convergence targets. The convergence criteria, set out in a protocol attached to the TEU, set out four tests that member states had to meet to join the single currency. First, the average rate of inflation in the country over the past year must not exceed 1.5 per cent of that of the three best performing member states. Second, the budgetary situation must be stable, and the state must not be subject to a Council of Ministers decision on an excessive deficit. Third, the currency must have remained within normal fluctuations of the Exchange Rate Mechanism (ERM) within the past two years with no devaluations, and, finally, in the past year, the nominal long-term interest rate must not have exceeded 2 per cent of that of the three best performing states.[1] States that met these criteria were invited to join phase three of EMU, which, on 1 January 1999, established a single currency, the euro, together with a European Central Bank and fixed exchange rates.

Created in the German model of central banks, the ECB is one of the most politically independent central banks in the world. Together with the European System of Central Banks (ESCB), it is responsible for defining and implementing monetary policy, conducting foreign exchange operations, managing the official foreign reserves of the member states, and operating the payments system. The independence of the ECB and the ESCB is affirmed in Article 130 TFEU, which declares that they will not "seek or take instructions from Union institutions, bodies, offices or agencies, from any government of a Member State or from any other body." Its formal independence, grounded in the treaties and the ECB's statutes, is further reinforced by an organizational culture that heavily values expert consensus in its decision-making in monetary policy (McNamara 2005, 153). Although the ESB operates insulated from political pressure, it is bound by the treaties to a mandate of pursuing price stability as the goal of monetary policy (Article 3(3) of the TEU).

By 1999, monetary union had emerged as one of the most supranational policy areas in the European Union, despite the fact that EMU was not initially included in the Treaty of Rome, which founded the European Community. How can this development be explained? One way to view the development of monetary union is in terms of neo-functionalist theory. From this perspective, EMU is the result of functional spillover, the natural extension of integration in the single market. Increased trade created demands to reduce transaction costs across jurisdictions through the introduction of a single currency. It was the logical next step to exchange rate coordination and monetary policy cooperation in the 1970s through the "snake in the tunnel" fixed exchange rate system in 1973 and its successor, the 1979 European Monetary System (EMS), which created the Exchange Rate Mechanism. Monetary policy was in many ways suitable for integration in the EU. Like other highly supranational policy areas in the EU, it is regulatory, rather than distributive or dealing with areas of "high" politics. It is non-majoritarian and involves delegated power to arms-length experts.

The creation of EMU can also be understood in terms of the role of ideas and policy entrepreneurs. Here, the European Commission played an important role in persuading European governments of the need for EMU through its authorship of two influential reports, the 1970 Werner Report and the 1989 Delors report, which made the case for economic and monetary union. Intergovernmentalists would also argue that the introduction of EMU can be understood in realist terms: member states agreed to EMU in treaty negotiations because it was in their national interest to do so. For countries like Italy and Spain, joining EMU made a commitment to low inflation credible. Both countries had been dealing with falling currencies in the early 1990s and high interest rates on government debt. For Germany, giving up the deutschmark for monetary union was a way to demonstrate its commitment to Europe in the wake of German reunification. For Germany, the design of EMU, with a strong and independent central bank committed to price stability, also reflects German interests.

Macroeconomic and Fiscal Coordination

The 1992 Maastricht Treaty created an uneven architecture of EMU: it created monetary union, but it did not create common economic and budgetary rules. There is no single European finance minister. Instead, national budgets fall to national governments. This is a problem with the economic governance policies created by the Maastricht Treaty. A single currency requires some degree of macroeconomic and fiscal coordination. Without this, there is a risk that states with lax budgetary discipline can free-ride on the fiscal discipline of the others, ultimately undermining the stability of the currency. Long-term budgetary deficits can put a strain on the currency, causing markets to lose confidence in the currency.

When a single currency or monetary policy is applied across a diverse group of countries or regions, these regions have the potential to experience asymmetric economic shocks—such as upward or downward changes in prices, unemployment rates, or demand for goods. This can make it difficult for a single monetary policy to suit the needs of all the regions in the common currency area. With a single currency, member states (or the states or provinces of a federation) can no longer devalue their exchange rate as a tool of adjustment to respond to external economic shocks and instead must rely on more painful modes of adjustment, such as downward wage adjustments. A high degree of macroeconomic coordination in the EU can help promote general economic convergence, which may help reduce the asymmetric economic shocks that eurozone member states experience.

Most currency unions in the world, including Canada, go further than macroeconomic coordination, and couple a single currency with fiscal federalism—provisions for the central or federal government to use taxes and transfer payments in countercyclical ways, sending transfer payments to regions with slow growth to help boost demand in order to stabilize economies in the currency union. While the European Union has redistributive policies such as the Common Agricultural Policy (CAP) and the structural funds, the small size of these spending programs mean they are inadequate as a tool of fiscal federalism. There is little political will among member states to develop a supranational level system of taxes and transfers. Under the TEU, fiscal policy remained a competence of the member states. National budgets were to be drafted by national finance ministries and debated and approved by national parliaments, albeit with an eye to their duty to coordinate economic policies with other European countries.

Without the tools of fiscal federalism to help maintain stability in the currency, the European Union uses measures of economic coordination to encourage budgetary discipline and help prevent asymmetric shocks. While monetary policy is highly supranational, with institutional rules entrenched in the treaties, the policy framework for economic coordination, while referenced in the treaties, is essentially an intergovernmental policy area. Article 121 TFEU declares that member states should "regard their economic policies as a matter of common concern and shall coordinate them in the Council."

Membership in the eurozone created a need for economic policy coordination among these member states. Finance ministers of the eurozone member states started meeting informally in 1998. They now meet regularly in advance of the meetings of the Economic and Finance Committee of the Council of Ministers (ECOFIN), an institution for policy coordination where eurozone finance ministers discuss matters related to the single currency. The Commission and the ECB take part in these meetings, which are chaired by a president of the eurozone elected for a two and a half year term. (This is affirmed in the protocol on the Euro Group attached to the Lisbon Treaty). ECOFIN is the formal institution for economic policy coordination. The Lisbon Treaty created provisions for eurozone-only voting on certain provisions that affected only the eurozone.

This process of closer economic coordination began before the first euro notes and coins were issued. In order to join the eurozone, member states needed to meet the convergence criteria, demonstrating that they were maintaining budget deficits of less than 3 per cent of Gross Domestic Product (GDP), debt of less than 60 per cent of GDP, maintaining exchange rate stability, and converging on EU benchmarks for inflation.

After countries adopt the euro, macroeconomic and fiscal coordination is carried out through both preventive and corrective forms of surveillance in the form of the Stability and Growth Pact (SGP) and the Excessive Deficit Procedure (EDP). The SGP is the "preventive arm" of fiscal surveillance. The SGP developed from the December 1996 Dublin European Council where member states, following a proposal from German finance minister Theo Waigel, decided that some form of fiscal policy surveillance was necessary for the stability of the euro. The SGP requires that member states whose budget deficits exceed 3 per cent of GDP or whose public debt exceeds 60 per cent of GDP take action.

The EDP forms the "corrective arm" of multilateral fiscal surveillance. It is set out in Article 126 of the Treaty on the Functioning of the European Union. This procedure is triggered if a eurozone member state's budget deficit exceeds 3 per cent of GDP. If this happens, the European Commission submits a report to ECOFIN, which then formulates an opinion on the report. The Commission, bearing in mind the ECOFIN opinion, sends an opinion to the member state.

The effectiveness of the SGP has been hampered in the past by its failure to insulate its operation from political pressure. In 2003, the Council voted not to apply Commission recommendations of penalties for Germany and France under the EDP, while the previous year proceedings were initiated against Portugal. In 2004, a ruling by the European Court of Justice affirmed that the Council had the legal right to do this. Heipertz and Verdun argue that this effectively put the SGP into abeyance, and as a result, "[d]ue to the politicized nature of the EDP, the essence of the Pact seems to be not so much a mechanism of 'quasi-automatic sanctions' but rather the institutionalisation of a political pledge to aim for low deficits" (Heipertz and Verdun 2010, 6–7). The Council's record of selective application of the EDP damaged the credibility of the SGP and the overall legitimacy of the EU's budgetary surveillance policies.

The March 2005 European Council meeting reformed the SGP by increasing its flexibility, including more justifiable reasons for member states to miss budgetary targets. The problem was that to effectively promote budgetary discipline, the SGP needed to be flexible, yet impartially applied and not politicized. It was especially important that it not be perceived to be selectively enforced. Following the 2005 reforms, some felt that the SGP had been left too flexible to be useful. After the sovereign debt crisis underscored the importance of effective measures to monitor and enforce budgetary discipline, the SGP was further reformed. The 2011 reforms introduced greater flexibility into the EDP mechanism, both increasing the reach of surveillance as well as retaining and improving flexibility to allow the EU to better distinguish between budgetary imbalances due to poor fiscal management and those due to unforeseen events.

The new EDP is aimed at preventing and correcting structural deficits, not those due to exceptional circumstances or predicted to be temporary. For this reason, if a deficit greater than 3 per cent occurs due to unforeseen or unusual events or from a severe economic downturn, then the deficit is considered to be exceptional. The Commission considers whether economic forecasts predict there will be a temporary deficit. Crucially, however, application of the EDP was reformed so that penalties under the EDP are more automatic. Now, under the "reverse QMV" (qualified majority voting) method, a qualified majority of member states is needed to overturn or withhold a Commission recommendation to sanction a member state, instead of being needed to enforce or apply such a recommendation. This and other post-crisis reforms will be discussed further below.

Structural Policies

Finally, economic governance can also include those policies intended to help stimulate economic growth. These include structural reforms to labour markets, investment in research and development, and other policies targeted at increasing competitiveness. These are policy areas where the European Union has attempted to achieve closer coordination, but because these areas still fall under national control the EU lacks the legal competence to achieve this and faces political obstacles to coordination.

The Lisbon Strategy for growth and jobs was launched in 2000 by the European Council with the aim of stimulating jobs and growth. It was later replaced by Europe 2020, a 10-year growth strategy for the EU that includes targets on employment, education, research and innovation, social inclusion and poverty reduction, climate, and energy. Without policy competence to introduce binding legislation in these areas, the Union must rely on "softer" policy coordination measures.

In summary, while a highly centralized and supranational institutional order developed in the policy area of monetary policy, integration has not proceeded as smoothly in other areas of economic coordination. Macroeconomic and fiscal coordination, integral to the stability of the single currency, has been subject to a looser form of integration, with an intergovernmental rule framework with variable norms of enforcement.

Compared to integration in monetary policy, integration in economic governance and fiscal policy is incomplete, both in the strength of integration (an intergovernmental framework with variable enforceability) as well as a limited reach of rules (surveillance tools before the crisis were limited to budgetary deficit and debt levels). Structural reforms, which deal with highly political issues such as labour market and welfare state reforms that are both distributive in nature and contested political issues at the domestic level, are particularly difficult to coordinate at the supranational level. Hence, we have seen only limited coordination to date, because of a weak intergovernmental framework with limited enforcement capacity.

The answer to the question of whether we have seen the development of a supranational legal and institutional order, as neoliberal views would predict, or a regime in which member states remain in charge, as neorealists would predict, depends on the policy area. We find an interesting contrast between the entrenchment or constitutionalization of monetary union, but not of policies relating to growth and fiscal policy. The rules that guide monetary policy are entrenched in the treaties, with strong enforceability.

Financial Crisis, Bailout, and Reforms

Crisis created the opportunity and demand for reforming the European Union's economic governance policies. When the sovereign debt crises hit eurozone economies, raising the real possibility that eurozone countries might default on their debt payments and perhaps be forced to exit the eurozone, the EU and International Monetary Fund (IMF) responded with emergency bailouts tied to strict policy conditionality. From 2010 to 2012 five eurozone states were bailed out by the EU and IMF for a total of 540 billion euro—Greece in May 2010 and

March 2012, Ireland in November 2010, Portugal in May 2011, and Spain and Cyprus in June 2012.

The sovereign debt crisis threatened the existence of monetary union, and in response, the European Union undertook a number of reforms to its economic governance policies. These reforms have attempted to extend the reach of economic governance policies by broadening the scope of macroeconomic surveillance, by regulating the financial sector, and by creating a fund that can serve as a firewall between failed banks and sovereigns. The new rules are designed to create greater fiscal discipline and address the uneven and political nature of the application of the EDP. While the reforms rely heavily on intergovernmental rule frameworks, they try to achieve greater effectiveness while retaining democratic legitimacy by anchoring fiscal discipline measures in national law.

The European Council, the intergovernmental body representing the heads of member state governments, established a task force in March 2010 to investigate reform of the SGP and tighten up budgetary discipline. The Commission, the supranational executive body of the European Union, also undertook its own search for reforms, which led to the six-pack reform proposals.

Reform of the Stability and Growth Pact: the "Six-Pack" of Reforms

The bailouts of the indebted eurozone periphery economies raised a call for new measures to impose fiscal discipline. Without this, it was feared that bailouts would create a moral hazard, rewarding lax budgetary policies. Reforming the Stability and Growth Pact was a key priority for ensuring greater fiscal discipline. The Stability and Growth Pact was reformed in December 2011 as part of the "six-pack" of reforms (so-named because it contained six pieces of legislation for economic governance). These reforms are designed to strengthen fiscal coordination in the eurozone. Crucially, the

six-pack reforms make the application of the Excessive Deficit Procedure more automatic. Under the new rules, a qualified majority vote is required in the Council to overturn Commission recommendations, rather than adopt them. This will make it more difficult for political influence to be brought to bear on the application of the EDP. The six-pack reforms try to introduce some flexibility that would distinguish between deficit and debt outcomes resulting from general economic circumstances out of the member state's control rather than structural deficits.

The reforms also extend surveillance beyond deficit and debt levels to include a wider range of macroeconomic indicators through the Macroeconomic Imbalance Procedure (MIP). The MIP includes a set of 10 economic indicators that capture international competitiveness and labour productivity, the housing market, private sector debt, pension funding, and current account deficits. These are some of the indicators that would have served as warning signs of economic problems ahead for Ireland and Spain. Under the MIP, the Commission assesses economic conditions and can issue country-specific recommendations (CSR) to member states. The MIP provides the economic governance framework with an excessive imbalance procedure in its toolkit, in addition to the excessive deficit procedure. If the Commission determines that an excessive imbalance exists, it can make recommendations to the member state to address it.

Coordination among national governments was also strengthened through the introduction of a new intergovernmental mechanism to strengthen economic governance. The Euro Plus Pact (EPP) was agreed to in March 2011 by the European Council. The EPP, which includes eurozone member states as well as Denmark, Poland, Latvia, Lithuania, Bulgaria, and Romania, is intended to address the shortcomings of the growth and stability pact. The pact focuses on structural reform measures to increase growth and competitiveness.

Alongside these reform measures, the European Union strengthened its framework for economic policy monitoring and coordination through the development in 2010 of the "European Semester," a synchronized timetable for all member states that provides a framework for policy coordination concerning structural reforms (such as growth and employment policies), and fiscal and macroeconomic imbalances.

The Fiscal Compact (Treaty on Stability, Coordination, and Governance)

By 2011, the costs of bailouts mounted and soaring bond yields on Italian and Spanish debt raised the possibility of default, calling the continued existence of the euro into question. Germany found itself facing the prospect of financing further bailouts to save the euro. To sell this to a hostile domestic electorate that already viewed the bailouts as financing the profligate spending habits of the periphery, the Germans demanded tougher measures to enforce budgetary discipline. This ushered in a set of reforms, the Fiscal Compact of 2012 and the "two-pack" reforms of 2013, which together signified an erosion of member states' budgetary sovereignty.

These measures were introduced in March 2012 by the Treaty on Stability, Coordination, and Governance, otherwise known as the "Fiscal Compact," which further strengthened economic and budgetary rules in the European Union, as provided by the SGP and the Euro Plus Pact. The Fiscal Compact imposes even tougher fiscal requirements than those in the SGP because it requires national budgets to be in balance or in surplus. One of the problems in the past for economic and budgetary rules has been that they have relied on member state compliance and the Council has

been ineffective and uneven in backing the enforcement of budgetary discipline rules. The Fiscal Compact addresses this problem by using national-level law to secure enforcement. The treaty requires member states to entrench this rule in national law, preferably in national constitutions. It retains some flexibility in applying the rules to target structural deficits and taking account of extraordinary circumstances, and makes use of automatic corrective actions (negative QMV).

There was strong pressure from Germany to entrench strict rules on budgetary discipline, yet reforming the EU treaties to achieve this was politically too difficult—doing so would have required unanimous consent from the member states. In the end, an intergovernmental solution was adopted: the Fiscal Compact is a separate intergovernmental treaty that was signed by all member states except the UK, the Czech Republic, and Croatia. (In March 2014, the Czech Republic reversed its position and announced its intention to sign the treaty).

Economic and budgetary policy has traditionally been the preserve of intergovernmental coordination among member states. While the Budgetary Pact enhances this through biannual summit meetings of eurozone heads of government, it also introduces an innovation for national democracy by attempting to foster interparliamentary coordination as well. Article 13 of the treaty creates a conference of national and European parliamentary committees that will discuss budgetary policies. Though it remains to be seen whether the interparliamentary committee will develop into a forum of substantive importance, this move represents, at least in symbolic terms, a counterweight to a potential hollowing out of national-level budgetary policy debate.

The Two-pack of Reforms

In May 2013, as signs of economic growth started to tentatively emerge across the EU member states, reforms further strengthened budgetary surveillance and coordination among the eurozone member states, but also highlighted, at least in symbolic terms, how European economic coordination is curtailing the power of national parliaments. The two-pack of reform, intended to increase budgetary transparency, creates a common budgetary timeline and rules for euro-area member states, starting in 2014. Under the framework, member states submit their budgets to the European Commission by 15 October. The Commission scrutinizes these budgets for compliance with the country's budgetary obligations under the Stability and Growth Pact. The two-pack was designed to more closely monitor countries that are facing financial problems. It also applies enhanced surveillance to member states that are emerging from bailout programs.

Banking Regulation

One of the problems with the EMU's macroeconomic oversight mechanisms before the financial crisis was that it focused narrowly on budget deficits and government debt, overlooking private sector financial imbalances, in particular ignoring banking and financial oversight (Eichengreen 2012, 128). As the events of the financial crisis proved, this was a crucial missing element in the eurozone's economic governance architecture. As the collapse of Lehman Brothers in September 2008 illustrated, the contagion effects of a bank failure can have catastrophic impacts on global financial markets. In the eurozone, the precarious financial situation of, especially, small- and medium-sized banks, and their subsequent failure, had devastating effects on some countries during the financial crisis. Yet banking union, including agreeing on common rules for winding down failed banks, proved to be one of the most politically difficult elements of the reform package, and as the recession began to wane in late 2013, member

states struggled to agree on rules for banking union.

Troubled banks were at the centre of the origins of financial crises in Ireland and Spain. In contrast to excessive public sector debt in countries such as Greece and Italy, public sector finances in Ireland and Spain, when measured in terms of debt and deficit levels, were strong in the years leading up to their bailouts. For Ireland, Spain, and Portugal, the dangers lay instead in their private sector balance sheets, the result of an overheated real estate market, dangerously overleveraged banks in Ireland and Spain, and high consumption levels in Portugal (Eichengreen 2012, 128).

Banks in Ireland and Spain lent heavily to finance property construction during the boom years. When the property bubble burst, the banks were left with massive holes in their balance sheets, triggering some of the largest bailouts in the countries' histories. For Ireland, the precarious state of Anglo-Irish Bank in 2008 led to its nationalization and an injection of over 30 billion euros in capital by the Irish government. This resulted in a massive transfer of debt from Anglo-Irish to the public balance sheet, leading the country to seek an 85 billion euro bailout from the IMF and European Union in 2010. Similarly, in Spain, the collapse of Bankia in May 2012, and its subsequent rescue by the Spanish state—the largest in Spain's history—triggered a 100 billion euro mini-bailout for Spain by the EU and IMF.

In response to these events, banking reform and banking union have been important yet problematic elements of the European Union's postcrisis economic governance reform efforts. The goal of banking reform was to amend the relationship between states and financial markets. Specifically, banking union sought to sever the link between weak banks and weak sovereigns and prevent contagion from the collapse of private banks.

This ambitious goal has been difficult for the EU to achieve, and over the course of negotiations on banking union, the EU downgraded its ambitions somewhat. Tellingly, in a May 2013 speech, EU Economic Commissioner Olli Rehn shifted the language used to describe the goal of banking union policy, replacing the term "sever the link" with "dilute the link."

Agreeing on rules for banking union has been a difficult task for the European Union. Banking union represents the creation of EU-level rules that, contentiously, would share risk and control over wind-downs and bailouts of failing banks. Among member states the greatest agreement has been on the need to reduce risk and on defining acceptable levels of risk. It has been much more difficult to agree on what the European Union should do when things go wrong—such as who should shoulder the burden when banks require recapitalization, and what role national governments and the European Commission should play in the event of a bank collapse. This debate centres on who bears the losses in the event of a bank collapse, with strong German resistance to taxpayer-funded bailouts of failing banks.

Member states have disagreed on the bank bail-in rules. Germany sought rules that would exclude or minimize fiscal federalism and risk-sharing. Together with the Commission, it wanted bank failure to automatically lead to creditors shouldering some of the loss—an automatic "bail-in" that would induce banks to behave more responsibly. France, meanwhile, resisted a strong supranational role for bank supervision, preferring an intergovernmental model that preserved state power and discretion in banking (*Financial Times*, 11 Dec 2013).

EU members have also disagreed about whether to create a single resolution authority that would be responsible for restructuring and bailing out failed banks. The European Commission sought to have strong authority granted to the Commission and ECB on this matter. Germany argued that the treaties do not grant the EU the authority for this.

Germany resisted Commission proposals to centralize banking resolution rules—and did not want the Commission to have powers to wind up failing banks (*Financial Times*, 11 Dec 2013). There has also been political resistance to banking union from member states, notably Germany and Spain, which have small regional banks with connections to regional politicians. These countries successfully lobbied to limit direct banking supervision by the ECB to the 200 largest banks in the eurozone (*Financial Times*, 11 Dec 2013).

The deal finally reached on banking union in negotiations in late 2013 and 2014 created a single resolution authority with the power to wind up failing banks. While potentially this could mean a significant surrender in sovereignty for national governments, the member states have maximized their control by creating this authority through an intergovernmental agreement with a simple majority threshold for overturning the board's recommendations. Coupled with this is a 55 billion euro fund that can be drawn from to wind up failing banks, funded in part by contributions from banks. While Germany agreed to the mutualization of risk through the creation of a common bailout fund, it demanded in return an increase in intergovernmental power, specifically that EU finance ministers, not the European Commission, retain the final say on closing banks.

As with the fiscal compact, the member states again turned to an intergovernmental agreement, rather than amending the EU treaties, to develop this policy framework. Using an intergovernmental agreement means that member states do not have to reform the EU treaties, a process that risks ratification failure in some member states. It also maximizes member state control over this policy area, limiting the role of EU institutions such as the Parliament, the European Central Bank, and the Commission.

Firewall and Lender of Last Resort

The eurozone crisis revealed one of the flaws in the architecture of economic and monetary union. Central banks normally act both as a force of monetary stability as well as a lender of last resort, providing emergency liquidity for the banking system and thereby preventing a run on the banks. The treaties do not provide this role for the ECB, and Article 125 of the TFEU—the "no bailout" clause—specifically prohibits the Union from taking on the debts of the member states. Article 123 of the Treaty further prohibits the ECB from purchasing debt directly from member state governments. Recent efforts to take on such a role have generated resistance. Germany has opposed proposals for the mutualization of debt in the Union through the issue of "eurobonds."

The European Stability Mechanism (which in 2013 replaced the European Financial Stability Facility), created a limited firewall. Its purpose is to serve as a fund that troubled sovereigns can draw on, ensuring financial stability for the eurozone. With a lending capacity of only 500 billion euros, however, it may only be suited to protecting states with smaller economies.

To strengthen the ECB's ability to stabilize the eurozone, ECB President Mario Draghi announced in the summer of 2012 that the ECB would do "whatever it takes" to defend the euro, through a controversial bond-buying program called "Outright Monetary Transactions" (OMT) designed to calm financial markets by purchasing the debt of troubled eurozone countries in secondary markets. (Purchasing the debt already in the markets, rather than directly from governments, gets around the treaty prohibition on the ECB buying government debt). The announcement of the program delivered

the desired effect and bond yields across the eurozone periphery fell as markets perceived these debt instruments to be safer. This in turn reduced borrowing costs for indebted eurozone governments, banks, and corporations.

The OMT program restored confidence and stability to debt markets but faced a challenge in the German Federal Constitutional Court over concerns that it breached treaty provisions prohibiting the EU from financing member state budgets and that it would expose Germany to financial risks that its parliament could not control. The European Court of Justice later ruled that the OMT program conformed to the treaties.

Debates

Economic governance in the European Union and its reform highlights a number of debates. First, does the European Union have a sufficient *demos* or political community to sustain further integration needed for a stable eurozone, including fiscal federalism? Second, how does the combination of supranational integration and the power of international financial markets affect the economic sovereignty of member states? How does the debate about austerity- or growth-oriented economic policies highlight divisions among member states as well as difficulties with the democratic process of economic policy-making?

Monetary Union Needs Fiscal Federalism—but does Fiscal Federalism Need a Demos?

Neither Canada nor the European Union may be optimal areas for a single currency. Canada's regional economic diversity means that the Canadian dollar does not always deliver an optimum exchange rate for all regions of the country: exporters might be hurt by a strong dollar while importers benefit. However, when asymmetric shocks affect regions of Canada, relatively high labour mobility across provinces provides one natural adjustment mechanism. The government can also use taxes and transfer payments, the tools of fiscal federalism, to help provinces respond to unequal economic conditions. In the European Union, reforms have attempted to enhance fiscal and macroeconomic coordination and remove barriers to the movement of labour, but the EU still stops short of fiscal federalism.

As the European Union sought to reform its economic governance in the wake of financial crisis, the thorniest debates were those that centred on issues of redistribution and the pooling of risk. These have highlighted the limits of political will in the EU for deeper integration in these areas and raise the question of whether the EU has a sufficient demos or political community that would allow for the redistributive politics of full fiscal federalism, with supranational taxation and transfers.

Where the development of supranational rules has proceeded most swiftly and smoothly in the European Union is in highly technical and regulatory areas, such as monetary policy, which is managed with relatively little controversy, by the highly independent European Central Bank. While willing to face common supranational rules on monetary policy, member states and their citizens are much more reticent to subject themselves to a supranational taxation regime that could redistribute resources from one member state to another through transfer payments. While Canada has a national political community or demos sufficient to support the contentious politics of federal-level redistribution, we do not see this to the same degree in the European Union.

Germany, long the paymaster of Europe, has objected to policies such as the mutualization of debt that would amount to transfer payments to the struggling economies of the eurozone periphery. In this view, sharing risk as well as the bailouts without strict conditionality create a moral hazard by rewarding weak budgetary discipline. One of the most contested proposals that ultimately failed to win support was the mutualization of eurozone debt by issuing eurobonds, an idea which would have required treaty revision, and which would have involved pooling risk or liability at the EU level.

Normative Debates over Austerity versus Growth Policies

The global financial crisis has triggered a normative debate worldwide over whether austerity or growth policies offer the best prescription for countries struggling with recession. Advocates of austerity measures argue that strict budgetary discipline is key to restoring the confidence of the financial markets. Proponents of growth policies argue that austerity measures strangle growth and warn of the economic, social, and political consequences of prolonged high unemployment levels, especially among youth, that risk creating a "lost generation" in countries such as Spain and Greece.

The European Union's policy response has primarily focused on austerity rather than growth. This policy approach is consistent with German policy preferences that emphasize monetary stability over growth policies and that support strict conditionality due to the concern that bailouts will create a moral hazard by rewarding profligate spending. The economic and political power of Germany has allowed it to be influential in shaping EU economic governance policy. We see German preferences for stability over growth and austerity measures reflected in the overall framework of the Stability and Growth Pact as well as in the eurozone crisis response, including the strict conditionality attached to EU bailouts, the strengthening of the Stability and Growth Pact, and the adoption of balanced budget measures through the fiscal compact.

The growth and austerity debate has pitted contrasting ideological visions for economic policy in Europe. The Christian Democrats in Germany have remained steadfastly committed to the austerity vision whereas the election of the socialist French president François Hollande in May 2012 signified a rejection of austerity politics by French voters and support for growth-oriented strategies.

The austerity and growth debate also divides member states, pitting the more prosperous northern states of the EU against the slower growth southern states, in a debate imbued with moral overtones. States that have undertaken structural reforms and have maintained budgetary discipline have limited patience for bailing out what they regard as profligate states with lax budgetary discipline. Rather than supporting measures that would mutualize debt or pool risk, they support tougher budgetary rules for all member states.

The single currency has distributive consequences that complicate this somewhat simplified moral view of the eurozone bailouts. Germany's large trade surpluses create a beggar-thy-neighbour policy. It benefits from an exchange rate that is artificially low for its economic conditions. Meanwhile, the less competitive southern European countries, unable to devalue their currency, only have the tool of lowering their wages during a recession.

The EU's austerity policy focus has gradually shifted, in line with shifting political sentiment in the member states. Support for austerity policies has waned in the Netherlands, once a strong supporter of austerity policies. Both trade unions and business associations have called for an end to austerity measures mandated by the European Commission to meet the country's deficit target. Growing opposition to economic policies mandated by the European Commission make the governing coalition increasingly fragile, as voters flee to the extreme right and left as well as euroskeptic

populist parties. By May 2013, the EU had shifted away from its austerity focus when it allowed France, Spain, and the Netherlands to miss their 3 per cent budget deficit target in exchange for labour market reforms.

The strongest proponents of growth strategies came from member states hit hardest by the crisis, such as Spain, where youth unemployment in 2013 exceeded 50 per cent. Public sector layoffs, tax increases, and record high unemployment levels triggered mass protests in Athens, Lisbon, Madrid, and Rome and electorates responded through support for euroskeptic populist parties, and extremist parties.

The Impact of Markets and Integration on Sovereignty and Democracy

Member states have emerged from the financial crisis and from economic governance reforms with less autonomy over their national budgets. From 2013, member states have been required to submit their national budgets to the European Commission for review before they are approved by national parliaments. This represents a creeping supranational control over the budgetary autonomy of states in a way that imposes constraints on their fiscal policies. At the same time, there has been little development of supranational fiscal policy tools that might compensate for this loss of room to manoeuver at the national level. Instead, supranational policy development has focused on regulation due to the political difficulty of integrating in redistributive policy areas.

The eurozone crisis and the reform of economic governance resulted in the further erosion of sovereignty for member states by both markets and EU policy. For the member states at the receiving end of EU and IMF bailouts, the limitations on sovereignty were sharply visible through strict conditionality: accepting rescue funds committed governments to implement a series of reforms, including drastic public sector cuts, tax increases, and structural reforms. As already noted, this generated a significant public backlash in numerous European capitals. Although supranational bodies have set the terms of conditionality, global financial markets have been a powerful force behind the scene, as anticipated market reactions have influenced the policy conditions attached to bailouts.

The influence of the markets and supranational bodies can be felt beyond economic policy. They can also influence decisions over who holds office. For example, when former Greek prime minister George Papandreou pledged in October 2011 to hold a referendum on the second bailout package Greece had agreed to with its international creditors, the markets reacted with panic. A month later, Papandreou abandoned this plan and shortly after stepped aside to allow for the creation of a technocratic national unity government, led by former European Central Bank vice-president Lucas Papademos. Italy also saw the installation of a technocratic leader, Mario Monti, who served as prime minister from 2011 to 2013.

The crisis context has opened opportunities for policy change, but has in some cases limited participation in debate and decision-making. The deals struck over bailouts favour elite power rather than direct democracy because they require leaders to be able to negotiate credible policy commitments in return for rescue funds. This limits public debate in a policy area that can have deep and painful social, economic, and political consequences.

Reforms have reduced the policy autonomy of member state governments, but at the same time there is limited development at the supranational level of both policy capacity and debate. The use of intergovernmental agreements rather than treaty reform, a pragmatic choice that acknowledges the difficulty of ratification during a period of integration fatigue, has the additional consequence of limiting the involvement of the European Parliament and the European Court of Justice, bodies that can represent a broad range of voices in the European polity.

Conclusion

The European Union is an example of uneven and incomplete integration across different areas of economic governance. We find most supranational policy-making in regulatory and highly technical areas, such as monetary policy, where rules tend to be enshrined in the treaty and backed by strong supranational institutions. Fiscal policy, by contrast, is a much more contested area, where we find increased policy coordination over time, underpinned by less formal institutions with sometimes contested legitimacy.

Recent reforms to economic governance in the EU have attempted to address the key weaknesses that made it vulnerable to the sovereign debt crises. The EU has imposed stricter requirements for budgetary discipline, expanded its macroeconomic monitoring to include a wider range of indicators, including trade and private debt, and it has introduced banking union to break the link between weak banks and weak sovereigns, although in a less ambitious and less supranational form than initially proposed. It has pursued these reforms through intergovernmental agreements, rather than through treaty change that would create deeper supranational integration. This reflects the reluctance of the member states to cede control over economic policies that have redistributive elements, such as sharing the costs of winding up failed banks. Some have criticized the EU for taking too long to respond to the economic crisis, and ultimately delivering too little in the way of reforms.

A key vulnerability remains: the European Union is a monetary union without fiscal union.

The introduction of supranational fiscal policy through taxes and transfers remains stalled by significant political hurdles. The weakness of a European-wide political community or "demos" also limits the ability of the union to undertake collective debate on economic policy. While recent reforms have attempted to bolster the role of national parliaments in economic policy-making, a key future challenge for the European Union will be to develop European-level democratic debate in economic policy in supranational institutions like the European Parliament.

Note

1   The Protocol on the convergence criteria is referred to in Article 109j TEC.

Key Terms

Economic and Monetary Union
supranational policies

intergovernmental rule frameworks
European Central Bank

Questions for Review

1. How does a currency union limit the ways in which its members can respond to economic shocks?
2. Why does a single currency require coordination of fiscal policies?
3. Why has the development of supranational policies occurred more slowly in redistributive than regulatory areas in the European Union?

4. How did the causes of the sovereign debt crises in Ireland and Spain differ from those in Greece and Italy? How have economic governance reforms addressed this?

Further Resources

Brunila, A., Buti, M., and Franco, D. (Eds). (2001). *The stability and growth pact: The architecture of fiscal policy in EMU*. Basingstoke: Palgrave.

Cameron, D. (1997). "Economic and monetary union: Underlying imperatives and third-stage dilemmas," *Journal of European Public Policy 4*, 455–85.

Eichengreen, B. "European monetary integration with benefit of hindsight."

Heipertz, M. and Verdun, A. *Ruling Europe: The politics of the stability and growth pact*.

McNamara, K. (1999). *The currency of ideas: Monetary politics in the European Union*. Ithaca: Cornell University Press.

Sandholtz, W. (1993). "Choosing union: monetary policy and Maastricht." *International Organization 47* (1) (Winter), 1–39.

For more detail on economic governance policies in the European Union, see www.eurozone.europa.eu/home/.

References

Eichengreen, B. (2012). "European monetary integration with benefit of hindsight." *Journal of Common Market Studies 50*, S1, 123–36.

Financial Times. (2013). "EU sets out framework for banking union," 11 Dec.

Heipertz, M. and Verdun, A. (2010). *Ruling Europe: The politics of the stability and growth pact*. Cambridge: Cambridge University Press.

McNamara, K. (2005). "Economic and monetary union." In H. Wallace, W. Wallace, and M. Pollack (Eds), *Policy-making in the European Union*, 5th edition. Oxford: Oxford University Press.

Mundell, R. (1961). "A theory of optimal currency areas." *American Economic Review 51*, 657–65.

Sandholtz, W. (1993). "Choosing union: Monetary policy and Maastricht." *International Organization 47*(1) (Winter), 1–39.

13 North America

Three Steps Forward, Two Steps Back?

Geoffrey Hale

"Does North America exist?" For veteran Canadian political scientist Stephen Clarkson, the nuanced answer after almost 500 pages of analysis published in 2008 could be paraphrased as "that depends." As a "geographical entity," certainly. As a "community" with broadly shared social ties, not really. As a set of legal and institutional relationships, quite weakly. As a market—"one region in the world," as opposed to "a self-contained region *of* the world, depending on the extent to which (mainly) US (and Canadian)-based multinationals have developed integrated operations across North America, in particular industries and economic sectors.[1]

Twenty years after the initial implementation of the North American Free Trade Agreement (NAFTA), North America remains three distinct, internally diverse sovereign nations whose governments, unlike those of Western Europe before 1990, have consciously and deliberately avoided developing shared political institutions to manage the processes of economic integration and societal interdependence. Despite hopes for greater economic convergence between Mexico and its more economically advanced neighbours, wide disparities remain both within and among the nations of North America. Both the Mexican and Canadian economies remain heavily integrated with that of the United States—even if shifts in economic activity have limited US–Canada integration since 2000. International trade and economic relations increasingly parallel one another in dealings with countries outside North America, and cooperation on security and regulatory issues has grown significantly in the past decade.

However, most such developments have been expressions of **dual bilateralism**: the development of separate, bilateral arrangements between the United States and its two neighbours, and to a much lesser degree, between Canada and Mexico, rather than *trilateral* initiatives pointing to closer continental integration. Even when the three countries participate in wider trade negotiations, as with those aimed at concluding a "Trans-Pacific Partnership" since 2012, they do so as independent actors with sometimes overlapping agendas.

This chapter examines the political economy of North America as the product of interactions among three distinct political systems, and evolving, interdependent economies shaped by a mix of domestic, North American, and broader international factors. It reviews the institutional processes that contribute to economic integration and the significantly greater diversity of policy relations among nation-states. It summarizes historical developments since the early 1980s, together with major factors that have cultivated and constrained North American integration during this period. It then considers two major policy arenas that reflect these forces: competitive liberalization in national trade policies and interwoven conflicts over migration, border management, and security.

Regional Economic Integration, Trade Policies, and Multi-Level "Games"

Processes of regional economic integration are the products of broader trends intended to facilitate enhanced economic activities across national borders and reciprocal intergovernmental cooperation in pursuit of broadly shared objectives. They also maintain domestic political legitimacy via national institutions, often involving various forms of economic redistribution. Regional integration has taken very different paths in Western (and subsequently, post-Soviet) Europe, North America, and other parts of the world.

Europe's path has moved along the continuum of integration (see Figure 13.1) beginning with the Treaty of Rome (1958), a free-trade agreement among six nations followed by a series of steps toward economic union over 40 years—the "widening" and "deepening" of Europe—culminating (for now) in the 1992 Maastricht Treaty and, after 2000, the European Economic and Monetary Union.

In contrast, the negotiation of the Canada–US (CUSFTA) and North American (NAFTA) Free Trade Agreements between 1986 and 1993 may have contributed to significant, largely market-driven economic integration. But shared North American institutions remain "shallow" as a result of the different priorities, agendas, and domestic institutional constraints facing US, Canadian, and Mexican governments. Mexican political scientist Isidro Morales describes the result as "open regionalism": a US-led model for market-opening between major economic regions within the broader international trading system that projects

Deep Integration/ Economic Union	Customs Union	Common External Tariff	Free Trade Agreements	Sectoral Agreements (e.g., Auto Pact)	Independent National

Free Trade Agreement	Reciprocal elimination of tariffs and other trade barriers, with specified exceptions.
Common External Tariff	Harmonization of tariff rates among participating countries on imports from third countries.
Customs Union	Removal (for trade purposes) of internal borders among participating countries; common trade policy in dealing with other countries.
Economic Union	Agreement to harmonize fiscal, monetary and other economic policies among participating countries, including provisions for labour mobility among members, regulatory coordination in competition, financial sector, and other specified policy fields.

Figure 13.1 The Economic Integration Continuum

market-based norms, disciplining domestic economic governance within specified limits.[2]

These processes have not replaced national governments as principal actors in international economic relations, but they have contributed to the emergence of complex, multi-layered arrangements—multilateral, regional, sectoral, and issue-specific—that involve successive and overlapping processes—"multi-level games"—of bargaining between and among state bureaucracies and various domestic constituencies.[3]

National decision-makers typically cultivate international and domestic constituencies for negotiations intended to assist closer trade relations and to impose rule-based disciplines on the unilateral application of power politics. Trade agreements are likely to create both winners and losers in each country. A major goal of international negotiations is to create the prospect of sufficient gains ("win-sets") in each participating country so that expanding industries will generate increased economic growth and prosperity—both for the country as a whole and for a majority of its citizens and communities. Economic growth should also expand the revenues available to governments to maintain existing services and help them adjust to increased international competition. This sometimes includes the "compensation" of prospective losers—although such actions require varying degrees of flexibility in the use of regulatory and other policy tools.

Such "games" may also take place through the parallel conduct of negotiations in multiple settings in which individual countries (and trading regions such as the EU) compete for international investment and comparative advantage by institutionalizing reciprocal market access to assorted trading partners and related efforts at trade promotion. This process has been described as **competitive liberalization**.[4] Competitive liberalization may enable major and emerging economic powers to project their interests and influence the agenda of broader multilateral trade negotiations. It can also allow smaller countries to avoid being marginalized in such games by negotiating their own networks of trade agreements.

However, despite the fact that some sectors—notably automotive and information technology—function as North American industries, this level of integration remains the exception rather than the rule, because independent national regulatory systems govern most industry sectors. Other industries, such as railways, airlines, financial, and (for the US and Canada) oil and gas sectors and telecommunications, have extensive cross-border operations and are interdependent but within distinctively national (or sub-national) systems of regulation—often involving, in Canada and Mexico, significant barriers to foreign ownership.

One result of such arrangements is a policy continuum of integration, as noted by Gattinger and Hale (see Figure 13.2), resulting in varied "**intermestic**" sectoral policy arrangements in which traditional distinctions between domestic and international policies are blurred by the realities of interdependence.[5] At one extreme, bilateral

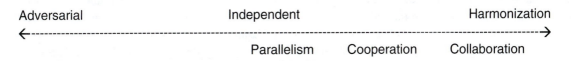

Figure 13.2 The Binational or Regional Policy Continuum

Source: From *Borders and Bridges* by Monica Gattinger and Geoffrey Hale, Oxford University Press, 2010. Reprinted with permission.

policy relations are conflictual or adversarial. With independent policy relations, each country forms its policy without direct reference to others. **Policy "parallelism"** involves the pursuit of similar policy goals, but often using different "tools"—methods that reflect separate legal histories, institutional arrangements, and patterns of interest group competition or accommodation. Policy "cooperation" involves largely informal arrangements to pursue complementary goals in ways that involve recognizing, accommodating, and reducing the effects of specific national differences. These processes become progressively more formalized under policy "coordination," potentially leading to "harmonization," with participating countries negotiating a jointly binding policy framework, or smaller countries simply adapting the policies and legal requirements of their larger trade partner(s).

The political dimensions of trade (and investment) policies do not function in isolation. Rather, they interact with domestic and broader international business cycles, responding to external ("exogenous") factors that influence sectoral competitiveness and economic growth, including patterns of business (including financial) innovation, price cycles for major commodities, and the diffusion of new technologies, production, and distribution networks. These realities have been visible in the relative decline in intra-North American trade since 2000, the deep structural shifts in regional energy markets, and the ongoing effects of the financial crisis of 2008–09, especially in the United States and the European Union. Taken together, these factors create a dynamic but highly uncertain environment for ongoing economic adaptation and adjustment at national, sectoral, and regional levels. They have also demonstrated the practical difficulties of building "shared" governance institutions, given persistent differences in the economic interests and domestic political constraints facing the three nations of North America.

Negotiating and Implementing NAFTA

The current era of North American integration may be said to have evolved in four phases: separate domestic choices and bilateral processes, leading to the negotiation of NAFTA (1982–93), NAFTA's initial implementation (1994–2001), sporadic efforts to engage its contradictions (2001–10), and current adaptations to a changing global environment (2010 –).

The first era began with separate Canadian and Mexican efforts to adapt to growing international interdependence and instability. The recession of 1981–82 demonstrated to both countries their relative vulnerability to international economic shocks, and the potential benefits of greater openness to regional and broader international markets. Although the Reagan administration showed little interest in the initial Canadian overtures, it was more receptive to the Mulroney government after 1985 to complement its agenda in the new Uruguay Round of GATT negotiations. The Canada–US free trade negotiations of 1986–87 served the interests of both governments by locking Canada "in" to the US-led agenda for international trade liberalization, and, with support from most provincial governments and organized business interests, locking "out" a reversion to nationalist and statist policies such as the National Energy Program of 1980–83.

Mexico's initial steps toward liberalization included joining GATT in 1986. President George H.W. Bush welcomed overtures from Mexico's Carlos Salinas de Gortari to reinforce Mexico's path toward economic liberalization as a prospective example to other Latin American countries at different stages of economic development. Canada's participation in subsequent negotiations was largely defensive, to protect formal gains from CUSFTA in accessing US markets, particularly its bilateral dispute resolution mechanism.[6] NAFTA negotiations generated greater controversy in the US than in Canada due to the novelty of negotiating reciprocal market access between a major developed, "high-wage" economy and a large developing, "low-wage" one. Their success ultimately depended on negotiating side agreements on labour and environmental issues between the US and its two neighbours—providing newly elected Democratic President Bill Clinton with the necessary political cover to secure enough Democratic support for ratification by Congress.

NAFTA's implementation was complicated by a financial crisis in Mexico in 1994–95, triggered by the Mexican government's decision to "float" the peso. Despite the subsequent US-led bailout, the resulting economic disruption intensified a wave of migration to the United States—pointing to the larger challenges of integrating the two economies without greater cooperation in managing the broader societal effects of policy shocks.[7] In comparison, CUSFTA/NAFTA's facilitation of the rapid growth of Canadian exports to the US—almost 40 per cent of GDP by 2000—provided a significant economic safety valve for fiscal restructuring and other domestic policy adaptations.

Efforts to broaden and deepen NAFTA came to a shuddering halt in the aftermath of the terrorist attacks on the United States in September 2001. Broader American security concerns were reinforced by a political backlash against the rapid increase in illegal migration since 1994, provoking the "rebordering of North America."[8] These issues are discussed further in this chapter's section on migration, border management, and security. Despite efforts to renew trilateral cooperation on issues of security and economic integration after 2004, competing and diverging policy priorities in each country have generally trumped proposals for closer state-led North American integration. Major factors have included the different impacts of and

responses to intense competition from China and other Asia-Pacific countries, political rigidities in responding to the changing context for energy and related environmental policies, continuing security concerns arising from Mexico's narco-insurgency, and finally, the varied effects of the 2008–09 financial crisis and recession on each country.

The twentieth anniversary of NAFTA's initial implementation provides a useful opportunity to examine the major characteristics of North America in 2015 in order to understand why economic integration has not been paralleled by movements toward greater political integration.

NAFTA at 20: North America in 2015

North America functions as a variably integrated economic region, with several distinct regional sub-cultures, as described in Garreau's *The Nine Nations of North America*[9]—although some of his regional boundaries have shifted in response to internal and external population movements (see Figure 13.3). However, its evolution in other respects continues to be defined by the disproportionate size and power of the United States, the global scope and preoccupations of its foreign and international economic policies, and the strategic and tactical responses of the Canadian and Mexican governments to these realities.

US policies toward North America have long been subsets of American domestic politics, and on occasion, of its broader foreign and international economic policies as well.[10] This overriding reality distinguishes North American integration and governance from the European experience. Robert Pastor had noted three persistent factors that have hindered both the development of coherent North American policies or strategies in Washington and the deepening of

Figure 13.3   The Nine Nations of North America

North American institutions: the independent policy-making role of Congress, the decentralization of responsibilities and high turnover of senior policy-makers within the US executive branch, and a consciousness of American power and "exceptionalism" among policy-makers and public that encourages unilateralism in policy-making and limited consultation with its neighbours.[11]

Both Pastor and Isabel Studer emphasize that these realities, which have deep historical, institutional, and cultural roots, create a strong bias against commitments to international or supranational institutions within the American political system, usually privileging domestic politics over international cooperation. This culture feeds protective attitudes toward national sovereignty and the maintenance of policy discretion in both

Canada and Mexico, along with preferences for bilateral over trilateral policy processes as more likely to accommodate their respective interests.[12]

The presence of more than 54 million Hispanic-Americans, over 60 per cent of Mexican birth or heritage, gives Mexico greater salience than Canada in American political life—although this reality produces as many difficulties as opportunities, notably deep American divisions over border management and immigration reform. Canada remains almost an afterthought in the US, despite long having been the latter's largest trading partner and source of energy imports.[13]

Canada's enduring preoccupation with managing its relations with the United States, its growing efforts to diversify its trade and investment relations outside North America, and its growing demographic linkages with East and South Asia have limited the growth of Canada–Mexico economic and political relations. Mexico is only the eighth largest destination for Canadian direct investment in the Western Hemisphere, far behind not only the US, but offshore financial centres (and tax havens) such as Barbados, the Cayman Islands, and Bermuda, along with the mining-intensive and industrial economies of Chile, Peru, and Brazil.[14]

Although North American leaders, foreign ministers, and other cabinet officials usually meet annually, and sometimes more often, the dominant reality of intergovernmental relations remains one of dual bilateralism: maintaining separate bilateral relationships on a wide range of policy issues reflecting historic differences in US relations with its two neighbours and the persistent differences in bilateral agendas. The Obama administration has reinforced this pattern by pursuing separate bilateral processes with Mexico and Canada to manage border-related security and trade facilitation efforts, along with separate regulatory cooperation processes.

These realities reflect multiple asymmetries among the three countries, the most obvious being their differences in size, wealth, and power (see Table 13.1). The United States remains among the world's largest, most prosperous economies although increasingly sharing economic leadership with other major economies. Both Canada and Mexico remain far more heavily dependent on trade with their American neighbour than the latter is with them—sending 75 and 78 per cent of their respective exports to the US in 2013.

Table 13.1   North America in Context

		United States		Mexico		Canada	
		Million	%	Million	%	Million	%
Population	1990	248.7	69.6	81.3	22.7	27.5	7.7
	2014	318.9	67.3	120.3	25.4	34.8	7.3
		United States		**Mexico**		**Canada**	
		USD	%	USD	%	USD	%
GDP	1990	5,801	86.8	288	4.3	595	8.9
	2014	16,720	84.1	1,327	6.7	1,825	9.2
		United States		**Mexico**		**Canada**	
		USD		USD	% of US	USD	% of US
GDP per capita	1990	23,198		7,358	31.7	20,204	87.0
PPP basis	2013	52,800		15,600	29.5	43,100	81.6
		United States		**Mexico**		**Canada**	
		% of GDP	% of trade with NAFTA partners	% of GDP	With US	% of GDP	With US
Trade	1990	21	19.2	39	52.0	52	56.6
	2012	31	25.8	63.6	71.0	62.6	60.2

Source: World Economic Forum, World Bank, CIA World Factbook, national statistical agencies; Ferguson et al. (2013); author's calculations.

As a result, though each country may selectively adapt its domestic policies to strengthen its comparative advantage within limits set by NAFTA and WTO agreements, domestic political sensitivities often require them to make such adjustments independently unless accompanied either by some American policy concession or, more frequently, greater support than opposition from strong cross-border (or domestic) coalitions of stakeholder groups. The result is a "variable geometry" of integration that varies widely by policy sector and, often, by the different contexts for various aspects of US–Canada and US–Mexico relations.[15]

Although overall US trade dependence has increased significantly since 1990, along with chronic current account deficits, it remains about half that of Canada or Mexico. Canada and Mexico may be the largest and third-largest US trading partners, respectively, but they still only account for about one quarter of the latter's overall trade. As a result, American policy-makers typically assess trade and regulatory initiatives within North America for their precedent-setting effects on US global trade relations. Key considerations include their contribution to broader US objectives such as promoting intellectual property rights and American regulatory standards, or in making further market-opening conditional on reciprocity by major trading partners.[16] These realities have been reinforced by the relative decline of intra-North American trade since 2000, as noted in Table 13.2.

A second critical asymmetry is that both the United States and Canada are advanced industrial countries, although the latter's exports have been weighted more heavily toward resources and industrial materials in recent years, whereas Mexico is still a developing country whose living standards remain substantially below those of its northern neighbours. These disparities reinforce American tendencies toward unilateralism and Mexican (and Canadian) tendencies toward defensiveness in bilateral relations.[17]

The United States has long been a major source of foreign direct investment (FDI) in other countries—although its net capital inflows have grown in recent years to finance chronic budget and current account deficits. Although Canada remains heavily dependent on foreign capital for economic development and growth, Canadian direct investment abroad has usually exceeded foreign direct investment in Canada since 1997. A relatively closed economy until the 1980s, Mexico has become a significant net importer of capital—although FDI accounts for a significantly higher proportion of Canadian corporate assets (see Table 13.3).

Mexico's status as a source of relatively low-wage labour may serve the comparative advantage

Table 13.2   Intraregional Trade as a Share of Total Two-Way Trade

	European Union	North America	(East) Asia
1980	53.2	32.6	28.8
1990	60.6	42.8	35.0
1999	61.7	54.6	39.1
2010	71.0	48.7	52.6*

* "Asia" for 2010.

Sources: Robert A. Pastor (2001), *Towards a North American community*, (Washington, DC: Institute for International Economics); World Trade Organization (2012), *International Trade Statistics: 2011* (Geneva.)

Table 13.3   Foreign Direct Investment Stocks as percentage of GDP

	2000			2013		
	Outbound	Inbound	Ratio	Outbound	Inbound	Ratio
Canada	32.8	29.3	1.117	40.1	35.3	1.136
United States	26.2	27.1	0.968	38.0	29.5	1.287
Mexico	1.4	17.5	0.081	10.8	29.3	0.370

Source: UNCTAD at http://unctadstat.unctad.org/EN/Index.html; author's calculations.

of both countries by lowering overall net labour costs on the assembly of many products, leading some recent observers to characterize it as America's "China next door."[18] However, Mexico's broader strategy of using NAFTA as a platform for economic modernization and competitiveness has been undermined by three major factors: the slow pace of domestic policy reforms within Mexico after 1997; tightened US border security since 2001, addressed later in this chapter; and disruptions from Mexico's painful adjustment to NAFTA.

The latter have strengthened internal political resistance to needed reforms within Mexico, creating a "chicken and egg" conundrum in which needed restructuring of, for example, the energy and education sectors, cannot be achieved without additional revenues to finance both structural reforms and "compensatory" distributive measures, particularly under conditions of divided government (see below). These structural rigidities increased Mexico's vulnerability to China's rapid rise as a source of low-cost imports to the United States until major policy changes introduced by the Peña Nieto administration elected in 2012.[19]

In recent years, Mexico's federal budget has depended heavily on Pemex, the national oil company, for up to 40 per cent of its budget. This reality, combined with strong political constraints either on loosening state monopolies on energy production and distribution, or on joint-venture operations with foreign firms deeply rooted in

Mexican nationalism, substantially constrains Mexico's capacity to invest in the renewal of its rapidly depleting offshore reserves. However, Pemex's 25 per cent decline in production between 2004 and 2012 threatened to place state revenues at significant risk. Significantly, the Peña Nieto administration elected in 2012 was able to persuade Congress to enact constitutional changes that eluded its predecessors to expanding opportunities for Pemex to engage in joint ventures with foreign investors.[20]

Moreover, migration and labour mobility issues remain highly controversial for Americans—whose household incomes (except for those in the top quintile) have never recovered to 1990s levels. By contrast, average pre-tax and after-tax incomes have grown for all income groups in Canada since 2000.[21] These realities have made NAFTA deeply suspect among many Americans, transcending partisan and ideological differences.[22]

These pressures have led advocates of closer integration such as Robert Pastor to advocate the creation of structural adjustment funds by the US and Canada to facilitate economic adjustment in Mexico, and rebalance some of the economic incentives that led millions of Mexicans to migrate to the United States in search of economic opportunities between 1995 and 2008.[23] However, political support for such proposals appears to be minimal.

A third area of asymmetry emphasized by Mexico is the closer cultural and intergovernmental linkages between the US and Canada due to their greater similarities in language and culture, and long-standing cooperation in bilateral and international relations. This distinction is mostly reflected in American public opinion, which is far more likely to see Canada as a close ally and friend than to see Mexico in these terms (see Table 13.4).[24] However, Canadian governments have come to recognize that American engagement with bilateral issues usually takes place in the context of American domestic politics—requiring careful management to frame preferred policies in ways beneficial to the interests of both countries while avoiding appearances of "meddling."[25] The Harper government's aggressive lobbying for the Keystone XL pipeline may have stretched these boundaries, but without changing the essentially domestic focus of American policies.

The combined effects of these asymmetries greatly increase the relevance of domestic politics and institutions to the ability and willingness of each country's government and political classes to manage ongoing issues of regional integration. Key structural factors include regionalized economies, political cultures, and related variations in income levels and patterns of party competition in each country, as well as the different dynamics through which their respective federal systems mediate or exacerbate these issues. The variables have been magnified by the prevalence of divided government in the US and at least one of its neighbours since 1994. These dynamics prevent all three countries from functioning as "unitary actors" in their cross-border policies, encouraging segmentation of issues and limiting the scope of policy changes they can address at any particular time.

Regionalism, Federalism, and Divided Government

Canada, Mexico, and the United States are three large, regionally diverse countries. However, divergences in geography, regional economic disparities, and federal and political systems have affected the two smaller countries' adaptation to NAFTA in different ways. US and, particularly, Mexican federal systems manage regional differences through "intrastate" federalism: political brokerage involving their respective federal executive branches and Congresses. Canada's highly decentralized ("interstate") federal system also requires regional and intergovernmental trade-offs that require sensitivity to the distributive effects of federal policies.

Table 13.4   American Views of "The Neighbours"

		Very favourable	Mostly favourable	Mostly unfavourable	Very unfavourable	No opinion
2013	Canada	53	38	3	2	3
	Mexico	8	39	34	15	3
2009	Canada	39	51	4	2	4
	Mexico	7	44	28	15	6
2005	Canada	38	48	8	2	4
	Mexico	15	59	16	5	5
2001	Canada	51	39	4	3	3
	Mexico	17	50	17	9	7

Source: Frank Newport and Igor Himelfarb (2013), "Americans least favorable towards Iran," (Princeton: Gallup, February).

Table 13.5   Relative Centralization of Federal Systems in North America

	Index of Decentralization[1] (20 point scale)	Central Government Pre-transfer Revenues (% of government total) (2000–04)	Federal Transfers as Share of Provincial/State Revenues (2000–04)
Canada	16.5	47.2	12.9
United States	14.5	54.2	25.6
Mexico	5.0	91.3	87.9

[1]Ferran Requejo (2010), "Federalism and Democracy: The Case of Minority Nations – A Federalist Deficit," in *Federal Democracies*, ed., M. Burgess and A. Gagnon (London: Routledge), 275–98.
Source: Michael M. Atkinson, Daniel Beland, and Gregory Marchildon (2013), *Governance and public policy in Canada: A view from the provinces.* (Toronto: University of Toronto Press), 11–12.

These domestic political constraints create substantial barriers to the kinds of large-scale changes to North American institutions advocated by some business and academic critics.[26] Table 13.5 provides metrics on the relative centralization of each country's federal system.

Geography has facilitated Canada's adaptation to NAFTA, allowing the seven provinces (with 95 per cent of its population) sharing land borders with the United States to adapt to varied regional conditions. Arguably, with only 18 per cent of its population living in the 6 (of 31) states along the American border, both physical and economic geography have increased Mexico's difficulty in adapting to NAFTA. American experiences have been more complex, reflecting not only its proximity to borders but major differences in regional political cultures and variations in NAFTA's economic impact. Each country's constitutional systems of checks and balances, together with the practical constraints of divided government noted later in this chapter, impose important constraints on formal policy coordination, limiting the scope for major policy changes.

Despite democratic reforms introduced in the 1990s, the Mexican federal system remains the most centralized of the three countries, reflecting 71 years of single-party rule under the Institutional

Revolutionary Party (PRI) (1929–2000) and the resulting effects of a strongly clientelistic political culture. These factors, exercised through a tradition of strong, centralized executive government, enabled the Salinas administration to mobilize the full resources of the Mexican state to build domestic support for NAFTA before 1994[27]—but not to cope with the subsequent economic and political challenges.

Mexican democratization emerged in the 1990s after the defection of the PRI's left-nationalist wing in the late 1980s to form the PRD (Partido de la Revolutión Democrática), President Ernesto Zedillo's recognition of the need for reforms to Mexico's often corrupt political system, and the economic and social disruption resulting from the 1994–95 peso crisis and adaptation to NAFTA. Vicente Fox's centre-right Partido Acción Nacional (PAN) exploited these changes in 2000 to achieve the first peaceful transition of power between parties since the 1911 revolution.

Regional and sectoral interests in the United States are frequently brokered through the historically decentralized committee systems of Congress. Brokerage politics and divided government frequently impose constraints on the federal executive. Negotiating and ratifying the CUSFTA and NAFTA required cooperation between Republicans and centrist Democrats under the Reagan, George H.W. Bush, and Clinton administrations. However, subsequent partisan and ideological polarization has limited the common political ground necessary to pursue deeper integration.

The constitutionally entrenched decentralization of Canada's federal system is reinforced by the perpetual challenges of balancing regional and linguistic interests—reflected in persistent autonomist sentiment in Quebec, the related weakening (and, since 1993, regionalization) of national political parties, and the growing capacities (and sometimes, ambitions) of provincial governments. Broad provincial support was vital to the Mulroney government's successful negotiation of CUSFTA in 1987–88, and its de facto ratification in the 1988 election.[28] Accommodating diverse regional economic interests remains a major factor in Canada's trade, investment, and other economic policies.

Mexico's centralized federal system is accompanied by regional economic disparities far greater than in either the US or Canada—even though federal transfers provide almost 90 per cent of state revenues.[29] The Federal District (Mexico City) has more than three times the average Mexican GDP per capita. Apart from Mexico City, the wealthiest areas of the country are the six northern states bordering the United States, and the oil-producing and tourism-based regions bordering the Gulf of Mexico. There is also substantial manufacturing activity in central Mexican states, including Jalisco,

Mexico State, Puebla and, more recently, Aquascalientes—much of it fed by heavy investments by multinational automobile companies to service North American markets. This trend has been reinforced by the phasing-out of Mexican domestic incentives to develop export-oriented manufacturing in export zones in its northern border states.[30] Since 2008, there has been a substantial southward shift of production both within the United States and toward Mexico (see Table 13.6), reinforced by the long-term depreciation of the Mexican peso (see Table 13.8, Figure 13.5).[31] Current trends suggest that Mexico will become the largest source of US auto imports by 2016, surpassing both Canada and Japan.[32] However, almost half of Mexico's population lives in 12 states whose average GDP per capita is less than 70 per cent of the national average—roughly that of Mississippi or Prince Edward Island, the poorest jurisdictions in the US and Canada respectively (see Table 13.7). These factors, which predate NAFTA, have been reinforced by clientelistic political cultures with limited incentives for state governments to escape the trap of fiscal and economic dependence.[33]

Although foreign investment in Mexico has grown significantly from 9.2 per cent of GDP in 1993 to 29.3 per cent in 2013, 75 per cent of inward FDI between 2000 and 2012 went to four jurisdictions: Mexico City (55 per cent), its neighbour Mexico state (5 per cent), and the northern states of Nuevo Leon (10 per cent) and Chihuahua

Table 13.6   North American Production of Cars and Light Trucks: 2000–14

	Canada		Mexico		United States		North America	
	Million	%	Million	%	Million	%	Million	%
2000	3.0	16.7	2.0	10.9	12.8	72.3	17.7	100.0
2004	2.7	16.7	1.6	9.7	12.0	73.7	16.3	100.0
2008	2.1	16.1	2.2	16.7	8.7	67.2	12.9	100.0
2014	2.4	13.7	3.4	19.3	11.7	67.0	17.4	100.0

Source: International Organization of Motor Vehicle Manufacturers at http://www.oica.net/category/production-statistics/; author's calculations.

Table 13.7 Regional Disparities within North America—2011

GDP/capita	United States		Mexico		Canada	
% of National Average	#	% of population	#	% of population	#	% of population
>120	8+	10.6	5+	17.1	5*	15.7
100–120	15	41.8	7	12.9	1**	0.1
80–99	21	40.9	7	17.9	5	81.0
<80	7	6.7	12	52.1	2	3.1
Total States, Provinces, and Territories	51	100.0	32	100.0	13	100.0

+ Includes District of Columbia, Federal District (Mexico City).
* includes Yukon and Northwest Territories.
** Nunavut Territory.
Sources: national statistical agencies; author's calculations.

(5 per cent)—generating fewer benefits for poorer states in the country's south and southeast.[34] Ironically, part of this gap has been filled by remittances by migrants in the US to relatives located largely in rural Mexico.

Weintraub and others have suggested that, until recently, these realities have combined with the effects of divided governance, noted below, to hinder the ability and willingness of Mexican governments to "make the structural changes that are necessary for economic growth"—including reforms to education, the justice system, and fiscal and tax policies—particularly those relating to the energy sector, and related issues of combating poverty.[35] The persistence of rural poverty, in particular, has provided considerable incentives for migration in search of greater economic opportunity—both internally within Mexico and to the US. President Peña Nieto's Pact for Mexico is an ambitious effort to create cross-partisan consensus to support structural changes to fiscal, competition, energy, and education policies, among others, to address these challenges.[36]

The effects of Canadian regionalism have less to do with relative regional income disparities, although these persist, and more with differences among provincial industrial structures and resource endowments which affect the relative prosperity and competitiveness of Canada's varied regional economies. Unlike Mexico, Canadian provinces retain sovereign jurisdiction over the ownership and development of most natural resources within their boundaries, often precluding unilateral federal action. The redistributive effects of Canada's tax-transfer system have reduced overall and regional disparities in family incomes—both in absolute terms and in comparison with the US.[37]

CUSFTA, NAFTA and other neoliberal policies introduced after 1985 resulted in Canada's economic axis pivoting from an emphasis on East–West (interprovincial) trade to international (largely North–South) trade. In 2010, seven of ten Canadian provinces exported more to foreign countries, mainly the US, than to other provinces.[38] These factors, combined with the post-2000 commodity boom and growing trade links with Asia, have reinforced the **regionalization** of the Canadian economy—both within North America[39] and in building economic links beyond it.

Canada's exchange rates typically reflect shifts in the prices of major traded commodities—with

Table 13.8 North American Exchange Rates: 1990–2013

					Average annual exchange rates				
	1990	1994	1997	2002	2007	2009	2011	2014	% change 1994–2014
MXN→USD	0.356	0.296*	0.126	0.103	0.092	0.074	0.080	0.075	− 74.7%
CND→USD	0.862	0.732	0.722	0.637	0.931	0.876	0.989	0.906	+ 23.8%
USD→€			(1999) 1.058	0.945	1.371	1.391	1.391	1.329	(1999–2014) − 25.5%

* Year of Mexican Peso Crisis
Source: www.data360.org; author's calculations.

significant regional effects. The loonie's substantial depreciation against the American dollar between 1990 and 2002 (see Table 13.8), though initially boosting export sales for Canadian manufacturers centred in Ontario, Quebec, and Manitoba, also reflected sustained price declines for resource and some agricultural commodities. Sharp increases in global commodity (especially oil) prices after 2000 have strongly reinforced economic growth in Western Canada and Newfoundland, whereas higher exchange rates and increased international competition have increased the competitive challenges facing many central Canadian industries. Rising global energy prices between 2000 and 2013 (except for 2008–09) have increased energy products' share of Canadian exports from 8.1 per cent to 22.7 per cent in 2012, peaking at 25.7 per cent in 2008—almost entirely to the US, with most production centred in Alberta, British Columbia, Saskatchewan, and Newfoundland.[40]

Canada's bitumen and heavy oil exports sell at a discount compared with lighter grades of oil. However, the uncertain, cyclical character of oil prices and the availability of surplus refining capacity in the US Gulf states have created incentives for most producers to send their product south for further refining rather than adding value in Canada. Pervasive opposition by American environmental groups to Canadian oil sands imports has slowed the expansion of cross-border pipelines, as noted in Monica Gattinger and Rafael Aguirre's chapter (chapter 22). The resulting regional glut has encouraged Canadian governments to pursue diversified export markets by building or expanding pipeline capacity to both coasts, while integrated North American rail networks have carried rapidly growing volumes of oil since 2009.[41] However, building new infrastructure has been greatly complicated by regional political dynamics and Supreme Court judgments expanding Aboriginal rights over lands intended to serve as pipeline rights-of-way.[42]

Canada's continued dependence on American export markets ensures Ottawa's preoccupation with maintaining market access secured through FTAs and the pervasive networks of business and economic interdependence they have reinforced, while attempting to balance regional interests in various economic sectors. One sign of the extensive integration of manufacturing supply chains within North America, blurring national distinctions between companies, is that protectionist "trade remedy" actions by US producers against Canadian-based firms have virtually evaporated since 2004.[43] McKinney notes that US exports currently make up about 40 per cent of value-added in Mexican manufactured exports to the United States, and 25 per cent from Canada.[44] However, although claims against Mexican-based firms remain well below their share of American trade, entrenched US domestic interests have been exploiting trade remedy laws to limit imports of Mexican cement, sugar, and tomatoes in protracted disputes—as well as preventing access to US trucking markets beyond a narrow border strip—as well as, until January of 2015—preventing access to US trucking markets beyond a narrow border strip.

Regional interests in the United States are usually subsumed within the broader category of interest-group politics and the protection of local interests in Congress and through administrative law processes of the executive branch. Highly decentralized congressional committee structures have traditionally provided a significant check on presidential authority in international trade negotiations, as well as the capacity for international regulatory cooperation.[45]

Divided Government

The challenge of divided government has emerged from two major developments: growing partisan and ideological polarization in the United States, particularly in Congress since 1994, and the progressive democratization of Mexico since 1997, particularly electoral reforms that have forced successive presidents to negotiate for support for their legislative initiatives with opposition parties in Congress.[46] After 20 years of successive majority governments broadly committed to progressive trade liberalization, three Canadian elections, in 2004, 2006, and 2008, also resulted in minority governments.

Mexico has experienced divided government for 17 of the 20 years since 1994, the United States for 13½ years, and Canada for seven (see Figure 13.4). Combined with asymmetrical electoral cycles—the only year during which national elections for the three countries have largely coincided was 2000—and a series of polarizing issues affecting cross-border cooperation between 2000 and 2010, these developments have narrowed the political mandates and "windows" for introducing major initiatives.

American observers are inclined to view divided government in Mexico as a recipe for gridlock.[47] It certainly provides strong incentives to manage incremental change through regional and intra-party brokerage involving issue-by-issue coalitions—as the US congressional system does.

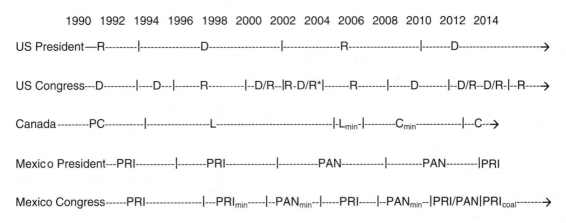

Figure 13.4 Divided Governments in North America since NAFTA

Electoral reforms introduced in 1997 have provided mixed incentives for cooperation between a centrist party (usually the PRI), and one or both of the other two major parties.[48] The electoral system encourages the development of varied national and state-level electoral coalitions, sometimes cutting across ideological lines, such as periodic PAN/PRD collaboration to contain local PRI dominance. These incentives have encouraged the emergence of three major parties within a multi-party system, while undermining party discipline as party factions and minor parties jockey for inclusion on coalition slates used to "top up" representation from single member districts of the Chamber of Deputies. Smaller parties have elected 29.5, 20, and 30 per cent of federal deputies respectively in the past three elections (2006–12). However, the Peña Nieto administration has shown great skill in passing several major elements of its "Pact for Mexico" reforms through Congress by means of a series of issue-by-issue deals with individual opposition parties.[49]

Divided government in the United States is not new. But it has taken on new dimensions as both parties have become more ideologically polarized, particularly in the House of Representatives. These patterns are reinforced by the use of gerrymandering to produce a majority of single-party-dominant districts in many states, and by state-level nomination rules that frequently reinforce the influence of each party's ideological core vote. As a result, it has become more difficult to secure the kinds of cross-party (or House–Senate) deal-making necessary to obtain approval for major legislation that involves bridging major ideological fault lines—let alone pan-North American governance approaches independent of Congress.[50]

The practical effects of divided government on North American governance may be seen in the design of major trilateral and bilateral efforts at cross-border cooperation since 2005. The Security and Prosperity Partnership (SPP), a trilateral effort to combine security cooperation with improved border facilitation, was designed to function within areas of exclusive executive jurisdiction in each country—generally avoiding measures requiring congressional or parliamentary authorization. However, the SPP's diffuse bureaucratic agenda lacked effective political coordination, signalling the lack of effective political will necessary to override bureaucratic inertia. As a result, rather than reducing the SPP's political profile, it triggered suspicions from both American and Canadian nationalist groups of a "hidden agenda" intended to promote "integration by stealth" without adequate public consultation or attention to constitutional norms.[51]

The Obama administration abandoned the SPP in 2009, later replacing it with separate bilateral processes on border security and facilitation and on regulatory cooperation with Canada and Mexico between 2010 and 2012. The two border facilitation processes initially showed signs of improved inter-agency and intergovernmental coordination, along with some improvements in stakeholder (if not necessarily public) engagement, although some observers suggest declining momentum resulting from limited political commitment. However, without effective congressional engagement, regulatory cooperation measures are heavily dependent on the broader international agendas of particular American regulatory agencies, and their congruence with the agendas of their Canadian and Mexican counterparts.[52]

Political constraints on cross-border cooperation imposed on minority governments in Canada were more significant during the administration of the highly unpopular George W. Bush than that of Barack Obama, whose popularity has generally diffused the tactical anti-Americanism to which Canadian political parties often resort when it serves their purposes.[53] The return to majority government in 2011 helped the Harper government to engage in broader negotiations under the Trans-Pacific Partnership (TPP). This process may ultimately provide an "easier" road toward regulatory coordination by making it more likely to reduce regulatory barriers to trade beyond North America more than would have been possible otherwise.

However, any such progress must address three major sets of issues that have emerged to complicate the evolution of North American integration, and their effects on public support for further integration: competitive liberalization; the emergence of security and migration issues as competitors to trade facilitation; and competing national contexts for energy policies and their integration with environmental issues.

Competitive Liberalization

Competitive liberalization—the parallel pursuit of multiple, overlapping bilateral and regional trade agreements—poses a major challenge for both Canadian trade policies and North American governance. Success in negotiating FTAs with an expanding network of partners makes it easier to be included in international investment and supply networks and can provide a source of comparative advantage. Exclusion from—or marginalization within—such networks can create a form of comparative disadvantage, both in pursuing foreign direct investment and from risks of securing access to such networks *after* major trading partners have designed these institutions to serve their interests.

CUSFTA and NAFTA were negotiated to provide Canada with secure access to US markets—at least in those areas covered by CUSFTA—in the hope of protecting that access against marginalization by emerging "hub and spoke" arrangements centred on the United States. Both the US and

Mexico subsequently pursued strategies of competitive liberalization as part of what Schott describes as a "three-dimensional trade strategy" involving parallel global, regional, and bilateral FTA negotiations.[54]

Although negotiations for a Free Trade Agreement of the Americas (FTAA 1998–2003) ultimately failed, largely due to differences between the US and Brazil, the Bush administration used the restored "Trade Promotion Authority" provided by a temporarily Republican-controlled Congress in 2001 to initiate successful FTA negotiations with several Latin American countries and "strategic" partners on other continents (see Table 13.9).

Anticipating these events, Mexico's Zedillo administration negotiated a series of bilateral FTAs with Latin American neighbours in the late 1990s, subsequently negotiating FTAs with the European Union (EU) and Japan by 2005. This strategy was intended to make Mexico a secondary hub for hemispheric integration, and a platform for firms from outside North America seeking large-scale entry into North American markets. However, as noted above, tighter US border security, intense Chinese competition, and the constraints placed by divided government on domestic reforms limited the strategy's overall effectiveness.[55]

Canada has been a comparative latecomer to the politics of competitive liberalization. Canadian trade policies in 2003–08 were focused primarily on protecting access to US markets and engaging in the multilateral WTO Doha Round process. Since 2009, Ottawa's two-tiered strategy has combined ongoing bilateral processes with Washington with the pursuit of a series of trade agreements outside North America.

Bilateral initiatives include the "Beyond-the-Border" process to streamline border management, facilitate cross-border trade, and develop a bilateral security perimeter with the US, while pursuing sectoral regulatory cooperation as extensions

Table 13.9 Competitive Liberalization Within North America
Additional Preferential Trade Agreements Negotiated by Each NAFTA Country

Separate Treaties with 3 NAFTA Countries	Mexico		United States	Canada
Chile	Argentina	Bolivia	Australia	EFTA
Colombia	Brazil	Cuba	Bahrain	Jordan
Costa Rica	El Salvador-	Ecuador	CA-4*	Panama
Israel	Guatemala-	Guyana	Dominican Republic	Oman
Peru	Nicaragua	Morocco	Jordan	European Union**
South Korea	Paraguay	Trinidad/Tobago	Panama	
	Uruguay	Venezuela	**Singapore**	
	EFTA	EU		
	Macedonia	Serbia		
	Algeria	Benin		
	Cameroon	Egypt		
	Ghana	Libya		
	Morocco	Mozambique		
	Nigeria	Sudan		
	Tanzania	Zimbabwe		
	Bangladesh	India		
	Indonesia	Iran		
	Iraq	**Japan**		
	Malaysia	Myanmar		
	North Korea	Pakistan		
	Philippines	**Singapore**		
	Sri Lanka	Thailand		
	Turkey	**Vietnam**		
+++++	+++++	+++++		+++++
Under Negotiation				Caricom
Trans-Pacific Partnership	South Korea			CA-4
(countries in **bold** print)				Dominican Republic
				India
				Japan
				Morocco
				Singapore
				Ukraine

*CA-4 — El Salvador-Guatemala-Honduras-Nicaragua
** Awaiting ratification
Sources: World Trade Organization, "Regional Trade Agreements"; Foreign Affairs, International Trade and Development Canada.

of similar post-NAFTA and SPP processes. Washington is engaged in a parallel regulatory cooperation process with Mexico. The Harper government's broader trade liberalization strategy has paralleled previous US initiatives in Latin America and the Middle East, with one major exception: negotiations for a 2013 Comprehensive Economic and Trade Agreement (CETA) with the European Union, currently awaiting ratification by contracting states.

Harper's majority election victory in 2011 freed Ottawa to participate in Trans-Pacific Partnership (TPP) negotiations with the US, Mexico, and eight other Asia-Pacific countries (nine if Japan joins the talks). Like the Canada–EU CETA talks, TPP negotiations are aimed at a "twenty-first century" agreement to reduce barriers to agricultural trade and many domestic policies (including those of subnational governments) not covered by previous agreements. Mexico has also joined the TPP talks—marking the first occasion since the demise of the FTAA that all three North American countries have participated in the same plurilateral negotiating process.

Some observers in both the US and Canada have suggested that the wider regional agreement provides a broad enough forum to provide each country with incentives for addressing the remaining barriers to trade liberalization—particularly in domestic regulatory systems and agricultural trade—that were politically untouchable in the context of NAFTA. However, many barriers remain, not least President Obama's challenges in securing Trade Promotion Authority (TPA) from Congress, lapsed since 2007, which would allow for a single ratification vote by each house of Congress, and the challenge of determining how to reconcile the "noodle bowl" of previously negotiated bilateral or regional agreements within the framework of an eventual TPP Treaty.[56]

A critical factor in managing ongoing trade liberalization processes, both in the US and in its relations with Mexico and Canada, is the development of coordinated or complementary approaches to managing border security, travel, and migration issues.

Migration, Terrorism, and Insecurity: "Security Trumps Trade" after 9/11

Both the US and Canada have long welcomed immigrants—with periodic exceptions based on varied mixtures of economic and racial insecurity. In 2000–05, official net migration to the United States totalled 6.5 million, and just over 1 million

to Canada. American policies have typically leaned toward family reunification whereas Canadian policies since the 1990s have emphasized economic criteria.[57]

In contrast, Mexico's comparative underdevelopment has encouraged periodic waves of outmigration, usually to the US. Sometimes, the two countries have managed these issues through bilateral guest worker agreements, such as the *bracero* program of 1943–64. However, social disruption created by major devaluations of the Mexican peso in 1982–83 and again in 1994–96 triggered ongoing surges in both legal and illegal migration.[58]

The terrorist attacks of 11 September 2001 effectively ended the presumption of open borders intended to facilitate economic integration, trade, and travel that had characterized US–Canadian and, to a lesser extent, US–Mexican relations since the ratification of CUSFTA and NAFTA. Within several months of 9/11, the Bush administration had negotiated detailed bilateral agreements on border management and security with Canada and Mexico. However, partisan competition to mobilize and respond to public opinion on "homeland security" issues as well as intense competition within the US federal bureaucracy provided strong incentives for unilateral policy-making.[59]

These events resulted in the creation of the new Department of Homeland Security (DHS) from 22 legacy agencies. Congress passed legislation in 2004 implementing the recommendations of the voluminous 9/11 Commission report, including unilateral measures for securing borders and new "safe ports" legislation that required mandatory screening of all shipping containers entering the US. Canadian governments introduced some parallel measures.[60]

The cumulative impact of these measures was greatest on companies with deeply integrated supply and distribution chains *within* North America, which often faced multiple border processing requirements and often unpredictable delays, while benefiting imports from China and other Asian countries, which usually faced one customs review rather than several. These measures also reduced the relative competitiveness of Mexican manufacturing and assembly plants as low-cost alternatives to Asian suppliers.

Border security issues became deeply enmeshed with US immigration policy debates. As noted earlier, the dislocations of Mexico's NAFTA transition fell most heavily on that country's rural poor. The Mexican peso's value against the US dollar dropped by 52 per cent between 1993 and 1996, 75 per cent by 2004 (see Figure 13.5). Reductions in trade barriers resulted in major structural changes to Mexican agriculture, including rising imports, falling prices, and a shift away from communal subsistence farming to commercial agriculture, with predictable effects on small-scale farming families.[61]

Rising American demand for unskilled and semi-skilled labour, combined with poorly enforced border and employer documentation controls, encouraged persistently high levels of illegal migration—more than 500,000 annually between 1996 and 2006. By 2000, some economists estimated that as many as 30 per cent of Mexicans with "formal sector" employment were working in the US. Weintraub notes that between 2002 and early 2008, "more Mexicans found jobs in the United States than in formal employment in Mexico."[62]

These trends provided a major safety valve for Mexican society, providing employment opportunities north of the border, *and* sharp increases in remittances to migrants' families—largely in rural Mexico. Remittances increased from $US 8.9 billion in 2001 to $ 25.1 billion in 2008 before declining during the subsequent recession.[63]

But efforts to enhance cooperation on border security and facilitation with Canada and Mexico after 9/11 and through the SPP were largely ineffective—partly due to growing American public resistance to integration with Mexico, partly due to sizeable differences in "threat perceptions" and the

Figure 13.5 Foreign Exchange Rate Mexico/US

range of domestically acceptable policy responses available to American officials and their Canadian and Mexican counterparts.[64] Neither the US nor Canada has been willing to cede sovereign control over their respective immigration policies, apart from a few areas of reciprocal accommodation. Canada's visa requirement for Mexican visitors, imposed in 2009 in response to a rising number of refugee applications resulting from narco-violence in Mexico, has also eroded bilateral relations, despite recent efforts to harmonize trusted-traveller programs among the three countries.[65]

The Calderón administration's commitment to disrupting the activities of drug smuggling cartels—a long-standing goal of US policies toward Mexico—led to a bloody "narco-insurgency" by criminal syndicates, many led by defectors from the Mexican police and military, which claimed close to 50,000 lives between 2006 and 2012. These developments led to much closer cooperation between US law enforcement and Mexican military authorities under the Meridá Initiative of 2008. At the same time, they demonstrated the challenges to American unilateralism created by drug-related corruption and other governance problems in fostering mutual trust and cooperation.[66] It remains to be seen how policy shifts introduced by President Peña Nieto since 2012 toward the drug war will affect the bilateral relationship.[67]

The US–Canada Beyond-the-Border process, initiated in 2011, has extended previous bilateral cooperation between law enforcement and other security agencies in each country, as well as providing a framework for joint security measures to facilitate cross-border commerce and travel and manage border bottlenecks. Although business groups in both countries have strongly supported these processes (and a parallel process with Mexico), progress remains slow.[68]

However, such measures only begin to address the *mutual* insecurity that has hindered closer US-Mexican and trilateral North American cooperation on labour mobility. Prospects for bipartisan agreement on immigration reform remain remote despite the sharp drop in illegal migration since the 2008–09 recession and increased enforcement both of border and employer hiring practices.

Conclusion

North America remains an amorphous concept in 2015. Its economies remain substantially more integrated and interdependent than in 1994 but societal divisions remain deep, as much within as between the three nations of North America. Collaboration among its national governments remains uneven across policy sectors. It is generally conditional on perceptions of mutual interest in each country arising from that interdependence, but also on the willingness of national governments and political systems to engage in the mutual accommodation of different political systems and varied sectoral regulatory regimes. Broader international negotiations, such as those associated with the Trans-Pacific Partnership or separate US and Canadian negotiations with the European Union, may create incentives for such cooperation—although their outcomes are far from certain. More likely is a continued pattern of pragmatic incremental adaptation by fragmented political systems to changing circumstances, punctuated by periodic crises that force national governments to collaborate more closely. As with the French proverb, *plus ça change, plus c'est la même chose.*

Notes

1   S. Clarkson, (2008), *Does North America exist? Governing the continent after NAFTA and 9/11*, 454.

2   I. Morales, *Post-NAFTA North America*, 1–2, 38–42.

3   H. V. Milner, *Interests, institutions, and information: Domestic politics and international relations*. Morales, *Post-NAFTA North America*, (20–2, 40–1); Geoffrey Hale, *So near yet so far*.

4   F., Bergsten, "Competitive liberalization and global free trade: A vision for the Early 21st Century, Working Paper 96-15; Jeffrey J. Schott (2007), "Trade Negotiations among *NAFTA* Partners," 77ff.

5   M. Gattinger, and G. Hale, "Borders and bridges: Canada's policy relations in North America," 7ff.

6   B. W. Tomlin, Norman Hillmer and Hampson, F. O., *Canada's international policies: Agendas, alternatives and policies*, 90–5.

7   R. Rubin, and J. Weisberg, *In an uncertain world*, 3–39; J. Passel, D. Cohn, and A. Gonzalez-Barrera, "Net migration from Mexico falls to zero—and perhaps less,"; Pastor, *Toward a North American community*.

8   Morales, *Post-NAFTA North America*, 123–6; P. Andreas, and T. J. Biersteker, *The rebordering of North America*; Edward Alden, *The closing of the American border*.

9   J. Garreau, *The nine nations of North America*.

10 Hale, *So Near Yet So Far*, 3–4, 55–64; Morales, *Post-NAFTA North America*.

11 R. A. Pastor, *Toward a North American community: Lessons from the old world for the New*, 149–50.

12 Ibid.; I. Studer, "Obstacles to integration," 53–75.

13 Hale, *So near yet so far*, 84–90.

14 Statistics Canada, "International investment position, Canadian direct investment abroad and foreign direct investment in Canada, by country."

15 G. Hale, and M. Gattinger, "Variable geometry and traffic circles," 361–80; see also Davidow, J. *The bear and the porcupine: the U.S. and Mexico*.

16 I. M. Destler, *American trade politics*.

17 Pastor, *Toward a North American community*, 157–8; J. Davidow, *The bear and the porcupine*; S. Weintraub, *Unequal partners: The United States and Mexico*.

18 Rapoza, K., "For American exporters, Mexico is the China next door."

19 Ibid.; Energy Information Administration, *Country reports: Mexico*; Weintraub, *Unequal Partners*; Iliff, L., "Mexico makes sweeping changes at energy regulator."

20 C. Wise, "Unfulfilled Promise," 84–8.

21 Villareal, M. A. (2012), "U.S.-Mexico economic relations: Trends, issues and implications"; Alexander, C. and Fong, F., "Income inequality under various income metrics."

22 For example, see "Americans and Canadians feel they have lost out with NAFTA," *Angus Reid Public Opinion*, 17 May (2012.

23 Pastor, *Toward a North American community*; R. A. Pastor, *The North American Idea*, 169–72.

24 Hale, *So near yet so far*, 88; Newport and Himelfarb, "Americans least favorable toward Iran"; Chicago Council on Global Affairs and Woodrow Wilson Center, "New Chicago Council Survey Finds American Opinion of Mexico Mixed."

25 Hale, *So near yet so far*, 99–174.

26 For example, see Pastor, *The idea of North America*.

27 Weintraub, *Unequal Partners*, 32.

28 G. B. Doern, and B. Tomlin, *Faith and fear: The free trade story*.

29 L. F. Cabrera-Castellanos, and R. Lozano-Cortes, "Decentralization and fiscal federalism in Mexico"; see also T. Courchene and A. Diaz-Cayeros, "Transfers and the nature of the Mexican federation," (200–36).

30 T. Payan, "Cross border flows—achieving security by opening, liberalizing and deregulating."

31 D. DesRosiers, "North American auto industry review"; D. Flavelle, "Auto manufacturing in Canada in long-term decline: report warns."

32 A. Gomez Licon, "Mexico to trump Japan as No. 2 car exporter to U.S. by year-end 2014."

33 Courchene and Diaz-Cayeros, "Transfers and the Nature of the Mexican Federation"; Cabrera-Castellanos and Lozano-Cortes, "Decentralization and Fiscal Federalism in Mexico." One recently cited example of the perverse facilitation of clientelism through poorly structured transfer systems is the 160,000 "shadow" teachers kept on state payrolls through the corrupt influence of the national teachers' union (SNTE). D. V. Negroponte, "Mexico's Enrique Peña Nieto confronts the challenges of federalism, fiscal reform, and education."

34 Weintraub, *Unequal partners*, 11–12. United States. U.S. Embassy—Mexico City (2013), "Foreign Direct Investment Factsheet" (Washington, DC: Department of State, April).

35 Weintraub, *Unequal partners*, 11ff; see also G. H. Hansen, "Understanding Mexico's economic underperformance."

36 A. I. Martinez, and S. Gardner, "Left's backing boosts Mexico tax plan chances, right skeptical"; C. Helman, and A. Fontevecchia, "Mexico's Enrique Pena Nieto is leading an oil revolution worth billions."

37 Alexander and Fong, "Income inequality under different income metrics," Statistics Canada (2012), "Median total income by province and territory," *CANSIM Table* 111-0009 (Ottawa: 27 June); United States. Bureau of Economic Affairs (2013), "Median Household Income by State" (Washington, DC: May).

38 The exceptions were Manitoba, Nova Scotia, and Prince Edward Island. Statistics Canada (2012), "Interprovincial and international trade," Cat. 13-518-X, (Ottawa).

39 Canada. Policy Research Initiative, The emergence of cross-border regions between Canada and the United States: Final report.

40 Hale, G., "In pursuit of leverage: The evolution of Canadian trade and investment policies in an increasingly multipolar world," (20106-19; Statistics Canada (2013), "Exports of goods and services on a balance-of-payments basis, by product," *CANSIM Table* 228-0059 (Ottawa: 3 July).

41 G. Hale, "'In the pipeline' or 'over a barrel'? Assessing Canadian efforts to manage U.S.-Canadian energy interdependence"; Y. Hussain, "Crude by rail gathers steam."

42 B. Hutchinson, "Ruling a 'game changer.'" (20

43 Hale, *So near yet so far*, 68; U.S. International Trade Administration (2013), "Antidumping and Countervailing Duty Investigations Initiated after January 01, 2000," (Washington, DC); online at: ia.ita.doc.gov/stats/inv-initiations-2000-current.html; accessed 26 June 2013.

44 J. A. McKinney, "NAFTA at 20 in the context of a changing world economy."

45 R. A. Pastor, and R. F. de Castro, (Eds), *Congress: The controversial pivot*; G. Hale, "Congress: Nobody's partner," 269–301.

46 For example, see Geoffrey Hale (forthcoming), "'Exceptional,' immovable, adaptable: Congress and the limitations of North American governance," in Brian Bow and Greg Anderson, eds. *Building without architecture: Understanding the new North America*, eds. (New York: Routledge); Benito Nacif (2005), "Congress Proposes and the president disposes," in A. B. Peschard-Sverdrup, and S. R. Rioff (Eds), *Mexican governance: From single party rule to divided governance* (Washington, DC: Center for Strategic and International Studies), 1–26.

47 Wise, "Unfulfilled promise," 41–2; Weintraub, *Unequal Partners*, (20–2).

48 Nacif, "Congress proposes, the president disposes," 3.

49 Martinez and Gardner (2013), "Left's backing boosts Mexico tax plan chances," *Reuters*, 9 September; D. Wood, "Raising Lazaro."

50 Hale (forthcoming), "'Exceptional,' immovable, adaptable."

51 G. Anderson, and C. Sands *Negotiating North America: The security and prosperity partnership.*

52 G. Hale, "The U.S.-Canada Regulatory Cooperation Council: Opportunities, outcomes, options."

53 M. Milke, "Limits on deliberative democracy."

54 Schott, "Trade negotiations among NAFTA partners," 77ff.

55 J. Zabludovsky, and S. Gomez-Lora, "Beyond the FTAA," 91–107; Hansen, "Understanding Mexico's economic underperformance," Wise, "Unfulfilled promise.

56 Fergusson et al., *The Trans-Pacific partnership: Issues for Congress*; N. Scheiber, (2014), "Obama is foundering on trade because he's too much like Bill Clinton, not too little."

57 T. M. Woroby, (2010), "Canadian migration policy in a North American framework," in Gattinger and Hale (Eds), *Borders and bridges* (Toronto: Oxford University Press), 214–17.

58 P. Martin, (2005), "Mexico-U.S. migration," 441–7.

59 P. Cellucci, (2005), *Unquiet diplomacy*, 15ff; R. B. Manaut, and C. Rodriguez Ulloa, (2006), "Homeland security in the new North America," in J. Jorge Díez, (Ed.), *Canadian and Mexican security in the new North America* (Montreal &Kingston: McGill-Queen's University Press), 25–38; Alden, *The Closing of the American Border*, 80–146.

60 United States. National Commission on Terrorist Attacks on the United States. *The 9/11 Commission Report.* Washington, DC: July (2004; P. J. Smith, "Anti-terrorism in North America: Is there Convergence or Divergence in Canadian and US Legislative Responses to 9/11 and the US-Canada border." In *Borderlands: Comparing border security in North America and Europe*, E. Brunet-Jailly, (Ed.), 277–310. Ottawa: University of Ottawa Press, 2007.

61 G. C. Hufbauer, and J. J. Schott, *NAFTA revisited*, 283–9, 331–8.

62 Passel et al, "Net migration from Mexico falls to zero"; Martin, "Mexico-U.S. migration," 253; Weintraub, *Unequal partners*, 98.

63 Villareal, "U.S.-Mexico economic relations," 9.

64 G. Hale, and C. Marcotte, "Border security, trade and travel facilitation," 100-19.

65 K. Mackrael, "Tensions rise with Mexico as Harper defends visa limits."

66 J. Davidow, *The Bear and the Porcupine*; Grayson, G. W., *Mexico: Narco-violence and a failed state?*

67 D. Priest, "U.S. role at a crossroads in Mexico's intelligence war on the cartels."

68 United States. The White House, and Canada. Privy Council Office. *United States-canada beyond the border: a shared vision for perimeter security and economic competitiveness.*

Key Terms

competitive liberalization

dual bilateralism

economic regionalization

intermestic(ity)

policy parallelism

Questions for Review

1. What were the major external and domestic factors contributing to the Canadian, American, and Mexican decisions to pursue free trade agreements within North America in the 1980s and 1990s?

2. What major factors have limited the deepening of the North American economic system—in the United States? Canada? Mexico? Why have processes of "dual bilateralism" often become a substitute for closer trilateral policy coordination?

3. What factors help to explain the frequent prevalence of domestic politics in each country in shaping the evolution of bilateral and trilateral North American policy relations?

4. How have US domestic debates over immigration and border security affected political and economic cooperation within North America since 2001? To what extent do these developments reflect competing cross-cutting policy agendas and societal responses to North American integration in each country?

Further Resources

Alden, E. *The closing of the American border: Terrorism, immigration and security since 9/11.*

Clarkson, S. *Does North America exist: Governing the continent after NAFTA and 9/11.*

Gattinger, M. and Hale, G. (Eds). *Borders and bridges: Canada's policy relations in North America.*

Hufbauer, G. and Schott, J. J. *NAFTA revisited: Achievements and challenges.*

Morales, I. *Post-NAFTA North America: Reshaping the economic and political governance of a changing region.*

Pastor, R. A. *The North American idea: A vision of a continental future.*

Studer, I. and Wise, C. (Eds). *Requiem or revival? The promise of North American integration.*

References

Alden, E. (2008). *The closing of the American border: Terrorism, immigration and security since 9/11.* New York: Harper.

Alexander, C. and Fong, F. (2012). "Income inequality under various income metrics." Toronto: TD Economics, 18 December.

Anderson, G. and Sands, C. (2007). *Negotiating North America: The Security and Prosperity Partnership.* Washington, DC: Hudson Institute, September.

Andreas, P. and Biersteker, T. J. (2003). *The Rebordering of North America*, ed. New York: Routledge.

Atkinson, M. M., Beland, D., and Marchildon, G. (2013). *Governance and public policy in Canada: A view from the provinces.* Toronto: University of Toronto Press.

Benitez Manaut, R. and Ulloa, C. R. (2006). "Homeland security in the new North America." *Canadian and Mexican security in the new North America: Challenges and Prospects.* Jordi Diaz (Ed.). Kingston, ON: School of Policy Studies, Queens University and McGill-Queens University Press, 25–38.

Bergsten, F. (1996). "Competitive liberalization and global free trade: A vision for the early 21st century, Working Paper 96-15 (Washington, DC: Peterson Institute for International Economics).

Cabrera-Castellanos, L. F. and Lozano-Cortes, R. (2008). "Decentralization and fiscal federalism in Mexico," MPRA Paper No. 10572; online at: http://mpra.ub.uni-muenchen.de/10572/; accessed 19 June 2013.

Canada. Department of Finance. (2012). *Fiscal reference tables.* Ottawa: October.

Canada. Policy Research Initiative. (2008). The emergence of cross-border regions between Canada and the United States: Final Report. Ottawa: November; online at: publications.gc.ca/collections/collection_2009/policyresearch/PH4-31-2-2008E.pdf; accessed 3 July (2013.

Canada. Supreme Court of Canada. *Tsilhqot'in Nation v. British Columbia*, (2014) SCC 44.

Cellucci, P. (2005). *Unquiet diplomacy.* Toronto: Key Porter.

Clarkson, S. (2008). *Does North America exist? Governing the continent after NAFTA and 9/11.* Toronto: University of Toronto Press.

Courchene, T. and Diaz-Cayeros, A. (2000). "Transfers and the nature of the Mexican federation," in M. Guigale and S. B. Webb (Eds), *Achievements and Challenges of Fiscal Decentralization: Lessons from Mexico.* Washington, DC: World Bank, 200–36.

Davidow, J. (2005). *The US and Mexico: The bear and the porcupine.* Princeton, NJ: Marcus Weiner.

Desrosiers, D. (2008). "North American auto industry review." *Observations 22:3* (Windsor: Dennis Desrosiers and Associates).

Destler, I. M. (2005). *American trade politics*, 4th ed. Washington, DC: Institute for International Economics (20.

Doern, G. B. and Gattinger, M. (2003). *Power Switch: Energy regulatory governance in the twenty-first century*. Toronto: University of Toronto Press.

———. and Tomlin, B.. (1991). *Faith and fear: The free trade story* (Toronto: Stoddart).

Fergusson, I. F., Cooper, W. H., Jurenas, R., Williams, B. R. (2013). *The Trans-Pacific Partnership negotiations: Issues for Congress. CRS Report # 42694*. Washington, DC: Congressional Research Service, Library of Congress, 17 June.

Flavelle, D. (2013). "Auto manufacturing in Canada in long-term decline: report warns," *The Toronto Star*, 19 April.

Garreau, J. (1981). *The nine nations of North America*. New York: Houghton Mifflin.

Gattinger, M. and Hale, G. (2010). "Borders and bridges: Canada's policy relations in North America," in M. Gattinger and G. Hale (Eds), *Borders and bridges: Canada's policy relations in North America* (Toronto: Oxford University Press), 1–18.

Gomez Licon, A. (2014). "Mexico to trump Japan as No. 2 car exporter to U.S. by year-end (2014," *Associated Press*, 21 February

Grayson, G. W. (2010). *Mexico: Narco-Violence and a Failed State?* New Brunswick, NJ: Transaction.

Hale, G. (2011). "Congress: Nobody's Partner." In *Forgotten partnership redux: U.S.-Canada relations in the 21st century*, Greg Anderson and Christopher Sands, eds. Amherst, NY: Cambria Press, pp. 269–301.

———. (2011). "'In the pipeline' or 'over a barrel'? Assessing Canadian efforts to manage U.S.-Canadian energy interdependence, *Canadian-American Public Policy* 76, May.

———. (2012). *So near and yet so far: The public and hidden worlds and Canada-U.S. Relations*. Vancouver: UBC Press.

———. (2012). "In pursuit of leverage: The evolution of Canadian trade and investment policies in an increasingly multipolar world." *Canadian Foreign Policy Journal* 18:1, March: 106–19.

———. (2013). "The U.S.-Canada Regulatory Cooperation Council: Opportunities, outcomes, options," paper presented to joint annual meeting of the Western Social Science Association and Association of Borderland Studies, Denver, CO, 11 April.

———. (2013). "CNOOC-Nexen, state-controlled enterprises, and the growing challenges facing Canadian foreign investment policies," paper presented to annual meeting of Canadian Political Science Association, 6 June.

———. Forthcoming. "'Exceptional', immovable, adaptable: Congress and the limitations of North American governance." In *Building without architecture: Understanding the new North America*, eds. B. Bow and G. Anderson. New York: Routledge.

——— and Gattinger, M. (2010). "Variable geometry and traffic circles: Navigating Canada's policy relations in North America." In *Borders and bridges*, M. Gattinger and G. Hale (Eds). Toronto: Oxford University Press Canada, pp. 361–80.

——— and Marcotte, C. (2010). "Border security, trade and travel facilitation." In *Borders and bridges: Navigating Canada's policy relations in North America*, M. Gattinger and G. Hale (Eds). Toronto: Oxford University Press, pp. 100–119.

Hansen, G. H. (2012). "Understanding Mexico's economic underperformance." Washington, DC: Woodrow Wilson Center for Scholars and Migration Policy Institute, August.

Helman, C. and Fontevecchia, A. (2013). "Mexico's Enrique Pena Nieto is leading an oil revolution worth billions," *Forbes*, 18 November.

Hufbauer, G. C. and Schott, J. J. (2005). *NAFTA revisited*. Washington, DC: Institute for International Economics.

Hussain, Y. (2014). "Crude by rail gathers steam," *Financial Post*, 10 January, FP1.

Hutchinson, B. (2014). "Ruling a 'game changer,'" *National Post*, 27 June, A1.

Iliff, L. (2014). "Mexico makes sweeping changes at energy regulator," *The Globe and Mail*, 25 February, B11.

Mackrael, K. (2014). "Tensions rise with Mexico as Harper defends visa limits," *The Globe and Mail*, 19 February, A1.

Martin, P. (2005). "Mexico-U.S. Migration." In *NAFTA Revisited: Achievements and Challenges*, G. C.

Hufbauer and J. J. Schott (Eds). Washington, DC: Institute for International Economics, 441–66.

Martinez, A. I. and Gardner, S. (2013). "Left's backing boosts Mexico tax plan chances, right skeptical," *Reuters*, 9 September.

McKinney, J. A. (2013). "NAFTA at 20 in the context of a changing world economy," paper presented to Association for Canadian Studies in the United States, Tampa, November.

Mendelsohn, M., Wolfe, R., and Parkin, A. (2002). "Globalization, trade policy and the permissive consensus in Canada." *Canadian Public Policy* 28(3), 351–71.

Milke, M. (2008). *Limits on deliberative democracy: A study of Canadian political culture and how attitudes toward the United States shape Canadian political debates*. PhD thesis, University of Calgary.

Milner, H. V. (1997). *Interests, institutions, and information: Domestic politics and international relations.* Princeton, NJ: Princeton University Press.

Morales, I. (2008). *Post-NAFTA North America: Reshaping the economic and political governance of a changing region.* New York: Routledge.

Negroponte, D. V. (20120). "Mexico's Enrique Peña Nieto confronts the challenges of federalism, fiscal reform, and education." Washington, DC: Brookings Institution, 30 November.

"New Chicago council survey finds American opinion of Mexico mixed." Chicago: Chicago Council on Global Affairs and Woodrow Wilson Center, 29 April 2013.

Newport, F. and Himelfarb, I. (2013). "Americans least favorable toward Iran," Princeton: Gallup, 7 March.

Passel, J., Cohn, D., and Gonzalez-Barrera, A. (2012). "Net migration from Mexico Falls to zero—and perhaps less." Washington, DC: Pew Hispanic Center 23 April.

Pastor, R. A. (2001). *Toward a North American community: Lessons from the old world for the new.* Washington, DC: Institute for International Economics.

———. (2011). *The North American idea: A vision of a continental future.* New York: Oxford University Press.

——— and Fernandez de Castro, R. (Eds). 1998. *Congress: The controversial pivot.* Washington, DC: The Brookings Institution.

Payan, T. (2013). "Cross border flows—Achieving security by opening, liberalizing and deregulating," paper presented to Association for Canadian Studies in the United States, 21 November.

Priest, D. (2013). "U.S. role at a crossroads in Mexico's intelligence war on the cartels," *The Washington Post*, 28 April, A1.

Rapoza, K. (2013). "For American exporters, Mexico is the China next door," *Forbes*, 25 January.

Rubin, R. and Weisberg, J. (2003). *In an uncertain world: Tough choices from Wall Street to Washington.* New York: Random House.

Scheiber, N. (2014). "Obama is foundering on trade because he's too much like Bill Clinton, not too little," *The New Republic Online*, 23 February.

Schott, J. J. (Ed.). (2004). *Free Trade Agreements: US strategies and priorities.* Washington, DC: Institute for International Economics.

———. (2007). "Trade Negotiations among NAFTA Partners." *Requiem or revival: The promise of North American integration*, I. Studer and C. Wise, (Eds). Washington, DC: The Brookings Institution), 76–88.

Smith, P J. (2007). "Anti-terrorism in North America: Is there convergence or divergence in Canadian and US legislative responses to 9/11 and the US-Canada border." In *Borderlands: Comparing border security in North America and Europe*, E. Brunet-Jailly (Ed.). Ottawa: University of Ottawa Press, 277–310.

Statistics Canada. (2012). "Interprovincial and international trade," Cat. 13-518-X, Statistics Canada, Ottawa.

Statistics Canada. (2013). "International investment position, Canadian direct investment abroad and foreign direct investment in Canada, by country." *CANSIM Table 376-0051.* Ottawa: May 2013; accessed 25 June 2013.

Studer, I. (2007). "Obstacles to integration." In *Requiem or revival: The promise of North American integration*, I. Studer and C. Wise, (Eds). Washington, DC: The Brookings Institution, 53–75.

Tomlin, B. W., Hillmer, N., and Hampson, F. O. (2008). *Canada's international policies: Agendas, alternatives and policies*. Toronto: Oxford University Press.

United States. Embassy to Mexico. (2013). "Foreign direct investment factsheet." Washington, DC: Department of State, April; online at photos.state.gov/libraries/310329/docs/FDI/pdf; accessed 4 July 2013.

United States. National commission on terrorist attacks on the United States. (2004). *The 9/11 Commission Report*. Washington, DC: July.

United States. The White House, and Canada. Privy Council Office. (2011). *United States-Canada beyond the border: A shared vision for perimeter security and economic competitiveness*. Washington and Ottawa: December.

Villareal, M. A. (2012). "U.S.-Mexico economic relations: Trends, issues and implications", *CRS Report # RL32934*. Washington, DC: Congressional Research Service, Library of Congress, 9 August.

Weintraub, S. (2010). *Unequal partners: The United States and Mexico*. Pittsburgh: University of Pittsburgh Press.

Wise, C. (2007). "Unfulfilled promise." In I. Studer and C. Wise (Eds), *Requiem or revival: The promise of North American integration* (Washington, DC: The Brookings Institution), 27–52.

World Trade Organization (WTO). (2012). *International Trade Statistics, 2011*. (Geneva: WTO).

Zabludovsky, J. and Gomez-Lora, S. (2007). "Beyond the FTAA." in I. Studer and C. Wise (Eds), *Requiem or revival: The promise of North American integration*. Washington, DC: The Brookings Institution, 91–107.

14 Japan and China
The Role of the State in Regional Dynamics

Jennifer Y.J. Hsu

Asian economies have weathered the current financial crisis relatively well. The dominance of East Asia and more recently, China, in terms of economic growth since the end of the Second World War, makes the region one of the most dynamic in the global political economy in the twenty-first century. East Asia's dominance—that is, Northeast Asia, and to a lesser extent Southeast Asia—is mainly due to its overwhelming economic success. Despite lower growth rates since the 2008 financial crisis, countries in the East and Northeast Asia regions experienced growth rates of 0.5 per cent in 2009 due to a heavy reliance on exports, compared with 2.9 per cent in 2008, whereas Europe experienced −4.2 per cent in 2009 (UNESCAP 2011, 105).

The role of the state in economic development is one of the key reasons for this stability. To understand the political economy of the region, it is important to comprehend the individual development trajectories of Japan and China post-Second World War. The postwar reconstruction period has shaped the domestic institutions and subsequently affected the political and economic development of both nations and the region.

Efforts to reform the education system, the agricultural sector, and other such institutions have contributed to the economic growth of both nations. Reforms were undertaken with the active involvement of the state and many have thus argued that the success of both economies can be attributed to their heavy state involvement. In comparing Japan and China, it is important to note that state involvement in economic development has led to very different outcomes. Japan has had an impressive postwar recovery whereas China experienced an economic disaster and the ensuing famine of China's Great Leap Forward of the 1950s.

Nonetheless, China's rapid economic growth of the last 35 years, while still state-led, marks a distinct break from the type of state involvement of the Mao Zedong era. Strong state involvement in national economic policy is one reason why the region has lagged behind in regional integration. Related institutions serve broader domestic political and economic interests rather than regional linkages. Although international institutions such as the World Bank, the International Monetary Fund (IMF), and the WTO have had a substantial impact in the region (for example, the Asian Financial

Crisis of 1997 where adherence to the IMF's policies had disastrous social consequences for nations such as Thailand) the state still remains an active and present stakeholder. China, in fact, has sought to ignore much of the advice given by the World Bank and IMF and proceeded to undertake its own development, financial, and monetary policies.

Historical tensions between two major powers, for example, China and Japan, also undermine potential movement toward deeper integration. Thus, this chapter will examine Japan and China in-depth, to understand how domestic institutions, including the state, have come to shape developments. As the title of the chapter suggests, the focus will be on China and Japan, not Asia as a whole, but it will also consider regional developments, such as the Association for Southeast Asian Nations (ASEAN). However, by focusing on China and Japan this discussion will attempt to avoid the tendency of some observers to homogenize the experience of what is one of the most distinct cultural and political regions in the world. In doing so, it will highlight domestic and inter-regional factors that have come to shape "Asia" or more specifically "East Asia." The rationale of such an approach is that China and Japan have a tremendous impact on the region. The first section will focus on the post-Second World War economic changes which will then inform the second section's concentration on the role of the state in Japan and China's economic development. The third section will examine the different types of state behaviour through an analysis of two key frameworks: the **developmental state** and the **corporatist state**. The fourth section will outline the regional cooperation that is evident in East Asia today, with reference to the impact of domestic institutions and concerns on regional dynamics. The case studies of Japan and China will demonstrate that the state, along with domestic stakeholders, has influenced regional dynamics.

Post-Second World War Developments

Japan

The post-Second World War period saw the rebuilding of the East Asian economies, including Japan's, with assistance from the United States. The strategic positioning of Japan in the Cold War, as a bulwark against the tide of communism from China, meant that the reconstruction of the region and its economies was critical. In this section, focus will be directed at Japan's reconstruction, the substantial support it received from the US, and the rapid rise of its economy, which eventually challenged that of the US in the late 1980s and early 1990s. The subsequent section demonstrates China's economic experience today, reflecting some of the concerns and anxieties of an earlier era.

Japan's defeat in the Second World War and subsequent postwar reconstruction efforts meant almost a complete rebuilding of not only its economy, but also its political and educational institutions. Such macro-level changes further affected institutions at the micro-level, for example, family relations. Japan's defeat in the war led to seven years of American occupation under the Supreme Command of the Allied Forces. During this time a number of institutional changes occurred, including the rewriting of Article 9 of the Japanese constitution prohibiting the settlement of international disputes by military means. Furthermore, the US-Japan Security Treaty (1952) allowed American forces to occupy strategic bases in Japan for regional defence purposes and also to quell internal disturbances if called upon by the Japanese government. Although the majority of the population supported the treaty, many pro-American Japanese conservatives still felt it seriously compromised Japanese independence. But given that the treaty was negotiated under American occupation, the Japanese had little choice but to accept.

A new education system was implemented in 1947 with the direct consultation of the Americans. Changes were guided by the *Fundamental Law of Education* (1947), which shifted to a single track system or 6–3, 3–4 (six years of elementary, three years of middle school, three years of high school, and four years of college). It also called for an extension of universal education to nine years; coeducational schools; the creation of educational boards at the prefectural and municipal levels; and the establishment of a university-based teaching training system. In 1950, the extension of the compulsory nine years of education was nearly complete. In 1950, only 42.5 per cent of lower-secondary graduates had been enrolled in high school, but by 1975 this figure had jumped to 91.9 per cent (UNESCO 2000). Education had thus become the great standardizer of Japanese social experience. Consequently, jobs were increasingly awarded based on merit rather than on status. Moreover, the education system, with its emphasis on discipline, also led to a more standardized and disciplined workforce. A more educated workforce was to become a central element in Japan's **industrialization**.

The introduction of a coeducational system postwar provided Japanese women with educational opportunities. Prior to the war, women had no property or civil rights; thus the new educational system not only provided education but also served to elevate the status of women in Japanese society. Furthermore, Article 14 of the new Japanese constitution guaranteed "essential equality of the sexes," and Article 24 clarified women's status with regard to marriage. In a few short years, women's rights were brought to the forefront of politics but not without opposition from male members of the Diet—Japan's parliament. Opposition to Article 9 and Article 14 remains strong today, especially among conservative political elites. The Liberal Democratic Party (LDP), Japan's current ruling party, has consistently targeted Article 9, but opposition from Japan's religious groups, pacifists, moderates, and liberals has thus far prevented the LDP from acquiring the two-thirds majority needed to amend the constitution (Métraux 2007). The institutional changes that occurred at the macro-level filtered down to affect the experiences of individuals, particularly Japanese women. Reforms to the education system, coupled with the elevation of women's status in the constitution, provided Japanese women the opportunity to advance socially and economically. Thus, to understand the regional developments of East Asia or any region requires attention to the domestic institutions, as, clearly, without such changes, Japan would not have had the capacity to develop its economy. Postwar developments dramatically changed various aspects of Japanese society and politics due to the American occupation. In China, the scale of changes were similar but of a totally different nature.

China

The traumas of the Japanese occupation (1937–45) and the protracted civil war between the Chinese Communist Party (CCP) and the Guomindang (GMD) that resumed after Japan's defeat in the Second World War led to the destruction of many Chinese social, political, and economic institutions. The victory of the CCP under Mao Zedong over the GMD in 1949 led to the establishment of the People's Republic of China and the rebuilding of the nation. The embracing of communist ideology and subsequent Mao Zedong thought pervaded all aspects of individual life and determined how society operated, including the abolition of private property and a move toward farming and industrial **collectivization**. The prominence of ideology was critical to the reconstruction of the nation. Notions such as self-reliance, class struggle, voluntarism, and anti-intellectualism were espoused by Mao in his writings and speeches. They provided a framework for the

Anti-Rightist campaign in the 1950s, the Great Leap Forward (1958–61), and the Cultural Revolution (1966–76), destroying the foundations of specialist knowledge across a number of sectors. Thus initial advances in the rebuilding of China and subsequent political campaigns relied heavily on Mao's ability to mobilize the masses.

Educational reform was also central to national redevelopment efforts post-1949, and emphasis was placed on addressing the different needs of the economy. As a result, the secondary education system was divided into different schools: general education, secondary technical, secondary teacher training, secondary vocational, and secondary skilled workers (Tsang 2000). Some leaders of the Cultural Revolution charged that the diversified structure of the secondary school system bred student elitism, and that schools did not tend to the interests of the proletariat. During the height of the Cultural Revolution, secondary skilled and technical schools were closed or converted to factories (ibid.). Mao also mobilized students and young adults throughout China to serve as "Red Guards," or agents of the Revolution. School children were asked to mimic the official criticisms of "revisionism" in China and instructed by teachers to think of situations where they had come across counter-revolutionary thoughts or actions. Initially, students copied criticisms published in newspapers but soon became bolder and singled out their teachers. Workplaces mirrored similar developments, where workers were asked to critique their employers. Eventually, the movement turned children against parents.

The Cultural Revolution led to the destruction not only of institutions that had been rebuilt, but also institutions at the micro-level, such as families and individual relationships. Unlike Japan, where nine-year compulsory education was near completion in 1950, China witnessed a regression during the Cultural Revolution, despite Mao's insistence in promoting social equality through expanding primary education to the peasant and working classes. For example, between 1967 and 1970, universities had no new entrants. Urban youth were regularly sent to the countryside for "education," effectively disrupting their formal education and impeding their lifelong employment earnings (Giles et al. 2008) and human capital development (Han et al. 2009). The cases of Japan and China demonstrate that development in regional political economies cannot be understood without first looking at domestic institutional change. In the next section, we will seek to further analyze the role of the state—a significant factor for the economic development of all East Asian nations.

The Role of the State in Economic Development

Japan

To understand the economic development of East Asia and its future trajectory requires a careful analysis of the state. The activist nature of the state in East Asian economies is characterized by the notion of the "developmental state." As we have seen thus far, state reforms of the education system in the 1950s for both Japan and China were in part related to feeding into the needs of the economy. However, Japan and China's strategies and type of state involvement in economic development differed sharply. The building of a communist China under Mao, and its modernization and industrialization, included the mobilization of all levels of society from both rural and urban areas. Japan, on the other hand, focused on policy instruments for its economic reforms. Both cases demonstrate that domestic institutions are key factors, but that the outcomes of state management can have vastly different results. In tracing China's economic development over the last three decades, it becomes clear that the East Asia region has been and will continue to be shaped by China.

Similar to China, Japan implemented its own land reforms after the Second World War. Land reforms were an important first step to economic reconstruction and resulted in a greater distribution of wealth and social stability. The reforms limited the amount of land a family could own to the amount of land a family could farm themselves without outside labour. The Japanese prefectural governors purchased land back from landlords on behalf of the state and then sold it to those willing to work the land. Farmers were permitted to own roughly 2.5 acres, which they could rent to others, and any excess had to be sold back to the government. The ratio of owner–farmers in the agricultural population increased from 32.6 per cent to 61.9 per cent. Part-tenant and tenant farmers decreased from 48.5 per cent to 30.7 per cent, and tenants from 28.7 per cent to 5.1 per cent. As a result, Japan's Gini coefficient declined from roughly 0.5 in the pre-war period to 0.35 after the reforms in 1950 (Kawagoe 1999, 2). Reforms thus helped to abolish social hierarchy based on land ownership and contributed to Japan's democratization process. Japan's agricultural reform success fuelled government confidence as it moved into reforming other sectors.

Several government ministries, including the Ministries of International Trade and Industry (MITI), Finance, Post and Telecommunications, and the Transport and Economic Development Agency also played a leading role in economic development by targeting certain industries for support and development. In many cases, these firms were essentially co-opted to serve the government's economic agenda. The Ministry of International Trade and Finance provided Japanese companies with tools and substantial resources for development. During the American occupation the *zaibatsu* (large Japanese industrial and business

firms) were dismantled because they were seen as strong supporters of Japan's military establishment. After the Americans departed, the top four conglomerates (Japan Toshiba Electric, Matsushita Electric, Toyota Motors, and Yawata-Fuji Steel) re-emerged to capture a substantial proportion of industrial capital.

Japan's industrial policy was driven by four key factors: ideology, institutions, interests, and instruments (Krauss 1992). First, there was ideological consensus on the legitimacy of the state. The unbroken rule of the Liberal Democratic Party (LDP) from 1955 to 1993 provided public legitimization of the party's interventionist economic policies. The "iron triangle" of the LDP, bureaucrats, and big business, also facilitated Japan's rapid economic recovery and growth. Second, the political institutions facilitated the growth of Japan's economy by centralizing business–government relations, which were often free from partisan influence and challenges to the LDP's economic agenda. This did not go unchallenged. Massive protests erupted in 1960 over the renewal of the US-Japanese Security Treaty and were followed by the Miike Union coal mining strike between the unionized mine workers and the Miike management over job cuts, some 2,000, from 13,000. Subsequent strikes, such as the public sector unions' strike of 1975, failed to generate public support and the strike was called off within a week. The government took disciplinary action against over 1,000 leaders and participants of the strike, which led to the slow decline of unions in Japan. Finally, the discriminatory policy instruments adopted by the likes of MITI enabled the rapid growth and development of Japan's private companies. By 1967, Japan had the second largest GDP in the world.

Japan's impressive postwar economic performance saw the economy grow at over 10 per cent annually in the 1960s. High growth rates also led to high personal savings rates. Savings in Japan increased steadily from 10 per cent in 1950, to 15 per cent in 1960 and 20 per cent in 1970. The high savings rates were used by development and private banks to back the expansion of private firms, who invested money in equipment and plants. Meanwhile, private corporations in the 1960s sought, through material incentives, to convince workers that the productivity movement was essential to Japan's competitiveness in an increasingly integrated economy, thus reducing antagonism between workers and management. While Japan's economic growth was in part stimulated by domestic consumption, consumers did not benefit from the lower prices of imported goods or budget surpluses. Instead, companies invested into *zaitech*: investing borrowed money at low interest rates, to show higher profits rather than through business activities alone.

The government also expanded foreign direct investment, mostly in US and European manufacturing plants (Gordon 2003, 294). By the 1980s, Japan was experiencing high growth rates, low unemployment, and high corporate profits. The flow of excessive funds fuelled a rise in stock and land prices, creating an economic bubble (Ito 1996, 214). Such growth could not be sustained. Stock prices started a precipitous decline in 1990, and by 1992 the Nikkei index[1] had lost 60 per cent of its value. Land prices also steadily declined during the period, creating serious financial difficulties with high rates of default on interest payments, and saddling banks with large numbers of nonperforming loans. By 1992, the Japanese economy was well into recession, lasting into the next decade, which became known as the "lost decade." In many ways, these troubles remain today, with the nominal GDP rate remaining stagnant over the last two decades and the Nikkei dropping below 10,000 points after the 2008 financial crisis. It also lost 10 per cent of its value following the 2011 earthquake.

Along with the Americans, the Japanese state played a critical role in coordinating Japan's postwar recovery. The impact of external factors such as the Cold War and the Korean War also ensured Japan's sustained growth. However, the onset of the recession of the 1990s and the financial crisis of 2008 have put into question the role of the state in economic development; that is, questioning whether a state-led economy is as beneficial as a market-driven one. Whether we subscribe to either a state- or market-led idea of economic growth, what is clear is that state-led development is not unique to Japan. In the next section, we will see how the Chinese state has led its economy since 1978 into a sizeable economic power, similar to the Japan of the 1980s, although the Chinese political and governing structure is clearly different.

China

Post-1949 China embraced the Soviet model of economic development: reliance on a centrally planned economy. Mao moved quickly into agricultural reforms following the CCP's victory. During collectivization, land was confiscated from landlords and redistributed to peasants until the process was complete in 1952. Collectivization occurred in three stages, with the first stage consisting of only five or six families in Mutual Aid Teams (MAT). Families in the MAT would work cooperatively during busy periods but each family would retain whatever their own land harvested. By 1952, 40 per cent of households were in MAT. The second stage of collectivization moved into "elementary cooperatives" where a small village or a section of a village consisting of 20–30 households would amalgamate assets and resources and work the land together. A management committee led the elementary cooperative, assigning work points to each family based on the work conducted and thus distributed grain and income according to the work points accumulated at the end of each year. The third stage was the "advanced coopera-tive," consisting of 150 to 200 households where all production was collectivized and all households were remunerated based on their work points. By 1956, 96.3 per cent of China's rural families were organized into 750,000 collectives of which 88 per cent were advanced cooperatives. Mao further advocated for the establishment of "people's com-munes," where a dozen advanced cooperatives were amalgamated, consisting of some 25,000 people. With 26,000 communes in place by 1958, communes became the new system for organizing the economy, politics, administration, and all social functions.

Mao believed that industrialization could be funded by agricultural surpluses. In 1958, over 16 million peasants were relocated to the cities to sup-port industry and construction. In the winter of 1957–58, the government mobilized 100 million peasants for large land reclamation and irrigation projects and the building of "backyard furnaces" in the drive to produce steel for construction. Local cadres carried out these projects with zeal but often ignored the expertise required. The Great Leap Forward (1958–60) signified China's industrializa-tion ambition and efforts. But the dependency on local small-scale initiatives resulted in the inefficient and wasteful use of resources. Simultan-eously, diverting agricultural labour to indus-trialization was to have dire consequences. Between 1957 and 1958, 38 million agricultural labourers left the land, thus leading to the neglect of the sec-tor. Although 1958 was a bumper year for harvests, local officials sometimes reported much higher fig-ures, as much as 2.5 times more. Grain retention in rural areas decreased from 273 kg per capita in 1957 to 193 kg in 1959 and to 182 kg in 1960. These reductions, due to the reduced labour force, gov-ernment procurement of grain based on high and inaccurate figures, and subsequent natural disas-ters, resulted in major famines in rural areas.

During this period, rural residents were allotted less than 500 grams of grains per day (Peng 1987, 657). It is estimated that some 30 to 40 million people died during the famine, a direct conse-quence of Mao's failed Great Leap Forward. The years following the Great Leap Forward saw other mass campaigns, including the Socialist Education Movement (1963–68) and the Down the Country-side Movement (1968–78) with the Cultural Revo-lution punctuating both the 1960s and 1970s. These political campaigns created further eco-nomic instability, despite China's Five Year Plans and new agricultural policies, such as contracting farm production to households in the early 1960s.

Thus, by the end of 1978, dissatisfaction among the CCP's leadership with the socialist eco-nomic system was apparent. The Third Plenum of the CCP in December 1978 saw a distinct break from past economic policies. It also marked the return of Deng Xiaoping, purged twice under Mao, as paramount leader of the CCP and China. Reforms in the early period saw a great deal of experimentation, with agriculture among the foremost items on the economic agenda. In fact, collectivization was eventually abolished and indi-vidual households given responsibility for their own production. Moving from a quota system to a contract system, one preferred by farmers, not only allowed greater choice as to what farmers produced but also enabled the accumulation of surplus cap-ital and labour, which had been instrumental in the growth of the non-farm sector. The move to the household responsibility system led to an increase in grain production, the courting of foreign invest-ment, and the establishment of special economic zones along China's eastern borders, all seeking to transform the economy.

The transfer of agricultural responsibility to the household level also generated a vast pool of rural surplus labour. Such a transformation allowed many to pursue non-farm activities. This went hand-in-hand with the expansion of state industries in the urban areas. The State Council's 1983 *Regulations Concerning Cooperative Endeavours of City and Town Labourers* saw a relaxation of the government's previous stance on migration. Even though the Regulation authorized rural residents to move into towns, they had to maintain their rural *hukou*[2] status and provide their own grains for consumption. The following year, the *Central Committee's Notice on Rural Work Document 1*, allowed further freedom of movement for rural workers to solve labour shortages. Unfortunately, the liberalization of migration into small towns in 1984 did not lead to better treatment of peasants working in these areas. Rural residents were granted urban registration in these small rural towns with the proviso that they would provide food, housing, and employment for themselves. Rural workers were also not entitled to receive benefits such as housing and medical services, as would an urban worker.

The boom and opportunities experienced in the first decade of economic reforms faltered, however, especially for peasants. By the end of 1984, grain production had stagnated and farmers' incomes began to decline, despite the initial increase. Waning government investment in agriculture coincided with the deterioration of rural incomes. Agricultural investment declined from a 30-year average of 11 per cent to only 5.1 per cent in capital construction. Between 1986 and 1988, this figure dropped even further to 3 per cent (Solinger 1999, 159). To counter the possibility of mass rural–urban migration, the government encouraged rural residents to invest in non-agricultural production within their villages or small rural towns. The slogan: "*litu bulixiang*" or "leave the land but not the countryside" summarizes the government's intent for its policy toward rural–urban migration.

The number of rural labour migrants continued to rise toward the end of the 1980s despite the depressed economy. The soaring inflation of the mid-1980s also forced the government to cancel many of its construction projects and close rural enterprises. This caused urban authorities to take decisive actions to limit migrants' entry. Rural migrants now represented more than 21 per cent of the urban population in 1989, a 5 per cent increase from 1968–78 levels, creating significant financial pressures (Mallee 2003, 92). As a result, the State Council, the Ministries of Civil Affairs, and the Public Security Bureau all issued circulars to limit the entry of migrant workers into the cities in 1989. Furthermore, in March 1989 the State Council issued guidelines directing local governments to restrict rural labour migration. This was followed up by guidelines issued separately by the Ministry of Civil Affairs and Ministry of Public Security in April 1989.

Economic conditions did improve after 1992, but subsequent growth led to widespread regional inequality between China's coastal and inland provinces. The decline in rural income as experienced in the 1980s also reappeared again in the mid- to late 1990s, this time due to the overproduction of grain for export markets and uncompetitive prices. As a result, peasant grain-related income dropped between 1998 and 2000, decreasing by 2.3 per cent in 1998, 4.5 per cent in 1999, and by 4.7 per cent in 2000 (Huang and Pieke 2003, 12). The insecurity of agricultural incomes further increased migration to large cities for employment. A second factor contributing to urban migration was expanded foreign direct investment (FDI), especially along the Eastern seaboard, which contributed to China's manufacturing base. Consequently, rural labour migrants in the urban areas increased from 60 million in 1994 to 88 million in 2000 and 94 million in 2002 (Huang and Zhan 2005). Presently, there are some 120–200 million permanent and temporary migrants. Figures relating to migrant numbers in urban areas vary[3], but there is no doubt that the number of migrants working in China's cities has risen dramatically over the last two decades.

Not surprisingly, the recent global financial crisis in 2008 made a sizable dent in the Chinese economy. A decline in exports, imports, and FDI inflows since 2008 has affected the Chinese economy. China's GDP slowed to 7.8 per cent in 2012, indicating the wearing off of the effects of the US $586 billion economic stimulus package (Morrison 2013, i). The Chinese state attempted to ward off the effects of the global financial crisis through a series of monetary policies and encouragement of domestic investment and consumption. These efforts resulted in a spike in GDP to 10.4 per cent in 2010 from 9.2 per cent in 2008, but was followed by a drop to 9.2 per cent again in 2011 (ibid., 4). The Chinese economy is also predicted to slow to 7 per cent in 2016, its slowest since 1999 (World Bank 2015). Such figures indicate that the future of the Chinese economy will increasingly become affected by global trends.

Understanding the State: China and Japan

The experiences of economic development for both Japan and China since the late 1940s indicate a clear role for the state, although the outcomes were very different, as the above sections show. This section will evaluate two frameworks that may best illuminate different aspects of Chinese and Japanese state-led initiatives. These are the developmental state and the corporatist state, which both incorporate domestic actors in their analysis.

The Developmental State

The developmental state is perhaps the best choice to highlight Japan's postwar development strategy.

Adrian Leftwich (1993, 401) defines the developmental state as having:

> sufficient power, autonomy and capacity at the centre to shape, pursue and encourage the achievement of explicit developmental objectives, whether by establishing and promoting the conditions and directions of economic growth, or organising it directly, or a varying combination of both.

The East Asian developmental state has been heavily linked to industrialization and government policy. For Chalmers Johnson (1982), the Japanese developmental state exercised policy regulations through key ministries to regulate private firms for the purpose of economic development. This resulted in dramatic industrial transformations in a few short decades. Reforms in the agricultural sector resulted in increased efficiency. Fewer workers were needed in that sector, translating into more labourers available to work in manufacturing. The influx of labourers allowed for rapid growth and investment in manufacturing. For example, between 1960 and 2005, annual employment growth in Japan's agricultural sector averaged negative 3.4 per cent, whereas the manufacturing sector averaged 0.4 per cent (OECD 2009, 24). The success of Japan's land and agricultural reforms, as noted previously, not only decreased inequality but also gave the Japanese government the confidence to progress with reforms in other sectors, notably the move toward industrialization. Changes to the education system provided the Japanese economy with a more educated workforce to meet the demands of industrialization. Coupled with investments by firms to train their employees, domestic policy changes ensured that Japan's economy was able to meet the needs of economic development. Furthermore, the demands of the Japanese economy also meant increased participation of women in the labour force. Women comprised 45.7 per cent of the total workforce in 1970 and 50.3 per cent in 1995 (Renshaw 1999, 22).[4]

The accumulation of capital allowed Japan to pursue import-substitution industrialization (ISI). It was implemented to nurture and protect chosen industries through the supply of credit and subsidies, adopting quotas and high tariffs for imported goods. The rapid expansion of manufacturing sectors throughout East Asia and Japan as a result of ISI allowed these economies to shift into technology-intensive industries where profit margins were much higher. State intervention in the case of Japan, as observed through MITI and other related ministries, was able to economically transform Japan in less than 50 years. Moreover, the unbroken rule of the LDP from 1955 to 1993 enabled the government and its ministries to carry out its economic plans and solidify the role of government in leading economic development.

Although state intervention did stimulate growth across East Asia, including the availability of cheap credit to large national firms, it also contributed to the East Asian financial crisis of 1997–98. The allocation of capital to declining industries throughout these high-performing East Asian countries by governments and banks did not boost productivity or efficiency, and ultimately created increasingly high corporate debt, triggering the contagion (Wade 1998). Others saw states as not doing enough to regulate the flows of short-term capital.

Regardless, the model of the developmental state in the contemporary global political economy has come under attack from a number of sources. First, the increasing convergence of national economies and globalization is seen as a factor in undermining state-driven interventionist policies. A second critique is a lack of "good governance" and the need to focus on issues beyond economic

development such as transparent government, a reduction of corruption, and respect not just for economic rights but also for the social and human rights of citizens. Furthermore, the end of the Cold War has also relegated the developmental state—as a concept for understanding state behaviour—as a product of history, particularly as US aid to the region dwindled as the threat of communism faded.

Nonetheless, Richard Stubbs (2011) argues that the current global recession reinforces the continued validity of the developmental state. The historical context is crucial to understanding the effect of the recession and the ensuing state response, that is, the lessons learned from the neoliberalization of East Asian economies in the 1980s and the Asian Financial Crisis in the mid-1990s. Furthermore, Stubbs (2011) argues that the impact of the recession demonstrates the evolving nature of developmental states like Japan, where they embrace both developmental state and neoliberal policies. Although Japan did undergo liberalization of its economy in the 1980s, Andrew Walter (2006) argues that the extent of neoliberal reforms were far from entrenched, particularly in the banking and financial sectors. The Financial Reconstruction Commission, for example, has minimal power or independence, because the Ministry of Finance still wields substantial control. Takashi Tsukamoto (2012), noting Tokyo as an example, also cites the political power exerted by local political leaders as further evidence of the developmental state. On the other hand, Japan's "lost decade" can also be assigned in part to the slow adaptation of the state in an increasingly integrated world. But most notable are the events that have occurred over the last two decades, the bursting of the Japanese economic bubble and the current financial crisis, which have forced the Japanese developmental state to become a mix of guiding and laissez-faire policies.

The Corporatist State

The strength of the local state in Chinese politics suggests that the developmental state is inadequate for analyzing China's development experience. Alternatively, the corporatist lens suggests that the central state is able to coordinate divergent interests through a:

> system of interest representation in which the constituent units are organized into a limited number of singular, compulsory, noncompetitive, hierarchically ordered and functionally differentiated categories, recognized or licensed (if not created) by the state and granted a deliberate representational monopoly within their respective categories in exchange for observing certain controls on their selection of leaders and articulation of demands and supports. (Schmitter 1974, 93–4)

In a typical corporatist system, only one national organization is recognized by the state, and this system of interest coordination can be seen in all economic and social realms. An interventionist state often assists by organizing and establishing sectoral associations. However, within this mode of operation some autonomy is allowed for the association, as we shall see below.

Decentralization of state power,[5] largely within the economic arena, has given local authorities the opportunity to exert their own influence over social organizations, associations, and other groups within their purview. Since the start of economic reforms in 1978, local authorities have had much greater power than under the rule of Mao Zedong, where economic planning was highly centralized, as evidenced in land collectivization. The economic disaster of centralized planning as witnessed in Mao's Great Leap Forward encouraged early reformers to adopt an experimental approach and involve the local authorities in rural reforms. Decollectivization and moves toward the household responsibility system allowed local economic initiatives to be tested, emboldening local authorities in the process. The rise of local authorities in economic development since 1978 is in part tempered by the central state's coordination. For example, the entry of rural labour migrants into the cities in search of employment, while initially restricted by the local urban authorities, was later coordinated at the central level through various circulars and regulations.

Jean Oi's (1995) study of rural township village enterprises (TVEs), convey this sense of localism in China's economic development. Local officials treat the TVEs within their realm of administrative responsibility and thus the TVEs are seen as only a segment of the whole. Oi regards the economic growth of local regions as a result of local—not central—state coordination. As such, the local corporatist structure sees an intimate relationship between banks, finance and tax offices, and township and village authorities, where each would cooperate and assist the other to maximize their revenues. What we see here is a fragmentation of the centre and that economic coordination at the local level has resulted in a redefining of relationships between local groups, whether they are associations or businesses, and the state—that is, the local state. Similarly, local economic associations representing Chinese entrepreneurs are often co-opted by the local authorities to meet the needs of the region rather than representing the interests of their constituents (see e.g., Nevitt 1996; Unger 1996; Yang 2013). By granting certain economic groups the legitimacy to represent specific interest groups we see China's economic development taking on a much more heterogeneous character than that of Japan. Furthermore, the decentralization process in China has given local states greater power and leeway to experiment with socio-economic policies (see e.g., Hsu 2012), hence Howell's (2006) reference to a "polymorphous" Chinese state. This leeway has also translated into high rates of land appropriation by local officials. Residents are forced from the land with minimal compensation, and the land is sold to property developers at above-market rates, thereby bringing in huge financial returns for the local state. The corporatist lens allows the observer to account for the local state in China's economic development, particularly since 1978.

Both the Japanese and Chinese state (since 1978) have transformed the economic prospects of their nations, but the different strategies used and the prominence of certain domestic stakeholders (see Breslin 2007) show that the political economy of the region will be shaped not only by nations but that the interests of economic or political domestic groups will be critical to any assessment. Though Japan's economy was able to remain relatively insulated for 50 years, its integration into the world economy also meant that the Japanese state could not protect the economy from nearly two decades of depressed economic growth. Yet, as we continue to observe China's development, we see that the Chinese state is not retreating but making active attempts to remain the torchbearer in national development strategies. China's strong economic performance has meant increasing integration into the regional economy. However, China's growth, as well as an active state in all aspects of politics and economy, has affected opportunities in regional cooperation.

Regional Cooperation

The historic role of the United States in the region highlights the importance of the Japanese developmental state as a foundation for future region-building (see Beeson 2007). Support for Japan as the foundation of capitalist development in the region ensured Japan's impressive postwar recovery and also assisted Japanese firms' expansion into Southeast Asia, whereby these nations were intricately connected to Japanese production networks (Beeson 2009). However, regionalism was not initially driven by Japan. In fact, Japan, China, and South Korea did not become members of the Association of South East Asian Nations (ASEAN) until 1999 (ASEAN + 3), as a response to the Asian Financial Crisis of 1997. Although critics label ASEAN as ineffective and sympathetic to authoritarian regimes, others see it as important to giving "political expression to what had hitherto been a fairly arbitrary geographical space" (Beeson 2009). Both Japan and China are now part of that process, and as members of ASEAN + 3 have supported greater economic cooperation in the region. The Chiang Mai Initiative, for example, agreed to lend financial exchange reserves to the distressed economies of participating member states. Trade has also fortified cooperation. Increases in intra-East Asian trade grew between 1988 and 2004 at the rate of 14 per cent per annum (compared to 9 per cent in the European Union). Concomitantly, East Asia's share of world exports increased by 6 per cent during the same period (Brooks and Hua 2008, 10). Between 1991 and 2009, trade between ASEAN and China grew at an average rate of 15 per cent annually (Aslam 2012, 46).[6] Finally, Stubbs (2002, 445–6) has suggested that the East Asian form of capitalism has the capacity to reinforce a sense of Asian identity and consciousness.

At the same time, however, Japan and China are also barriers to further cooperation, once again emphasizing the need to understand the impact of domestic policies on regionalism in Asia. The 2010 China-ASEAN Free Trade Area (CAFTA), for example has been criticized as simply eliminating tariffs on goods, and doing little to generate extra trade or investment in the region. Moreover, China's pursuit of other preferential trade agreements

(PTAs) is also viewed as part of its competition with Japan "to establish leadership credentials in east Asia [and] securing privileged influence in other regions" (Sally 2010, 22). The proposed Trans-Pacific Partnership, a regional free trade agreement involving nine member countries[7] is touted as a possible mechanism for greater East Asian integration. However, without strong domestic political and administrative support, and the exclusion of China, the TPP may create further regional divisions rather than integration (see Cheong 2013). Regional tensions are also being exacerbated by the Sino-Japanese dispute over the Senkaku/Diaoyu Islands in the East China Sea. In 2010, Japanese coast guards seized a Chinese trawler and its crew after the boat collided with two coast guard vessels near the islands. In April 2012, Tokyo's mayor, Shintaro Ishihara, also announced plans to acquire the islands from their private owners with public money, sparking a diplomatic row. Finally, in November 2013, China announced its East China Sea Air Defense Identification Zone (ADIZ) which challenges Japan's administration and sovereignty over the islands. Not surprisingly, these events escalate the potential for conflict between Japan and China and undermine the success of regional cooperation over the last decade. Thus, the combination of historical events, territorial disputes, and increasingly nationalist sentiments as exhibited by both governments and their citizens has the ongoing potential to jeopardize the security and stability of the region.

Conclusion

The rise of China to become the second largest economy in the world, a position recently held by Japan, demonstrates that the ascendency to such a position for both nations required substantial involvement and investment of the state and domestic institutions. Thus, to understand the political economy of the region, careful attention must be given to domestic conditions. Interestingly, China and Japan have the potential to both increase and diminish regional cooperation, further emphasizing the need to understand the impact of domestic developments in these two states in relation to ASEAN. In recent years China has sought to re-engage with members of the Association of Southeast Asian Nations, most notably with CAFTA, but its resulting increase in cheap Chinese imports to ASEAN nations, as well as ongoing Chinese state subsidies, has eroded the competitiveness of smaller states in the region. In addition to Sino-Japanese tensions over the Senkaku/Diaoyu Islands in the East China Sea, China has territorial disputes with the Philippines in the South China Sea. Attempts to counter China's role in the region were also evident in January 2013 when Japan's newly elected nationalist prime minister, Shinzo Abe, made his first state visits to ASEAN nations, rather than to the US. Furthermore, the recent "pivot" of US interests in the direction of Asia (see Manyin et al. 2012) suggests that the re-emergence of the US as a stakeholder in the region will undoubtedly affect Sino-US relations, strengthen US-Japanese relations, and potentially strain Sino–Japanese relations. Both Japan and China's rapid economic growth and transition, in different time periods, clearly demands an understanding of the internal forces that have contributed to their strengths and weaknesses.

Notes

1   The Nikkei 225 index is the price weighted average (in Japanese yen) of Japan's top 225 listed companies in the First Section of the Tokyo Stock Exchange.

2   The *hukou* system—during the Maoist period and early days of reform—essentially prevented people from moving between rural areas and the cities, and vice versa, without prior permission from the local public security bureau. The *hukou*, which categorizes people on the basis of "agricultural" and "non-agricultural," also served in the government's distribution of economic resources. While the monitoring of the *hukou* has relaxed to some extent in China's urban areas, government benefits are still tied to one's status and the status is transferrable to one's offspring.

3   There is inconsistency in the definition of "migrant"; this therefore affects any survey of the migrant population. Researchers and government bodies often employ different definitions and this may underestimate or overestimate the numbers.

4   However, much of the work undertaken by women was in the low-skilled and low-waged category and was highly flexible.

5   Decentralization often refers to three types: administrative, political, and fiscal.

6   China's ascension into the WTO has led to China becoming the world's biggest exporter however, China's has had a varied record of WTO implementation and is involved in various rounds of litigation.

7   Australia, Brunei Darussalam, Canada, Chile, Japan, Malaysia, Mexico, New Zealand, Peru, Singapore, the United States, and Vietnam are currently negotiating the TPP.

Key Terms

collectivization

corporatist state

developmental state

industrialization

Questions for Review

1.   What are the advantages and disadvantages of state-led economic development?

2.   How do Japan and China's experience in their economic development contribute to a new understanding of capitalism?

3.   To what extent does state-led development in Japan and China prevent greater East Asian cooperation?

4.   What insights can the past offer toward the emergence of a viable regional order in East Asia?

Further Resources

Beeson, M. *Regionalism and globalization in East Asia: Politics, security and economic development.*

Breslin, S. *China and the global political economy.*

Cheong, I. "Negotiations for the Trans-Pacific Partnership agreement: Evaluation and implications for East Asian regionalism."

Howell, J. "Reflections on the Chinese state."

Johnson, C. *MITI and the Japanese miracle.*

Krauss, E. "Political Economy: Policymaking and industrial Policy in Japan."

Stubbs, R. "The East Asian developmental state and the great recession: Evolving contesting coalitions."

References

Aslam, M. (2012). "The Impact of ASEAN-China Free Trade Area Agreement on ASEAN's manufacturing industry." *International Journal of China Studies* 3(1), 43–78.

Beeson, M. (2009). "East Asian regionalism and the end of the Asia-Pacific: After American hegemony." *The Asia-Pacific Journal*, 2 Available at: www.japanfocus.org/-Mark-Beeson/3008#sthash.bwP8mdy9.dpuf [Accessed 30 November 2013]

———. (2007). *Regionalism and globalization in East Asia: Politics, security and economic development*. New York, Palgrave.

Breslin, S. (2007). *China and the global political economy*. New York: Palgrave.

Brooks, D. H. and Hua, C. (2008). "Asian trade and global linkages," ADB Institute Working Paper No. 122, December.

Cheong, I. (2013). "Negotiations for the Trans-Pacific Partnership Agreement: Evaluation and Implications for East Asian regionalism." Asian Development Bank Institute Working Paper 428.

Giles, J., Park, A., and Wang, M. (2008). "The great proletarian cultural revolution, disruptions to education, and returns to schooling in Urban China." World Bank Development Research Group, Policy Research Working Paper 4729.

Gordon, A. (2003). *Modern history of Japan: From Tokugawa times to the present*. Oxford: Oxford University Press.

Han, J., Suen, W., and Zhang, J. (2009). "Picking up the losses: The impact of the cultural revolution on human capital reinvestment." Hong Kong Institute of Economics and Business Strategy Working Paper 1189.

Howell, J. (2006). "Reflections on the Chinese state." *Development and Change 37*, 273–97.

Hsu, J. (2012). "Layers of the urban state: Migrant organizations and the Chinese state." *Urban Studies 49*, 3513–30.

Huang, P. and Pieke, F. N. (2003). *China migration country study*. Paper presented at Regional Conference on Migration, Development and Pro-Poor Policy Choices in Asia. Dhaka, Bangladesh, 22–4 June.

Huang, P. and Zhan, S. (2005). *Internal migration in China: Linking it to development*. Paper presented at Regional Conference on Migration and Development in Asia. Lanzhou, China, 14–16 March.

Ito, T. (1996). "Japan and the Asian economies: A 'miracle' in transition." *Brookings Paper on Economic Activity 27*, 205–72.

Johnson, C. (1982). *MITI and the Japanese miracle*. Stanford: Stanford University Press.

Kawagoe, T. (1999). "Agricultural reform in postwar Japan: Experiences and issues." World Bank Policy Research Paper, 1–43.

Krauss, E. (1992). "Political economy: Policymaking and industrial policy in Japan." *PS: Political Science and Politics 25*, 44–56.

Leftwich, Adrian. (1993). "Governance, democracy and development in the Third World." *Third World Quarterly 14*, 605–24.

Mallee, H. (2003). "Migration, hukou and resistance in reform China." In *Chinese Society: Change, Conflict and Resistance*, edited by E. Perry and M. Selden. London: Routledge.

Manyin, M. E., Daggett, S., Dolven, B., Lawrence, S. V. Martin, M. F., O'Rourke, R., and Vaughn, B. (2012). *Pivot to the Pacific? The Obama Administration's "rebalancing" toward Asia*. Congressional Research Service, 28 March, R42448. Available at: www.fas.org/sgp/crs/natsec/R42448.pdf [accessed 8 July 2013]

Métraux, D. A. (2007). "Religion, politics, and constitutional reform in Japan: How Sōka Gakkai and Kōmeitō have thwarted conservative attempts to revise the 1947 constitution." *Southeast Review of Asian Studies 29*, 157–72.

Morrison, W. M. "China's economic rise: History, trends, challenges, and implications for the United States." Congressional Research Service, 4 March 2013. RL33534. Available at: www.fas.org/sgp/crs/row/RL33534.pdf [accessed 5 July 2013].

Nevitt, C. E. "Private Business associations in China: Evidence of civil society or local state power?" *The China Journal 36* (1996), 25–43.

OECD. *Evaluation of agricultural policy reforms in Japan*. Paris: OECD, (2009).

Oi, J. C. (1995). "The Role of the local state in China's transitional economy." *China Quarterly 144*, 1132–49.

Peng, X. (1987). "Demographic consequences of the Great Leap Forward in China's provinces." *Population and Development Review 13*, 639–70.

Renshaw, J. (1999). *Kimono in the boardroom: The invisible evolution of Japanese women managers*. New York: Oxford University Press.

Sally, R. (2010). "Chinese trade policy after (almost) ten years in the WTO: A post-crisis stocktake." Pacific Trade and Development Paper 34.

Schmitter, P. "(1974). Still the century of corporatism?" *The Review of Politics 36*, 85–131.

Solinger, D. J. (1999). *Contesting citizenship in urban China: Peasant migrants, the state and the logic of the market*. Berkeley, CA: University of California Press.

Stubbs, Richard. (2011). "The East Asian developmental state and the Great Recession: evolving contesting coalitions." *Contemporary Politics 17*, 151–66.

———. (2002). "ASEAN plus three: Emerging East Asian regionalism?" *Asian Survey 42*, 440–55.

Tsang, M.C. (2000). "Education and National Development in China Since 1949: Oscillating Policies and Enduring Dilemmas," *China Review 2000*, 579–618.

Tsukamoto, T. (2012). "Neoliberalization of the Developmental State: Tokyo's bottom-up politics and state rescaling in Japan." *International Journal of Urban and Regional Research 36*, 71–89.

UNESCAP. *Statistical Yearbook for Asia and the Pacific 2011*.

UNESCO. *The EFA 2000 Assessment: Country Reports: Japan*. (2000). Available at: www.unesco.org/education/wef/countryreports/japan/rapport_1.html [accessed 26 June 2013]

Unger, J. (1996). "'Bridges': Private Business, the Chinese Government and the Rise of New Associations." *The China Quarterly 147*, 795–819.

Wade, R. (1998). "The Asian Debt-and-Development Crisis of 1997–?: Causes and Consequences." *World Development 26*, 1535–53.

Walter, A. (2006). "From developmental to regulatory state? Japan's new financial regulatory system." *The Pacific Review 19*, 405–28.

World Bank. (2015). "Global Economic Prospects: Forecast Table." Available at: https://www.worldbank.org/en/publication/global-economic-prospects/summary-table [accessed 20 June 2015]

Yang, K. (2013). "Keep business for business: Associations of private enterprises in China." In J. Y. J. Hsu and R. Hasmath (Eds), *The Chinese Corporatist State: Adaption, survival and resistance*. New York: Routledge, 66–82.

15 African Political Economies Beyond 2015

Diversity, Growth, Partnership, and Poverty

Adam Sneyd

"Politics na big business".

Femi Kuti[1]

Africa's poverty problems were front-page news in the lead-up to the Group of 8 (G8) meeting held at Gleneagles, Scotland, in 2005. The efforts of numerous civil society groups had contributed to pushing a diverse range of African political economy challenges onto the international agenda. Campaigners for increased aid, debt relief, trade justice, and other issues of interest to Africa were united in calling for global action to end **poverty**. Academics, including Jeffrey Sachs, and celebrities such as Bob Geldof, Bono, Angelina Jolie, and Chris Martin, prominently encouraged the G8 to address these concerns. The Gleneagles Summit outcome document ultimately endorsed the relief of debts owed to the World Bank and the International Monetary Fund (IMF), and the doubling of aid to Africa. Though a few civil society luminaries worried about the limited nature of the G8 response, many development experts remained confident that these actions would help African countries to realize the United Nations Millennium Development Goal (MDG) of halving extreme poverty by 2015.

Narratives on the challenges and opportunities facing Africa's political economies have shifted since Gleneagles despite the fact that many of them will fail to reach the MDG poverty reduction targets.[2] This new storyline was consolidated between 2012 and 2014. In the financial press, for example, rose-coloured accounts of African opportunities replaced anti-poverty outrage and Afro-pessimism. *The Economist* ran a special report on "Emerging Africa," while the *Financial Times* presented a series on "Africa Inc.," and the *Jeune Afrique* media group consolidated its English-language presence through the success of *The Africa Report*. This upbeat treatment homed in on economic growth. Soaring growth rates and returns to investors in Ghana, Kenya, Nigeria, and elsewhere led the press to rebrand some African economies as "frontier markets" or "lion economies." As media voices played up the fact that Africa was the world's second-fastest growing region in 2012, the 14th Summit of La Francophonie was held at Kinshasa, Democratic Republic of Congo (DRC). Also in 2012, the *Africa CEO Forum* took place in Geneva, and Libreville, Gabon played host to a gathering of business and political leaders known as the *New*

York Forum Africa. These one-off conferences subsequently became annual events.

A new culture of **partnership** between African political economies and their creditors, investors, and trade networks underpinned this developing-growth story. Chinese President Xi Jinping's first overseas visit was indicative of this trend. To enhance his country's ongoing partnerships with Africa through the *Forum on China–Africa Cooperation,* Xi travelled to Tanzania, South Africa, and Congo-Brazzaville. Africa's other emerging partners had also scaled up their engagements. These were evident on the sidelines of the March 2013 summit of the BRICS (Brazil, Russia, India, China, and South Africa) group held at Durban, South Africa. That year Brazil agreed to cancel (write off) or restructure (relieve) nearly $900 million in African debt, and African governments strengthened their ties to India through the *Africa–India Framework for Cooperation.* And the following year the BRICS launched a new development bank that aimed to offer clients in Africa and in other developing areas an alternative to World Bank lending. Morocco, Qatar, Saudi Arabia, and South Korea also made notable efforts to support the new connections that their agri-businesses, banks, construction firms, and development agencies were forging across Africa.

Not to be outdone, many of Africa's "traditional" development partners had also scaled up their engagements. Japanese leaders pledged $32 billion in development assistance and new investments over the next five years at the conclusion of the fifth Tokyo International Conference on African Development. That same month, in June 2013, $100 million was reportedly spent to enable US President Obama to travel for one week to visit Sénégal, South Africa, and Tanzania. France also hosted an Africa summit in December 2013, and the Obama administration followed suit in August 2014 with a US-Africa summit that trumpeted the

$14 billion in new investments that US firms had made across the continent. Within Africa, new partnerships between established international organizations were also formed. On this front, the Commission of the African Union (AU), the African Development Bank (AfDB), and the UN Economic Commission for Africa (UNECA) agreed to rationalize their efforts. These organizations established a new division of labour to better reflect their respective specializations in peace and security issues (AU), in the financing of development projects (AfDB), and in research and economic analysis (UNECA).

In the context of higher growth and the development of new partnerships, the diversity of political economic conditions and challenges in Africa nonetheless remained stark. Kenneth Kaunda, the first president of Zambia, underscored these divergences in his May 2013 remarks to the 50th anniversary celebration commemorating the establishment of the Organization for African Unity (OAU) (now the African Union (AU)). Although the annual *African Economic Outlook* portrayed most African countries as on generally stronger paths than they had been a decade ago, Kaunda was not the only authority to constructively contest excessive Afro-optimism during the 2012 to 2014 period. The annual reports of the *Africa Progress Panel* of highly connected and influential personalities, for instance, identified the diverse challenges associated with the poor governance of natural resources and illicit financial flows.[3]

Similarly, UNECA's flagship *Economic Reports on Africa* focused on the diversity of the continent's commodity export specializations and industrialization challenges. These reports showed that specializing in the production and export of different types of agricultural and extractive commodities required distinct approaches to the pursuit of industrialization and economic transformation. The outbreak of diverse civil conflicts in 2012 and

2013 also reinforced the limitations of narratives on "African" growth and progress. The conflicts in Mali, the Central African Republic, and South Sudan were very different from one another. Likewise, the ideologies and interests behind the 2013 attacks and subsequent hostage crises at the Tigantourine gas facility near In Amenas, Algeria, and at Nairobi's Westgate Mall, were not entirely alike. Additionally, labour strife, including the wildcat strike and the ensuing massacre of miners at Lonmin's Marikana platinum mine near Rustenburg, South Africa, belied stories of universal "progress." The 2014 Ebola virus outbreak and health crises in Guinea, Liberia, and Sierra Leone afforded Africa's leaders a further opportunity to differentiate themselves from one another. At the US-Africa Business Summit, for instance, Tanzania's President Jakaya Kikwete reminded attendees that "Tanzania was in East Africa" and that Ebola was in West Africa. The African reality remained diversity.

To shed light on the current complexity of Africa's political economies the chapter begins by engaging at greater length with the growth narrative noted above. It briefly discusses the possible ways of differentiating "types" of political economies in Africa, and details how these frameworks capture Africa's diversity and also draw attention to numerous pan-African commonalities. The chapter then recounts how new partnerships and engagements are facilitating or detracting from the fight against African poverty. This section presents three dynamic aspects of the complex interactions between African and global actors (including governments, corporations, and civil society groups). Here the focus is on ongoing African "revolutions" in (i) finance, (ii) information and communications technology (ICT), and (iii) agriculture. The concluding section details resurgence and change in the continent's cultures and cultural industries, and brings home what this complexity might mean for Africa's political economies after 2015.

Africa's Political Economic Diversity and Commonalities

As the attention of the global media has turned toward the African continent, the idea that we are witnessing an African "renaissance" rooted in a common African economic condition has been popularized. In this context, media consumers who have no direct interest in Africa should be forgiven if they make the mistake of inaccurately referring to Africa as a "country." Students of Africa, for their part, should be wary of downplaying commonalities as they grasp the complexity that Dr Timothy M. Shaw has captured with his notion that there are "varieties of Africas."[4]

This diverse reality in no way precludes similarities in the political and economic challenges African governments face. It must be recalled that Africa has a shared history. Imperial ventures and colonial rule bequeathed the economic structures that today's leaders seek to transform. This topic—Africa's "structural transformation"—was the theme of the AfDB's annual meetings in 2013 held at Marrakech, Morocco. Calls for **pan-Africanism**—for Africans to recognize their shared history and to unite to overcome external sources of political economic oppression and thereby uplift the continent—continue to resonate. Those who make such calls should not simply be dismissed for glossing diversity. The push for pan-African solutions to common challenges should also not be confused with an effort to foster cultural homogeneity or to "disappear" difference. Rather, it is rooted in an effort to liberate Africa, but is not always and everywhere a throwback to African socialism. The United Nations Conference on Trade and Development's (UNCTAD) *Economic Development in Africa Report 2013*, for instance, expressed the view that stronger intra-African trade and economic cooperation could enable greater private sector dynamism and African empowerment. Several of Africa's new philanthropist billionaires, including Nigerian banker Tony Elumelu and South African mining magnate Patrice Motsepe, have asserted that the pan-Africanism of the twenty-first century will be "Africapitalism": a socially oriented and transformative capitalism driven by private sector leadership and complemented by corporate giving.[5] This business-friendly spin on African unity also has powerful overseas backers, including so-called "philanthropreneurs" or "philanthrocapitalists." Private equity groups, pension funds, and other people who wield financial or political power advocating and executing "social investments" in African ventures tend to convey the "Africapitalist" orientation of doing good through doing more business.

African governments, international organizations, civil society groups, philanthropists, and the media use a number of methods to distinguish countries that reveal Africa's diverse political economic realities. Each of these ways of knowing can enhance understanding of Africa's diversity *and* of its continuing commonalities. The World Bank's system for classifying countries, for example, homes in on gross national income (GNI) per capita.[6] Using this criterion the Bank distinguishes countries by income group, including: low income ($1,025 or less); lower-middle income ($1,026–$4,035); upper-middle income ($4,036–$12,475) and high income ($12,476 or more). According to the 2012 classification, diversity was evident even between the two Congos. At $2,250 GNI per capita that year, Congo-Brazzaville fell into the lower-middle income category, whereas the equivalent figure for the Democratic Republic of Congo of $220 placed it at the bottom of the low-income grouping.

The World Bank's approach to categorization can also be used to contextualize the conventional wisdom on Africa's economic "success" stories by showing that economic reality has a tendency to be more diverse or complex than first-glance perceptions. GNI per capita in Botswana, for instance, a country popularly held to be an economic model for Africa to emulate, fell only into the upper-middle income ($7,720) level in 2012. By contrast, GNI per capita in Equatorial Guinea came in at the high-income level ($13,560) that year. The common perception is that the latter country is notable for its regime's kleptocratic approach to governance, and the corruption charges that US and French authorities have levelled at President Obiang's son. This viewpoint captures an aspect of the story of inequality in Equatorial Guinea, but not all of it. Equatorial Guinea was also Africa's only high-income country in 2012, and had a much higher GNI per capita than South Africa. Botswana might be a model, but attention to this classification shows that it is not the richest country in Africa. That distinction goes to an oil-rich country with a tiny population which in 2014, disturbingly, arrested Javier Blas, then Africa editor of the world's leading business newspaper, the *Financial Times*. Beyond diversity, however, the Bank's classification system also reveals a nasty pan-African commonality. Most of the 36 countries in its low-income category are African states.

Continuing with the theme of similarities, a brief glance at the United Nations Development Programme's (UNDP's) approach to measuring the average level of human development in particular countries is in order. To move beyond income-centric understandings of "progress" or development, the UNDP annually builds a human development index (HDI), a composite statistic of education, income, and life expectancy levels. To better capture the ways that average people experience human development, the UNDP also adjusts this statistic for inequality (the "IHDI"). Through doing so it has come to light that in more unequal societies, the "real" or "lived" IHDI of the average person is often lower than the traditional HDI. Africa's commonalities are unambiguous by this measure. Whereas IHDI rates in Mauritius and Gabon were 50th and 65th in the world respectively in 2013, of the 133 countries for which an inequality-adjusted HDI statistic was produced that year, 30 African countries fell into the bottom 33 places on the list.

The pattern of several high-ranking African outliers and a concentration of African laggards at the bottom of the heap holds for other country rankings compiled by the World Bank, by Transparency International (TI) and by a civil society–media partnership. According to the World Bank's annual *Doing Business* report in 2013, Mauritius was the 19th easiest place to do business in the world, and Rwanda had moved up to 52nd position. Of the 185 countries ranked that year, however, most African countries fell in the bottom quarter of the pile, and nearly all of the countries ranked between numbers 150 through 185 were African. Drawing upon governance and business climate data compiled by independent research institutions, TI's *Corruption Perceptions* index in 2012 told a similar story. Botswana and Mauritius fell at the 30th and 43rd positions, whereas Guinea (154), Zimbabwe (163), Chad (165), Sudan (173), and other resource-rich African states plagued by governance challenges were at the back of the pack. Unfortunately, the low rankings of African countries on indexes of good governance are mirrored in their list-topping status on the *Failed States* index produced by the Washington, DC-based Fund for Peace and *Foreign Policy* magazine. Seven of the ten political economies that topped the failed states list that year were in Africa, including Somalia (1) and Africa's newest state, South Sudan (4).

The continent's "success" stories are nonetheless real, and these demonstrate its diversity *and* the extent of its common challenges. Recipients of the Mo Ibrahim prize for achievement in African leadership, for example, cut through the notion that African political economies are always and everywhere governance basket cases. By receiving this prize, the contributions that former presidents Joaquim Chissano (Mozambique), Festus Mogae (Botswana), and Pedro Pires (Cape Verde) have made to the pursuit of better governance practices have been prominently recognized. Nevertheless, better or even "good enough" governance remains far from the African norm. The Ibrahim prize, which provides a $5 million disbursement to the winner over 10 years and subsequent $200,000 annual payments for life, was not awarded in 2009, 2010, 2012, or 2013 because no suitable candidates could be found.[7] Even so, more and more African governments have shown an interest in breaking out of this worrying, all too common fact of political and economic life. Since African heads of state and government forged the *New Partnership for Africa's Development* (NEPAD) in 2001 under the auspices of the African Union, more governments have begun monitoring their governance practices. As part of NEPAD's good governance agenda, 33 of the AU's 54 members have voluntarily signed up for the African Peer Review Mechanism (APRM). The APRM seeks to ensure compliance with a range of international civil, political, economic, social, and cultural rights norms. Countries that join the APRM produce self-assessments on these matters, and share reflections on their governance challenges.[8]

Beyond classifications, indices, prizes, and reviews, Africa's political economies share many other relevant commonalities and divergences. For those interested in the ecological and climatic zones that shape the limits of possible political economic activities on the continent, a 2013 production of the natural history unit of the BBC—Sir David Attenborough's *Africa*—offers a wealth of information. Africa's diverse agro-ecological zones, and its varying soil and sub-surface geological profiles can also provide a snapshot of difference or useful parallels. Demographics are also a helpful lens. The continent's population is projected to rise to two billion by 2050, but this growth could be very unevenly distributed. Likewise, similarities and differences in languages and culture are a valuable entry point for analysis. The extent of linguistic and cultural changes associated with the colonial encounter and its aftermath is not always and everywhere the same. In just one country—Cameroon—there are over 200 distinct ethnolinguistic groups, and the legacies of British, French, *and* German colonization continue to be evident. Gender empowerment also remains an important entry point. African women have attained prominent official positions. Malawi's Joyce Banda, Liberia's Ellen Johnson Sirleaf, and the Central African Republic's Catherine Samba-Panza each ascended to the presidency of their country, and South Africa's Nkosazana Dlamini-Zuma currently chairs the AU Commission. Yet even a cursory review of the work of the United Nations and in particular UN Women on Africa reveals a more mixed and troubling picture on gender.

Taken together, similarities and differences between African political economies demand nuanced treatment. Some African countries certainly experienced fast economic growth rates as the MDG completion date loomed, but the glowing coverage of Africa's "renaissance" could not be described as subtle. This chapter offers a more balanced presentation of the obstacles and possibilities facing Africa after 2015 by applying a political economy framework to assess the progress and pitfalls of efforts to address Africa's poverty challenges, below. Although this represents only one possible approach to capturing the complexity of Africa's political economies, the poverty orientation remains relevant.[9] Nearly half of the continent's population continues to subsist on the equivalent of $1.25 per day, and population growth threatens to outstrip the capacity of Africa's leaders to address the income aspect of poverty, or its other dimensions.

Africa's Fight Against Poverty

A comprehensive account of the political economy of impoverishment and of the ways and means to overcome poverty in Africa is a topic that is far too vast for an introductory survey chapter. All the same, a cursory treatment of this subject can draw attention to some of the biggest dynamics shaping Africa's political economic futures after 2015. Focusing on contests of ideas, on the development of institutions, and on the exercise of power across three issue areas—finance, telecommunications, and agriculture—reveals some important features of the spaces for stasis and change in Africa. However, in narrowing the discussion to only these sectors, not all of the continent's notable attributes are covered. Other sectors or challenges are equally worthy of further study and student investigation, including the continent's burgeoning energy, mining, oil and gas, and transportation sectors, and its education, health, piracy, and post-conflict challenges.

Financial Revolutions

A generation ago, Africa's financial story was one of persistent public deficits and indebtedness, inefficient or ineffective state-run banks, and a lack of foreign interest in disbursing loans or making investment commitments.[10] In the 1980s, the IMF sought to make further lending to African governments conditional upon the latter's acceptance of more market-oriented policies. At that time, African leaders such as Tanzania's Mwalimu Julius K. Nyerere strongly contested the imposition and acceptance of economic management ideas backed by Washington. With the downturn in the world economy, the prices of primary commodities of export interest to Africa stagnated and trended lower. In this milieu many governments agreed to take the IMF's "medicine." Across Africa, state ownership was rolled back, investment was liberalized, regulations deemed overly market-impeding were removed, and public expenditures were retrenched. African currencies that had previously been pegged to "hard" currencies at elevated levels were also adjusted. High currency valuations had formerly enabled Africans seeking to procure US, European, or Asian-produced capital or technological goods to do so on favourable terms. The downsides of these rates nonetheless prompted the IMF, and subsequently the World Bank, to promote currency devaluation. Inflated exchange rates had permitted Africa's political economic elite to excessively import luxury goods and stow money abroad. They had also undermined the continent's export competitiveness at a time when demand for its commodities was weak.

The extent of financial sector "friendliness" fostered by the uptake of these governance "innovations" nonetheless varied considerably. When governments chose to privatize their state banks, for example, former public bankers with close ties to key officials often benefited directly from privatization processes. Wherever and whenever these personalities retained control of new, nominally private banks, cronyism took hold in ways that circumscribed the intent of privatization. Their supporters often gained access to soft loans or other favours, and the risks and costs of mismanagement or total failure in "private" banking continued to be socialized. More broadly, in the context of retrenchment and budgetary austerity, a monetary policy shift in the United States contributed to stagnation in African banking, and compounded the continent's deficit and debt problems. As the US Federal Reserve targeted inflation and deprioritized employment generation, the associated punishingly high interest rates raised the costs of debt service across Africa, and had the knock-on effect of keeping domestic banking in Africa largely an elite affair.

It would be a stretch to argue that these challenges are "ancient" history. The legacies of the 1980s continue to be felt by African savers who have not saved enough to be "banked" or to access property loans through formal channels. Central bankers across the continent continue to target inflation and keep interest rates high despite strong evidence that higher inflation rates did not preclude the development of several of the Asian Tigers, including Taiwan and South Korea. The budgetary constraints African governments have faced have also continued to hit the headlines. When conflicts have emerged with western creditors over expenditure priorities, and allegations of bad governance have been levelled, the gloomy vestiges of conditionality have been in plain view. After excessively re-indebting itself to facilitate the development of its oil sector in 2014, for instance, Ghana sought out another dose of the IMF's medicine. Moreover, while the West and Central African franc zone (CFA) currencies remain pegged to the euro, inhabitants of the 14 countries in these zones have continued to experience the repercussions of a particularly painful devaluation. Rumours that the Banque des États de l'Afrique Centrale and the Banque Centrale de l'Afrique de l'Ouest were considering further devaluations also persisted in the aftermath of the global financial crisis in 2011.

Despite these continuities, financial innovation in Africa has boomed over the past decade. Africa's emerging development "partners" have challenged North–South norms of development cooperation. The Chinese approach has shaken up business-as-usual in creditor disbursements to debtors by being rooted in a doctrine of "non-conditionality." Chinese leaders have touted what they term the "win–win" and "non-political" aspects of the various African deals that their state-run lenders have cut. According to an analysis conducted by the *Financial Times*, China's Exim

Bank and the China Development Bank signed loans in 2009 and 2010 that were worth more than the loan commitments the World Bank's private sector and non-concessional lending arms entered in to over those years.[11] As emerging market financial institutions beyond China have also scaled up their involvement in Africa, questions have been raised about the implications of this lending surge. Western development institutions have expressed concern over the sustainability of the new debt service and repayment commitments that African governments have entered into. High-level officials, including Lamido Sanusi—the former governor of Nigeria's central bank who prominently resigned in 2014 after exposing billions of dollars of missing oil revenues—have emphasized the "neo-colonial" aspects of Africa's relations with its new creditors. And civil society groups across the continent have flagged the possible dangers of hastily executed debt-heavy energy, and extractive and infrastructure projects. The costs of extending, maintaining, or fixing these schemes could skew future public investment priorities away from areas of demonstrable social development need. At present there are no easy answers to the short-run impacts of Africa's emerging lenders on poverty. There continues to be a significant research gap on this topic, but new knowledge is slowly emerging that could help to cut through popular conjectures or speculation about the possible long-term consequences of these engagements for Africans.

The poverty-reduction strengths and weaknesses of other recent financial innovations are a little less hypothetical. Ten years ago few global financial gurus would have dabbled in African bonds or stocks, considered the development of private equity partnerships, or have even known the names of Africa's big banks. Today investment professionals around the world consider knowledge of these areas to be essential. As central banks flooded the system with cheap money in response to the global crisis, the fund management industry, private bankers, and independent investors turned increasingly to emerging markets, and then to Africa in search of higher yields. From 2007 through February 2013, 10 different African governments followed Ghana's lead in seeking to take advantage of investor greed to raise funds. Over that period Angola, Côte d'Ivoire, Namibia, Zambia, and others issued a total of $8.1 billion in sovereign bonds denominated in foreign currencies at coupon (interest) rates that averaged an exceedingly high 6.2 per cent. As a result, these countries entered into debt obligations where borrowing costs were in many cases four times higher than those associated with the debt stock they had previously accumulated.[12] In the context of a future downturn these governments could now become targets for "vulture funds": investment funds that buy bonds at risk of imminent default on the cheap with the hope of reaping large returns in the aftermath of debt defaults.

Recognizing the potential risks of bonds, in the context of heightened global interest in Africa's commodity exports, several countries embraced an alternative approach to securing public finances. Angola, Ghana, and Nigeria launched state-owned funds to set aside, invest, and actively manage some of their commodity export revenues. Aiming to model their operations on the $700 billion fund that Norway has built from its oil export revenues, the professional management of these new sovereign wealth funds (SWFs) could help these countries to mitigate "boom–bust" commodity cycles. Doubts have nevertheless been raised about their potential to adhere to the global voluntary guidelines on the governance of SWFs. Known as the Santiago principles, these guidelines on industry best practices seek to ensure that SWFs are transparent and well managed. Media and civil society alarm bells went off in 2013, for example, when the son of the president of Angola, José Filomeno dos

Santos, was tapped to chair the Angolan SWF. His sister, Isabel, is globally renowned for being the richest woman in Africa. Critics such as the Open Society Institute have been troubled by the prospect that a $5 billion SWF could be managed as a family affair in one of the "most unequal societies" on the planet.

The possible costs and risks of the burgeoning interest in stocks listed in "frontier" markets such as Ghana, Kenya, and Nigeria are similarly unambiguous. The Nigerian stock exchange's all-share index grew by 35 per cent in 2012, but in doing so the country was exposed to the risk that foreign investors could quickly reverse their new portfolio investments in entities such as Nigerian Breweries, United Bank for Africa (UBA), and Zenith Bank Nigeria. Although Nigeria has the resources necessary to impose capital controls such as taxes or other requirements that aim to prevent outflows of hot money, the viability of this precautionary strategy in other lesser-developed "frontier" markets is questionable. Unscrupulous short-term investors aiming to "pump" and subsequently "dump" shares can thrive when weak governments are unable to legitimately threaten to introduce exchange controls or minimum stay requirements for investors.

The nascent interest of private equity funds in Africa raises similar concerns vis-à-vis the long-term fight against poverty. According to an analysis by Ernst & Young, private partnerships raised at least $10 billion from institutional investors and multilateral development banks to pursue investments in Africa between 2007 and 2012.[13] Funds as diverse as the buyout specialist Carlyle Group's Sub-Saharan Africa Fund and anti-poverty campaigner Bob Geldof's social-impact-oriented 8 Miles Fund sought to acquire stakes in or outright control of budding private sector standouts. The extent to which this new interest could lead to the asset stripping of targeted firms, the ratcheting up

of their debt levels, or the imposition of corporate practices inappropriate to Africa's level of development is simply not yet known. There have also been several prominent failures, including the implosion of the highly publicized New Star Heart of Africa Fund. At the height of the global crisis, the New Star fund experienced a classic liquidity crunch. It could not sell its assets and consequently ran out of cash. New Star's failure stung its backers, and pulled the rug out from under the African businesses that it had invested in.

Beyond the growing financial interest in Africa, considerable innovation has also taken place in finance within Africa. Several large pan-continental banking conglomerates have emerged over the past decades. In the 1980s, the dearth of such entities convinced the federation of West African chambers of commerce and industry and the Economic Community of West African States (ECOWAS) to foster the development of a pan-African private sector bank. The result was Ecobank, a transnational entity headquartered in Togo, now with operations in 33 countries. Other African banks that are even bigger than Ecobank have also cultivated interests across the continent, including South Africa's Standard Bank Group and ABSA, Nigeria's UBA and Zenith, and Morocco's Attijariwafa and BMCE banks, among others.[14] These private banks aspire to provide industry-leading services, but have not been immune from the challenges and shortcomings exposed by the financial crisis. Bad governance allegations, for instance, forced the Chair of Ecobank Transnational to step aside in 2013, and pushed its CEO out the door the following year. Africa's private banks have also had to navigate serious adversities. A spate of brazen robberies of Ecobank's subsidiary in Cameroon between 2010 and 2013, for instance, was allegedly connected to shadowy political and military figures.

In sum, new ideas, institutions, and power relations are shaping Africa's financial futures and their prospects of working for the poor. Regarding the former, in policy and business circles, the idea that a welcoming stance toward a diverse array of new debt and equity investments is needed to realize the continent's emerging market aspirations has been ascendant. Other ideas linked to the ICT (information and communications technology) revolution, including the crowdsourcing of funds and microcredit, have also shot to prominence and are detailed in the section below. Institutions as wide-ranging as private equity and foreign state-owned banks are making considerable contributions to establishing investment priorities and to providing finance. African governments command the power to attract a diverse array of investors. They can also exercise more degrees of freedom in the financial partnerships that they establish than was possible during the era of conditionality. The corollary of this reality is that more types of corporate and public financial institutions wield power over the potential for African poverty reduction than ever before. The power of finance—as everywhere else—is more apparent in the day-to-day life of the continent, and ongoing investor attractions to Africa are not limited to portfolio (bonds, stocks) or non-physical interests. Even in the context of a global downturn in foreign direct investment (FDI) flows in 2012, according to UNCTAD's *World Investment Report 2013*, Africa was the only global region where inward FDI flows increased. FDI in new operations or takeovers in Africa that year, including speculative direct investments, topped $50 billion.

ICT Revolutions

The scaling up of Africa's connectivity with the rest of the world has also permitted new ideas, institutions, and power relations to flourish. The development of cellular networks, for example, has enabled considerable innovation. Networks have been established, extended, and consolidated to the extent that the World Bank estimates that there are more than 650 million mobile telephone subscribers south of the Sahara. Since Mo Ibrahim sold Celtel in 2005 and launched his foundation, intense competition has developed continent-wide between subsidiaries of India's Bharti Airtel, South Africa's MTN, France's Orange, and many other local and regionally based network operators. Airtime costs in some cases have trended lower, but in many places have remained stubbornly high, especially for international calls and for SMS. Protests linked to popular unease with high airtime prices in South Africa in 2013 underscored the notion that cell phones have not been the unidirectional "liberators" that they were once touted to be. Although they have clearly made communications more accessible and have facilitated a profusion of income-generating activities and efficiencies, they continue to have numerous political economic and social costs.

For example, efforts to build, maintain and upgrade Africa's cell networks have relied heavily upon imported technologies. North–South and South–South technology flows in this area to date have resulted only in the transfer of the knowledge and skills necessary to use current machines or equipment. Little attention has been paid to enabling Africans in Africa to learn more about, invent, or produce the components that could underpin future mobile networks. The turn away from landlines has also undercut a potential source of demand for copper from Zambia or from the DRC's Katanga province.

Demand has nonetheless emerged for another African extractive commodity. The electrolytic capacitors essential to the circuitry of cell phones require tantalite or coltan anodes. Africa is the principal source of the global supply of newly mined coltan, and significant amounts continue to be produced in the DRC provinces of Maniema, North Kivu, and South Kivu.[15] As supply from the eastern DRC ramped up in the 2000s, civil society groups identified and drew attention to linkages between coltan production and the financing of the persistent conflicts that have plagued that region. Global consumer boycotts of cell phones, tablets, and other electronic devices containing DRC-origin coltan were also initiated. Concern over this "conflict mineral" and others eventually spilled into the US Senate. Section 1502 of the Dodd-Frank Wall Street Reform act that President Obama signed into law in 2010 specified that electronics firms were responsible for reporting that they were not sourcing coltan and other minerals from the DRC or its nine neighbouring countries.

Other problems with the production, sale, and operation of handsets also have the potential to limit employment generation and economic diversification. The largest global handset producers have not moved their production facilities to Africa. Consumers across the continent also typically purchase dated or used models from Asian-origin resellers, or buy pirated or knock-off "Iphonies." A prime beneficiary and driver of the low-cost handset revolution, China's Tecno Telecom, has expressed an interest in ending Africa's dependence on imported phones by establishing local production facilities. In so doing, its commitment to Africa stands out from global brands that have continued to view the continent primarily as a source of raw materials and a sink for obsolete or cheaper units. Turning to software applications, with a few notable exceptions, including development "apps" such as mPedigree, M-Farm, and Frontline SMS, Africans have continued to rely primarily on foreign apps to execute their mobile web needs.

Nonetheless, Africa's mobile networks have made communications more accessible. Although many operators have had to come up with costly solutions that help their networks to weather frequent power cuts, they have also become platforms for the development of employment-generating economic activities. Kenya's Safaricom, for instance, has famously built a mobile phone-based money transfer and microfinance service that generates considerable revenues. Known as M-Pesa, this for-profit service enables subscribers to make electronic payments and send money home and abroad, and has spawned copycats within Africa and elsewhere. M-Pesa's paperless banking service, M-Shwari, directly challenges the power that traditional banks have held over consumer credit and savings. More broadly, cellular networks have become the backbone of Africa's microfinance boom. Aiming to support entrepreneurs and existing small- and medium-sized enterprises (SMEs), private lending institutions of all types and qualities have rapidly entered this market. The African Microfinance Network of practitioners in this area and the African Microfinance Transparency Forum aim to professionalize this burgeoning business and ensure that it does not degenerate into cell phone-enabled predatory lending or loan sharking.

ICT has also been at the core of new trends in western engagement with Africa, and has been a key focus of infrastructure investments. It has become trendy for western-based institutions to support SMEs and social entrepreneurship ventures in Africa by crowdsourcing funds.[16] These pooled or collective venture capital efforts aim to close what institutions such as the Rockefeller Foundation refer to as Africa's start-up funding "gap." They aspire to facilitate social or environmental "impact" investments that will also have sound financial returns. However, crowdsourcing requires considerable data transmission, so it would not have thrived under Africa's formerly creaking and in many cases broken telecommunications infrastructure. In the past, calls from urban centres as close as Lomé, Togo, and Cotonou, Bénin, were routed through Europe, and Internet traffic ground to a halt on a daily basis as oversubscribed satellite networks frequently overloaded. Since 2010, several submarine fibre-optic cables off Africa's East and West coasts have freed up data transmission. Business ideas—and political ideas—have flowed more freely over the enhanced networks.

Overall then, ICT is unshackling innovation in Africa, but it is not doing so evenly or without costs. Technologies have made it possible for new institutions, including a raft of online importers, to thrive. As a direct result of the levelling of access to ICT, more rural Africans know more about global commodity prices than at any previous time. Governments, for their part, have at their disposable enhanced means to push public service information, such as agricultural advice, to the masses. Yet here too ICT has been a mixed blessing. African governments and companies have the capacity to collect more data on citizens and on consumers than ever before. Several public authorities have asserted draconian powers over more rapid and intensive transnational and domestic information flows. In the immediate aftermath of the Arab Spring revolutions in Tunisia, Egypt, and Libya, for example, the Government of Cameroon temporarily shut down the Twitter social network. Where enhanced ICT has taken the form of cheap handsets and improved access to data and to finance, it has worked in the service of income growth and poverty alleviation. Where it has destroyed industries or prevented the development of new types of ICT business within Africa, such as components or equipment manufacture, or mobile and web applications development, its long-run effects on poverty have been less clear-cut.

Agricultural Revolutions

A generation ago the introductory story of the ideas, institutions, and power relations of agriculture in Africa could be quickly summarized. After formal political independence, Adam Smith's famous "invisible hand" simply did not govern African agricultural production and trade. Instead, it was the very visible "fist" of state intervention that was evident in the many countries in Africa that retained heavy-handed colonial systems of agricultural administration. Colonial powers had established tight control in part to ensure continuous flows of agricultural raw materials such as cotton back to Europe to bolster their industrial revolutions. The colonial commodity export model also drew African agriculturalists into the money economy, and subjected them to taxation. New African nations embraced the old idea that the agricultural sector needed to be governed to maximize returns to the state. Private competition forward and backward from African farms was consequently shunned. Backward from production, state-run organizations controlled the import and distribution of agricultural inputs such as fertilizers, pesticides, and seeds to farmers. Forward from the farm gate, crop development or marketing boards were typically the only government-sanctioned buyers, and were often the sole sellers of crops onto the world market.

State-run entities often made deliberate efforts to get agricultural prices "wrong" during this period. Farmers of export crops such as cocoa, coffee, cotton, sugar, tea, and tobacco, and of food crops for domestic markets, were frequently poorly paid. In theory, low farm gate prices enabled governments to use more of their export revenues to support industrial development, and to subsidize urban food consumption. From the 1980s, the inequities associated with these non-market-based systems fostered a World Bank-led push to get prices "right." Evidence of the impoverishing fallout from how the countryside was being asymmetrically "milked," and of the perversely excessive enrichment of "insiders" along the input distribution and marketing chains, informed this policy shift.[17] A report on this topic—*Accelerated Development in Sub-Saharan Africa*—now commonly referred to as the *Berg Report*, popularized the notion that the structure of agricultural production and marketing in Africa needed to be adjusted to enable market liberalization.

In the context of lower commodity prices, higher interest rates, and the rise of policy-based or conditional lending in the 1980s, cash-strapped African governments acceded to this structural adjustment of agriculture. However, the extent to which the ideal of liberalization was subsequently embraced varied considerably. Wherever and whenever competition to provide inputs or to buy crops was introduced, for example, former price-makers or gatekeepers sometimes became "private" barons of the countryside. In the case of Tanzania after structural adjustment, extensive research showed that regulators and private buyers had not fully embraced more liberal principles or practices.

The impacts of day-to-day "illiberal" realities at the domestic level in Africa nonetheless paled in comparison to the devastating effect that protectionist policies elsewhere continued to have on the competitiveness of the continent's key agricultural exports. The lavish subsidies that the United States and European Union continued to offer their cotton farmers, for instance, pushed global cotton prices lower and by the early 2000s had reduced returns from cotton to specialists, including Bénin, Burkina Faso, Chad, and Mali. These cotton-dependent countries subsequently sought redress by launching an initiative on the issue within the WTO's Doha Round of trade negotiations.[18] Other North–South initiatives beyond the WTO, including the EU's Economic Partnership Agreements (EPAs) and the US and African Growth and Opportunity Act (AGOA), promised and in some cases delivered more open export markets for Africa. The EPAs were nevertheless criticized for locking Africa into its commodity-heavy export specializations. Similarly, AGOA made concessional access to the US market conditional upon the maintenance of democracy. In the aftermath of the 2009 political crisis in Madagascar and that country's prolonged failure to return to constitutional rule, this stipulation devastated the Malagasy textile sector.

Illiberal trade also had South–South dimensions. Among other unwelcome effects, intra-African trade barriers continued to impede cross-border flows of food from surplus to deficit countries. Talk of trade liberalization within ECOWAS, the Communauté Économique et Monétaire des Etats de l'Afrique Centrale (CEMAC), and the Southern African Development Community (SADC) increased throughout the 1980s and 1990s. However, trade barriers persisted into the 2000s, and ambitious liberalization projects such as the Common Market for Eastern and Southern Africa (COMESA) faltered. Like their counterparts in the West, many African governments seemingly found it easier to preach free trade than to actually practise it.

As agriculture has continued to be the principal source of employment and of rural income generation, and as food insecurity and poverty challenges have continued, global efforts to inform the future of farming in Africa have intensified. Faced with evidence of the limits of pure market fundamentalism, the World Bank prominently shifted its position in the 2000s. In its *World Development Report 2008: Agriculture for Development*, the Bank recognized that government interventions could make agriculture work better for farmers in certain cases. Even so, this moderation was limited: the Bank simultaneously called for a big push for private investments in large-scale agriculture projects. Other development agencies also scaled up their attention to this topic before the global food crisis of 2007–09. They funded initiatives such as the Future Agricultures Consortium, and after the crisis, homed in on food security in response to the G8 initiative on this theme launched at L'Aquila in 2009. Philanthropists had also thrown their weight around on this issue before the crisis. The Bill and Melinda Gates Foundation and the Rockefeller Foundation funded the Alliance for a **Green Revolution in Africa** (AGRA). Chaired by former UN secretary general Kofi Annan, AGRA seeks to transform African agriculture through funding initiatives that aim to build farmer capacity, including the development of improved seed varieties. The former UN Special Rapporteur on the Right to Food, Dr Olivier De Schutter, encouraged African governments to engage more with domestic sources of food insecurity. De Schutter called for national strategies for growth and poverty reduction, and for agricultural sector and rural development strategies, to include more language and measures about the right to food. His work emphasized the ways and means to enhance: (i) the physical *availability* of food, (ii) social and economic *access* to food, and (iii) the cultural, nutritional, and safety or *adequacy* of food.

Booming interest in African agriculture has made it much more difficult to capture and represent a brief snapshot of developments in this dynamic area. Nonetheless, it can be said with certainty that several distinct rural "revolutions" are now playing out across Africa. These divergent revolutions are rooted in very different ideas, and have generated dissimilar power relations. Their possible contributions to poverty reduction and to the realization of food security are consequently dissimilar. The first "revolution" emerged as governments and public and private firms responded to the implications of the 2003–13 price boom known as the global commodity "super-cycle" for food security and profitability by making more direct investments in African agriculture. Land acquisitions soared as investors linked to food-insecure emerging market economies sought to use Africa as a platform for the production and export of cheap food. Other investors, including commodity specialists Cargill and Olam, found Africa's newly welcoming stance toward FDI in agriculture to be conducive to their needs to hedge supply chain risk, or to mitigate regulatory risks beyond Africa. Development advocates strongly criticized the poverty reduction potential of land "grabbing," and the cheap land lease rates, low levels of employment generation, and environmental despoliation that plagued numerous acquisitions in places as diverse as Ethiopia, Gabon, Sierra Leone, and Uganda. To ensure that future large-scale acquisitions would not unduly benefit foreign investors, in 2012 the UN Committee on World Food Security endorsed a set of voluntary (non-binding) guidelines on land tenure governance.

By focusing on building the capacity of smallholders, the AGRA is advancing a fundamentally different type of agricultural revolution. This second "revolution" was comprehensively spelled out in the UNDP's 2012 *Africa Human Development Report*. It aims to enrich independent family farms by enhancing their access to improved seeds, fostering gender empowerment, strengthening producer organization, and enhancing marketing infrastructure, such as storage and roads. In contrast to the extensive growth of agriculture associated with large-scale projects, this vision seeks to intensify African agriculture by keeping traditional, locally controlled farming systems intact. However, to do so it advocates the increased use of conventional petrochemical-based input technologies. This stands in stark contrast to a third widespread revolution in African agriculture.

In many African contexts, experimentation with agro-ecological methods and certified organic production systems has been ongoing for two decades. In most cases, these systems have durably enhanced sustainability, and have also had numerous other social and economic benefits. As a United Nations Environment Programme (UNEP)-UNCTAD task force presented in a report on *Organic Agriculture and Food Security in Africa*, the use of botanical pesticides, organic fertilizers, trap crops, nitrogen-fixing legumes, and the development of other on-farm organic innovations has generated new input industries and employment opportunities. It has also augmented food security and thereby reinforced the conclusion of the International Assessment of Agricultural Knowledge, Science and Technology for Development (IAASTD) report, that diversified fields of sustainably cultivated food crops have a greater potential to enhance food security than monocultures and conventional methods. Organic has not been a silver bullet in places where previously excessive applications of petrochemical pesticides and synthetic fertilizers have depleted soil productivity nor has it had powerful financial backers to trumpet its successes.

Taken together, all of the new interest in African agriculture ensures that more actors of more origins are exerting more power over life on African farms. The context-specific and contingent exercise of power in this milieu makes it difficult to make universal claims about the potential for agriculture to work better for poverty reduction after 2015. Although some farmers, in some places, might benefit from how power has been exercised to create any of the three "revolutions" noted above, each of these approaches could potentially oppress other farmers in different contexts. For students, when it comes to the future of agriculture in Africa, easy answers are unfortunately unavailable.

Conclusions

As the financial, ICT, and agricultural "revolutions" detailed above continue to play out they will contribute to ongoing processes of cultural change and resurgence. Cultures of consumption are shifting across Africa. Shopping centres and retail developments linked to hotel complexes and modelled on the West have sprung up or are planned in locations that are remote from the global tourist circuit, including the capitals of Mauritania, Niger, and The Gambia. This uptick is linked not only to the resource "boom," but also to the growth of Africa's middle class and its heightened demand for consumer goods. Satellite TV, status updates, and more frequent international travel have exposed this new class to global consumer culture and cultivated brand recognition and new tastes. In this context, high-flying footballers, including Didier Drogba of Côte d'Ivoire and Cameroon's Samuel Eto'o, the A-list movie stars of Nigeria's "Nollywood," and top-selling bands such as Magic System set pan-continental trends.

Aiming to serve emerging African consumers, several global brands have rapidly scaled up their interests. Walmart, for example, has acquired South African retailer Massmart. Giant European food retailers Tesco and Carrefour have also sought to emulate Groupe Casino's past African successes in supermarkets. Other global firms have increasingly catered to Africa's wealthiest. In Lagos, Nigeria, high-end clothing retailer Ermenegildo Zegna has opened a shop, and a Porsche dealership seeks to serve the booming market for luxury automobiles. Foreigners have also launched exclusive sushi restaurants in Djibouti, Italian eateries in Yaoundé, and members-only private nightclubs in Abidjan.

Yet the extent of the impact that elite and middle-class consumption is having on consumer cultures across Africa should not be overplayed. Though Ethiopian Airlines might have been the first African airline to take delivery of Boeing's 787 Dreamliner, most Ethiopians could not possibly dream of being able to afford to hop on a Dreamliner to visit Kensington High Street shops in London or duty-free in Dubai. To meet their needs, they typically rely on imports of used televisions and clothing, and also on imports of low-end and in some cases pirated consumer-durable, soft, and household goods. Imports of used and cheap clothing, and of household items such as plastic buckets have certainly enabled consumer choice. In many African cases they have also undercut the development or viability of job-creating light manufacturing industries.

The dynamism of the continent's cultural industries has nonetheless soared. As more foreign partners have been attracted to the fight against poverty or to Africa's new role as a "pole" for global growth, interest in the outputs of Africa's diverse artists, craftspeople, musicians, and writers has surged. The older writings of the late Chinua Achebe and Ngugi wa Thi'ongo, and those of a new generation, including Teju Cole, NoViolet Bulawayo, and others have reached new audiences. Musicians have also honed original and fusion sounds that have resonated around the world, including Cheikh Lô and Tinariwen. The troubling realities of Africa's political economies have also continued to inform the development of a musical style that seeks to liberate Africa. The politically charged anti-poverty lyrics of the late Fela Kuti infuse the new recordings of his sons Femi and Seun, and his Afrobeat sound is widely emulated and has gone global. Growth in the celebration of African cultures has also been rapid. The Pan-African Film and Television Festival held annually at Ouagadougou attracts global attention, as have Mali's annual literary festival, and the Festival au Desert world music showcase held near Timbuktu. And the cultural resurgence continued in the wake of the 2013 conflict in Mali, as the latter two festivals were successfully

moved to Burkina Faso and to Brazzaville that year.

In sum, Africa is diversity. Its economic growth is rapid yet uneven, and its new partnerships are many, but varied. Looking after 2015, it consequently makes little sense to talk about a common African "condition." As Tim Shaw reminds us, there are varieties of Africas. Still, the common challenges remain stark. On this front, faltering progress on the Millennium Development Goals is just the tip of the iceberg. Climate variability and change, wildlife conservation, deforestation, forest degradation, desertification, watershed management, urban sprawl, and a host of other shared problems persist at the intersection of the environment and political economic development. Difficulties at the peace and security nexus are equally glaring. Africans face the challenge of coordinating their efforts on all of these tests, and of managing the engagements of all of their partners to maximize poverty reduction. They also confront and are actively entertaining new ideas about the development of institutions that could become new centres of power. Some of these ideas would draw the continent even closer together. The idea of an African monetary union and common "Afro" currency, for example, might remain an integrationist pipedream after 2015, but could become a source of considerable governance innovation and change if it takes institutional form.

As a diverse growth pole subject to the variously self-interested and well-intentioned engagements of its many expanding partnerships, Africa after 2015 will be anything but poor. The ultimate and as yet unanswered question is whether its political economies will be able to embrace the ideas and institutions necessary to counterbalance the financial and other power asymmetries that have entrenched poverty up to the present.

Notes

1 Femi Kuti, 2013, "Politics Na Big Business," *No place for my dream*. New York: Knitting Factory Records.

2 United Nations Development Programme, *MDG Report 2013: Assessing progress in Africa toward the millennium development goals*. New York: UNDP, 2013.

3 Africa Progress Panel, *Africa Progress Report 2013: Equity in Extractives—Stewarding Africa's natural resources for all* (Geneva: APP, 2013). In late 2013 the IMF also warned about the potential risks associated with the growth of sovereign bond (debt) issuance across Africa and the continent's increasing links to the global economy. See IMF, *Regional economic outlook: Sub-Saharan Africa—Keeping the pace*. Washington, DC: IMF, October 2013.

4 T. M. Shaw, (2011), "Africa's quest for developmental states: Renaissance for whom?," *Third World Quarterly 33*(5), 837–51.

5 R. Edwards, 2013, "Can Africapitalism save the continent" (London: *The Guardian*), 12 July. Electronic edition.

6 World Bank, "How we classify countries" (Washington, DC: World Bank). http://data.worldbank.org/about/country-classifications.

7 To learn about the underpinnings of poor governance see Göran Hydén, 2006, *African politics in comparative perspective* (Cambridge: Cambridge University Press).

8 For a critical take on NEPAD, see Patrick Bond (Ed.), 2002, *Fanon's warning: A civil society reader on the new partnership for Africa's development* (Trenton, NJ: Africa World Press).

9 An equally relevant approach would be to foreground peace, security, or post-conflict challenges. See Ian Spears, 2011, *Civil war in African states: The search for security*. Boulder: Lynne Rienner.

10 T. Mkandawire and C. Soludo, 1999, *Our continent, our future*. Ottawa: IDRC.

11 G. Dyer et al., 2011, "China's lending hits new heights." London: *Financial Times*, 18 January, 1.

12 J. Stiglitz and H. Rashid, 2013, "SSA's eurobond spending spree gathers pace," London: *The Guardian*, 26 June, Economics blog.

13 Ernst & Young, 2012, *Private Equity Roundup—Africa*. London: E&Y.

14 See *Jeune Afrique*, 2013, "Spécial finance," 15e edition. Paris: Groupe JA.

15 M. Nest, 2011, *Coltan*. Cambridge: Polity Press.

16 For more on the approaches larger or more established firms have taken with respect to their social or environmental impacts in Africa, see S. Ponte et al. (Eds), 2011, *Governing through standards*. Basingstoke: Palgrave Macmillan.

17 See P. Gibbon et al., 1993, *A blighted harvest*. London: James Currey.

18 Adam Sneyd, 2011, *Governing cotton: Globalization and poverty in Africa*. Basingstoke: Palgrave Macmillan.

Key Terms

partnership

poverty

green revolution in Africa

pan-Africanism

Questions for Review

1. Who are some of Africa's "traditional" and "emerging" partners? How do they engage with African governments, civil society organizations, businesses or individuals?

2. What are some of the key innovations in African finance since the era of policy-based or conditional lending?

3. Where and in what ways has ICT contributed to poverty reduction and/or the entrenchment of poverty?

4. When have models of agricultural governance in Africa shifted, and why are several distinct agricultural revolutions ongoing in Africa?

5. Why are changes in Africa's consumer culture or in its capacity to produce culture relevant to a discussion of the political economy of poverty in Africa?

Further Resources

Achebe, C. (1958). *Things fall apart*. Oxford: Heinemann.

Bulawayo, N. (2011). *We need new names*. New York: Reagan Arthur Books.

le Carré, J. (2001). *The constant Gardener*. London: Hodder & Stoughton.

Cole, T. (2007). *Every day is for the thief*. New York: Random House.

Leys, C. (1996). *The rise and fall of development theory.* Bloomington: Indiana University Press.

Malan, R. (1990). *My traitor's heart.* New York: Grove Press.

Saul, J. (2009). *Revolutionary traveler.* Winnipeg, Arbeiter Ring.

Vassanji, M. G. (2003).*The In-between world of Vikram Lall.* Toronto: Random House.

Wa Thiong'o, N. (1977). *Petals of blood.* London: Heinemann.

Websites

http://africasacountry.com/

http://ny-forum-africa.com/en/home#!prettyPhoto

www.institutions-africa.org/

www.focac.org/eng/

www.jeuneafrique.com/

https://web.archive.org/web/20150314212920/http://thinkafricapress.com/

www.cnn.com/video/shows/anthony-bourdain-parts-unknown/episode8

References

AfDB (African Development Bank) et al. (2013). *African economic outlook 2013.* Paris: AfDB, OECD Development Centre and UNECA, 2013.

AGRA (Alliance for a Green Revolution in Africa). (2013). *Africa agriculture status report: Focus on staple crops.* Nairobi: AGRA.

APP (Africa Progress Panel). (2013). *Africa progress report 2013: Equity in extractives—Stewarding Africa's natural resources for all.* Geneva: APP.

Campbell, B. (Ed.). (2009). *Mining in Africa: Regulation and development.* Ottawa: IDRC and Pluto Press.

Cornelissen, S., Cheru, F., and, T. M. (2011). *Africa and international relations in the 21st century.* Basingstoke: Palgrave Macmillan.

Ernst & Young. (2012). *Private equity roundup—Africa.* London: E&Y.

Gibbon, P. et al. (1993). *A blighted harvest.* London: James Currey,

Harrison, G. (2010). *Neoliberal Africa: The impact of global social engineering.* London: Zed Books.

Hydén, G. (2006). *African politics in comparative perspective.* Cambridge: Cambridge University Press.

IAASTD (International Assessment of Agricultural Knowledge, Science and Technology for Development). (2009). *Agriculture at a crossroads: Synthesis report.* Washington, DC: IAASTD.

IMF (International Monetary Fund). (2013). *Regional economic outlook: Sub-Saharan Africa—Keeping the pace.* Washington, DC: IMF, October.

Jeune Afrique, Les 500 premières entreprises Africaines, Paris: Groupe JA, (2013).

Jeune Afrique, "Spécial finance," 15th edition. Paris: Groupe JA, 2013.

Jerven, Morten. (2013). *Poor numbers: How we are misled by African development statistics and what to do about it.* Ithaca: Cornell University Press.

Leys, C. (1994). "Confronting the African tragedy," *New Left Review* (204), March–April.

Maharaj, B., Desai, A., and Bond, P. (2011). *Zuma's own goal: Losing South Africa's "War on poverty."* Trenton, New Jersey: Africa World Press.

McKinsey Global Institute. (2013). *Africa at work.* Washington, DC: McKinsey Global Institute.

Mkandawire, T. and C. Soludo. (1999). *Our continent, our future.* Ottawa: IDRC.

Nest, M. (2011). *Coltan.* Cambridge: Polity Press.

Ponte, S. et al. (Eds). (2011). *Governing through standards: Origins, drivers, limitations.* Basingstoke: Palgrave Macmillan.

Power, M. et al. (2012). *China's resource diplomacy in Africa: Powering development?* Basingstoke: Palgrave Macmillan.

Shaw, T. M. (2011). "Africa's quest for developmental states: Renaissance for whom?," *Third World Quarterly 33*(5), 837–51.

Sneyd, A. (2011). *Governing cotton: Globalization and poverty in Africa.* Basingstoke: Palgrave Macmillan.

Spears, I. (2011). *Civil war in African states: The search for security.* Boulder: Lynne Rienner.

TI (Transparency International). (2012). *Corruption perceptions index*. Berlin: TI.

UNCTAD (United Nations Conference on Trade and Development). (2013). *Economic development in Africa report 2013*. Geneva: UNCTAD.

UNCTAD. *World investment report 2013*. (2013). Geneva: UNCTAD.

UNDP (United Nations Development Programme). (2012). *Africa human development report 2012: Towards a food secure future*. New York: UNDP.

UNDP. *MDG report 2013: Assessing progress in Africa toward the Millennium Development Goals*. (2013). New York: UNDP.

UNECA (United Nations Economic Commission for Africa). (2013). *Economic report on Africa 2013: Making the Most of Africa's Commodities*. Addis Ababa: UNECA.

UNEP (United Nations Environment Programme) and UNCTAD. (2008). *Organic agriculture and food security in Africa*. New York and Geneva: United Nations.

World Bank. (2007). *World development report 2008: Agriculture for development*. Washington, DC: World Bank.

World Bank. (2013). *Doing Business 2013: Smart regulations for small and medium-size enterprises*. Washington, DC: World Bank.

PART V

Levels of Analysis

International regional pressures are not the only factors influencing state activity in the global political economy. It is also important to remember that domestic considerations can have a direct impact on the foreign economic policies of states. International trade, for example, rarely fulfills the needs of all interests, especially if the state includes a wide range of sectors and regional economies, all with different export and import needs. Contemporary international trade agreements also tend to intrude on domestic areas of jurisdiction, creating potential problems for central governments as they implement and enforce these commitments. In addition, foreign investment creates international priorities for states as domestic investors accumulate tangible assets in other countries (foreign direct investment) or invest in short-term, volatile, portfolio investments, such as stocks, bonds, and other forms of securities. Exchange rates can further affect the foreign activity of government and non-government actors due to the purchase power of a state's currency vis-à-vis its counterparts in other domestic economies. Finally, the institutional actors within states can have a significant impact on foreign economic policy due to the changing priorities of the executive, legislative, and bureaucratic branches of government, as well as sub-federal governments in federal states and municipalities (Hiscox 2011, 98–121).

Added to this list is a wide range of non-institutional domestic and transnational actors that also influence international economic activity. For example, transnational corporations and corporate interests, typically from western developed states, invest heavily and have subsidiaries in numerous foreign states, many in the developing world. Many of these corporations also establish supply chains that are difficult for central governments to monitor and control. In addition, other domestic interests, such as the media, labour and ethnic groups, political parties, and other domestic advocacy organizations and coalitions, can mobilize to raise awareness, support, and/or opposition to foreign trade and investment practices. When examining domestic pressures it is also important to take into consideration "non-legitimate" actors that engage in trade and investment activity in both legitimate and "black" markets, such as individual criminals, organized crime, terrorists, and national liberation movements (Willetts 2011, 330–4). Many of these considerations are discussed in Part V, but also in other sections of the volume, most notably in Part VI.

All of these considerations highlight the importance of domestic politics, institutions, and non-state economic actors in international bargaining, especially with other states and multilateral and bilateral institutions. This is often referred to as the "level of analysis" problem in IPE. During the Cold War, international relations scholars began adopting economic-based "rational actor" models and "bureaucratic politics" frameworks to better understand the relevance of domestic institutional actors in the formulation of foreign policy (Allison 1971; Simon 1982). Eventually, however, a number of new contributions began exploring levels of analysis using a broader sample of variables. One attempt was the "second-image reversed" approach, offered by Peter Gourevitch, who suggested there was a reciprocal relationship between domestic politics and developments in the international system (Gourevitch 1978). Robert Putnam also attempted to incorporate domestic actors in his study of "two-level games." In this theory of international bargaining, it was generally assumed that government officials attempted to manipulate both domestic and international politics at the same time (Putnam 1988).

On the surface, these contributions appeared to represent significant progress in addressing theoretical weaknesses related to the gap between domestic and international politics, the separation of politics and markets, and the centrality of the state as a unitary rational actor. In reality, however, the "second-image reversed" approach was essentially a state-centric analysis of domestic interests in areas of foreign policy. Gourevitch, despite recognizing the impact of the bureaucracy, the perceptual set of leaders, and the importance of transnational actors, eventually relied on a "strong state" (limited domestic influence) versus "weak state" (strong domestic influence) framework. Further, Putnam essentially focused on domestic "win-sets" and the opportunities and constraints these imposed on international negotiators. As some critics suggested, this simply reinforced the common argument that international and domestic pressures shape policy outcomes at both levels of analysis (Goldstein and Keohane 1993). Putnam, much like Gourevitch, also tended to concentrate on domestic as opposed to relevant international developments.

Although not directly related to the level of analysis problem there was another branch of literature that focused specifically on international relations and federal states. One early attempt to understand this sub-federal activity centred on the concepts of "trans-sovereign" linkages and "perforated sovereignty" (Duchacek, Latouche, and Stevenson 1988). Developed in the late 1980s these terms reflected the increasing decentralization of federal states as a result of expanding economic interdependence. It also noted the increasing institutionalization of cross-border regional cooperative frameworks. These themes were subsequently explored using the concept of "paradiplomacy" (Michelmann and Soldatos 1990). Despite a specific emphasis on economic relations, this comparative analysis offered observations related to culture, electoral politics, human rights, and the environment. Although these contributions highlighted the global role of sub-federal governments studies of "perforated sovereignty" tended to be atheoretical and "paradiplomacy," ultimately concluded that sub-federal activity posed little threat to state sovereignty. Both frameworks also paid limited attention to institutional factors, such as constitutional issues, bureaucratic capacity, party structure, political leadership, and cooperative federalism.

The chapters in this section of the volume touch on many of these themes. Hans Michelmann begins by focusing on the "constituent diplomacy" of Alberta and Quebec

(Canada), Baden-Württemberg (Germany), and Flanders (Belgium), and argues that, despite intergovernmental tensions, both orders of government in all four countries demonstrate a remarkable degree of cooperation, especially in terms of foreign economic policy. Trevor Harrison's examination of global cities and finance capital, however, focuses on the importance of the financial districts of London and New York and their impact on contemporary capitalism, as well as the possible emergence of new municipal centres in the future, especially in Asia. Laura Macdonald and Jeffrey Ayres then shift the discussion to the rapidly changing, but impressive, impact of civil society on both the practice and study of global politics since it first exploded onto the streets in the late 1990s. Finally, Anil Hira takes on the complicated practice of industrial policy and the growing tension between open markets and the politics of economic policy both within and between states.

References

Allison, G. (1971). *Essence of decision: Explaining the Cuban missile crisis*. New York: Harper and Row.

Duchacek, I. D., Latouche, D., and Stevenson, G. (Eds). (1988). *Perforated sovereignties and international relations: Trans-sovereign contacts of subnational governments*. New York: Greenwood Press.

Goldstein, J. and Keohane, R. O. (Eds). (1993). *Ideas and foreign policy: Beliefs, institutions, and political change*. Ithaca: Cornell University Press.

Gourevitch, P. (1978). "The second image reversed: The international sources of domestic politics." *International Organization 32*(4) (Autumn), 881–912.

Hiscox, M. J. (2011). "The domestic sources of foreign economic policies." In John Ravenhill (Ed.). *Global Political Economy*, 3rd ed. Oxford: Oxford University Press.

Michelmann, H. J. and Soldatos, P. (Eds). (1990). *Federalism and international relations: The role of subnational units*. Oxford: Clarendon Press.

Putnam, R. D. (1988). "Diplomacy and domestic politics: The logic of two-level games." *International Organization 42*(3) (Summer): 427–60.

Simon, H. A. (1982). *Models of bounded rationality*. Cambridge MA: MIT Press.

Willetts, P. (2011). "Transnational actors and international organizations in global politics." In J. Baylis, S. Smith, and P. Owens (Eds), *The globalization of world politics*, 5th ed. Oxford: Oxford University Press.

16 Constituent Diplomacy in Federal Countries

Hans J. Michelmann

Government representation of their citizens' interests abroad is generally considered a responsibility of national governments. This has never been exclusively the case because other orders of government have long engaged in international activities. In an age in which economic activities and other human interactions are less and less confined within national boundaries, an age of ever-increasing globalization, these other orders of government have been increasingly motivated to look abroad to serve the interests of their citizens. This chapter discusses the international activities of constituent units in three highly developed federal countries, two Canadian, one German, and one Belgian, to provide an overview of such activities, which in this chapter will be called **constituent diplomacy**.[1] The analysis will be informed by the conceptual framework developed for an edited volume, *Foreign Relations in Federal Countries*, and will also rely to some extent on its country chapters.[2]

Constituent diplomacy is affected by, among other factors, the responsibilities entrusted to constituent units by national constitutions and the relations between orders of government that have developed over time; the geographical/regional setting in which it takes place; ethnic/linguistic factors, in some instances; and, of importance in all contexts, the nature of constituent unit economies, especially the degree to which their prosperity is dependent on international trade and commerce.

Constituent diplomacy comprises a wide range of internationally oriented governmental actions. The pursuit of economic interests is of major, if not paramount, importance. In a world marked by economic interdependence, and given citizens' expectations of governments at all levels to further their prosperity, policies and actions aimed at attracting foreign investment and providing assistance to firms in selling their products abroad to augment such efforts by national governments are crucial, especially since constituent units are more knowledgeable about and likely to be more sensitive to the needs of business in their jurisdiction. In all economically highly developed federations, constituent units participate in national foreign policy decision-making to varying degrees, depending on constitutional provisions and intergovernmental practices that have developed over time. They also participate in international and regional organizations, again in a range from very limited involvement to participation as fully recognized members. When it comes to projecting their interests internationally, their constituent diplomacy involves such actions as missions abroad by premiers and senior ministers if such visits promise to contribute significantly to effectively promote, for example, trade and investment, or when such visits serve broader political interests. In some instances, provincial premiers have even met with prime ministers or presidents of national governments. Governments advertise abroad, engage commercial agents in foreign countries or domestically, provide advice in house or through private organizations to local firms about conducting business, even representing these businesses abroad, and provide tax and other incentives to attract or retain foreign firms. The promotion abroad of tourism is very common in various media, and constituent units participate or subsidize their firms to participate in trade shows. Cultural and educational constituent diplomacy is universally practised, and the constituent units of many developed-world federations provide technical as well as capacity-building assistance to strengthen governance in the underdeveloped world and in countries undergoing the transition to democracy. Some have surprisingly generous foreign aid programs that they execute, often in cooperation with their federal government and/or international organizations. And, as shall be demonstrated later in this chapter, some constituent units also engage in more politically oriented constituent diplomacy, meant to enhance their image and presence abroad as political actors in their own right with a mission that transcends economic, cultural, educational, and other, less ambitious, concerns.

The resources deployed at home to launch and direct constituent diplomacy, largely but not exclusively government ministries and agencies, vary in prominence and reflect the emphasis given constituent diplomacy. Some constituent units have employed private-sector organizations to represent their firms abroad and counsel them on how to conduct business there, as well as providing advice to foreign firms wishing to establish themselves in their jurisdiction. To enhance these efforts, some constituent units have established offices abroad on their own or sometimes in cooperation with their national government to represent their political and economic interests in countries they feel are of strategic importance to them. These offices also become involved in outreach activities in other fields such as education, culture, scientific exchanges, and, from time to time, governance capacity-building efforts abroad, to enhance or supplement such efforts originating from the home government or even the national capital. Their duties include assisting firms and individuals to engage in business ventures abroad and to seek investment capital. They also engage in gathering information and in establishing contacts with private and public sector actors. In the pages that follow these facets of constituent diplomacy will be illustrated and elaborated on.

The Choice of Constituent Units

The choice of constituent units for this study was made to highlight the range of phenomena on the dimensions of comparisons identified above. A Belgian, a German, and two Canadian constituent units were chosen because they demonstrate a range of experiences with constituent diplomacy that permits a comprehensive overview of the phenomenon. The experience in other constituent units of our sample countries or those in other federations will occasionally be addressed when it becomes instructive.[3]

Quebec is the Canadian province most actively engaged in constituent diplomacy, and *Alberta* is in the next tier of Canadian provinces in this regard. They operate in the same constitutional context, which is not very permissive of constituency diplomacy, and are located in a similar geographic matrix (bordering the United States). Both have export-dependent economies, a fact that motivates their constituent diplomacy. Quebec's ethno-cultural composition provides added impetus to its efforts as it seeks to forge ties with francophone countries worldwide to build and enhance relations, even political relations, with culturally and linguistically similar polities in a bid to strengthen its cultural and ethnic identity.

The rationale for the choice of *Baden-Württemberg* is best stated by quoting from the Land's website:

> For decades, Baden-Württemberg has cultivated intensive relations to its partners around the world. These close ties have come about as a result of its central position within Europe, its export-oriented economy and its leading position in the field of science and technology. Baden-Württemberg borders with France to the west, with Switzerland to the south and—across Lake Constance—with Austria. All of Europe's capital cities are just a few hours' flight away. With a population of around 10.7 million, and one of the highest per-capita income levels in Europe, Baden-Württemberg is bigger and economically more powerful than many of the European Union's member states.[4]

Baden-Württemberg was also chosen because of its constitutional setting which permits the German Länder considerable scope for constituent diplomacy on their own account and allows them to participate in the national foreign policy decision-making process through their membership in the German upper house (Bundesrat). In addition, the

Land, like Flanders, participates intensively in the EU institutions and in the national decision-making process on EU affairs. But it is also engaged far beyond the European continent. Among the German Länder, it is one of the most actively engaged in constituent diplomacy.

The fourth constituent unit discussed in the chapter is *Flanders*, also with a very active constituent diplomacy. Like Baden-Württemberg, it participates actively in European Union (EU) institutions as well as in Europe-wide regional organizations. Its economy is heavily export-oriented, and Flanders has built much of its prosperity on international business. It was also chosen because the constitutional provisions that apply to its constituent diplomacy are polar opposites of those to which Quebec and Alberta are subject because Flanders operates in a very permissive constitutional environment, one in which the resulting system of intergovernmental relations is particularly conducive to constituent diplomacy.

The Constitutional and Intergovernmental Relations Settings

The degree of involvement by constituent units in foreign policy decision-making varies, ranging from minimal consultation to regular though only partly institutionalized consultation; to legally or even constitutionally mandated consultation with the national government; to participation in national legislative institutions in forging foreign policy; to almost co-equal partnership in the conduct of foreign policy in the sense that constituent unit governments are formally empowered to conduct business abroad independently of their federal government on matters under their jurisdiction. Negotiating and signing international treaties is normally the responsibility of national governments, though, as shall be demonstrated later, Belgium is an exception because its constituent units are empowered to do so on their own behalf, as are German Länder. Formal treaties are not the only instruments employed by governments to forge agreements with partners abroad. Numerous agreements that fall short of treaty status, some simply memorandums of understanding, are concluded by constituent units with foreign jurisdictions. Constituent units also participate to various degrees in both regional and more broadly international IGOs. In the European Union federations this encompasses participation in the EU decision-making processes at both the national and supranational levels. Constituent diplomacy in this context is regulated by highly formalized domestic agreements, in Germany by provisions that resulted from a constitutional amendment. Because of its very nature, EU decision-making makes it difficult to differentiate between the national and supranational process because many policy sectors are highly integrated, though member states usually arrive at a domestic position before proceeding to Brussels. As a result, constituent unit relations with the EU transcend the usual demarcation between the domestic and the international that applies to relations with other IGOs in both federations and non-federal countries because many important decisions, which would be domestic decisions in other countries, are made in Brussels, the EU capital, including such matters as international trade that directly affect constituent diplomacy.

The interaction between federal and constituent units when it comes to constituent diplomacy varies significantly among federations, depending in part on constitutional provisions and in part on **intergovernmental relations**, i.e., structures and practices that have evolved over time to regulate the interaction between the federal government and its constituent units. Intergovernmental relations

play a major role in shaping the practices and strategies adopted by constituent units in carrying out their international activities. The Canadian, German, and Belgian patterns demonstrate the range of constitutional and intergovernmental provisions that regulate the relationship between constituent units and national governments. The Canadian pattern demonstrates a highly restrictive constitutional and loosely structured intergovernmental relations setting; the German one demonstrates highly integrated decision-making involving the two levels of government, due to constitutional provisions and established practices; the Belgian one demonstrates a very permissive constitutional and a structured intergovernmental relations setting.

Canada

The Canadian constitution does not assign provinces treaty-making powers. Nor, given the provisions for selecting the members of the Canadian Senate, are the provinces represented in federal institutions in any meaningful way; hence, they do not formally participate in national foreign policy decision-making. However, a judicial ruling, the 1937 Labour Conventions case, stipulated that implementing the provisions of international treaties on matters falling under provincial jurisdiction domestically is a provincial responsibility. This provision goes nowhere near to meeting the demands of Quebec as outlined in the Gérin–Lajoie doctrine for powers to engage polities abroad in its own right in all policy sectors under its jurisdiction. The federal government has the constitutional responsibility for representing Canada's political interests abroad and to negotiate agreements with the force of international law, although, despite these provisions, as will be demonstrated below, Quebec's constituent diplomacy is very extensive.

Intergovernmental relations in the Canadian foreign policy decision-making process differ significantly from those of many other federations in that there are no formally institutionalized structures to deal with these matters. However, the need for consultations and negotiations between the two orders of government on foreign relations is self-evident: technical and political expertise in policy sectors under provincial jurisdiction reside with the provinces and implementing international agreements in these sectors is their responsibility. Hence provincial input is essential to forge a well-considered Canadian position in international negotiations and to help ensure provincial compliance in the implementation of these agreements. Thus there exist agreements about consultation between the two orders of government in the various policy sectors that have a strong foreign relations component; for example, agriculture, trade, and the environment. However, these agreements have often left provinces dissatisfied with the degree of access afforded them as well as the extent of the impact that their views have on the position the federal government takes in negotiating with its international partners. In the past, there had traditionally been more or less regular consultations between the provinces and the federal government before and during negotiations of international agreements, involving meetings of first ministers in areas of high politics and ministers responsible for departments when important matters affecting their portfolio were under negotiation. Committees of public servants from both orders of government met for ongoing consultation during the course of negotiations, but the federal government did not allow direct participation by the provinces in negotiations with foreign partners. Since coming to power, the present Harper government has de-emphasized the degree of federal–provincial coordination favoured by previous federal governments in the various policy sectors.

However, operating procedures may be changing in the negotiation of international agreements that affect provincial jurisdiction. Most recently, this practice has been altered when, at the insistence of Canada's EU partner in the Comprehensive Economic and Trade Agreement (CETA) negotiations, the provinces were direct participants.[5] The government of Canada signed an agreement in principle with the EU on 18 October 2013 to which all provinces have consented, though the agreement's provisions have yet to be worked out in detail. Whether such a practice persists remains to be seen.[6] As compared to other federations, however, intergovernmental relations between the provinces and the federal government are marked by the absence of formal, institutionalized structures, a state of affairs the provinces wish to remedy.[7]

Germany

The German constitution (*Grundgesetz* or Basic Law) allocates the Länder a substantial role in managing relations between Germany and the world, permitting them to negotiate international treaties on matters that fall under their jurisdiction.[8] Hence they can become active in international relations in their own right. Before such treaties are concluded, however, the federal government's assent is required, which means that much consultation and negotiation must take place before that. In the event, such treaties have been modest in number, with Baden-Württemberg accounting for only about 30. The Basic Law does not state clearly whether the federation can negotiate treaties in matters falling under Länder jurisdiction nor does it state clearly whether Länder must implement treaties concluded by the federal government on these matters. An agreement between the two orders of government in 1957 obliges the federal government to consult with the Länder, represented in specially established committees, at the earliest possible instance after deliberations begin domestically on the position to be taken by Germany and well before such treaties are negotiated.[9] Hence, there is a long-institutionalized structure within which this aspect of German intergovernmental relations is conducted. Practical considerations necessitate such a procedure because of the Länder's policy expertise and because the Länders implement most domestic federal government legislation, including obligations arising from international treaties.

The Länder participate actively in the conduct of German foreign policy in yet another way. Their governments constitute the membership of the Bundesrat, Germany's upper house. Article 50 of the Basic Law mandates that international treaties regulating political relations between Germany and foreign states require its consent. Hence the Länder participate directly in the treaty-making processes that involve both their constitutional responsibilities and those of the federal government. Negotiations between the two orders of government on such matters take place in Bundesrat committees and are thus constitutionally mandated.[10]

In the decades since the beginning of the European integration process that has resulted in an ever-increasing transfer of their powers to the European Union institutions, the Länder, like their Belgian counterparts, insisted that they become integrally involved in the EU decision-making process on matters that are under their jurisdiction, in part to help offset the loss of their powers. As the result of a constitutional amendment, an article of the Basic Law stipulates that the federal government keep both houses of the federal government comprehensively informed on EU initiatives. The Länder are actively and on an ongoing basis engaged in domestic, largely Bundesrat-based, deliberations about EU matters of concern to Germany. What is quite remarkable in this context is that, as a result of constitutional changes both in Germany and at the EU level in the 1990s, Länder representatives at both the political and public service levels negotiate on behalf of Germany in EU Council deliberations affecting culture, education, and broadcasting. The process has become another aspect of the highly institutionalized system of intergovernmental relations that characterizes German federalism.

Another example of the close cooperation between the two orders of government is found in Germany's relations with international organizations. Länder, regularly at the invitation of the federal government, actively participate in Germany's delegations to such international organizations as the OSCE, IMF, and UNESCO, especially when matters subject to their jurisdiction are at issue. Länder are active participants in the German foreign policy process in a manner that extends well beyond the participation of their counterparts in many other federations, though their Belgian counterparts play an equally prominent part in their nation's foreign policy.

Belgium

The Belgian constituent units enjoy what Quebec aspires to in its relationship with Ottawa: the right to conduct foreign relations in policy fields under their jurisdiction, including the negotiation and conclusion of treaties.[11] To make this quite explicit, Article 167 of the Belgian constitution stipulates that the federal government conduct its foreign relations without prejudicing the right of the constituent units to conduct theirs, including the right to make treaties in policy fields under their jurisdiction.[12] These treaties can be entered into "with sovereign states, with international organizations that have international legal personality and with federated states that have competences which, according to their internal laws, they may execute at an international level."[13] Like constituent units in other federations, Flanders can negotiate and has negotiated, a large number of agreements with partners lacking international legal personality (e.g., Quebec), such as cooperation agreements and statements of intent. These commit Flanders to cooperation in various policy fields with partners abroad, but the ability of Belgian constituent units to conclude treaties with states and international organizations in their own right in fields falling under their jurisdiction is an important feature of their constituent diplomacy.

The Belgian constitution makes provisions for the conduct of foreign relations in areas of concurrent jurisdiction such as trade policy, development policy, and the environment that result in so-called mixed treaties. All parliaments must ratify mixed treaties, which engage the jurisdiction of both the national and constituent unit governments. Thus, constituent units can block their ratification. As demonstrated in the discussion of Baden-Württemberg, whose interactions with the EU are not as extensive as those of Flanders with its jurisdiction over a much broader range of policies, the breadth of scope and complexity of the EU decision-making process makes a clear division of responsibilities for policy sectors very difficult. Much of the affected subject matter, if not already falling in policy sectors explicitly identified as such in the constitution, thus effectively becomes treated as if it were subject to concurrent jurisdiction.[14] The constituent units are participants in negotiating Belgian agreements and treaties with the EU as well as other international organizations whose mandate affects their jurisdiction, and they formally ratify these legal instruments; in other words, constituent unit legislatures must ratify treaties concluded by the national government if their subject matter impinges on their jurisdiction.

However, the constitution also stipulates that constituent diplomacy "cannot contradict the broad orientation of the commonly agreed foreign policy of the Belgian federation."[15] To help ensure that this provision is honoured, the constitution mandates that constituent units must keep the federal government informed of international agreements they enter into and define their international activities more broadly. Under special circumstances the federal government can suspend the constituent units' treaty-making procedures, though it is unlikely to do so given, among other reasons, partisan political and national unity considerations. When implementing treaties, each order of government ensures compliance with obligations that it has undertaken. The constitution does make the provision that the federal government must take responsibility for the obligations undertaken by a region (though not vice versa) if that region is found to be in contravention of international agreements.

Such complexities necessitate specifying provisions and creating processes and structures that bring some clarity and coherence to the conduct of Belgian foreign relations. A unit of the Belgian Foreign Affairs Ministry organizes the process of arriving at a common, consensus-based position on EU matters under constituent unit jurisdiction, normally at the public service level, or, in instances when such a consensus is not reached, at the ministerial level. Hence federal officials and officials of constituent units participate in a highly institutionalized intergovernmental process with constituent units as equal partners of the national government.

Coordinating foreign relations in other policy sectors takes place in what is known as a *Concertation* Committee that operates at various levels, from first ministers to 15 inter-ministerial conferences, including one on foreign policy, again on the basis of consensus, such that any party has a veto.[16] The resulting coordination/cooperation agreement procedures serve to govern Belgium's foreign relations. The constituent units, without federal participation, have also established committees to address matters of mutual concern in conducting their foreign relations; for example, cooperation in establishing commercial attaché offices abroad so that constituent units not represented in a foreign location are represented on a part-time basis by attachés of the other unit. It should be noted that many of these attachés are lodged (co-located) in Belgian embassies and consulates abroad, a fact that demonstrates the cooperation between the two orders of government even in a federation as loosely coupled as Belgium's.

There is no structure to prepare a Belgian position for negotiations in other multilateral organizations such as UNESCO, the WTO, and the Council of Europe. Cooperation agreements regulate the interactions between the federal and constituent unit governments on negotiations in these organizations, in which constituent units participate directly, often as associate members. Flanders and Wallonia represent and speak for Belgium in organizations such as the UNESCO General Conference, though in most other multilateral contexts they participate as part of the Belgian delegation.[17] Hence, the Belgian system of intergovernmental relations is somewhat less highly structured than its German counterpart, but significantly more so than that of Canada. The relationship between Belgium's constituent units and its federal government in this regard has been characterized as follows:

> the conduct of Belgian foreign relations can be characterized in terms of cooperative federalism because practical arrangements have been devised to ensure the country's foreign policy remains coherent by virtue of the coordinating role of the federal government.[18]

As in Baden-Württemberg, Belgian constituent units represent Belgium in the EU Council of Ministers and other EU institutions when matters falling under their jurisdiction are considered there. But because the Belgian constituent units have much more comprehensive constitutional competences than their German counterparts, they speak for Belgium more frequently in these

contexts than representatives of the German Länder speak for Germany.[19]

Implementation of Constituent Diplomacy

Domestic Organizational Infrastructure

Quebec and Flanders have impressive governmental structures to anchor their international activities. Those of Alberta are less elaborate; those of Baden-Württemberg are modest, as the Land devolves the implementation of many functions to private-sector organizations.

Quebec's constituent diplomacy is administered by its Ministère des relations internationales et de la Francophonie et Commerce extérieure, a large and complex organization headed by a cabinet minister. The Ministère had a budget of some $150 million and employed 638 persons at home and abroad in 2013.[20] Quebec's financial commitments are some ten times those of Alberta and are evidence of a major international effort.

Alberta's organizational infrastructure is modest compared to Quebec's. It comprises a division of the Ministry of International and Intergovernmental Relations whose primary responsibility is for domestic intergovernmental relations and is headed by a cabinet minister. The division's 2011–12 budget was $15,138,000. This sum was divided between the Head Office: ($9,094,000) and the 10 Alberta International Offices: ($6,044,000).[21] The division is composed of five directorates (four with a geographical focus).[22]

Constituent diplomacy's importance to *Flanders* is reflected in the government structure through which it is conducted and organized. The Flemish Department of Foreign Affairs is a full-fledged ministry reporting to the Flemish Minister-President, and advised by the Flemish Foreign Affairs Council, a policy research centre.[23] The

Department's responsibilities include tourism, development cooperation, and foreign trade; furthering the internationalization of the Flemish economy; and even the import and export of strategic goods as well as dual-use technologies, including the monitoring of such trade.[24] Its foreign affairs and policy divisions focus on Flemish bilateral and multilateral relations as well as its relations with the EU, all reflecting the importance of relations with the world of a constituent unit whose export ratio exceeds 100 and which accounts for more than 80 per cent of Belgium's trade. In 2007, some 495 persons were employed in Flanders's foreign relations establishment at home and abroad and total expenditures were €163,533,000.[25]

Baden-Württemberg's constituent diplomacy is managed by the office of the minister in charge of the Bundesrat, Europe and International Affairs, and involves only a small number of officials in that setting. The sectoral ministries are heavily involved in the policy process especially for EU matters but also for constituent diplomacy more generally. Their participation in the preparation for EU negotiations as well as their participation in the foreign policy process on other matters is facilitated by the Länder representative offices in Berlin which coordinate their dense network of relations with the federal government at both the bureaucratic level, and, when it comes to sensitive political matters, at the highest political levels. Given the international dimensions of much of German domestic policy, foreign relations are often at play even when this appears at first glance not to be the case.

Baden-Württemberg is among the most active German Länder on EU matters. The heavy emphasis on the EU in its international activities is facilitated by its representative office to the EU in Brussels where, like the offices of the other Länder and those of Austrian Länder, its civil servants keep track of the legislative and broader decision-making process by interacting regularly with the EU Commission,

Council, Parliament, and the Economic and Social Committee.[26] Baden-Württemberg's membership in the Committee of Regions, an EU advisory institution that represents EU regional and local authorities, also facilitates this work. Monitoring the EU institutions has become essential not only because of their role in the domestic implementation of the ever-increasing number of policies made in Brussels but also because, though very modest when compared to national finances, European constituent units and regions have become beneficiaries of EU program funding and hence have an interest in decisions about its allocation.

Bilateral and Regional Constituent Diplomacy

The management of cross-border relations with adjacent countries or subnational polities, including constituent units of federations or regions in countries with unitary governments, is an important feature of constituent diplomacy. "Housekeeping" activities, such as the management of border-spanning infrastructure like highways and water supply systems, cooperation on pollution control, and providing mutual access to health care infrastructure adjacent to national borders are examples of cross-border cooperation between constituent units and adjacent foreign partners. Beyond such quotidian cooperation is cooperation in more significant functions: *Quebec*, for example, is engaged with Vermont in the Quebec–Vermont Joint Commission to "strengthen cooperation in economic development, energy, the environment, security, justice, tourism, transportation and education,"[27] and the Quebec–New York Economic Summits exist to foster cooperation between scientists, government officials, and business people on trade, transportation, renewable energy, and science and technology.[28] *Flanders* borders only one foreign jurisdiction, the Netherlands, with which it has a number of agreements to manage cross-border relations. One of the most noteworthy is a treaty on cooperation in the areas of culture, education, science, and welfare. Alberta has a transboundary partnership agreement with Montana to address mutual economic concerns such as agriculture, firefighting, the environment, and transportation.

Regional constituent diplomacy is also practised multilaterally—many regional organizations affiliate adjacent and proximate non-adjacent subnational polities in addressing common concerns. North America provides numerous examples: cooperation with foreign jurisdictions over "housekeeping" matters is straightforward and uncomplicated. But weightier matters are also the object of regional constituent diplomacy. *Alberta*, for example, participates in a number of transboundary organizations such as the Pacific North West Economic Region (PNWER) which affiliates Alaska, Idaho, Montana, Oregon, and Washington in the US, and British Columbia, Alberta, and Yukon in Canada. In that context they focus on such matters as cooperation in agriculture, energy transmission, transportation, security and disaster resilience, and telecommunications, as well as trade and economic development. The Canadian American Border Trade Alliance (Can/Am BTA) seeks, among other goals, to enhance tourism and commerce between Canadian provinces and American states, and is dedicated to the resolution of US–Canada border issues, needs, and concerns.[29] Alberta also participates in US state government organizations such as the Western Governors Association and Council of State Governments, and has formal consultative links with Montana and Alaska.

Quebec participates in numerous regional organizations that affiliate it with American states and provide further examples of the typical content of such regional constituent diplomacy. For example, the Southeastern United States–Canadian Provinces Alliance, is an "economic forum dedicated to increasing trade, promoting bilateral investment, and stimulating technological and scientific exchanges"; the Eastern Regional Conference of the Council of State Governors "addresses common problems, creates joint programs and exchanges information"; the Conference of New England Governors and Eastern Canadian premiers "brings together the governors of all six New England states (Connecticut, Maine, Massachusetts, New Hampshire, Rhode Island, and Vermont) and the premiers of Quebec and the four Atlantic provinces" to discuss topics of shared interest. The conference "encourages cooperation in energy, environment, trade and transportation."[30]

Baden-Württemberg is situated in a region of Europe that is densely populated and highly developed economically. The Land participates in four organizations that foster cooperation among constituent units and regions in adjacent countries, France, Switzerland, and Austria, as well as with Liechtenstein, to coordinate the many housekeeping functions necessary to manage a common space and to promote such shared interests as tourism and regional development both regionally and internationally. The Land was instrumental in establishing the "four motors of Europe region" involving Lombardy in Italy, Catalonia in Spain, Rhône-Alpes in France, und Baden-Württemberg, with its affiliates Flanders, Wales, and even Ontario, to further common interests in high technology and postsecondary education.[31] There are also numerous bilateral agreements with neighbouring jurisdictions to manage practical matters of mutual concern, for example with Upper Austria. Equally important is its membership in organizations such as INTERREG,[32] the Congress of Local and Regional Authorities of the Council of Europe, and REG-LEG,[33] which affiliate subnational governments to study and pursue common concerns. Baden-Württemberg, like other Länder and Belgian constituent units that are also members of these networks, has a role to play in participating in the implementation of the Schengen and other agreements that serve to regulate interactions among EU member states on matters such as immigration, the control of EU external borders, and combatting international crime. In short, it is heavily engaged in multilateral regional organizations with functional and political concerns.

However, constituent unit bilateral relations are not limited to adjacent or even regionally proximate neighbors. Each of the four constituent units has relations with constituent units of other federations or subnational governments of unitary states worldwide, and Flanders even has bilateral relations with nation states. These bilateral relationships encourage cooperation in such fields as trade promotion, foreign direct investment, economic development, environmental protection and cooperation in the development of new technologies, as well as cultural, educational, and scientific exchanges and, in the case of Quebec, Baden-Württemberg, and Flanders, foreign aid, including assistance in government capacity building.

Alberta has sister province relationships that affiliate the province with one subnational polity in South Korea, Japan, and China, and two in Ukraine, as well as one constituent unit in Germany and Mexico, and three in Russia.

The Government of *Quebec* describes its bilateral constituent diplomacy as follows:

> The Government of Quebec maintains bilateral relations with some thirty federated states and regions around the world, mainly in Western Europe and North America, but also in Asia and South America. Trade, education, culture, the environment, science and innovation are at the core of the relations between Quebec and its partners. These relations allow the parties to share knowledge on issues for which they are responsible, exchange best

practices and create linkages between economic and social actors.[34]

Baden-Württemberg is affiliated bilaterally with two subnational polities in China, one in Japan and one in Burundi, as well as a province in South Africa, a region in Russia and two Russian cities. *Flanders* has bilateral agreements, some in the form of international treaties, with the Czech Republic, Poland, Hungary, Estonia, Latvia, Lithuania, Bulgaria, Romania, and South Africa.[35]

Representation Abroad
Representative Offices

Though this cannot be said to the same extent for Alberta and Baden-Württemberg, Flanders and Quebec have established a visible international presence as political entities well beyond their regional settings. The rationale for establishing offices abroad and travel by constituent government politicians is in most instances much the same as that for the other forms of constituent diplomacy discussed earlier. In addition to these more functional motivations, however, constituent diplomacy often entails political/representational considerations in that they demonstrate the presence of constituent units as political entities and can provide international visibility that other forms of constituent diplomacy may not.

Three constituent units, *Alberta*, *Flanders*, and *Quebec*, have established representative offices abroad. *Baden-Württemberg* has adopted a different strategy. Its government supports the international interests of its industrial and commercial sector through the "Baden-Württemberg Internationale Gesellschaft für internationale wirtschaftliche und wissenschaftliche Zusammenarbeit mbH (bw-i)" (Baden-Württemberg Society for International Economic and Scientific Cooperation) a private-sector firm established in cooperation with the Land's federation of chambers of commerce and other corporate interests. Its role is to support small- and medium-sized enterprises to open up export markets and also to provide assistance to universities in promoting Baden-Württemberg as an attractive centre of learning and research: Baden-Württemberg focuses heavily on promoting its high-tech industries and its universities.

In addition, Wirtschaftsfördergesellschaften, private-sector economic development agencies, and the Deutsche Industrie und Handelskammertag (German Chamber of Industry and Commerce) support the international interests of Baden-Württemberg businesses both domestically and abroad in its 120 Deutsche Auslandshandelskammern offices in 80 countries.[36] Its office in Brussels, which monitors and lobbies the EU institutions on behalf of the private sector, enhances the efforts of the Land government to represent Baden-Württemberg private-sector interests in that setting that is so important for European economic interests. It thus enhances the work of Baden-Württemberg's own office in Brussels. German Länder governments not infrequently employ these organizations to undertake special projects of benefit to their business sectors.[37] Political relations are channelled through German embassies and consulates. Most other activities, such as cultural, educational, capacity building, and foreign aid efforts directed abroad are administered by the various government ministries.

Alberta has ten offices abroad, the majority in Asia.[38] Most are co-located in Canadian embassies or consulates. Canada's embassy in Washington harbours Alberta's most important office, with its mandate of furthering Alberta's policy interests in the US, whereas the others are responsible for the more focused tasks such as trade promotion and investment attraction, and offering Alberta businesses help in their commercial endeavours abroad. These offices are lightly staffed, most with

no more than two persons. All are charged with helping to organize travel abroad by the Alberta premier, ministers, members of the legislative assembly and senior public servants; providing intelligence about economic and political developments; helping Alberta businesses pursue their interests; encouraging foreign direct investment in the province; assisting foreign firms wishing to do business in Alberta; and facilitating cooperation in cultural, educational, and scientific exchanges. Unlike Quebec's international offices, they are not meant to project a political presence abroad; its offices present Alberta as a province in Canada and do not sell themselves as part of a network of quasi-embassies, as is more nearly the case for those of Quebec.

Flanders's network of offices is much more elaborate. There are eleven Representatives of the Flemish Government whose mission is to represent its "general political interests." They have diplomatic status in the host country, a status unique among the constituent units considered in this chapter. Flanders has concluded treaties with many of these countries.[39] A number of their offices are co-located in Belgian embassies and permanent representative offices to multilateral organizations. Some of these representatives are accredited to more than one partner country or institution. For example, Flanders's Paris office, in addition to its responsibilities for France, also represents Flanders in three international organizations, UNESCO, the OECD, and the Council of Europe, and its Pretoria office is responsible for South Africa as well as six other southern African countries to help manage its relations with countries in a region it has chosen to emphasize in its constituent diplomacy.

The geographical location of these, the most important of Flanders's offices abroad, is quite circumscribed: they are found in Europe and southern Africa. Flanders's emphasis on Central and Eastern Europe reflects a long-standing interest in these regions and involves projects in such fields as the environment, education, vocational training, and governance capacity building, though Flanders's economic interests are also pursued.[40] Some 60 Flemish Economic Representatives (FER) and five technological attachés, among many officials, work in these foreign posts.

Flanders's economic representation abroad is undertaken by a specialized agency, Flanders Investment and Trade (FIT). That organization has over 90 foreign offices,[41] 21 of which work in cooperation with those of Wallonia, its sister constituent unit. They are much more widely dispersed geographically than the Department of Foreign Affairs outposts. FIT provides assistance to companies engaged in foreign trade and seeking foreign investment as well as foreign firms seeking commercial ties with Flanders. In addition, there are 11 Flanders Tourist Offices (most situated in Europe but also in New York, Tokyo, and Beijing), two offices of the Flanders Agricultural and Marketing Board and two cultural centres (in Amsterdam and Osaka). Many of Flanders's foreign aid efforts are concentrated on southern Africa and are administered there by three offices of the Flemish International Cooperation Agency in South Africa, Malawi, and Mozambique. These offices cooperate with several United Nations agencies.[42] Flanders's development aid programs reflect the UN's Millennium Development Goals: "(t)he Flemish contribution focuses on extreme poverty and hunger (MDG 1), health care (MDG 4–6), ecological sustainability (MDG 7) and the partnership for development (MDG 8)."[43]

The total network of *Quebec's* offices abroad is impressive, larger by far than Alberta's and, if one excludes the FIT offices that are focused on trade and commerce, larger even than that of Flanders.[44] The délégations générales (the most important offices abroad)[45] are responsible for representing Quebec in all sectors of activity under its constitutional jurisdiction.[46] Many of these are functional and practical responsibilities (for example, promoting trade and investment and attracting immigrants) but they also have political/representational responsibilities in the sense that their aim is to represent Quebec as an international actor with a distinct cultural and political identity. This is demonstrated by a report of the ministry's activities in the 2009–10 reporting period stating that its officials not infrequently met with national officials, occasionally even ministers.[47] These visits, then, are meant to establish Quebec as an international actor of some visibility and to project Quebec as a political entity, not focus primarily on its economic, educational, and cultural interests.

The responsibilities of offices with less prominence, five delegations (four in the US, one in Rome) and 10 bureaus on four continents address economic concerns, culture, and education, and in some instances also focus on immigration, though they are not entirely without political/representational functions toward regional and even national governments or international organizations.[48] Some are responsible for representing Quebec in their host and in adjacent countries.[49] They constitute, then, a network with responsibilities that transcend functional concerns, as might be expected given the at times latent, at other times, and especially under separatist governments, more pronounced attempts by the Quebec provincial government to create an international profile separate from that of the Canadian federal government.

Premiers, Ministers, and Officials Represent their Government Abroad

Premiers and cabinet members often travel abroad to represent their constituent unit's interests. Such visits abroad by politicians are a regular feature of constituent diplomacy. They are meant to highlight the importance to a constituent unit government of the concerns addressed in these visits. Often constituent unit politicians head a delegation of business leaders who engage with their counterparts in the foreign destination and, of course, constituent unit governments host delegations from abroad.

In *Alberta*, constituent diplomacy conducted by political leaders is modest, though it has increased recently. In 2012, 22 missions of various kinds were undertaken abroad. Eight were led by the premier, six to the US and two to China. Ministers led five missions: two to the US, one to China, one to the Middle East, and one to Europe. Members of the legislative assembly led eight missions, all to the US. Of these missions, nine focused on economic matters alone and 13 on multiple matters, among which economic matters predominated.[50] In 2013, Premier Alison Redford had visited the US three times by October. These visits served the purpose of promoting the sale of Alberta's energy, especially the export of oil sands bitumen to the United States, to lobby for the controversial Keystone XL pipeline that is to carry the bitumen to refineries in the Gulf of Mexico region, and to attempt to convince environmentalists and their political allies that Alberta's environmental record is sound, that the Keystone pipeline project is a safe way to transport bitumen, and that increased bitumen extraction in the Alberta oil sands would not lead to an environmental catastrophe. These visits, in addition to the work of Alberta's offices in the US, demonstrate Alberta's strong emphasis on enhancing Alberta–US economic relations.[51] The premier also visited China, India, and other countries to further trade and foreign investment. Politicians and senior civil servants have led foreign missions with representatives of Alberta organizations, primarily representatives of business, to meetings focusing on trade and investment, environmental concerns, and technological developments, most frequently in the oil and gas sectors.

Quebec's international profile is also enhanced by its politicians and civil servants' missions abroad. For the 2009–10 reporting year, Quebec launched 66 ministerial missions abroad. Among these were 12 led by Premier Charest (six to the US, five to Europe, and one to India) to meetings of international and intergovernmental organizations; various conferences, including the Copenhagen Climate Change Conference and the Davos World Economic Forum, and also to visit heads of government: the premier's travels give an important indication of the emphasis the Quebec government places on its visibility abroad. These were primarily political and representational visits though they also touched on such matters as climate change and economic concerns. Missions by ministers, most frequently the minister of international relations but almost equally as frequently by the minister responsible for the Francophonie (who travelled as often as not to non-francophone countries, often in tandem with the minister of international relations) took place on all continents. Few visits had a primarily economic focus—they, like those of the premier, were clearly directed at representing Quebec at conferences on cultural, educational, and environmental themes and to establish or maintain relations with subnational governments. The missions by other ministers were more frequently aimed at economic, cultural, and educational concerns, but also served to highlight Quebec's international presence. More recently, in October 2012, Quebec's Premier Pauline Marois visited the Congo for a meeting of the Organisation internationale de la Francophonie. In December 2013, on a visit to Paris to discuss the promotion of trade, investment, innovation and research, and the Canada–EU Comprehensive Economic and Trade Agreement, Marois met with France's President François Hollande and other French officials, demonstrating the political/representational focus in Quebec's constituent diplomacy.[52]

When *Baden-Württemberg* politicians make state visits abroad, they are almost always accompanied by delegations composed of representatives of the many export-oriented Baden-Württemberg industries. They travel widely afield, reflecting the Land's global economic interests. A recent delegation to India led by the Land's vice-premier and minister of finance and further composed of representatives of chambers of commerce, business interest groups, firms, and postsecondary education institutions, provides an example of these missions. Members explored the potential for cooperation between local and Baden-Württemberg firms invested in India, discussed investment, and visited postsecondary institutions to explore research cooperation and student, as well as faculty, exchanges. Similar missions have been undertaken to Saudi Arabia, Brazil, China, and other destinations worldwide.

Intergovernmental Cooperation Abroad

Constituent diplomacy is conducted within the context of constitutional provisions and systems of intergovernmental relations practices and structures. Though these vary in the four constituent units discussed in this chapter, in all four of them there is clear evidence of cooperation between the two orders of government and among constituent units in their international activities; for example, co-locating constituent unit offices abroad in embassies and consulates of the national government, as is practised by Flanders and Alberta. As noted above, Alberta's international offices provide clear evidence that they do not challenge the federal government in its roles by noting that they are offices of Alberta, *Canada*. Constituent diplomacy and the international efforts of national governments can quite naturally enhance each other by increasing the overall resources available for international activities for both partners, given the different types of expertise that representatives of the two orders of government can bring to bear. Constituent unit representatives are knowledgeable about their home turf and experienced in the policy sectors under their jurisdiction, and national diplomats are knowledgeable about the federal setting and economic and political conditions on-site abroad. Representatives of the two orders of government can and do share intelligence as they become aware of information relevant to each other's goals and concerns.

This type of cooperation abroad takes place among constituent units as well, as demonstrated by the practice of Flanders and Wallonian representatives formally representing the interests of their sister constituent units abroad and sharing information, thus making each of their international efforts more effective and efficient. Similarly, there is information sharing between representatives abroad of Canadian provinces. What is more, constituent units frequently cooperate with or act as agents for their national governments in projects abroad that require their expertise; for example, in the education policy field in foreign aid projects funded by their federal government.

Cooperation between national governments and constituent units can have its ups and downs, as demonstrated by the friction between Ottawa and Quebec City in the past as Parti Québécois governments worked to carve out a greater niche for themselves in the world preparatory to what they hoped would be separation from Canada. Over time the relationship has become much less tense as, for example, Ottawa has consented to Quebec participation on its own behalf in the organizations and functions of the Organisation internationale de la Francophonie and in UNESCO. There is also much cooperation between the federal government and Quebec on economic and other functional concerns.

Similarly, on occasion, relations between Berlin and Länder capitals have become frosty when Land leaders make statements abroad that go counter to German foreign policy, or when they become engaged in political activities with foreign governments or politicians unsavoury to the federal government. But such conflicts are rare, and when they occur are not infrequently motivated by partisan considerations or by the aspirations of political leaders at the Land level to attempt to increase their profile for electoral purposes, possibly to jockey for national office.[53] Overall, however, the actions of both orders of government in the four settings discussed demonstrate that they recognize the importance of cooperation in a world that is becoming increasingly globalized and in which prosperity depends on positive relations with foreign public and private-sector partners.

Notes

1   Constituent unit is a term commonly used to describe the component polities that constitute a federation: states, provinces, Länder and so on. Constituent diplomacy, a term introduced by John Kincaid, (elsewhere also referred to as paradiplomacy and sub-national diplomacy) entails the foreign relations of constituent units of federal countries, including their participation in national foreign policy making and the actions directed at foreign public and private sector actors, as distinguished from foreign policy and diplomacy as it is conventionally understood, the internationally directed activity of national governments involving foreign and security policy and other matters of high politics as well as foreign trade and commercial policy. As will be demonstrated later, however, in some contexts these two concepts overlap insofar as constituent units in some federations become more or less directly involved in the national foreign policy decision-making process.

2   H. Michelmann, (Ed.). (2009). *Foreign Relations in Federal Countries.* On Belgium: P. Bursens, and F. Massart-Piérard, "Kingdom of Belgium," 90–113; On Canada: A. Lecours, "Canada,"115–40; On Germany: R. Hrbek, "The Federal Republic of Germany," 142–67.

3   Constituent diplomacy in less developed and developing world federations will be excluded because its range and intensity in these settings is limited due to the nature of their economies and resource constraints and because national governments tend to keep tight rein on the international activities of their constituent units.

4   Baden-Württemberg, www.baden-wuerttemberg.de/en/In_Europe_and_the_world/86227.html, accessed January 2011

5   The EU demand for participation by the provinces arose from the fact that some provinces had refused to implement some provisions of agreements made in the past between Canada and the EU and its predecessor, the European Community.

6   Interview with a Government of Saskatchewan official, November 2013. The agreement provides for opening of public procurement markets, elimination of industrial and some agricultural tariffs, allows greater access to the EU for Canadian automobiles, liberalizes trade in services, allows for the easier temporary movement of company personnel, liberalizes trade in agricultural commodities and the auto sector, makes provisions for establishing mutual recognition of professional qualifications, and includes provisions liberalizing investments. Clearly, these matters affect the jurisdiction of the provinces and their lack of input and consent would hamper the implementation of the Agreement.

European Union Delegation to Canada, http://eeas.europa.eu/delegations/canada/index_en.htm, accessed November 2013.

7   Indeed, after an 6 August 2010 meeting of the Forum of the Federation the following communiqué was issued, part of which reads: Foreign relations is a subject also addressed in meeting of the Council of the Federation: Premiers feel very strongly about the need to open and deepen international trade relations particularly in Europe and Asia. Premiers reiterated the need for provinces and territories to be able to fully participate in Canada's international negotiations and forums that impact their jurisdiction. Premiers stressed the importance of establishing a formal federal-provincial-territorial agreement on the role of provinces and territories in international negotiations, agreements and forums.

Council of the Federation, www.councilofthefederation.ca/meetings/meetings2010.html, accessed January 2011.

8   Similar powers are provided for Swiss cantons and Austrian Länder.

9   The agreement goes by the name of Lindauer Abkommen.

10   A similar provision applies in Austria, where treaties affecting the powers of the Länder must be referred to the Federal Council which, like the German Bundesrat, represents Länder governments at the federal level.

11   The designation of the Belgian constituent units is complex, there being both "communities" that manage such functions as cultural policy, education, and welfare; and regions that manage the economy, environmental policy, employment, and infrastructure. For Flanders community and region have been fused for some time. In the case of the French communities there has been an amalgamation of foreign affairs administrative units such that the foreign relations of the Walloon Region and the French Community have been administered jointly since 2009 (Criekemans, "Regional sub-state diplomacy from a comparative perspective," 42.

12   Flanders has concluded 33 full-fledged treaties in the period from 1993–2008, rather few in comparison with the Wallon region's 67 and the French Community's 51 between 1993 and 2008 (Criekemans, 48).

13   Government of Flanders, www.flandre.be/servlet/Satellite?c=Page&cid=1278906673798&context=1166590833692--EN&p=116659083 7362&pagename=flanders_site%2FView, accessed January 2011.

14   For evident reasons, the present section will not replicate the treatment of the EU institutional structures and processes outlined in the previous section on Baden-Württemberg since these apply to

Flanders as well, though some slight differences between the two contexts will be noted.

15 Bursens and Massart-Piérard, 98.

16 Bursens and Massart Pierard, 101.

17 Criekemans, 53.

18 Bursens and Massart-Piérard, 107.

19 During Belgium's presidency of the EU in 2010, for example, Flanders represented Belgium in the education, youth, sports, environment, and fisheries policy fields, as well as agriculture in cooperation with the Walloon Region. Government of Flanders, www.flanders.be/servlet/Satellite?c=Page&cid=1278906504677&context=1166590833692--EN&p=1166590837362&pagename=flanders_site%2FView, accessed January 2011.

20 Government of Quebec, www.mrifce.gouv.qc.ca/content/documents/fr/rapportannuel.pdf, accessed December 2012.

21 Communication with a senior officer of the Ministry, 11 March 2011.

22 www.international.alberta.ca/933.cfm, accessed 18 February 2011.

23 www.vlaanderen.be/int/en/organigram.

24 Responsibility for the last of these functions is an indicator of the important role of Belgian constituent units in relations between Belgium and parties abroad. While there have been disputes with the federal government in this policy field these have been generally resolved.

25 Bursens and Massart-Piérard, 107. This was the equivalent of some $250,000,000 Canadian dollars.

26 H. J. Michelmann, (2012). *Paradiplomacy in the EU*, 91–100.

27 www.mrifce.gouv.qc.ca/en/Relations-du-Quebec/Ameriques/Etats-Unis/Relations-bilaterales/Quebec-Vermont

28 www.mrifce.gouv.qc.ca/en/Relations-du-Quebec/Ameriques/Etats-Unis/Relations-bilaterales/Sommet-Quebec-New-York.

29 Canadian/American Border Trade Alliance, http://canambta.org/about-us/our-purpose/ accessed December 2013.

30 Relations Internationales, Francophone et Commerce extérieur, www.mrifce.gouv.qc.ca/en/relations-du-quebec/ameriques/etats-unis/relations-bilaterales, accessed December 2013.

31 Four Motors of Europe and Associates, www.anella.cat/web/4motors/, accessed December 2013. This organization, in turn, cooperates in the organization and carrying out of joint missions abroad to such countries as Russia and Morocco.

32 An EU-founded organization to foster cooperation among EU regions.

33 REGLEG is a political network for EU regions with legislative power. It comprises representatives of regional governments who work together on issues of common concern. Interestingly, Quebec is an affiliate member.

34 Relations Internationales, Francophone et Commerce extérieur, www.mrifce.gouv.qc.ca/content/documents/fr/rapportannuel.pdf, accessed January 2014.

35 Government of Flanders, http://nadia-burger.vlaanderen.be/nadia/repertorium/openindex.do?index=02.01, accessed December 2013.

36 Deutscher Industrie und Handelstag, www.dihk.de/wir-ueber-uns, accessed January 2014. These offices have developed working relationships with chambers of industry and commerce in host countries thus enhancing their reach in these settings.

37 Baden-Württemberg is home to some very large firms, which on their own represent their interests abroad, but the Land has many export-oriented small and medium size enterprises which benefit from such assistance.

38 China, Hong Kong, Taiwan, Japan, Shanghai, South Korea, the UK, Germany, Mexico, and Washington, DC.

39 Criekemans, 48.

40 Criekemans, 51–2.

41 Flanders Investment and Trade, www.flanderstrade.com/site/internetEN.nsf/vPAG/About+-+Us__About+-+Us+-+Homepage?opendocument, accessed December 2013.

42 In 2009 Flanders's ODA budget came to some 50 million euros.

43 Flemish Department of Foreign Trade, www.vlaanderen.be/int/en/development-cooperation, accessed January 2014.

44 Though it should be noted that the heads of Flanders's offices have diplomatic status and in that sense the Flanders's offices are a weightier presence than those of Quebec.

45 Located in Brussels, London, Mexico City, Munich, New York City, Paris, and Tokyo.

46 Relations www.mrifce.gouv.qc.ca/en/ministere/representation-etranger

47 Relations Internationales, Francophone et Commerce extérieur, www.mri.gouv.qc.ca/fr/pdf/rapport_annuel_2009-2010.pdf, accessed March 2011.

48 Barcelona, Beijing, Berlin, Mumbai, Sao Paolo, and Washington. Its Shanghai, Hong Kong, and Vienna offices have exclusively immigration responsibilities, each for a large number of countries, and the office in Stockholm is responsible for "investment prospecting and promotion" in the Scandinavian countries.

49 There are also four trade branches (staffed by local employees) in Milan, Santiago, Seoul, and Taipei.

50 Alberta International and Intergovernmental Relations, http://international.alberta.ca/556.cfm, accessed January 2014.

51 By far the largest share of Alberta's exports go to the United States and that country is the origin of more than half of foreign direct investment, as well as more than half of tourists visiting the province.

52 Relations Internationales, Francophone et Commerce, www.mrifce.gouv.qc.ca/en/salle-de-presse/actualites/13487, accessed January 2014.

53 Länder politicians not infrequently make the jump to national politics where a number of them have become Chancellor.

Key Terms

constituent diplomacy

intergovernmental relations

Questions for Review

1. What is the most important motivation for constituent diplomacy?
2. Identify the importance of the regional setting for constituent diplomacy.
3. Which key features of the Belgian, Canadian, and German constitutions most affect the conduct of constituent diplomacy in their respective settings?
4. Why are intergovernmental relations of central importance to the conduct of constituent diplomacy?
5. Compare the participation by Baden-Württemberg in the German foreign policy decision-making process to that of Alberta and Quebec in the Canadian process.

Further Resources

Blatter, J., Kreutzer, M., Rentl, M., and Thiele, J. (2008). "The foreign relations of European regions: Competences and strategies." *West European Politics* 31(3), 464–90.

Callanan, M. and Tatham, M. (2013). "Territorial interest representation in the European Union: actors, objectives and strategies." *Journal of European Public Policy 21*(2).

Criekemans, D. (Ed.). *Regional sub-state diplomacy today.*

Fry, E. (2005). "Federalism and the evolving cross border role of provincial, state and municipal governments." *International Journal 60*(2), 471–82.

Kukucha, C. T. (2005a). "From Koyoto to the WTO: Evaluating the legitimacy of the provinces in Canada's foreign trade and environmental policy." *Canadian Journal of Political Science 38*(1), 129–52.

LaChapelle, G. and Paquin, S. (Eds). (2005). *Mastering globalization: New sub-states governance and strategies.* London & New York: Routledge.

Michelmann, H. (Ed.). *Foreign relations in federal countries.*

Mingus, M. (2006). "Transnationalism and subnational paradiplomacy: Are governance networks perforating sovereignty?" *International Journal of Public Administration 29*(8), 577–94.

Paul, D. E. (2005). *Rescaling international political economy: Subnational states and the regulation of the global political economy.* London: Routledge.

References

Alberta, International and Intergovernmental Relations. (2014). "About the Ministry" (23 November). Available at www.international.alberta.ca/572.cfm.

Alberta, International and Intergovernmental Relations. (2014). "International Missions" (23 November). Available at http://international.alberta.ca/556.cfm.

Baden-Württemberg. (2011). "International Relations" (January 22). Available at www.baden-wuerttemberg.de/en/In_Europe_and_the_world/86227.html.

Bursens, P. and Massart-Piérard, F. (2009). "Kingdom of Belgium." In H. J. Michelmann (Ed.). *Foreign relations in federal countries.* Montreal & Kingston: McGill-Queen's University Press, 90–113.

Canadian/American Border Trade Alliance. (2013). "Our Purpose" (5 December). Available at http://canambta.org/about-us/our-purpose/.

Council of the Federation. (2010). "Summer Meeting 4–6 August 2010—Winnipeg Manitoba" (10 November). Available at www.councilofthefederation.ca/en/meetings-events/39-2010/97-summer-meeting-august-4-6-2010-winnipeg-manitoba.

Criekemans, D. (2010). "Regional sub-state diplomacy from a comparative perspective: Québec, Scotland, Bavaria, Catalonia, Wallonia and Flanders." In D. Criekemans (Ed.). *Regional sub-state diplomacy today.* Leiden: Martinus Nijhoff Publishers.

Deutscher Industrie und Handelstag. (2014). "Chambers of Commerce and Industry" (17 January). Available at www.dihk.de/wir-ueber-uns.

Flanders Department of Foreign Affairs. (2014). "Development Cooperation" (20 January). Available at www.vlaanderen.be/int/en/development-cooperation.

Flanders Department of Foreign Affairs. (2014). "Organigram" (24 November). Available at www.vlaanderen.be/int/en/organigram.

Flanders Investment and Trade. (2013). "About Us" (13 December). Available at www.flanderstrade.com/

Four Motors of Europe and Associates. (2014). "Four Motors for Europe" (20 November). Available at www.anella.cat/web/4motors/.

Government of Flanders. (2011). "International Treaties" (5 January). Available at www.flandre.be/servlet/Satellite?c=Page&cid=1278906673798&context=1166590833692--EN&p=1166590837362&pagename=flanders_site%2FView.

Government of Flanders. (2013). "Catalogus Overeenkomsten" (12 December). Available at http://nadia-burger.vlaanderen.be/nadia/repertorium/openindex.do?index=02.01.

Hrbek, R. (2009). "The Federal Republic of Germany." In H. J. Michelmann (Ed.). *Foreign relations in federal countries*. Montreal & Kingston: McGill-Queen's University Press, 42–167.

Lecours, A. (2009). "Canada." In H. J. Michelmann (Ed.). *Foreign relations in federal countries*. Montreal & Kingston: McGill-Queen's University Press, 115N40.

Michelmann, H. J. (2012). *Paradiplomacy in the EU: Austria, Belgium and Germany*" in C. Plilip et al. (Eds). *Réalisations et défis de l'Union européenne: Droit-politique-économie. Mélanges en hommage au Professeur Panayotis Soldatos*. Brussels: Bruylant, 91N100

Michelmann, H. J. (Ed.). (2009). *Foreign relations in federal countries*. Montreal & Kingston: McGill-Queen's University Press.

Québec, Relations Internationales et Francophonie. (2013). "Pauline Marois meets with François Hollande" (18 December). Available at www.mrifce.gouv.qc.ca/en/salle-de-presse/actualites/13487.

Québec, Relations Internationales et Francophonie. (2013). "Bilateral and regional relations" (16 March). Available at www.mrifce.gouv.qc.ca/en/relations-du-quebec/ameriques/etats-unis/relations-bilaterales.

Québec, Relations internationales, francophone et commerce extérieur. (2013). "Annual Report" (20 December). Available at www.mrifce.gouv.qc.ca/content/documents/fr/rapportannuel.pdf.

Québec, Relations Internationales et Francophonie. (2012). "Québec's international policy: Working in concert" (14 December). Available at www.mrif.gouv.qc.ca/en/Grands-dossiers/Politiques-et-Strategies/Politique-internationale/Presentation.

Québec, Relations internationales et Francophonie. (2012). "Québec-Vermont Joint Committee" (16 December). Available at www.mrifce.gouv.qc.ca/en/Relations-du-Quebec/Ameriques/Etats-Unis/Relations-bilaterales/Quebec-Vermont.

Québec, Relations internationales et Francophonie. (2012). "Québec-New York economic summits" (16 December). Available at www.mrifce.gouv.qc.ca/en/Relations-du-Quebec/Ameriques/Etats-Unis/Relations-bilaterales/Sommet-Quebec-New-York.

Québec, Relations internationales, francophone et commerce extérieur. (2010). "Annual Report 2009–2010" (20 November). Available at www.mri.gouv.qc.ca/fr/pdf/rapport_annuel_2009-2010.pdf.

17 A Tale of Two (Global) Cities

London, New York, and the Rise of Finance Capital

Trevor W. Harrison

Conventional political economy has centred on the nation-state. Academic and popular examinations of globalization beginning in the 1980s reinforced this focus, even when they discussed whether states were "withering away" amid the rise of corporate capital or non-state counter-movements. Coincident with these debates, however, has been increased attention to the role of global cities in contemporary capitalism.

This chapter briefly reviews the global cities literature and examines a set of global cities indexes, noting the repeated placement of London and New York at their apex. With reference to the economic history of these two cities, this chapter argues that their dominance in global indexes reflects the specific role of their financial districts (The City and Wall Street) in the development of modern capitalism. Inadvertently, global cities indexes provide a way of thinking about the origins and the role of finance capital within the world economy; and its power and influence, as revealed during the recent world recession, at which The City and Wall Street held front-row seats.

Urban Sociology, Global Cities, and Globalization

Nineteenth-century European scholars viewed the rise of cities as a prominent feature of modernity. By the early twentieth century, cities had become objects not only of philosophical speculation but intense study, both in Europe and North America, particularly in the United States, where the Chicago School constructed an urban sociology/ecology based on the social disorganization paradigm (see Walton 1993, 301; also, Gottdiener and Feagin 1988). However, critics in the 1960s assailed this approach, viewing cities within a broader political economy framework that later also embraced culture (see Castells 1977; Harvey 1973; Ribera-Fumaz 2009).

Often labelled the "new urban sociology," this new approach attracted urban planners, political scientists, geographers, and economists, as well as sociologists (Gottdiener and Feagin 1988, 163; Walton 1993). Influenced by European scholarship, it argued that modern cities had to be understood in their historical context, specifically their relationship to the state and their place within the global system of capitalist exchanges (Harvey 1985; Zukin 1980; also Walton 1993). Far from imposing a single focus, the new urban sociology spurred a series of methodological innovations that included historical, spacial, ethnic, and community studies, as well as examinations of the possibility of new forms of social and political action, and comparative approaches (Walton 1993). One of the comparative approaches that emerged was the study of global cities.[1]

John Friedmann (1998, 26), one of the best known and earliest exponents of the approach, defined global cities as "a class of cities that play a leading role in the spatial articulation of the global economic system or designate a dimension of all cities that in varying measure are integrated with this system" (see also Friedmann and Wolff 1982). Saskia Sassen (1991) likewise argued that the functions of finance and control of the economy under globalized capitalism had become centralized in a few cities, particularly London, New York, and Tokyo. She described these global cities as nodal points within the emerging global economy (Sassen 1991), "strategic places" (Sassen 2000) that are part of a growing transnational network (including other major cities) that service global capital and its respective class (see also Sassen 2005). Similarly, Yusuf and Wu (2002, 1214) have contended that London, New York, and Tokyo constitute global cities based on "the current size of their economies," "their favoured location within their respective countries," "their past impetus from a broad industrial base and their role as regional—or national—transport hubs," their abilities to "exploit the commercial opportunities offered by communications technology," and "the strength of market institutions and economic openness in all three countries." According to Taylor et al. (2002, 233), this network of cities is "linked together by the communications of information, ideas, knowledge, and infrastructure through virtual and material flows within service office networks." These operate at three levels: the network level, that of the world economy; the nodal level, the cities themselves; and the sub-nodal level, the service firms.[2]

The global cities literature first emerged amid contentious debates about globalization. Globalization's advocates viewed efforts to expand trade while breaking down regulations and privatizing services positively; for them, globalization was not only unreservedly good and necessary, but inevitable. In contrast, critics of globalization argued it was a reterritorialization of power (Brenner 1998); indeed, not a new phenomenon, but instead old-fashioned colonialism and imperialism in different garb (Robertson 2003). Although some argued that the traditional state was being "hollowed out" or was "withering away," others contended that it was merely undergoing a series of displacements, of which it was the author. Still others debated whether power was moving upward, outward (to new state or non-state actors), downwards, or perhaps each of these in a process of "glocalization"—a reconfiguration and reterritorialization of capitalist relations that merged the national, the international, and the local (Robertson 1995). For obvious reasons, the global cities perspective played an important role in these debates.

Since then, however, global cities arguments have themselves been criticized on several fronts, including privileging certain cities as "global," while ignoring the degree to which the nexus of globalization–urbanization is occurring in all cities (McCann 2004); that the concept in fact reifies certain cities (Smith 1998; Taylor et al. 2002; see also McCann 2004), while also ignoring "the role of the state and national interest in the formation of all world cities" (Hill and Kim 2000, 2187), as well as local political actors (Robinson 2005). Each of these criticisms is valid. Despite these and other criticisms, however, the examination and ranking of global cities has become a kind of growth industry in recent years. It is to a set of these indexes that we now turn.

London, New York, and Global Cities Indexes

A host of indexes examine and rank global cities.[3] Prominent among these indexes are the Global Cities Index (GCI); the Cities of Opportunities Index (COI); the Global Power City Index (GPCI); the Global Cities Wealth Report (GCWR); and the Global Competitive Cities Index (GCCI).[4] Table 17.1 (below) assembles the top 20 global cities ranked by these five indexes, a total of 31 cities.

All of these indexes rely heavily upon economic criteria, sometimes repeatedly (e.g., GCCI's listing of "financial maturity"). Four indexes (GCI, COI, GCWR, and GCCI) list human and intellectual capital and knowledge, whereas the fifth index

Table 17.1   Global City Rankings

Index Rank	GCI 2012	COI 2012	GPCI 2012	GCWR 2012	GCCI 2012
1	New York	New York	London	New York	New York
2	London	London	New York	London	London
3	Paris	Tokyo	Paris	Paris	Singapore
4	Tokyo	Paris	Tokyo	Tokyo	Hong Kong
5	Hong Kong	Hong Kong	Singapore	Hong Kong	Paris
6	Los Angeles	Chicago	Seoul	Singapore	Tokyo
7	Chicago	Singapore	Amsterdam	Sydney	Zurich
8	Seoul	Shanghai	Berlin	Washington	Washington
9	Brussels	Los Angeles	Hong Kong	Toronto	Chicago
10	Washington	Zurich	Vienna	Zurich	Boston
11	Singapore	Seoul	Beijing	Berlin	Frankfurt
		Boston			
		Beijing			
12	Sydney		Frankfurt	Brussels	Toronto
13	Vienna		Barcelona	Seoul	Geneva
14	Beijing	Washington	Shanghai	Boston	San Francisco
15	Boston	Osaka	Sydney	Beijing	Sydney
16	Toronto	Brussels	Stockholm	Vancouver	Melbourne
		Rhine-Ruhr			
17	San Francisco		Osaka	Chicago	Amsterdam
18	Madrid	Toronto	Zurich	Vienna	Vancouver
		Shenzhen			
19	Moscow		Brussels	Amsterdam	Los Angeles
20	Berlin		Copenhagen	Los Angeles	Seoul

(GPCI) lists the related area of "research and development"; three of the indexes (GCI, GPCI, and GCCI) include culture; three (COI, GPCI, and GCWR) list criteria related to quality of life issues; two (GCI and GCWR) specifically mention politics; two (GPCI and GCCI) include the environment; two (COI and GCCI) mention cities' global connectivity; one (COI) lists "transportation and infrastructure."

There is a broad consistency across the indexes' top 20 cities. Seven cities are listed in all five indexes (Hong Kong, London, New York, Paris, Tokyo, Seoul, and Singapore) whereas nine cities appear in four of the indexes (Beijing, Boston, Brussels, Chicago, Los Angeles, Sydney, Toronto, Washington, and Zurich).

Several large cities play a major role in the global economy. The McKinsey Global Institute (2013) contends that, "only 600 urban centers generate about 60 per cent of global GDP." In consequence, there is also an unsettling competitiveness about these indexes (Robinson 2005, 760), ignoring the earlier "project of world cities research . . . not merely to classify cities within world-scale central place hierarchies, but [to] examine the new international division of labour" (Brenner 1998, 4).

Although some of the dimensions and criteria used in ranking the indexes vary, economic power is a central element in all the indexes, a major consequence of which is the consistently high score given to London and New York. Their high ranking is not merely ordinal, however; it is substantive, a point also noted by several global cities scholars. No other cities present a genuine challenge to the dominance of London and New York. Of Tokyo, for example, both Freidmann (1995) and Sassen (1999) acknowledge that it does not entirely fit their paradigm of a global city (see Walton 1993, 311).

Taylor et al.'s (2002) study of the relative power of cities further emphasizes the singular importance of London and New York among global cities. The study examined the power of cities according to three different notions of power: power as capacity through connections; power as domination and command; and power through the network. On each of these measures, and their sub-scales, London and New York stood out far above other world cities. In terms of world city connectivity, for example, Taylor et al. describe London and New York as the only "global cities," while at the level of international financial centre connectivity, only Tokyo comes close (and still third). Likewise, London and New York stood out as "mega" dominant centres, global command centres, and (along with Miami and Hong Kong), regional command centres. Clearly, many other cities throughout the world are important to global capitalism, often as "gateway cities" for expansion. But London (after two hundred years) and New York (after one hundred) remain the epicentres of global capitalism, so much so that Peter Taylor, founder of the Globalization and World Cities Research Network, argues that the United States and London make up "a single central region of economic globalisation," that can be termed "USAL" (quoted in Knight Frank 2013, 19).

Though it is undoubtedly correct, as Hume (2004, 2) states, that, "global cities can exist anywhere, but must exist somewhere," the fact is that London and New York are that privileged "somewhere." Yet, their importance—and why they are important—is insufficiently noted by this ranking.

What makes London and New York distinctive? In brief, it is the place that finance capital holds within them; more specifically, their financial districts. Of course, other global cities also have important finance districts, but London and New York have had a unique historic role in the development of global capitalism, most particularly in their role of protecting, promoting, and even valorizing finance capital as distinct from industrial capital, a differentiation that requires brief comment.

Recent literature has dealt with a range of types of capital: human, social, natural, and cultural, as well as economic. Economic capital can be divided in turn into industrial and finance capital. Harvey (2011, 40) argues that industrial or productive capital (e.g., raw materials, machinery, the physical plant) has dominated since the eighteenth century. Such capital is necessarily rooted in national territories.

By contrast, finance capital not being a real thing—indeed, as Polanyi (2001) argued, fictitious—gains its legitimacy through a process of valorization and legitimation by powerful actors; the belief that gold has a value provides an example. The nature, however, of finance capital is international, even as national states and popular elements within them have often attempted to control it.

The quest of finance capital has always been to assert its sovereignty, while simultaneously using the national state for its own ends. The story of London and New York is the story of finance capital's efforts at liberation, orchestrated within the financial districts of these cities.

The City of London and "The City of London"

The Romans founded London (Londinium) around 50 CE. It grew over the next centuries into a sprawling and disorderly town, housing roughly 50,000 inhabitants in 1500—easily the largest in England—and 187,000 in 1600. The middle of the seventeenth century witnessed the English Revolution, during which London's economic, political, and cultural power within the expanding nation-state grew immensely. By 1700, London's population had grown to 550,000; by 1750, 676,000; and by 1800, 861,000—the largest city in all of Europe and, by further comparison, dwarfing any city in the United

States at that time: Philadelphia had 68,000 inhabitants then, New York, 63,000 (all figures from Chandler 1987: 19–22; see also Inwood 1998).

Around 1800, the term "London" became somewhat less than distinct. Mogridge and Parr (1997, 98) describe a series of progressively larger "Londons" beginning at that time. These include The City of London (the financial district), the Central Area, Inner London (in 1800, a "very compact [city] with a number of small outlying centres"), the London metropolis, the southeast and London regions, and finally Great Britain itself. Their analysis shows that as the built area of London expanded, the population within this area first grew and then declined, moving outward to the receding parts of the metropolitan area. Most striking in this regard, however, is that the population of the City of London in 1851 was the same as in 1648, just before the Great Fire, at which point it began a "precipitous fall which reached a geometric rate of 30% per decade, so that by 1991 its population . . . was less than 5% of the 1851 value" (Mogridge and Parr 1997, 101). Thereafter, the City's residential population began to slide.

Just before the First World War, in 1911, Greater London's population was more than 7.2 million, whereas the City of London's residential population was 20,000, augmented every day by the arrival of roughly 364,000 commuting workers. By 1939, Greater London's population had reached 8.7 million, but The City's residential population had dropped to 10,000, replenished daily by roughly a half million migrating workers. The ensuing war sped up the process by which The City was depopulated, even as its purpose became more clearly that of finance and trade to the global economy. By 1966, The City's residential population stood at 4,900 (all figures taken from Dunning and Morgan 1971, 34; more generally, 31–5).

London's prosperity in the early nineteenth century was based on manufacturing, transportation, shipping, and financial services (banking, insurance, etc.), earning its reputation by century's end as the "richest city in the world" (Inwood 1998). By the mid-twentieth century, however, The City as a distinct geographical area within Greater London owed its economic prosperity primarily to international finance.[5] And, although The City remained interdependent with its immediate environs, that is, located *in* the city, it was increasingly not *of* the city, but rather, of the world.

The splitting off of the financial district from Greater London is not entirely dissimilar to what occurred in other large cities. The particular relationship of The City and the city to the English state requires at least passing comment, however.

The few world cities that arose early on in human history, in Europe and elsewhere, were places of trade and protection, a few of which became city-states. The development of city-states was an uneven and differentiated process, however, hindered in part by continuous wars that, as in Greece, preserved their autonomy (Polanyi 2001, 6), but also slowed the development of larger geographic states. Nonetheless, some city-states, notably in Italy, expanded outward during the eleventh century in efforts to secure food supplies and trade, a process of expansion that occurred much later in the cities of Northern Europe, though these cities did exercise considerable economic influence over their surrounding territories (Scott 2012) and often formed military and trade alliances between cities, such as the Hanseatic League. The next two centuries saw a proto-capitalism emerge in several cities, including Amsterdam and Bruges (Murray, 2005). But, as Braudel (1983) argues, the result remained essentially "city-centred economies."

Only in the seventeenth century did the modern European state emerge, based on a "territorial economy," none more so than in England. Why was this the case?

Although the causes of the English Revolution (alternatively, the civil wars) of the seventeenth century remain disputed, there is little doubt that these events coincided with and to some degree resulted in a series of political, economic, ideological, and social changes that paved the way for modern capitalism. Politically, the revolution established the rights of property and, not inconsequentially, the political rights of the propertied (Manning 1991); in other words, as Skocpol (1979, 141) notes, it was a bourgeois revolution that did not transform England's class and social structures, but instead "furthered social-economic development" along lines commensurate with the interests of a nascent capitalist class, made up of aristocratic landowners, industrialists, and merchants.

Economically, the new bourgeois order benefited from the start of the industrial revolution (begun the following century), a development in which England faced few competitors; and world trade (promoted through both diplomacy and the British navy), the latter given ideological justification by Adam Smith and David Ricardo. Socioculturally, the period following the English Revolution also witnessed a series of related changes, including increased urbanization, and the rise of new class formations, notably an urban proletariat that replaced, though not wholly, agrarians and craft workers.

Yet, whereas the other European cities—even those that became capitals—were embedded within the national territorial states, London retained its autonomy. This remained the case, even as it became the centre of a strong, centralized state. Inwood (1998, 6) notes that, "For centuries, governments have feared the size and power of London, and tried to develop policies to minimize the city's threat to authority and order." He adds (ibid.),

[I]t is often difficult to avoid crossing the line between London's history and England's.

The two are so closely intertwined that to separate them is sometimes virtually impossible, in economic, social and cultural affairs as well as political ones. London has been the home of national government, and the city in which many of England's most important political struggles have been fought, for close on 1,000 years.

Ghosh (2012) similarly notes:

London clearly exercized (and exercizes) both economic and political dominance over a large region, and had (and continues to have) a massive influence on lifestyles, economies, prices, supply-lines, demographic and settlement patterns—and is also the centre of governance. And that last is perhaps why London is not a city-state: it is a capital instead.[6]

Why did London become so dominant within the British realm? First, London was the capital, a political advantage that it used over any other city. Second, it was overwhelmingly the largest city in the Isles. Unlike Europe, it had few competitors in terms of population. As earlier noted, London's population in 1800 was 861,000; the second largest city in Britain at the time was Dublin, with a population of 165,000 (Chandler 1987, 23). Third, it also had geographical advantages, notably the Thames River and the port system, which made London a conduit for goods, services, people, and money both entering and leaving the country.

But it was not simply London that dominated England and the United Kingdom. More specifically, it was The City, whose primary power was financial.[7] This circumstance too requires an explanation.

In the early days of capitalism, industrialists, merchants, and bankers—though perhaps personally competitive—were not structurally at odds.

Over time, however, fault lines appeared between big and small capitalists and, more especially, between industrial capitalists (in coalition with provincial elites and landed interests) and finance capitalists, the former being more inclined to protectionism, the latter to laissez-faire policies (Alford 1996, 103). The political expression of this fracture, and of finance capital's subtle elevation over industry within the state, was Britain's abandonment of mercantilism and its gradual adoption of free trade policies in the first part of the nineteenth century (McMichael 1987, 191–2). But the geographic expression of finance capitalism's growing might was The City of London whose wealth had already increased markedly as a result of the revolutions of the late eighteenth century and the continuing political uncertainty that marked the following century. The City, itself protected by the British Empire, offered a safe haven for wealth at a time when the French Revolution and the subsequent Napoleonic Wars were threatening the privileged classes throughout Europe.

The City embraced three inter-related elements of finance capital: insurance, centred on Lloyd's of London; market exchanges, regulated primarily through the London Stock Exchange (LSE); and banking (the Bank of England).

Lloyd's was founded in the late seventeenth century as a marine insurance company, over which it held a corporate monopoly two centuries later, advanced by strong political and banking connections. By the late nineteenth century—it was formally incorporated as the Society of Lloyd's (of London) in 1871—its reach extended internationally, particularly into the United States, even as its financial interests spread well beyond marine insurance alone and into such areas as brokerage (Cockerell 1984).

The origins of the London Stock Exchange lie with the Royal Exchange founded in 1571. As trade and commerce expanded, the Royal Exchange proved inadequate to regulating the buying and selling of stocks which often took place in alley-ways and coffee houses. The London Stock Exchange was thus founded in 1801 with a set of new regulations designed to organize the growing market. After 1840, the LSE became an international exchange, facilitated by the emergence of several technologies (e.g., telegraph, later the telephone and tickertape) that allowed for the development of global markets. The LSE was at the heart of this trade and soon became the world's largest player: by 1913, £5 billion, or one-half of the world's overseas investments, resided on the LSE (Inwood 1998, 480).

Of these three great institutions, however, the most important was the Bank of England. Founded in 1694, it is the world's second oldest central bank. The Bank of England thus played a key role in the development of much of the institutional framework that guides modern banking, and was influential in establishing the gold standard in the eighteenth and nineteenth centuries (see Grossman 2010, 169). Alford's (1996, 22–3) description of the Bank of England, and its relationship to The City, is worth quoting at length:

> The City was private enterprise par excellence. The Bank of England, no less, was a private institution, though it was banker to the government. From the 1870s onwards, the Bank recognized that it stood in a particular relationship to the rest of the banking system and that this involved certain responsibilities for maintaining financial stability, [including that of] lender in the last resort to the banking system. . . . Moreover, the Bank acted independently of the government, and its governor and directors (the Court) were drawn exclusively from the leading financial institutions in the City. The overriding interest of members of the Court, in common with the other leading financiers and traders in the City, was the maintenance of London's dominant role in international trade and commerce.

Inwood (1998, 475) notes the particular importance of London's banks: "Victorian London dealt in many things, but the commodity which brought it the greatest profits, and through which it achieved its position of unique international importance, was money. During the nineteenth century London became the world's greatest money market, the supreme international centre of banking, commercial credit, overseas loans, commodity transactions, share-dealing and insurance."

London—more accurately, The City of London—thus became, by the late nineteenth century, the undisputed centre of the "new international order" of global capitalism (Polanyi 2001, 14). Through its political power within the British state, The City—"the clearinghouse of international finance and the source of sterling as the world's currency" (McMichael 1987, 192)—fashioned the conditions necessary for the creation of an open world market that was monetarily stable during the period 1875–1914 (Block 1977, 5), albeit politically quite unstable, as subsequent events showed. Though centred in London, The City financiers, as Alford (1996, 87) notes, operated "outside Europe and the USA, particularly in the empire, South America, the Middle and Far East," fostering the "movement of commodities around the globe." Of course, other sites were also important to the network: Paris, Berlin, New York, and Boston, as well as others emergent, such as Tokyo. But no city stood taller than London; and within its environs, The City, protected by geography, political and military power, and the benefits of being the earliest capitalist country.

As the First World War began, the City of London remained high among the cities that

Polanyi (2001, 221) termed the "brain centres" of world capitalism. But its relative importance at the head of international finance was already in decline, a decline accentuated by the war that followed and growing competition from other financial centres, especially New York (Alford 1996, 120–1). Indeed, both symbolically and practically the war signalled the transfer of empire and the role as chief protector of global capitalism from the United Kingdom to the United States. Before the war, American capitalists were content to expand their influence in London; after the war, they took steps to make New York the world's financial centre (Panitch and Gindin 2012, 57).

The Empire's embers, though diminished, continued to glow, however; indeed, they can still be seen today in the creative use of financial instruments, crafted to meet the letter if not the spirit of the law; in the entrenchment of Greenwich Mean Time, by which London is the starting point for every trading day, with New York close behind[8]; and in the widespread use of English as the lingua franca of international business, by which the torch of Anglo financial dominance could so easily be passed to its former colony.

Islands Unto Themselves: New York, Manhattan, and Wall Street

New York's ascent to financial power was not pre-ordained. Its European origins began in 1626 with the purchase of Manhattan Island from an Aboriginal tribe by Peter Minuit, working on behalf of the Dutch West India Company. In 1653, Peter Stuyvesant built a barricade in lower Manhattan to protect local merchants and traders, as they set about buying and selling, from attacks by the members of the local Lenape tribe. Behind this "walled street" soon emerged a new market, conducted in coffee houses and side streets, which approximated the stock exchanges found in Antwerp and London. Thus began an institution that facilitated the investment of European capital eager for new markets (Geisst 2012, 5), and which continued after 1664 when, following Dutch defeat at the hands of the English, New Amsterdam was renamed New York.

Though it grew slowly, New York had advantages that over time resulted in its regional economic dominance. Glaeser (2005) notes three particular elements: geography, transportation costs, and scale economies, and the subsequent attraction of new immigrants to the developing city. Like London, New York was a port city, benefiting in the early years from the lucrative fur and slave trades. Unlike London, however, New York was not the nation's capital and at first faced a number of urban challengers, notably Boston (known for its shipping and banking) and Philadelphia (the home of the first stock exchange) (Geisst 2012, 4). New York's dominance was established only in the period 1790–1860, during which its population grew from 33,131 to 813,669 (Glaeser 2005, 10). Glaeser (ibid.) argues that New York's rise to prominence was the result of two "closely related growth processes" during this period: its role in shipping and immigration and its development as a manufacturing town based on sugar, publishing, and the garment trade. But New York also had superior qualities as a port, compared with Boston and Philadelphia, as well as economic and social attributes that made it a hub of manufacturing.

Within Manhattan, in the area now formally known as Wall Street, financial services, especially in insurance and banking, emerged early on. In 1792, however, the bankruptcy of a prominent merchant caused a scandal, the result of which was increased regulation of the market and the formal creation of the United States' first exchange, though the location of the New York Stock and Exchange Board was not finalized until 1817 (Geisst 2012).

Shortly thereafter, New York's population rose to 170,000, the largest in the United States. By the end of the century, New York housed 4.2 million people, far surpassing Philadelphia (1.4 million) and Boston (1.1 million) (all figures from Chandler 1987, 536 and 567).

New York's increased population was due in part to its natural endowments. Like London, however, it also benefited, albeit slowly, from national expansion. The American Revolution, like its counterpart in England, was bourgeois; political, not social. The new state's republican impulses hindered imperial ambitions, but—somewhat more than in England—its political culture embraced the Lockean notions of private property, possessive individualism, and upward social mobility so essential to modern capitalism, as well as to the American myth; and which, after 1776, gave also ideological and moral justification to westward expansion. As a growing city on the eastern seaboard, an entrepôt for European capital and labour, New York and the financiers of Wall Street benefited from American expansion; indeed, the New York Exchange and private banks funded much of this expansion, including the Louisiana Purchase.

Although the United States grew rapidly after 1776, during the nineteenth century American capitalists were, by and large, unable to conquer or otherwise pacify their internal market. The Civil War (1861–65) resolved the problem of competing modes of production, but the United States remained fragmented along racial, class, religious, political, and ethnic lines. Exacerbated by an abundance of free land, social fragmentation prevented the immediate formation of a capitalist labour market (Gordon et al. 1982). But most telling was the United States' continued support of protectionism during the nineteenth century and after—a clear sign of the strength of industrial capitalists—at the same time as the US banking system remained decentralized and dominated by commercial banks (Grossman 2010).[9] This situation is properly contrasted with Britain's adoption of free trade earlier in the century in defiance of mercantilist interests.

While expanding throughout the nineteenth century, US imperialism remained mostly confined to the Americas until the Spanish-American War of 1898 when the United States annexed Puerto Rico, the Philippines, and Guam, and established a permanent American naval base in Guantánamo Bay, Cuba. The American Empire began just as its British counterpart was in decline, a development heralded also by the transfer of influence from London to New York, from The City of London to Wall Street. The deeper meaning of the First World War that began shortly thereafter—that financial power was shifting from the United Kingdom to its former colony—was not lost on Britain's finance capitalists. As Panitch and Gindin (2012, 117) note, "London's merchant bankers—the financial praetorian guard of the old empire—made a bold move to switch allegiance to the U. S. dollar." The British pound formally remained the **international reserve currency** until 1944, but the trend towards US dominance was clear.

Why did the United States replace Britain at the head of the capitalist table? First, the United States' vast resources and burgeoning population made it a growing industrial power. Second, its geographic location (even isolation)—far from the seemingly endless troubles afflicting Europe and Asia—and military might—exemplified in the war with Spain—made it the obvious successor to Britain as the world's policeman and protector of capital. But, third, we must also consider the role of elite cultural affinity.

Beginning especially in the late nineteenth century, as the United States grew in power, notions of an Anglo-Saxon race, spreading over time and space, from India to Germany to Britain and now to the Americas, took hold among the American and British elite. Financiers, aristocrats, writers, and politicians spoke of a bond bred of cultural and racial superiority found in the values and political institutions among English-speaking peoples (Kramer 2002). These imagined notions of superiority—and of imperial destiny—were nurtured through business and personal connections, including marriage, while also solidifying, if not confirming, elite fears of threat to their wealth and status; hence, the need for a safe haven, as the United States—and New York—offered.

By the turn of the century, New York was the clear financial centre of the United States. Historically, American financiers, despite occasional scandals, had been more conservative than their more freewheeling and creative British counterparts. This began to change, however, in the years immediately after the First World War, leading to rampant speculation that found its apogee in the years leading up to 1929 (see Galbraith 1997). The Great Depression was sobering, the Second World War that followed even more so.

The end of that war saw the United States take on the fallen mantle of the British Empire as the chief protector of global capitalism, an especially important role in the subsequent Cold War context of the Communist threat. Within this broader role, the United States also played an important part in rebuilding and stabilizing the world economy. This was achieved primarily through the Bretton Woods system. This system, established at the end of the Second World War, was largely the product of John Maynard Keynes, a British economist and a director of the Bank of England. It balanced the interests of finance (money) capital and industrial capital through a system of international monetary exchanges capital based on the American dollar (Fennema and van der Pijl 1987) overseen by the US-led International Monetary Fund (IMF) and the World Bank. Given their obvious political importance in the postwar world, Washington was made the headquarters of both these institutions.

Bretton Woods lasted roughly 25 years. Ironically, when it collapsed, it did so at the hand of American finance capitalists, though certainly not this class alone. The early postwar years provided ample opportunities for finance capitalists to make a profit. But the Keynesian welfare state that had emerged put restraints on capital—finance capital in particular—in the name of the domestic economy and national interests. By the early 1960s, finance capitalists, headquartered within the major global cities, were bridling at the regulatory restraints and costs imposed upon them by this system (Block 1977, 203). International by its nature, finance capital—housed in the major banking institutions in London, New York, and elsewhere—finally gained the upper hand in the early 1970s when a series of technological, sociological, and ideological revolutions, combined with the OPEC crisis and the onset of **stagflation** throughout the western world, unravelled the Keynesian compromise. The period of neo-globalization that ensued freed up finance capital for expansion, in many instances breaking up the national states in which it had previously been embedded, while simultaneously giving rise to new city-states—the global cities—able to provide "services directly to the global economy" (Hobsbawm 1995, 280–1). But the new imperialism that emerged was not like the old imperialism. Previous empires had relied on direct power or the collaboration of local elites. In contrast, the new, informal type of empire practised by the US, though still capable when needed to exercise force, imposed its will in hegemonic fashion through institutions such as the World Bank and IMF and, after the 1980s, through a series of trade agreements that expanded the reach of finance capital (Mann 2008). Unrestrained, however, finance capital soon found itself the victim of over-reach.

Finance Capital and the Great Recession

At first successful in restoring capitalist profitability, neoliberalism itself soon ran into difficulties. The age-old problem of financial bubbles resulted in a series of comparatively small, but significant, crashes beginning in 1987. As Keen (2011, 22) notes, central bankers, notably the US Fed, rescued the finance capitalists, as they did "in the other crises that followed—the Savings and Loans crisis, the Long Term Capital Management crisis, and finally the DotCom crisis"; but, thus, also encouraged "the speculative excesses of Wall Street to continue," leading to the much graver crisis that occurred in 2007 (Keen 2011).

The Great Recession—as it is now widely termed—began, as with most financial crises, with a bank run, in this case on Northern Rock, a British bank. Faced with collapse, Northern Rock sought and obtained a financial bailout from the Bank of England in September of 2007. When this failed to stabilize it, Northern Rock was nationalized. But the problems facing the world financial markets were only beginning.

The following year a host of US investment banks went bankrupt, were merged, or were transformed into commercial banks and overseen with increased regulations, while the United States' largest mortgage corporations, colloquially known as Fannie Mae and Freddie Mac—which were blamed for the housing bubble that had burst— were placed under the conservatorship of the Federal Housing Finance Agency.

Elsewhere, governments in several countries, including Ireland, the Netherlands, Spain, and Switzerland followed the lead of the United Kingdom in nationalizing banks; likewise, the UK, through the Bank of England, did not stop with Northern Rock. It took on substantial ownership of several institutions, including the Bank of Scotland and Lloyds. The instability in financial markets spread quickly: personal bankruptcies and foreclosures increased; unemployment reached double digits in nearly every developed country.

The causes of the recession are much debated. The identified culprits include income inequality (Reich 2010); class conflict more generally (Panitch and Gindin 2010); lax regulation and enforcement; the psychology of risk among bankers and traders; and new technologies that have enhanced the speed with which reckless behaviour and outright criminality[10] can be practised (Blinder et al. 2012).

Tying together all of these explanations, however, is the role of finance capital. On a strictly empirical level, finance capital is not the largest element of capitalist production, but it is the system's most unstable element, and it has grown in size and influence since the onset of neoliberal globalization.

Worldwide, Hoggarth et al. (2010) estimate that between 2002 and 2007, a period of rapid expansion, gross international capital flows increased from 5 per cent to 17 per cent of GDP, plummeting in 2008 to 1 per cent. This enormous volatility says something in its own right about the consequences of the power of finance capital. Panitch and Gindin (2010, 9) argue, however, that, by the 1980s and 1990s, a new period of capitalism—"predominantly financialized capitalism"— had emerged; a term capturing "the greater mobility of **financial capital** across sectors, space and time (especially via **derivatives**)—that is, financial capital's quality as general or 'abstract' capital."

Financialized capitalism was not "merely speculative or parasitic, or rentier," however; it was not separate or isolated from productive capital, as was often the case in earlier capitalist development; rather, it had insinuated itself into the goods-producing sectors and non-financial services, as described by Radice (2010, 30):

The new world of financial power and influence is thus emphatically not one in which the financial sector has become "detached" from the real economy. Rather, it is one where the so-called real economy of businesses, households and governments has been thoroughly "financialized." We all make money now, not things.

Globalization meant that the recession was also globalized; yet even after the recession began, finance capital continued to grow. A report by the German newspaper, *Der Spiegel* (2011), reports that the global total of goods and services produced in 2010 was US$63 trillion. By comparison, however, the value of shares and bonds traded that year was US$87 trillion, the off-exchange trading of derivatives was US$601 trillion, and the total value of currency exchange transactions was US$955 trillion. According to Lord Adair Turner, chair of Britain's Financial Services Authority, however, much of what happens on Wall Street and in The City is "socially useless," the values created neither real nor of use to society.

But, as Polanyi (2001) warned, financialization has also meant that finance capital has captured other elements of society, including culture and, most especially, the state and its political institutions. This is no more evident than in Britain and the United States, where links between finance capital and government are well documented.

A report conducted by the Bureau of Investigative Journalism in the UK (Mathiason, Newman, and McClenaghan 2012) found that Great Britain's financial industry, through the City of London Corporation (the local authority) directly, industry bodies, "banks, insurers, hedge funds and private equity firms," and political contributions, spent £93 million on lobbying in 2011 alone, by which the industry obtained privileged access to the Chancellor of the Exchequer and other senior Treasury ministers. According to the report, these efforts paid off, among other things, in "[t]he slashing of UK corporation tax and taxes on banks' overseas branches" and the halting of government plans to create "a new corporate super-watchdog to police quoted companies." In the words of Andrew Simms of the New Economics Foundation think tank, "This looks like full-scale mobilisation for an economic war of attrition in which the finance industry is on one side, and the rest of the society, business and industry on the other."

The links between Wall Street and the US government are perhaps even more obvious. For example, Henry Paulson, Treasury Secretary for President George W. Bush, was once head of Goldman Sachs. Alan Greenspan, chair of the US Federal Reserve from 1987–2006, has been a director of several corporations, including JP Morgan. Lawrence Summers, a top economic adviser to both President Clinton and President Obama, who was instrumental during the former administration in designing the policies that loosened financial regulations, has strong financial connections with several corporations. Tim Geithner, who served as President Obama's Treasury Secretary between 2009–13 and who was president of the Federal Reserve Bank of New York, became president of Warburg Pincus, a Wall Street private equity firm, in the spring of 2014. Lobbying Washington to enact policies favouring Wall Street is not difficult given the revolving door of central figures in both the governmental and economic spheres.

The onset of the Great Recession and its aftermath revealed the political clout of finance capital; although some notable financial institutions failed, in the larger sense finance capital escaped unscathed. The immediate problem of the seizing up of private credit was solved by central banks, the Federal Reserve and, if somewhat more reluctantly, the European Central Bank, which resorted to "quantitative easing," by which the central banks purchased the financial assets (many of them of sub-par value) from private banks "in order to provide cash that [could] be lent to businesses and households" (Radice 2010, 41, fn20). In effect, private debt was transferred to the public ledger. By 2010, governments had bailed out the private sector to the tune of $20 trillion (McNally 2010), money that western governments have since attempted to claw back through various austerity measures (cuts to the welfare state) and attacks on the wages and benefits of public sector workers.

Back to London and New York

London and New York are not the world's largest cities in population: New York is eighth, whereas London is thirty-fourth.[11] And they are not the wealthiest cities in terms of gross domestic product, though they rank highly: New York is second to Tokyo; London, in fifth place behind Los Angeles and Seoul.[12] They are not even the number one place of residence for the world's billionaires: that accolade goes to Moscow (84, with a total worth of US$366 billion), though New York is second (62 billionaires), with London and Hong Kong tied for third (43 billionaires each) (Forbes 2013).

Yet London and New York still rank above any other cities, by a wide margin, as the two foremost global cities. They remain so due to the particular importance of their financial districts within the international system of capitalist exchange. The organization of this exchange is a vital aspect of capitalism; it must be planned, coordinated, and executed. This role, for the better part of two hundred years, has fallen to The City and, subsequently, to Wall Street.

How large is the financial industry in these cities? In the decade before the collapse, the UK's financial services sector, located primarily in The City, grew at a rate twice that of the country's GDP

(Burgess 2011). Before 1982, Wall Street's financial sector claimed 12 per cent of pre-tax profits, but by 2008 had garnered 34 per cent. Wall Street's financial assets, equal to 462 per cent of the US GDP in 1982, were 1,058 per cent of GDP in 2007 (both figures from Henwood 2010, 84).

A report by McKinsey and Company (2007), commissioned by the City of New York and the United States Senate just before the recession, stated that the financial industry accounted directly for 318,000 jobs in London and 328,000 jobs in New York. In the latter case, although financial services made up 8 per cent of the US economy, it represented 15 per cent of New York's real gross GDP, of which the securities industry was the largest sector (171,000 of the direct jobs in that city) (ibid., 35–6).

Today, New York remains the headquarters for the top five investment banks in the world (JP Morgan Chase, Bank of America Merrill Lynch, Goldman Sachs, Citigroup, and Morgan Stanley) whereas London is home to the seventh largest investment bank, Barclays.[13] But the importance of these cities' financial districts lies not so much in the size of their investments or of their workforces, but in their role in coordinating the flow of finance capital at the heart of a global network (Friedmann 1998 and Sassen 1991; 2000; 2005).

The financial districts of London and New York were thus at the geographic centre of the Great Recession. In London, the service sector declined by 10 per cent from its peak, though it has since recovered (Burgess 2011). But several UK financial institutions, many of them subsidiaries of US banks, collapsed, among them HBOS (acquired by Lloyds) and several banks associated with the UK building societies. Among the many prominent New York-based financial institutions that collapsed during the recent crisis were Merrill-Lynch, Countryside Financial, and Lehman Brothers, which were listed on the New York Stock Exchange, and Bears Stearns, likewise headquartered in New York before its collapse.

Today, the financial crisis has passed for The City and Wall Street. The money lost between 2007 and 2010 has been more than recovered. Because of mergers and takeovers, the institutions of finance capital would seem more than ever "too big to fail."

Conclusion

This chapter has examined the specificity of London and New York at the apex of global cities. It has argued that their prominence is due primarily to their financial districts (The City and Wall Street) and their role in coordinating the flow of finance capital within the global economy. Examining the historical development of London and New York tells us much about how finance capital has come to dominate the global economy. But it also raises questions about the importance of ethno-cultural affinity in shaping economic relations, the role of historical contingency in global financial systems, and the limits of liberal democracy within a liberal economic system.

Will The City and Wall Street remain at the centre of finance capital? Globalization's current epoch has resulted in a real transfer of productive forces and wealth from the industrialized North to the undeveloped South; this would suggest challengers to London and New York in the future. Yet, countering this, the McKinsey Global Institute (2013) has argued that, while the centre of gravity of the urban world will move South and East, primarily to China (e.g., Beijing), through 2025 New York will continue to have the highest GDP, whereas London will slip only marginally, to fourth place behind Tokyo and Shanghai.

But we may also consider a third option, as Marx once averred: that finance capital will continue to grow beyond the precincts of The City and of Wall Street, or of any other global city, nestling and settling everywhere, an abstraction that, once confronted—as the Occupy Movement has discovered—melts into air.

Acknowledgement

The author thanks Greg Anderson for his very helpful comments on an earlier draft of this chapter; and Dan Konecny who researched materials of use in the writing.

Notes

1 Following Sassen (2005: 28) the term "global cities" is used throughout this chapter as opposed to "world cities."

2 For a summary of the major theses underpinning the global cities hypothesis, see Hill and Kim (2000: 2169–71).

3 The first comparative global cities index was devised in 1998 by researchers at Loughborough University in the UK, and resulted in the Globalization and World Cities Research Network (GaWC). The network's most recent rankings are not presented here as they involve a system not entirely comparable with the others used. For the purposes of this chapter, however, it is worth noting that London and New York are also the top two cities in the GaWC report.

4 Further details about the indexes can be found at: (GCI) www.atkearney .com/research-studies/global-cities-index; (COI) www.pwc.com/ us/en/cities-of-opportunity/; (GPCI) www.mori-m-foundation .or.jp/english/index.shtml; (GCWR) www.knightfrank.com/ wealthreport; (GCCI) www.economist.com/blogs/graphicdetail/ 2012/03/daily-chart-8?zid=292&ah=165a5788fdb0726c01b1374d8e 1ea285

5 In 1971, Dunning and Morgan (1971: 62) noted that over half of the city's workers were in "professional services and insurance, banking and finance."

6 The journalist Larry Elliott (2013: 21) argues that London should become an independent city state given that "the disparity between a thriving London and the rest [of the UK] has never been greater."

7 Though the heartland of English industry, Manchester's population in 1800 was only 81,000 (Chandler, 1987: 23).

8 Barrows (2011: 45) argues that Greenwich Mean Time was devised by "transnational investors" who used the international conference in 1884 in order to "synchronize countries to precisely coordinated capital flow." He argues further that (p. 46),

What is particularly modern about standard time is that it facilitates the unification of global markets to the penetration of capital. The "dread international conference" sanctioned the coordination of capital flow with transcontinental railways, telegraphy, Pace or "Empire-girdling" cables, and imperial intelligence bureaus. . . .

The importance of the time zone was made critically apparent in the aftermath of the recent recession. Investigators into the causes of the crisis found that the 60-second trading window surrounding the fixing of the day's benchmark exchange rate (at 4:00 p.m., London time), could be manipulated by currency traders (Slater, 2014).

9   The failures of the First and Second Banks of the United States in the early nineteenth century were only remedied in 1913 with the creation of the Federal Reserve, which became headquartered in Washington.

10   Since the crisis, US and British fraud investigators, as well as regulators from dozens of other countries, have been looking into price-rigging in currency markets at some of the world's biggest banks and on financial exchanges. As of summer 2014, at least 30 traders in Europe and elsewhere had been fired or suspended (Slater, 2014).

11   www.worldatlas.com/citypops.htm. Downloaded December 1, 2013. Tokyo is first with 37 million people; New York has 20.4 million; and London, 8.6 million.

12   www.therichest.com/rich-list/world/the-top-10-richest-cities-in-the-world/. Downloaded December 1, 2013.

13   http://finance.mapsofworld.com/investment/banks/top-10-bank.html

Key Terms

derivatives
financial capital

international reserve currency
stagflation

Questions for Review

1.   What are the central tenets of the global cities perspective?

2.   What is the relationship of London to its financial district and to the rest of Britain?

3.   What factors underpinned The City's development as a bastion of finance capital?

4.   What factors led to New York's emergence as the dominant US city?

5.   What role did finance capital play in the Great Recession that began in 2007?

Further Resources

Ferguson, N. (2008). *The ascent of money: A financial history of the world*. Toronto: Penguin.

Foster, J. B. and Magdoff, F. (2009). *The great financial crisis*. New York: Monthly Review Press.

Galbraith, J. K. (1997). *The great crash of 1929*. Boston: Mariner.

Galbraith, J. K. (1990). *A short history of financial euphoria*. Toronto: Penguin.

Klein, N. (2008). *The shock doctrine: The rise of disaster capitalism*. Toronto: Vintage.

Naylor, R. T. (2004). *Hot money and the politics of debt*, 3rd ed. Montreal & Kingston: McGill-Queen's University Press.

Reich, R. (2012). *Beyond outrage: What has gone wrong with our economy and our democracy, and how to fix it*. Toronto: Vintage.

References

Alford, B. W. E. (1996). *Britain in the world economy since 1880*. London: Longman.

Barrows, A. (2011). *The cosmic time of empire*. Berkeley, California: University of California Press.

Blinder, A. S., Lo, Andrew, W., and Solow, R. M. (Eds.). (2012). *Rethinking the financial crisis*. New York: Russell Sage.

Block, F. L. (1977). *The origins of international economic disorder.* Berkeley: University of California Press.

Braudel, F. (1983). *The perspective of the world.* New York: Collins.

Brenner, N. (1998). "Global cities, glocal states: Global city formation and state territorial restructuring in contemporary Europe." *Review of International Political Economy* 5(1): 1–37.

Burgess, S. (2011). "Measuring financial sector output and its contribution to UK GDP." Bank of England *Quarterly Bulletin* Q3, 234–46.

Castells, M. (1977). *The Urban question: A Marxist approach.* A. Sheridan, trans. Cambridge: The M.I.T. Press.

Chandler, T. (1987). *Four thousand years of urban growth.* St. David's: St. David's University Press.

Cockerell, H. (1984). *Lloyd's of London: A portrait.* Homewood, Illinois: Dow Jones-Irwin.

Der Spiegel. (2011). "Out of control: The destructive power of the financial markets." 22 August. www.spiegel.de/international/business/out-of-control-the-destructive-power-of-the-financial-markets-a-781590.html Downloaded 11 January 2014.

Dunning, J. H. and Morgan, E. V. (1971). *An economic study of the City of London.* London: Ruskin House.

Elliott, L. (2013). "London is a separate country." *The Guardian Weekly,* 21.

Fennena, M. and Pijl, K. van der. (1987). "International bank capital and the new liberalism." In M. S. Mizrucki, and M. Schwartz (Eds.), *Intercorporate Relations: The Structural Analysis of Business.* Cambridge: Cambridge University Press.

Forbes. (2013). "Forbes top 10 billionaire cities— Moscow beats New York again." www.forbes.com/sites/ricardogeromel/2013/03/14/forbes-top-10-billionaire-cities-moscow-beats-new-york-again/ Downloaded 23 September 2013.

Friedmann, J. (1995). "The world cities hypothesis." In P. L. Knox and P. J. Taylor, (Eds), *World cities in a world system.* Cambridge: Cambridge University Press.

——. (1998). "World city futures: the role of urban and regional policies in the Asia Pacific region." In Y. Yeung (Ed.), *Urban development in Asia:*

Retrospect and prospect. Hong Kong: Chinese University of Hong Kong Press.

——, and Wolff, G. (1982). "World city formation: An agenda for research and action." *International Journal for Urban and Regional Research* 6, 309–44.

Geisst, C. R. (2012). *Wall Street: A history* (Updated edition). New York: Oxford University Press.

Ghosh, S. (2012). Review of T. Scott's, "The city-state in Europe, 1000–600. Hinterland, territory, region." *Reviews in History,* 1252.

Glaeser, E. L. (2005). "Urban colossus: Why is New York America's largest city?" *Economic Policy Review,* (December), 7–24.

Gordon, D., Edwards, R., and Reich, M. (1982). *Segmented work, divided workers: The historical transformation of labor in the United States.* New York: Cambridge University Press.

Gottdiener, M., and Feagin, J. R. (1988). "The paradigm shift in urban sociology." *Urban Affairs Review* 24, 163–87.

Grossman, R. (2010). *Unsettled account: The evolution of banking in the industrialized world since 1800.* Princeton: Princeton University Press.

Harvey, D. (1973). *Social justice and the city.* London: Edward Arnold,

——. *The urbanization of capital.* (1985). Baltimore: Johns Hopkins Press.

——. *The enigma of capital and the crises of capitalism.* (2011). Oxford: Oxford University Press.

Henwood, D. (2010). "Before and after crisis: Wall Street lives on." In L. Panitch and S. Gindin (Eds), *The crisis this time. The Socialist Register 2011.* Halifax: Fernwood.

Hill, R. C., and Kim, J. W. (2000). "Global cities and developmental states: New York, Tokyo, and Seoul." *Urban Studies* 37(12), 2167–95.

Hobsbawm, E. (1995). *Age of extremes: The short twentieth century 1914–1991.* London: Abacus.

Hoggarth, G., Mahadeva, L., and Martin, J. (2010). "Understanding international bank capital flows during the recent financial crisis." Bank of England Financial Stability Paper 8.

Hume, C. (2004). "What makes a global city?" *Toronto Star,* 1 November.

Inwood, S. (1998). *A history of London.* New York: Carroll and Graf.

Keen, S. (2011). *Debunking economics,* 2nd ed. London: Zed Books.

Knight Frank Research. (2013). *The wealth report.* London: Knight Frank.

Kramer, P. A. (2002). "Empires, exceptions, and Anglo-Saxons: Race and rule between the British and United States empires, 1880–1910." *The Journal of American History,* March, 1315–53.

Mann, M. (2008). "American empires: Past and present." *Canadian Review of Sociology* 45(1), 7–50.

Manning, B. (1991). *The English people and the English revolution.* London: Bookmarks.

Mathiason, N., Newman, M., and McClenaghan, M. (2012). "Revealed: The £93m city lobby machine." *The Bureau of Investigative Journalism,* 9 July.

McCann, E. J. (2004). "Urban political economy beyond the 'Global City.'" *Urban Studies* 41(12), 2315–33.

McKinsey and Company. (2007). *Bloomberg/Schumer Report: Sustaining New York's and the US' global financial services leadership.*

McKinsey Global Institute. (2013). "Urban world: Mapping the economic power of cities."

McMichael, P. (1987). "State formation and the construction of the world market." *Political Power and Social Theory* 6, 187–237.

McNally, D. (2010). *Global Slump: The Economics and Politics of Crisis and Resistance.* Oakland, California: PM Press.

Mogridge, M., and Parr, J. B. (1997). "Metropolis or region: On the development and structure of London." *Regional Studies* 31(2), 97–115.

Murray, J. M. (2005). *Bruges: Cradle of capitalism.* Cambridge: Cambridge University Press.

Panitch, L. and Gindin, G. (2012). *The making of global capitalism.* London: Verso.

Polanyi, K. (2001). *The great transformation: The political and economic origins of our time.* Originally published 1944. Boston: Beacon Press.

Radice, H. (2010). "Confronting the crisis: A class analysis." In L. Panitch and S. Gindin (Eds.), *The crisis this time. The Socialist Register 2011.* Halifax: Fernwood.

Reich, R. (2010). *After-shock: The next economy and America's future.* New York: Alfred A. Knopf.

Ribera-Fumaz, R. (2009). "From urban political economy to cultural political economy: Rethinking culture and economy and beyond the urban." *Progress in Human Geography* 33(4), 447–65.

Robertson, R. (2003). *The three waves of globalization.* London: Zed Books.

Robertson, R. (1995). "Glocalization: Time-space and homogeneity-heterogeneity." In M. Featherstone, S. Lash, and R. Robertson (Eds), *Global Modernities.* Thomas Oaks, CA: Sage.

Robinson, J. (2005). "Urban geography: world cities, or a world of cities." *Progress in Human Geography* 29(6), 757–65.

Sassen, S. (1991). *Global City: London, New York, Tokyo.* Princeton: Princeton University Press.

———. (1998). *Globalization and Its Discontents.* New York: New Press.

———. (1999). "Global financial centers." *Foreign Affairs* 78, 75–87.

———. (2000). *Cities in a World Economy,* 2nd ed. Thousand Oaks: Pine Forge.

———. (2005). "The global city: Introducing a concept." *Brown Journal of World Affairs,* Winter/Spring, XI(2), 27–43.

Scott, T. (2012). *The city-state in Europe, 1000–1600. Hinterland, territory, region.* Oxford: Oxford University Press.

Skocpol, T. (1979). *States and social revolutions.* Cambridge: Cambridge University Press.

Slater, J. (2014). "Currency markets probe expands to U.K." *Globe and Mail,* 22 July: B1 and B5.

Smith, M. P. (1998). "*The global city: Whose social construct is it anyway?*" *Urban Affairs Review* 33(4), 482–8.

Taylor, P. J., Walker, D. R. F., Catalano, G., and Hoyler, M. (2002). "Diversity and power in the world city network." *Cities* 19(4), 231–41.

Walton, J. (1993). "Urban sociology: The contribution and limits of political economy." *Annual Review of Sociology* 19, 301–20.

Yusuf, S. and Wu, W. (2002). "Pathways to a world city: Shanghai rising in an era of globalization." *Urban Studies* 39(7), 1213–40.

Zukin, S. (1980). "A decade of the new urban sociology." *Theory and Society* 9, 575–601.

18 Civil Society and International Political Economy

Laura Macdonald and Jeffrey Ayres

For ordinary individuals, civil society is the most frequent site of contact with the international political economy (IPE). Whether through the international charitable activities of mainstream churches and charities, or the actions of more radical groups like Greenpeace, the World Social Forum, and the Occupy movement, civil society is the most common way for individuals to connect to the global economy. Even phenomena and actors that might be perceived as indelibly local have a transnational dimension. Local food movements, for example, are usually inspired by the tactics and visions of international counterparts, and may participate in **transnational social movements (TSMs)** like Via Campesina. Students daily may purchase fair trade coffee certified by international social movement organizations, collaborate in campus fossil fuel divestment campaigns, or participate in anti-sweat-shop campaigns that have a strong transnational dimension.

Despite the ubiquity of civil society actors on international terrain, international political economy theories often downplay or ignore the role of civil society actors in the international system. These "Davids" of the international political economy appear dwarfed by the IPE Goliaths: states and markets that occupy most of IPE theorists' attention. In this chapter we argue, however, that an understanding of the role of civil society is essential to an understanding of the broader global political economy, for several reasons. First, states and markets cannot be understood separately from civil society, and the role of civil society is either implicitly or explicitly recognized in all theoretical traditions of IPE. The complex and evolving nature of power in the global political economy cannot be understood without reference to the discursive, symbolic, and cognitive power of civil society, and civil society is also central to any potential norms-driven transformation of the international system. Second, civil society actors are increasingly influential and important internationally, and their role has expanded in tandem with the forces of globalization—to some extent in reaction against globalization, but also sometimes in support of it. An important aspect of the study of globalization involves an analysis of the concept of "globalization from below"—the transnational alliances of actors challenging the elite-driven phenomenon of neoliberal globalization through what is now referred to as the "alter-globalization movement." Civil society also provides a useful way of overcoming the arbitrary distinctions of traditional international theory between the local, the national, and the international. An analysis of civil society requires a move toward multi-scalar modes of analysis and an understanding of how these different scales are interconnected. Finally, the concept of civil society is an essential opening to any discussion of democratization of the global political economy and the array of institutions of global economic governance.

Theories of **civil society** have a long intellectual tradition dating back to the Greeks and Romans, and it is only in recent years that theorists have grappled with how to understand the international dimensions of the concept.[1] In this chapter, we first review some of the main theoretical traditions of international political economy and how they grapple with the concept of civil society. In the second half of the chapter, we review how the international activities of civil society actors have evolved in recent years, with special reference to debates around regionalization, globalization, and contentious politics in the North American context. We adopt a broad definition of civil society as a realm of associational activity located between the market and formal political institutions of the state. Like Jan Aart Scholte, we emphasize how civil society actors "deliberately seek to shape the rules that govern one or the other aspect of social life."[2] Cross-border ties between civil society actors may take a variety of forms, adding to the complexity of the theoretical challenge of understanding them. Some types of international action may take the form of loose networks, based largely on informal ties and the diffusion of ideas and information, with little formal organizational substance. Other forms of cooperation, such as transnational social movements, show higher levels of institutionalization, coordination, and consensus.[3] In short, all of

the major theories of IPE, whether the traditional approaches discussed by Axel Hülsemeyer in chapter 2 of this volume or the "challengers" discussed by Rob Aitken in chapter 3, contain basic assumptions about the nature of civil society, even if they do not always explicitly recognize it.

Civil Society and Theories of IPE

The theoretical approach that seems most resistant to incorporating civil society is that of *economic nationalism*, or *mercantilism*, which is based on a statist approach to IPE. This approach assumes that nation-states are, and should be, the fundamental actors in the international political economy. Mercantilist approaches provide an important critique of liberal IPE theories, which assume that all state intervention is the result of self-interested action by rent-seeking individuals and groups, and that such state intervention inevitably results in inefficient and uncompetitive economic outcomes. After years of neoliberal hegemony, these approaches are seeing a resurgence in the era of the post-Washington Consensus, in which there is increasing recognition of the potentially beneficial and positive role of state intervention in the economy, and of the widespread existence of market imperfection. The rising economies of the BRICs (Brazil, Russia, India, and China) are frequently seen as the products of neomercantilist or developmentalist states, and are based to different degrees on extensive state intervention in pursuit of economic growth and prosperity. In the context of the widespread perception of the failure of neoliberal strategies to promote growth, the states that are seen to be most successful in overcoming underdevelopment in the contemporary global economy are developmentalist states.

Theorists of the neomercantilist or developmentalist state often base their prescriptions on the experiences of East Asian states like South Korea, Taiwan, and Singapore. These countries achieved high levels of growth in the 1960s and 1970s based on effective programs of state intervention. However, it is not just any state that can adopt these strategies successfully. According to Peter Evans, the success of these developmental states is not based on pure state strength and extreme autonomy, but rather on their "embedded" character. Because of the absence of strong landlord and capitalist classes, these states were in the position to:

> orchestrate a concrete national project of development, built on a dense set of concrete interpersonal ties that enabled specific agencies and enterprises to construct joint projects at the sectoral level. This "embeddedness" was as central to the success of the 20th century developmental state as bureaucratic capacity.[4]

Strong developmentalist states in East Asia thus emerged based on their capacity to harness the forces of civil society in support of a national project. Similarly, the developmentalist New Left regimes currently in place in much of Latin America (Brazil, Argentina, Venezuela, Ecuador, Bolivia, etc.) have come to power with the support of broad-based civil society movements that emerged in opposition to the impact of neoliberalism on the poor and middle classes.[5]

Finally, it is important to note that although the anti-globalization movement is frequently described as a transnational social movement, much of the strength of opposition to free trade agreements and neoliberal policies is based on economic nationalism. Moreover, the roots of the protest campaigns against neoliberalism remain largely state-centric, with actual transnational social movement collaboration a much more ephemeral development. As we will see below in our discussion of opposition to the Canada–US Free Trade

Agreement (CUSFTA) and NAFTA, civil society actors across North America framed much of their critique of free trade with support for sovereignty and national identity.

Liberal and neoliberal approaches to IPE also seem to frequently downplay the importance of civil society in their analyses. Certainly some versions of neoliberalism are based on a radical individualist view (Margaret Thatcher once famously said, "There is no society"). Karl Polanyi criticizes the tendency of the forces of market liberalism to break asunder the traditional ties between individuals and groups that hold societies together.[6] Liberal international political economy often takes the form of objective analysis of the purportedly apolitical functioning of the international economy, and assumes that the market operates autonomously to produce the optimal outcomes for the majority of society. However, other versions of liberalism, such as social liberalism (associated with John Stuart Mill) and **cosmopolitan liberalism** (associated with Immanuel Kant) accept and celebrate the role of a strong civil society as a necessary complement to a strong market economy.

Several versions of IPE theory draw upon these liberal traditions in their analysis of the role of civil society in the global political economy. Authors like David Held and Mary Kaldor are associated with cosmopolitan international relations theory that advocates the spread of universal liberal values through the operations of global civil society. This analysis is based on a liberal view of civil society as an autonomous sphere where "activities . . . are undertaken for the public good by groups or individuals in the space between the family, the state and the market."[7] These authors also believe in the existence of a global civil society operating beyond all nation-states, which performs a role at the international level similar to that played by civil societies in the domestic realm. According to Mary Kaldor, "[g]lobal civil society . . . is about 'civilizing' or democratizing globalization, about the process through which groups, movements and individuals can demand a global rule of law, global justice and global empowerment."[8] Despite the diversity of these groups and movements, they are united by shared, universal cosmopolitan values.

Even if these cosmopolitan liberals criticize the excesses of globalization, they also believe that globalization has given rise to other processes that pave the way for the taming of these excesses by transnational social movement organizing. Louis Kriesberg argues, for example, that the growth and nature of transnational social movement organizations (TSMOs) are characterized by four trends that shape the contemporary world: "growing democratization, increasing global integration, converging and diffusing values, and proliferating transnational institutions."[9] Kriesberg recognizes that diversity exists among these TSMOs and that although some TSMOs may be advocating for change, others are engaging in actions that can be seen as reinforcing existing inequalities. However, referring to the classic liberal theorist Alexis de Tocqueville, Kriesberg argues that a pluralistic global civil society is necessary for developing a legitimate, egalitarian, and democratic international system.

Although this cosmopolitan liberal literature is openly normative, other more objective social science approaches to studying TSMOs implicitly share some liberal assumptions. This literature often draws on social movement theories developed within comparative politics literature, and transfers some of these lessons to the international context. Smith, Pagnucco, and Chatfield refer, for example, to the use of mobilizing structures; the existence of political opportunities in national, intergovernmental, and non-governmental contexts; and to the use of resource mobilization strategies.[10] Although the challenges faced by TSMOs may be more intense because of the difficulties of long-distance communication and coordination, they are not different in kind, and the same theoretical tools that have been developed to analyze domestic social movements in western democracies can be used for transnational organizing. These authors thus share fundamentally liberal pluralist notions about the nature of state–society relations and their work provides valuable tools for categorizing and understanding TSMO campaigns. It remains open to challenge, however, by more radical interpretations of the nature of power in the contemporary global economy, and the limitations of liberal strategies.

Finally, liberal institutionalism represents another variant of liberalism that places considerable emphasis on the increasingly important role of civil society at the international level, particularly when western liberal democracies are involved. Liberal institutionalism presents a challenge to realism and neorealism. Its proponents argue that, in practice, states are constrained by the rules and norms of the international system, and they emphasize the importance of international organizations and international regimes. Although these organizations are made up of state actors, Robert Keohane and Joseph Nye, the most influential authors in this school, have argued that the international system is becoming more complex in the context of globalization.[11] In particular, scholars such as O'Brien et al. see a new form of global governance emerging—"**complex multilateralism**"—which is based on the more robust participation of civil society, and differentiated from older state-centric multilateralism in three ways: (1) the new multilateralism is still in an emergent form based on multiple interactions between civil society groups around the world; (2) this new complicated multilateralism is developing "from the bottom up" through the efforts of **civil society organizations (CSOs)** that are independent of the state; and (3) the new multilateralism is explicitly "post-hegemonic;" it respects cultural diversity and promotes alternate means of civil society organizing.[12]

In the era of complex multilateralism, then, non-state actors are pushing for greater influence in international decision-making and the line between the domestic and the foreign has become blurred.[13] With regard to international trade, Keohane and Nye state that the construction of global trade rules and agreements was traditionally dominated by the "club model" in which agreements were made behind closed doors by state negotiators with technical expertise in economic issues. Increasingly, however, as they, and others working in a post-hegemonic, complex multilateralism framework, argue, in the contemporary world we are seeing this club model come under challenge based on its lack of democratic legitimacy, and the increased incorporation of civil society actors into decision-making in powerful international institutions.[14] Like other liberal theories, however, this approach tends to overlook the structural forces that shape the participation of civil society actors. International society is not a level playing field, but a sharply uneven terrain in which powerful actors, whether state or non-state, have access to greater material, symbolic, and discursive resources that give them disproportionate influence over the way the global political economy is evolving.

In this respect, critical theories provide an important series of analytical tools that can be drawn upon to provide insight into the ways in which the role of civil society in the global political economy is shaped by existing inequalities of race, class, gender, and sexuality. Indeed these approaches may be more likely to provide insightful analysis into the dynamics and role of civil society actors at the global level than their nationalist and liberal competitors, since they tend to highlight the importance of struggle and resistance to the dominant social order.

Nevertheless, these approaches, too, sometimes downplay the role of civil society, or fail to develop careful empirical analysis of the composition and dynamics of the groups comprising civil society. Marxists are often optimistic about more radical versions of TSMOs, like the so-called "anti-globalization" movement that began to emerge in Canada in the late 1980s with the opposition to the Canada–US Free Trade Agreement. We discuss this movement in more detail below. Some Marxists are optimistic about what Barry Gills calls the "politics of resistance" to "neoliberal economic globalization,"[15] whereas others are critical of this movement's insufficient working class character. Some neo-Gramscian authors draw upon the work of Italian Marxist theorist Antonio Gramsci to analyze the counter-hegemonic potential of this resistance.[16] Eschle and Maiguashca argue, however, that "the practices and significance of 'the anti-globalisation movement' remain undertheorised" within Marxist international relations theory, possibly because these writers tend to spend more energy "mapping structural relations of power and domination than on theorizing the logic and nature of resistance or counter-hegemony."[17] Even feminist IPE authors, who devote considerable attention to the effect of changes in the global economy on the lives and work of women, have paid less attention to the implications of the anti-globalization movement and other forms of TSMOs for feminist politics.[18]

Post-colonial theory represents another important strain of critical theory that provides a more skeptical view of the operations of global civil society actors than in the liberal or realist version. Within this school, David Slater raises important challenges to dominant liberal understandings of the nature of globalization, which tend to emphasize increased homogenization and convergence of societies and economies toward a western liberal norm. Post-colonial theorists emphasize instead the unevenness of this process and the persistence of strong local cultures and epistemologies. Though globalization may bring increased wealth and mobility to a few, others encounter new barriers to movement and experience new fragmentation and processes of social and political disintegration.[19] Citing Mosquera, Slater argues that

> While the word "globalization" may evoke the idea of a planet in which all points happen to be interconnected in a web-like network, in actual fact connections occur inside a radial and hegemonic pattern around the centres of power, while the peripheral countries tend to remain disconnected from one another, or are only connected indirectly via and under the control of the centres.[20]

TSMOs are not immune from this dynamic and tend to be dominated by NGOs and social movements located in the global North, whereas the voices of groups in the global South are often muted and disarticulated. Post-colonial authors thus call for TSMOs to introduce different political practices based on internal democratization of the organizations themselves to provide greater participation by marginal voices, particularly voices from the South. Boaventura de Sousa Santos argues that spaces like the World Social Forum (WSF) also need to reject false universalisms and represent the "wide multiplicity and variety of social practices of counter-hegemony that occur all over the world."[21] In the place of universalisms, he argues, the WSF should pursue a praxis of translation, which allows actors from diverse locations to understand one another. This, he argues, will require an enormous effort of "mutual recognition, dialogue, and debate" among the diverse social actors that make up the movement of movements: feminists, Indigenous peoples, environmentalists, pacifists, and others. Post-colonial theory thus proposes a

radical democratization of the practices of transnational civil society activism.

Overall, critical IPE provides useful theoretical tools. First, Marxist, neo-Marxist, and neo-Gramscian approaches present a useful corrective to the rather voluntarist assumptions of liberal IPE about the origins of transnational civil society activity by offering a structural analysis of changes in the global civil society that stimulate the contradictions that give rise to protest. Also, critical approaches in general offer tools for critical analysis of the dynamics of power that operate within and across "global civil society." They criticize liberal analysis that locates civil society as an autonomous and self-organizing realm of activity located between state and market (and family). Eschle and Maiguashca note that "this framing has the effect of masking the role of multiple power relations within civil society and social movements, and of representing movements as intrinsically and uniformly progressive."[22] Though these critical approaches provide a useful corrective to these oversights, they usually pay less attention to the messy details of organizing and the factors that influence movement success or failure than the liberal theories based on social movement theory.

Waves of Civil Society Contentious Politics[23]

Debates about the role of civil society and international political economy are influenced not just by theoretical tendencies but also by changes that have occurred in international politics in recent years. The role of civil society is particularly difficult to analyze because of the sometimes ephemeral and often cyclical nature of social movement contentious politics. In this section, we review the nature of the interaction between globalization and civil society over the last several decades through a "waves of contentious politics" conceptual approach. We argue that globalization or, more broadly, the international political economy and civil society, have interacted through three different cycles of protest, spanning the last several decades of global politics. The first wave of contentious politics largely affected the global South during the 1970s and 1980s. The second wave unfolded mostly in the global North in the 1990s through a series of regional protests against neoliberal trade agreements and institutions. The third wave takes the form of a series of protests, ranging from the Occupy movements to student and Indigenous movements in Quebec and Canada to anti-austerity protests in Europe following the outbreak of the global financial crisis in 2008–09, to protests against mining projects in the Americas. Unlike the protests of the last two cycles, this cycle is not characterized by a great deal of cross-border coordination between social movements. To some extent, there has been a retreat from the transnational sphere by elements of global civil society. Nonetheless, we argue that these movements remain transnational in the sense that they continue to protest against neoliberal globalization, and we often see processes of political learning and emulation occurring across borders as movements learn from the successes and failures of their counterparts in other countries. This cycle of contentious politics is thus more globally dispersed and multi-scalar than previous cycles.

Cycles of Protest and Contention

Sidney Tarrow, an influential social movement theorist, provides the concept of a "**cycle of contention**," defined as "a phase of heightened conflict across the social system, with rapid diffusion of collective action from more mobilized to less mobilized sectors, a rapid pace of innovation in the forms of contention employed, the creation of new or transformed collective action frames, a combination of organized and unorganized participation, and sequences of intensified information flow and interaction between challengers and authorities" (Tarrow 2011, 199).[24] Almost inevitably, a phase of heightened contestation and protest is followed by a phase of decline and dispersal of protest activities. However, over time, the knowledge, ideas, organizational linkages, and social capital developed in each phase may be contributing to the transformation of the international system. These cycles are often discussed in purely national terms, but also occur at the international level. We argue that the current and distinct cycle of protest has emerged from what Val Moghadam describes as two earlier cycles of transnational collective action and protest.

The first cycle of contention was mostly located in countries of the global South in response to the neoliberal structural adjustment programs (SAPs) imposed on those countries by the International Monetary Fund and other international financial institutions in the 1980s and 1990s. These policies led to a wave of protests and riots across the developing world. These protests were not originally coordinated across borders but emerged more or less spontaneously in response to the devastating impact of neoliberal policies on populations. However, eventually a transnational civil society campaign emerged, composed of organizations, groups, and individuals from across the world that came together in opposition to the policies of the international financial institutions. This campaign did not achieve all of its objectives, but it did result in the cancellation of some of the debt of the highly indebted states, particularly in sub-Saharan Africa.[25] In addition, the continued failure of the SAPs to generate sustained growth or reduce poverty, as well as the theoretical critiques levelled against these programs by social movement activists as well as intellectuals inside and outside the IFIs (international financial institutions) protest, also eventually resulted in the shift toward a post-Washington-Consensus period in which the virtues of the market are not taken for granted.

The second phase of mobilization against neoliberal globalization occurred in the 1990s and was mostly located in the global North, with some notable exceptions. In this cycle, activists targeted a series of international financial and trade agreements, such as NAFTA, the Maastricht Treaty of the European Union, the proposed Multilateral Agreement on Investment (MAI), the creation of the World Trade Organization (WTO), which replaced the General Agreement on Tariffs and Trade in 1994,[26] and the proposed Free Trade Area of the Americas (FTAA). Social movement theory would suggest that this cycle emerged in response to an opening in the political opportunity structure provided by the signing of these free trade agreements, which provided a clear target for critique and protest. In this period, relatively strong transnational coalitions emerged, made up of a diverse range of social movements, including trade unions, environmentalists, women's groups, social justice organizations, and others.[27] These movements stimulated a great deal of optimism, if not romanticism, about the power of global protests among students of global civil society and inspired much of the theorizing discussed in the last section.

Some of these transnational alliances were successful in derailing agreements or meetings, such as the MAI and the Seattle WTO conference, and they may have contributed to the move away from more ambitious multilateral trade agreements toward the current "spaghetti bowl" of bilateral and regional agreements. However, the shift toward a multitude of bilateral and regional agreements has dispersed political energies and fragmented the organizing frame of many cross-border protests, resulting in a decline of transnational organizing against free trade. In parts of the South,

especially Latin America, this phase also gave rise to some new post-hegemonic forms of regional trade agreements, such as the ALBA (Bolivarian Alliance for the Peoples), composed of developmentalist states. These new regional groupings challenge some of the assumptions of neoliberal trade agreements and incorporate some civil society participation as well as drawing on economic nationalist and anti-neoliberal sentiments.[28]

The third distinct cycle of contentious protest that we see still unfolding globally targets a wide range of phenomena. Some of these targets of citizens' anger are apparently domestic, like the Canadian government's neo-colonial policies toward Indigenous peoples or the decision of the Quebec government to raise tuition rates. However, they are all, we argue, part of a third global protest cycle against neoliberal policies, including trade and financial liberalization, deregulation, tax cuts, and cuts to social spending, which result in growing inequality and economic insecurity, and in growing discontent with the lack of channels for democratic representation in political structures nationally and transnationally.

Cycles of Transnational Civil Society Protest in Canada and North America

North America is an excellent testing ground for the concepts discussed above, especially in terms of the changing interactions between civil society and the international political economy. All three of these cycles of contentious civil society activity have played out across this continent over the last several decades. As the first regional trade agreement to incorporate a developing country (Mexico), the case of the North American Free Trade Agreement (NAFTA) illustrates particularly well some of the dilemmas of neoliberal globalization that give rise to civil society responses, as well as the challenges of cross-border organizing. Moreover, North American civil society responses to neoliberal globalization and maneuverings within the IPE illustrate the changing character of civil society influence and power as well as the post-hegemonic character of globalization from below across the continent.

First Cycle of North American Contention: Mexico and the IPE of the 1980s

Mexico was one of the first countries to experience the implementation of neoliberal policies in the 1980s since it was the first country to declare that it could not pay its debts during the Latin American debt crisis of the early 1980s. Mexico received support from the United States, Canada, and the International Monetary Fund to restructure its debt, but in return was required to adopt a series of structural adjustment programs that resulted in extensive cutbacks to subsidies and social programs, a rapid increase in poverty, unemployment, and inequality, and the dismantling of the corporatist developmentalist state that had been constructed after the Mexican revolution.

The emergence of Mexican social movement opposition to neoliberal policies was constrained by the history of state control over civil society. After the revolution, a dominant party emerged, eventually named the Institutional Revolutionary Party (PRI), which ruled Mexico for 71 years. The PRI established corporatist sectors to represent different social sectors (labour, peasants, the "popular classes," and, early on, the military). Members of these groups received benefits from the state in return for their political support. The corporatist organizations lacked autonomy from the state, and other forms of organization of civil society

were discouraged or prohibited (Mackinley and Otero).[29] This system, and the high rates of growth that occurred under state-sponsored import substitution policies, guaranteed PRI hegemony for many decades. Protests were thus sporadic, disarticulated, and occasionally brutally repressed, as in the Tlatelolco massacre of 1968 in which the military opened fire on student protesters, killing hundreds.

The Mexican government's implementation of neoliberal economic policies in the early 1980s led to the emergence of a new, more autonomous form of civil society organizing, part of the first cycle of global contentious politics. During the 1970s, after the Tlatelolco massacre, activist groups had changed their tactical approach, away from direct challenges to the state toward promoting a broader protest movement based on grassroots democracy and coalitions between the urban poor, peasants, and workers in unions independent of the state's corporatist structures.[30] A key element of these new movements was the participation of lower-class women, especially in the urban and teachers' movements. Women were radicalized by the precipitous decline of their living standards during the economic crisis, and by the failure of the state to meet basic needs like food, infrastructure, and basic services.[31]

These new social movements located in civil society were not able to change the Mexican government's economic and social policies, but they did contribute to broad-based pressure for democratization. Important elements of civil society, like the official trade unions, remained tied to the governing party, however, limiting their capacity to push for change. Mexican social movements and non-governmental organizations (NGOs) also participated in international fora and alliances opposed to IMF structural adjustment policies, and ultimately contributed to the second cycle of

North American contention, in opposition to NAFTA.

Second Cycle of North American Contention: The Backlash Against Free Trade

For over a decade, blurring into the heyday of the alter-globalization movement protests at the beginning of the twenty-first century, dramatic, influential, and unprecedented civil society mobilizing took place nearly anywhere international economic meetings were taking place (mostly across the global North). The coordinated anti-free-trade protests arguably began in Canada in the late 1980s against the Canada–US Free Trade Agreement, and continued for a decade, climaxing at the 1999 Seattle WTO Ministerial protests, marking the second global protest cycle of contentious politics against neoliberalism. The Canadian protests against the CUSFTA, though national in origin, campaign, and intended target, had an impact on the style of civil society organizing that would shape the protest cycle for the entire decade. Three characteristics of the protest cycle that began in the anti-CUSFTA campaign stand out in particular: the CUSFTA served as a political opportunity structure for civil society mobilizing; the major vehicle or style of organizing was cross-sectoral—a prelude to cross-border organizing between civil society groups that would soon emerge; and the character of the groups collaborating was post-hegemonic, in that women's, Aboriginal, student, senior, labour, and environmental groups forged an unusually non-hierarchical coalition to collaborate in opposition to the CUSFTA. The Pro-Canada Network—a cross-sectoral and cross-country coalition of groups opposed to the CUSFTA—shaped the political strategies of the Canadian opposition New Democratic and Liberal parties, and encouraged a groundswell of public opposition against the accord, which nearly killed it.

The cross-border anti-NAFTA protests that swept across North America from 1990–93 borrowed heavily from the anti-CUSFTA campaign. NAFTA shaped both national protests and transnational coalition-building and collaboration. As an international political opportunity structure shaping the protest strategies of civil society groups in three countries, NAFTA encouraged unprecedented cross-border collaboration between Canadian, US, and Mexican civil society groups, including cross-border coalition-building and protests along the US–Mexico border, joint conferences between Canadian, US, and Mexican groups, and the creation of similar cross-sectoral coalitions in the US and Mexico. Specifically, the organization form of the Pro-Canada Network clearly influenced the strategies of civil society groups in the US and Mexico, who created the Alliance for Responsible Trade (ART), the Citizens Trade Campaign (CTC), and the Mexican Action Network on Free Trade (RMALC). Although these coalitions coordinated national opposition and protests against NAFTA, they also cooperated strategically to plan joint conferences, road shows, and lobbying campaigns. In this instance, civil society mobilizing clearly affected the debate in the United States over the ratification of NAFTA, and encouraged then-President Clinton to propose the side agreements on labour and the environment to ensure NAFTA's passage through the US Congress. These side agreements, moreover, became, for a time, focal points for both national and transnational civil society protests to promote greater awareness of labour and environmental abuses in all three NAFTA states.

Beyond the CUSFTA and the NAFTA, North America was the setting for a number of other notable civil society protest campaigns against neoliberalism during the late 1990s. US-based groups, including the CTC and ART, mounted a successful campaign to derail the renewal of presidential fast-track negotiating authority in 1997–98; tens of thousands of civil society groups descended on the streets of Seattle in 1999 for the WTO Millennial Round; while thousands of eclectic civil society groups massed in the streets of Quebec City in April 2001 against the proposed Free Trade Area of the Americas. In each of these instances, activists targeted neoliberal arrangements and summits, challenging the TINA (There Is No Alternative) orthodoxy of the Washington Consensus and demanding greater democratic openness and access for civil society groups during negotiations. Their power was less material than symbolic and cognitive—civil society groups brought tremendous research expertise and organizing experience to these campaigns, disseminating knowledge and understandings of the proposed trade agreements through the Internet, email, and other forms of electronic communication.

Third Cycle of North American Contention: Occupy and Anti-Austerity

Some of the most dramatic manifestations of civil society contestation and engagement over the past several years can be illustrated in what we see as an ongoing third wave of global protests against neoliberalism and domestic and international democratic deficits. From the rubble-strewn European streets of Madrid, Rome, Lisbon, and especially Athens, to the rallies on Moscow's streets against ever-encroaching oligarchic rule in Russia, to massive, spontaneous, and widespread protests across Brazil against government corruption, to the phenomenal global diffusion of Occupy protests, to the tens of thousands of Quebec students who participated in the surprising *"printemps érable,"* or "maple spring," since late 2010, the world has been experiencing a new cycle of unrest against corporate power, inequality, austerity, and neoliberal democracy. Moreover, we differentiate two notable characteristics in this third wave of global protests

from the first two: there is a clear break across these globally and geographically dispersed protest campaigns from the "usual" connections to the political system, thus limiting the value of traditional political opportunity structure theory; and the content of these protests—the frames that are shaping the meanings inherent in these campaigns—and the styles of organizing, are frequently "post-hegemonic," demonstrating protestors' preference for non-hierarchical and leaderless decision-making.

Across North America, the student and Occupy protests were clearly connected to a growing and widespread sense that the representative institutions and the voting processes available to citizens had become irreparably constrained by 20 years of neoliberal policies. Neoliberal democratic deficits could mean many things to different constituencies but some of the key themes that have linked protests across North America in recent years are an appreciation of the huge income inequalities and concentrations of wealth characteristic of North American society, the undermining of governments by the corporate sector, and the sense that decision-making has been displaced to an increasingly unpredictable, and for many citizens, unfathomable global sphere.[32] There was a palpable sense that young people in both Canada and the US—clearly not unaware of the high rates of unemployment for those who at the same time had graduated college with immense debt—were facing a new austere era much different from that of their parents, one characterized by weak, slow growth economies and tight labour markets that seemed designed only to protect the jobs of their aging parents, not provide paths to economic betterment.[33]

Whether being pepper-sprayed on the campus of the University of California–Davis, roughed up by police on the streets of New York City at the City University of New York, or engaging in massive street protests against the government of Quebec Premier Jean Charest, students were protesting real or perceived cutbacks to educational access that undermined the affordability of a higher education, encouraged students to take on greater and greater debt, and seemed to further limit access to a higher standard of living and better quality of life.[34] The Occupy protest movement, which began in New York City, spread across most major cities in Canada and the US, and ultimately gained followers around the world, attempted to turn itself into genuine democratic constituent processes in the encampments that sprouted up in city parks and squares.[35] As Giroux put it:

> Both the Occupy Movement and the Quebec student resistance have ignited a new generation of young people who now face the ongoing challenge of developing a language and a politics that integrate a meaningful consideration of public values and imagine the possibilities of a democracy not wedded to the dictates of global capitalism.[36]

Although this third cycle of contention has been less characterized by strong cross-border coalitions than the protests of the first two phases, it does display strong tendencies toward cross-border emulation of tactics, symbols, and analyses that have spread rapidly across the globe in response to local, national, and global crises and austerity policies.

Conclusion

This brief review of the relationship between international political economy and civil society reveals the ways in which thinking about civil society is integral to every tradition of IPE theory, even if this dimension of the international system is not always explicitly addressed. The intensification of global interconnections over the last several decades, driven in part by the adoption of neoliberal policies by governments, has given rise to several cycles of contentious political action. As our review of IPE theories shows, all of the major theoretical traditions provide useful tools for analyzing the nature, impact, and driving forces behind global civil society organizing, even if they differ about the relative importance of civil society actors and their capacity to achieve change. In many ways, North America has been a crucible for transnational civil society organizing. Even if the heady days of organizing against free trade agreements are past, civil society actors continue to play an important role in identifying inequalities and injustices, and in envisioning alternative local, national, and global social orders.

Notes

1 See L. Macdonald, "Globalising civil society: Interpreting international NGOs in Central America." *Millennium 29*(2).

2 J. A. Scholte, "Civil society and governance," in M. Ougaard and R. Higgott (Eds), (2002), *Towards a global polity* (London: Routledge), 146. See also Jeffrey Ayres and Laura Macdonald (Eds), *Contentious politics in North America*, 6.

3 J. Smith and J. Bandy, (2005), "Introduction: Cooperation and conflict in Transnational Protest," in Joe Bandy and Jackie Smith (Eds), *Coalitions across borders: Transnational protest and the neoliberal order.* Lanham: Rowman & Littlefield, 3.

4 P. B. Evans, (2010), "Constructing the 21st century developmental state: Potentialities and pitfalls," in O. Edigheje, *Constructing a Democratic Developmental State in South Africa, Potentials and Challenges.* Cape Town, HRSRC Press, 46–7.

5 See F. Ignacio Leiva, (2012), *Latin American neostructuralism: The contradictions of post-neoliberal development* (Minneapolis: University of Minnesota Press), 2008; E. Silva, "Exchange rising? Karl Polanyi and contentious politics in contemporary Latin America. *Latin American Politics and Society 54*(3), 2–32.

6 K. Polanyi. *The great transformation.*

7 Naidoo (2003), 2, cited in C. Berry and C. Gabay, "Transnational political action and 'global civil society' in practice: The case of Oxfam." *Global Networks 9*(3), 2009, 339–58.

8 Kaldor (2005), cited in Berry and Gabay, 340.

9 L. Kriesberg, (1997), "Social movements and global transformation," in J. Smith, C. Chatfield, and R. Pagnucco (Eds), *Transnational social movements and global politics: Solidarity beyond the state.* Syracuse: Syracuse University Press, 4.

10 J. Smith, R. Pagnucco, and C. Chatfield, (1997), "Social movements and world politics: A theoretical framework," in J. Smith, C. Chatfield, and R. Pagnucco (Eds), *Transnational social movements and global politics: Solidarity beyond the state*. Syracuse: Syracuse University Press, 60.

11 R. Keohane and J. Nye, (1972), *Transnational relations and world politics*. Cambridge, MA: Harvard University Press.

12 R. O'Brien, A. M. Goetz, J. A. Scholte and M. Williams, (2000), *Contesting global governance: Multilateral economic institutions and global social movements*. Cambridge: Cambridge University Press, 4–5.

13 J. Ayres and L. Macdonald, (2009), "Introduction: Conceptualizing North American contentious politics." In J. Ayres and L. Macdonald (Eds), *Contentious politics in North America: National protest and transnational collaboration under continental integration*. Basingstoke: Palgrave Macmillan, 8.

14 R. Keohane and J. Nye, (2001), "Between centralization and fragmentation: The club model of multilateral cooperation and challenges of democratic legitimacy," John F. Kennedy School of Government Harvard University, Faculty Research Working Papers Series, February.

15 B. Gills, "Introduction." In Barry Gills (Ed.), *Globalization and the Politics of Resistance*. London: Macmillan, 3–11.

16 R. Germain and M. Kenny, "Engaging Gramsci: International relations theory and the new Gramscians," *Review of International Studies 24*(1), 3–21; S. Gill, "Toward a Postmodern Prince? The Battle in Seattle as a moment in the new politics of globalisation." *Millennium: Journal of International Studies 29*(1), 131–41; A. Morton, "Mexico, Neoliberal Restructuring and the EZLN: A Neo-Gramscian analysis," in B. Gills (Ed.) *Globalization and the politics of resistance*. London: Macmillan, 255–79.

17 C. Eschle and B. Maiguashca, (2005), "Introduction." In C. Eschle and B. Maiguashca (Eds). *Critical theories, international relations and 'the anti-globalisation movement': The politics of global resistance*. London: Routledge, 3.

18 Ibid., 4–5. See, however, L. Macdonald, (2004), "Gendering transnational social movement analysis: Women's groups contest free trade in the Americas," in J. Bandy and J. Smith (Eds), *Coalitions across borders: Transnational protest and the neo-liberal order*, Lanham: Rowman and Littlefield, 21–41; D. Caouette, D. Masson and P. Dufour, 2010, *Solidarities beyond borders: Transnationalizing women's movements*, Vancouver: UBC Press.

19 D. Slater, (1998), "Post-colonial questions for global times." *Review of International Political Economy 5*(4).

20 Ibid., 650.

21 B. de Sousa Santos, (2013), "The World Social Forum: Toward a counter-hegemonic globalisation (Part II), www.boaventuradesousasantos.pt/media/wsf_Jai%20senPart2.pdf on 6 November.

22 Ibid., 4.

23 This section draws upon content in Jeffrey Ayres and Laura Macdonald, "Transnational Protest," paper presented at the annual meeting of the Canadian Association of Latin American and Caribbean Studies, Ottawa, May 3–5, 2013.

24 S. Tarrow, (2011), *Power in movement: Social movements and contentious politics*, 3rd ed., New York: Cambridge University Press.

25 E. Friesen, (2012), *Challenging global finance: Civil society and transnational networks*. Basingstoke: Palgrave Macmillan.

26 J. Ayres, (1998), *Defying conventional wisdom: Political movements and popular contention against North American free trade*. Toronto: University of Toronto Press; J. Shoch, 2000, "Contesting globalization: Organized labor, NAFTA, and the 1997 and 1998 fast track fights," *Politics and Society 28*(1), 119–50; P. Smith and E. Smythe, 1999, "Globalization, citizenship and technology: The MAI meets the Internet." *Canadian Foreign Policy 7*(2), 83–105.

27 Ayres, *Defying Conventional Wisdom*.

28 P. Riggirozzi and D. Tussie (Eds), (2012), *The rise of post-hegemonic regionalism: The case of Latin America*. Dordrecht: Springer.

29 H. Mackinlay and G. Otero, (2004), "State corporatism and peasant organizations: Towards new institutional arrangements," in Gerardo Otero (Ed.), *Mexico in transition: Neoliberal globalism, the state and civil society*. New York: Zed Books.

30 Mi. Díaz-Barriga, (1998), "Beyond the domestic and the public: *Colonas* participation in urban movements in Mexico City," in S. E. Alvarez, E. Dagnino, and A. Escobar, (Eds), *Cultures of politics, politics of cultures: Re-visioning Latin American social movements*. Boulder: Westview, 225.

31 J. Foweraker, (1990), "Popular movements and political change in Mexico," in J. Foweraker and A. L. Craig (Eds), *Popular movements and political change in Mexico*. Boulder: Lynne Rienner, 7.

32 V. Moghadam, (2013), *Globalization and social movements*, 2nd ed. Lanham, MD: Rowman and Littlefield.

33 R. Sears, (2011–12), "From Cairo to Canada, a very big year." *Policy Options*, December–January, 17–23.

34 E. Pineault, (2012), "Quebec's red spring: An essay on ideology and social conflict at the end of neoliberalism." *Studies in Political Economy 90* and Andrei Cherny, 2011, "American spring." *Democracy Journal* (Fall).

35 M. Hardt and A. Negri, "The fight for 'real democracy' at the heart of Occupy Wall Street." *Foreign Affairs*, available at: www.foreignaffairs.com/print/98542.

36 H. Giroux, (2013), "The Quebec student protest movement in the age of neoliberal terror." *Social Identities 19*(5), 515–35.

Key Terms

civil society

civil society organizations (CSO)

complex multilateralism

cosmopolitan liberalism

cycle of contention

transnational social movements

Questions for Review

1. How do different theoretical approaches to international political economy conceptualize the role of civil society in the global arena?

2. How has the role of civil society in the global system changed since the 1980s?

3. What role has civil society played in political debates in Canada and North America regarding trade liberalization and globalization?

4. Do you think civil society actors should play a greater role in global decision-making regarding economic issues? What problems or obstacles do these actors face when they attempt to influence on this type of decision-making?

Further Resources

Ayres, J. *Defying conventional wisdom: Political movements and popular contention against North American free trade.*

Ayres, J. and Macdonald, L. (Eds). *Contentious politics in North America: National protest and transnational collaboration under continental integration.*

Bandy, J. and Smith, J. (Eds). *Coalitions across borders: Transnational protest and the neoliberal order.*

Moghadam, V. M. (2013). *Globalization and Social Movements*, 2nd ed. Lanham, MD: Rowman and Littlefield.

O'Brien, R., Goetz, A. M., Scholte, J. A., and Williams, M. *Contesting global governance: Multilateral economic institutions and global social movements.*

Van Rooy, A. (2004). *The global legitimacy game: Civil society, globalization and protest.* New York: Palgrave.

Scholte, J. A. (Ed.). (2011). *Building global democracy? Civil society and accountable global governance.* Cambridge: Cambridge University Press.

Smith, J. (2007). *Social movements for global democracy.* Baltimore, MD: John's Hopkins University Press.

19 Understanding Industrial Policy

Anil Hira

This chapter introduces students to the topic of industrial policy from the perspective of political economy. We can think of any economy as being made up of a series of different types of industries, loosely defined as any productive money-making activity. Industrial policy is a somewhat subjective term, in the sense that it is used differently by different people at different times. However, there is a common thread—namely the idea that government can promote certain industries through policy. By definition, therefore, **industrial policy** is about domestic policies. However, this chapter will also cover the implications for international political economy (IPE) by discussing three main issues. The first concerns the central debate about the effectiveness of the role of government in promoting industrial policy. In other words, can the state really promote industries? As we shall see, this debate has deep and lasting historical reverberations, including whether industrial policy has damaging effects on the possibility for trade and investment. The second issue is, if industrial policy can make a difference in some circumstances, what types of policies make sense for which types of situations? This overlaps with the third

main issue, which is, in a world of globalizing production, can industrial policy still be effective? As we work through the chapter, we will see that regardless of the theoretical merits, industrial policy is omnipresent, and that the true answers to these questions depend in good part on the time, place, and industry in question.

Definition of Industrial Policy

Like most social science terms, industrial policy varies in its usage. However, we can suggest that it usually refers to policies that affect the operating environment for businesses within an industry(ies) for a social purpose. Generally speaking, the social purpose is the creation of employment, revenues, new businesses, and new technologies by improving the competitiveness of local industries.

Debate 1: Is Industrial Policy Effective?

The debate over whether industrial policy is effective ramps up in the nineteenth century, based upon the work of the classical political economy thinkers mentioned in the introductory chapter. They are the foundation for the emerging discipline of economics, and with it, the battle over industrial policy that reaches its climax in the middle of the twentieth century, with the emergence of communism as an alternative to capitalism as a means of organizing an economy. Once that battle ended, the debate about industrial policy largely disappeared from general US/UK political economy discussions about economic policy, with the exception of those who study development. With the dominance of the Anglo-American laissez-faire approach to economic policy, it is no wonder that the anti-industrial policy camp has dominated decision-making, even if the approach is limited, in practice, by pragmatic considerations.

Industrial Policy Is Ineffective

Any discussion of industrial policy has to begin with the father of modern economics, Adam Smith. Adam Smith's book, *The Wealth of Nations* (1776), provides the core argument behind our conceptions about the optimality of market forces for deciding upon the allocation of resources rather than states. We have to remember that Smith was writing at a time when state intervention under the colonial era policy of mercantilism was the central feature of economic policy. By mercantilism, we refer to the policies by European colonial powers during the fifteenth to the early twentieth centuries to privilege production of their own goods, using primary product resources from their colonies to produce and consume the finished products, and creating barriers such as tariffs (taxes on imports) for goods from their competitors. As Smith correctly points out, these sets of policies reduced trade, and often led to production inefficiencies, as higher cost countries entered into industries in which they were less competitive. National competitiveness, according to Smith, rested only partly

on natural endowments of resources, such as climate and land. It also depended upon the "skill, dexterity and judgment with which its labour is generally applied (8)." Smith points out that using money that is readily exchangeable as a store of value is behind the ability of countries previously mired in feudalism to develop rapidly (265). Currency allows for the exchange of different products and services as well as being a store of value that can be invested into larger projects, thus enabling trade.

Perhaps the most important idea from Smith is the division of labour. Smith pointed out that, even in the simplest situation, producing a metal pin, breaking the production process down into its various components and allowing different people with different sets of skills to focus on each component leads to much more efficient production than one person trying to complete the process by themselves (13–16). Specialization of labour comes from the fact that every person and every country is naturally endowed with a different set of resources, skills, and talents, as well as the knowledge acquired over time from doing the same task. As Smith states, (293) "[I]f a foreign country can supply us with the commodity cheaper than we ourselves can make it, better buy it off them with some part of the produce of our own industry employed in a way in which we have some advantage." He goes on to say that through specialization, the capital of the country and its resources can be put to its "greatest advantage." This notion is the core idea behind absolute advantage, that is, the idea that some nations are better at producing some things than others, which in turn is the foundation for our ideas behind the superiority of free trade. David Ricardo extended Smith's analysis to show quite plainly that "comparative advantage," that is relative efficiency in producing one type of product versus another (versus absolute amounts, as Smith contended) provided an even stronger logical argument for free trade. Smith refers specifically to "bounties" (subsidies) that were given by governments at that time to local manufacturers (313) and which go against comparative advantage. He points out that the net result of this was to create market distortions that benefited a few people but at higher prices and costs for everyone else. Moreover, he introduced the idea that such favouritism helps local manufacturers, "not by their own improvement, but by the depression of those of all our neighbors (376)," reinforcing the idea that barriers to trade hurt the general welfare, and implying that it would lead to reciprocal actions on the part of other countries. *The laissez-faire point of view concludes that industrial policy destroys the natural efficiency gains of fair trade through specialization and trade based upon comparative advantage.*

Although Smith laid the foundations, certainly the most important thinker behind the skepticism about industrial policy is Friedrich Hayek. Hayek's *The Road To Serfdom*, written in 1944,[1] inspired a generation of future economists, including Milton Friedman, who developed a very strong case for allowing markets to choose "winners" and "losers." Hayek was writing in the context of the rise of both communism and fascism, when central planning was viewed as a possible alternative method of organizing the economy. Hayek believed that there was no middle ground between planning the entire system and making it open to competition (90). He believed that planning is bound to fail, because managing an economy is very different from managing the war, in which there is one clear goal. In an economy there are "different needs of different people" (106). Planning, in turn, inevitably leads to a form of political dictatorship, as someone must decide what should be produced and when, adjusting to circumstances as they arise (110 & 113). To counteract dictatorship, Hayek recommends having the rule of law, which levels the playing field and allows for fair competition (120). Moreover, the idea of making private property public only exacerbates inequality because concentration of power leads to concentration of resources, and the idea that we could all agree upon what a fair wage is for each occupational task is impractical given the range of effort and quality of skills of individuals (135 & 140–1). Although he is not against "adequate security against severe privation," it should be provided in such a way that it does not interfere with markets and competition, which, while not perfect, offers the best combination of individual freedom and opportunity for improvement (156). Hayek's ideas continue today in the economic school of public choice, which suggests in part that special interests engage in **regulatory capture**, that is, companies and organizations can rig the rules of the market or government interests for their own pecuniary interests. *Hayek is a key thinker in the century-long battle between communism and capitalism. His perspective highlights the negative effects of states picking "winners" as opposed to the benefits of competition as an indictment of industrial policy.*

Industrial Policy is Effective

The other side of the debate has at its foundation the work of John Maynard Keynes, a contemporary of Hayek. It is also important to understand the context in which Keynes's masterwork, *The General Theory of Employment, Interest, and Money*, was published in 1936—the height of the Great Depression. It was an era when classical economics had seemingly failed, and the threat of both fascism and communism as alternative economic systems was quite real. Keynes pointed out that there could be structural glitches in the economy that could prevent adjustment during downturns. For example, wages could be "sticky" downwards, meaning that wage rates would reduce much more slowly than prices during downturns, thus unemployment could continue to be a problem. If prices declined faster, businesses could not afford to pay workers higher wages. The essential problem of downturns came, according to Keynes, from a crisis of confidence in which investment dried up along with economic activity, even if savings continued. As investment declined, employment and wages would also decline, leading to a "liquidity trap." During such periods, it is necessary for the government to use spending to "pump the prime," or to reignite business activity and investment to get out of the trap. Government spending goes well beyond the formal amounts because of the "multiplier effect." By multiplier effect, Keynes refers to the idea that money spent in one transaction, for example, payment for a good, will then be spent multiple times because a person receiving payment will then purchase another good or service. Therefore, money spent today will lead to rising wages and employment tomorrow. It is interesting to note that Keynes's analysis is based in part on the idea that we are partly motivated by emotion, what he called "animal spirits"; thus government can restore confidence. The premise of emotion-based economic decision-making has generally been ignored in the rational choice direction of much of the IPE literature as noted in the introduction. Keynes's ideas are largely credited with "saving" capitalism as economies recovered going into the Second World War, largely through the stimulus of large public investment, as well as war expenditures. *Keynes therefore contributes the idea that during severe economic downturns, government intervention may be necessary to rescue the economy, thus legitimizing the prioritization of domestic over global policies.*

Although Keynes is the most important scholar for government intervention during crises, other thinkers lay the foundations for a more active and ongoing intervention that has more commonly been associated with industrial policy. Foremost among these is Friedrich List. A German scholar, List wrote *The National System of Political Economy* in 1885, in direct response to Adam Smith. List's argument is more subtle than has been subsequently depicted. He points out, foremost, that the proponents of free trade are centred in England, and sees this as no coincidence. He mentions a number of times that because England is predominant in manufacturing a move toward free trade locks in those advantages. This argument has been echoed over time in regard to the global North–South divide. Thus List underscores the all-important issue of timing. Although he supports free trade within a nation, and at the onset of industrialization, to reduce the costs of initial inputs and equipment, he believes that there is an intermediate stage in which some protection is necessary to provide an atmosphere conducive to national manufacturing. Through historical studies of Italy, Germany, England, and the US, he seeks to show that this has been the pattern where manufacturing has taken hold. He thereby accuses the English of hypocrisy (25).

His argument has evidence behind it. The English protected agricultural interests in the nineteenth century through the Corn Laws, the profit of which List claims was used to fund the initial move toward manufacturing, and, on achieving independence, the Americans set high tariffs to protect their nascent manufacturers. List also claims, interestingly, that industrialization, in transforming the economy, goes hand-in-hand with individual liberty and strong social institutions (107). In this direction, he directly confronts the Smithian vision of society. He criticizes Smith's philosophy as leading to an overemphasis on individualism and materialism to the detriment of the collective, particularly national, interests (136–7). Instead, he suggests that the "productive powers" for aggregate production of the nation are far more important than the "values of exchange" or level of trade (170). List goes on to state that, therefore, in times of war, agricultural producers are vulnerable to the cost of trade, while manufacturing nations are more self-sufficient (244), reflecting the differential powers of the South and North in the US Civil War and another ongoing debate in the IPE of development. List also has an interesting idea about the sources of economic growth ultimately lying in "mental capital," referring to the level of education of the country (140), which appears later as the term "human capital" in the economic growth and development literatures. If we accept the notion of human capital, such as education and health expenditures increasing productivity, then we have already gone beyond the Smithian and Ricardian notion that natural endowments should determine what a country should produce.

The justification for state intervention via industrial policy ultimately comes down to the idea that there are barriers to entry in a number of sectors, and that the natural industrial organization is not perfect competition, as Smith and Hayek presupposed, but oligopoly, thus calling into question both the natural hand of market discipline and the idea that consumers have the ultimate power. In fact, we see oligopolies in large manufacturing industries such as the auto industry, and often even in many agricultural sectors such as coffee, where four roasters dominate global production. The key implication is that state subsidization (whether direct or indirect, see below) to overcome barriers to entry can be justified because real competition in the long run is about market share, not price. If a company can push out rivals, it will enjoy consistent oligopoly rents, and be in a position to use those rents to maintain its position through further developing the product, tailoring it for niche markets, buying out upstarts, etc.

List presages much of the discourse of development, including the ideas that developing countries are disadvantaged because of their late industrialization; that the state is the only actor capable of promoting collective national economic interests; and that protectionism may be necessary for countries seeking to "catch up." List's criticism of Britain's "kicking away the ladder" for those industrializing later reflects the dynamic between the North and the South in multilateral negotiations (see below). Most international agreements now contain differential clauses for developing countries.

Industrial Policy to Promote Innovation

If we see industrial policy as intimately tied to sources of economic growth, then there is considerable overlap with the debate about the relation between innovation and growth. Joseph Alois Schumpeter is the key scholar on this topic. His masterwork, *Business Cycles* (1939), deals with a most vexing problem in economics, the fact that our economies go through occasional up- and downturns. For Marxists, this is proof of the volatility and eventual self-destruction of the capitalist system, as owners of capital increasingly squeeze workers. In contrast to Keynes's diagnosis of liquidity traps, Schumpeter coined the term "**creative destruction**" to refer to the idea that new innovations in product or process could shake up markets. The phenomenon seems obvious to us now, for example seeing the movement from the vinyl record to the CD to the MP3, with different companies getting shaken out along the way.

Schumpeter suggested that there are two modes by which innovation wreaks havoc. The first, mode 1, refers to individual entrepreneurs who achieve breakthroughs that then shake up markets. We often think of Steve Jobs of Apple in this way. The second, mode 2, refers to the increasingly complex and costly processes of research and development in some fields, such as pharmaceuticals. In these fields, Schumpeter argues that there is something akin to economies of scale, the idea that producing larger amounts reduces per unit costs in research and development (R&D). Schumpeter suggests that R&D on a large scale requires large organizations, and could quite possibly lead to oligopolies. In this matter, he was also prescient, as we are equally concerned today about the market power and concentration of companies like Microsoft and Apple. In later works, Schumpeter warned that such oligopolies could come to wield dominating political influence, something we are all too aware of. In sum, Schumpeter saw innovation breakthroughs as creating business cycles as old companies fall behind and new ones are created. *Schumpeter's contribution is to link innovation with economic growth. Therefore the state has a role through industrial policy to promote entrepreneurship and to support large scale research and development.*

Case 1: When does Industrial Policy Succeed? The Case of the Argentine vs. Brazilian Aerospace Industries

In the 1950s, under President Juan Perón, Argentina developed advanced planes with the help of former Nazi engineers recruited for that purpose. This early head start gave Argentina the possibility of developing an airplane manufacturing industry, one that could create a number of jobs and positive spillover effects. Argentina's jet fighters, though state-of-the-art at one time, never led to commercial success for a variety of reasons. One reason was the volatile political situation within the country, which led to inconsistent support, including frequent changes in management and an inability to provide insulation from unpredictable financial shifts. Another reason was the lack of long-term vision for the industry, as well as how it could be shifted into self-sustainability. Where Argentina failed, Brazil was able to support, both directly and indirectly, Embraer, now the third-largest international aircraft manufacturer. Brazil struggled for several decades with issues similar to Argentina's;

however, it was far more consistent in developing industrial policies over the long term to support Embraer's success. Part of these policies included setting up a research centre to continually improve its designs. Moreover, like the US and Europe, Brazil has used defence contracts to cross-subsidize its commercial aviation industry, something Argentina did only inconsistently. In the 1990s, Embraer was privatized and grew into a successful commercial enterprise. However, perhaps as a sign of future industrial policy, the Brazilian government still maintains a strong influence on the company's board. It is inconceivable to think of Embraer as a successful private aircraft manufacturer without Brazilian industrial policy (Hira and de Oliveira 2007).

How the Debate about Industrial Policy Played Out in Canada: Addressing the Staples Issue

Any review of Canadian industrial policy has to begin with the work of Harold Innis. Innis's staples theory matches that used by many development economists, such as Raúl Prebisch, to try to explain why there is so much divergence in levels of development both globally and within regions. The **staples** approach begins with the idea that regions that focus on commodity production to the exclusion of other activities are likely to suffer from recurring development issues. These include continually fluctuating prices for commodities, an inability to develop large numbers of stable, middle-class income and employment, and an inability to maintain pace with manufacturing regions. Fluctuating prices can have devastating effects on the ability to plan for the long term, and to make long-term investments. In technology-intensive resource extraction sectors such as mining, the levels of employment created at the middle levels of income are extremely limited. Moreover, such enterprises can suffer from the "Dutch disease" whereby during booms, a currency is likely to soar in value, making imports much cheaper, thus wiping out other industries. Last, over time, we expect that the increasing sophistication of products through technological and design breakthroughs, such as the movement from film to digital cameras, means that the overall value of most products relies much less on the raw materials and unskilled labour, and more on the "value added" aspects of production, which transform those materials into consumer and business products. A computer, for example, is worth far more than the value of the raw materials used to build it. Therefore, the staples theory expects that since the nature of raw materials does not change, and since demand for them is limited (as opposed to luxury goods or services), as income rises, the relative price of them vis à vis manufactured goods will decline.

Thus, the history of Canada as a source of raw materials, from the fur trade to the more recent petroleum boom in Alberta, is the central problematique for understanding the difficulties of creating an industrial policy at the national level where commodities play such a significant role, as is the case in most of the developing world. On top of this central issue axis, we can overlay the secondary axis of regional differentiation. Of course, regional differentiation has linguistic, cultural, and historical components too; for example, in regard to the separatist movement in Quebec. Nonetheless, many of the core claims of the separatist movement had to do with perceived discrimination against francophones, leading to differential economic fortunes. The fact that Canada is run as a federation both reflects and reinforces regional differences, which has played out in terms of "equalization payments" designed to reduce regional

inequalities. Some of the equalization took the form of industrial policies to diversify and support local economies that lagged, such as Newfoundland when the fisheries collapsed. As such, they have generally been criticized by Canadian economists as being boondoggles, futile in changing natural comparative advantage and a waste of taxpayer resources.

In practice, Canadian industrial policy has largely been a secondary interest given the high level of economic dependence on foreign investment, with political and social considerations to maintain national unity largely trumping developing new industries. Ironically, this avowedly laissez-faire approach has historically accompanied consistent support of private enterprise, from private railroad consortia to the more recent (2008) bailout of US auto branch manufacturers. There have, nonetheless, been occasional periods and ongoing pockets of more direct industrial policy activity, as we discuss below.

As Brodie (1990) points out (16), one way to understand the different groups in the equation is to differentiate resource-consuming from resource-producing regions. Ontario, as the industrial heartland of Canada, is the main province in the former category. Thus, the suggestion is that political confederation in Canada was motivated in part by the need to create strong East–West transportation links, particularly railway links, in order to further develop the frontier as well as to ensure that the US would not effectively control Western Canada. Canada's first industrial policies arguably begin with the National Policy of 1879, when the Macdonald government created a high tariff to protect nascent manufacturing (Howlett, Netherton, and Ramesh 1999, 298). The same government provided subsidies and monopoly rights to a private consortium to build the Canadian Pacific Railroad, linking Central Canada to the West (Hale 2006, 115). The railways were eventually consolidated under the Canadian National Railway in 1919 when many faced bankruptcy (Howlett, Netherton, and Ramesh 1999, 299). These efforts paralleled the development of the strong wheat production built in the Canadian prairies, as well as the beginnings of resentment from that region and Western Canada. The development of the wheat economy rested on industrial policies, ones that developed frost-hardy wheat and created pro-immigration settlement policies for the Prairies. Resentment in Western Canada derived from the sense that the National Policy favoured Ontario and Quebec manufacturing and services because of revenues from their commodity production. For example, the Canadian Pacific Railway charged higher rates for goods per kilometer from the Prairie provinces compared with the rates in Eastern Canada in the late nineteenth century (Brodie 1990, 114). During this time, an important precedent was set with the creation of provincially controlled energy providers, such as Ontario Hydro, setting aside at least one sector that continues to be in public hands.

By 1929, much of the industry in Quebec had moved to Ontario. The First World War also brought with it a huge influx of US direct investment, leading to the setting up of a number of branch plants for American manufacturing in Ontario. In part, this was a reflection of growing American economic power, and in part a desire to gain access to Canadian markets and through them, the preferential treatment of Canadian exports throughout the Commonwealth (Brodie, 138–9). However, the onset of the Great Depression led to the Second National Policy in 1940. In the context of collapsing exports, the federal government vastly increased the provision of social welfare and employment policies. In terms of industrial policies, by the late 1940s the Canadian government had moved back to championing economic integration with the US, with the idea of embracing Canada's role as a natural resource provider (Brodie, 149 & 152).

In 1957, the Gordon Commission issued an influential report that criticized the growing influence of foreign investment and pointed out the fact of increasingly uneven regional development (Brodie, 162–3). This was despite the fact that the pro-free trade St Laurent government had created Trans-Canada airlines (later Air Canada) and built the Trans-Canada pipeline (Hale 2006, 136). The report laid the groundwork for a new axis of industrial policy, paralleling provincial equalization payments. The latter refers to the postwar transfer payments from "have" to "have not" provinces, relating in part to the collapse of the fisheries economy in Atlantic Canada during this time. From the 1960s, the federal government, working through the provinces, offered significant development funds for new industries or to revive old ones, such as investments in rural development in Atlantic Canada (Brodie, 171).

The peak of economic nationalism occurred during the Trudeau administration in the 1970s. These efforts reflected a general breakdown in trust between business and government leaders (Hale 2006, 151). The breakdown was a result of the perceived deterioration of Canadian competitiveness from the late 1950s, including increases in imports; slowing of productivity growth; increasing competition for Canadian manufacturing from emerging economies; and a lack of economies of scale to compete in global markets (Howlett, Netherton, and Ramesh 1999, 300). The combination of these factors suggests two possible logical solutions—either to develop stronger national champions who could compete or integrate with multinational companies, primarily from the US. Both options have met resistance, though by the 1980s the second had won. Resistance comes in good part from Canadian history, reflecting the close ties between the Canadian state and local and US business interests. Such relations are critically examined in a strain of Canadian academic writing that was distrustful, and remains so, of long-standing links between the Canadian government and local business elites. Such critics point to concentration in key economic spheres as favouring connected groups, such as air transport (Air Canada) and telecommunications, where a few large media companies dominate, and in areas such as energy and automobiles, where they feel that national interests have been sold out to foreign ownership (Brownlee 2005).

Trudeau created the Canadian Development Corporation to fund entrepreneurs, developed the national industrial strategy, announced in 1972, and established the Foreign Investment Review Agency (FIRA) to review and potentially reject new foreign investments unless they were of "significant benefit to Canada." The crown jewel of state intervention was the creation of Petro-Canada. As oil prices began to soar in the 1970s, and large parts of Canada began suffering from related inflation, Trudeau introduced the National Energy Policy (NEP), which sought to promote new exploration and further develop Petro-Canada's position of asserting Canadian control over local resources. Furthermore, through price controls and changes in revenue sharing from oil rents, the federal government sought to redistribute wealth from producing to consuming provinces. The end result was a rebellion on the part of the western producing provinces and the conclusion that Canada could not compete alone as a manufacturer in an increasingly global market (Brodie 1990, 188 & 209).

The idea of the exploitation of the resource-producing provinces, as implied by the staples theory, has never been wholeheartedly accepted (Brodie, 24). Rather, the predominant mode of thinking in Canada is more along the lines of Smith's idea of laissez-faire liberalism. As Howlett and Ramesh (1992, 234–5) remark, the conclusion

reached by most Canadian economists was that manufacturing industries established as a result of protection never fully outgrew their infancy. Competitiveness was even less likely with the onset of new manufacturing powers from East Asia by the 1970s, by which time Canadian radio, television, and rubber manufacturers had been wiped out by foreign competition. On top of this was a growing and continuing skepticism about the effectiveness of Canadian industrial policy, both from the point of view of capture by special interests, and of bureaucratic efficacy (Atkinson and Powers 1987). Therefore, the above episodes, such as Trudeau's NEP, can be understood more as deviations than course corrections. The Third National Policy under the Mulroney government of the 1980s went back to the predominant paradigm, making a free trade agreement with the US its centrepiece. The influential Macdonald Commission delivered its report in 1985, providing the deathblow for interventionist strategy, and embracing continental integration (Brodie 1990, 189 & 219). These movements in Canada parallel the rise of neoliberalism in the US and the UK under Reagan and Thatcher, and can be seen as part of a broader international shift toward the Hayekian vision of economics. The signing of the North American Free Trade Agreement (NAFTA) in 1992 virtually sealed in the strategy of continental integration.

The current Canadian approach towards industrial policy remains eclectic given the overt acceptance of laissez-faire approaches. There are some elements of supporting companies that help to improve political aims, such as the support for Quebec-based Bombardier. On the provincial level, there are still important assets operated as Crown corporations. Most provinces still have government monopolies in charge of electricity generation, such as BC Hydro, and all except Alberta (where only the retail level has been privatized) monopolize liquor sales. Various reasons have been given to justify continuing these efforts, from natural monopoly regulation (BC Hydro) to infrastructure development (BC Ferries) to stabilization of income during economic transition (Cape Breton Development Corporation, which ran the coal industry until 2000) to control of externalities (provincial liquor boards) (Eckert and West 2005, 13–14). Skepticism about the benefits of privatizing such assets abounds; the privatization of Ontario Hydro was reversed in the early 2000s when prices skyrocketed.

Most industry supports policies from the federal government that are oriented toward R&D subsidies given out with the help of provincial agencies. There are a number of programs that seek to improve Canadian competitiveness in both declining and emerging industries through R&D, given a general consensus that Canada lags in innovation by standard measures, such as patents. These include, for example, the National Research Council of Canada, Genome Canada, and Western Economic Diversification. A relatively new agency, Sustainable Development Technology Canada, seeks to provide venture capital for new technology start-ups. Nonetheless, by OECD measures, the level of resources offered is below that of other competitors in a comparable situation, such as the Scandinavian countries. The spreading of resources across a wide variety of sectors that changes over time, such as a recently announced program for research into new technologies that will help to revive the Canadian auto manufacturing industry, reflects the lack of consensus as well as the inability to create national champions that can compete globally. Where there are glimpses of success, such as Blackberry, they have been too mercurial to capture policy-makers' imagination.

As Howlett and Ramesh state (1992, 245): "There has been no dearth, then of industrial policies in Canada. But a collection of policies does not necessarily make an industrial strategy." They go on to point out that (251) there are severe institutional constraints for developing an industrial policy in Canada. These go beyond the limited size of Canada and its resource-based economy. The nature of federalism, the fragmentation of national labour unions, and the long-standing penetration of the business sector by US interests all constrain the possibilities for a coherent long-term strategy. The end result, as we have seen, is a set of industrial policies that are situationally based, and reflect political compromise and interesting but often fleeting initiatives (Howlett, Netherton, and Ramesh 1999, 314).

The debate over the effectiveness of industrial policy continues despite the interventionist theories developed through the twentieth century. There are always examples of government debacles in trying to develop industries, such as Japan's failure to develop an aerospace industry despite many millions of dollars and multiple efforts. Canada has also had its share of failures, such as the collapse of one-time telecom giant Nortel in the early 2000s. Answers to the question have never been definitive. For those who fall into the positivistic camp informed by mainstream economics, it seems clear that global efficiency is diminished by industrial policy intervention. However, the question becomes much more convoluted when we start to look at relative (national and local) long-term gains vs. absolute short-term gains for the world economy, particularly if we consider innovation. It is thus impossible in practice to find an economy or company where industrial policy has not played some role (Hira 2007); even the Internet, the backbone of free-flowing entrepreneurship was developed by the US Defense Advanced Research Projects Agency (DARPA). Qualitatively and historically oriented scholars, in turn, point to the development of East Asia through active industrial policies as proof that late developers need industrial policy to catch up. If we conclude that industrial policy can play a useful role, then we arrive at a set of secondary debates. These include issues of timing, such as can government lead the economy into new industries or only play a supportive role? There are few, if any, cases where a government has created an industry; Cuba's generic pharmaceutical industry is one. If the government is to play a supportive role, what type of role does that entail? To answer these questions, we turn to policy instruments.

Debate 2: Which Policy Instruments?

Policy instruments refer to the tools that governments can use to regulate and support industries. We say regulate, meaning the rules of markets, because, as in the wider debate about industrial policy, there is a parallel debate about policy instruments. Some see market-reinforcing instruments as the way to go, while others believe more direct interventions are sometimes justified.

Indirect Instruments

Those who fall into the market camp see the government's role as being primarily one of regulating markets. A government could ensure that there is adequate and reliable information on market prices. We see this in terms of the regulation of stock market and commodity exchanges where the government enforces the posting of accurate pricing information and may even create the exchange itself. A government indirectly influences the business environment in a myriad of ways. For example, when governments operate in deficit, they tend to "crowd out" private investment by soaking up some of the available capital for financing. They may thus raise the costs for businesses to borrow. Governments that impose environmental regulations are often accused of creating an additional burden on companies, which they claim is unfair if their competitors outside the system do not have to abide by them. Thus, for a market-oriented person, industrial policy is really about making sure that the market is functioning well. This could include taking care of "market failures." For example, there were a number of lawsuits in the US and Europe about Microsoft's bundling of Internet Explorer with its dominant Windows operating system. The successful suits claimed that Microsoft was using its market power to constrain and unduly push out competition in the Internet browser market. Scholars in this vein are generally fine with the government providing financing for basic R&D. What government should not do is to "pick winners" as this disrupts and distorts the ability of the market to seek efficiency through competition, and for entrepreneurs to develop innovations.

Direct Instruments

Whereas market-oriented scholars prefer the use of indirect instruments when necessary, the other perspective is that the government can and should pick winners, even if some of them end up losing. This perspective is built on the idea that there are barriers to entry for any industry. These could, for example, be based on late entry into an industry, requiring knowledge catch-up; economies of scale of production, finance, supply, or buyer chains; and predatory practices of incumbent firms, such as a coffee chain purchasing local upstarts to put the competition out of business. Thus scholars in this camp often refer to infant industries, meaning industries trying to break into an established business, that need government support. The expectation is that once they have reached a certain level of production, they can "grow up," meaning they can be weaned off support. There are numerous examples of infant industries that both failed and succeeded, yet we have no clear theory about why.

A rich literature for that task focuses on the industrialization of East Asia (Hira 2007). This literature points to the synergy of public and private sectors in promoting national export champions. Authors like Robert Wade claim that East Asian governments were able to "govern" markets in the sense of intervening without undermining competition. This was done in part though offering subsidies to national companies tied to the achievement of explicit targets; supporting multiple national companies and letting them compete for future support; and protecting those companies domestically but forcing them to compete in world markets through export targets. Under what conditions and in what situations do such interventions work, and what types of interventions are best for what types of situations is an agenda for future research in industrial policy.

National Innovation Systems and Clusters Approaches

Building on Schumpeter, Richard Nelson's work (1993) on **national innovation systems (NIS)** is the latest instalment in the theoretical foundations for innovation and industrial policy. NIS sees the possibility for creating the institutional foundations of innovation, thus maintaining the lead in competitiveness, and thus capturing the main rents from production. The NIS literature suggests that for any industry there are knowledge, production, and regulatory inputs; these can be seen as the primary elements of an innovation system. That is, any industry needs know-how and continual innovation in product and process; production agents who are continually improving through profit-seeking; and government to help coordinate and support those agents. The NIS approach suggests therefore that there should be a coordinated effort of researchers (including but not exclusive to academics); producers (the private sector); and government.

Although the NIS was originally conceived of in national terms, it has also been very useful in explaining regional situations like Silicon Valley, the centre of US information technology (IT) activity, where a cluster of producers are geographically concentrated. Clusters such as this are impossible to explain in terms of comparative advantage; anyone who sees the astronomical real estate prices in Silicon Valley can see that. But there are two world class research universities in the area, UC Berkeley and Stanford; historical government support through defence contracts; and a reasonably well-organized set of industry associations.

Clusters are one example of what are called "spillover effects" or "positive externalities" in industrial policy. Spillover effects refer to the indirect benefits of developing a local industry. Direct benefits, of course, include employment, tax revenues, and earnings from the sale of the production and services. Indirect benefits could include any economic development related to having that industry in a certain locale. In developing a wine industry, for example, tourism for other local attractions can be expected to boom along with the wine industry. Similarly, the development of expertise in advanced agro-industrial techniques related to the wine industry could lead to improvement in productivity and other local agricultural sectors. Even if one accepts the potential effectiveness of either indirect or direct policy instruments, there is increasing skepticism about whether such policies can be effective given the globalization of production for most products.

Case 2: The Rise of Nokia as a Cell Phone Manufacturer

In the 1990s, an unlikely new company came to dominate a new, but eventually almost universal, consumer product, the wireless cell phone. Nokia is a Finnish company that began as a pulp and wood mill, moved into rubber boots, and at one time even produced TVs. Finland is not a place we would ordinarily think of as a hotbed for high-tech manufacturing. Though the story is complicated, the long distances of the Finnish frontier led to military contracts that created the initial technology for Nokia's cell phones. However, industrial policy also played a vital role. It is interesting to note that after Nokia's initial success, the Finnish government openly adopted the NIS approach. It began to invest serious resources into producing engineers, and subsidizing research and development for wireless technology. The government also helped the company to survive a financial crisis. Among other things the government helped to create European standards for cell phone transmissions which gave its national champion a decided competitive edge. Although the company is currently on the wane, the lessons of its rise in a most unlikely place reinforce the possibility that in certain sectors many different countries could develop the sources of dynamic comparative advantage around human capital and specialization in technologies. The key factor from this case is to recognize the importance of timing, what I call "innovation windows" (Hira 2012).

Debate 3: Is Industrial Policy Still Effective Under Globalization

Raymond Vernon's seminal work can be seen to work with Schumpeter's ideas and begin to explain why location still matters in a global world. In a recent article, I tried to merge the two theories (Hira, Wixted, and Arechavala 2012). Vernon was trying to explain the location of production, and helps us to understand how innovation can trump comparative advantage. In particular, he helps us to solve the mystery of why not all labour-intensive manufacturing moves to places in the developing world where wages are cheapest. Vernon points out that there is a cycle by which innovation is developed and spreads globally. In the initial stage, an innovator, being the only one producing the new product, enjoys a brief stint as a monopolist. Prices are high and a small number of customers are willing to pay a lot for the novelty and performance of the innovative product. We can point to the recent Tesla Motors roadster, an electric sports car introduced in the early 2000s that costs over $100,000, and was bought by a few very rich executives and actors. In the second stage, which Tesla hopes to enter by 2015, the production process becomes more standardized, and costs can be brought down. In this stage, Vernon's model suggests that we are likely to see oligopolistic (a few large producers) structures of production. In the final stage, the production process is so well hashed out, that many producers can compete. This is the stage of mass production when prices bottom out. If we think of t-shirts, they are at this stage. Vernon suggests that since the North has strong design and innovation advantages, it is able to capture the first two stages of the production cycle (innovation and oligopolistic production). Mass production, such as t-shirts, moves to the developing world for lower labour costs. We are also seeing some parts of more advanced industries, such as electronics and cars, move overseas.

Why doesn't everything else move? The answer, if we follow Vernon's model, goes back to innovation. If we consider cars, we see continual improvement in gas mileage, electronics, reliability, etc. Therefore, the North is able to keep large parts of the production process at home through the high requirements of design, improving production process, and skilled labour. If we add in Keynes's idea of the multiplier effect, then we see that there is a virtuous circle, in the sense that the largest and richest consumer markets are also in the North.

Still, the increasing integration of global markets potentially weakens the interventionist hand. If we think about the basic costs of organizing production, in terms of coordinating different raw material and component providers as well as workers, capital, and knowledge; in terms of the information that needs to flow among suppliers and buyers; and finally in terms of the physical movement of people and materials to make this happen, we can see all of these as transaction costs. Transaction costs of information, organizing, and negotiating can be significant. If we think about where industries are located, transactions would appear to play a large role. Financial firms agglomerate around ultra-expensive Wall Street because that is where the stock exchange is. Steel mills developed around Pittsburgh at the turn of the century in part because of the proximity to iron ore, river transportation, and the financial capital and steel markets of the East Coast. Corporations can thus be explained as large organizations in part because they can develop managerial expertise and in part through reducing transactions costs by internalizing them. By the latter, we mean that there will not have to be negotiations or changes in price if suppliers of raw materials, components, and producers are all part of the same organization, which we refer to as vertical integration. Beyond this, of course, is that large organizations have economies of scale, the ability to raise larger amounts of finance, and the legal aspect of corporations as entities with liability separate from the individuals working within them.

Globalization theorists posit that transaction costs have decreased. The General Agreement on Tariffs and Trade (GATT) and the World Trade Organization (WTO), among other trade agreements, have reduced trade barriers and helped to improve standards. The development of transportation revolutions, from supertankers to container shipping, has similarly reduced costs for exports and imports. The revolutions in communications technology, culminating in the Internet, allowing near instantaneous messaging across the globe, have further reduced transaction costs. All of these changes have created the possibility of global supply chains. When we buy a car or computer, the different components have usually been made all around the world. The implication is that the reduction in transaction costs reduces the power of economies of scale and the advantages of concentration. More important, it suggests that aiding a large national company, such as Ford, which is, effectively, transnational, may not lead to any increase in benefits in the giving country. In fact, companies will play off countries for tax breaks, promising to locate production there on that basis. Thus critics often call for critical examination of whether such subsidization leads to net benefits for the consumer. A spectacular example is the emerging solar panel industry that Chinese companies, heavily subsidized by the government, entered into the market in the late 2000s. Their efforts dropped costs in the industry dramatically, wiping out more established competitors in North America and Europe. The response of the latter was partial support of their companies, but the change happened too fast for policy-makers to respond. As of this writing, the critics of intervention point to the fact that many Chinese companies have also gone bankrupt with the collapse of prices, and that same collapse has spurred on greater purchase of solar panels in the North (at Chinese expense).

At the same time, the Doha Round of trade liberalization has appeared to be "stuck" for the past decade, with developing countries desiring more concessions from the North to reduce agricultural subsidies, but at the same time resisting a level playing field principle for opening up their own markets to services and financial capital. The global trade and investment negotiations therefore revolve around industrial policy issues, in this case the promotion of agriculture, but also around related questions, such as intellectual property rights enforcement. For example, ongoing disputes about the development of generic drugs in the developing world pit those who claim it is a matter of social justice versus those who conclude that reducing rents for innovation will slow the development of new drugs (Hira 2009).

Despite the purported levelling effects of globalization, many critics see the rise of transnational corporations as threatening in the sense that they no longer seem beholden to any particular country. There does seem to be some evidence that companies are merging with rivals across national boundaries, such as Fiat's purchase of Chrysler, to meet global competition. Moreover, there are a few isolated examples of industrial policy that reaches across borders, principally in the European Union, such as Airbus's regional strategy toward production of airplanes. Transnational companies enjoy not only the advantages of incumbency and global economies of scale, but also economies of scope. By the latter, scholars refer to the possibility of linking similar industries to spread knowledge across them. For example, Samsung produces a wide range of electronics requiring similar business and technology know-how, from cell phones to TVs. Nonetheless, a mapping out of major companies in any given industry shows that the most important parts of the manufacturing process for most industries still have a strong geographic concentration. Pharmaceutical companies, for example, are still concentrated in the US and Switzerland. Samsung is still a South Korean company, despite its global reach. For the moment at least, even key service industries, such as software in Silicon Valley, have a "stickiness" to certain areas that requires complementary industrial policies, particularly efforts to promote higher education and R&D. One could also argue that many of the highest-paying jobs related to services are still tied to manufacturing location, such as the design, testing, and integration work in aerospace and automobiles.

Yet, other insightful authors such as Richard Langlois see the possibility for a mode 1 revival in the future. They suggest that modularizing (breaking into standardized pieces) the global production process is reducing the advantages of vertical integration. They can point to the development of outsourcing, such as software coding in India, as an example of how the advantages of large organizations may be shrinking as global transactions continue to decline. One of the most interesting topics for further research is the general shift in world production and consumption toward services. This brings up the need for adapting industrial policy strategy which has traditionally been based on promoting manufacturing. If we consider, further, that the vast majority of the world's population lives in the developing world, and that parts of the developing world have the highest economic growth rates and potential, then it is quite possible that much of future industry and innovation will slowly shift there.

Case 3: Are Global Trade Agreements Shrinking the Space for Industrial Policy? Bombardier v. Embraer

In direct response to some of the East Asian strategies, new regulations on the multilateral level, principally through the WTO, sought to clamp down on government support along these lines. Gallagher (2005, 10) points to a number of areas where the policy space of state intervention has shrunk through multilateral agreements, namely:

- Trade-Related Investment Measures Agreement—which restricts the performance and local content requirements on investment;
- Trade-Related Aspects of Intellectual Property Rights (TRIPS) Agreement—which seeks

to protect intellectual property, including patented research, thus restricting reverse engineering and thereby the cost-effective diffusion of the latest technology;

- Subsidies and Countervailing Measures Agreement—which reduces the scope for states to put targeted subsidies toward R&D, regional inequality, and environmental protection

These multilateral provisions are often marked by similar or more onerous provisions in the bilateral agreements that have proliferated over the past two decades as multilateral trade talks have stalled. One example is the infamous Chapter 11 provision of the NAFTA, which allows private parties, under some circumstances, to sue national governments for unfair regulation.

On the other hand, one can respond to such alarmism by pointing out that multilateral agreements are voluntary; usually have safeguard provisions, giving nations some ability for temporary opt-outs; have generally recognized the principle that developing countries deserve more generous treatment; and have very limited enforcement capability. The development of generic AIDS drugs in India and South Africa, for example, flies in the face of the movement toward greater intellectual property enforcement.

An interesting case related to Case 2 was the Bombardier-Embraer WTO case from the late 1990s. As we related, Embraer entered the regional jet market in full force in the 1990s, taking on the incumbent, Bombardier, a Canadian company that had dominated this niche, which had emerged from US air travel deregulation in the 1980s. Both governments correctly accused each other of subsidizing their national champions. However, the type of support differed. Whereas Brazil's export promotion agency, Proex, subsidized exchange rates, Canada supported loans for product

development. In 1999, a WTO dispute panel found that the Canadian program violated subsidies and countervailing measures by conferring an unfair market advantage. However, in the same year, a different WTO panel found that Brazil was also in violation (Goldstein and McGuire 2004; Lawton and McGuire 2001). Although the case was never formally resolved, both countries seem to have moved on. It is interesting to note that Boeing and Airbus engaged in a similar skirmish at the WTO, which began shortly after this case.

Conclusion

Industrial policy is a central axis of debate in international political economy. The question of state intervention to promote industries remains controversial. Though, in practice, all states intervene, whether such intervention is effective or efficient, and whether it can sometimes create benefits that outweigh collective losses in trade and finance on the global level remains hotly contested. The question of how best to intervene, whether through direct or indirect promotion, and which industries to target and when, is another question about which there is even less consensus. With the fact of ongoing globalization of production and investment, the industrial policy debate is bound to remain a key issue of IPE. The claims of developing countries for exemptions to pursue more direct industrial policies have deep historical roots. Contention over what are legitimate industrial policy interventions occurs on a regular basis between a wide variety of states around the globe, and is reflected in ongoing discussions, negotiations, and disputes around trade and financial flows. Although these debates will continue, the fact is that industrial policies, both direct and indirect, are ubiquitous, and deserve closer scrutiny and evaluation.

Note

1   This section refers to the following version: F.A. Hayek. (2007. *The road to serfdom: Text and documents—The definitive edition*, Bruce Caldwell (Ed.), Chicago: University of Chicago Press.

Key Terms

industrial policy
creative destruction
NIS (national innovation systems)

regulatory capture
staples

Questions for Review

1. Consider the argument between free trade theorists such as Smith, Hayek, and Ricardo and interventionists such as Keynes and List in historical perspective. To what extent are these thinkers reflecting the situation of their times?

2. Entrepreneurs such as Bill Gates and Steve Jobs are celebrated examples of individuals making a difference. Do a brief biographical search for them or other entrepreneurs. What complementary elements do you think entrepreneurs need to succeed?

3. Why does industrial and innovation policy in Canada seem like an afterthought compared with other large developed countries, such as the US and the European Union? What are the political, economic, social, and other barriers to a national industrial strategy in Canada? Are there advantages to Canada's decentralized approach?

4. The Nokia case study seems to disprove the theory of natural comparative advantage given the shift in the Finnish economy from resource to high-tech producer. Or does it? Consider the recent decline of Nokia as a cell phone manufacturer as a result of Asian rivals and why this might have happened.

5. There is a push by some activist groups to promote local production, particularly of food. What do you think the merits are of the argument that we should reject globalization and only consume local production? What would be the results of such a shift on a significant scale?

Further Resources

Hayek, F.A. *The road to serfdom: Text and documents—The definitive edition*.

Hira, A. (2007). *The new path: An East Asian model for Latin American success*. Burlington, VT: Ashgate.

Innis, H. A. *Problems of staples production in Canada*.

List, F. *National system of political economy*.

Nelson, R. R. *National innovation systems: A comparative analysis*.

Schumpeter, J. A. *Business cycles: A theoretical, historical, and statistical analysis of the capitalist process*.

Vernon, R. *International investment and international trade in the product cycle*.

Wade, R. H. *Governing the market: Economic theory and the role of government in East Asian industrialization*.

References

Atkinson, M. M. and Powers, R. A. (1987). Inside the industrial policy garbage can: selective subsidies to business in Canada. *Canadian Public Policy 13*(2), 208–17.

Brodie, J. (1990). *The political economy of Canadian regionalism*. Toronto: Harcourt Brace Jovanovich.

Brownlee, J. (2005). *Ruling Canada: Corporate cohesion and democracy*. Halifax: Fernwood Publishing.

Eckert, A. and West, D. S. (2005). *Canadian supplement for industrial organization*, 2nd ed. Toronto: Pearson.

Gallagher, K. P. (2005). Globalization and the nation-state: Reasserting policy autonomy for Development, 1–15. In Gallagher (Ed.), *Putting development first: The importance of policy space in the WTO and IFIs*. NY: Zed Books.

Goldstein, A. E. and McGuire, S. M. (2004). The political economy of strategic trade policy and the Brazil-Canada export subsidies saga. *The World Economy 27*(4), 541–66.

Hale, G. (2006). *Uneasy partnership: The Politics of business and government in Canada*. Peterborough, ON: Broadview Press.

Hayek, F.A., (2007). *The road to serfdom: Text and documents—The definitive edition* Bruce Caldwell (Ed.), Chicago: University of Chicago Press.

Hira, A. (2009). The political economy of the global pharmaceutical industry: Why the poor lack access to medicine and what might be done about it, *International Journal of Development Issues 8*(2), 84–101.

Hira, A. (2012). Secrets behind the Finnish miracle: The rise of Nokia. *International Journal of Technology and Globalisation 6*(2), 38–64.

Hira, A. and Oliveira, G. de. (2007). Take off and crash: Lessons from the diverging fates of the Brazilian and Argentine aircraft industries, *Competition and Change* (Nov.) *11*(4), 329–47.

Hira, A., Wixted, B., and Arechavala-Vargas, R. (2012). Explaining sectoral leapfrogging in countries: Comparative studies of the wireless sector. *International Journal of Technology and Globalisation 6*(2), 3–26.

Howlett, M., Netherton, A., and Ramesh, M. (1999). *The political economy of Canada: An introduction*, 2nd ed. Don Mills, ON: Oxford University Press.

Howlett, M. and Ramesh, M. (1992). *The political economy of Canada: An introduction*. Toronto: McClelland & Stewart.

Innis, H. A. (1933). *Problems of staples production in Canada*. Toronto: Ryerson.

Keynes, J. M. (2007). *The general theory of employment, interest and money*. London: Palgrave Macmillan.

Langlois, R. N. (2007). *The dynamics of industrial capitalism: Schumpeter, Chandler, and the new economy*. NY: Routledge.

Lawton, T. C. and McGuire, S. M. (2001). Supranational governance and corporate strategy: The emerging role of the World Trade Organization. *International Business Review 10*, 217–33.

List, F. (1964). *National system of political economy*. NY: Augustus M. Kelley.

Nelson, R. R. (Ed.). (1993). *National innovation systems: A comparative analysis*. NY: Oxford U. Press.

Ricardo, D. (1996). *Principles of political economy and taxation*. Amherst, NY: Prometheus Books.

Schumpeter, J. A. (1964). *Business cycles: A theoretical, historical, and statistical analysis of the capitalist process*. NY: McGraw-Hill.

Smith, A. (1993). *An inquiry into the nature and causes of the wealth of nations*. Kathryn Sutherland (Ed.), NY: Oxford University Press.

Vernon, R. (1966). International investment and international trade in the product cycle. *Q J Econ 80*, 190–207.

Wade, R. H. (1990). *Governing the market: Economic theory and the role of government in East Asian industrialization*. Princeton: Princeton University Press.

PART VI

Issues in the Twenty-first Century

The post-Cold War era has been witness to several cross-cutting, contradictory impulses. On the one hand, a global economic system seems to be inexorably shrinking distances, erasing borders, and linking societies together in ways unimaginable just a couple of decades ago. At the same time, some of the same processes that are pushing societies closer to one another are infringing on sensitive areas of culture, economics, and politics, upending traditional sources of power and stability, frequently exposing deep societal fissures. These same dynamics are transforming many of the traditional areas of focus for scholars of IPE and bringing new ones to the fore.

In late 2010, a series of anti-government street protests in Tunisia led to the ouster of long-time president Zine El Abidine Ben Ali. Aided by the widespread use of social media, those protests quickly spread to other parts of the Arab Middle East—Egypt, Libya, Yemen, Bahrain, and Syria among them. The final outcome of those protests remains uneven in many locations, particularly Syria, where protests evolved into all-out civil war that threatens to tear the country apart. At the same time, as forces within threaten to pull these countries apart, many are also some of the newest members of the World Trade Organization, with Yemen joining in late 2013.

In each of these situations, we see several of the overlapping and contradictory impulses that have come to characterize important parts of the international system. On the one hand, the dynamics of globalization have reduced time and distance as principal impediments to interaction between different parts of the globe, facilitated the integration of economies, stimulated the growth of new institutions such as the WTO, and opened new avenues for a host of sub-state and non-state actors to enter the governance game. Yet, these same dynamics have also brought about significant pressure on traditional governance structures rooted primarily in states, fragmenting the nodes of governance authority, and, some argue, undermining the utility of the state itself (Rodrik 1997; Wolf 2001).

Political scientists love to coin new terms and catchphrases in the hope that they will catch on. In recent years, a host of terms have been invented attempting to describe contemporary forms of governance: multi-level governance, multi-dimensional governance, subsidiarity, intermesticity, the perforated state, or the disaggregated state are just a few (Burgess 2006; Krasner 1999; Lake 2003; Slaughter 2002).

Another such term, coined by James Rosneau (2000), fits comfortably alongside these other bits of disciplinary jargon. However, it also usefully attempts to reconcile two separate phenomena that scholars have been wrestling with for years: integration and fragmentation.

Economists celebrate Adam Smith and David Ricardo for highlighting the benefits of trade and the international division of labour anchored in comparative advantage. Coupled with innovation in information technology and the sharp reduction in transportation costs, our increasingly globalized and integrated economic system has dramatically reduced the importance of time and space, helped linkages of all kinds to be established between diverse sets of people, and rendered national boundaries less and less significant.

The same pressures that increasingly globalized processes are bringing to bear on economic and political systems around the world are also helping to relocate authority centres away from the traditional nodes of state-based government, and toward a range of institutional arrangements such as the World Trade Organization (WTO), the International Monetary Fund (IMF), or the European Union (EU). The proliferation of governance entities competing with states at an international level also includes a broad range of non-governmental, for-profit and not-for-profit associations, industry groups, and environmental organizations. Many of these groups are not even groups in the sense of a formal organization, but are instead best characterized as networks (Hooghe and Marks 2003), whose coordination has been greatly assisted by the Internet. Yet, governance is not being uniformly dispersed upward toward multilateral institutions with a focus on international issues. We also see governance fragmenting, taking place in the devolution of authority downward to ever more localized, often non-government forms of governance. This kind of localized authority includes everything from the devolution of federal authority to sub-state levels of government, to the plethora of non-government organizations that organize locally.

In fact, as Rosenau (2000) argues, contemporary global governance is actually characterized by three overlapping polarities—globalization and localization, centralization and decentralization, and integration and fragmentation.

These competing polarities and the forms of governance they have spawned have rendered traditional state-centric government merely one of many focal points of authority. Though it is premature to begin writing obituaries for the state (Wolf 2001), the growing importance of other levels of governance, as well as their proliferation, has vastly complicated the policy process for a whole range of issues. Rosenau identifies at least six different kinds of contemporary governance collectivities (Rosneau 2000, 12):

1. public subnational and national governments
2. for-profit private transnational corporations
3. international governmental organizations
4. subnational or national not-for-profit NGOs
5. international or transnational not-for-profit NGOs
6. markets that have a range of formal and informal structures

As Rosenau argues, these broad "fragmegrative dynamics have added to the crises of states by relocating their authority in diverse directions, upward to supranational institutions, downward to subnational entities, sideward to social movements, non-governmental organizations, corporations, and a wide range of other types of collectivities" (Rosenau 2000, 7). Many of these collectivities are held together and connected through horizontal, rather than traditionally vertical, flows of authority. In other words, the links between information, decision-making, and governance all flow between some of these new collectivities rather than to and from governments. In contrast to the types of governance that flow vertically up or down, newer forms of governance (formal and informal networks, for example) are pervaded by nuance, by interactive and multiple flows of influence that may either pass through or bypass the halls of government, pushing the tasks of governance beyond the boundaries of the state while also complicating the completion of those tasks (Rosenau 2000, 15).

The postwar integration of economies via trade liberalization always presented policymakers with these kinds of challenges. However, as stakeholders in different parts of the world have come into deeper and more frequent contact with one another through a greater number of pathways, such challenges have proliferated. Trade liberalization is inherently involved in the production of winners and losers. Yet, until the end of the Tokyo Round of GATT negotiations in 1979, negotiations were relatively straightforward since they mainly involved tariffs (Anderson 2012a) and the impact tariff reduction had on narrowly focused sectors (the losers). However, the post-Tokyo Round agenda increasingly dealt with a whole range of so-called behind-the-border, or non-tariff, barriers to trade, that were inherently much more difficult to negotiate away because they reached ever more deeply into domestic governance, that is, sovereignty (Anderson 2012b).

These broad complex processes are creating new, dynamic, and sometimes unexpected, governance demands from a variety of stakeholders at multiple levels. Moreover, the range of issues that are now the subject of considerable study in IPE are no longer self-contained, neatly defined issue areas. Most, as is the case with every chapter in this section, involve a complex web of cross-cutting sub-issues and spillovers, along with a complicated and ever-changing constellation of stakeholders.

For example, Patrick Leblond's essay on the global financial crisis describes the evolution of a financial bubble that originated in houses on Main Street but exploded into systemic risk on Wall Street. The contagion then spilled across borders, infecting economies all over the world, generating one of the deepest and longest-lived recessions since the Great Depression. Similarly, this section features pieces on what are arguably going to be the two most important, divisive, and intertwined issues of the early twenty-first century: the environment and energy. First, Michael Howlett and Jeremy Rayner examine the prospects for international forest governance which, if done right, would set a precedent for other areas of international environmental governance. Monica Gattinger and Rafael Aguirre then examine the dramatic changes that have shaken up the Canada–US energy picture.

The challenges of development are not new, but the focus of the international community on them is as acute as ever. One recent, and understudied, phenomenon has been the use of large sporting events, like the World Cup or the Olympics, as vehicles for development, particularly where infrastructure is concerned. David Black and Katelynn Northam look closely at the role of mega-sporting events in the growth strategies of the developing world. Ellen Gutterman then takes on the political economy of corruption and bribery by looking at some of the variability in worldwide norms and governance regimes. Finally, Yasmeen Abu-Laban tackles the growing and complex set of pressures swirling around migration all over the world. While our attention to these issues is often focused in places like the US–Mexican border or Southern Europe, Abu-Laban highlights the many similarities with which they play out in Canada as well.

References

Anderson, G. J. 2012a. "Securitization and sovereignty in post-9/11 North America." *Review of International Political Economy* 19(5), 711–41.

———. 2012b. "Did Canada kill fast track?" *Diplomatic History* 36 no. 3: 583–624.

Burgess, M. 2006. *Comparative federalism: Theory and practice*. London and New York: Routledge.

Hooghe, L. and Marks, G. 2003. "Unraveling the central state, but how? Types of multi-level governance." *American Political Science Review* 97(2) (May), 223–43.

Krasner, S. 1999. *Sovereignty: Organized hypocrisy*, Princeton: Princeton University Press.

Lake, D. A. (2003). "The new sovereignty in international relations." *International Studies Review* 5(3), 303–23.

Rodrik, D. 2000. "How far will international economic integration go." *Journal of Economic Perspectives 14* (Winter), 177–86.

———. 1997. *Has globalization gone too far?* Washington, DC: Institute for International Economics.

Rosenau, J. N. 1997. *Along the domestic-foreign frontier: Exploring governance in a turbulent world*. Cambridge: Cambridge University Press.

———. 2000. "The governance of fragmegration: Neither a world republic nor a global interstate system." Unpublished paper presented at the Congress of the International Political Science Association, Quebec City, August 1–5.

Slaughter, A. M. 2002. "Global government networks, global information agencies, and disaggregated democracy." *Michigan Journal of International Law 24*, 1041–76.

20 The Global Financial Crisis

Patrick Leblond

Not since the Great Depression of the 1930s has the world economy suffered a crisis like the one that shook it in the late 2000s. That is why this global financial crisis (GFC) has become known as the Great Recession, precisely because central banks and governments adopted monetary and fiscal policies that helped avert a depression. Although the crisis was relatively well managed, it did not prevent the world economy from stagnating at lower levels of growth afterward, in line with the historical record (Reinhart and Rogoff 2009). In the case of Europe, the GFC morphed into a sovereign debt crisis for the euro area. In Asia, there was no financial crisis per se, unlike the one experienced in 1997–98, but those economies were nonetheless significantly affected as exports to and investment from North America and Europe slowed down, though they avoided recessions for the most part. On the other side of the Pacific, Canada was in a similar situation (no financial crisis) but was unable to prevent its economy from plunging into recession, given its heavy reliance on the EU and the US for trade and investment.

Except for a few Cassandras (e.g., Rajan 2005; Roubini 2006; White 2006), nobody saw the crisis coming until it was too late, which is as it should be since the crisis would not have happened otherwise: manias, panics, and crashes, to use Charles Kindleberger's terms (Kindleberger and Aliber 2005), should not occur in a context where economic actors and policy-makers are able to foresee market excesses and act accordingly to correct them before they become unsustainable. So why were those market and policy (or regulatory) corrections not made in time so as to avoid the crisis? And why were financial market excesses able to build up in the first place? Finally, what has been done since the crisis to prevent new excesses from building up in the future, and are those reforms likely to work?

To answer the above questions, the chapter is structured as follows. First, it provides a brief history of the crisis and how it was managed. Second, it aims to situate an explanation of the crisis in broader, global terms. Third, it reviews the progress made in governing international financial markets so that the risk of another global financial crisis is lessened, if not prevented, in the future. Finally, the chapter concludes with a discussion about the added value of using an international political economy perspective, as opposed to an exclusively economics one, in analyzing the crisis.

The Global Financial Crisis and Its Aftermath

The global financial crisis began in the winter of 2007 when a number of US **mortgage** lenders, most notably New Century Financial and IndyMac Bancorp, began experiencing serious financial difficulties as they reported losses on their mortgage holdings, eventually leading to bankruptcy in many cases. That is because these firms specialized in or were heavily exposed to subprime (i.e., low-quality) mortgages, a market that had boomed in the preceding five years or so.[1] It did not take long for these negative pressures to spread to other parts of the American financial system through **mortgage-backed securities (MBSs)**. For instance, Bear Stearns, the once-prominent US investment bank, ended up having to close two of its hedge funds (heavily invested in subprime MBSs) in June 2007 because investors were taking their money out so they could protect themselves from the losses afflicting the US subprime mortgage market. Unable to regain the confidence of investors and the financial market in general, Bear Stearns eventually ran out of money—or **liquidity**, to be more accurate—and had to be rescued by JP Morgan Chase in March 2008 to avoid bankruptcy.[2]

The instability that plagued the US financial system continued throughout 2008. This situation reached its apex in the fall, when a high degree of uncertainty as to which institution was solvent led financial institutions to stop lending to each other (Brunnermeier 2009). This credit crunch caused another venerable US investment bank to face bankruptcy: Lehman Brothers.[3] In the latter's case, however, there was no white knight that came to the rescue because none could be found (Paulson 2010, 216).[4] Lehman's failure caused panic in the

US and global financial systems, which basically froze: everyone was now waiting to see what would happen next, which meant that nothing was happening. This caused Citigroup and AIG, respectively the world's largest bank and insurer at the time, to be next in the insolvency line.[5] But, given their size and importance for the global financial system, the US government decided to come to their rescue with hundreds of billions of dollars in early October 2008 through the Troubled-Asset Relief Program (TARP), which authorized the US Treasury to purchase or insure up to $700 billion of "troubled" financial **assets** such as mortgages, shares, bonds, and derivatives. Other prominent financial institutions like Goldman Sachs and JP Morgan Chase, even though not faced with insolvency, also received funds from TARP to stabilize the US financial system.[6]

It did not take long for the US financial crisis to cross the Atlantic and hit Europe's shores. Many European banks had invested in the US **securitization** market. For instance, in the summer of 2007, BNP Paribas, a French bank, prevented investors from redeeming their units in three of its investment funds, arguing that the uncertainty in the US **asset-backed securities (ABSs)** market was such that it could no longer value the funds in question (European Commission 2009a). In addition, and more significantly, many European banks leveraged their **balance sheets** and invested heavily in mortgages, just like their American counterparts did. The countries that were hardest hit initially were Ireland and the United Kingdom, because, as in the US, the Irish and UK real estate markets had seen the creation of significant price bubbles in their respective housing markets.

The grim financial situation of banking leverage and real estate prices in Ireland and the UK was not, however, altogether different in the euro area, according to Carmassi et al. (2009). Hence, as in the US, as the interbank credit market froze, European banks found it more and more difficult to roll over their short-term debts,[7] which accounted for a large portion of their total **liabilities**, while at the same time they saw the value of their assets decline. In fact, banks found themselves in the same "vicious circle" as their American counterparts (Quaglia et al. 2009, 66). The more they attempted to rebuild their liquidities by selling assets to pay back short-term liabilities, the greater the downward pressures on asset values; as a result, more and more assets had to be sold off to raise the amounts of liquidities. What had also started out as a crisis of liquidity in Europe (i.e., financial institutions did not have enough liquid assets to pay back their short-term debts) was quickly turning into a crisis of solvency, whereby the value of banks' assets was declining to a level deemed insufficient to cover all of the banks' liabilities and **capital**. The only option to prevent bank failures, therefore, was for European governments to intervene, just as the US government had done with TARP.

According to Quaglia et al. (2009, 66), EU governments injected a total of $380 billion into European banks' capital between June 2007 and January 2009. As at the end of February 2010, cumulative capital injections by eurozone governments amounted to 2 per cent of GDP; in comparison, total bank recapitalization had reached 5 per cent and 2 per cent of GDP in the UK and the US, respectively (ECB 2010b, 79). European governments also extended loans as well as loan guarantees to struggling banks. These support measures were even more important as a percentage of GDP than capital injections (ECB 2010b, 79). Finally, in cases where banks had difficulty selling assets in order to cover their liabilities, governments would intervene and either buy these assets directly from the banks or insure them so they could be used as collateral against new loans (ECB 2010b, 85–6).

Another key source of emergency financing for banks is the central bank, where they can borrow, against collateral, on a very short-term basis, to fund liquidity gaps. The majority of this financing occurs overnight; nevertheless, central banks can also lend for longer periods of time, though they do not usually extend beyond three months. In the context of the GFC, however, central banks in the EU and the US began to provide banks with longer-term refinancing operations with longer maturities (Chailloux et al. 2008; Minegishi and Cournède 2010). They also accepted a wider array of financial assets eligible as collateral against their lending to banks, thereby allowing banks to refinance more of their assets, thus maintaining the latter's value in a panicked market. According to Jean-Claude Trichet, former head of the European Central Bank (ECB), "[t]he primary aim of these non-standard measures is to support the short-term funding of banks in order to alleviate the potential negative impact of liquidity risk on the availability of credit to households and companies across the euro area economy" (Trichet 2010, 12). In other words, with these measures central banks were temporarily replacing the frozen interbank credit market so that banks could stay in business.

To lower the cost for banks of borrowing funds from them, central banks also reduced their refinancing rates. For instance, the US Federal Reserve (the Fed) decreased its fed funds rate from 4.75 per cent in September 2007 to the unprecedented level of 0 to 0.25 per cent in December 2008, where it has remained to this day (March 2015). The ECB, for its part, was slower than the Fed in recognizing the scale of the crisis that was taking place. In fact, it kept increasing its leading interest rates throughout 2007. It was not until July 2008 that it began lowering interest rates. Between then and May of the next year, however, the ECB reduced its rate for refinancing operations from 4.25 per cent to 1 per cent. Surprisingly, given the severe economic pressures faced by the euro area as a result of the debt crises (see below), the ECB increased its refinancing rate by 0.25 percentage points in April and July of 2011, only to lower it back to 1 per cent by the end of the year. In July 2012 and May 2013, the ECB once again reduced its refinancing rate by 0.25 percentage points each time to a level of 0.5 per cent, moves that were welcomed by banks in particular and financial markets in general.

If stabilizing banks and the financial system, through bank rescue plans and central bank financing, was necessary to prevent a depression from settling over North America and Europe, governments felt that fiscal stimulus would help their economies sink less deeply into recession and, they hoped, help them get back on their feet more quickly. In the US, it was not until Barack Obama took over the White House and a new Congress was in place that a fiscal stimulus became possible. In mid-February 2009, Obama signed the American Recovery and Reinvestment Act of 2009 (ARRA) into law. This legislation represented a multi-year package of federal government spending and tax incentives amounting to approximately US$800 billion. This fiscal impulse was in addition to the mitigating effects of the so-called automatic stabilizers that adjust in size according to the state of the economy (e.g., employment insurance and other social security benefits). The end result was that the ARRA, in combination with the financial bailouts and the Fed's rapid monetary easing and non-standard policies, helped the US economy step out of recession in June 2009, 18 months after it began in December 2007. The recovery was feeble, however, as American households and financial institutions continued their **deleveraging** process while Europe entered its own crisis's second phase (i.e., the euro area's debt crisis [see below]).

The European Commission published its European Economic Recovery Plan (EERP) in late November 2008 (European Commission 2008). This plan was adopted a couple of weeks later by EU governments at the European Council's meeting of 11–12 December. The EERP called for an economic stimulus of €200 billion or 1.5 per cent of EU GDP, with €170 billion coming from member states' budgets and €30 billion coming from EU and European Investment Bank budgets. According to the European Commission (2009b), the fiscal stimulus measures adopted by member states in their 2009 and 2010 budgets amounted to about 2 per cent of GDP. This is the target that was agreed to at the first G20 meeting of heads of state and government in Washington in mid-November 2008. In total, the Commission estimates that the EU economy received a fiscal boost of 5 per cent of GDP (European Commission 2009b, 13). According to the ECB (2010b), the EERP has contributed to supporting economic output and employment but at the cost of rapidly deteriorating fiscal balances and rising government indebtedness, thus setting the stage for the euro area's debt crisis.

Bank bailouts and stimulus packages usually end up creating significant pressures on the fiscal front, according to Reinhart and Rogoff (2009, 162–71). This is why, in June 2010, the European Commission (2010) expected the EU's public debt-to-GDP ratio to increase by 25 percentage points between 2007 and 2011, to an average of 84 per cent of GDP (88.5 per cent in the euro area). Such a grim fiscal outlook had already been anticipated in the Commission's June 2009 report (European Commission 2009a). For their part, market actors had begun reacting to euro-area member states' fiscal situations even earlier. Already in January 2009, Standard and Poor's, the credit rating agency, downgraded its ratings for Greece, Portugal, and Spain while issuing a warning to Ireland (Johnson and Oakley 2009), whose credit rating was finally downgraded on 30 March 2009. This corresponded to increases in the differences (known as spreads) between the **yields** on German sovereign bonds (considered the safest) and those of other eurozone countries (Attinasi et al. 2010). As such, sovereign bond investors were becoming more discriminating in their pricing as a result of the financial crisis. The prices of **credit default swaps (CDSs)**, which act as insurance against sovereign default, also increased rapidly for euro area government bonds as banking rescue and fiscal stimulus packages were put together in the fall of 2008 (Attinasi et al. 2010, 36). By the spring of 2009, sovereign bond yields and CDS premia were returning to more normal levels as crisis management measures restored some degree of confidence in financial markets. By September 2009, they had reached levels that were lower than those found before the crisis; the only exceptions to this state of affairs were Greece and Ireland (Attinasi et al. 2010, 38).

In December 2009, all the main credit rating agencies (Fitch, Moody's, and Standard & Poor's) downgraded Greece's sovereign debt to only a couple of grades above junk status.[8] These downgrades followed a surprise announcement by Greece's newly elected PASOK government that the 2009 fiscal deficit would not be 3.6 per cent of GDP, as the previous government originally forecast, but 12.8 per cent instead (Featherstone 2011, 199). Although the new government of George Papandreou committed itself in a mid-November budget to reducing the fiscal deficit to 9 per cent of GDP in 2010, credit rating agencies and sovereign bond investors deemed the effort insufficient to put Greece's public finances back on a sustainable path (*The Economist*, 19 December 2009: 89 [US edition]). It was at this moment that the eurozone's debt crisis (the second leg of Europe's financial crisis) began in earnest. The spreads between the yields of German debt on the one hand and Greek, Irish, and Spanish debt on the other soared to new highs, dragging Italy and Portugal down along with them. Only a strong commitment to keeping

the eurozone intact through government bailouts and the ECB's unlimited monetary support would end up calming down sovereign bond investors, thereby restoring some degree of economic stability to the euro area (Chang and Leblond 2014).

Although euro area governments had agreed in principle to come to Greece's rescue as early as February 2010, it was only in mid-April that they finally took action to match their rhetoric. Such a bailout became necessary since words and promises were ultimately not enough to calm sovereign bond investors, especially after Greece's fiscal deficit for 2009 was again announced to be higher than previously thought: 13.6 per cent rather than the 12.8 per cent estimated in December.[9] In exchange for further budgetary cutbacks, eurozone member states and the IMF ultimately committed €110 billion to help Greece's government pay back debt that was maturing over the next three years as well as pay for deficits incurred during that period.[10]

Once the May 2010 Greek rescue package was in the bag, sovereign bond investors shifted their attention to other euro area countries experiencing fiscal difficulties. As a result, volatility in financial markets didn't let up and the cost of refinancing sovereign debt for countries such as Ireland, Italy, Portugal, and Spain made it impossible for them to get back onto the path of fiscal sustainability. To end this destructive panic, eurozone member states had to take immediate and bold action. In May 2010, eurozone governments and the IMF delivered a massive rescue package plan of €750 billion, which was meant to be at the disposal of EU member states facing public finance difficulties. The ECB again contributed to this rescue operation by putting together a "securities markets program" whereby it would purchase government bonds on financial markets to maintain (not increase) liquidity in eurozone credit markets.

Ireland was the first beneficiary of these new rescue measures. In November 2010, the Irish government officially requested financial assistance from the EU and the IMF. Such a bailout became necessary when Ireland's public debt was forecast to reach 99 per cent of GDP at the end of 2010, from only 25 per cent of GDP before the financial crisis began. This large increase in indebtedness was mainly caused by the failure of Irish banks as a result of the bursting of a real estate bubble. For 2010 alone, the Irish government's budget deficit was more than 30 per cent of GDP, two thirds of which were due to financial injections into the banking system. As a result, Ireland saw the yields on its long-term government bonds reach levels above 8 per cent in November 2010, a level considered unsustainable (i.e., too costly) for the Irish government to support the banking system with public funds raised on international capital markets. The Irish bailout package totalled €85 billion: €45 billion from the EU, €22.5 billion from the IMF, and €17.5 billion from Ireland itself (by using cash reserves and the National Pension Reserve Fund).

In early April 2011, it was Portugal's turn to request financial assistance from the EU and the IMF. The request came on the heels of the fall of the Sócrates government, after it lost a parliamentary vote on austerity measures, and credit ratings downgrades by Standard & Poor's and Fitch of Portugal's main banks as well as its sovereign debt, to one level above junk status. As a result, yields on 10-year government bonds continued their upward path to surpass the unsustainable rate of 8 per cent, from around 4 per cent at the beginning of the year. At the beginning of May 2011, the EU and the IMF thus agreed to grant Portugal a total of €78 billion in financial assistance, of which €12 billion was earmarked for aiding the banking sector.

For their part, Italy and Spain also saw the yields on their sovereign debt increase substantially in the fall of 2010, albeit at much lower rates than Greece, Ireland, and Portugal's, which is why they did not require official bailouts from the EU and the IMF. In Spain's case, in spite of the country's low public debt as a percentage of GDP, investors were concerned with the medium-term sustainability of the debt because they feared the government would be unable to resolve the country's banking crisis, thus eventually finding itself in Ireland's position. This pressure from the bond market caused the Spanish government to respond with measures to reduce the fiscal deficit and reforms to its banking system, including merging and closing many of the regional savings banks (the *cajas*) that were highly exposed to the collapsed domestic real estate market. For Italy, the concern was not so much the banking system but the government's already high debt level (higher than Greece's before the crisis). Given that the Italian economy had generated little growth since its entry into the eurozone, sovereign bond investors feared that in a weak European economy it would not be able to sustain its indebtedness. The fact that the Berlusconi government seemed unable, if not unwilling, to bring about the necessary economic reforms to contribute to stimulating the Italian economy only accentuated investors' concerns. This is why Berlusconi was eventually forced to resign in November 2011, amid financial market pressures on Italy's sovereign debt and the fear that it might have to ask for a bailout, for which the existing EU-IMF rescue measures were inadequate. A caretaking technocratic government, under the leadership of former European commissioner Mario Monti, replaced the Berlusconi government until April 2013, when a new government was finally formed (two months after the elections) under Enrico Letta. Monti's government immediately got working on a set of long overdue reforms to improve the Italian economy's productivity, managing to calm investors down a little. As a result, Italy and the eurozone were able to avoid the potentially catastrophic scenario of a default.

In the summer of 2012, under the threat of the escalating crisis in Spain, the European Council, eurozone leaders, and the ECB took decisive steps to ensure the integrity of the euro's membership by strengthening its institutional framework (particularly financial integration) and creating a credible financial backstop that would obviate the need for a country to default on its debt. At the end of June, a euro area summit set the stage for a genuine banking union across the eurozone, something that was considered necessary to help prevent future financial crises in Europe. But the biggest "game-changer" of the crisis was Mario Draghi's (the ECB president) promise in July 2012 to do "whatever it takes to preserve the euro." This resulted in the outright monetary transactions (OMT) program in which the ECB promised to buy an unlimited amount of a country's sovereign bonds in financial markets (i.e., only bonds that were already issued) as long as those countries were operating under an official adjustment agreement with the EU and/or the IMF. Draghi praised OMT as "probably the most successful monetary policy measure undertaken in recent times" (*Financial Times*, 6 June 2013). With OMT, which, in the end, did not need to be tapped, the sovereign debt crisis abated as the slope of sovereign bond yields in the Euro-Med countries tilted downward for good. This is because only the ECB's unlimited firepower could satisfy investors that major countries such as Italy and Spain would remain inside the eurozone and prevent the euro area from disintegrating. By the summer of 2013, there were even signs that the region's economy was slowly coming out of a prolonged recession, as the eurozone economy experienced positive growth (0.3 per cent in the second quarter) for the first time in 18 months.

In Canada, the situation could not have been more different than those in the EU and the US. During the period of transatlantic turmoil, Canada remained an oasis of financial stability: Canadian financial institutions did not suffer the kind of meltdown that their American and European counterparts experienced. As a result, the Canadian government did not have to inject one cent into banks' capital to keep them afloat. In fact, Canadian banks' asset writedowns represented only about 0.75 per cent of GDP in 2008 (IMF 2009, 4), one quarter that of their American and European counterparts. Moreover, Canadian banks remained profitable throughout the global financial crisis (Bank of Canada 2011, 6). The main reason behind the Canadian banking system's superior performance is that it relied to a much lesser extent on market-based financial innovations for its operations, especially securitization, than American and European banks (Leblond 2013), thus less exposed to the uncertainties of financial markets. Because of tighter regulation and supervision, Canadian banks' balance sheets were also less leveraged (and therefore less risky) than their counterparts in Europe and the United States (Leblond 2013). Nevertheless, the Canadian economy was not spared by the shocks that hit its two main economic partners, since it experienced an economic recession between the fall of 2008 and the summer of 2009. However, compared to the EU and the US, the Canadian recession was milder, both shorter and less severe.

Explaining the Crisis

Opaque and complex financial instruments, inappropriate incentives for bankers and consumers, transnational lending and investing, monetary imbalances, easy monetary policy, overindebtedness, and inadequate regulation and supervision: the causes of the global financial crisis are by now well understood, though their relative importance remains open for debate.

As mentioned in the above section, the bursting of price bubbles in housing markets in Europe and the United States acted as the trigger for the global financial crisis. In the US, for instance, the housing bubble formed because (1) credit was cheap for both consumers and financial institutions as the Fed lowered interest rates in the wake of the 11 September 2001 terrorist attacks and (2) countries such as China, Japan, and Saudi Arabia were investing their growing reserves of dollars in the United States (Schwartz 2009). Ben Bernanke (2005), the former Fed chairman, referred to this abundance of liquidity in world financial markets as the global "savings glut," because, he argued, there were too much savings from East Asia and the oil-producing countries chasing too few investment opportunities around the world. The end result of these global monetary imbalances is that foreign savings were, in good part, paying for Americans' indebtedness (Dunaway 2009), which went into housing and the consumption of non-perishable goods (e.g., cars, electronics, furniture).

The irony is that many of the goods consumed by Americans were imported from East Asia, with China serving as the conduit through which Japanese, Korean, Taiwanese, and even US products, for example, would flow because this is where they were assembled into final consumer goods.[11] So, in essence, a large share of savings in East Asian countries, which were being generated from the manufacturing of products for export to the US market, was actually being used to finance US consumers. This situation was compounded by the fact that many East Asian governments, most notably in China, had adopted undervalued exchange rate policies by fixing, more or less formally,[12] the value of their national currency to the US dollar to keep their country's exports relatively cheap in western markets (especially the US).[13] As a result, they had to invest their large accumulation of foreign currency reserves in the United States, since most of the reserves were denominated in US dollars.

A similar situation took place in oil-producing countries. The latter were also rapidly accumulating US dollars as the price of a barrel of oil jumped from about US$35 in 2000 to more than US$100 in 2007. Oil consumption adjusts slowly to changes in price. These countries were thus unable to integrate all these surpluses into their domestic economy without fuelling large-scale inflation, because it was impossible to find enough quality (i.e., productive) investment projects to plough the oil revenues into. As a result, the excess funds had to be invested abroad, mostly in the US economy. This situation was reminiscent of the 1970s when petrodollars from the Middle East were being invested in Latin America via the American banking system, eventually leading to a major debt crisis across the region.[14]

The resulting increases in the supply of credit in US financial markets caused the cost of borrowing to drop significantly, with a corresponding rise in the demand for credit. However, as more and more people sought to borrow money to buy into the booming housing market, the quality of the borrowers declined (i.e., credit risk rose). As people came to believe that house prices could not fall, households, financial institutions, and institutional investors became reckless with mortgages, believing that higher credit risk—i.e., the risk of home-owners not repaying their mortgages—would nevertheless be covered by rising house prices. Lenders thus began issuing mortgages to households that were considered subprime (i.e., with mediocre and bad credit profiles). And because the higher risk of these mortgages was thought to be passed on to others through securitization, mortgage lenders felt even less compelled to remain vigilant in assessing their customers' credit worthiness.[15] Mortgage-backed securities were most often transformed into **collateralized debt obligations** (CDOs). In addition, the top tranche of a CDO would sometimes be insured through CDSs, issued by insurance companies, like AIG, or investment banks, like Bear Stearns and Goldman Sachs, to secure a top credit rating. CDOs became very popular among institutional investors, especially the more risk-averse ones, because they offered returns that were superior to those offered by government securities while having the same top credit rating (for details, see Coval et al. 2009).[16] According to Carmassi et al. (2009), such financial innovation is the key main ingredient of the speculative bubbles behind the global financial crisis. Since credit was cheap and plentiful, investors borrowed heavily to buy more CDOs, pushing lenders to generate more subprime mortgages. By using **leverage**, the whole financial system could thus generate high profits, though only as long as house prices continued to increase. These required low interest rates and a strong economy. Carmassi et al. (2009) consider unsustainable leverage to be the third and final key ingredient for speculative bubbles to arise.

In spite of the fact that overall credit quality was declining in the United States, with the rise of subprime mortgages and banking leverage, credit rating agencies (CRAs) maintained their ratings on CDO tranches. According to Colva et al. (2009), this is because CRAs' models for pricing risk were inadequate in a world of structured or securitized finance; they underestimated the risk of CDOs, especially the AAA-rated senior tranches. Whether this was done by design, to gain more fees from banks issuing CDOs, or by mistake remains unclear. The US Financial Crisis Inquiry Commission (2011) found that it was more by design that CRAs issued so many CDO senior tranches and mortgage-backed securities with AAA ratings, which is why the Commission concluded that "[t]his crisis could not have happened without the rating agencies" (Financial Crisis Inquiry Commission 2011, xxv).

Colva et al. (2009) are reluctant to blame CRAs for the crisis because ultimately financial regulators and investors did not make different risk assessments than the CRAs. Even so, the authors (2009, 22) mention that Wall Street executives realized that the credit-fuelled real estate boom would eventually come to an end but that they had to keep going until the "music stopped."[17] Similarly, Best (2010a) argues that the limits of financial risk management were such that it would have been presumptuous for those involved to think that they could value structured finance products correctly (see also Milne 2008). First, given an economy's complexities and uncertainties, it is very difficult, if not impossible, to devise financial models that are capable of calculating risk accurately. Second, to facilitate the measurement and calculation of risk, it made sense to fragment risk into its different components but at the cost of ignoring the links between them. Finally, structured finance has made financial transactions more abstract to the system in the sense that they are removed from the direct contractual relationship between lender and borrower. Consequently, the borrower or lender believes that the responsibility for the risk of a given financial transaction lies elsewhere since the resulting financial assets will be repackaged and sold to someone else in the system. Due diligence and information sharing thus becomes wholly inadequate.

The US real estate bubble ultimately burst because of increases in interest rates that eventually made mortgages and other debts (such as credit cards) too onerous for subprime borrowers, who ended up defaulting in greater and greater numbers because their debts were contracted at variable interest rates (Mayer et al. 2009).[18] Trying to keep inflation under control while the US economy was growing rapidly, the Fed raised the federal funds rate from 1 per cent in 2003 to 5.25 per cent in 2006. As a result, investors holding MBSs and other ABSs (like those backed by credit cards) saw the value of their investments decline rapidly because the stream of payments was flowing in decreasing volumes. Because, in return, these investors were also highly leveraged, it became more and more difficult for them to service and pay back their own, often short-term, debts (to other investors). As a result, the entire US financial system was at risk of crumbling.

In addition to global monetary imbalances, financial innovation, flawed incentives, and hubris on the part of borrowers and lenders, financial deregulation has also been blamed for the US financial crisis.[19] The gradual demise of the Glass-Steagall Act during the 1980s and 1990s, culminating in its repeal in 1999, is seen as one of the root causes behind the crisis. The US Congress passed the Glass-Steagall Act in 1933 in response to the Great Crash of 1929. In addition to establishing the Federal Deposit Insurance Corporation and strengthening the Fed's remit over credit issuance, the Act prohibited commercial banks from underwriting securities. Commercial banks (taking deposits and lending) now had to be separated from investment banks (underwriting equities and bonds) and brokerage firms.[20] Financial conglomerates were banned so as to avoid the conflict of interests that were deemed to have led to the 1929 stock market crash (banks were accused of promoting stocks that benefited them directly to individual investors). In the mid-1980s, the Fed, which was responsible for enforcing the Glass-Steagall Act, began reinterpreting the Act to allow commercial banks to underwrite some securities. The limit on revenues generated from underwriting securities was initially set at 5 per cent of a bank's gross revenues in 1986. It was later raised to 10 per cent (1989) and 25 per cent (1996). With the latter limit, the Glass-Steagall Act was effectively rendered useless in terms of separating the activities of commercial and investment banks from one

another. In 1997, the Fed further weakened the Glass-Steagall Act by allowing commercial banks to acquire securities firms. In 1998, it allowed Citicorp to merge with Travelers, the insurance group that had bought Salomon Brothers, a well-known Wall Street investment bank, the year before. Finally, in 1999, the US Congress passed the Financial Services Modernization Act (also known as the Gramm-Leach-Bliley Act), which officially repealed the Glass-Steagall Act. According to Stiglitz (2010, 15), this gradual erosion of financial regulation in the US led to the financial industry's consolidation, with the emergence of financial firms that had become "too big to be allowed to fail," thereby causing excessive risk-taking by these firms' managers (the so-called moral hazard problem).[21]

It should not be surprising that European banks suffered fates similar to their American counterparts. After all, real house prices in the eurozone (excluding Germany) and the UK increased even more than in the US over the 2000–09 period (European Commission 2009a, 12). Furthermore, European banks followed US banks in acquiring or developing investment banking, hedge fund, and private equity activities, both at the national and international levels (Hardie and Howarth 2013). Securitization in Europe also increased rapidly between 2000 and 2006, though less so than in the US (Véron 2007, 4). The result was that the average leverage level of eurozone banks was even higher than that of US investment banks, which were at the heart of the US financial crisis. For instance, the eurozone's banking sector assets-to-capital multiple reached highs above 30 (summer of 2008), whereas that of the US banking sector as a whole came close but never actually reached the 30 mark. In the case of the UK banking sector, the leverage multiple was also high, reaching slightly above the 25 mark in the summer of 2008 (Bank of Canada 2008, 24). European banks were thus even more vulnerable to a crisis of confidence in financial markets than US banks.

Similar to the situation in the US, monetary imbalances created the conditions for European banks' troubles; however, in the EU's case, it was not the imbalances with Asia and oil-producing countries that were so much at fault but those that were actually taking place inside the EU, especially inside the euro area (Berger and Nitsch 2013; Chen et al. 2012). Countries in the North, like Germany and the Netherlands, with current account (or trade) surpluses, were financing spending and indebtedness in the South and the East, where countries were running current account deficits. In other words, savings in the North were financing consumption and investment in the rest of the EU and these funds were channelled through Europe's banking system. In Greece and Italy, cheap funds served mostly to finance public indebtedness whereas in Ireland and Spain they were directed at private consumption, especially housing, with Portugal standing somewhere in the middle.[22]

Monetary policy in the eurozone contributed to fuelling the imbalances between the North and the South that developed after the euro's inception. In fact, as Bayoumi and Eichengreen (1997) concluded more than a decade ago, the eurozone is made up of two core optimum currency areas (OCAs),[23] one centred on France and Germany (with Austria, the Benelux countries, and Slovenia) and another on southern European countries. Contrary to what Frankel and Rose (1998) argued, an OCA for the eurozone did not arise endogenously following the introduction of the single currency (Willett et al. 2010). Thus, given that the ECB's monetary policy is targeted to the entire euro area rather than specific countries and that the Franco-German core is the most significant part of the eurozone economy, the common monetary policy was better suited to the economic situation of northern countries than that of the Euro-Med

ones. For instance, between 2001 and 2005 the German economy pretty much stagnated, with an average annual real GDP growth rate of less than 0.5 per cent. At the same time, Greece, Ireland, and Spain were experiencing rates of growth above 3 per cent of GDP. Hence, for them the eurozone's monetary policy should have been much stricter than it actually was. Interest rates should have been much higher in order to slow down growth and inflation, which was running at over 3 per cent annually, compared with less than 2 per cent in Germany. Loose monetary policy in Greece, Ireland, and Spain only fanned the flames of cheap credit that was available to these countries.

The only option left for countries facing inflationary pressures and a common monetary policy that is too loose is to use fiscal policy to cool the economy down. However, this is politically difficult to justify: how can a government raise taxes or decrease public spending when the economy is booming, especially if public debt is itself declining? In fact, Ireland and Spain were already running budget surpluses during that period. The Greek case is the most conspicuous since fiscal deficits were averaging 5 per cent of GDP at a time when the economy was booming. Clearly, the government was adding fuel to the fire when it should have been trying to put it out, which explains why Greece's public finances exploded when the global financial crisis hit. The egregious Greek situation is one that the EU's Stability and Growth Pact was supposed to prevent but did not, because it was politically difficult to enforce, with the member states having to vote to impose sanctions on each other as well as themselves (Heipertz and Verdun 2010).[24] As a result, financial markets were counted on to exercise the necessary pressures on governments whose finances were not sustainable (Leblond 2006). But they did not. Until early 2009, sovereign bond investors (led by European banks) were happy to treat eurozone countries as if they were all Germany, on the assumption that no member state would ever be allowed to default and give up the euro (Chang and Leblond 2014).

If fiscal policy was not politically feasible, from compensating the inability of the eurozone's monetary policy to dealing with the economic disparities that existed between member states, what about regulation? For example, the supply of credit to consumers and firms could have been restricted by limiting banks' leverage. As in Canada, the regulators could have imposed a ceiling on the amount of leverage that banks were allowed to undertake (Leblond 2011).[25] Alternatively, they could have required banks to hold more capital against the mortgages that they were underwriting as the level of household indebtedness increased and real estate markets were booming, an approach known as countercyclical provisioning. They could also have made the purchase of housing with debt more difficult by lowering allowable loan-to-value ratios,[26] as Canada has done in recent years. The problem in the EU and the eurozone more specifically was that there was no single supranational financial supervisor that could make such regulatory changes. Under a broad regulatory framework set at the EU level, national supervisors were responsible for applying financial rules to banks under their jurisdiction.[27] However, they have tended to adopt measures that were favourable to their national banking systems and economies (Grossman and Leblond 2011). It was politically difficult, if not impossible, for national financial supervisors to impose stricter rules on the banks they regulated if the ultimate outcome was an economic slowdown or customers taking their business to another member state's banks, where no such regulatory restrictions applied.[28]

In sum, the GFC was the result of an explosive cocktail: monetary imbalances fanned by loose monetary policy, financial innovations whose risks were not well-understood by market participants and regulators, financial supervisors who were reluctant to tighten the screws on banks to take away the punchbowl before the party was over, and individuals who believed (or were led to believe) that "this time was different," so the good economic times would last. When the providers of credit (i.e., the investors) began to doubt, too late, that all was well, the party was effectively over.[29] But by then the partygoers' excesses made for a rude hangover, tempered with monetary and fiscal medicine. So, ultimately, this crisis was no different than the ones that took place before it (Reinhart and Rogoff 2009, Roubini and Mihm 2010). The cycle of manias, panics, and crashes associated with rapid credit expansion followed by even faster contraction, so well analyzed by Kindleberger and Aliber (2005), repeated itself once again in Europe and the United States.

Preventing the Next Crisis

Although history has taught us that completely preventing financial crises is very difficult, if not impossible,[30] it did not take long for the machinery of global financial governance to get to work to redress the weaknesses highlighted by the global financial crisis. It began with the G20 meeting of heads of state and government that was held in London in early April 2009.[31] This is when the Financial Stability Forum was upgraded to the Financial Stability Board (FSB), and charged by G20 leaders with the task of spearheading and co-ordinating the efforts to reform the rules governing international finance as well as to comply with them.[32] At the same time, the Basel Committee on Banking Supervision (BCBS), which was expanded to include all G20 national regulatory agencies, began revising the Basel II banking standards, which were in the process of being implemented nationally. Finally, at the April 2009 G20 summit in London, the IMF was given significantly more financial resources to intervene in crisis-ridden countries to help stabilize financial markets with sovereign loans, which it eventually did in the eurozone as well as in Iceland and Central and Eastern Europe; however, it was not given new responsibilities per se in terms of crisis prevention, but more an enhancement of existing surveillance initiatives. Many of these were put in place in the aftermath of the Asian financial crisis, some dating even further back (e.g., Best 2010b; Pauly 2008).[33]

In light of the central role that monetary imbalances played in the global financial crisis, whether in the US or in the EU, they should have been given the highest level of attention by G20 leaders in their attempt to reform the rules of the international financial system. The IMF is the best-placed international organization to deal with such an issue given that it has been dealing with balance of payments disequilibria since its creation. For this reason, the G20 asked the IMF to provide it with technical analysis for the mutual assessment process (MAP) that the leaders agreed to in November 2009 at their Pittsburgh summit. The IMF's role is to analyze G20 members' medium-term economic plans to determine their aggregate effect on the world economy, including whether global monetary imbalances are likely to improve or worsen. In response, the IMF was expected to develop policy suggestions for G20 members, at the individual as well as the collective level. The issue here has been for the IMF and the G20 members to agree on a common framework for measuring imbalances (Eichengreen 2011). In addition, the IMF has decided to pay more attention to monetary imbalances in its multilateral surveillance responsibilities (i.e., those based on its own data and not those provided by G20 members), as in its flagship publications: *World Economic Outlook* and *Global Financial Stability Report*. Finally, the IMF also began publishing an external sector report in July 2012, which "contains

a multilaterally consistent assessment of members' external balances, currencies, and policies" (IMF 2013, 2).

Although the above surveillance endeavours are useful in highlighting the extent of global monetary imbalances and how they can be corrected, the problem will persist as long as G20 members are not willing to prioritize them over domestic interests so they can coordinate their efforts in view of fostering a more stable world economy.[34] According to Pettis (2013), this will be very difficult to achieve in an orderly way. For example, Germany's leaders are unlikely to adopt policies that encourage Germans to consume more and save less, including possibly the government increasing its own consumption and, as a result, running fiscal deficits. This would be a major policy reversal for German leaders and a cultural shift for the population, which is therefore unlikely to support it. The ongoing battle between the White House and Congress in the US over reducing the federal government's deficit is another example of the challenge that the G20 faces in resolving global monetary imbalances. In China, moving from an export- and investment-led growth model to one based on consumption and innovation is also likely to be a difficult process and one that will take a long time, given the leadership's aversion to rapid economic change and the risk of political instability that may arise as a result. And there is not much that the IMF can do about it since its role is limited to identifying the extent of the problem and offering various policy solutions (Guerrieri 2010); it cannot force its largest member states, such as the US, Germany, and China, to adopt these solutions. It has no leverage over them because they do not borrow from it.

Financial innovation, namely securitization and derivative products such as CDSs, has been blamed for the global financial crisis. However, G20 members have refrained from regulating the creation of new financial products and thereby impeding financial innovation directly. As such, they have heeded two of the basic principles of financial regulation identified by Davies and Green (2008): (1) there should be a balance between financial system stability and risk-taking by financial firms; (2) competition is necessary for risk-taking. This was stated most clearly in the communiqué issued at the leaders' first G20 summit in Washington in November 2008: "Regulators must ensure that their actions support market discipline, avoid potentially adverse impacts on other countries, including regulatory arbitrage, and support competition, dynamism and innovation in the marketplace" (G20 2008). The logic is that regulation must provide the boundaries in which competition and innovation in financial markets take place. It must ensure that the potential costs of competition and innovation in terms of financial system instability are taken into account when financial firms' managers and traders make decisions.[35]

Financial regulation involves key measures such as minimum capital adequacy requirements, limits on leverage, minimum liquidity ratios, as well as more transparency in terms of the information available to financial market participants. These measures are the responsibility of the BCBS, which rapidly developed the Basel III standards in light of the crisis. In December 2010, the BCBS issued its regulatory standards on banks' capital and liquidity requirements. The objective was to raise banks' capital requirements so that they would have lower leverage and thus be less risky for the financial system. The Basel III framework also now includes minimum levels of liquidity for banks, something that was absent in the previous Basel standards. This is to ensure that banks have sufficient liquidities in case they face difficulties in rolling over debt or must pay back depositors who may be concerned with the safety of their money.

This measure is not meant to prevent a full-blown run on banks or a credit freeze but to buy time for the central bank (as lender of last resort) and the government to react reasonably to the situation at hand.

Lall (2012) argues that Basel III (and Basel II for that matter) fell short of the BCBS's original objectives, meaning that the new rules for capital and liquidity are not as stringent as initially intended (see also Admati and Hellwig 2013). The reason for this absence of significant change is that large multinational banks were able to "hijack" the negotiations because they have superior information about the regulatory agenda, which allows them to be "first at the decision-making table, giving them disproportionate influence over the substance of new rules" (Lall 2012, 618). Lall also argues that the fact that negotiations at the BCBS take place behind closed doors and are not subject to ratification by national parliaments provides an institutional environment that allows large multinational banks to have a "first-mover" advantage. Looking specifically at Basel II, Young (2012) challenges the view that large multinational banks have "captured" the BCBS. He argues that, although these banks have access and influence, the regulators who sit on the BCBS do not always accept their demands. Young argues that national banking regulators have significant resources and discretion to stand up to the banks, and sometimes do so. Nevertheless, Admati and Hellwig (2013, 194–9) point out that banks as well as regulators and politicians constantly argue that global competition in banking requires a level playing field. This is simply an excuse for fighting rules that they dislike and gaining advantages for their industry.

If the Basel III accord is less than originally intended, its implementation at the national (or regional, in the EU's case) level has not been without tampering, often in a way that weakens the standards agreed to in Basel. For instance,

Howarth and Quaglia (2012) argue that, following pressures from France and Germany, the European Commission issued a draft legislation (known as the Capital Requirement Directive [CRD] IV) that softened some of the Basel III provisions, to take into account the particularities of EU banking systems. In the US, Blinder (2013) describes how the implementation of the Dodd-Frank Wall Street Reform and Consumer Protection Act, which aims to reform the US financial system and its regulation, was delayed and weakened as a result of bank lobbying and Republican opposition in Congress.[36]

> Through all this, one group has kept its eye squarely on the ball. That's the financial industry and its legion of lobbyists, aided immensely by the U.S. Supreme Court's 2010 landmark *Citizens United* [italics in original] decision, which, in effect, allows corporations to make unlimited political contributions (Blinder 2013, 318).

Lavelle (2013, 217) also argues that the Dodd-Frank Act, although it went much further than initially anticipated, did not actually "change institutional behavior" because the system and its leadership had not really changed; all parts (industry and regulators) had strong vested interests in preserving the status quo.

In addition to increasing capital requirements and imposing liquidity minima for banks, legislators in the UK and the US have adopted structural measures aimed at reducing contagion in the system. The Dodd-Frank Act includes a provision known as the Volcker Rule,[37] which bans commercial banks from proprietary trading (i.e., trading with the bank's own money to generate speculative revenues); only trading on behalf of customers is allowed. This constitutes a partial return to the Glass-Steagall era, when commercial and investment banking were separate, because only investment banks and hedge funds would be allowed to do proprietary trading. The problem with this rule, however, is that it is very difficult to differentiate proprietary trading from market making on behalf of clients (Blinder 2013, 274–5). Moreover, it is likely to move a large share of trading activities to a less regulated area of the financial system, which may end up making the system less stable (Blinder 2013, 273). Across the Atlantic, UK legislators, following recommendations from the Independent Commission on Banking (also known as the Vickers Commission), decided to ring-fence retail banking from other (riskier) activities conducted by banks. This means that retail banks will be limited mostly to collecting deposits and making loans.[38] The EU is also considering some form of banking activity separation. In October 2012, a high-level group of experts chaired by Erkki Liikanen, governor of the Bank of Finland, produced a report that recommended a complete ban on trading by commercial banks in the EU, thereby avoiding the Volker Rule's need to distinguish between types of trading (Vickers 2012, 16–17). Following the report's publication, the European Commission was tasked with drafting legislation to be adopted by EU member states and the European Parliament.

In the aftermath of the global financial crisis, the above makes clear that institutional and regulatory reforms have taken place at the international as well as the national (or regional) level. The key issue, however, is not so much that change has happened, since it was expected,[39] but how much has really changed given the severity of the crisis. Kahler (2013, 48) states that changes in institutional innovation at the G20, FSB, BCBS, and IMF, are "limited." This is because the changes represent upgrades to the existing system of global financial governance rather than a restructuring of the system (e.g., the creation of a global financial regulator). As for regulatory reforms, significant changes have been made to make the global financial system more resilient but it is still too soon to determine how effective they will be in practice given that they will not be completely implemented at the national level until the end of the decade. As mentioned above, there are certainly doubts when it comes to US financial reforms under Dodd-Frank. But such concerns also apply to the international level. For example, Kahler (2013, 47) writes that "resistance to effective international surveillance on the part of the major economic powers is likely to persist." Thus, many scholars believe that financial regulation after the global financial crisis is likely to be characterized by a large degree of continuity rather than systemic restructuring (e.g., Helleiner 2014, Helleiner et al. 2010), as was the case after the Great Depression (Kahler 2013).

There are, however, other analysts who argue that a new global financial order will emerge in the aftermath of the crisis (Drezner and McNamara 2013). According to Germain (2010), the state will become the central "locus of regulatory authority" and the world economy will experience a period of "deliberalization" (i.e., the process of globalization will reverse). For Helleiner and Pagliari (2011), a period of organized regulatory divergence (what they call "cooperative decentralization") is in store for global financial governance, leading to a weakening of international standards in favour of national (or regional) ones. The authors argue that this is, first, because interstate power will be more diffuse in the future, because regional powers such as Brazil, China, and India are now members of the key international financial standard-setting bodies, such as the BCBS and the FSB. Second, they suggest that the politicization of financial regulation will make it more difficult for regulators to find an international consensus. Finally, it is likely that regulators will conclude that adopting a one-size-fits-all approach will most probably not work since countries have different financial systems (see also Germain 2010). As we saw above, the EU has certainly adopted this position when it comes to transposing the Basel III rules into EU law.

Whether a new global financial order is emerging or not, what is clear is that G20 governments and the international financial institutions that support them have adopted regulatory and surveillance measures that address the main causes behind the global financial crisis: monetary imbalances, leverage, and liquidity. It remains to be seen how effective these measures will be once they are fully implemented at the national level, for the devil is obviously in the details when it comes to financial regulation and supervision. But, at the very least, the reforms have so far been in the right direction, at least in the case of banks, which will find themselves operating in a more constraining regulatory environment in the foreseeable future.

Conclusion

The global financial crisis is the result of the interplay of: (1) domestic policy decisions in Europe, the United States, and East Asia; (2) the structure of the world's oil market; (3) the structure of international trade and production; and (4) the unfettered flow of capital across borders. Therefore, to gain a full understanding of the global financial crisis and its aftermath, one needs to analyze three contexts together: domestic, interstate, and transnational (Helleiner and Pagliari 2011). But "few scholars succeeded in drawing together the politics of the macro story of the global imbalances with the politics of the micro-level market and regulatory failures" (Helleiner 2011, 85). This is why there was a general failure to foresee the crisis, even though many scholars got parts of the story right (Helleiner 2011).

But one might question the extent to which it is realistic to expect scholars to develop "more comprehensive analytical tools to explain global financial crises" while at the same time "[open] the black box of global finance to explore the specific practices and products, institutions and rules, as well as ideas and culture that make up global markets" and, finally, "[pay attention] to the links between global markets and financial practices at more local and everyday-life levels" (Helleiner 2011, 84–5). Given such a gargantuan task, scholars might have an easier time focusing their time and energy on efforts to prevent the next crisis.

The debate about the future of the international financial architecture seems to oppose a scenario of continuity to one of cooperative decentralization. In the first case, there is incremental change in favour of more regulation but the governance structure itself does not really change. The reforms are not, however, considered sufficient to make much of a difference in the way that global financial markets conduct themselves. This means that the likelihood of a crisis occurring in the near future is high. In the second case, it is not at all clear whether the system will be more resilient and stable, because there is technically more discretion for national-level regulators. If it shares similarities with the embedded liberalism compromise of the Bretton Woods era, then decentralized cooperation may have a positive impact on the global financial system. In any event, regardless of how the international financial architecture evolves, financial crises will not be a thing of the past because global financial orders contain the seeds of their own demise, in what Drezner and McNamara (2013) refer to as a Kuhnian life-cycle framework: a crisis is a necessary (though apparently not sufficient) condition for moving from one global financial order to another.

Notes

1 In 2006, subprime mortgages accounted for close to one quarter of the US residential mortgage market, compared to less than 10 per cent 5 years earlier. In Canada, subprime mortgages never represented more than 5 per cent of the market (IMF 2008, 15).

2 For a detailed account of the failure and rescue of Bear Stearns, see Cohan (2009).

3 For a detailed account of Lehman Brothers' bankruptcy, see McDonald and Robinson (2009).

4 At the same time, Merrill Lynch, another important US investment bank facing financial problems, managed to sell itself to Bank of America.

5 AIG was also heavily exposed to the US subprime mortgage market. First, it had issued a large number of credit default (CDSs) swaps on subprime (mortgage) collateralized debt obligations (CDOs) (see glossary). According to Lowenstein (2010, 55), although AIG stopped writing CDSs on subprime CDOs at the end of 2005, it was still exposed to some of the riskiest CDOs, for a total amount of US$80 billion by the time the crisis hit. Second, AIG had invested billions of US dollars in MBSs, with an average maturity of 10 to 12 years, using cash that it had to pay back to clients in 20 to 30 days (Lowenstein 2010, 154). This maturity mismatch caused AIG grave liquidity problems, in addition to the liabilities arising from the CDSs it had issued. That is why it had to be rescued by the US government.

6 For details on the US government's rescue of the financial system, see Sorkin (2009).

7 Short-term liabilities do not necessarily mean that banks repay those debts when they come due. In fact, they often take out new debt to repay the old debt, which is why we speak of debt rollover.

8 If a financial asset (e.g., a bond) is rated "junk," then it means that certain investors—most especially conservative institutional investors like insurance companies and pension funds—can no longer buy such an asset. As a result, there is less demand for this asset, which leads to a decrease in its price and an increase in its yield.

9 The figure was again revised by Eurostat in November 2010, to 15.4 per cent of GDP.

10 The same day, not by coincidence, the ECB announced that it was suspending, in the case of Greek government debt, its requirement that debt instruments accepted as collateral in refinancing operations satisfy a minimum credit rating threshold. This measure ensured that eurozone banks would be able to continue offering Greek sovereign debt as collateral against loans from the Eurosystem even if credit ratings on Greek debt were falling below the ECB's minimal requirement.

11 This is a result of globalized supply and production chains (also known as global value chains) that firms, large and small, have come to rely upon to compete effectively in world markets (see Van Assche 2012).

12 Many East Asian countries had no official policy of fixing their exchange rates but Calvo and Reinhart (2002) found that they did so anyway.

13 For an excellent analysis of the domestic politics behind China's undervalued exchange rate, see Steinberg and Shih (2012).

14 For details on the Latin American debt crisis that took place in the 1980s, see Ffrench-Davis (2000) and Kahler (1985).

15 As it happened, many financial institutions that securitized their mortgages ended up taking them back onto their balance sheet as a result of liquidity and credit enhancements that were attached to these securities to entice investors to buy them. Even in the absence of such enhancements, some banks bought back the securitized mortgages at their nominal value to maintain good business relations with their clients.

16 The fact that an investment vehicle offered higher rates of returns for a level of risk that was supposedly equal to that of a US government bond should have made investors sceptical.

17 However, Cohan's (2009) detailed description of Bear Stearns' demise demonstrates that such a view was not pervasive across Wall Street.

18 Rajan (2010, chapter 1) argues that US politicians have supported policies in favour of easy credit for households, especially for housing, as a way to deal with growing income inequalities.

19 Inadequate financial supervision has also been blamed for the global financial crisis, though contradictory arguments have been made (Masciandaro et al. 2011). In the US, for instance, the large number of financial supervisors has been blamed because no one agency had a complete view of the financial system and financial firms could play off supervisors against each other (Baily 2009). A similar argument has been made about the EU since there was no single supranational financial supervisor to deal properly with the growth in cross-border banking in Europe (see Leblond 2011, 173). Surprisingly, Masciandaro et al. (2011) find that having multiple financial supervisors does not make financial systems less resilient (or more prone to crises); the issue is not so much how many supervisors there are but what they do.

20 In 1956, the Bank Holding Act further restricted banks' activities. Commercial banks could not enter into non-banking activities such as insurance or equity investment (i.e., banks could not invest in company stocks). Furthermore, they could not buy banks in another state.

21 Stiglitz (2009) called this situation ersatz capitalism: "the privatizing of gains and the socializing of losses."

22 It is important to note that before the crisis, Ireland and Spain had public debts that were among the lowest in Europe.

23 An OCA is deemed to exist if its members (countries or subnational regions) possess at least one of three characteristics. First, they must face similar shocks to their economies and react to these shocks in the same way. Second, in the absence of such symmetry, an OCA occurs if the member states have sufficient labour and capital mobility between them so that factors of production can move from one country experiencing an economic downturn to another enjoying an upturn. Finally, if both symmetry and factors of production mobility are inexistent, then an OCA exists if there is a high level of price flexibility (especially wages) in member states. For further details, see Kenen and Meade (2008).

24 The Stability and Growth Pact (SGP) was reformed in 2011 to address many of its shortcomings, which the eurozone debt crisis made only more obvious. For instance, it is now harder for EU member states to block the imposition of sanctions following non-compliance with the SGP's rules (for details, see Seng and Biesenbender 2012).

25 The maximum leverage multiple that Canadian banks could have on their balance sheet was 20, with some exceptions that allowed it to go up to 22. As mentioned above, banking leverage in Europe and the US was often well above a multiple of 30.

26 In many places throughout the EU, individuals were able to purchase housing solely with debt (i.e. a loan-to-value ratio of 100 per cent). In some cases, like the UK, banks would lend more than the actual value of the house or apartment, assuming that its value would continue increasing rapidly in the future.

27 National regulatory agencies were expected to coordinate their activities and share information at the EU level under the aegis of the Committee of European Banking Supervisors; however, the latter's effectiveness was very limited since it had no authority to impose rules and regulations on pan-European banking groups, let alone national ones, or to require national agencies to undertake certain actions (Véron 2007).

28 Customers did not even have to cross borders to do business with banks benefiting from less stringent regulations since branches of banks from other EU member states were regulated and supervised by their home (not host) national regulatory agency under the EU's passport (i.e. mutual recognition) system: once a bank is licensed in one member state it can operate in the rest of the EU by setting up branches (separate legal subsidiaries are subject to host-country supervision and regulation).

29 This is the self-fulfilling nature of financial markets.

30 Financial crises may not be avoidable but their intensity and frequency can be reduced with financial regulation and supervision.

31 For an analysis of the G20's enhanced role in the international economic governance's architecture and the challenges that it faces, see Cooper and Bradford (2010).

32 For an analysis of the FSB's creation, role and challenges, see Helleiner (2010).

33 The IMF has been severely criticized for failing to identify the vulnerabilities that led to the global financial crisis, including in a report by its own Independent Evaluation Office (for details, see Bossone 2011).

34 This problem of international cooperation is not limited to global monetary imbalances. It also applies to financial regulation and supervision (Davies 2010). This should not be surprising as it is a general feature of international relations.

35 It presupposes that both market participants as well as regulators understand and adequately measure the distribution of risks of financial products, both individually as well as collectively. As we saw above, this is easier said than done.

36 In the Congress's case, delays occurred with regards to nominations to financial regulatory agencies as well as funding (appropriations) increases for agencies like the Securities and Exchange Commission and the Commodities Futures Trading Commission, which are not self-financed unlike the Federal Reserve and the Federal Deposit Insurance Corporation.

37 US President Obama coined the term because Paul Volcker, former chairman of the Federal Reserve and advisor to the president at the time, was the measure's main advocate. For details on the measure's adoption, see Blinder (2013, 311–12).

38 For an analysis of the UK's retail ring-fencing measure in the context of other structural reform alternatives like the Volcker Rule, see Vickers (2012).

39 The recent historical record suggests that financial crises are followed by institutional and regulatory reforms. For instance, the

Great Depression was followed by the creation of the Bretton Woods institutions based on the idea of embedded liberalism (Ruggie 1982). The stagflation of the 1970s along with the economic recession that affected the developed world in the late 1970s and early 1980s, which contributed to the decade-long Latin American debt crisis, saw a long period of economic and financial liberalization in their wake (Abdelal 2007, Helleiner 1994). Finally, the East Asian financial crisis of 1997–98 also led to changes in the international financial architecture (Kenen 2001).

Key Terms

asset-backed securities (ABSs)
assets
balance sheet
capital
collateralized debt obligation (CDO)
credit default swap (CDS)
deleveraging

leverage
liabilities
liquidity
mortgage
mortgage-backed securities (MBSs)
securitizaton
yield

Questions for Review

1. Why did so few people foresee the global financial crisis?
2. What are the main causes of the global financial crisis in Europe and the United States? Do they differ from one side of the Atlantic to the other?
3. Why did Canada not experience a financial crisis in 2008–09?
4. Why did the global financial crisis not cause another Great Depression (just a Great Recession)?
5. Is the global financial system safer as a result of Basel III and the other global financial reforms that have been adopted under the G20's auspices in the aftermath of the global financial crisis? Are financial crises now a thing of the past?
6. Why is it necessary to analyse the domestic, interstate, and transnational contexts together in order to gain a full understanding of the global financial crisis and its aftermath?
7. What is the role of the state in the post-crisis international financial architecture? Is it different than in the pre-crisis period?

Further Resources

Davies, H. and Green, D. *Global financial regulation: The essential guide.*

Drezner, D.W. *The system worked: How the world stopped another Great Depression.*

Hardie, I. and Howarth, D. (Eds). *Market-based banking & the international financial crisis.*

Helleiner, E., Pagliari, S. and Zimmermann, H. (Eds). *Global finance in crisis: The politics of international regulatory change.*

Kindleberger, C. and Aliber, R. (1996). *Manias, panics, and crashes: A history of financial crises,* 3rd ed. New York: John Wiley & Sons.

Lane, P.R. (2012). "The European sovereign debt crisis." *Journal of Economic Perspectives* 26(3), 49–68.

Mishkin, F.S. (2011). "Over the cliff: From the subprime to the global financial crisis." *Journal of Economic Perspectives* 25(1) 49–70.

Reinhart, C.M. and Rogoff, K.S. *This time is different: Eight centuries of financial folly.*

References

Abdelal, R. (2007). *Capital rules: The construction of global finance*. Cambridge, MA: Harvard University Press.

Admati, A. and Hellwig, M. (2013). *The bankers' new clothes: What's wrong with banking and what to do about it*. Princeton, NJ: Princeton University Press.

Attinasi, M. G., Checherita, C. and Nickel, C. (2010). "Euro area fiscal policies and the crisis: The reaction of financial markets." In A. van Riet, (Ed.), "Euro area fiscal policies and the crisis," Occasional Paper Series No. 109, April. Frankfurt: European Central Bank 35–43.

Baily, M. N. (2009). "Strengthening and streamlining prudential bank supervision." Fixing Finance Series No. 2009-05. Washington, DC: Brookings Institution.

Bank of Canada. (2008). "Financial system review." December. Ottawa. Available online at www.bankofcanada.ca/wp-content/uploads/2010/04/fsr_1208.pdf.

Bank of Canada. (2011). "Financial system review." June. Ottawa. Available online at www.bankofcanada.ca/wp-content/uploads/2011/06/fsr_0611.pdf.

Bayoumi, T. and Eichengreen, B. (1997). "Ever closer to heaven? An optimum-currency-area index for European countries." *European Economic Review* 41(3–5) 761–70.

Berger, H. and Nitsch, V. (2013). "Bilateral imbalances in Europe." *CESifo Economic Studies* 59(3) 559–75.

Bernanke, B. S. (2005). "The global saving glut and the U.S. current account deficit." Remarks delivered at the Sandridge Lecture, Virginia Association of Economists, Richmond, Virginia, 10 March. Washington, DC: Federal Reserve Board. Available online at www.federalreserve.gov/boarddocs/speeches/2005/200503102/.

Best, J. (2010a). "The limits of financial risk management: Or what we didn't learn from the Asian crisis." *New Political Economy* 15(1), 29–49.

Best, J. (2010b). "Bringing power back in: The IMF's constructivist strategy in critical perspective." In Abdelal, R., Blyth, M., and Parsons, C. (Eds). *Constructing the international economy*. Ithaca, NY: Cornell University Press, 194–210.

Blinder, A.S. (2013). *After the music stopped: The financial crisis, the response, and the work ahead*. New York: The Penguin Press.

Bossone, B. (2011). "At the shrink's bed: The IMF, the global crisis and the Independent Evaluation Office report." VoxEU.org, 11 February. Available online at www.voxeu.org/index.php?q=node/6099.

Brunnermeier, M. K. (2009). "Deciphering the liquidity and credit crunch 2007–2008." *Journal of Economic Perspectives* 23(1), 77–100.

Calvo, G. A. and Reinhart, C. M. (2002). "Fear of floating." *Quarterly Journal of Economics* 117(2), 379–408.

Carmassi, J., Gros, D. and Micossi, S. (2009). "The global financial crisis: Causes and cures." *Journal of Common Market Studies* 47(5), 977–96.

Chailloux, A., Gray, S., Klüh, U., Shimizu, S., and Stella, P. (2008). "Central bank response to the 2007–08 Financial Market Turbulence: Experiences and lessons drawn." IMF Working Paper No. WP/08/210. Washington: International Monetary Fund.

Chang, M. and Leblond, P. (2014). "All in: Market expectations of eurozone integrity in the sovereign debt crisis." *Review of International Political Economy*, advance online publication.

Chen, R, Milesi-Ferretti, G.M. and Tressel, T. (2012). "External imbalances in the euro area." IMF Working Paper No. WP/12/236. Washington, DC: International Monetary Fund.

Cohan, W. D. (2009). *House of cards: A tale of hubris and wretched excess on Wall Street*. New York: Doubleday.

Cooper, A. F. and Bradford, C. (2010). "The G20 and the post-crisis economic order." CIGI G20 Paper No. 3. Waterloo, ON: Centre for International Governance Innovation.

Coval, J., Jurek, J. and Stafford, E. (2009). "The economics of structured finance." *Journal of Economic Perspectives* 23(1), 3–25.

Davies, H. (2010). "Global financial regulation after the credit crisis." *Global Policy* 1(2), 185–90.

Davies, H. and Green, D. (2008). *Global financial regulation: The essential guide*. Cambridge: Polity Press.

Drezner, D. W. and McNamara, K. R. (2013). "International Political Economy, global financial orders and the 2008 financial crisis." *Perspectives on Politics* 11(1), 155–66.

Dunaway, S. (2009). "Global imbalances and the financial crisis." Council Special Report No. 44, March. New York: Council on Foreign Relations.

ECB. (2010a). "Measures taken by euro area governments in support of the financial sector." *Monthly Bulletin* April. Frankfurt: European Central Bank, 75–90.

ECB. (2010b). "The effectiveness of euro area fiscal policies." *Monthly Bulletin* July. Frankfurt: European Central Bank, 67–83.

Eichengreen, B. (2011). "The G20 and global imbalances." VoxEU.org, 26 June. Available online at www.voxeu.org/article/g20-and-global-imbalances.

European Commission. (2008). "A European economic recovery plan." COM(2008)800, 26 November. Brussels.

European Commission. (2009a). "Economic crisis in Europe: Causes, consequences and responses." *European Economy* 7. Brussels: Directorate-General for Financial and Economic Affairs.

European Commission. (2009b). "Public finances in EMU—2009." *European Economy* 5, June. Brussels: Directorate-General for Economic and Financial Affairs.

European Commission. (2010). "Public finances in EMU—2010." *European Economy* 4, June. Brussels: Directorate-General for Economic and Financial Affairs.

Featherstone, K. (2011). "The Greek sovereign debt crisis and EMU: A Failing State in a Skewed Regime." *Journal of Common Market Studies* 49(2), 193–217.

Financial Crisis Inquiry Commission. (2011). *The Financial crisis inquiry report: Final report of the National Commission on the causes of the financial and economic Crisis in the United States*. Washington, DC: U.S. Government Printing Office. Available online at www.gpo.gov/fdsys/pkg/GPO-FCIC/pdf/GPO-FCIC.pdf.

Frankel, J. A. and Rose, A. K. (1998). "The endogeneity of the optimum currency area criteria." *Economic Journal* 108(449), 1009–25.

Ffrench-Davis, R. (2000). *Reforming the reforms in Latin America: Macroeconomics, trade and finance*. Basingstoke: Macmillan Press.

Germain, R. (2010). *Global politics & financial governance*. New York: Palgrave Macmillan.

G20. (2008). "Declaration of the summit on financial marketsand the world economy." November 15. Washington. Available online at www.g20.utoronto.ca/2008/2008declaration1115.html.

Grossman, E. and Leblond, P. (2011). "European financial integration: Finally the great leap forward?." *Journal of Common Market Studies* 49(2), 413–35.

Guerrieri, P. (2010). "Multipolar governance and global imbalances." *International Affairs* 86(3), 681–92.

Hardie, I. and Howarth, D. (Eds). (2013). *Market-based banking and the international financial crisis*. Oxford: Oxford University Press.

Heipertz, M. and Verdun, A. (2010). *Ruling Europe: The politics of the stability and growth pact*. New York: Cambridge University Press.

Helleiner, E. (1994). *States and the reemergence of global finance: From Bretton Woods to the 1990s*. Ithaca, NY: Cornell University Press.

Helleiner, E. (2010). "What Role for the New Financial Stability Board? The politics of international standards after the crisis." *Global Policy* 1(3), 282–90.

Helleiner, E. (2011). "Understanding the 2007–2008 global financial crisis: Lessons for scholars of international political economy." *Annual Review of Political Science* 14, 67–87.

Helleiner, E. (2014). *The Status Quo Crisis: Global financial governance after the 2008 meltdown*, New York: Oxford University Press.

Helleiner, E. and Pagliari, S. (2011). "The end of an era in international financial regulation? A postcrisis research agenda." *International Organization* 65(1), 169–200.

Helleiner, E., Pagliari, S. and Zimmermann, H. (Eds). (2010). *Global finance in crisis: The politics of international regulatory change*. New York: Routledge.

Hodson, D. and Quaglia, L. (2009). "European perspectives on the global financial crisis: Introduction." *Journal of Common Market Studies* 47(5), 939–53.

Howarth, D. and Quaglia, L. (2012). "Banking on stability: The political economy of the new capital requirements in the European Union." *Journal of European Integration* 35(3), 333–46.

IMF. (2008). "Canada: Selected Issues." IMF Country Report No. 08/70. Washington, DC: International Monetary Fund.

IMF. (2009). "Canada: 2009 Article IV consultation—Staff Report; staff statement; and public information notice on the executive board discussion." IMF Country Report No. 09/162. Washington, DC: International Monetary Fund.

IMF. (2013). "Strengthening surveillance—Lessons from the financial crisis." Factsheet, March 26. Washington: International Monetary Fund. Available online at www.imf.org/external/np/exr/facts/pdf/refsurv.pdf.

Johnson, M. and Oakley, D. (2009). "Spate of downgrades raises fears a big economy could be next." *Financial Times*, 23 January.

Kahler, M. (1985). "Politics and international debt: Explaining the crisis." *International Organization* 39(3), 357–82.

Kalher, M. (2013). "Economic Crisis and Global Governance: The stability of a globalized world." In Kahler, M. and Lake, D. (Eds). *Politics in the new hard times: The great recession in comparative perspective*. Ithaca, NY: Cornell University Press, 27–51.

Kenen, P. B. (2001). *The international financial architecture: What's new? What's missing*. Washington, DC: (Peterson) Institute for International Economics.

Kenen, P. B. and Meade, E. E. (2008). *Regional monetary integration*. New York: Cambridge University Press.

Kindleberger, C. P. and Aliber, R. (2005). *Manias, panics, and crashes: A history of financial crises*, 5th ed. Hoboken, NJ: John Wiley & Sons.

Lall, R. (2012). "From failure to failure: The politics of international banking regulation." *Review of International Political Economy* 19(4), 609–38.

Lavelle, K.C. (2013). *Money and banks in the American political system*. New York: Cambridge University Press.

Leblond, P. (2006). "The political stability and growth pact is dead: Long live the economic stability and growth pact." *Journal of Common Market Studies* 44(5), 969–90.

Leblond, P. (2011). "A Canadian Perspective on the EU's financial architecture and the crisis." In K. Hübner, (Ed.). *Europe, Canada and the comprehensive economic partnership*. New York: Routledge, 165–79.

Leblond, P. (2013). "Cool Canada: A case of low market-based banking in the Anglo-Saxon world." In Hardie, I. and Howarth, D. (Eds). *Market-based banking and the international financial crisis*. Oxford: Oxford University Press, 201–17.

Lowenstein, R. (2010). *The end of Wall Street*. New York: The Penguin Press.

Masciandaro, D., Vega Pansini, R. and Quintyn, M. (2011). "The economic crisis: Did financial supervision matter?." IMF Working Paper No. WP/11/261. Washington, DC: International Monetary Fund.

Mayer, C., Pence, K. and Sherlund, S.N. (2009). "The rise in mortgage defaults." *Journal of Economic Perspectives* 23(1), 27–50.

McDonald, L. G. and Robinson, P. (2009). *A colossal failure of common sense: The inside story of the collapse of Lehman Brothers*. New York: Crown Business.

Milne, F. (2008). "Anatomy of the credit crisis: The role of faulty risk management systems." Commentary No. 269, July. Toronto: C.D. Howe Institute.

Minegishi, M. and Cournède, B. (2010). "Monetary Policy Responses to the Crisis and Exit Strategies," OECD Economics Department Working Papers No. 753. Paris: Organisation for Economic Cooperation and Development.

Paulson, Jr., H. M. (2010). *On the brink: Inside the race to stop the collapse of the global financial system*. New York: Business Plus.

Pauly, L. W. (2008). "The Institutional Legacy of Bretton Woods: IMF Surveillance, 1973–2007." In Andrews, D.M. (Ed.). *Orderly change: International monetary relations since Bretton Woods*. Ithaca, NY: Cornell University Press, 189–210.

Pettis, M. (2013). *The great rebalancing: Trade, conflict, and the perilous road ahead for the world economy.* Princeton, NJ: Princeton University Press.

Quaglia, L., Eastwood, R. and Holmes, P. (2009). "The financial turmoil and EU policy co-operation in 2008." *Journal of Common Market Studies* 47(Annual Review), 63–87.

Rajan, R. G. (2005). "Has financial development made the world riskier?" NBER Working Paper No. 11728. Cambridge, MA: National Bureau of Economic Research.

Rajan, R. G. (2010). *Fault lines: How hidden fractures still threaten the world economy.* Princeton, NJ: Princeton University Press.

Reinhart, C. M. and Rogoff, K. S. (2009). *This time is different: Eight centuries of financial folly.* Princeton, NJ: Princeton University Press.

Roubini, N. (2006). "The BW 2 regime: an unstable disequilibrium bound to unravel." *International Economics and Economic Policy* 3(3–4), 303–32.

Roubini, N. and Mihm, S. (2010). *Crisis Economics: A crash course in the future of finance.* New York: The Penguin Press.

Ruggie, J. G. (1982). "International regimes, transactions, and change: Embedded liberalism in the postwar economic order." *International Organization* 36(2), 379–415.

Schwartz, H. M. (2009). *Subprime nation: American power, global capital, and the housing bubble.* Ithaca, NY: Cornell University Press.

Seng, K. and Biesenbender, J. (2012). "Reforming the stability and growth pact in times of crisis." *Journal of Contemporary European Research* 8(4), 451–69.

Sorkin, A. R. (2009). *Too big to fail: The inside story of how Wall Street and Washington fought to save the financial system from crisis—and themselves.* New York: Penguin.

Steinberg, D. A. and Shih, V. C. (2012). "Interest group influence in authoritarian states: The political determinants of Chinese exchange rate policy." *Comparative Political Studies* 45(11), 1405–34.

Stiglitz, J. E. (2009). "Obama's ersatz capitalism." *The New York Times*, 31 March.

Stiglitz, J. E. (2010). *Freefall: America, free markets, and the sinking of the world economy.* New York: W.W. Norton & Co.

Trichet, J.-C. (2010). "State of the union: The financial crisis and the ECB's response between 2007 and 2009." *Journal of Common Market Studies* 48(Annual Review), 7–19.

Van Assche, A. (2012). "Global value chains and Canada's trade policy: Business as usual or paradigm shift." IRPP Study No. 32, June. Montreal: Institute for Research on Public Policy.

Véron, N. (2007). "Is Europe ready for a major banking crisis?." Policy Brief No. 2007/03, August. Brussels: Bruegel.

Vickers, J. (2012). "Some economics of banking reform." Department of Economics Discussion Paper No. 632, November. Oxford: University of Oxford. Available online at www.economics.ox.ac.uk/materials/papers/12467/paper632.pdf.

White, W. (2006). "Financial globalisation." Opening remarks, BIS Fifth Annual Research Conference on "Financial Globalisation," Brunnen, 19 June. Available online at www.bis.org/speeches/sp060619.htm.

Willett, T. D., Permpoon, O. and Whilborg, C. (2010). "Endogenous OCA analysis and the early euro experience." *The World Economy* 33(7), 851–72.

Young, K. L. (2012). "Transnational regulatory capture? An empirical examination of the transnational lobbying of the Basel Committee on Banking Supervision." *Review of International Political Economy* 19(4), 663–88.

21 Improving Global Natural Resource and Environmental Regimes

Policy Failures in Weak Governance Complexes

Michael Howlett and Jeremy Rayner

Introduction

Distinguishing between international institutional design problems and national implementation ones is a subject of some concern in the area of international natural resource and environmental policy. Many observers, for example, have traced the failings of existing global governance architectures to the lack of hard law at the international level. However, recent work on **international regimes**, especially that dealing with regime fragmentation and the interplay between different regimes, suggests that the "failure" of a regime to develop hard law may simply reflect the lack of a need for such efforts. This work has highlighted the corresponding need to deal with an issue at a national or local level rather than an international one. Efforts at these levels, however, have also often failed, in large measure due to the inability of national governments to control private-sector actors.

Both experiences suggest the correct approach to the problem is to focus on **multi-level governance (MLG)** and the tools and instruments required to put an effective multi-level policy and governance architecture in place. Natural resource and environmental policy-making may be better served by regional agreements than by efforts to develop national or international regimes. Much can be learned in this area from the experiences of the European Union and its principle of "**subsidiarity**" in institutional policy design.

The Challenge of Global Policy Integration: Strong vs. Weak Regimes in International Political Economy

International regimes that attempt to govern the use of natural resources face many challenges. On the one hand, most states regard the disposition of natural resources within their jurisdiction (including those found in and under oceans) as a purely domestic policy question and often resent international actors that attempt to deal with this issue because these are seen as an affront to national sovereignty. On the other hand, how to use the world's natural resources raises complex problems of international coordination as questions relating to trade, biodiversity conservation, climate change, the rights of indigenous peoples, development, and many others intersect and interact in the resource area, requiring some form of transnational cooperation.

Some of these issues, like climate change, can plausibly be represented as problems of the global commons affecting all nations; but others, such as conservation of migratory fish stocks or the preservation of water quality in a large river basin affected by mining, may concern only a few countries at most. As a result, though global governance arrangements for natural resources vary in size and scale they often strike observers as imperfect.

Though often lamented, this is not all that unusual a circumstance in international affairs. The existence of international regimes, broadly defined as "sets of implicit or explicit principles, norms, rules, and decision-making procedures around which actors' expectations converge in a given area of international relations" (Krasner 1985, 2), is not an automatic process or occurrence. And as the scope and ambition of global governance arrangements and issues have increased over the past three decades, the relatively simple issue areas tackled by early international regimes, such as the regulation of discrete activities like whaling or the production of ozone-depleting substances, have given way to much more complex policy problems. This has resulted in both more complex regimes and additional difficulties in creating and managing them.

Moreover, not all areas of social, political, economic, or cultural life, of course, are governed through the use of well-integrated international regimes. Such arrangements are, in fact, quite rare. Many prominent areas of concern, such as international migration, lack either or both of the binding international agreements and institutions, or the common sets of norms and expectations that

form the basis of traditional international regimes, such as those found in banking and trade. Such "non-regimes," as Radoslav Dimitrov (2005) terms them, are issue areas characterized by the absence of multilateral institutions for ordering actors' interactions where there are issues about which states have raised concerns but have done little to address them; there are networks of states that have attempted and failed to sign a binding agreement but have endorsed non-binding policy initiatives; and there are issues about which no transnational advocacy groups exist even though observers identify them as problem areas (5).

What to do about this situation is uncertain. Helen Briassoulis (2005), for example, has argued that, faced with this situation, domestic policy-makers should try to integrate existing policies, reconcile overlaps and duplications, and seek consistency and coherence when they create governance strategies that address interrelated policy problems using existing policy tools and techniques. On the other hand, Richard Tarasofsky (1999, 10) has argued overlaps and duplication in cross-sectoral issues like agriculture and mining, combined with uncertainties linked to patterns of trade and other similar factors, requires the creation of more integrated treaty regimes (hard-law regimes) in these areas if domestic policy-making is to successfully address transnational issues.

In this chapter, we argue **policy integration** through hard-law treaties is neither the only nor necessarily the best way of improving global governance arrangements for natural resource governance, not least because the governance arrangements that have already emerged in many of these areas are complex multi-level institutional structures with multiple goals and means. In many cases, these have developed incrementally over many years and are not only difficult to change but are already having some success in dealing with transnational issues. In practice, existing complex multi-level international regimes have very much resisted efforts to reorganize and integrate their apparently disparate elements (McDermott et al. 2007; Puzl 2009; Tarasofsky 1999). Simply because a regime with a legally binding basis might be more "logical" or "functional" in no way ensures that it will be developed or promote better policy integration (Wellstead, Rayner, and Howlett 2013). This chapter discusses why this has been the case and what can be done about it.

The Need for Better Policy Integration: International Regimes and Regime Complexes

Policy-making at all levels, from the local to the international, involves the attempt to match policy goals and means, preferably in such a fashion that high-level policy goals and program-level objectives, as well as general sets of policy instruments and their more precise calibration, are coherent, consistent, and cohesive (Hall 1993; Howlett and Cashore 2009; Howlett and Rayner 2006). The challenge of policy-making, however, is multiplied when complex multi-level governance situations exist. These can occur in domestic–international trade and other situations, and are especially difficult to handle when developing new policies involves reforming or replacing elements in an existing policy mix where existing arrangements are cemented or "locked" in place by legal, social, political, or other factors (Cashore and Howlett 2007; Howlett and Rayner 2006).

Efforts to create better integrated governance architectures, both at the domestic and international levels, involve efforts to (re)construct such **policy mixes** to better match the relationships between multiple policy goals and means across

levels of government (Briassoulis 2005), and are specifically intended to address the perceived shortcomings of previous, often more ad hoc regimes. This is usually attempted by "rationalizing" multiple goals and combining policy instruments in new ways, so that these instruments support rather than undermine one another in the pursuit of policy goals, as often happens in mixes developed incrementally over time (Grabosky 1995). Both hard- and soft-law efforts to improve policy-making and outcomes are thus attempts to better *integrate* existing, and sometimes competing, policy initiatives into a cohesive strategy; to better *coordinate* the activities of multiple agencies and actors; and, generally, to substitute a more *holistic approach* to a problem for one that has decomposed policy into a set of multiple and loosely linked problems and solutions (Briassoulis 2004, 2005; Meijers and Stead 2004; Stead et al., 2004). This can be done by treaty or by other means such as intergovernmental agreements or independent state action. Often, however, such efforts at better integration are not completely successful or even fail entirely. This sometimes results in new policy goals and instruments simply being added on top of older ones, adding confusion to an already complex policy mixture.

In many cases at the international level, "regimes" centred on treaties never developed. Rather "**regime complexes**," "an array of partially overlapping and non-hierarchical institutions governing a particular issue area," exist (Raustiala and Victor 2004). Such "complexes" are a feature of many natural resource and environmental sectors, such as those involved in dealing with climate change, forests, and many other issue areas (Colgan, Keohane, and Van der Graf 2012; Keohane and Victor 2011).

In a useful effort to add greater precision to the regime complex idea, Orsini, Morin, and Young focused on the tendency of regime complexes to overlap and coexist, especially when treating a novel or emergent issue area. They found "divergence regarding the principles, norms, rules or procedures of their elemental regimes" (2013, 29) characterized such complexes.

This is indeed a feature of many international natural resource and environmental policy areas. In evaluating these complexes, Howlett and Rayner (2006) focused attention on the manner in which existing mixes retain or do not retain coherent goals and consistent means. The extent of consistency and coherence must be evaluated on a case-by-case basis, but policy goals are typically considered *coherent* if they are logically related to the overall policy aims and objectives and can be achieved simultaneously without any significant trade-offs. They are *incoherent* if they contain major contradictions, i.e., goals that cannot be achieved simultaneously and lead to the attainment of only some or even none of the original objectives; for example, simultaneously promoting both large-vehicle sales to encourage employment and fuel efficiency standards to enhance energy conservation. Policy tools are *consistent* when they work together to support a policy goal. They are *inconsistent* when they work against each other and are counterproductive; for example, providing simultaneous incentives and disincentives toward the attainment of stated policy goals, such as enacting both rent controls and construction subsidies in attempting to provide housing for lower-income citizens.

This way of thinking about regimes and regime complexes highlights the critical importance of how regime elements emerge. It suggests global governance studies can usefully converge with the study of how institutions evolve which has been a feature of recent work in comparative politics.

Kathleen Thelen and others, for example, have identified several typical processes through which complex policy mixes have evolved over time

(Thelen et al. 2003; Hacker 2004a, 2004b, 2004c, 2005). These can be applied equally to international institutions such as regimes and regime complexes.[1]

Layering is one such process whereby new goals and instruments are simply added to old ones in an existing regime without abandoning previous ones, typically leading to both incoherence among the goals and inconsistency in the instruments used (Beland 2007). *Drift* is a second type, which occurs when new goals replace old ones without changing the instruments used to implement them. These instruments can then become inconsistent with the new goals and most likely ineffective in achieving them (Torenvlied and Akkerman 2004). *Conversion* involves the reverse situation, whereby new instrument mixes evolve while old goals are held constant. If the old goals lack coherence, then changes in policy instruments may either reduce the level of implementation conflicts or enhance them, but they are unlikely to succeed in better matching means and ends of policy. *Replacement* is a fourth variation that occurs when there is a conscious effort made to recreate or fundamentally restructure policies by replacing old goals and means with new ones so that they both become more consistent, coherent, and congruent (Eliadis, Hill, and Howlett 2005; Gunningham and Sinclair 1999). Replacement sometimes comes about from recognizing that previous institutional arrangements have *exhausted* their problem-solving capacities, leading key actors to support new arrangements.

Although replacement is often the aim of reform efforts at the international level, the existence of regime complexes means that many **policy mixes** have either developed haphazardly through less well-coordinated processes of policy layering, or through repeated bouts of policy conversion or policy drift, in which new institutional arrangements have been piled on top of older ones, creating a palimpsest-like mixture of divergent policy elements (Carter 2012). Colgan and his colleagues, for example, have demonstrated the effects of the operation of these processes in the evolution of the global energy regime complex between 1950 and 2010, identifying no fewer than 11 institutional arrangements with overlapping memberships in a layered configuration.

Frank Biermann et al. (2009) have argued that the governance architectures of different international regime complexes can be ranged along a continuum from integrated to fragmented. To simplify, they present the competing architectural "styles" as synergistic, cooperative, or conflictual (Table 21.1).

Biermann and his colleagues are careful to note that any existing governance architecture is likely to have elements of all three architectural styles and that the concepts of architecture and fragmentation are proposed as value free. That is, that these styles come about as the result of the unintended consequences of long-term processes, and fragmentation may have positive as well as negative consequences.

Fragmentation is a key aspect of such regime complexes, however (Young 1999). And unmanaged conflict may result in the failure of an existing regime or the movement of a fragmented non-regime from a synergistic mode to a conflictive one (Dimitrov 2006; 2007). More typically, however, fragmentation is accepted as a fact of life in such complexes and is more or less managed.

Disorganized (and often exhausted) policy mixes have been widely observed in both international and domestic policy regime complexes (Bode 2006). This often becomes the starting point for attempts to reimpose coherence and consistency in a domain through policy replacement. These forms of regime complexes are not restricted to natural resource and environmental policy issues, but are very common in these areas given the physical location of most resources and their control by national states. Efforts since the 1980s to expand the spatio-temporal range of policy concerns to those involved with complex ecosystem-level interactions such as the desire to attain intergenerational equity or "sustainability" (Fischer et al. 2007; Johannesen 2006; Vince 2007; Witter et al. 2006), for example, have often resulted in additional layering or the conversion of existing regime elements in older resource sectors.

International Natural Resource and Environmental Policy as Fragmented Regime Complexes

What then is the general situation for international environmental and resource regimes? International environmental agreements exist in many forms. Each resource sector—covering activities such as fisheries, wildlife, mining, oil and gas, water, forestry, energy, and agriculture—is covered by many

Table 21.1 Types of International Regimes			
	Synergistic	Cooperative	Conflictive
Institutions	One core institution; others integrated	Multiple core institutions; others loosely integrated	Multiple, largely unrelated institutions
Norms	Core norms integrated	Core norms not conflicting	Core norms conflict
Actors	All relevant actors support the core institution	Some actors outside core institutions but supportive	Major actors support different institutions

Source: Adapted from Biermann et al. 2009a, 2009b, 2008.

different treaties affecting aspects of their activities. Many of these treaties are bilateral but the major multilateral ones are included in Table 21.2. These mainly cover environmental areas such as air, biodiversity and ecosystems, chemicals, climate change, environmental cooperation, freshwater, hazardous wastes, meteorology, and marine/oceans. Others cover areas such as the Arctic or Antarctic, deserts, and other fragile ecosystems. However, very few can be characterized as the centrepieces of natural resource "regimes" in the sense described above.

Table 21.2 International Multilateral Environmental Agreements and Treaties

Agreement on International Humane Trapping Standards (AIHTS)

Agreement on the Conservation of Polar Bears and Their Habitat

Basel Convention on the Control of Transboundary Movement of Hazardous Wastes and Their Disposal (Basel Convention)

Cartagena Protocol on Biosafety

Convention on Biological Diversity

Convention on International Trade in Endangered Species of Wild Fauna and Flora (CITES)

Convention on the Prevention of Marine Pollution by Dumping of Wastes and Other Matter (LC72)

Convention on the Transboundary Effects of Industrial Accidents

Convention of the World Meteorological Organization

Convention on Wetlands of International Importance Especially as Waterfowl Habitat (Ramsar)

Declaration of Intent for the Conservation of North American Birds and their Habitat

International Convention for the Control and Management of Ships' Ballast Waster and Sediments

International Convention for the Prevention of Pollution from Ships (MARPOL)

International Convention on Civil Liability for Oil Pollution Damage (CLC)

International Convention on Oil Pollution Preparedness, Response, and Cooperation (OPRC)

International Convention on the Control of Harmful Anti-fouling Systems on Ships (AFS)

International Convention on the Establishment of an International Fund for Compensation for Oil Pollution Damage (FUND)

International Treaty on Plant Genetic Resources for Food and Agriculture

North American Agreement on Environmental Cooperation

Rotterdam Convention on the Prior Informed Consent (PIC) Procedure for Certain Hazardous Chemicals and Pesticides in International Trade

Stockholm Convention on Persistent Organic Pollutants (POPs)

UNECE Convention on Long-Range Transboundary Air Pollution (LRTAP):

Protocol to Abate Acidification, Eutrophication, and Ground-level Ozone (Gothenburg Protocol)

Protocol Concerning the Control of Emissions of Volatile Organic Compounds (VOCs) or their Transboundary Fluxes

Protocol Concerning the Control of Nitrogen Oxides or their Transboundary Fluxes

Protocol on Further Reductions of Sulphur Emissions

Protocol on Heavy Metals

(continued)

Table 21.2 (*continued*)

Protocol on Long-Term Financing of the Co-operative Programme for Monitoring and Evaluation of the Long-range Transmissions of Air Pollutants in Europe (EMEP)

Protocol on Persistent Organic Pollutants (POPs)

Protocol on the Reduction of Sulphur Emissions or their Transboundary Fluxes by at Least 30 Percent

UNECE Convention on Environmental Impact Assessment in a Transboundary Context (Espoo Convention)

Protocol on Pollutant Release and Transfer Registers under the UNECE Convention on Access to Information, Public Participation in Decision-making and Access to Justice in Environmental Matters (Aarhus Convention)

United Nations Framework Convention on Climate Change (UNFCCC)

United Nations Framework Convention on Climate Change (UNFCCC)–Kyoto Protocol

United Nations Convention on the Law of the Sea (UNCLOS)

United Nations Convention to Combat Desertification

Vienna Convention for the Protection of the Ozone Layer

Vienna Convention for the Protection of the Ozone Layer–Protocol on Substances that Deplete the Ozone Layer (Montreal Protocol)

Source: Environment Canada http://ec.gc.ca/international/default.asp?lang=En&n=0E5CED79-1

On the other hand, there are many more treaties in the natural resources sector. Table 21.3, for example, sets out the major multilateral ones affecting a sector such as the fishery whereas Table 21.4 shows the much larger number that exist covering specific crops and products in a sector like agriculture. And Table 21.5 shows the large number of agreements that can affect a specific industry with significant security and environmental dimensions, such as the nuclear industry.

Table 21.3   Fisheries

- **United Nations Convention on the Law of the Sea** (UNCLOS) a comprehensive legal text that establishes jurisdiction and governance parameters of key issues related to the world's oceans.

- **United Nations Agreement on Straddling and Highly Migratory Fish Stocks** (commonly called the UN Fish Stocks Agreement, or UNSFA) provides the framework for the conservation and management of straddling and highly migratory fish stocks in high seas areas regulated by Regional Fisheries Management Organizations (RFMOs).

- **The United Nations Food and Agriculture Organization** (FAO) has developed the following agreements to reinforce international legal instruments by providing guidance that can be incorporated into national and regional fisheries management activities.

  - Code of Conduct for Responsible Fisheries

  - International Plan of Action for the Management of Fishing Capacity

  - International Plan of Action to Prevent, Deter and Eliminate Illegal, Unreported and Unregulated Fishing

  - International Plan of Action for the Conservation and Management of Sharks

  - International Plan of Action for Reducing Incidental Catch of Seabirds in Longline Fisheries

Source: http://www.dfo-mpo.gc.ca/international/dip-trt-eng.htm.

Table 21.4 Agriculture

1. International Agreement on Olive Oil, 1956. Opened for signature at the Headquarters of the United Nations from 15 November 1955 to 15 February 1956.

4. International Coffee Agreement, 1962. New York, 28 September 1962.

5. International Coffee Agreement, 1968. New York, 18 and 31 March 1968.

6. International Sugar Agreement, 1968. New York, 3 and 24 December 1968.

7. Agreement establishing the Asian Coconut Community. Bangkok, 12 December 1968.

8. Agreement establishing the Pepper Community. Bangkok, 16 April 1971.

9. International Cocoa Agreement, 1972. Geneva, 21 October 1972.

10. International Sugar Agreement, 1973. Geneva, 13 October 1973.

11. Agreement establishing the Asian Rice Trade Fund. Bangkok, 16 March 1973.

14. International Cocoa Agreement, 1975. Geneva, 20 October 1975.

15. International Coffee Agreement, 1976. London, 3 December 1975.

16. Agreement establishing the International Tea Promotion Association. Geneva, 31 March 1977.

17. Agreement establishing the Southeast Asia Tin Research and Development Centre. Bangkok, 28 April 1977.

19. Agreement establishing the International Tropical Timber Bureau. Concluded at Geneva on 9 November 1977.

20. International Natural Rubber Agreement, 1979. Geneva, 6 October 1979.

21. Agreement establishing the Common Fund for Commodities. Geneva, 27 June 1980.

22. International Cocoa Agreement, 1980. Geneva, 19 November 1980.

24. International Agreement on Jute and Jute Products, 1982. Geneva, 1 October 1982.

26. International Tropical Timber Agreement, 1983. Geneva, 18 November 1983.

28. a). International Wheat Agreement, 1986: (a) Wheat Trade Convention, 1986. London, 14 March 1986.

28. b). International Wheat Agreement, 1986: (b) Food Aid Convention, 1986. London, 13 March 1986.

30. International Agreement on Olive Oil and Table Olives, 1986. Geneva, 1 July 1986.

31. International Cocoa Agreement, 1986. Geneva, 25 July 1986.

32. International Natural Rubber Agreement, 1987. Geneva, 20 March 1987.

36. International Agreement on Jute and Jute Products, 1989. Geneva, 3 November 1989.

37. International Sugar Agreement, 1992. Geneva, 20 March 1992.

38. International Cocoa Agreement, 1993. Geneva, 16 July 1993.

39. International Tropical Timber Agreement, 1994. Geneva, 26 January 1994.

40. International Coffee Agreement, 1994. 30 March 1994.

41. a) Grains Trade Convention, 1995. London, 7 December 1994.

41. b) Food Aid Convention, 1995. London, 5 December 1994.

41. c) Food Aid Convention, 1999. London, 13 April 1999.

42. International Natural Rubber Agreement, 1995. Geneva, 17 February 1995.

Source: http://www.un.org/millennium/law/titles.htm

Table 21.5   Energy: Nuclear, Oil and Gas etc.

IEA ID#	Signature Date	Agreement Title (link to text) Reverse Chronological	Lineage (related agreements)	Secretariat
2601	1923-12-09	Convention Relating To The Development Of Hydraulic Power Affecting More Than One State	Hydraulic Power	United Nations Department of Economic and Social Affairs, Programme of Technical Cooperation
2670	1957-12-20	Convention On The Establishment Of A Security Control In The Field Of Nuclear Energy	Security Control in the Field of Nuclear Energy	International Atomic Energy Agency
2693	1960-07-29	Convention On Third Party Liability In The Field Of Nuclear Energy	Third Party Liability Nuclear Energy	Organisation for Economic Cooperation and Development
2708	1962-05-25	Convention On The Liability Of Operators Of Nuclear Ships	Liability Operators Nuclear Ships	No known secretariat
2717	1963-01-31	Convention Supplementary To The Paris Convention On Third Party Liability In The Field Of Nuclear Energy	Third Party Liability Nuclear Energy	Organisation for Economic Cooperation and Development
2721	1963-05-21	Convention On Civil Liability For Nuclear Damage	Civil Liability for Nuclear Damage	International Atomic Energy Agency
3748	1963-05-21	Optional Protocol Concerning The Compulsory Settlement Of Disputes to the Convention On Civil Liability For Nuclear Damage	Civil Liability for Nuclear Damage	International Atomic Energy Agency
2799	1971-12-17	Convention Relating To Civil Liability In The Field Of Maritime Carriage Of Nuclear Material	Maritime Carriage Nuclear Material Civil Liability	International Maritime Organization (IMO)
2835	1974-11-18	Agreement On An International Energy Programme	International Energy Program	International Energy Agency
2836	1974-11-18	Implementing Agreement On The Technical Exchange Of Information In The Field Of Reactor Safety Research And Development To The Agreement on an International Energy Programme	International Energy Program	International Energy Agency
2838	1975-01-14	Agreement Concerning A Joint Project For Planning, Design, Experiment, Preparation, Performance And Reporting Of Reactor Safety Experiments Concerning Containment Response	Reactor Safety Experiments	No known secretariat
2911	1980-03-03	Convention On The Physical Protection Of Nuclear Material	Physical Protection of Nuclear Material	International Atomic Energy Agency

Table 21.5 *(continued)*

IEA ID#	Signature Date	Agreement Title (link to text) Reverse Chronological	Lineage (related agreements)	Secretariat
3003	1986-09-26	Convention On Early Notification Of A Nuclear Accident	Nuclear Accidents	International Atomic Energy Agency
3004	1986-09-26	Convention On Assistance In The Case Of A Nuclear Accident Or Radiological Emergency	Nuclear Accidents	International Atomic Energy Agency
3034	1988-09-21	Joint Protocol Relating To The Application Of The Vienna Convention On Civil Liability For Nuclear Damage And The Paris Convention On Third Party Liability In The Field Of Nuclear Energy	Third Party Liability Nuclear Energy	Organisation for Economic Cooperation and Development
3050	1989-09-21	Protocol For The Protection Of The Southeast Pacific Against Radioactive Contamination	Permanent Commission South Pacific–renumber	Permanent Commission of the South Pacific
4652	1992-01-16	Agreement about joint and coordinated efforts of member states of the CIS in minimizing and overcoming the consequences of the Chernobyl disaster	CIS Environmental Agreements	No known secretariat
4653	1992-02-08	Agreement of heads of governments of the CIS on coordination of intergovernmental relations in the area of electric energy of the CIS	CIS Environmental Agreements	No known secretariat
3170	1993-11-12	Amendment Regarding Radioactive Wastes To The Convention On The Prevention Of Marine Pollution By Dumping Of Wastes And Other Matter	Dumping of Wastes and Other Matter	London Convention Secretariat
3197	1994-09-20	Convention On Nuclear Safety	Nuclear Safety	International Atomic Energy Agency
3202	1994-12-17	Energy Charter Treaty	Energy Charter	Energy Charter Secretariat
3203	1994-12-17	Protocol On Energy Efficiency And Related Environmental Aspects To The Energy Charter Treaty	Energy Charter	Energy Charter Secretariat
3264	1997-09-05	Joint Convention On The Safety Of Spent Fuel Management And On The Safety Of Radioactive Waste Management	Safety of Spent Fuel Management and Radioactive Waste	International Atomic Energy Agency
3265	1997-09-12	Protocol To Amend The Vienna Convention On Civil Liability For Nuclear Damage	Civil Liability for Nuclear Damage	International Atomic Energy Agency

(continued)

Table 21.5   *(continued)*

IEA ID#	Signature Date	Agreement Title (link to text) Reverse Chronological	Lineage (related agreements)	Secretariat
3266	1997-09-12	Convention On Supplementary Compensation For Nuclear Damage	Civil Liability for Nuclear Damage	International Atomic Energy Agency
3292	1998-10-16	Protocol For The Implementation Of The Alpine Convention Concerning Energy	Alps	Permanent Secretariat for the Alps Convention
4577	2001-07-11	Convention of the African Energy Commission	African Energy Commission	African Union (formerly Organization of African Unity)
4648	2004-02-12	Protocol To Amend The Convention On Third Party Liability In The Field Of Nuclear Energy	Third Party Liability Nuclear Energy	Organisation for Economic Cooperation and Development
4649	2004-02-12	Protocol To Amend The Convention Supplementary To The Convention On Third Party Liability In The Field Of Nuclear Energy	Third Party Liability Nuclear Energy	Organisation for Economic Cooperation and Development
4508	2005-07-08	Amendments To The Convention On The Physical Protection Of Nuclear Material	Physical Protection of Nuclear Material	International Atomic Energy Agency
4558	2009-01-26	Statute of the International Renewable Energy Agency	International Renewable Energy Agency	International Renewable Energy Agency

Source: Data from Ronald B. Mitchell. 2002–2015. *International Environmental Agreements Database Project* (Version 2014.3). Available at: http://iea.uoregon.edu/ Date accessed: 12 June 2015. See also, Ronald B. Mitchell, 2003. "International environmental agreements: A survey of their features, formation, and effects." *Annual Review of Environment and Resources* 28:429–61.

As these tables show, rules and treaties that can develop in a particular sector can be complex, but often lack a central treaty and organization, and can display considerable overlap and duplication, as well as significant gaps in coverage.

Both the actors within these regimes and outside observers have expressed a significant degree of frustration with the performance of these complexes to date (Humphreys 2001, 1996; Puzl 2009). These kinds of regimes have been labelled as "fragmented" or even "non-regimes" by observers such as Biermann et al. (2009 and 2008), Dimitrov (2005, 2006), and Dimitrov et al. (2007).

The case of the international forest regime (or non-regime) illustrates the issues involved with one such agreement in the global political economy. It is a good example of a natural resource regime that has resisted rationalization through treaties or other forms and is better characterized as a regime complex than as an international regime (Overdevest and Zeitlin 2012).

The International Forestry Regime Case

In the case of forests, as noted above, critics such as Richard Tarasofsky (1999) have argued the centrepiece of a more highly integrated arrangement should be a legally binding convention ratified by a significant number of states and administered by a secretariat hosted by a well-regarded international organization, such as the United Nations. However, it is by no means obvious that effective policy-making in this sector requires a traditional "hard-law"–based policy regime of this type (Florini and Sovacool 2009). And regime reconstruction efforts at the international level have proven to be very challenging projects with a mixed track record of success.

The history of the development of the international forest situation, in fact, is one in which a weak and fragmented regime complex has developed a conflictual rather than a cooperative architecture (Braatz, 2003; Giessen 2013; Humphreys 1996; Puzl 2009; Tarasofsky 1995, 1999). Resistance to the idea that forest issues are global rather than local (Betsill et al. 2007; Dimitrov 2005), continuing opposition to the norms of Sustainable Forest Management (SFM) by many influential NGOs, for example (Humphreys 2001, 2004), and the parallel development of the Convention on Biological Diversity (CBD) and climate change regimes (Gehring and Oberthur 2009), all have posed significant challenges to the various elements of the forestry "non-regime complex."

As is well known, efforts to negotiate a legally binding international instrument to better integrate the conservation and sustainable management of the world's forests have failed repeatedly. In the forestry case, there have been three such failed attempts to negotiate a binding international convention on forest protection and management. But there also has been significant convergence on international norms of sustainable forest management outside of a treaty framework (Humphreys 1996 and 2001). These norms have been expressed, for example, in a growing movement for third-party certification of "sustainable" forestry, and in a number of government-sponsored regional initiatives to develop criteria and indicators of sustainable forest management.

A number of legally binding international instruments also do make explicit mention of forests and constitute, by implication, an inchoate global governance architecture for forests. Several important international environmental conventions, for example, are relevant to forest management, including the Convention on Biological Diversity and the Ramsar Convention on the Conservation of Wetlands.

To complicate matters further, however, there is also a host of other initiatives at the international and regional levels that address forests, such as climate change negotiations, which propose to add additional elements and features to this architecture. These treaties and activities have an impact on the national level by prescribing or demanding detailed objectives and plans to implement specific aspects of forest-related industrial and other activity at both the international, national, and local levels.

Against Tarasofsky, some observers have argued all is well and the development of a better integrated forest regime is proceeding apace:

> Today there is a rich mix of "soft law" and legally-binding commitments on forests at the global level. . . . Over the past decade, many legally binding global conventions and agreements related to forests have been ratified. There has been a strengthening of regional agreements on forests in recent years. . . . Steps have been taken to increase collaboration and cooperation among these bodies. The development of multi-stakeholder processes in various international policy fora and new partnerships are providing increased opportunities for non-governmental, scientific, business, indigenous peoples and other organizations to participate in international

decision-making and implementation of commitments. (Braatz 2003)

However, most, like Puzl (2009), have argued the opposite; that the forest regime at the international level is a failure or at best only very partially successful in some areas and in need of much reform:

> No forest convention could be agreed to as the definition of tropical forests as global commons was linked to their availability and not to global functions (e.g., for example like in the discussion on biodiversity), or to the terms of utilisation and in this sense it was closely linked to sovereignty issues. The definition of tropical forests as global commons can thus be understood as the execution of Foucauldian power. The problem definition (tropical forests as global commons) did not fit the envisaged problem solution (protection of tropical forests by global instrument) and thus lead to a north/south division among countries. (Puzl 2009, 11)

None of this is especially unusual in the international sphere, however, and international forest relations should not be singled out as presenting unique challenges of global governance design (Florini and Sovacool 2009; Sending and Neumann 2006). Unlike the situation with regimes in areas such as world trade and finance, coordination in many natural resource and environmental sectors may be better served by the kind of de-centralized, regional, or national-level initiatives found in this sector (Biermann et al. 2008 and 2009; Dimitrov 2006; Weiss 1998 and 1999). That is, improved management may take the form of (a) creating a new international governor (rare) or (b) a set of institutions and instruments that allow positive "interplay" among regime elements (Oberthur

2009; van Asselt 2007). Where conscious efforts are made to design integrated governance architectures without a central treaty or organization, the challenge is to achieve genuine policy integration with a clear "nested" division of competencies rather than overlap, ambiguity, and gaps (Alter and Meunier 2006; Nilsson et al. 2009). As discussed below in the EU case, effective "regime interplay" can be achieved by careful use of procedural policy instruments and other techniques of network management (van Asselt 2007; Hafner 2003; Gehring and Oberthur 2000)

The Failure of Purely National Solutions: The NFP Experience as a Regional Alternative

The existing fragmented international regime complex in the forest sector, as in many other resource sectors, has resulted from continued multiple layering processes which ultimately produced arrangements of policy elements that are both complex and costly to administer and often contain counterproductive instrument mixes and incoherent goals. While "illogical," these are nevertheless very difficult to change, since even the dysfunctional elements of existing regimes can confer benefits on well-entrenched interests who may resist their alteration or elimination (Beland 2007; Grabosky 1995; Pierson 1993).

Although efforts to promote a hard-law international regime in forestry have failed to overcome fragmentation and generate integrated policy outcomes, a multi-level perspective on regime complexes suggests many issues can be dealt with at a national level, bilaterally among nations, or at a multilateral, regional, level. The forestry experience is also a good illustration of the problems of purely national policy integration initiatives and the need for regional designs. This is the case, for example, with 1990s efforts to create National Forest Policies or strategies (NFPs or NFSs) in Europe.

NFPs are instances of "next-generation" policy instrument mixes or "natural resource new governance arrangements" adopted as part of national governments' responses to the weak international forest regime. In this case, new governance arrangements were proposed as a response to decades of piecemeal adjustment, layering, and drift that had combined to create a patchwork of overlapping and ambiguous regulations and perverse incentives in many countries.

The formal adoption of an NFP, in itself, however, is only a minimum measure of policy effectiveness. It tells us nothing about the extent to which a country had actually managed to produce substantively altered policy outputs as a result of its creation. A great deal of skepticism has been expressed on this score. European NFPs, for example, have been criticized for perpetuating the dominance of traditional forest sector interests and failing to attract political commitment to change from governments (Papageorgiou et al. 2005). Nonetheless, most European countries continue to experiment with some form of strategic direction for forest policy, continuing to attempt better intersectoral and intergovernmental coordination in the face of cross-cutting issue areas such as climate change or biodiversity conservation.

In one sense, this story of the European experience with NFPs is a familiar one: they are examples of convergence on a common "new governance" solution to national government capacity loss caused by globalization, in the absence of a robust international regime. It is no surprise that smaller countries with significant exposure to global markets in a policy sector like forestry should be at the forefront of the development of new natural resource governance arrangements. This new "governance" relationship, in which states attempt to steer loose networks of private and public actors toward common policy goals, emerged in the context of an internationalized trade environment that restricted states' ability to control national actors involved in international commodity production and exchange.

The solution to such problems of international fragmentation and national-level capacity loss involves better efforts at creating effective or integrated multi-level governance (MLG) arrangements across subnational, national–regional, and international levels. Recent initiatives in this direction include multinational regional agreements, public–private partnerships, and schemes for private governance, such as forest certifications. Some of these arrangements are explicitly designed to implement intergovernmental agreements; others are not.

Toward a Multi-level Governance Alternative to National and International Action: Moving Natural Resource and Environmental Governance Architectures Toward More Polycentric Forms of Governance

The forestry case described here is a good example both of the failure of existing national- and international-level initiatives to promote better regime coherence and of the benefits of smaller-scale regional reform efforts.

EU policy-making in this way provides a good example of how a multi-level system can operate in practice to promote policy integration, even in the absence of hard law. First, the EU level provides a political arena for coordinating national policies and positions. Second, although the European Union treaties make no provision for common EU policies in many resource and environmental sectors, there is a large body of EU policies in other areas that affects these sectors either directly or indirectly. Community actions about the forests in the EU, for example, are linked to goals pursued in other sectors, in particular the Common Agricultural Policy, environment, and rural development policies. Third, the evolution of a multi-level system of joint decision-making has brought about substantial changes in the logic of influence for domestic actors. The supra-national level comprises new actors and institutionalized arenas, provides additional points of access, and requires national actors to broaden their perspectives.

Conclusion: Repairing and Upgrading International Governance Architectures in Natural Resource and Environmental Sectors

At this point, improving existing regime complexes is an issue that has come onto the policy agenda not just as a nice idea but as the solution to the widely perceived problem of a failure of both national and international actors to deal with issues such as resource depletion and climate change. Disorganization in such complexes is the outcome of long periods of incremental policy change characterized by layering and drift. Although it opens up space for local innovation, disorganization frustrates effective implementation, fuelling demands for more integrated strategies that can allow multiple stakeholders to operate in a more credible policy framework.

Although the difficulties of coordinating government responses across sectors in the effort to promote integration are well-known (see for example Martinez de Anguita et al. 2008; Saglie et al. 2006; Witter et al. 2006), they have not been effectively addressed. As a result much debate continues to centre on hard-law options or strictly national-level initiatives rather than with the complexities of more effective multi-level arrangements.

Of course, attaining requisite levels of multi-sectoral coordination is not easy in multi-level system of governance with relatively fixed jurisdictional limits between levels of government (Fafard and Harrison 2000; Hogl 2002; Hooghe and Marks 2001 and 2003; Mackendrick 2005; Torenvlied and Akkerman 2004; Westcott 2002). But themes that are worth exploring in the development of multi-level alternatives to traditional national- and international-level action in the resource sector include the importance of governance at the appropriate scale, regional agreements and the possible role of making more of the principle of subsidiarity as a tool to promote positive non-regime interaction (Carozza 2009; Hogl 2000; van Kersbergen and Verbeek 2007).

Responsive policy-making on large-scale complex international resource and environmental policy issues *requires* problems to be dealt with on a multi-level and multi-sectoral basis (Gerber et al. 2009; Weber et al. 2007). For the reasons noted above, efforts in this direction at the regional level are more likely to bear fruit than the many efforts over the past half century that have been designed to create "hard"-law treaty regimes in these sectors or enhance purely national level industries, that have both failed to produce tangible results.

Note

1 Studies of institutional reform efforts in complex policy arenas such as healthcare, pensions, and urban transportation have revealed that existing policy mixes typically emerge through one or more of four common processes: "drift," "conversion," "layering," and "exhaustion/ replacement" (Beland 2007; Thelen et al. 2003; Hacker 2004a, 2004b, 2004c; Stead and Meijers 2004; Evers and Wintersberger 1990; Evers 2005; Briassoulis 2005).

Key Terms

international regimes

multi-level governance

policy integration

policy mixes

policy regimes

regime complexes

subsidiarity

Questions for Review

1. Discuss the differences between an international treaty regime and a regime complex. What difference does this make for the substance and processes followed in international policy-making in general and in areas dealing with resources and the environment?

2. What is "hard law"? How does this concept apply in the international sphere and how does it differ from "soft" law? Which technique is most prevalent in international resource and environmental policy?

3. How do institutions, both domestic and international, evolve? How do development processes such as "layering" or "drift" affect policy content?

4. What is a policy mix? Are some mixes better than others? What role do criteria such as coherence, consistency, and congruence play in evaluating and designing policy mixes?

5. Describe the development of the international forest regime since 1945. How does this case illustrate the problems that exist in the international sphere coordinating the actions of governments? How can this situation be improved?

Further Resources

Alter, K. and Meunier, S. "Nested and overlapping regimes in the transatlantic banana trade dispute."

Biermann, F. et al. "The fragmentation of global governance architectures: A framework for analysis."

Dimitrov, R. S. et al. "International nonregimes: A research agenda."

Giessen, L. "Reviewing the main characteristics of the international forest regime complex and partial explanations for its fragmentation."

Hafner, G. "Pros and cons ensuing from fragmentation of international law."

Hooghe, L., and Marks, G. *Types of multi-level governance.*

Humphreys, D. "Forest negotiations at the United Nations: Explaining cooperation and discord."

Papageorgiou, A., Mantakas, G., and Briassoulis, H. "Sustainable forest management in the European Union: The policy integration question."

Young, Oran R. *The effectiveness of international environmental regimes: Causal connections and behavioral mechanisms.*

References

Alter, K. and Meunier, S. (2006). "Nested and overlapping regimes in the transatlantic banana trade dispute." *Journal of European Public Policy 13*(3), 362–82.

Bauer, J. (2006). *International forest sector institutions and policy instruments for Europe: A source book.* Geneva: FAO/UNECE.

Beland, D. (2007). "Ideas and institutional change in social security: Conversion, layering and policy drift." *Social Science Quarterly 88*(1), 20–38.

Betsill, M. M., Corell, E., and Dodds, F. (2007). *NGO diplomacy: The influence of nongovernmental organizations in international environmental negotiations.* Cambridge, MA: The MIT Press.

Biermann, F. et al. (2008). "Fragmentation of Global Governance Architectures: The case of climate policy." Paper presented to the International Studies Association, San Francisco.

Biermann, F. et al. (2009). "The fragmentation of global governance architectures: A framework for analysis." *Global Environmental Politics 9*(4), 14–40.

Biermann, F., Davies, O., and Grijp, N. (2009). "Environmental policy integration and the architecture of global environmental governance." *International Environmental Agreements: Politics, Law and Economics 9*(4), 351–69.

Bode, I. (2006). "Disorganized welfare mixes: Voluntary agencies and new governance regimes in western Europe." *Journal of European Social Policy 16*(4), 346–59.

Braatz, S. (2003). *International forest governance: International forest policy, legal and institutional framework.* Quebec City. XII World Forestry Congress.

Bressers, H., and Bruijn, T. de. (2005). Conditions for the success of negotiated partnerships for environmental improvement in the Netherlands. *Business Strategy and the Environment 14*, 241–54.

Briassoulis, H. (2004). Policy integration for complex policy problems: What, why and how. In *2004 Berlin Conference on the Human Dimensions of Global Environmental Change: Greening of Policies— Interlinkages and Policy Integration*, 1–30. Berlin.

Briassoulis, H. (Ed.). (2005). *Policy integration for complex environmental problems: The example of mediterranean desertification.* Aldershot, UK: Ashgate.

Bridge, L., and Salman, A. (2000). *Policy Instruments for ICZM in nine selected European countries. Final study report prepared for the Dutch National Institute for Coastal and Marine Management RIKZ.* Leiden: EUCC.

Brueckner, M. (2007). The Western Australian Regional Forest Agreement: Economic rationalism and the normalisation of political closure. *The Australian Journal of Public Administration 66*(2), 148–58.

Carozza, P. "Subsidiarity as a structural principle of international human rights law." *SSRN eLibrary.* Available at: http://papers.ssrn.com/sol3/papers.cfm?abstract_id=984743 [Accessed 1 December 2009].

Carter, P. (2012). "Policy as palimpsest." *Policy & Politics 40*(3), 423–43.

Cashore, B., and Howlett, M. (2007). Punctuating which equilibrium? Understanding thermostatic policy dynamics in Pacific Northwest forestry. *American Journal of Political Science 51*(3), 532–51.

Colgan, J. D. Keohane, R. O., and Van der Graf, T. (2012). Punctuated equilibrium in the energy regime complex." *Review of International Organizations 7*, 117–43.

Counsell, D., and Haughton, G. (2006). Sustainable development in regional planning: The search for new tools and renewed legitimacy. *Geoforum 37*, 921–31.

Dimitrov, R. (2005). "Hostage to norms: States, institutions and global forest politics." *Global Environmental Politics 5*(4), 1–24.

Dimitrov, R. S. (2006). *Science & international environmental policy: Regimes and nonregimes in global governance.* Lanham, MD: Rowman & Littlefield.

Dimitrov, R. S. et al. (2007). "International nonregimes: A research agenda." *The International Studies Review 9*, 230–58.

Eliadis, P., Hill, M., and Howlett, M. (Eds). (2005). *Designing government: From instruments to governance.* Montreal: McGill-Queen's University Press.

Elsasser, P., and Pretzsch, J. (2004). "Germany: A sociopolitical dialogue to promote sustainable forest management within the framework of sustainable development." In *Forests for the future: National forest programmes in Europe—Country and regional reports from COST Action E19*, D. Humphreys, (Ed.), 113–26. Brussels: European Science Foundation.

Evers, A. (2005). "Mixed welfare systems and hybrid organizations: Changes in the governance and provision of social services." *International Journal of Public Administration 28*, 737–48.

Evers, A., and Wintersberger, H. (1990). *Shifts in the welfare mix: Their impact on work, social services and welfare policies.* Frankfurt/Boulder: Campus/Westview.

Fafard, P. C., and Harrison, K. (2000). *Managing the environmental union: Intergovernmental relations and environmental policy in Canada.* Kingston: Queen's University Institute of Intergovernmental Relations.

Fischer, A., Petersen, L., Feldkötter, C., and Huppert, W. (2007). Sustainable governance of natural resources and institutional change—An analytical framework. *Public Administration and Development 27*, 123–37.

Fischer, F. (2007). "Policy Analysis in Critical Perspective: The epistemics of discursive practices." *Critical Policy Analysis 1*(1), 97–109.

Florini, A., and Sovacool, B.K. (2009). "Who governs energy? The challenges facing global energy governance." *Energy Policy 37*(12), 5239–48.

Gehring, T., and Oberthur, S. (2000). *Exploring regime interaction: A framework of analysis.* Barcelona November 9–11: Paper Presented to the Final Conference of the EU-financed Concerted Action Programme on the Effectiveness of International Environmental Agreements and EU Legislation—Fridtjof Nansen Institute.

Gehring, T., and Oberthur, S. (2009). "The causal mechanisms of interaction between international institutions." *European Journal of International Relations 15*(1), 125–56.

Gerber, J-D., Knoepfel, P., Nahrath, S., and Varone, F. (2009). "Institutional resource regimes: Towards sustainability through the combination of property-rights theory and policy analysis." *Ecological Economics 68*, 798–809.

Giessen, L. (2013). Reviewing the main characteristics of the international forest regime complex and partial explanations for its fragmentation." *International Forestry Review 15*(1), 60–70.

Grabosky, P. (1995). "Counterproductive regulation." *International Journal of the Sociology of Law 23*, 347–69.

Grande, E. (1996). The state and interest groups in a framework of multi-level decision-making: The case of the European Union. *Journal of European Public Policy 3*(3), 318. doi:10.1080/13501769608407037.

Guenette, S., and Alder, J. (2007). "Lessons from marine protected areas and integrated ocean management initiatives in Canada." *Coastal Management 33*, 51–78.

Gulbrandsen, L. H. (2003). "The evolving forest regime and domestic actors: Strategic or normative adaptation?" *Environmental Politics 12*(2), 95–114.

Gulbrandsen, Lars H. (2004). "Overlapping Public and Private Governance: Can forest certification fill the gaps in the global forest regime?" *Global Environmental Politics 4*(2), 75–99.

Gunningham, N., and D. Sinclair. (1999). "Regulatory Pluralism: Designing policy mixes for environmental protection." *Law Policy 21*(1), 49–76.

Gunningham, N., and D. Sinclair. (2002). *Leaders and Laggards: Next generation environmental regulation.* Sheffield: Greenleaf Publishing.

Hacker, J. S. (2004). "Review Article: Dismantling the health care state? Political institutions, public policies and the comparative politics of health reform." *British Journal of Political Science 34*, 693–724.

Hacker, J. S., Levin, M. A., and Shapiro, M. (2004). "Reform without change, change without reform: The politics of US health policy reform in comparative perspective." In *Transatlantic policymaking in an age of austerity: Diversity and drift*, 13–63. Washington DC: Georgetown University Press.

Hacker, J. S., W. Streeck, and K. Thelen. (2005). "Policy drift: The hidden politics of US welfare state retrenchment." In *Beyond continuity: Institutional change in advanced political economies*, 40–82. Oxford: Oxford University Press.

Hafner, Gerhard. (2003). "Pros and cons ensuing from fragmentation of international law." *Michigan Journal of International Law 25*, 849.

Hall, P. A. (1993). "Policy paradigms, social learning and the state: The case of economic policy making in Britain." *Comparative Politics 25*(3), September, 275–96.

Hänninen, H., Ollonqvist, P., and Saastamoinen, O. (2004). "Finland: Sustainable welfare courtesy of diverse forests." In *Forests for the future: National forest programmes in Europe—Country and regional reports from COST Action E19*, D. Humphreys (Ed.), 87–99. Brussels: European Science Foundation.

Hogl, K. (2000). "The Austrian domestic forest policy community in change? Impacts of the globalisation and Europeanisation of forest politics." *Forest Policy and Economics 1*(1), 3–13.

Hooghe, L., and Marks, G. (2001). Types of multi-level governance. *European Integration Online Papers 5*(11).

Hooghe, L., and Marks, G. (2003). Unraveling the Central State, but How? Types of multi-level governance. *American Political Science Review 97*(2), 233–43.

Howlett, M., and Cashore, B. (2009). "The dependent variable problem in the study of policy change: Understanding policy change as a methodological problem." *Journal of Comparative Policy Analysis: Research and Practice 11*(1), 33–46.

Howlett, M., and Rayner, J. (2006a). "Globalization and governance capacity: Explaining divergence in national forest programmes as instances of 'next-generation' regulation in Canada and Europe." *Governance 19*(2), 251–75.

Howlett, M., and Rayner, J. (2006b). "Convergence and divergence in 'new Governance' Arrangements: Evidence from European integrated natural resource strategies." *Journal of Public Policy 26*(2), 167–89.

Humphreys, D. (1996). *Forest politics: The evolution of international co-operation*. Earthscan.

Humphreys, D. (2001). "Forest negotiations at the United Nations: Explaining cooperation and discord." *Forest Policy and Economics 3*, 125–35.

Humphreys, D. (2004). "Redefining the issues: NGO influence on international forest negotiations." *Global Environmental Politics 4*(2), 51–74.

Johannesen, A. B. (2006). "Designing integrated conservation and development projects (ICDPs): Illegal hunting, wildlife conservation and the welfare of the local people." *Environment and Development Economics 11*(1), 247–67.

Keohane, R.O. and Victor, D.G. (2010). *The Regime Complex for Climate Change*. The Harvard Project on International Climate Agreements, Discussion Paper 10-33. Boston: Harvard Kennedy School.

Keysar, E. (2005). "Procedural Integration in support of environmental policy objectives: implementing sustainability." *Journal of Environmental Planning and Management 48*(4), 549–69.

Krasner, S. (1985). "Structural causes and regime consequences: Regimes as intervening variables." In *International regimes*, Stephen Krasner (Ed.). Ithaca: Cornell University Press, 1–21.

MacKendrick, N. A. (2005). "The role of the state in voluntary environmental reform: A case study of public land." *Policy Sciences 38*(1), 21–44.

Martinez de Anguita, P., Alonso, E., and Martin, M. A. (2008). "Environmental economic, political and ethical integration in a common decision-making framework." *Journal of Environmental Management 88*, 154–64.

McDermott, C. L., O'Carroll, A., and Wood, P. (2007). *International forest policy—The instruments, agreements and processes that shape it*. New York: UN Forum on Forests Secretariat, Department of Economic and Social Affairs.

Meijers, E., and Stead, D. (2004). Policy Integration: What does it mean and how can it be achieved? A multi-disciplinary review. In *2004 Berlin Conference on the human dimensions of global environmental change: Greening of policies—Interlinkages and policy integration*, Berlin, 1–15.

Meijers, E., Stead, D., and Geerlings, H. (2004). Policy integration: A literature review. In *Policy integration in practice: The integration of land use planning, transport and environmental policy-making in Denmark, England and Germany*, 9–24. Delft: Delft University Press.

Monni, S., and Raes, F. (2008). "Multilevel climate policy: The case of the European Union, Finland and Helsinki." *Environmental Science and Policy 11*, 743–55.

Nilsson, Måns, Pallemaerts, Marc, and Homeyer, Ingmar. (2009). "International regimes and environmental policy integration: Introducing the special issue." *International Environmental Agreements: Politics, Law and Economics 9*(4), 337–50.

Orsini, Amandine, Morin, Jean-Frederic, and Young, Oran. (2013). "Regime complexes: A buzz, boom or a boost for global governance." *Global Governance 19*, 27–39.

Overdevest, Christine and Zeitlin, Jonathan. (2012). "Assembling an experimentalist regime: Transnational governance interactions in the forest sector." *Regulation and Governance*. doi:10.1111/j.1748-5991 .2012.01133.x.

Papageorgiou, A., Mantakas, G., and Briassoulis, H. (2005). "Sustainable forest management in the European Union: The policy integration question." In *Policy integration for complex environmental problems: The example of mediterranean desertification*, Helen Briassoulis (Ed.), 269–310. Aldershot, UK: Ashgate.

Pierson, P. (1993). When effect becomes cause: Policy feedback and political change. *World Politics 45*, 595–628.

Puzl, H. (2009). "The politics of forests: The (non-)governance of natural resources within the United Nations." In *Paper prepared for the 5th ECPR General Conference*, Potsdam Germany 10–12 Sept. 2009.

Raustiala, K. and Victor, D.G. (2004). "The Regime Complex for Plant Genetic Resources." *International Organization 58* (Spring), 277–309.

Saglie, I-L., Rydin, Y., and Falleth, E. (2006). *Fragmented institutions: The problems facing natural resource management*. Cheltenham: Edward Elgar.

Sending, O. J. and Neumann, I. B. (2006). "Governance to governmentality: Analyzing NGOs, states, and power." *International Studies Quarterly 50*(3), 651–72.

Stead, D., and Meijers, E. (2004). Policy Integration in Practice: Some experiences of integrating transport, land-use planning and environmental politics in local government. In *2004 Berlin Conference on the Human Dimensions of Global Environmental Change: Greening of Policies—Interlinkages and Policy Integration*, Berlin, 1–13.

Stead, D., Geerlings, H., and Meijers, E. (2004). *Policy integration in practice: The integration of land use planning, transport and environmental policy-making in Denmark, England and Germany*. Delft: Delft University Press.

Tarasofsky, R. (1999). *Assessing the international forest regime*. IUCN.

Tarasofsky, R. (1995). *The international forests regime*. ([Cambridge, UK], Gland, Switzerland): IUCN—the World Conservation Union, World Wide Fund for Nature. Available at: http://openlibrary.org/b/OL612156M/international_forests_regime [Accessed 1 December 2009].

Thelen, K., Mahoney, J., and Rueschemeyer, D. (2003). "How institutions evolve: Insights from comparative historical analysis." In *Comparative historical analysis in the social sciences*, 208–40. Cambridge: Cambridge University Press.

Torenvlied, R., and Akkerman, A. (2004). "Theory of 'Soft' Policy Implementation in multilevel systems with an application to social partnership in the Netherlands." *Acta Politica 39*, 31–58.

van Asselt, H. (2007). *Dealing with the fragmentation of global climate governance: Legal and political approaches in interplay management*. Amsterdam: Vrije Universiteit.

Van Kersbergen, K., and Verbeek, B. (2007). "The politics of international norms: subsidiarity and the imperfect competence regime of the European Union." *European Journal of International Relations 13*(2), 217–38.

Vince, Joanna. (2007). "Policy transfer in oceans governance: Learning lessons from Australia's oceans policy process." *Ocean Yearbook 22*, 159–81.

Weber, E. P., Lovrich, N. P., and Gaffney, M. J. (2007). "Assessing collaborative capacity in a multidimensional world." *Administration & Society 39*(2), 194–220.

Weiss, L. (1999). "Globalization and national governance: Autonomy or interdependence." *Review of International Studies 25*, no. supplement, 59–88.

Weiss, L. (1998). *The myth of the powerless state: Governing the economy in a global era.* Cambridge: Polity Press.

Wellstead, A., Rayner, J., and Howlett, M. (2013). "Beyond the black box: Forest Sector vulnerability assessments and adaptation to climate change in North America." *Environmental Science & Policy* doi:10.1016/j.envsci.2013.04.002.

Westcott, G. (2002). "Integrated Natural resource management in Australia: The opportunity offered by a national coastal policy." *Australian Journal of Environmental Management* 9(3), 138–40.

Witter, J. V., v Stokkom, H. T. C., and Hendriksen, G. (2006). "From river management to river basin management: A water manager's perspective." *Hydrobiologia 565*, 317–25.

Young, O. R. (1999). *The effectiveness of international environmental regimes: Causal connections and behavioral mechanisms.* Cambridge, MA: The MIT Press.

22 The Shale Revolution and Canada–United States Energy Relations

Game Changer or Déjà Vu All Over Again?

Monica Gattinger and Rafael Aguirre[1,2]

Google the terms "shale revolution" and "game changer" and the number of results is staggering—over 200,000 hits. The so-called "shale revolution" refers to the rapid, dramatic, and largely unanticipated expansion of oil and gas production in the United States owing to technological developments that permit oil and gas to be economically produced from shale deposits. The twin technologies of hydraulic fracturing ("fracking") and horizontal drilling have unlocked the potential to profitably produce oil and gas from vast shale reserves in North America. The remarkable surge in American oil and gas production is the so-called "game changer" for the US, broader North American, and global energy landscapes. Several short years ago, concerns over US energy security and its mounting dependence on foreign energy imports dominated policy debates in that country. Now, focus has abruptly turned to heretofore unimaginable discussions of US energy independence, as projections predict that the US is positioned to become self-sufficient in net energy terms in the coming decades.

Needless to say, given the highly interconnected energy systems of the US and Canada, this rapid transformation of American energy markets has the potential to radically alter Canada's energy relations with the United States. It has generated significant debate, discussion, and market response in Canada as the "shale revolution" calls into question the size and viability of the US market for Canadian energy resources, now and into the future. Inherent in these changes is the prospect that the US might shift from customer to competitor for Canadian oil and gas. In this context, it is not surprising that there is a mild amount of panic in industry and government circles in Canada, and an increasingly wide-ranging debate and growing number of major energy infrastructure project proposals aimed at getting Canadian oil and gas "to tidewater" for shipment to new (i.e., non-American) export markets. There has even been talk about, and concrete moves toward, developing a Canadian "national energy strategy," a remarkable turn of events given that national approaches to energy have been tantamount to a "third rail" in Canadian politics, following the federal government's much-reviled National Energy Program of 1980 (see Gattinger, in press).

All told, it would appear, to borrow from the iconic Bob Dylan, that "the times they are a-changin'" for Canada–US energy relations. But this is far from the first time that Canada has had to fundamentally rethink its energy relations with the United States. In the postwar period, there have been no less than four such **critical junctures** in bilateral energy affairs, all primarily in response to changing market conditions: the "Great Pipeline Debates" of the 1950s, as Canadian oil and gas production surged; the energy crises of the 1970s that ultimately led the federal government of Prime Minister Pierre Trudeau to enact the protectionist National Energy Program of 1980; the decline in energy prices in the 1980s and the roll-back of NEP provisions with the Canada–US Free Trade Agreement, which institutionalized free trade in energy between the two countries; and bilateral relations in the 1970s over the development of oil and gas resources in the Arctic (debates that emerged again at the turn of the century due to changing market conditions).

This chapter assesses whether the current juncture in Canada–US energy relations marks a revolution in Canada–US energy affairs, or, if placed in historical perspective, a mere evolution. We seek to identify the drivers of pivotal energy junctures and the factors that shape Canadian governments' responses to them. In brief, we argue that changing market conditions generate pivotal moments in bilateral energy relations and that Canadian government responses to them are shaped by the prevailing ideas about energy in a given period: ideas about energy as a policy sector and its relationship to the broader economy and society, and ideas at the macro level about the role of the state in the economy writ large. Although changing market conditions are the common denominator of pivotal junctures, ideas about energy and the role of the state have evolved considerably in the postwar period, expanding in scope and diversity: from national energy self-sufficiency and the development of the Canadian-owned and -controlled

industry in the 1950s, 1960s, and 1970s, to the rise of neoliberalism in the 1980s, which favoured trade liberalization and deregulation, to the emergence of environmental and other social concerns about energy exploration, production, distribution, and consumption in the 1990s and beyond. Government responses at pivotal moments are shaped in significant ways by such ideas, but they are also influenced by the policy measures and decisions taken during previous critical periods. Past decisions can serve as "policy legacies" that inform the nature or constrain the scope of government policy responses at subsequent junctures.

In short, this analysis reveals that the current juncture in Canada–US energy relations is arguably the most complex that Canadian governments have faced to date, and, depending on how governments and industry respond, may well represent a game changer in Canada–US energy relations—a revolution, not an evolution, in bilateral energy affairs.

The chapter proceeds as follows: Section one provides an overview of the Canadian energy landscape in institutional, geological, and environmental terms, including the division of powers in the Canadian constitution over energy and related areas, and the distribution of energy reserves, production, and GHG emissions throughout the country. Section two fleshes out the analytical framework, specifying the role of energy markets in generating critical junctures in Canada–US relations, and the influence of ideas and previous policy measures on Canadian government responses. In the third section, we apply this analytical lens to four key junctures in bilateral energy relations mentioned earlier: the 1950s pipeline debates, the NEP, the negotiation of the Canada–US Free Trade Agreement, and debates over northern gas resources in the 1970s. Section four analyzes the current juncture in Canada–US energy relations in light of the framework and the historical experiences with past junctures. Section five discusses key findings and offers conclusions.

A Brief Overview of the Canadian Energy Landscape

The energy sector and energy policy-making in Canada are characterized by the country's constitutional, geological, demographic, economic, and GHG-emissions profiles. Canada has one of the most divided and decentralized constitutional energy arrangements among western industrialized countries (Doern and Gattinger 2003). The provinces are dominant players in the field, but the federal government also possesses significant powers in the energy sphere and related areas. This produces a multifaceted, multidimensional, and complex context and generates policy decisions that fly in the face of the conception of the nation-state as a unified actor—that is, one that pursues fixed and easily identifiable interests in a unified way over time.

Provinces have constitutional jurisdiction over non-renewable natural resources, including exploration, development, management, royalties, and intra-provincial energy trade and commerce. They also have jurisdiction over the generation, production, transmission, and sale of electricity within their boundaries (nuclear is an exception in some respects, as discussed below). The federal government's powers derive from its jurisdiction over interprovincial and international trade and commerce (including foreign direct investment), international treaty-making, taxation, fisheries, and energy development offshore and on frontier lands.[3] Ottawa also intervenes in the energy sector via the federal spending power (e.g., loan guarantees for major energy infrastructure projects) and equalization (the extent to which energy royalties are counted—or not—in equalization formulae).

The federal government also possesses important powers when it comes to energy resources and infrastructure on or crossing Aboriginal lands, given its jurisdiction over Aboriginal reserves, and when it negotiates land claims or other agreements with Aboriginal communities (provinces can also be involved in these arrangements). Provinces have jurisdiction over the conservation of energy resources within their boundaries as well as intra-provincial environmental energy impacts. The federal government has jurisdiction over transboundary environmental impacts, as well as fisheries, navigation and shipping, agriculture, criminal law, and the power to legislate for peace, order, and good government. The federal government retains a key role when it comes to the security dimensions of energy by protecting critical energy infrastructure, and in nuclear safety and security, the latter via the Canadian Nuclear Safety Commission, which regulates nuclear power facilities.

Canada is endowed with vast energy resources and is a major energy producer.[4] As shown in Table 22.1 (see appendix), established reserves and production are significant but concentrated regionally, with Alberta the largest reserve-holder and producer of oil, followed by Saskatchewan and East Coast offshore. Alberta, British Columbia, and Saskatchewan possess the largest natural gas reserves and are also the major gas producers, followed by Atlantic Canada offshore. As discussed below, Canada also possesses sizable reserves of unconventional natural gas (shale gas), but, given environmental concerns over the hydraulic fracturing process, shale gas production is only taking place in British Columbia and Alberta (there is a moratorium in Quebec, Newfoundland and Labrador, and Nova Scotia while studies of the practice are underway in each province, and there is fierce opposition to shale gas development in New Brunswick). As Table 22.1 reveals, energy reserves and production tend to be at a distance from major population centres: reserves are predominantly in the West, North, and East whereas major population concentrations are in the central provinces of Ontario and Quebec. This amplifies the differences in provincial greenhouse gas (GHG) emissions, with major hydrocarbon-producing provinces emitting the highest volumes of GHGs either in absolute (Alberta) or per capita (Saskatchewan) terms.

The economic and demographic contexts, combined with the location of energy reserves and production in Canada, have tended to produce North–South energy flows: the closest major population centres to which western energy producers ship their products have tended to be in the United States.[5]

Critical Junctures in Canada–US Energy Relations: Markets, Ideas, Policy Legacies, and Canadian Policy Responses

In recent years it has been impossible to watch the news or read a newspaper without running across coverage of the multitude of major pipeline proposals intended to carry Canadian energy resources within or beyond North America. There is TransCanada's Keystone XL to bring bitumen from Alberta to refineries on the American Gulf Coast; Enbridge's Northern Gateway pipeline to carry oil from Alberta's oil sands to Kitimat for export to Asian markets; Kinder Morgan's Trans Mountain project to expand an existing oil pipeline from Alberta to the Vancouver area; TransCanada's Energy East project, which would convert an existing natural gas pipeline to carry oil and expand the pipeline substantially to ship oil from Alberta and Saskatchewan to Quebec and New Brunswick; and

Enbridge's Line 9 Reversal, which seeks to expand an existing pipeline between Montreal and Sarnia and reverse its flow to carry domestic oil to Eastern Canada rather than imported oil from Montreal to Sarnia. The number and size of these proposed projects is staggering: collectively, they would have the capacity to carry an additional 2.8 million barrels of crude oil per day (Hoberg 2013, 3). One would have to return to the 1950s (as we do below) to find another period in which such a large number of major pipeline proposals were under consideration. Then, as now, market conditions generated this state of affairs.

The Origins of Critical Junctures: Changing Energy Markets

Major changes in energy markets generate pivotal moments in Canada–US energy affairs. Large shifts in energy prices, energy supply, and/or energy demand produce powerful pressures and incentives for government and industry to respond—whether by policy changes to strengthen energy security, affordability, or market access, or by business strategies proposing new energy projects (often infrastructure) to pursue profitability in a changing market context. In the postwar period in Canada and the United States, energy markets—oil and gas prices, reserves, supply/demand, and imports/exports—have been marked by periods of significant and often fast-paced change. In recent years, the rise of demand for oil and gas in Asia has also reshaped the context for energy production in North America, notably with growing export markets beyond the United States.

Changes in oil prices are primarily a function of global demand and supply. Economic crises can affect demand, lowering prices, whereas periods of economic growth will have the opposite effect. On the supply side, decisions to curtail production—notably those undertaken by OPEC nations—or uncertainty and sudden interruptions due to non-economic conditions like geopolitical instability or warfare can increase prices and price volatility. Conversely, excess capacity or oil supply "gluts" serve to lower prices. Oil prices are also shaped when states intervene in the market to limit or enhance supply with such mechanisms as import substitution, quotas, or tariffs. The combination and interaction of these various factors make price dynamics a complex issue, more amenable to retrospective explanation than to prognosis. In contrast to oil prices, gas prices have historically been defined on a regional, not global basis. The possibilities of global transportation of natural gas by tanker in liquefied form have only developed relatively recently, working against the emergence of a global market and price for natural gas.

It is worth noting that, in comparison to other regions in the world, the extent of trade liberalization for natural gas between Canada and the US constitutes a singular—rather than a typical—case. The structuring of the sector between the two countries favours flexible trade of the commodity (Doern and Gattinger 2003). On the other hand, in North America, natural gas has not been a lever of power games in international relations, as has been the case in other regions—for instance, between Russia and Europe (Kropatcheva 2011).

The early postwar period (1950s to 1960s) was characterized by stability and low oil and gas prices, especially when compared with the ensuing decade (see Figures 22.1 through 22.3 in appendix). In the US, production capacity—but also demand and imports—rose steadily and the country's profile transformed from net energy exporter to net importer (Cochrane and Griepentrog 1981, 691). As for Canada, oil and gas production grew significantly in the 1950s and 1960s, from 30 million barrels of oil in 1950 to 190 million in 1960, and from 70 million to more than 500 million cubic feet of natural gas over the same period (McDougall 1982, 58). Canadian domestic demand, however, grew

more modestly given that economic growth in the country was slower and less steady during this time (Frank and Schanz 1978). This propelled great interest in exporting Canadian energy supplies to the United States, and, as discussed in the following section, policy to support development of the industry (Grey 2000; McDougall 1982).

Geopolitical events and accommodations in the early postwar period (e.g., the Suez crisis, the Arab–Israeli war of 1967) were weathered without serious disruption to supply or increase in prices. Price and supply stability were also supported by production levels that generally lagged well below capacity, both in the United States and in Canada (Frank and Schanz 1978, 7). In the United States, the Mandatory Oil Imports Program (MOIP) of 1959 also generated excess capacity, as it sought to preclude external shocks with incentives to domestic producers to reduce their reliance on supply from politically insecure sources in the Middle East. Although its oil sector was exempt from these protectionist measures, Canada deployed a substantial diplomatic effort to avoid being affected by the policy. Of interest to an IPE reading of energy trade relations, the bifurcated intentions of policies like the MOIP reveal the intertwining of interests on the global geopolitical scale with those at the level of the domestic economy (Grey 2000; Nemeth 2008 and 2010).

The 1970s and 1980s would mark an abrupt end to this relative stability in oil and gas markets. The Arab oil embargo of 1973 and the Iranian revolution of 1979 saw world oil prices soar from less than five (nominal) dollars a barrel in the early 1970s to over \$30 by the early 1980s[6] (see Figure 22.2 in appendix). Natural gas prices also climbed, jumping from several (nominal) dollars per thousand cubic metres in the early 1970s to close to \$100 per thousand cubic metres in the first half of the 1980s[7] (see Figure 22.3 in appendix). Over this period, US dependence on foreign energy imports continued to climb, including continued growth in imports from Canada—albeit with the notable exception of the years immediately following the National Energy Program (see Tables 22.2 and 22.3 in appendix).

By the mid-1980s, energy prices had fallen from their previous heights and, following the 1985 Canada–US Free Trade Agreement, held relatively steady from the late 1980s to the mid-1990s. Prices reached historical lows in the late 1990s because of a glut in production, addressed by OPEC with coordinated cuts in member state production beginning in 1999. The 1990s ended with a recovery of oil prices, which hovered around the $27 per barrel mark (National Energy Board 2008, 4), and agreements between OPEC and non-OPEC nations to incentivize production. Rapid economic growth in Asia (predominantly China and India, but also in Indonesia, Thailand, Malaysia, and South Korea) was a major contributor to commodity price changes worldwide during this period, with the impact on oil prices beginning to show in the late 1990s. In natural gas, prices held at just over $50 per thousand cubic metres until the mid-1990s, at which point they began to rise owing to tightening supplies in North America (see Figure 22.5 in appendix). American dependence on foreign energy imports continued to climb during this period (see Tables 22.2 and 22.3 in appendix) along with growing concerns in the country about its energy security. Canadian energy exports continued to expand, recovering to their pre-NEP levels by the mid-1980s (gas) and early 1990s (oil), and climbing rapidly thereafter.[8]

The early to mid-2000s saw significant price volatility in oil and gas once again. Throughout the first decade of the 2000s, oil prices increased as a general trend, pushed strongly by demand in emerging economies, of which Asia's China and India are the most notable. Between 1990 and 2011, the former increased its share of world oil consumption by nearly 400 per cent, the latter by 283 per

cent (IEA 2012, 85). Whereas China consumed 3 per cent of world oil in 1990, by 2011 it was consuming 10 per cent—second only to the US, which comprised 20 per cent of oil demand in that year (ibid.). Demand for natural gas also grew, fuelled in large measure by growing demand in emerging economies. Measured as a proportion of global demand, between 1990 and 2010 China increased its consumption of natural gas by 734 per cent, and India and Brazil by 492 and 675 per cent, respectively. In the same period, in contrast, US consumption grew by 102 per cent and world demand increased by 162 per cent (IEA 2012, 128). In the North American natural gas market, gas prices continued their climb in the early years of the twenty-first century owing to rising demand and tightening supplies, and only began their rapid descent post-2008, as the financial crisis and the ensuing economic downturn dampened demand and the "shale revolution" began to pick up steam.

Canadian Policy Responses to Critical Junctures: The Role of Ideas and Policy Legacies

We propose here that government responses to changing market conditions are shaped primarily by the ideas surrounding energy that prevail at the time. They are also shaped by past policy decisions, which influence, inform, or constrain subsequent policy choices.

Social constructions of energy as a policy field have changed over time, with new (or evolving) ideas progressively layering over one another through the years. This progressive layering has resulted in four key ideas (or imperatives) characterizing contemporary energy policy: markets, environment, security, and social acceptance.[9]

When it comes to markets, ideas about energy markets and the role of the state in the energy sector have changed substantially in the postwar period. From the 1950s to the 1970s, energy markets and governments' role in the sector were understood primarily from a nationalist and interventionist perspective that placed emphasis on direct government intervention to support the growth of the industry and to reduce energy prices for consumers in the face of rapid price hikes. Beginning in the 1980s, the advent of neoliberalism portended major transformations in ideas about the functioning of energy markets and the state's role therein. Getting energy markets to work more efficiently and competitively and reducing the role of the state in the energy sphere were the watchwords of this period. In oil and gas, this included price deregulation, introducing competition into various segments of the upstream and downstream markets, trade liberalization, and the unbundling of various functions within energy firms to establish open nondiscriminatory access to their services and facilities[10] (see Plourde 2005). The result was, and is, a context in which governments intervene much less readily and much less directly in energy markets, although regulatory frameworks structure the business context in which firms operate (Gattinger 2005). Regulators ultimately decide which infrastructure projects will go forward (under what conditions) and which will not. Canadian governments also intervene indirectly to support the energy industry when it comes to accessing international markets through diplomatic or trade policy channels. Oil and gas policy choices made in the 1980s in response to changing ideas about the role of the state overall, and in relation to energy markets in particular, both inform and constrain subsequent policy choices in the energy field—for our purposes, most notably when it comes to responding to watershed moments in bilateral energy affairs.

A second idea shaping governments' responses to changing market conditions relates to the environment. In the 1980s and 1990s, environmental considerations increasingly came to accompany ideas about energy markets. Mounting concerns over the environmental impact of energy exploration, production, transmission, and consumption, expanded the purview of governments' energy policy decisions to such matters as biodiversity, ecosystem health, climate change, land use, and water quality. Given the transboundary nature of environmental matters, many of these issues have been the subject of international agreements (e.g., the Canada–US Air Quality Agreement of 1991 and the United Nations Convention on Biological Diversity in 1993). In Canada, the federal government and individual provinces have also pursued environmental policies in relation to energy. These include British Columbia's carbon tax in 2008, Ontario's Green Energy Act of 2009, and Quebec's cap-and-trade program with California. Action on the energy–environment interface at the federal level has often focused on international treaties (e.g., the United Nations Framework Convention on Climate Change in 1994, followed by the Kyoto Protocol of 1997), although these commitments have been followed up with only limited action domestically (Jaccard and Rivers 2007). In recent years, the federal government has adopted a number of American policies (e.g., tailpipe emissions standards and US commitments at Copenhagen), and made some progress on regulations for coal-fired generation in the electricity sector.

A third idea influencing governments' responses to critical junctures pertains to energy security. Although energy security has always been an undercurrent of energy policy in Canada, it has been understood differently over time. In the early postwar period, it was understood in the sense of ensuring that energy supplies for the country were adequate, reliable, and affordable, with a preference for domestic energy supplies. As Canada's oil and gas production grew over the 1950s and 1960s and policy decisions were taken that bolstered North–South energy flows (in oil, notably via the National Oil Policy of 1961), the preference for domestic supplies waned, but the importance of adequate, reliable, and affordable supplies continued. Following the terrorist attacks of 9/11, understandings of energy security broadened from security of supply to security of energy infrastructure, including the physical and cybersecurity of pipelines, nuclear facilities, refineries, and the like. The focus on critical energy infrastructure protection has also sharpened following revelations of sophisticated hacking efforts targeting energy firms and critical energy infrastructure in Canada and the United States, allegedly by the Chinese military (Sanger, Barboza, and Perlroth 2013).

Finally, beginning in the 1980s, the concept of **social acceptance** of energy development (sometimes referred to as "social license") has become progressively important in energy policy-making. Energy policy and regulation used to be relatively uncontroversial, but the last number of years has seen a significant and growing engagement—mostly opposition—of civil society (NGOs, Aboriginal communities, communities, individual citizens) to energy exploration, production, distribution, and use. Not only has public opposition intensified, it has also grown considerably in scope. Opposition in the 1980s and 1990s could predominantly be characterized as NIMBYism ("not in my backyard"), but in recent times, this has progressed to far more challenging forms of principled opposition, captured neatly by the acronyms BANANA ("build absolutely nothing anywhere near anyone") and NOPE ("not on planet earth"). Protests of proposed energy projects have become increasingly commonplace, and have begun to escalate to violent confrontations between protestors and police. These emerging forms of opposition cannot always—indeed, can rarely—be addressed by conventional responses in policy and

industrial toolkits (compensating affected parties, project relocation, etc.).

In sum, these four key ideas about energy—markets, environment, security, and social acceptance—have progressively layered upon one another over time and generated an increasingly complex and challenging set of imperatives shaping energy policy-making and, of particular interest for this chapter, Canadian governments' responses to critical periods in the country's energy relations with the United States. This is because ideas have broadened in scope and diversity, and also because the legacy of past policy choices informs, shapes, and constrains subsequent policy decisions.

Pivotal Moments in Canada's Policy Relations with the United States

With the above analytical framework in hand, this section explores four pivotal junctures in Canada's energy relations with the United States. Each juncture was produced by changing market conditions, and Canadian governments' policy responses were shaped in significant ways by ideas about energy prevailing at the time of the juncture and the policy legacies of previous responses.

The Great Pipeline Debates, the Borden Commission and the National Oil Policy (1950s–1961)[11]

The 1950s were a period of extensive and extended debates over Canadian energy policy, chiefly concerning the routing of oil and gas pipelines to take the country's burgeoning energy production to market. In the wake of the Leduc (1947) and Redwater (1948) oil strikes in Alberta and growing gas production in Alberta, British Columbia, and Saskatchewan, energy producers were eager to secure markets for their product, along with the pipeline infrastructure required to transport the oil and gas to market. Prior to the 1950s, Canadian oil and gas production was limited, and production was consumed in the provinces that produced it (Plourde 2012). The 1950s were a transformative period as the Canadian energy sector began producing oil and gas far beyond the requirements within the producing province. The federal government, in recognition of the changing market context, passed the Pipeline Act in 1949, which conferred authority on Ottawa over international and interprovincial pipelines. To ship oil and gas beyond provincial boundaries, pipeline companies required the approval of Parliament to become incorporated. Their proposals then had to be approved by the Board of Transport Commissioners.

The 1950s debates turned on which markets Canadian oil and gas should be sold to (domestic and/or American), which pipeline routes should be used to carry it there, and whether pipeline companies should be wholly Canadian owned and controlled. In the early 1950s, there were multiple major project proposals before Parliament. In oil, three major projects were under consideration: the Interprovincial Oil Pipe Line project, which would route western oil East to serve eastern Canadian markets, and the Transmountain and Border Pipeline projects, which would transport Alberta oil West to serve British Columbia and American West Coast needs. When it came to natural gas, there were four main project alternatives under consideration. Three of the projects would move gas west from Alberta to serve the Washington State, Oregon, and Vancouver markets (the Alberta Natural Gas, Prairie Transmission, and Westcoast projects). The Trans-Canada pipeline project, for its part, would carry gas from Alberta to Eastern Canada through an all-Canadian route passing through the Prairie provinces and Ontario to Montreal to serve Canadian markets.

Debate in Parliament on these various proposals was extensive, and projects routed primarily through the United States and/or serving US energy markets before Canadian needs received the harshest critique. In oil, the Border Pipeline proposal fell afoul of both of these fault lines, as its routing was almost exclusively in US territory on the way to British Columbia, and it would serve American markets before those in Canada. But even the Interprovincial project, whose sole aim was to serve Canadian energy needs and was primarily routed through Canada, ran into opposition for one leg of its route: to reduce construction costs, the proposed pipeline crossed into the US south of Winnipeg to a terminus in Superior, Wisconsin, to be shipped by tanker to refineries in Sarnia, Ontario. Not only was there concern that this routing would not serve northern Canadian communities, there was also fear that the pipeline would ultimately lead to growing oil exports to the United States. As for the gas pipeline projects, when it was first proposed, the Trans-Canada project was the least contentious given that it proposed an all-Canadian route to serve Canadian markets (the project became highly contentious later on because of its financing and ownership arrangements, as discussed below). Among the projects proposed to carry gas to western markets, debate focused on whether there was sufficient surplus in Canadian gas supplies to warrant each of the projects, with Westcoast eventually winning out because it sought to carry gas from Northwest Alberta, where supplies were more plentiful than in the southern part of the province, the point of origin for the other two pipeline proposals (Prairie Transmission and Alberta Natural Gas).

The projects that received approval were those that tilted the balance in favour of serving Canadian needs with primarily (or wholly) Canadian routing, that mainly required the export component to make the project economically viable, and whose exports themselves were surplus to Canadian supplies. Two projects were approved in each of oil and natural gas on these bases: Interprovincial and Transmountain to carry oil West and East, and Trans-Canada and Westcoast to do the same in natural gas. In 1953, the St Laurent government announced the Government Pipeline Statement to sum up its orientation to oil and gas infrastructure and exports. In oil markets, the government committed to supporting projects that would move oil to refineries in the most economically efficient way and that the surplus of Canadian supply could be sold to the highest bidder. In gas, the policy was firmer about ensuring that exports were surplus to Canadian needs, and confirmed the government's view that the Ontario and Quebec markets could only be reliably served with Canadian gas.

But this was far from the end of pipeline politics and debates over Canadian energy policy in the 1950s. The Trans-Canada project in particular proved to be controversial. Despite its all-Canadian route, the (American) company proposing the pipeline required financial support from the federal government to construct the project. Nationalist sentiment of the day, the high level of support Ottawa was willing to provide the company, and the government's willingness to go forward with financing in the face of significant opposition, led to major dissatisfaction with the St Laurent government, and contributed to its losing power to Diefenbaker's Progressive Conservatives in the 1957 general election. Almost immediately upon gaining power, the Diefenbaker government struck a royal commission to undertake an independent study of a host of energy policy issues.

The Royal Commission on Energy (more frequently referred to as the Borden Commission, for its chair, Henry Borden) focused on a number of key issues, notably the methods by which exportable surpluses should be calculated, the desirability of going forward with an Alberta to Montreal oil pipeline (a new project under consideration at the time), and the regulatory framework that should govern pipeline approvals and the setting of pipeline tolls, rates, and tariffs. The oil pipeline project proved politically charged, with independent producers (proponents of the project) pitted against oil majors, who were opposed to the project because it would deprive them of importing cheaper oil from international markets to their refineries in Eastern Canada.

The Commission's reports made a number of key recommendations: it proposed formulae for calculating surpluses; recommended that the Alberta to Montreal oil pipeline should not be built, and that the government should instead enact a policy dividing the Canadian oil market in two, with markets west of the Ottawa Valley supplied by Canadian oil and those east supplied by imports; and finally, that the government should create an independent regulatory commission to make decisions on interprovincial and international energy projects (pipeline construction, tolls, tariffs, and rates). Prime Minister Diefenbaker ultimately accepted these recommendations, creating the National Energy Board in 1959 and enacting the National Oil Policy in 1961.

Overall, in this first pivotal juncture in Canada–US energy relations, despite the nationalist sentiments of the time, the reality of economics meant that expanding Canada's oil and gas industry required a substantial degree of North–South continentalization of energy markets—provided that exports were surplus to Canadian needs that is, especially in gas. Canadian energy infrastructure projects connecting the country's production and consumption centres needed to serve US markets to be economically viable (Doern and Toner 1985; Frank and Schanz 1978). To support further development of the Canadian industry, the government created two markets: western oil production would not serve Eastern Canada at all—and would stay at prices conveniently higher than imports east of the Ottawa Valley (McDougall 1982). In sum, the orientation of the oil and gas industry toward exports was by no means a move that followed a pure logic of economic liberalism.

The Energy Crises of the 1970s and the National Energy Program of 1980[12]

As noted above, during the energy crises of the 1970s, world prices for oil and gas soared. Although in Canada developing domestic production capacity had been a major focus in the 1950s and 1960s, by the start of the 1970s demand in both the United States and Canada had grown significantly and the potential for energy shortages began to loom large, raising concern among policy-makers. In 1972, for the first time, the National Energy Board stated that a dilemma existed between serving domestic oil needs and US export markets (Grey 2000). Similar concerns arose in natural gas—would domestic supplies be sufficient to serve Canadian energy markets at affordable prices?

In response to increasingly dramatic price increases and mounting concerns over security of supply, the federal government's response was shaped first and foremost by energy security. Security was primarily understood in this period as the affordability and adequacy of Canadian supplies of energy for the country's needs. It was also understood in nationalist protectionist terms, with a major preoccupation about the extent of foreign ownership (mainly American) in the energy sector. The government sought to protect eastern consumers from world prices and foster Canadian energy security with domestic production and enhanced Canadian ownership and control in the energy sphere. Western energy producers went along with the federal government's moves up to a point, but as Ottawa's demands began to cut further and further into profits and royalties, western tolerance withered. Tensions ran particularly high

between Ontario and Alberta, with Alberta even threatening to cut off gas exports to the East and Ontario announcing in 1973 that it would test the constitutionality of the threat. As the energy crisis deepened, Ottawa, intent on shielding Eastern Canada from world oil prices, brought in the National Energy Program in 1980.

The NEP sought to achieve energy self-sufficiency in the coming decade through a range of measures, including increased Canadian ownership and control in the energy industry, a two-price policy for energy resources with preferential pricing for Canadian consumers, restrictions on energy exports, and a host of other protective measures to enhance domestic energy security and independence from world markets. The program curtailed oil exports and froze gas exports to the United States and aimed to increase federal revenues from the energy sector. Export taxes and subsidization of oil imports also sought to address imbalances between provinces that windfall revenues could have exacerbated (Courchene 2006).

The NEP was developed with virtually no provincial or industry input. Western producers, who felt entitled to receive the world price for oil, were enraged, and western provinces, notably Alberta, saw the NEP as the height of federal arrogance and interventionism in an area of provincial jurisdiction, given its direct impact on provincial capacities to develop, manage, and raise revenue from energy resources.[13] As for the United States, the Reagan administration denounced the policy as an attack on American energy security and US energy companies' operations in Canada.

The Decline in Energy Prices in the 1980s, Dismantling of the NEP, and Negotiation of the Canada–US Free Trade Agreement

The NEP's centralizing nationalizing vision was not to last for long. Western energy-producing provinces were adamant that the program be rolled back, and the early 1980s saw oil prices decline significantly, undercutting the NEP's assumptions of high prices going forward. In response, Ottawa negotiated a revenue-sharing agreement with Alberta in the years following the NEP and put in place the Western Accord, which deregulated oil prices and opened the sector to international trade. Following this, the election of the pro-market Mulroney Progressive Conservative government in 1984 signalled the permanent reversal of the NEP's protectionist measures, with Prime Minister Mulroney famously declaring that Canada was "open for business" shortly after becoming prime minister.[14]

The election of Mulroney heralded the turn to neoliberalism in Canada, with the government embarking on a broad program to reduce government intervention in the economy. This included deregulating a host of economic sectors, privatizing Crown corporations, reducing barriers to foreign investment, and liberalizing trade, notably with the United States. For energy-producing provinces, the energy sector, and American governments, the energy provisions of the Canada–US Free Trade Agreement (CUSFTA) were welcome news. These provisions prohibit the enactment of two-price policies for energy (i.e., different domestic and export prices) and prohibit governments from imposing discriminatory export restrictions on energy. In effect, CUSFTA's energy provisions institutionalized free trade in energy between Canada and the US: henceforth, market forces—not governments—would be the primary drivers of bilateral energy relations. Although governments still intervene in ways that affect the investment climate for business by regulating the conditions under which energy companies operate (e.g., requiring permits for cross-border energy infrastructure), the forces of energy supply and demand would henceforth be the primary drivers of energy

relations between Canada and the US, and the key cross-border interlocutors would be energy consumers and producers.

Overall, deregulation and trade liberalization would shape and constrain governments' responses to changing market conditions in bilateral energy relations for years to come, reducing the number and range of tools in policy-makers' toolkits.

Northern Pipeline Debates (1970s, Re-emerging in the Early 2000s)

The discovery of large deposits of oil and gas in the Prudhoe Bay and Beaufort Sea areas of Alaska and the Canadian Arctic in the late 1960s constitute a fourth key juncture in Canada–US energy relations—one that has known various twists and turns over time. It is also a juncture that reveals the role of ideas about the environment and social acceptance and support of energy development in shaping Canadian governments' responses to changing market conditions.

In the 1970s, one of the key projects proposed to develop northern oil was a pipeline system to carry Alaskan oil across Canadian territory. From Canada's perspective, this was supported on the basis that it would avoid the environmental risks associated with transporting Alaskan oil by tanker along the Pacific coastline (Kirkey 1997). From a market perspective, it also included a "**joint service**" rationale in that the project would support the Canadian energy industry through continental integration. But this project never saw the light. Ultimately, the US decided to transport Alaskan oil through the Trans-Alaska Pipeline System (TAPS), which runs south to the port of Valdez and then—just what the Canadian government had hoped to avoid—by tanker to the lower 48 states.

At the same time, Canada and the United States were considering various alternatives to develop natural gas reserves in the region. One of the proposed projects, the Mackenzie Valley

Pipeline, would have brought Alaskan gas from Prudhoe Bay down through Canada to southern markets. The project was to include a leg to bring Canadian gas from the Beaufort Sea and the Mackenzie Delta southward as well (the "Dempster Spur"). The domestic policy process in Canada surrounding this project resulted in what amounted to a 10-year moratorium on construction of the pipeline, owing to concerns over social acceptance and support. By the time the pipeline could have been back on the agenda, its initial economic attractiveness had dwindled due to changing market conditions. This threw it into a state of latency in the 1980s—and, despite a brief resurgence of interest in developing the pipeline in the early 2000s, market conditions are such that it is still in abeyance today.

Nonetheless, reviewing the distant and more recent pasts—and fates—of Canada–US relations in the development of northern energy resources offers valuable insights into the influence of ideas in shaping policy responses, along with their interplay with policy legacies, in particular market conditions. As noted above, the energy crises of the 1970s were met by the Trudeau Liberals with a nationalist (not continentalist) approach to energy security. In this context, it is rather surprising that the Mackenzie Valley project was not pushed through. But energy security was not the only idea of the time. Ideas of social acceptance were emerging in nascent but powerful forms at this juncture. With a view to undertaking a more detailed study of the Mackenzie Valley pipeline, Ottawa struck a Commission of Inquiry (the Berger Commission, named for its commissioner Justice Thomas Berger). The Commission has been identified as one of the most influential and important in Canadian history when it comes to the incorporation of non-expert opinion in and post-positivist approaches to policy decision-making (see Bradford 1999; Torgerson 1996). Aboriginal communities along the proposed pipeline route expressed deep concerns about the impact of the pipeline on their culture, environment, and way of life. Justice Berger recommended that the project not proceed until Aboriginal land claims had been settled in the area.

In the meantime, a number of companies were proposing alternative projects to the Mackenzie Valley route, including one, the Alaska Highway Pipeline, that would bring Alaskan gas south and avoid some of the more sensitive environmental and Aboriginal areas contemplated by the Mackenzie Valley Pipeline. In 1977, Canada and the US signed an agreement that led to the construction, in stages, of the Alaska Highway project. Only the first stage (the "Pre-Build"), was built between 1980 and 1982, linking southern Alberta gas markets to the United States. The remainder of the pipeline was not built. By the time regulatory approvals were received, natural gas prices had softened, and the project proponent announced in 1982 that it would not go forward with Stage 2 of the project.

More recent debates on developing and exploiting energy sources in the Arctic have taken place in a much different context, one that is governed by the market liberalization ideas of the post-CUSFTA period. When northern gas pipeline proposals ascended again on the Canadian and American policy agendas in the early 2000s, Canadian government responses illustrated the effect of the **policy legacy** of market liberalization. There were two pipeline routes under consideration at the time: the Alaska Highway project, which had been in abeyance since the early 1980s, and a renewed Mackenzie Valley project, to bring gas from the Beaufort Sea to southern markets. With respect to the latter, the decades since the 1970s have seen far greater support among local Aboriginal communities for development of the Mackenzie Valley pipeline (today, one of the key proponents of constructing a Mackenzie Valley gas pipeline is the Aboriginal Pipeline Group, a one-third project partner with Imperial, Royal Dutch Shell, Exxon Mobil, and ConocoPhillips).

In keeping with ideas of market liberalization, the Canadian federal government and the Bush administration in the United States both adopted route-neutral positions with regard to pipeline construction. In letters to the Bush administration, the media, and Congress, Ottawa expressed the position that the choice of route was ultimately one for the private sector to make (see, for example, Kergin 2001, 2002, and 2003).[15]

Although floor prices in natural gas render further development of northern gas resources for southern markets rather unlikely at present, market conditions in the long run may well make further exploration and production in the area an attractive prospect, even in the absence of state financial support (Lajeunesse 2013). Development could also include the possibility of exporting northern gas as liquefied natural gas (LNG) to Asian markets (Huffington Post 2013).

The Pipeline Debates of the 2000s: Déjà Vu All Over Again?

The last five years have seen substantial and rapid change in the North American energy scene: the discovery of massive reserves of **shale oil and gas**, along with the combination of fracking and horizontal drilling that permit their economic recovery, are transforming the energy picture in Canada and the United States. The United States's proved oil and gas reserves and technically recoverable oil and gas resources have soared in line with this change. In Canada, the change in picture is not as dramatic, particularly for oil, but the potential from shale gas is significant.

The so-called "shale revolution" has the potential to significantly alter Canada–US energy

relations: the United States has gone from being a net importer of natural gas (virtually all from Canada) to the very real possibility of becoming a net gas exporter. A similar change is underway for oil: even though the US will continue to import oil, it may be able to significantly reduce its oil imports. The country halved oil imports between 2006 and 2012 and a February 2013 Citigroup report projects that it could eliminate imports from Middle Eastern and hostile suppliers within five years (Soloman 2013). The International Energy Agency predicts that the United States will become the largest oil producer in the world by around 2020 and that its dependence on oil imports will decline from 50 per cent of consumption to less than 30 per cent by 2035 (International Energy Agency 2012, 76). The US is also projected to become a net exporter of natural gas by 2035 (International Energy Agency 2012, 76). The US Energy Information Administration has put forward similar projections, including a projected decline in net imports of natural gas from Canada between now and 2040 (United States Energy Information Administration 2013). Although long-range forecasting of energy production is notoriously challenging and US production increases of this scale might not materialize in the decades to come (particularly because shale deposits may prove less productive than their conventional counterparts but also because conventional oil production in the US is on the decline), there is no question that the size and viability of the US as an ongoing export market for Canadian energy has been called into question the last few years.

In oil, the challenge is especially daunting: given increased shale oil production and constrained refinery capacity in the US, the price of a barrel of oil in the US (West Texas Intermediate) has been selling at a discount to its European counterpart (Brent). Historically, the price spread between the two markets has been a few dollars, but since the end of 2010 it has increased significantly, to between $10 and $20, or even higher (YCharts 2013; see also Figure 22.4 in appendix). Canadian crude oil faces a "double discount": that between WTI and Brent, but also the price spread between Western Canadian Select (the price marker for oil in western Canada) and WTI. This spread more than doubled from an average of just under $10 in 2009 to $21 in 2012 (Baytex 2013), hitting a whopping $42.50 in December 2012 (Els 2013). The WTI/WCS owes its growing discount to increased US oil production and lack of sufficient pipeline capacity from Western Canada to refineries on the Gulf coast—this is the rationale for TransCanada's Keystone XL pipeline. For the oil sands, the situation is especially problematic. Given how heavy oil from the oil sands is, it is far more expensive to produce and refine than light/medium oil from shale formations like the Bakken basin in North Dakota, Montana, and Saskatchewan. Bakken oil has a much lower break-even point, and, given its geographic location, could be an obstacle to crude from the oil sands accessing pipelines into the US market (Els 2012).

In sum, oil from the Canadian oil sands sells at a substantial discount to both US and world prices and is increasingly landlocked in a hydrocarbon-rich North America. Even if the Obama administration approves the Keystone XL pipeline—which has turned out not to be, as Prime Minister Stephen Harper famously quipped, a "no-brainer"—it is not clear that this would entirely address the market challenges facing oil sands in North America or capitalize on market opportunities elsewhere. Oil sands crude would still face the discount between WTI and Brent to the extent that it persists, and, if the WTI declines further, the commercial viability of oil sands projects may weaken (Suncor and Total cancelled an upgrader planned for the oil sands in March 2013). The oil sands also face some stiff political opposition in the United

States, and potential regulatory challenges in the form of low carbon fuel standards in jurisdictions like California.

So where will oil sands oil go if the opportunities to go south begin to weaken? The main alternative market opportunities are east to eastern Canadian markets, refineries, and export markets, and west to British Columbia tidewater for export to Asian markets. Both of these options are being pursued at the time of writing: west via Enbridge's Northern Gateway pipeline proposal and Kinder Morgan's proposal to expand an existing pipeline into British Columbia, and east via reversals of Enbridge's Line 9 pipeline between Sarnia and Montreal, which would shift from carrying imported crude from international markets to transporting western Canadian crude to Ontario and Quebec. TransCanada also has an eastern-based proposal in the works: Energy East would reverse the flow of an existing pipeline from Alberta to Ontario and build a new stretch of pipeline to enable it to ship bitumen all the way from Western Canada to refineries in Quebec and New Brunswick. From there, bitumen could also be transported by tanker to the American Gulf coast for refining. Overall, these market dynamics are shifting the historical vertical North–South flows of oil from Canada to the United States and generating greater industrial and political interest in horizontal East–West flows within and beyond the country.[16]

In natural gas, the US may likewise be shifting from consumer to competitor for Canadian gas producers, and Canadian shale gas production in northeastern BC in the Horn River formation has yet to secure infrastructure to the West Coast for export (Lawrence 2013). In electricity, EIA projections also forecast a decline in imports of Canadian power. Long-time electricity analyst Jean-Thomas Bernard doubts that electricity from Quebec and Ontario will be able to compete against power in the US Northeast that is produced more cheaply from shale gas (Dufresne 2013). Nonetheless, gas pipeline infrastructure constraints in New England mean that considerable market opportunities for Canadian electricity exporters may remain. Hydro-Québec's Northern Pass project to sell hydroelectric power into the New England market is evidence of this, as is Nalcor's massive Lower Churchill Falls development, which will possess significant excess capacity to sell into New England after supplying Atlantic Canadian markets.

The question for the purposes of this chapter, then, is what are the responses of Canadian governments in this pivotal period and how are they likely to evolve over time? Are we witnessing an evolution or a revolution in Canada–US energy relations? Is the current period a game changer or, as Yogi Berra famously quipped, "déjà vu all over again"?

Governments have been responding in a range of fashions to the current juncture. At the federal level, the Conservative government of Prime Minister Stephen Harper has been a staunch supporter of the oil and gas sector, making regular trips to Washington and other locations in the United States to lobby in support of the Obama administration's approval of TransCanada's Keystone XL pipeline project. Ottawa has also come out strongly in favour of pipeline proposals to carry oil east and west within Canada, whether it be Enbridge's Northern Gateway pipeline proposal, TransCanada's Energy East, or the other pipeline proposals under consideration. The government also approved the takeover of oil and gas firm Nexen by CNOOC, China's state-owned offshore oil company, to further develop the energy industry. On the policy front, Ottawa has sought to streamline regulatory approval processes for major energy projects by reducing the scope of application of federal environmental reviews and putting shorter timelines on regulatory approval processes. It also, in a rather controversial move, altered the regulatory framework governing the National Energy Board, by requiring that applications rejected by the NEB come to cabinet for review and possible reversal of the decision, thereby leaving the ultimate fate of pipeline proposals directly in the hands of the prime minister and cabinet.

At the provincial level, premiers have been actively supporting the development of their respective energy sectors. Former Alberta premier Alison Redford has been the most vocal, travelling to Washington on a regular basis to lobby for approval of Keystone XL and spearheading efforts by the provinces to develop a "national energy strategy," a concept long demonized in the decades following the National Energy Program. Indeed, the potential reorientation of energy flows from cross-border vertical (North–South) to domestic horizontal (West–East) represents a sea change in Canadian energy politics and markets, and requires the provinces—which have been accustomed to developing their energy policies mostly independently of one another in the post-NEP period (see Gattinger, in press)—to collaborate and develop the political will to move forward on one or more of the major infrastructure projects on the table. On Northern Gateway, there has been conflict between the premiers of Alberta and British Columbia, with BC's Christy Clark declaring that the project must meet a range of conditions, including environmental safety and a "fair share" of economic returns for her province, in order to garner her support. Looking east, the premiers of Alberta, Quebec, and New Brunswick have been in talks regarding TransCanada's Energy East project, which would see crude oil from Alberta flow to refineries in Quebec and New Brunswick.

The degree of political attention on energy in Canada and the sheer number and scale of pipeline proposals under consideration harken back to the great pipeline debates of the 1950s, but much has changed in the last 60 years. Although there is still a strong focus on expanding the energy industry, ensuring Canadian energy needs are met with Canadian energy resources has become a far less salient consideration. Instead, environmental and social acceptance imperatives have come to the fore: debates over and opposition to the various pipeline proposals are increasingly framed with these ideas. Opposition to Keystone XL and Northern Gateway has turned primarily on their potential impact on the environment, whether these are concerns over pipeline leaks in sensitive areas (the Ogallala Aquifer for Keystone XL and pristine BC forest with Northern Gateway), tanker spills and the adequacy of marine response (Northern Gateway) or, more broadly, principled opposition to further development of Alberta's oil sands given their higher GHG emissions profiles in comparison to conventional crude. But although environmental NGOs actively oppose many of these projects—they have been particularly active on Keystone XL in the US—they are not the only ones with concerns. Many Aboriginal groups living along proposed pipeline routes have also been vocal in their opposition to the projects, raising concerns over damage from spills. Given governments' legal "duty to consult and accommodate" Aboriginal communities about projects that might adversely affect their existing or potential Aboriginal or treaty rights, social acceptance from an Aboriginal perspective is a very real and challenging matter.

All told, the current juncture in Canada–US energy relations is arguably the most complex that Canadian governments have ever faced. And they are facing it with a much more limited set of policy options at their disposal than in past decades. The creation of the National Energy Board at the end of the 1950s served to depoliticize decision-making about cross-border and interprovincial pipelines, calculation of surpluses, and the setting of pipeline rates, tolls, and tariffs. Deregulation in the energy sector (including removal of the surplus condition)

and the Canada–US Free Trade Agreement reduced the role of the state in energy, letting market forces—not policy—set energy prices, trade volumes, and trade flows. Governments still shape the market context in important ways—notably with regulations in or affecting the energy sector—but there is no question that the extent to which they can intervene directly in energy markets has shrunk considerably in the postwar period. In some ways, they have gone from "ringleader" to "cheerleader" in Canada's energy policy relations with the US, a shift perhaps best illustrated by the repeated trips Canadian politicians make to the United States to lobby for approval of the Keystone XL pipeline. At the same time, given the growing importance of environmental and social acceptance imperatives in the energy sphere, governments are called upon to serve (sometimes reluctantly) as mediators or facilitators between a much larger range and diversity of players (energy firms, NGOs, Aboriginal groups, etc.). In sum, governments face a far more complex policy context in the current juncture.

Given these realities, although parallels can be drawn between the current juncture and pivotal periods in Canada–US energy relations in the past, the "shale revolution" is more than just "déjà vu all over again." But will it lead to a revolution in bilateral energy relations between the two countries? The concluding section turns to this question.

The Shale Revolution: Evolution or Revolution in Canada–US Energy Relations?

It is too early to say whether the current period will be a revolution in bilateral energy relations, but there are a number of signs that suggest it might. First, in the postwar period, Canada has been a net energy exporter to the United States. Although

Canada does import energy from the US, the lion's share of energy flows north to south. The federal government's slogan, "We are your largest, most reliable, trusted and responsible energy partner," neatly captures this point. Throughout the postwar period, energy scarcity has dominated US thinking and policy on energy, including in its relations with Canada. The rapid transformation to being hydro-carbon-rich and potentially self-sufficient in net energy terms in the coming decades turns American thinking about energy policy on its head—and potentially its orientation to Canadian energy along with it.

Second, for Canada, this juncture represents the first in which debate focuses on diversifying the country's energy exports beyond the United States. Previous periods have focused largely on the relative merits of serving Canadian versus US energy needs, and the role of joint service (i.e., serving both markets) in energy infrastructure projects. Now, the parameters of debate have extended beyond the domestic/bilateral dichotomy to encompass domestic, bilateral, and international energy markets. The rise of Asia as a thirsty energy consumer represents considerable opportunities for Canadian energy, whether for oil or for natural gas (now that LNG has enabled the long distance shipment of gas by tanker). Indeed, in British Columbia, development of shale gas in the northeast of the province is being undertaken primarily with international—not American—markets in mind.

As noted above, this has even revived interest in the Mackenzie Valley pipeline, which is not economically viable when it comes to serving floor-priced North American gas markets, but might be viable if sales are being made into higher-priced international markets.

Finally, though the federal and Alberta governments have lobbied the US hard on the Keystone XL pipeline, there has been limited bilateral engagement on energy issues, the shale revolution, and what it might mean for North American energy relations writ large, now and into the future. At the turn of the century, there was much greater emphasis on Canada–US and North American approaches to energy issues through such mechanisms as the North American Energy Working Group or the Security and Prosperity Partnership. Now, governments' focus on energy in North America has waned. Paradoxically, at a time when uncertainty looms large and multi-billion-dollar energy infrastructure decisions that will be with us for decades to come are in the offing, there is not much political will at high levels for broader-based discussions on energy and the opportunities the shale revolution could represent for North America in economic and energy security terms.

Thus, the pivotal juncture created by the shale revolution may well lead to a revolution in Canada–US energy relations: one in which the countries pivot away from one another.

Notes

1 Monica Gattinger and Rafael Aguirre are, respectively, associate professor and doctoral candidate at the University of Ottawa's School of Political Studies.
2 An earlier draft of this chapter was presented at *Canada in the Hemisphere*, the 2013 Biennial Conference of the Association of Canadian Studies in the United States, 19–23 November 2013, Tampa, Florida. The authors thank conference participants for their insightful comments on the text. In particular, we would like to thank David Biette, Director of the Canada Institute at the Woodrow Wilson International Center for Scholars, who served as discussant for our paper.
3 The federal government has reduced or devolved a number of its powers by, for example, negotiating agreements with provincial and territorial governments to delegate or co-manage regulatory authority and royalties in offshore and frontier lands. With the Canada–US Free Trade Agreement, Ottawa liberalized international energy trade, thereby reducing its control over international energy flows.

4   The focus of this chapter is on oil and gas, but Canada also possesses large uranium and coal reserves, as well as significant potential in hydroelectric and other renewable power sources (e.g., wind, solar, geothermal, tidal).

5   The same holds true for electricity exports.

6   Given inflationary pressures during this period, in real terms, the price increases were even more dramatic.

7   Ibid.

8   As shown in Table 22.3 and discussed below, Canada's gas exports to the US began to drop in the mid-2000s.

9   What Gattinger has referred to in previous research as the energy MESS (acronym for important elements of energy policy: markets, environment, security, and social acceptance) policy-makers face (see Gattinger 2012).

10 Privatization of Petro-Canada followed in 1990.

11 This section draws primarily on Doern and Toner 1985; McDougall 1982; and Grey 2000.

12 This section draws primarily on Doern and Toner 1985; McDougall 1982; and Gattinger 2009.

13 Indeed, Alberta successfully challenged the constitutionality of the federal government's export tax on natural gas (Chalifour 2010, 179).

14 Despite the NEP's demise in practical policy terms, it continues to influence federal and provincial interests in the energy domain: provincial governments jealously guard their constitutional authority over energy resources and the federal government is ever-careful to tread softly in the energy sphere (see Gattinger, in press).

15 In this case, unfortunately the Canadian government's efforts were unsuccessful. The Alaska government pushed for the Alaska route and Congress was intent on mandating—and ultimately did mandate—this route.

16 Alberta is also exploring options to move oil north to Tuktoyaktuk in the Northwest Territories, to Alaska, or to Churchill, Manitoba to access export markets.

Key Terms

critical juncture

policy legacy

joint service

shale oil and shale gas

social acceptance

Questions for Review

1. To what extent has the rapid emergence of shale oil and gas changed overall energy relations between Canada and the United States? To what extent has it changed energy relations within Canada or between Canada and the rest of the world? Will the "shale revolution" lead to a "revolution" in Canada's domestic, bilateral, or international energy relations?

2. How has the geographical distribution of population and energy reserves in Canada, along with the country's political institutions, influenced the responses of Canadian governments to large and sudden transformations in energy markets (e.g., the discovery and development of Canadian oil reserves in the 1940s and 1950s, the energy crises of the 1970s, and the recent development of shale oil and gas in the US)? How have changing understandings of the role of the state in the energy sector over time informed or constrained policy responses?

3. Why have infrastructure projects for oil and transportation become so politically and socially contentious in recent years? How does the MESS framework (markets, environment, security and social acceptance) articulated in this chapter help to understand this change?

4. To what extent have the shifts of the 1980s and 1990s toward deregulation and market liberalization impinged on the capacity of Canada and the United States to jointly respond to new policy challenges like climate change and the availability of shale oil and gas? Are joint efforts on these or other areas desirable? Why or why not?

5. What could a "national energy strategy" resemble in the current period? To what extent does the National Energy Program of 1980 serve as a model—or counter-model—for such a strategy? How do ideas about the role of the state in energy markets, the environment, security, and social acceptance favour or militate against developing the political will needed to develop a national energy strategy?

Further Resources

Chastko, P. 2012. "Anonymity and ambivalence: The Canadian and American oil industries and the emergence of continental oil," *Journal of American History* 99(1), 166–76.

Frigon, M. and Perreault, F. 2012. *The economics of North American pipeline projects: The race to the sea*. Publication No. 2012-27-E. Ottawa: Library of Parliament, Parliamentary Information and Research Service.

Gattinger, M. "A national energy strategy for Canada: Golden age or golden cage of energy federalism?"

Hoberg, G. "The battle over oil sands access to tidewater: A political risk analysis of pipeline alternatives."

Nemeth, T. 2010, "From conflict to cooperation. Canada-U.S. oil and gas policy from the 1970s to the 1980s," in Michael Behiels and R.C. Stuart, eds., *Transnationalism. Canada–United States History into the 21st Century*. Montreal & Kingston: McGill-Queen's University Press.

Plourde, A. "The changing nature of national and continental energy markets." In *Canadian energy policy and the struggle for sustainable development*, ed. G. B. Doern. Toronto: University of Toronto Press.

Standing Senate Committee on Energy, the Environment and Natural Resources. 2012. *Now or never: Canada must act urgently to seize its place in the new energy world order*. Ottawa: Senate of Canada.

References

Baytex. (2013). "WCS pricing." January 2013, Available online at www.baytex.ab.ca/files/pdf/Operations/Historical%20WCS%20Pricing_January%202013.pdf.

Bradford, N. (1999). "Innovation by commission: Policy paradigms and the Canadian political system," in James Bickerton and Alain Gagnon (Eds). *Canadian Politics* 3rd ed. Peterborough: Broadview, 541–60.

Chalifour, N. (2010). "The constitutional authority to levy carbon taxes." In *Canada: The state of the federation 2009. Carbon pricing and environmental federalism*. T. J. Courchene and J. R. Allan (Eds). Montreal & Kingston: McGill-Queen's University Press, 177–95.

Cochrane, J. and Griepentrog, G. (1981). "U.S. energy. A quantitative review of the past three decades," in C. Goodwin (Ed.), *Energy policy in perspective*. Washington DC: Brookings Institution, 685–705.

Courchene, T. J. (2006). "Energy prices, equalization and Canadian federalism: comparing Canada's energy price shocks," *Queen's Law Journal 31*, 644–95.

Doern, G. B., and Gattinger, M. (2003). *Power switch: Energy regulatory governance in the 21st century*. Toronto: University of Toronto Press.

Doern, G. B., and Toner, G. (1985). *The politics of energy: The development and implementation of the NEP*. Toronto: Methuen.

Dufresne, J-M. (2013). "Against the current? The Quebec government is relying on the redevelopment of hydroelectric power to boost its revenues. Yet the economic outlook for this source of energy isn't rosy, says Jean-Thomas Bernard." In *Research perspectives: A Journal of Discovery and Innovation from the University of Ottawa*. Summer, 14–15.

Economist Intelligence Unit. (2013). *Diminishing energy dependence. Shrinking U.S. Imports*. Available online at www.economist.com.

Els, F. (2012). "Fire sale: Oil sands players now get $45 a barrel vs global price of $109." 14 December. *Mining.com* Available online at www.mining.com/oil-sands-players-now-get-only-45-a-barrel-vs-global-price-of-109-54211/.

———. (2013). "Welcome to Canada, land of the $63 barrel of oil." 14 March. *Mining.com* Available online at www.mining.com/welcome-to-canada-land-of-the-63-barrel-of-oil-90773/.

Frank, H. J. and Schanz, Jr., J. J. (1978). *US-Canadian energy trade: A study of changing relationships*, Boulder: Westview Press.

Gattinger, M. (2005). "From government to governance in the energy sector: The states of the Canada–US energy relationship," *American Review of Canadian Studies, 35*(2), 321–52.

———. (2009). "Multi-level energy regulatory governance in the Canadian federation: Institutions, regimes and coordination," in *Governing the energy challenge: Canada and Germany in a multilevel regional and global context*, B. Eberlein and G. B. Doern (Eds). Toronto, University of Toronto Press.

———. (2012). "Canada-United States energy relations: Making a MESS of energy policy." *American Review of Canadian Studies 42*(4), 460–73.

———. In press. "A national energy strategy for Canada: Golden age or golden cage of energy federalism?" in L. Berdahl and A. Juneau, eds. *Canada: The state of the federation 2012–2013*. Montreal & Kingston: McGill-Queen's University Press.

Grey, E. (2000). *Forty years in the national interest. A history of the National Energy Board*. Calgary: National Energy Board.

Hoberg, G. (2013). "The battle over oil sands access to tidewater: A political risk analysis of pipeline alternatives," *Canadian Public Policy 39*(3), 371–91.

Huffington Post. (2013). "Mackenzie Valley pipeline facing possible revival," *Huffington Post*, 25 October. Available online at www.huffingtonpost.ca/2013/10/25/mackenzie-valley-pipeline_n_4161962.html.

International Energy Agency. (2012). *World Energy Outlook 2012*. Paris: OECD/IEA.

———. (2000). *World Energy Outlook 2000*. Paris: OECD/IEA.

Jaccard, M. and Rivers, N. (2007). "Canadian policies for deep greenhouse gas reductions." In *A Canadian priorities agenda: Policy choices for economic and social well-being*, J. Leonard, C. Ragan and F. St-Hilaire (Eds). Montreal: Institute for Research on Public Policy, 75–106.

Kergin, M. (2001). *Ambassador Kergin's letter to [Secretary of Energy] Spencer Abraham*, 5 September.

———. (2002). "Trust the market (and Canada)," Letter to the Wall Street Journal, *Wall Street Journal*, 15 May.

———. (2003). *Ambassador Kergin's letter to Rep. W.J. Tauzin and Sen. P. Domenici*, 12 September.

Kirkey, C. (1997). "Moving Alaskan oil to market. Canadian national interests and the Trans-Alaska Pipeline, 1968–1973," *The American Review of Canadian Studies*, 495–522.

Kropatcheva, E. (2011), "Playing both ends against the middle: Russia's geopolitical energy games with the EU and Ukraine," *Geopolitics 16*, 553–73.

Lajeunesse, A. (2013). "The new economics of North American Arctic oil," *American Review of Canadian Studies 43*(1), 107–22.

Lawrence, D. (2013). "Canada faces hurdles joining shale gas revolution," *The Globe and Mail*. 21 February. Available online at www.theglobeandmail.com/report-on-business/industry-news/energy-and-resources/canada-faces-hurdles-in-joining-shale-gas-revolution/article8900288/.

McDougall, J. (1982). *Fuels and the national policy*. Toronto: Butterworths.

National Energy Board. (2008). *Global and Canadian context for energy demand analysis*, available online at www.neb-one.gc.ca/clf-nsi/rnrgynfmtn/nrgyrprt/nrgdmnd/glblcndncntxt2008/glblcndncntxt-eng.html#s4.

Nemeth, T. (2008). *Canada-U.S. oil and gas relations. 1958–1974*, PhD Dissertation, University of British Columbia.

———. (2010), "From conflict to cooperation. Canada-U.S. oil and gas policy from the 1970s to the 1980s," in M. Behiels and R. C. Stuart (Eds). *Transnationalism. Canada—United States history into the 21st century*. Montreal & Kingston: McGill-Queen's University Press.

Plourde, A. (2005). "The changing nature of national and continental energy markets." In *Canadian energy policy and the struggle for sustainable development*, ed. G. B. Doern. Toronto: University of Toronto Press, 51–82.

———. (2012). "Canada," in G. Anderson (Ed.), *Oil and gas in federal systems*. Toronto: Oxford University Press.

Sanger, D., Barboza, D., and Perlroth, N. (2013). "Chinese army unit is seen as tied to hacking against

U.S." *The New York Times*, 18 February. Available online at www.nytimes.com/2013/02/19/technology/chinas-army-is-seen-as-tied-to-hacking-against-us.html?pagewanted=all&_r=0.

Soloman, L. (2013). "Fight jihad, stop carbon taxes," *Financial Post*. 21 February (last updated February 22). Available online at http://opinion.financialpost.com/2013/02/21/lawrence-solomon-shale-means-security/.

Torgerson, D. (1996). "Power and insight in policy discourse: Post-positivism and problem definition," in L. Dobuzinskis, M. Howlett, and D. Laycock (Eds), *Policy studies in Canada*. Toronto: University of Toronto Press, 266–98.

United States Energy Information Administration. (2013). *International Energy Statistics* (Petroleum and Natural Gas Reserves). Available online at www.eia.gov/cfapps/ipdbproject/IEDIndex3.cfm.

YCharts. (2013). *Brent WTI spread*. Available online at http://ycharts.com/indicators/brent_wti_spread.

Appendix

Table 22.1 Canadian Population, Economic Activity, Energy Reserves/Production, and Greenhouse Gas Emissions

Province / Territory	Population (thousands, 2012)	GDP (billions of dollars, 2012)	Oil (Gas) Reserves (MMbl, 2010) (Tcf, 2010)	Oil (Gas) Production (MMbl, 2012) (Tcf, 2012)	GHG Emissions (megatonnes CO_2 equivalent, 2011)	GHG Emissions per capita (kt CO_2 equivalent per person, 2011)
British Columbia	4,622.6	217.7	117.4 (27.8)	7.7 (1.5)	59.1	12.9
Alberta	3,873.7	295.3	170,126.8 (38.8)	841.9 (4.3)	242.4	64.2
Saskatchewan	1,080.0	74.7	1,156.4 (2.3)	171.9 (0.2)	72.7	68.7
Manitoba	1,267.0	55.9	48.5 (–)	17.6 (–)	19.5	15.6
Ontario	13,505.9	654.6	9.9 (0.7)	0.5 (0.007)	170.6	12.8
Québec	8,054.8	345.8	– (–)	– (–)	80.0	10.0
New Brunswick	756.0	32.2	– (0.1)		18.6	24.6
Nova Scotia	948.7	37.0	East Coast Offshore 887.3 (0.3)	East Coast Offshore 72.2 (0.08)	20.4	21.5
Prince Edward Island	146.1	5.4			2.2	15.1
Newfoundland & Labrador	512.7	33.6			9.4	18.3
Yukon	36.1	2.7			0.4	11.3
Northwest Territories	43.3	4.8	408.3 (0.5)	4.8 (0.007)	1.6	20.6
Nunavut	33.7	2.0				
TOTAL	34,880.5	1,762.4	172,754.6 (70.4)	1,116.6 (6.0)	702.0	20.4

Notes: Most recent data available from these sources at time of writing. Totals may not add due to rounding or methodological approaches these sources use to calculate national figures. GDP figures are expenditure–based at current prices. Oil = crude oil and non–conventional oil. Reserves = remaining established reserves. Oil reserves for the territories include the Mackenzie/Beaufort. Natural gas reserves for the territories only include mainland reserves. Data for Alberta non–conventional oil reserves from 2011. MMbl = million barrels; Tcf = trillion cubic feet; TWh = terawatt hours.

Sources: Canadian Association of Petroleum Producers, *Technical Report: Statistical Handbook for Canada's Upstream Petroleum Industry*. Calgary: CAPP, June 2013; Environment Canada, *Greenhouse Gas Emissions Data*, available on–line at https://www.ec.gc.ca/indicateurs–indicators/default.asp?lang=en&n=BFB1B398–1; Statistics Canada, *Gross domestic product, expenditure–based, by province and territory*, available on–line at http://www.statcan.gc.ca/tables–tableaux/sum–som/l01/cst01/econ15–eng.htm; Statistics Canada, *Population by year, by province and territory*, available on–line at http://www.statcan.gc.ca/tables–tableaux/sum–som/l01/cst01/demo02a–eng.htm.

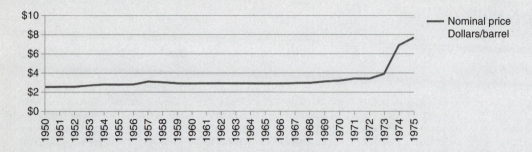

Figure 22.1   Oil Prices, 1950–1975

Source: United States Energy Information Administration. Table 9.1: *Crude oil price summary*, available online at http://www.eia.gov/beta/MER/index.cfm?tbl=T09.01#/?f=A

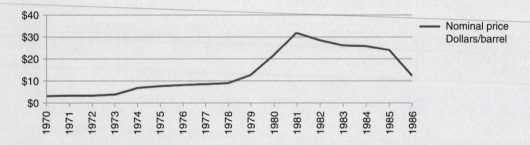

Figure 22.2   Oil Prices, 1970–1986

Source: United States Energy Information Administration. Table 9.1: *Crude oil price summary*, available online at http://www.eia.gov/beta/MER/index.cfm?tbl=T09.01#/?f=A

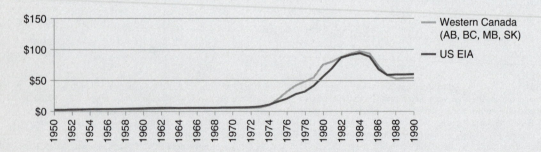

Figure 22.3   Natural Gas Prices, Canada and the United States, 1950–1990 (US $/ 1,000 m3)

Source: United States Energy Information Administration. *US Natural Gas Wellhead Price.* Available at: http://tonto.eia.gov/dnav/ng/hist/rngr11nus_1a.htm; and Canadian Association of Petroleum Producers, *Western Canada. Average prices of crude oil and natural gas.* Available at http://membernet.capp.ca/SHB/Sheet.asp?SectionID=5&SheetID=259

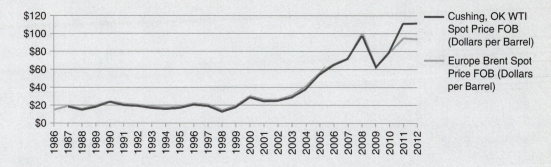

Figure 22.4 Oil Prices, 1986–2012

Source: United States Energy Information Administration. Petroleum and Other Liquids: Spot. Prices, available online at http://www.eia.gov/dnav/pet/pet_pri_spt_s1_a.htm

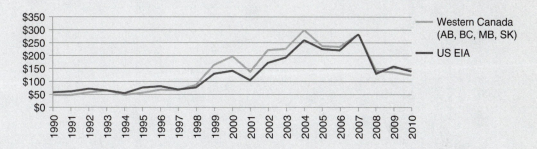

Figure 22.5 Natural Gas Prices, Canada and the United States, 1990–2010 ($/1,000 m3)

Source: United States Energy Information Administration. US Natural Gas Wellhead Price. Available at: http://tonto.eia.gov/dnav/ng/hist/rngr11nus_1a.htm and Canadian Association of Petroleum Producers, *Western Canada. Average prices of crude oil and natural gas.* Available at http://membernet.capp.ca/SHB/Sheet.asp?SectionID=5&SheetID=259

Table 22.2   Imports, Exports, and Supply of Oil for Canada and the United States, 1950–2012

Year	Total Oil Imports to the US from all trade partners (Mbbl/d)	Total Oil Exports from the US to all trade partners (Mbbl/d)	Total Oil imports to Canada from all trade partners (Mbbl/d)	Total Oil exports from Canada to all trade partners (Mbbl/d)	Total US Oil Supply (Mbbl/d)	Total Canadian Oil Supply (Mbbl/d)	Proved Oil Reserves US (MMbbl)	Proved Oil Reserves Canada (MMbbl)
1950	487	NA	NA	NA	5,894	NA	25,268	1,376
1955	782	NA	237	46	7,589	594	30,012	2,755
1960	1,015	202	344	113	8,051	877	31,613	4,215
1965	1,238	187	395	295	9,043	1,270	31,352	9,793
1970	1,324	259	571	670	10,961	1,952	39,001	18,328
1975	4,105	209	823	705	12,479	2,398	32,682	10,875
1980	5,263	544	554	206	13,859	2,095	29,805	8,698
1985	3,201	781	283	488	12,172	1,854	28,416	10,248
1990	5,894	857	537	654	13,250	2,204	26,254	10,927
1995	7,230	949	590	1,058	13,789	2,561	22,351	10,693
2000	9,071	1,040	914	1,384	14,892	3,116	22,045	13,403
2005	10,126	1,165	927	1,579	15,307	3,447	21,757	178,800
2010	9,213	2,353	771	1,949	14,684	3,620	23,267	174,577
2012	8,527	3,205	725	2,396	15,014	3,984	26,544	173,625

Notes: Mbbl/d = thousand barrels per day; MMbbl = million barrels; Oil exports from the US include refined petroleum products and crude oil. For Canada, oil = crude oil and equivalent.

Source: United States Energy Information Administration, Table 3.1. Petroleum Overview and Table 3.3b. Petroleum Trade. Imports and Exports by Type. Available online at http://www.eia.gov/beta/MER/index.cfm?tbl=T03.03B#/?f=A; Table: Crude Oil Proved Reserves Available at http://www.eia.gov/cfapps/ipdbproject/iedindex3.cfm?ti d=5&pid=57&aid=6&cid=r1,&syid=1980&eyid=2013&unit=MST; Statistics Canada. Total Oil imports to and from Canada to and from all partners, Table 126–0001 (from 1995 to 2012) and Table 126–002 (prior to 1995). Available online at http://www5.statcan.gc.ca/cansim/a05?lang=eng&id=1260001. Statistics Canada. Table 126–0002 Crude oil and equivalent supply and disposition, annual. Available online at http://www5.statcan.gc.ca/cansim/a26?lang=eng&retrLang=eng&id=1260002&t abMode=dataTable&srchLan=-1&p1=-1&p2=9.

Table 22.3 Natural Gas Production, Supply, Imports, and Exports between Canada and the United States, 1950–2012

Year	Proved Reserves United States (tcf)	Proved Reserves Canada (tcf)	Production United States (tcf)	Production Canada (tcf)	Imports into the US from Canada (bcf)	Exports to Canada from the US (bcf)
1950	184.59	NA	0.60	NA	0.00	3.17
1955	222.48	12.57	0.90	0.15	10.88	11.47
1960	262.33	23.31	1.22	0.47	108.66	5.76
1965	286.47	45.34	1.53	1.08	404.69	17.98
1970	290.75	57.86	2.10	1.79	778.69	10.88
1975	228.20	64.68	1.92	2.35	948.12	10.22
1980	199.02	88.15	1.94	2.47	796.51	0.11
1985	193.37	99.19	1.65	2.91	926.06	0.18
1990	169.35	96.50	1.78	3.77	1,448.07	17.36
1995	165.15	67.03	1.86	5.32	2,816.41	27.55
2000	177.43	60.70	1.92	6.09	3,543.97	72.59
2005	204.39	56.60	1.81	7.29	3,700.45	358.28
2010	304.63	61.95	2.13	6.25	3,279.75	738.75
2012	334.07	61.00	29.79	5.98	2,963.00	971.00

Notes: tcf = trillion cubic feet; bcf = billion cubic feet.
Sources: Reserves for US: United States EIA, *U.S. Dry Natural Gas Proved Reserves*. Available at http://tonto.eia.gov/dnav/ng/hist/rngr11nus_1a.htm. Reserves for Canada 1955—2000: Canadian Association of Petroleum Producers, *Marketable Natural Gas. Remaining Established Reserves in Canada*. Available at: http://membernet.capp.ca/SHB/Sheet.asp?SectionID=2&SheetID=153; Figures after 2000 are from US EIA, *Proved Reserves of Dry Natural Gas*. Available at: http://tonto.eia.gov/dnav/ng/hist/rngr11nus_1a.htm. Production figures: US EIA (http://www.eia.gov/dnav/ng/ng_prod_sum_dcu_nus_a.htm) and Canadian Association of Petroleum Producers. Exports and Imports of Natural Gas: US EIA, *Table 4.2 Natural Gas Trade by Country*. Available at: http://www.eia.gov/totalenergy/data/monthly/dataunits.cfm.

23 Mega-Events and "Bottom-up" Development

Beyond Window Dressing?

David Black and Katelynn Northam

In June of 2013 Brazil—South America's "miracle economy" for much of the past decade—was rocked by sustained mass protests coinciding with the Confederations Cup Football Tournament. Initiated in response to a hike in bus fares despite chronically poor bus service, the protests quickly became the outlet for broadly based discontent over the juxtaposition of the country's inadequate public services and vast inequalities with the tens of billions of dollars being invested in back-to-back sport mega-events—the 2014 FIFA World Cup and the 2016 Rio Summer Olympics. These events, greeted euphorically when they were announced, as unprecedented development opportunities and symbolic expressions of Brazil's global "arrival," had become graphic manifestations of the jarring clash between "top-down" and "bottom-up" development visions that sport mega-events highlight (Watts 2013).[1]

The relationship between sport and international political economy has been under-examined academically and yet the competitive nature of sport has served as a powerful metaphor for the ways in which states, international sport organizations like FIFA and the IOC, and multinational corporations attempt to use sport to gain economic and political power. The extraordinary visibility and branding opportunities associated with sport mega-events, in particular, have made them powerful focal points for political and economic interests— local, national, and international. Yet clashes like the ones described in Brazil clearly illustrate the tension between the promise that sport mega-events seem to offer and the real experiences of hosts.

During the past decade, two parallel trends concerning sport and the "developing world" have accelerated. First, sport mega-events have become a pivotal strategic policy priority for an increasing number of ambitious "rising states" in the global political economy. Typically, these events involve massive expenditures of scarce public resources in ways designed to impress global audiences with the sophistication and "modernity" of the host. Among other objectives, they are supposed to attract foreign direct investment (whether directly or indirectly) and signal that the host is "open for business." The concept of development that has been privileged in the planning and execution of these events is elite-driven or "top-down," often following a predominantly neoliberal logic. Various social or human development initiatives are typically undertaken in association with these events, but they have been widely critiqued as superficial sources of legitimation, or window dressing, for the principal beneficiaries—national, international, and corporate.

Second, however, projects, programs, and organizations associated with the Sport for Development and Peace (SDP) movement have grown dramatically, attracting new funding and followers at a rate far beyond that of the "development regime" as a whole (e.g., Beutler 2008; Darnell and Black 2011; Darnell 2012; Kidd 2008). Although the organizations and practices associated with this movement are diverse, diffuse, and under-theorized (see Coalter 2010), they have frequently reflected a more "bottom-up" or "grass-roots" approach inspired (consciously or otherwise) by "**alternative development**" thinking. In the broadest of brushstrokes then, these parallel movements highlight two distinct and long-standing development logics—one reflecting a more conservative or mainstream emphasis on growth, mega-projects, and aggregate benefits that are supposed to "trickle-down" to society as a whole, and another a more reformist preoccupation with poverty alleviation, equity, and inclusion.

Many critical scholars and activists (e.g., Lenskyj 2008; Shaw 2008) have long argued that in the context of **mega-events**, the former logic invariably trumps the latter and that society as a whole would be far better served by public policies that reallocated the resources devoted to the pursuit of event hosting to urgent social development priorities. Such arguments are even more compelling in still-developing countries marked by stark inequalities and widespread poverty. Indeed, an underexplored but important aspect of this calculus concerns the resources required to even *mount* a bid.[2] Although bids are often pursued by a combination of private and public actors, thus reinforcing

the tight integration of public with elite private actors, such efforts nonetheless involve tremendous financial risk. This risk is compounded for host cities in the global South, where poverty and inequality affect much of the population and resources are scarce. The opportunity costs of even bidding for a sport mega-event thus raise important moral and ethical dilemmas.

And yet, while this emphasis on "bread not circuses" is compelling in principle, it runs up against the dilemma that, in practice, resources can be mobilized and minds focused for the pursuit of mega-events in a way that no other imperative short of war can easily match. In other words, without the urgent stimulus provided by such events, it is unlikely that remotely comparable resources and collective energy will be "unlocked."[3] Anti-event activists must also reckon with what Chalip (2006) has analyzed as the powerful and extraordinary sense of shared community identity and purpose—the "feel-good factor" or what he identifies as "**liminality**"—associated with most mega-events. This dynamic creates a moment of opportunity for social re-imaginings and redirection that, if productively harnessed, can make exceptional projects possible.

Given these conditions, the question becomes: Could major games be recast as vehicles for a more frontal effort to tackle poverty, inequality, and marginality? To what extent, that is, can the critical or "alternative development" sensibilities associated with some in the SDP movement and in development studies be more fully integrated into bidding for, planning, implementing, and/or building on sport mega-events? To answer this question, this chapter proceeds as follows: We will first briefly discuss the major alternative currents of development thought and what is at stake in thinking about the developmental implications of mega-events. We will then survey a cross-section of mega-event experiences, mostly (though not exclusively) in the global South. This will be followed by a thought experiment, identifying some key features of a more truly developmental sport mega-event. We do this based on the constructivist view that it is only by articulating such imaginings that alternative possibilities can be brought into serious consideration by decision-makers and practitioners. Finally, we will outline some of the necessary conditions that could make this normatively preferable future possible (see Cox 1986), and the degree to which at least *some* mega-events could move toward greater emphasis on social equity and inclusiveness. Our argument is that by connecting bottom-up and top-down agents and dynamics, more broadly developmental outcomes are possible; but that both the range and effects of such outcomes are likely to remain limited.

Toward a Reformist Synthesis in Development Praxis

Virtually all sport mega-events are portrayed by their advocates as having important developmental dimensions and legacies (e.g., Black and van der Westhuizen 2004; Cornelissen 2009). The critical question is, what *concept* of development is invoked by these event boosters? This question takes us directly into the contested meanings of development.

Elsewhere, Black (2010) has written about the ambiguities of development and their ramifications for "development-through-sport" (see also Coalter 2010; and Levermore and Beacom 2009). These ambiguities include the prevalence of both top-down and bottom-up concepts of development; its characteristic manifestation (following Joseph Schumpeter) as a form of "creative destruction," with both progressive and destructive repercussions; and the co-habitation of both oppressive/disciplinary and emancipatory meanings and

practices. In practice, elements of all of these possibilities often coexist, both in the way we talk about development, and in the way we practise it.

Nevertheless, in the course of the past generation it has been possible to discern three broad tendencies in development thought and practice (Pieterse 2010, 182–220). The first tendency, dominant for most of this period, has been the neoliberal conceptualization privileging "market forces," private actors, a more limited state, and individual rationality and responsibility. Often referred to as "the Washington Consensus" (reflecting the central role of Washington-based governmental and international financial institutions in imagining, promoting, and enforcing it), this tendency has also shaped the dominant form of globalization. In this context, development policy has been largely conceived as a process by which governments enable their corporations and citizens to adapt and compete within increasingly competitive regional and global markets. Fostering individual opportunity has characteristically trumped concerns with community and social equity.

Throughout this period, however, this neoliberal "common sense" has been accompanied and challenged by a variety of reformist alternatives—the offspring of the more Keynesian, structuralist, and state-led development policies that dominated the postwar international development landscape until the 1970s. In the era of neoliberalism, ascendant since the early 1980s, this alternative tendency has taken a variety of forms, including alternative development ideas stressing bottom-up, community-led, and participatory development policies and methods, and human development (and human security) ideas privileging institutions and policies that foster broadly based social development, social equity, and capacity-building.

A third powerful current has been the "post-" or "anti-development" turn. Although this has frequently been manifested as a highly theoretical tradition inspired by postmodern, post-structural, and post-colonial ideas, it has had its real world analogue in various forms of anti-globalization activism and an emphasis on "alternatives to" development, often highly localized. In practice, this current has been far stronger at critique and deconstruction than at articulating feasible alternatives. In relation to development praxis, it risks throwing out the emancipatory baby with the disciplinary bathwater. But it has also stimulated critical reflection in development studies as a whole, and (through its trenchant critique of top-down neoliberal development and the propensity for co-opting progressive ideas) has widened the space for reformist alternatives.

In practice, these currents run along a fluid continuum of ongoing conversation and contestation. Neoliberal structural adjustment, for example, attempted to incorporate/appropriate more reformist tendencies by including ideas like "adjustment with a human face," "ownership," "participation," and "social inclusion" (e.g., Cornwall and Brock 2005; VanWynsberghe et al. 2012). The alternative/human development current has adapted to post-development critiques by articulating a more power-sensitive conceptualization of "critical modernism" (e.g., Hickey and Mohan 2004). As the model of neoliberal development has become more and more embattled however, most recently by the global financial crisis as well as mounting concerns over its ecological sustainability, Pieterse (2010, 200), among others, has argued that "the contours of a coherent (reformist) alternative to neoliberalism may gradually be taking shape."[4] This would involve, in line with Noel and Therien's (2008) broad articulation of persistent "Left and Right" tendencies in global politics, a greater emphasis on regulation at both national and transnational levels, aimed at rolling back widening inequalities, empowering impoverished communities, and promoting more participatory and democratic decision-making that increases the ability of poor people and communities to hold elites accountable.

Similar tendencies are evident in the world of sport generally, and the politics and planning of sport mega-events specifically (see Cornelissen 2009; Levermore 2009). Since the inception of the era of commercialized and professionalized sport, marked in the mega-event domain by the 1984 Los Angeles Olympics, the predominant developmental logic has been neoliberal (notwithstanding some important variations, addressed below). Indeed, it has been argued that a major reason for the growing popularity of such mega-events, notably in the global South, has been that they represent a uniquely apt strategic response to the competitive pressures of globalization (e.g., Black 2008; Dupont 2011; VanWynsberghe et al. 2012). At the same time, critics of mega-event hosts and the international sport organizations (ISOs) like the Fédération Internationale de Football Association (FIFA) and the International Olympic Committee (IOC) that oversee these events, have played on the "sport for good" ideological underpinnings of **Olympism** specifically, and sport more broadly, to promote reformist accommodations. Examples include incorporating environmental sustainability as a "third pillar" of the Olympic movement, and support to Sport for Development and Peace (SDP) initiatives and programs (see Peacock 2012). Meanwhile, alternative and grassroots development tendencies have been apparent in the explosive growth of SDP organizations at both state and non-state levels. Finally, dissenting from but also prodding this dynamic process have been the forceful critiques and activism of anti-Olympic and anti-elite sport organizations and movements.

The question, then, is what evidence can we find of a long-term shift—a new onus—toward considerations of equity, participation, and poverty-alleviation in mega-event planning, reflecting the broader, inchoate trend identified by Pieterse above? And, if we see this trend as normatively and politically desirable, what might it look like in practice?

Mega-events and Development: The Evidence to Date

Table 23.1 lists a range of first- and second-order sport mega-events that have informed the analysis in this section about the developmental aspirations, approaches, and legacies of previous and prospective hosts. Its purpose is to clarify key analytical themes that have characterized these events and their hosts. Most (but not all) of the events identified took place in what can be described as the period of "high globalization," following the debt crises and structural adjustment prescriptions of the 1980s and the collapse of the Soviet bloc at the start of the 1990s. Events cited prior to this (e.g., the Tokyo Summer Games of 1964 and the Mexican events of 1968 and 1970) are particularly significant as precursors and exemplars for the growing

Table 23.1 Selected Sports Mega-events in "Developing" Countries

	Latin America	Asia	Africa	Europe and Canada
1st Order Events	• Brazil (World Cup 2014) • Brazil/Rio (Olympics 2016) • Mexico (Olympics 1968) • Mexico (World Cup 1970)	• Japan/Tokyo (Olympics 1964, 2020) • Sapporo (Winter Olympics 1972) • Japan/Nagano (Winter Olympics 1998) • Seoul (Olympics 1988) • China/ Beijing (Olympics 2008) • Japan/Korea (World Cup 2002) • Korea/ Pyeonchang (Winter Olympics 2018) • Qatar (World Cup 2022)	• South Africa (World Cup 2010) • South Africa/Cape Town (failed Olympic bid 2004)	• Athens (Olympics 2004) • Vancouver (Winter Olympics 2010) • Toronto (failed Olympic bids 1996 & 2008) • Russia/Sochi (Winter Olympics 2014) • Russia (World Cup 2018)
2nd Order Events	• Brazil/Rio (Pan Am Games 2007) • Cuba/Havana (Pan Am Games 1991) • Dominican Republic/ Santo Domingo (Pan Am Games 2003) • Mexico City (Pan Am Games 1975) • Mexico/Guadalajara (Pan Am Games 2011) • West Indies (Cricket World Cup 2007)	• Malaysia/Kuala Lumpur (Commonwealth Games 1998) • India/Delhi (Commonwealth Games 2010)	• South Africa (Rugby World Cup 1995) • South Africa (Cricket World Cup 2003)	• Canada/Toronto (Pan Am Games 2015)

popularity of mega-events in late-developing countries. Table 23.1 also includes several Canadian and European examples that illustrate some dominant tendencies and alternative possibilities in mega-event hosting. The specific events from which examples are drawn include the truly "first-order" events of the Olympics[5] and the FIFA World Cup, along with a range of second-order events that incorporate both western liberal capitalist and non-western developing-country participants and hosts (the Commonwealth Games, the Pan American Games, and Cricket and Rugby World Cups).

Several broad observations can be drawn from these examples. First, there is a tendency for certain countries and cities to make a habit of mega-event hosting as a central feature of their development policies. Table 23.1 actually understates this tendency. For example, Japan's long-standing "mega-event habit" was firmly established well before the Second World War (see Low 1999); Brazil's (and Rio's) propensity toward mega-event hosting includes, among others, the World Cup of 1950 and the Pan American Games in Sao Paolo in 1963 as well as the more recent spate of events (see Curi et al. 2011; Gaffney 2010); and Mexico City hosted the 1955 and 1975 Pan Am Games, bookending the first Summer Olympics in the "developing world" as well as the 1970 World Cup. This clustering tendency can become a kind of mega-event addiction, with the "fix" of the next major event masking and distracting from underlying social and developmental challenges.

Second, the overall mega-event hosting pattern reflects the gradual transition in global wealth and power from the "old" West to the rising states of the global South, which have used mega-event hosting as a symbolic marker of their global ambitions and "arrival." Nothing symbolizes this more clearly than the divergent hosting patterns of Toronto and Rio. The latter, after two failed bids for the Summer Olympics, "set up" its successful bid

for the 2016 Games by hosting the 2007 Pan Am Games. Moreover, in the competition to host the 2016 event, Rio defeated bids from several well-established, "First World" global cities—Chicago, Madrid, and Tokyo. Toronto, on the other hand, twice failed in bids for the Summer Games and has now "settled for" hosting the 2015 Pan Am event—a mega-event consolation prize. Whether hosting such events will effectively consolidate the rising fortunes of ambitious Southern hosts, or delay (and possibly even reverse) them is less certain. Mexico's unhappy experience in 1968 (Zolov 2004) and Athens' in 2004 suggest that fragile rises can be symbolically and, at least to some degree, practically derailed by mega-event "overstretch."

Third, while there are some striking similarities in the aspirations of mega-event hosts across disparate regional and developmental categories (see Black 2007), there is also a need for more fine-grained comparative analyses of the developmental approaches and possibilities associated with different types of events, and hosts in different regional contexts. These reflect distinct development patterns that are associated with regional forms of capitalism and demonstration effects. For example, a succession of Asian late developers have adopted an approach to mega-event hosting that has not only emulated the example set by Japan (and later South Korea), but has also reflected the distinctive features associated with Asian "developmental states": intense economic nationalism; a high level of state intervention and leadership of the economy, associated with a high tolerance for large-scale public expenditures on what are perceived as strategic initiatives; and aggressive pursuit of a "hybridized" conception of modernity, combining western and indigenous ideas and practices (see Black and Peacock 2011). The Latin American pattern, by comparison, has shifted over time from the populist patterns of industrial modernism associated with the import substitution era in the first several postwar decades (see Gaffney 2010, 16; Zolov 2004), to the externally oriented and socially differentiated pattern of the post-adjustment ("high globalization") period in which disparities are not only tolerated but reinforced.

With regard to first- versus second-order events (as well as multi-sport, single-centred versus single-sport, multi-centred events) there is, first, a need to think more carefully about the suitability of certain types of events for prospective hosts, in terms of existing infrastructure, the popular base and social meaning of different sporting codes, the sequencing of event-centred strategies, etc. (see Black 2008; Cornelissen 2009, 92). In short, certain types of events are likely to generate more reliable benefits, and involve fewer risks for some hosts than others.[6] More broadly, with regard to maximizing the social/human development benefits of mega-events, there are particular kinds of dangers and distortions associated with the high stakes and visibility of first-order events, where fear of failure—particularly for developing-country hosts—can trump virtually all the more routine developmental priorities and produce major distortions in public spending (e.g., Cornelissen 2011, 525; Gaffney 2010, 20–5; Zimbalist 2010). On the other hand, that same heightened degree of visibility and scrutiny, both internally and externally, can combine with the "sport for good" ideological associations of first-order events to produce unprecedented incentives for social development initiatives. This dynamic was clearly present in both South Africa's 2004 Olympic bid and its 2010 World Cup (see Cornelissen 2011; Hiller 2000; Swart and Bob 2004), as well as Toronto and Vancouver's Olympic adventures (Kidd 1992; VanWynsberghe et al. 2012). Conversely, the lower visibility and public/media scrutiny associated with second-order events can make it easier for public officials and bid committees to abandon social development plans with political impunity,

and to engage in corrupt practices in the course of creating venues and infrastructure that serve local and international elites, while limiting popular accessibility. This dynamic is illustrated by the 2007 and 2011 Pan Am Games in Rio and Guadalajara, and the 1998 and 2010 Commonwealth Games in Malaysia and India, respectively (Doolittle 2011; Dupont 2011; Gaffney 2010; van der Westhuizen 2004;). In short, both the propensity for heightened social inequities and for more expansive social/human development possibilities are increased in the case of first-order events, whereas the constraints on abuses seem to be weaker in the case of second-order events.

Finally, it is apparent from the cases reviewed as well as the weight of academic analysis that, as noted in the introduction, the dominant developmental logic of mega-events has always been top-down, reflecting the aspirations and interests of political and economic elites and the popularizing potential of "booster coalitions." Nevertheless, the more specific nature of this elitist development logic has been malleable, reflecting different conceptions of development in different times and places. Thus, the predominantly neoliberal logic of many events in the last generation is a departure from the more statist and populist logic of earlier Latin American events (see Gaffney 2010; and Zolov 2004), and has always been modified in the case of East Asian hosts by their more state-led developmental approaches. Moreover, there has been growing pressure, and enthusiasm, to incorporate broadly based social development objectives, programs, and projects in the hosting plans for mega-events—echoing the growing popularity of the SDP movement (Coalter 2010; Kidd 2008) and its most prominent manifestations, such as the athlete–ambassadors associated with Right to Play.

The impact of this latter trend should not be discounted. To date, however, it has been distinctly limited, in three senses. First, where it has been most systematic and sustained, notably in the cases of Toronto's bids for the 1996 and 2008 Olympics and in Cape Town's bid for the 2004 Games, the bids have been unsuccessful. Moreover, in the case of Toronto, the advocacy that led to the heightened developmentalism of the bid was blamed by event supporters for the bid's failure. This underscores the historic indifference of the International Olympic Committee and other ISOs to the ramifications of the events they oversee for social equity and development, beyond their bedrock conviction concerning the elevating effects of international sport. Second, where developmental dimensions have been most prominent, notably in South Africa's breakthrough hosting of the 2010 World Cup, the plethora of SDP initiatives associated with the event were initiated comparatively late in the preparatory process, while social development initiatives received a small fraction of the public expenditures devoted to the event as a whole (see Cornelissen 2011, 520 and 525). And third, somewhat ironically, the civil society advocacy and relatively open, accountable governance structures that have underpinned a stronger social development focus are most robust in more developed countries such as Canada and the United Kingdom, or a country with a long history of democratic struggle like South Africa. This takes us back to our original core question: to what extent, and in what ways, could bottom-up development initiatives, explicitly concerned with poverty alleviation and social equity, become a higher priority in mega-event planning—beyond window dressing?

Towards More Truly Developmental Mega-events?

The first point to be made in this regard is that sport mega-events, no matter how well conceived, should not be oversold as a means of advancing human development objectives. The prevalence of breathless boosterist promises of "once-in-a-lifetime" benefits from such events, and other public investments in elite sport, is broadly matched by the weight of academic evidence underscoring the degree to which such promises have been habitually overstated. There are structural obstacles to a more comprehensive developmental approach to such events, rooted in their elite orientation and the powerful corporate, political, and organizational interests that surround and back them. As a result, there will always be a danger of creating unrealistic expectations about what they can achieve in the face of pervasive human need (e.g., Hiller 2000, 444–50). Similarly, as with other aspects of legacy analysis, developmental ramifications need to be assessed over a much longer time frame than has typically occurred (see Cornelissen et al. 2011, 315; Swart et al. 2011).

Past experiences combined with the accumulated understanding of developmental interventions in other contexts thus provide some crucial markers of what a more broadly based developmental mega-event could look like. They include the following:

A foundational commitment: A focus on maximizing the social/human development benefits of event hosting, specifically to historically marginalized communities, and on the distributional effects of such events (that is, how their costs and benefits are distributed among different social groups) would need to be built into bid processes from the outset—ideally as a prerequisite for candidate cities. This is a long-standing idea: Bruce Kidd (1992, 164), for example, argued, in light of Toronto's experience with its bid for the 1996 Summer Games, that the IOC should require each candidate city to conduct a social impact assessment and a public consultation before submitting Olympic bids. Harry Hiller noted Cape Town's innovative decision to conduct a "Strategic Environmental Assessment"—though he also noted that it came too late in the preparation process to significantly affect bid planning (Hiller 2000, 449). Hosts, particularly in developed countries like Canada and the UK, have increasingly undertaken wide-ranging consultations with representative groups and, notably under the auspices of the IOC-mandated Olympic Games Impact (OGI) studies, have tracked a lengthy list of indicators of Games impacts over an extended time period (see OGI–UBC 2011; Cornelissen 2009, 85–6).

There is, therefore, some movement upon which to build, but these experiences are relatively recent and not yet habituated within the international sporting community. Traditionally, mega-event hosts have not incorporated considerations of social impact into the bidding process; for example, Minnaert's (2012) analysis of Olympic Games from 1996–2008 found very little focus on "social sustainability" in any of the Games, though there was a small degree of focus on environmental sustainability. Although London 2012 did have some developmental aspirations, reflected in the choice to situate much of the Games infrastructure in London's poorer east end, the long-term outcomes of this effort remain to be seen. Aside from a commitment to diversity, the Games committee didn't articulate any overt commitment to the city's poor and marginalized (London 2012). Thus, a mega-event planning process that privileged distributional effects and poverty alleviation would be a departure, given the powerful incentives for both event organizers/boosters and ISOs to stress the breadth of popular support and the capabilities of the prospective host. Highlighting profound social problems, especially for southern bidders and hosts, runs counter to the "rising" image they seek to project through event hosting, and their interests in mounting a winning bid. Both motivations create a powerful incentive to minimize or gloss

over entrenched development challenges. The political foundations and incentives for a more explicitly "pro-poor" approach would therefore require careful attention—a point to which we will return in the final section of this chapter.

Community consultation: Closely related to a foundational commitment to social equity and broadly based development would be the need for early, systematic, and sustained community consultations, particularly with historically disadvantaged communities. Again, there are examples upon which to build. However, it is difficult, and time consuming, to structure and sustain meaningful consultations with representatives of the people whose interests one is seeking to address, particularly if they are historically marginalized. Development practice is replete with examples of "participatory" processes (most recently national Poverty Reduction Strategy Papers—PRSPs) that have been effectively co-opted to gain legitimacy and acquiescence for the development preferences of the powerful (see Cornwall and Brock 2005). How, then, to establish consultative processes that strengthen rather than distort democratic input, without compromising the urgent tasks of event preparation to rigid deadlines?

There are no easy formulas for addressing this challenge, especially in countries where traditions of democratic participation are limited. There will certainly be contextual variations in what is feasible and effective. Perhaps the most important practical suggestion is that ample time must be provided for meaningful consultation, which may require the typical timeline of a mega-event bid to be amended. Community leaders often underestimate the length of time needed to develop, facilitate, and analyze the results of participatory exercises. As Hiller (2000) points out in his analysis of Cape Town's Olympic bid, consultations and assessments undertaken too late have little chance of actually affecting the content of the bid. If consultations are to be taken seriously and to yield real results, they must occur in the earliest stages of the bid, not after major decisions have already been made. Hiller recounts how Cape Town officials simply presented their results to the public, rather than engaging in sustained discussions around them. Arnstein (1969) identifies this type of participation as essentially manipulative—an attempt by governments or elites to "sell" decisions they have already taken. Booster coalitions could improve the legitimacy of their plans for mega-event hosting by engaging in better public consultation, particularly since the IOC considers public support in their analysis of each host city.

The key point is that a developmental mega-event would aim to systematically expand consultation with, and participation by, historically marginalized communities. If this objective is not firmly entrenched from the beginning, consultative processes are likely to fall under the rubric of window dressing.

Transparent and accountable governance structures and processes: Cornelissen, Bob, and Swart (2011, 315) argue that, "Among the strongest predictive factors for how a host could be affected in the future are the governance relationships that exist in the host country or city, and the management structures that are set up to stage an event." The problem, of course, is that mega-event bidders and organizers cannot easily foster robust and accountable governance practices where they do not already exist—certainly not in the compressed time frame of an event cycle. Nor are they themselves particularly inclined toward routine exposure to public scrutiny. Quite the reverse: event organizing committees have typically taken the form of "public–private partnerships" (or, in the case of the Sochi organizers, a "state corporation"—Wisniewska 2008) that are, by design, at least partially shielded from the routine processes of accountability that public agencies would face. The objective, under the circumstances, should be to ensure that the organizing committee is itself broadly representative, particularly of communities that a "developmental games" is aiming to prioritize; that they are regularly answerable to elected representatives; and that there are regular and robust reporting requirements on plans, preparations, and expenditures.

The prospects for robust accountability are a function not only of the formal governance structures in the host country/city, but of the wider social structures of accountability within which both the government and the organizing committee are embedded. This includes dynamic and capable civil society organizations, of the sort that compelled Toronto to adopt the "Toronto Olympic Commitment" in a previous era (Kidd 1992), and a strong and independent mass media that can hold organizers and overseers to account (and that is not irredeemably incorporated into a pro-event-booster coalition). There are, however, profound imbalances in the capacities of such civil society groups and if mega-events are to have a strong developmental emphasis, they will have to make particular provision for groups that speak for poorer people and communities. Some of these groups will almost certainly remain opposed to such events; their advocacy can be crucial in pushing organizers and government toward a more developmental orientation.

There is also a key role in this process for researchers. Many scholars and researchers (in both development and sport studies) have a strong normative commitment to social equity, and can help both civil society groups and event organizers imagine what a more developmental and inclusive event can look like. Initiatives like the Sport Legacies Research Collaborative at the University of Toronto (http://physical.utoronto.ca/Sport_Legacies_Research_Collaborative/Research.aspx), initiated with the aim of scrutinizing the planning for and legacies of the 2015 Pan Am Games along with other mega-events, are potentially critical agents of accountability. A developmental mega-event would support, and respond to, research networks aiming to critically analyze and enable human/social development plans and possibilities.

Design: This is a very broad marker that encompasses venues (both competition and training), the new transportation and communication infrastructure that is a ubiquitous byproduct of mega-event planning and preparations, housing for athletes, officials, and media, the enhancement of public spaces, etc. Developmental design in this regard would and should be closely aligned with principles of sustainability (the "third pillar" of Olympism) in the conception and construction of the built environment associated with mega-events.

Hiller's discussion (2000, 444–50) of the plan for Cape Town's 2004 Olympic bid provides some excellent starting points for thinking about how a foundationally developmental event might proceed. First, venues would need to be designed in such a way as to improve access, opportunities, community services, and attractive public spaces for marginalized communities. In the case of Cape Town, this involved siting as many venues as possible in historically disadvantaged (and racially defined) areas of the Cape Town metropolitan area. It also involved developing transportation and community infrastructure plans that would use the occasion of the Games and the venues constructed for it to trigger the development of new community centres, public transportation links, and the like, that would enhance quality of life and access to crucial public services for marginalized communities—for example design principles that link venue development to health, education, housing, and other recreational facilities in such communities. One area where Hiller noted a serious risk of misplaced expectations was the critical

challenge of decent and affordable housing. In Cape Town, for example, even if all housing created for the event was "affordable" (a highly challenging proposition in economic terms), the resulting housing stock would not have made much of a dent in the acute shelter needs of Capetonians. Much the same could be said for the residents of the sprawling favelas of Rio. Nevertheless, these events can perhaps be used as opportunities to think in innovative ways about housing designs that could be replicated to have a larger impact on housing shortages and requirements.

With regard to event and training venues, a clear design brief seeking to ensure, to the greatest extent possible, that venues are accessible to community participants after the event, and/or that they are sufficiently modest and affordable to attract a wide range of tenants and "pay their way," is particularly critical. Alternatively, venues could be designed with an eye to how they might be feasibly and affordably modified to meet other community needs (Zimbalist 2010). The long history of mega-event "white elephants" (e.g., Horne 2004) should be avoidable with careful planning. Here, the London Games seems to offer some inspiration with their architectural emphasis on "touching the ground lightly," and their prioritization of sustainability principles in design, construction, and post-event use (Renzetti 2011). This would be accompanied by plans for community recreation and training programs that would seek to ensure that the venues were well and widely used, particularly by youth from poorer areas. Sport and community development organizations would be key partners in formulating such peri- and post-event plans.

The general point is that a developmental mega-event would require a different kind of design brief that would privilege accessibility, affordability, and sustainability at every turn, with a particular eye to providing more equitable access for disadvantaged communities. One can imagine some very interesting and innovative architectural and planning results from such an approach.

Employment: Hiller (2000, 446–7) notes that the Cape Town Olympic bid enjoyed higher levels of support from black than white South Africans, in part because of their acute need for, and expectation of, new employment opportunities. This is another area in which anticipated benefits are often substantially oversold. Nevertheless, there *are* new employment opportunities that are inevitably associated with mega-event preparations, construction, and hosting. To ensure that these benefits reach the widest possible range of citizens, and that skills training and transferable skills are maximized (an explicit aspiration of the Cape Town organizers), event planning would have to be coordinated with educational and training institutions and programs, as well as potential employers motivated by corporate social responsibility (CSR) incentives. This, in turn, assumes capable and responsive policy-making capacity, and the ability of training and educational institutions to respond to the resulting needs and opportunities. Again, these are capacities that cannot be quickly created if they are not already in place—but mega-events can create powerful incentives for institutional reform. These capacities may be developed too slowly to fully seize pre-event possibilities, but they could lead to program innovations and capacity enhancement that linger as key legacies after the event—an outcome that longer-term post-event analyses could capture.

Narratives: Sport has traditionally been considered, if not apolitical, at least transcendent of the economic, social, and geopolitical issues between peoples and nations. Sport mega-events in particular are often held up as opportunities for overcoming these challenges and fostering international and intercultural understanding. Hartmann and Kwauk (2011) deconstruct this common narrative of sport and development, arguing that sport is used as a tool to "maintain and reproduce established social functions" (286). The neoliberal underpinnings of the international sporting community emphasize hierarchy, expertise, competition, and the idea that improvement can be achieved by simply trying harder. This emphasis masks the underlying structures of inequality that permeate much of the world. These dominant narratives of sport and development, argue Hartmann and Kwauk, are thus fundamentally reproductive rather than emancipating.

If this is the case, broadly, for the SDP movement, Hartmann and Kwauk say that we need to focus more on empowerment. And, if this is the direction that SDP ought to move in, what role can mega-events play in this process? Such hegemonic narratives need not be taken for granted. Mega-events could articulate and "sell" a different story. What if host cities were to privilege their commitment to goals aside from economic growth, national pride, and the promotion of athleticism? Perhaps their websites could commit to and then highlight things such as community development or gender equality. A timely, if still controversial, step would be for an ISO to make a clear and strong statement in support of homosexual athletes—an issue placed into sharp relief by the Sochi Winter Games. Such efforts could give the story of these events a previously underexplored angle. Furthermore, if mega-event organizers took this approach, they might be able to attract an even broader assortment of community partners and supporters, interested in working to achieve these goals rather than criticizing the event from the sidelines.

Broadly, events such as the Olympics provide an unprecedented opportunity for governments, NGOs, and activists to bring attention to issues of human suffering. Human rights advocates took just such an opportunity in the run-up to the 2008 Beijing Olympic Games, and the human rights abuses of the Chinese government were widely discussed and highlighted by events like the Torch Relay prior to the Games.[7] Mega-events can therefore open doors to global conversations about human rights, poverty, and inequality that might otherwise be difficult to make heard. Although hosts are unlikely to want to highlight such issues, mega-events provide an extraordinary window of opportunity for NGOs to appeal to both their own governments and the international community—raising awareness, money, and the potential for political recognition and change within governmental (and sporting) organizations. This potential was highlighted, once again, by the June 2013 protests in Brazil.

Youth development: Sport mega-events are youth-centric. Not only are youth the primary competitors, they also stand to both benefit and suffer most from the effects of expenditures on such games. The legacy of any such event is, in effect, their legacy. In the context of the global South, youth represent the largest, and the most vulnerable, demographic. They therefore need to be included throughout the bidding process, incorporated into the event itself, and then kept in mind and regularly consulted as the recipients of post-event legacy projects. Unfortunately, the experience of youth in past sport mega-events has been mixed at best. Marginalized youth have tended to be negatively affected, particularly as a result of attempts to "clean up" cities in preparation for tourists and television cameras. Youth in both "developed" and "underdeveloped" cities have experienced forcible removal by security forces in tandem with mega-events (Kennelly and Watt 2011; van Blerk 2011). This reflects the impulse of hosts to remove distracting or embarrassing sights. A developmental mega-event would incorporate youth into the development of the bid, the design of spaces, legacy projects, and programs, as volunteers and workers during the event, and as recipients of related SDP programming.

This is an admittedly sketchy and incomplete list of factors that could help realize the potential of an explicitly developmental mega-event. What is the likelihood of such an approach being more widely and systematically adopted, particularly in the "rising states" of the global South that are hosting a growing share of contemporary mega-events?

The Politics of Promoting Developmental Mega-Events

Reflecting on these possibilities is both promising and sobering. Promising, because there has been significant movement even in the past decade and a half, from the time when Hiller (2000, 442) could argue that "the Cape Town bid [with its developmental focus] provided an entirely new variation of the rationale for utilizing a mega-event for urban development." Sobering, because mega-events with an explicitly human/social development rationale remain exceptional; because even where considerations of "social inclusion" and "empowerment" are explicitly pursued, these objectives have been relatively marginal and filtered through a de-politicizing neoliberal prism (VanWynsberghe et al., 2012); and because they have been most advanced in developed liberal capitalist settings, such as Vancouver and London, where the need (though still substantial) is least acute.

This leads us, finally, to the question of the political foundations upon which a more widespread, systematic, and sustained emphasis on bottom-up development priorities could be built into mega-event planning and legacies—particularly though not only in the global South. The general point to be made here is that advances in this regard will depend on the interplay of political dynamics at multiple levels: bottom-up progress will involve permissive and active conditions from elite and middle-level actors and processes as well as bottom-up pressures.[8]

Given the hierarchical and highly structured nature of sport governance, ISOs will be important in enabling or, alternatively, inhibiting a stronger developmental focus—none more so than the International Olympic Committee. This is because of the IOC's unique self-conception as the keeper of the ideology of Olympism, with its foundational commitment to the idea of "sport for good" and its pivotal role in shaping the norms and practices of other ISOs. Byron Peacock (2011, 478) has applied insights from a "world polity" approach to highlight the way in which the IOC has effectively adapted its sense of "social mission or purpose" through a process of absorbing and adapting the main normative influences and dominant ideas of successive historical periods. In so doing, it has continuously (re)defined its conception of "the good" that is served through sport generally, and the IOC specifically. This process has been critical, Peacock argues, to its institutional survival and its persistent—indeed growing—social and political influence in the world. In the past, for example, it was able to absorb and reflect changing ideas regarding amateurism, racial equality, gender norms, and environmentalism, among others. Of particular relevance to this chapter is the degree to which, in the same period that developing countries have become increasingly prominent as mega-event hosts, since 1980, the IOC has come to embrace "sport for peace and development" as its principle conception of "sport for good." In doing so, Peacock argues, it has "embraced the rhetoric and form of "grassroots," "participatory," or "empowering" development" (489), using its increasing wealth to forge partnerships with governmental, non-governmental, and corporate partners to do so. It now supports a plethora of development and humanitarian initiatives that specifically aim to support community-based efforts to tackle social ills such as "poverty, reconciliation, gender equality, or HIV/AIDS *through* sport" (Peacock 2011, 492).

Given the embedding of this bottom-up development conception of "sport for good" in the IOC's sense of social mission (however shallow or self-serving it may seem in practice), as well as growing global concern with social inequality highlighted by the "Occupy Wall Street" movement and its offshoots, it seems that the IOC *should be* sensitive to charges that its foundational event, the Games themselves, are indifferent or even detrimental to the social needs of marginalized communities in host jurisdictions. It *should be* a relatively small step, under the circumstances, to embracing (or even requiring?) a more actively developmental approach to Games preparations. This would be an important enabling condition for those who seek to push the Games in this direction. How, and how much, such a trend would "spill over" to other ISOs, beginning with FIFA but extending to other single- and multi-sport bodies (e.g., the Commonwealth Games Federation and the Pan American Sports Organization) would then become an interesting and important trend to track.

In practice, however, the IOC and other ISO's have multiple purposes and interests—most fundamentally the staging of successful, popular, and media-friendly mega-events, thereby ensuring their own vitality and enrichment. Indeed, ISOs are fascinating and powerful international actors in their own right—combining elements of inter-governmental, civil society, and corporate identities and behaviours (see Peacock 2011). Furthermore, it seems unlikely that the Games and other mega-events are in danger of being undermined by their lack of emphasis on developmental outcomes—though growing global awareness of the public policy distortions associated with these events and the costs and risks of hosting them may be altering this calculus.[9] Nevertheless, the impetus for ISOs to require such a focus would have to be reinforced from outside the organization's own sense that it is the socially responsible thing to do. Without sustained pressure to emphasize developmental needs and opportunities, more self-serving and "top-down" motivations are likely to continue to predominate given the powerful nexus between ISOs, host political and economic elites, and privileged corporate sponsors. Thus, bottom-up development priorities must also be emphasized and supported at the level of host states (national, regional, and local) and public policies. It is instructive in this regard to revisit Cape Town's "developmental" bid for the 2004 Olympics. The key point here is that the bid emerged in the immediate aftermath of the end of apartheid, when all elite sectors accepted the need to redress the racial injustices of the past, and the imperative of addressing inherited inequalities and deprivations as a prerequisite for social stability and reconciliation. Under the circumstances, it was virtually unimaginable that an Olympics bid could be mounted and sustained *without* a foundational focus on improving the life chances of the historically disadvantaged, and restructuring the "apartheid city." Whether the country's hard-pressed public sector institutions would have had the *capacities* necessary to successfully orchestrate such a process is questionable, but the *will* and *legitimating logic* underpinning such an approach was clear.

To what extent can similar public sector imperatives be generated and sustained in Brazil, for example, where comparable social needs and inequalities coexist with high levels of elite corruption, particularly in the sporting establishment (see *Economist* 2011)? What about state institutions in, for example, Russia or Qatar? In short, the public sector conditions for a stronger bottom-up orientation are often weak among political and bureaucratic elites in host countries/cities.

This highlights the importance of a mobilized "developmental coalition" in host societies. Such a coalition would stand in contrast (though not always in opposition) to the inevitable booster coalitions that mega-events generate. It would include capable and media-savvy civil society organizations and activists, along with socially engaged planners, architects, researchers, and politicians. An early exemplar would be the coalition that orchestrated the Toronto Olympic Commitment in the late 1980s, motivated by a keen sense of "the politics of the possible" and the "more humane Olympic [and sporting] tradition which was brought into the debate by progressive athletes and sports leaders" (Kidd 1992, 159–60). It would relate uneasily to hard-line anti-event activists, finding areas of common ground on social critiques and objectives, but diverging on strategic and tactical approaches. It would depend, however, on the pressure brought to bear by mega-event critics for the impetus to advance its own reform agenda.

The presence of, and space for, such a developmental coalition in prospective mega-event hosts will vary considerably. Typically, to reiterate a paradox noted earlier, their capacities and connections will be stronger in more "developed" societies with less acute developmental challenges. Recall, however, that many rising southern states (and prospective event hosts) have robust and sophisticated traditions of social mobilization and activism. Moreover, in the context of a growing, and increasingly transnational, Sport for Development and Peace "movement," experiences and capacities can and will be shared transnationally. In this regard, SDP activists and developmental coalitions can learn from the well-established literature on and experiences of transnational advocacy networks that have fostered social change in a range of issue areas, from human rights to the environment (see Keck and Sikkink 1998).

Finally, there is a critical role and opportunity for more genuinely grassroots and bottom-up initiatives. This brings us back to the characteristic "liminality" and collective exhilaration associated with mega-events (Chalip 2006), and the atmosphere of celebration and possibility they generate, however ephemerally. In these contexts, many community-based organizations of various kinds may be inspired to launch event-themed initiatives that can have important community development benefits. Swart et al. (2011) highlight an interesting example associated with the FIFA World Cup in South Africa. The Football Foundation of South Africa was established in 2008 in the racially divided, non-host community of Gansbaai, with just under 25,000 residents. The Foundation responded to the stimulus of the looming event, and the paucity of community recreation facilities, by initiating plans for a new multi-purpose recreation facility, linking the resulting facilities and opportunities to social development programming in education and health. The community was able to exploit the conjuncture of the World Cup to partner with corporate and governmental agencies to finance the facility. The authors summarize that: "The FFSA can be considered a sport-plus [in Fred Coalter's terms] non-governmental organization that focuses primarily on sport development but also emphasizes wider social benefits." Moreover, "the project would not have developed to the same extent had it not been for the World Cup. Increasing popular pressure on international sport federations and their commercial partners to demonstrate greater levels of accountability has obliged them to take the issue of the broader developmental significance of their events more seriously" (419, 420). Through survey data, the authors have tracked the positive effects of this initiative in the Gansbaai community, and the "solid foundation" it has built.

This case is instructive because it illustrates the catalytic possibilities of mega-events in potentially linking bottom-up initiatives to top-down interests and resources, through governmental, non-governmental, and corporate programs and support. It underscores the basic point that social/human development advances in mega-event hosts, while depending strongly on local initiative and participation, can achieve much more (in both scale and speed) by connecting with top-down agents and resources. It is the process of connecting these levels of initiative in a more systematic and sustained way that should be the focus of strategic consideration. It is also essential to establish policies and programs that will extend well beyond the event itself, to ensure sustainability. Swart et al. rightly emphasize the need to track the long-term impacts of the promising case of the FFSA. Similar processes of medium- and long-term assessment should become the norm in analyzing the developmental legacies of other mega-events. Likewise, there is a need for a more systematic study of comparable local or "grassroots" initiatives in various mega-event hosts. How representative is the experience of Gansbaai and the FFSA? Have other, similar initiatives enjoyed comparable levels of success? If not, why not? As promising as case studies like this one are, they need to be supplemented by larger-scale comparative analyses before we can begin to reach firmer conclusions regarding the transformative potential of national hosting experiences. Donnelly et al.'s argument (2011, 592) regarding SDP applies equally to the range of developmental initiatives associated with mega-events: "Perhaps more than anything else (what is needed is) a healthy dose of normal science—what is the size and shape of this "beast" we are studying? What are its characteristics? How might the various projects and programs be monitored and evaluated?"

Conclusion

The developmental initiatives and possibilities that have come to be stimulated by at least some mega-events should be understood as a kind of progress. Window dressing is, after all, an attractive *accoutrement* to any structure. But where they have gained a foothold, they typically fall well short of a sustained engagement with entrenched structures of poverty and inequity. Moreover, in many, particularly second-order events, even these limited gains have yet to materialize.

As more rising states seize the opportunity to host mega-events in the hopes of attracting a range of economic and political benefits, it is increasingly crucial to evaluate the full developmental possibilities of such events. We are beginning to understand the sorts of considerations that could lead to more broadly based developmental benefits from mega-events, bearing in mind the need for clear-eyed appraisals of these possibilities and the avoidance of inflated expectations stimulated by event-linked euphoria. We also understand some of the political dynamics and strategic calculations that could advance the prospects for this new orientation toward more developmental mega-events. Given the powerful countervailing factors and interests that continue to pervade mega-event preparation and implementation, it remains to be seen how far these possibilities can be realized.

Notes

1 For an excellent, ongoing account of Brazil's encounter with sport mega-events and International Sports Organizations (ISOs), see Chris Gaffney's blog, "Hunting White Elephants" (www.geostadia.com/search/label/Rio).

2 Chicago, for example, spent nearly $48 million and nearly four years in their losing bid for the 2016 Olympics (Badger 2013).

3 Black (2008) has argued elsewhere that this situation represents a collective failure of imagination and should *not* be accepted without considering alternative, more broadly beneficial, ways of "branding" the city/region/nation. Nevertheless, there is no denying the mobilizing power of sporting mega-events.

4 For an articulation of this emerging alternative, see the 2011 UNDP Human Development Report, on *Sustainability and Equity: A Better Future for All*.

5 Although the Winter Olympics are much more modest in their scale and reach.

6 Think here of the America's Cup in New Zealand, which was arguably a particularly good fit with the history and capacities of the host (though marked by jarring celebration of extreme wealth and high-tech hyper-competition).

7 Though, strikingly, these concerns were essentially ignored in the context of the event itself.

8 See Death (2011, 113–14) for a similar argument.

9 As reflected, for example, in the fact that only two cities—Beijing and Almaty, Kazakhstan—are left in the competition to host the 2022 Winter Olympics. Tellingly, both are located in authoritarian regimes, after all democratic governments pulled out of the race due to a lack of public support.

Key Terms

alternative development
liminality

mega-events
Olympism

Questions for Review

1. Why has sport been neglected as a focus of study in IPE?

2. What makes mega-events attractive as a strategic response to globalization?

3. What ideological meanings have been associated with Olympism, and how have they changed over time?

4. What patterns of development have been favoured by mega-events?

5. What would a "developmental" mega-event look like, and what conditions would be required to make it feasible?

6. Canadian cities have been regular mega-event hosts, including Summer and Winter Olympic Games, Pam American Games, and Commonwealth Games among others. What are the legacies and developmental effects of these events?

Further Resources

Black, D. and van der Westhuizen, J. (Guest editors). (2004). Special Issue of *Third World Quarterly* 25(7), on "Going global: The promises and pitfalls of hosting global games."

Bloyce, D. and Smith A. (guest editors). (2012). Special Issue of *International Journal of Sport Policy and Politics* 4(3), on "Olympic and Paralympic policy."

Chalip, L. "Towards social leverage of sport events."

Coalter, F. "The politics of sport-for-development: Limited focus programmes and broad gauge problems?"

Cornelissen, S. (2012). "Our struggles are bigger than the World Cup": Civic activism, state-society relations and the socio-political legacies of the 2010 FIFA World Cup, *British Journal of Sociology* 63(2), 328–48.

Darnell, S. *Sport for development and peace: A critical sociology.*

Horne, J. and Manzenreiter W. (Eds). (2006). *Sports mega-events: Scientific analyses of a global phenomenon.* Oxford: Blackwell Publishing.

Levermore, R. and A. Beacom (Eds). *Sport and international development.*

References

Alegi, P. (2007). "The political economy of mega-stadiums and the under-development of grassroots football in South Africa." *Politikon* 34(3), 315–31.

Arnstein, S. R. (1969). A ladder of citizen participation. *Journal of the American Institute of Planners* 35(4), 216–24.

Badger, Emily. (2013). What happens to the Olympic plans of cities that don't win them? *The Atlantic Cities*, April 15. Retrieved from www.theatlanticcities.com/neighborhoods/2013/04/what-happens-olympic-plans-cities-dont-win-them/5284/.

Beutler, I. (2008). "Sport serving development and peace: Achieving the goals of the United Nations through sport." *Sport in Society* 11(4), 359–69.

Black, D. (2007). "The symbolic politics of sport mega-events: 2010 in comparative perspective." *Politikon* 34(3), 261–76.

Black, D. (2008). "Dreaming big: The pursuit of "second order" games as a strategic response to globalization." *Sport in Society* 11(4), 467–80.

Black, D. (2010). "The ambiguities of development: Implications for 'development through sport.'" *Sport in Society* 13(1), 121–9.

Black, D. and Peacock, B. (2011). "Catching up: Understanding the pursuit of major games by rising developmental states." *The International Journal of the History of Sport* 28(16), 2270–87.

Black, D. and Van der Westhuizen, J. "The allure of global games for 'semi-peripheral' polities and spaces: A research agenda." *Third World Quarterly* 25(7), 2004, 1195–214.

Chalip, L. (2006). "Towards social leverage of sport events." *Journal of Sport and Tourism* 11 (2), 109–27.

Coalter, F. (2010). "The politics of sport-for-development: limited focus programmes and broad gauge problems?" *International Review for the Sociology of Sport 45*(3), 295–314.

Cornelissen, S. (2009). "A delicate balance: Major Sport events and development." In R. Levermore and A. Beacom (eds). *Sport and international development.* London: Palgrave Macmillan, 76–97.

Cornelissen, S. (2011). "More than a sporting chance? Appraising the sport for development legacy of the 2010 FIFA World Cup." *Third World Quarterly 32*(3), 503–29.

Cornelissen, S., U. Bob, and K. Swart. (2011). "Towards redefining the concept of legacy in relation to sport mega-events: Insights from the 2010 World Cup." *Development Southern Africa 28*(3), 307–18.

Cornwall, A. and Brock, K. "What do buzzwords do for development policy: a critical look at 'participation', 'empowerment', and 'poverty reduction.'" *Third World Quarterly 26*(7), 2005, 1043–60.

Cox, R. (1986). "Social forces, states, and world order: Beyond international relations Theory." In R. Keohane (Ed.), *Neorealism and its critics.* New York: Columbia University Press, 204–53.

Curi, M., Knijnik, J., and Mascarenhas, G. (2011). "The Pan American Games in Rio de Janeiro 2007: Consequences of a mega-event on a BRIC country." *International Review for the Sociology of Sport 46*(2), 140–56.

Darnell, S. (2012). *Sport for development and peace: A critical sociology.* Bloomsbury Academic.

Darnell, S. and Black, D. (2011). "Mainstreaming sport into international development studies." *Third World Quarterly 32*(3), 367–78.

Death, C. (2011). "'Greening' the 2010 FIFA World Cup: Environmental sustainability and the mega-event in South Africa *13*(2), 99–117.

Donnelly, P., M. Atkinson, S. Boyle, and Szto, C. (2011). "Sport for development and peace: A public sociology perspective." *Third World Quarterly 32*(3), 589–601.

Doolittle, R. (2011). "Learning from Guadalajara's mistakes." *The Star* (Toronto), 14 October.

Du Pont, V. (2011). "The dream of Delhi as a global city." *International Journal of Urban and Regional Research.*

Economist. (2011). "Own goals from Senhor Futebol," 1 October.

Gaffney, C. (2010). "Mega-events and socio-spatial dynamics in Rio de Janeiro, 1919–2016." *Journal of Latin American Geography 9*(1), 7–29.

Hartmann, Douglas and Kwauk, Christina. (2011). Sport and development: An overview, critique and reconstruction. *Journal of Sport and Social Issues 3*(3), 284–305.

Hickey, S. and Mohan, G. (2004). *Participation: From tyranny to transformation.* London: Zed Books.

Hiller, H. (2000). "Mega-events, Urban Boosterism and Growth Strategies: An analysis of the objectives and legitimations of the Cape Town 2004 Olympic bid." *International Journal of Urban and Regional Research 24*(2), 2000, 439–58.

Horne, J. (2004). "The global game of football: The 2002 World Cup and regional development in Japan." *Third World Quarterly 25*(7), 1233–44.

Kennelly, Jacqueline and Watt, Paul. (2011). Sanitizing public space in Olympic host cities: The spatial experiences of marginalized youth in 2010 Vancouver and 2012 London. *Sociology 45*(5), 765–81.

Keck, M. and Sikkink, K. (1998). *Activists Beyond Borders.* Ithaca: Cornell University Press.

Kidd, B. (1992). "The Toronto Olympic Commitment: Towards a Social Contract for the Olympic Games." *Olympika 1*, 154–67.

Kidd, B. "A new social movement: Sport for development and peace." *Sport in Society 11*(4), 370–80.

Lenskyj, H. (2008). "Olympic industry resistance." Albany: State University of New York Press.

Levermore, R. (2009). "Sport-in-international development: Theoretical frameworks." In R. Levermore and A. Beacom (Eds). *Sport and international development.* London: Palgrave Macmillan, 26–54.

Levermore, R. and Beacom, A. (Eds.). (2009). *Sport and international development.* London: Palgrave Macmillan.

London 2012 Olympic Games (n.d.). *About us.* Retrieved from www.london2012.com/about-us/

Low, M. "Japan, modernity and the Tokyo Olympics." *Humanities Research 2*, 1999, 33–52.

Minnaert, L. (2012). An Olympic legacy for all? The non-infrastructural outcomes of the Olympic Games for socially excluded groups (Atlanta 1996–Beijing 2008). *Tourism Management 33*(2), 361–70.

Noel, A. and Therien, J-P. (2008). *Left and Right in Global Politics.* Cambridge: Cambridge University Press.

OGI-UBC Research Team. (2011). "Olympic Games Impact (OGI) Study for the 2010 Olympic and Paralympic Winter Games—Games-time Report. 11 May.

Peacock, B. (2011). "'A Secret Instinct of Social Preservation': Legitimacy and the dynamic (re)constitution of Olympic conceptions of the 'good'." *Third World Quarterly 32*(3), 477–502.

Pieterse, J. (2010). *Development theory: Deconstructions/ reconstructions*, 2nd ed. Sage.

Renzetti, E. (2011). "The Lego Olympics." *The Globe and Mail* (Toronto), 24 September.

Shaw, C. (2008). *Five Ring Circus: Myths and Realities of the Olympic Games.* Gabriola Island, BC: New Society Publishers.

Swart, K. and Bob, U. (2004). "The seductive discourse of development: the Cape Town 2004 Olympic bid." *Third World Quarterly 25*(7), 1311–24.

Swart, K., Bob, U., Knott, B., and Salie, M. (2011). "A sport and sociocultural legacy beyond 2010: A case study of the Football Foundation of South Africa." *Development Southern Africa 28*(3), 415–27.

UNDP (United Nations Development Program). (2011). *Sustainability and Equity: A Better Future for All.* Human Development Report 2011.

Van Blerk, L. (2011). "Managing Cape Town's street children/youth: the impact of the 2010 World Cup bid on street life in the city of Cape Town." *South African Geographical Journal 93*(1), 29–37.

Van der Westhuizen, J. 2004. "Marketing Malaysia as a Model Modern Muslim State: The Significance of the 16th Commonwealth Games." *Third World Quarterly 25*(7), 1277–91.

VanWynsberghe, R., Surborg, B., and Wyly, E. (2012). "Neoliberalism, social inclusion, and mega-events: The case of 2010." *International Journal of Urban and Regional Research.*

Watts, J. (2013). "Brazil protests erupt over public services and World Cup costs." *The Guardian* (guardian. co.uk), 18 June.

Wisniewska, I. (2008). "State corporations: State property in de facto private hands." *Baltic Rim Economies 29*(2), 23–4.

Zimbalist, A. 2010. "Is it Worth It?," *Finance and Development*, March.

Zolov, E. (2004). "Showcasing the 'Land of Tomorrow': Mexico and the 1968 Olympics." *The Americas 61*(2), 159–88.

24 Corruption in the Global Economy

Ellen Gutterman

Big city mayors in Canada have been in a lot of trouble in recent years. In 2012 Toronto's Rob Ford made international headlines for his outrageous behaviour and dereliction of the public trust. That same year, the mayor of Laval, Quebec resigned amid allegations of bribery and other criminal practices, followed the next year by the arrest of the mayor of Montreal on similar charges; the Charbonneau Commission revealed widespread bribery, bid-rigging, illicit enrichment, and other criminal practices in the management of public construction contracts in Quebec; the RCMP raided several offices of the Canadian-based multinational construction and engineering firm SNC-Lavalin, in investigations into alleged bribery and other illicit practices in several of the firm's projects in Bangladesh, Libya, and Algeria; and three senators and the Prime Minister's Office have been embroiled in scandal because of improper expense reimbursements. Following on the heels of the "sponsorship scandal" of 2004 and other misuse-of-federal-funds scandals of the 1990s, these events draw attention to something that observers of Canadian politics have traditionally not focused on: corruption.[1]

Corruption is a complex, age-old, and universal phenomenon. The payment of off-the-books sums to get permits more quickly or to avoid safety inspections and other types of government regulation, secret consultant expenses and special "commissions" to gain business contracts, and the theft of a government's treasury by those in power are common manifestations of corruption around the world. Corrupt acts include bribery, extortion, nepotism, fraud, influence peddling, the use of "speed money," and embezzlement. Rent-seeking, black marketeering, money laundering, and transnational crime are also aspects of corruption. "Transactional corruption" involves exchanges between two or more parties; "auto-corruption" consists of the self-enrichment of leaders in kleptocratic regimes. Corruption can be systematic and organized at high levels or diffuse and decentralized at low levels. Virtually all forms of corruption are proscribed by virtually all countries, yet corruption remains endemic in most parts of the world.

Not too long ago scholars, business people, and policy-makers in Canada and other industrialized countries either ignored corruption or considered it to be a problem relevant only to poor, developing countries. Culturally relativist ideas about corruption held that, though unacceptable in the West, corruption in the global South was natural, to be expected, and in several respects beneficial to economic and political development. The political scientist Samuel Huntington, for example, argued that corruption in developing states can enhance political stability. In Huntington's view,

> Like machine politics or clientelistic politics in general, corruption provides immediate, specific, and concrete benefits to groups which might otherwise be thoroughly alienated from society. Corruption may thus be functional to the maintenance of a political system in the same way that reform is. Corruption itself may be a substitute for reform and both corruption and reforms may be substitutes for revolution. Corruption serves to reduce group pressures for policy changes, just as reform serves to reduce class pressures for structural changes.[2]

In international business the prevalent idea was that corrupt practices condemned in the West were necessary for doing business in the developing world. Many prominent industrialized countries (such as Australia, France, Germany, and the Netherlands) accepted bribes paid to foreign officials in the pursuit of international business contracts as a legitimate—and tax-deductible—business expense. Within such international organizations as the World Bank, the International Monetary Fund (IMF), and the United Nations (UN), the very topic of corruption was taboo. World Bank officials, in fact, would not explicitly mention corruption in public statements nor in internal memoranda, referring instead to "the C word."[3]

Ideas and practices permitting corruption began to change in the mid-1990s. The end of the Cold War removed strategic and geopolitical incentives in the West for supporting corrupt regimes in the Philippines, Indonesia, Nigeria, and elsewhere. The spread of democracy emboldened popular movements against corrupt leaders and accentuated the threats to democratization posed by corruption. An "eruption" of major corruption scandals in democratic, industrialized states including Belgium, France, Germany, Spain, Italy, and Japan, as well as in newly capitalist Russia, exposed the vulnerability of even wealthy and "advanced" polities to problems of corruption and showed that this could no longer be considered a "third world" issue.[4] A new wave of corruption research by economists, legal scholars, and political scientists also presented mounting evidence about the costs of corruption: countries with high levels of corruption displayed lower levels of investment, lower economic growth rates, lower scores in social development, harmfully skewed government expenditures, and other problems of serious concern to the international political and economic system.[5]

As a result, a diverse range of international, regional, and local political and economic institutions began to promote new anti-corruption policies. The World Bank identified corruption as "the single greatest obstacle to economic and social development" and committed to fighting against it.[6] The Organisation of American States (OAS), the Organisation for Economic Cooperation and Development (OECD), the Council of Europe, the IMF, and the UN, plus an array of private sector and non-governmental organizations produced legal conventions and recommendations, policy statements, codes of conduct, and new research all focused on curbing corruption in the global economy. Today, corruption is one of the principal issues of global governance. It is a core concern of the international political economy, as well as a paradigmatic issue for the academic discipline of

IPE: the very notion of "corruption" invokes values and ideals about what is good and appropriate in the international political economy, while such practices as transnational bribery directly affect the distribution of money, legitimacy, power, and security in the world.

This chapter considers corruption from this global perspective, asking: What is corruption, and why does it matter? What are some analytic tools and approaches that might help us to think about, describe, and explain corruption, particularly in its comparative and international dimensions? What current policies are in place to combat corruption in the global economy, and what is Canada's role in global anti-corruption efforts? The balance of the chapter addresses these important questions, before concluding with a discussion that places the global "corruption eruption" in a more critical perspective.

What is Corruption, and Why Does it Matter?

Simply put, *corruption is the abuse of entrusted power for private gain.*[7] Beyond this seemingly simple definition, corruption is a remarkably complex phenomenon and its definition is the subject of significant theoretical and empirical debate.

Consider the following "ripped from the headlines" examples of corruption:

- **Everyday Corruption in India.** Vishal is the owner of a small fried-chicken stand in Delhi, the bustling capital of India. Every other week he is stopped by a traffic officer demanding 100 rupees ($1.75) to avoid citation on a trumped-up offence. At lunchtime most days the local beat cops stop by the stand to receive free meals. More senior police officers with authority over opening hours take 10,000 rupees ($175) each month so Vishal can stay open late. Vishal also makes regular monthly payments to local authorities to avoid problems with health, safety, and hygiene inspections. Of 40,000 rupees ($700) he earns each month from his restaurant, Vishal says he pays at least a third in bribes.[8]

- **Kleptocracy in Equatorial Guinea.** Equatorial Guinea is a small West African coastal country with a tiny population and huge oil reserves. Because of its oil exports, by some measures Equatorial Guinea's GDP rivals that of the UK, France, and Germany. Yet more than half its population lacks access to safe drinking water.[9] At the same time, the president Teodoro Obiang is one of the world's richest men, with a personal fortune estimated at around $600 million. His son, Teodorin Obiang, leads a well-publicized playboy lifestyle in Europe and the United States, including a $30 million mansion in Malibu, California, $10 million worth of luxury cars, and a $33 million private jet.[10]

- **Corruption in humanitarian relief.** In the 1990s, when Iraq was the subject of highly restrictive trade sanctions following its 1991 invasion of Kuwait, the UN established a program known as "oil-for-food" that permitted Iraq to sell its oil and use the revenues to buy food, medicine, and other humanitarian supplies for its people. Under the program, however, Saddam Hussein was able to decide to whom the oil would be sold and from whom humanitarian supplies would be bought. Subsequent UN and US sponsored investigations revealed that nearly half of the 4,500 participating companies paid kickbacks and illegal surcharges to win lucrative contracts, and that Saddam Hussein personally enriched himself through "oil-for-food," to the tune of $1.8 billion. Benon Sevan, the head of the UN program, was also found to have "corruptly benefited" from kickbacks. Of the program's total official revenue of $64.2 billion, only $42.7 billion (67%) was spent on humanitarian relief.[11]

- *Corruption in an "emerging market."* Also in the 1990s, Walmart, the largest retailer in the United States, began to expand its operations into Mexico at a rapid pace. Today Walmart is the largest private employer in Mexico and one in five of its stores worldwide is located there. Walmart's Mexico subsidiary achieved this rapid growth in large part by resorting to widespread bribery, covered up by fraudulent accounting. As it built new stores at a break-neck pace Walmart de Mexico executives cultivated a vast bribery scheme involving government officials at various levels, including "mayors and city council members, obscure urban planners, low-level bureaucrats who issued permits—anyone with the power to thwart Walmart's growth."[12] By paying bribes, Walmart got zoning maps changed, made environmental objections disappear, received accelerated permits, and built hundreds of new stores—in some cases over the objection of powerless local communities.[13]

- *Transnational business bribery.* During the period 2001 to 2007 the giant German multinational Siemens made $1.4 billion in illegal payments to secure business and contracts around the world. Siemens's telecommunications unit alone maintained an annual budget of $40 to $50 million for the express purpose of paying bribes to win contracts, such as $12.7 million in payments to senior officials in Nigeria for government contracts and $5 million in bribes to the son of the prime minister and other senior officials, to win a mobile phone contract in Bangladesh. Other transnational bribes paid by Siemens included: in Argentina, at least $40 million to win a $1

billion contract to produce national identity cards; in Israel, $20 million to senior government officials to build power plants; in Venezuela, $16 million for urban rail lines; in China, $14 million for medical equipment; and in Iraq, $1.7 million to Saddam Hussein and his cronies.[14]

- *Transnational crime and corruption.* A UN report on human trafficking tells the story of "M," a young girl from Moldova who was trafficked to the Balkans and sexually exploited in a brothel before eventually being rescued by an international human trafficking task force. Her traffickers obtained fraudulent passports to ensure her passage through customs inspections at border crossings despite the obvious illegality of her documents (which were filled out incorrectly, and contained the wrong official stamps and other "glaring mistakes") and to evade police investigation at the brothel, which was in fact across the street from the local police station and which regularly serviced police officers as clients.[15]

These examples do not reveal all of the important features of corruption as it is commonly practised around the world. But together they shed some light on at least three notable aspects of corruption in the global economy. To begin with, *corruption ranges from the micro-level to the macro-level and involves many different types of actors.* Corruption involves powerless individuals and powerful groups; it occurs at the local and global levels and every level in between; it includes corporations in the private sector and governments and bureaucrats in the public sector; for-profit and non-profit organizations; and all levels of government and international institutions. Bribes paid in corrupt transactions range from the tiniest amounts to the millions and billions of dollars. It is important to note that the size of a bribe is a relative amount; a million dollar or even lesser bribe that is small potatoes to a multinational corruption can be a transformative sum and a huge incentive to its recipient. Conversely, even small amounts extorted from individuals can create a poverty trap.

Second, *transactional corruption involves a demand-side and a supply-side*. Extortion—when an official requests money to provide an official service—is the flip-side of bribery, and in practice it can be difficult to isolate one from the other. But not all corruption is explicitly transactional; it can also include ongoing relationships between criminals and corrupt public officials, as well as outright theft from the public purse. Finally, *corruption blurs the lines between the licit and the illicit global economies*. It is the key vulnerability for state authority and control vis à vis transnational crime and is a significant component of "illicit globalization."[16]

A few basic concepts can help us organize our analysis of the kinds of corruption illustrated in the examples above. These offer distinctions between **petty corruption** and **grand corruption**; *systemic corruption* and *sporadic corruption*; and **kleptocracy**. This chapter is chiefly concerned with grand and systemic corruption.

Petty corruption describes low-level administrative bureaucrats extracting personal benefits in transactions involving taxes, regulations, licensing requirements, and the discretionary allocation of government benefits, such as subsidized housing, scholarships, and jobs.[17] Where it is rife, this type of corruption often permeates the everyday lives of ordinary people in myriad and obvious ways.

Grand corruption occurs "at the highest levels of government, where political leaders, the bureaucracy, and the private sector all interact" and typically lies in government decisions that cannot be made without high-level political involvement. Examples include the procurement of large budget items such as military equipment, civilian aircraft, or infrastructure, or broad policy decisions about the allocation of credit or industrial subsidies.[18] Through grand corruption, political leaders and state agents use their authority to sustain their own power, status, and wealth.

Both petty and grand corruption can be systemic or sporadic. *Systemic corruption* describes a situation where corruption is endemic in society and "embedded in political and economic systems in ways that both reflect its impact and sustain its force."[19] It is a situation in which "the major institutions and processes of the state are routinely dominated and used by corrupt individuals and groups, and in which many people have few practical alternatives to dealing with corrupt officials."[20] Moreover, it is "embedded in a wider political and economic situation that helps sustain it."[21] Contemporary Zaire under the leadership of Mobutu Sese Seko is a prime example. Zaire, like Equatorial Guinea, also fits the description of a *kleptocracy*, a political system "dominated by those who steal from the state coffers and practice extortion as their modus operandi."[22]

As opposed to both systemic and kleptocratic corruption, *sporadic corruption* occurs irregularly. Although it can drain the economy of resources, it does not necessarily threaten the fundamental integrity of political, social, or economic institutions or their mechanisms of control.

The Costs of Corruption

Most contemporary research on corruption reveals that corruption is harmful, causing damaging outcomes across a range of concerns in the international political economy—which makes its control an important focus of international policy. Research shows that *corruption distorts markets, disrupts international flows of goods and capital, and reduces economic growth*. Some estimates show that the cost of corruption amounts to more than 5 per cent of global GDP (US$2.6 trillion), with more than US$1 trillion paid in bribes each year.[23] In international business, bribery impedes fair market competition and obstructs liberal international trade. By paying bribes, corrupt firms gain an unfair business advantage against more efficient firms and raise the cost of doing business for all. The cost of bribes can escalate, and the advantages gained became increasingly unreliable. Insofar as corruption includes the "capture" of public institutions and regulatory bodies by powerful private interests, it has been identified by some as the key underlying cause of the 2007–08 global financial crisis.[24]

Corruption impedes sustainable development and perpetuates poverty. Resources intended to assist development and alleviate global poverty are often diverted through corruption and aid does not reach its intended recipients. Corruption can lead to indiscriminate lending for development projects that fill the pockets of bureaucrats rather than the stomachs of the hungry. In his book *The White Man's Burden* William Easterly notes how trillions of dollars of foreign aid spent on grandiose development projects since the 1960s have been wasted, and billions stolen outright due to corruption, resulting in costs to democracy, human rights, global health, and the environment.[25] Corruption also degrades the quality of goods and services provided, with sometimes catastrophic social costs—substandard housing and public health systems, substandard medicine and health care, dangerous industrial conditions, and vulnerability to natural disasters. As the anti-corruption NGO Transparency International emphasizes, the poor and disempowered suffer the most from corruption, which often goes hand in hand with violence and persistent poverty.[26]

Corruption undermines democracy, human rights, and human security. Corruption feeds political instability, sustains inequality, undermines public trust in society's institutions of governance, leads to social unrest, and supports the proliferation of transnational crime. In her work on the "New Authoritarianism," Louise Shelley describes how corrupt and criminal organizations can supplant government authority, creating a new type of violent and authoritarian social control that is destructive of communities and human rights. Though fictional, the television series *The Wire* realistically depicted how corruption at a maritime port of entry enabled the criminal importation into the United States of illicit goods, including trafficked women and drugs. Corruption is an underlying feature of the ongoing drug wars in Mexico, the 2012 Arab Spring developments and continuing political instability in the Middle East, and international terrorism.

Thinking Theoretically about Corruption: Two Approaches

How can corruption be diminished? How can the taxing costs of corruption be mitigated and the human suffering that is its result alleviated? Different ways of conceptualizing the problem of corruption yield theoretical insights that can help explain the causes of corruption and suggest solutions for its control. Thinking theoretically requires abstracting away from specific instances and examples of corruption to discover core features that may be common across many instances. Conceptual "models" or approaches that highlight the core features of corruption across cases can then be useful analytic tools for considering the conditions under which corruption is more or less likely to flourish in various contexts, and for identifying appropriate policy responses. Two alternative conceptual approaches that are particularly useful for thinking theoretically about and explaining corruption are *principal-agent theory* and *network models* of corruption.

Principal-Agent Theory

Principal-agent theory (PA) derives from the discipline of economics, particularly neo-institutional economics, and has been well-developed in studies of public bureaucracies in the United States. In the international realm, scholars have used PA to explain the politics and policies of international organizations. Explanations of behaviour derived from PA theory focus on how actors (principals) delegate authority and tasks to agents, who are thus entrusted and empowered to act on their behalf.[27]

The key concepts of a PA model are *principal*, *agent*, and *delegation*. In a democracy, for example, legislators are the agents of the voting public (the principal) who have granted these lawmakers authority to develop rules on their behalf. Within governments, legislators and executives can be understood to be principals who grant authority to bureaucrats (agents) to act on their behalf. In both cases, a hierarchy of authority is in place such that the principal is empowered to monitor the agent, impose administrative checks, and terminate employment if the agent fails to carry out the principal's interests.[28]

One of the key assumptions of PA theory is that, although agents are supposed to act only on the principal's interests in fact agents and principals do not share the same interests, and under certain conditions an agent will be motivated to assert autonomy from the principal, using its delegated authority to pursue its own interests rather than fulfilling the demands of the principal. PA theories therefore explain the behaviour of agents as dependent on the willingness and capability of principals to monitor and control what agents do, whether through reward, sanction, or other means within a hierarchical environment.

In the PA model, *corruption* enters the picture when a *third party* whose gains or losses depend on the principal or the agent interferes with the appropriate principal-agent relationship. Third parties can try to influence principals directly, or they may bypass the principal altogether and focus on altering the incentives of agents directly.[29] In the PA model, corruption is defined as any unauthorized transaction between an agent and a third party—usually bribery.[30] Corruption is thus conceived as the result of an agent's individual action within an institutional context and is an instance of institutional failure.

Robert Klitgaard offers a complementary, and oft-cited, definition of corruption that summarizes its basic ingredients in the following formula:

$$\text{Corruption} = \text{Monopoly} + \text{Discretion} - \text{Accountability}^{31}$$

To elaborate on the formula's terms, we can read Klitgaard's definition as follows. Where an agent (or a principal) (1) is the sole provider of a desired good (*monopoly*, or lack of competition for the good); (2) possesses the authority, delegated or otherwise, to provide or not provide that good (*discretion*); and (3) perceives little monitoring of his or her decision or responsibility for its result (*accountability*); (4) *corruption* will occur.

A traditional form of corruption that can be usefully examined through the lens of this model is the bribery of bureaucrats by companies in the pursuit of government-offered contracts or permits. Walmart's bribery in Mexico and Siemens's transnational business bribery, described above, are prime examples. One of the advantages of this model of corruption is the clarity with which it suggests where anti-corruption measures may most usefully be employed to reduce opportunities for corruption. For instance, to resolve the institutional weaknesses that lead to corruption, the model suggests that anti-corruption reforms should strive to increase oversight and accountability mechanisms, increase the salaries of public agents, decrease government monopolies (i.e., reduce the size of the public sector by privatizing the provision of goods), and thereby decrease both opportunities and incentives for corruption.[32]

The PA model can be very useful for examining corrupt transactions and the individual choices that lead to them: the individual weighs the benefit of corruption against the cost of getting caught and behaves accordingly. It is a limited model, however, that leaves some important aspects of corruption unexamined. The PA model is not particularly good at explaining the *social-interaction* aspects of corruption. For instance, research has shown that when a leader is corrupt this affects subordinates' behaviour and may lead to systemic corruption. The question of how the actions of one individual can affect the actions of others is not addressed in typical PA models.[33] In addition, the PA model is not particularly helpful at explaining why we can observe more widespread corruption in some societies than others, nor the many varieties of corruption we can identify across societies.

Network Models

In contrast to the focus on individual decision-making and institutional failure in the principal-agent model, *network models* of corruption are *social* models. They focus on how informal institutions, such as culture, religion, social norms, and networks can influence the extent of systemic corruption in a society in ways that are not captured by PA theory.[34] They reveal the manner in which informal and exclusive networks based on mutual trust and reciprocity can conceal illicit activity within legitimate organizations and networks, and they highlight how corruption can flourish even in advanced democracies—not just in developing societies with presumably weaker bureaucratic institutions.[35]

For example, in France the Elf Aquitaine scandal in the late 1990s embroiled a broad swath of the political and economic elite of the country in allegations of widespread fraud, embezzlement, irregular campaign finance, payoffs, and transnational bribery in connection with the Paris-based oil multinational Elf, which had for decades maintained secret slush funds for illicit purposes. The Elf affair resulted in the convictions on various corruption-related charges of former French foreign minister Roland Dumas, former Elf chairman Loik Le Floch-Prigent, and others. In this case, elite social and political networks linked members of the French political class, created patterns of both formal and informal relationships, and permitted both legitimate and illegitimate pursuits within established institutions. In particular, a policy network of graduates of the elite French postgraduate schools, including the prestigious *École Nationale d'Administration* (ENA), overlapped with elite business and social networks. Illicit networks of associates across these spheres easily became nested within legitimate associations, enabling corruption in France to occur on a grand scale.[36] These illicit networks—informal institutions that acted both within and outside the boundaries of formal institutions—reduced the transparency and accountability of public institutions and allowed members to systematically conceal illicit activities for personal gain.

We can distinguish among at least three types of social network that may be conducive to widespread corruption in a society. Social networks based on primary interpersonal relationships such as family, kinship, and ethnicity can slant people's exchanges and communications and shape their norms to favour close relatives over the interests of the general public.[37] One specific kind of this type of social network is *patron–client networks*, which are defined by repeated, personalized exchange between patrons and clients, where the patron holds a status (social, economic, and/or political) superior to the client.[38] It is not unusual in many societies for locally powerful (usually male) elites to be responsible for the provisioning and well-being of subordinate (and otherwise vulnerable) clients in close-knit and exclusive ethnically based networks, in exchange for political support and position.[39]

A second type consists of social networks based on *secondary relations such as professional and religious ties*, as in the case of the Elf Aquitaine scandal in France. Another example is that of *guanxi* networks in China. **Guanxi** describes the presence of direct, particularistic ties between individuals or organizations, which in China draw on underlying moral principles derived from the Confucian heritage—including hierarchy, interdependence, and reciprocity.[40] In reform-era China, *guanxi* has served to fill in governance gaps during periods of uncertain transition, relative disorder, and social inequality and it often overrides the norms and desired outcomes of formal institutions.[41]

Criminal networks are a third type of social network conducive to systemic corruption. In contrast to the transactional emphasis on bribery in PA models, studies of criminal networks reveal how these often substitute bribery with violence, coercion, and terrorist-like activities to extract gains and exert influence in and from political institutions. Criminal behaviour and coercive methods, which have been especially important sources of corruption in the transition and post-transition Eastern European countries as well as in several African and Latin American countries, can have deep effects on democratic institutions that reach to the extent of systematically modifying the rules of public policy to favour illicit activity and personal gain, from *within* the regime.[42] In some cases, criminal organizations fully supplant the institutions of the state.[43]

In sum, corruption is not always as obvious as the payment of money in exchange for services rendered, the perversion of agency relationships by third parties, or "the abuse of entrusted power for private gain." It can be much more subtle (and also deeply societally entrenched), having to do with long-standing relationships of mutual benefit, exchanges of favours among people in advantageous positions, and expectations of reciprocity within ongoing relationships maintained by exclusive networks of trust—both licit and illicit. In such cases, anti-corruption policies that do not take into account the informal institutions of society that may sustain "corruption"—culture, religion, ethnic norms, or various types of social network—will fail.

Combating Corruption in the Global Economy: The Global Governance of Corruption

The **"global governance of corruption"** refers to the collection of governance-related activities, rules, and mechanisms in place at a variety of levels in world politics, aimed at cooperative anti-corruption problem-solving. Global governance, generally, is identified by what Margaret Karns and Karen Mingst have termed the "pieces of global governance": sets of international rules or laws; norms or "soft law"; and formal and informal structures, including intergovernmental organizations (IGOs), non-governmental organizations (NGOs), transnational advocacy networks, and ad hoc conferences and associations focused on particular problems.[44] In some instances, these "pieces" are linked together in what we can identify as an *international regime*: a set of explicit or implicit "principles, norms, rules, and decision making procedures around which actor expectations converge in a given issue-area."[45] The global governance of corruption includes each of the above pieces of governance as well as a robust international regime of anti-corruption. Three aspects of this regime are especially noteworthy: a proliferation of international anti-corruption treaties and IGO-driven anti-corruption programs; the prominence of transnational non-governmental advocacy in this area; and the growth of private governance initiatives.

International Law and IGOs

International law has been a main focus for international anti-corruption efforts by states and IGOs. In 1997, the states of the OECD—the IGO of rich, industrialized countries—agreed upon a new Convention on Combating the Bribery of Foreign Public Officials in International Business Transactions, the first binding international legal instrument to specifically target the *supply-side of transnational bribery*. Together with related recommendations, the Convention obligated its signatories to criminalize the bribery of foreign public officials, end the tax-deductibility of those bribes, and cooperate to monitor and enforce compliance. It is in many respects the legal centrepiece of the international regime of anti-corruption.

Transnational bribery—the practice of sending corrupt payments from one national jurisdiction into another to secure influence in the recipient jurisdiction—is a relatively new area in criminal law. Although the bribery of domestic public officials had long been outlawed in the developed world, paying bribes across borders to foreign officials in the pursuit of international business had not. For decades previous to this Convention, most OECD states—including the wealthiest and most highly industrialized countries in the world—permitted or even encouraged transnational business bribery as a strategic trade policy, particularly for industries with important impacts on a state's foreign policy goals, global influence, or GDP—such as the arms industry, natural resource extraction, and construction.[46] The

only country that did prohibit transnational bribery was the United States, with its **Foreign Corrupt Practices Act (FCPA)**, which criminalized foreign bribes in 1977. The FCPA originated in the aftermath of the Watergate scandal and it faced significant opposition from American companies, who argued that it placed them at a competitive disadvantage against international competitors who were permitted to bribe abroad in the pursuit of foreign business contracts.[47] In response to these concerns about trade competitiveness, the United States became the principal promoter of international rules to control transnational bribery and corruption in the 1990s, spearheading a pathbreaking Inter-American Convention Against Corruption in 1996, and then the process that led to the OECD's anti-bribery Convention.

Today, the United States vigorously enforces the FCPA, the OECD Convention's signatories have all adopted similar kinds of legislation, and the Convention parties have conducted three rounds of rigorous peer-review monitoring to evaluate members' compliance and enforcement of the rules. According to the OECD, since 1997 over 300 individuals and companies have been sanctioned for foreign bribery under national laws and hundreds more are under investigation.[48]

Another important international legal agreement is the United Nations Convention Against Corruption (UNCAC) which entered into force in 2005, the first universal such agreement. The UNCAC requires ratifying states to outlaw a wide range of corrupt activities, including the bribery of national and foreign public officials and officials of public international organizations; embezzlement and misuse of funds in both the public and private sector; laundering the proceeds of crime; obstruction of justice; and others. Significantly, the UNCAC denotes *corruption* as a crime, which "is a notion broader than bribery and extortion."[49] The UNCAC initiated a review mechanism in July 2010 that is currently in its third year of a five-year round of reviews evaluating criminalization and enforcement among the Convention's signatories. The review mechanism is proceeding steadily, but with delays and a lack of transparency that has been disconcerting to anti-corruption advocates.[50] To date, the extent of compliance and enforcement with the UNCAC across the member states remains variable and uncertain.

In addition to these instruments of international law, the World Bank has been a leading purveyor of anti-corruption research and policy on governance and development in the global South. Anti-corruption efforts at the Bank focus on increasing transparency, integrity, and "good governance" both internally, in its own program delivery systems, and in the institutions and development projects of its loan recipient countries. The Bank's anti-corruption and governance agenda has been the source of considerable controversy, both within the organization and among international development experts.[51] At question, in part, is whether or not the Bank should continue to lend money to projects and countries identified as "corrupt." On the one hand, proponents argue that the Bank should cease lending money to poorly governed projects and countries, where funds routinely have been siphoned by corrupt officials and where past projects have failed to demonstrate development gains. On the other hand, critics argue that withdrawing aid from poorly governed countries while channelling aid to those who are already comparatively better off is at odds with the Bank's mission to alleviate poverty and aid the world's most vulnerable people.

Transnational Non-Governmental Advocacy

Advocacy by non-state actors has been a leading driver of the international regime of anti-corruption, since the first years of its emergence. In particular, Transparency International, a transnational NGO (TNGO) based in Berlin with close to 100 national chapters around the world, has been the most prominent non-state advocate for anti-corruption efforts in the public and private spheres.[52] TI has been especially effective in raising awareness about corruption through its comprehensive anti-corruption web portal (www.transparency.org) and its extensive research, publications, and rankings of countries in its widely publicized Corruption Perceptions Index (CPI), Bribe Payers Index (BPI), and other reports. TI develops practical problem-solving tools for business and engages in direct policy advocacy specifically to pressure governments to adopt anti-corruption norms and comply with international anti-corruption commitments.

Transparency International is also one of the founders of the UNCAC Civil Society Coalition, which unites over 350 civil society organizations from over 100 countries in a global network aimed at promoting the ratification, implementation, and monitoring of the UNCAC. And TI is also one of the leading organizers of a long-standing series of International Anti-Corruption Conferences (IACC), a biannual forum for debate and exchange "that brings together heads of state, civil society, the private sector and more to tackle the increasingly sophisticated challenges posed by corruption." The conferences attract up to 1,500 participants from over 135 countries, serving as a leading global forum for anti-corruption advocacy and action on a global and national level, among citizens and institutions around the world.

Other notable anti-corruption TNGOs include Global Parliamentarians Against Corruption (GOPAC), headquartered in Ottawa, and Global Witness.

Private Governance

Alongside increased enforcement of anti-bribery legislation in the United States, United Kingdom, Germany, and elsewhere, an industry of anti-corruption compliance professionals, consultants, and programs in the private sector has become an increasingly prominent component of the international regime of anti-corruption. In this area of private governance, firms voluntarily establish anti-corruption standards either individually to ensure compliance with government standards, or in concert to alleviate dilemmas of collective action in private sector competition. The UN Global Compact, whose 10th principle is that "businesses should work against corruption in all its forms, including extortion and bribery," and the OECD Guidelines for Multinational Enterprises, which include standards on combating bribery, bribe solicitation, and extortion, provide policy frameworks within which firms voluntarily promote anti-corruption as part of a broader agenda of corporate social responsibility.[53] Recognizing that corruption is a strategic business risk, the World Economic Forum has also established a Partnering Against Corruption Initiative to promote a "zero tolerance" approach to bribery and corruption in international business.[54]

In a less organized way, anti-corruption experts in law firms, accountancies, management firms, and consultants profitably sell their services to help businesses navigate new and emergent anti-corruption regulatory environments in various national and international jurisdictions. For example, the paid advertisers on the private sector FCPA Blog (self-identified as "the world's biggest anti-corruption compliance portal") include, for instance, various global risk advisories, professional training institutes and seminars, due diligence investigative services, and others in the anti-corruption compliance industry. In the United States, especially, "anti-corruption" is a booming business.

Challenges in the Global Governance of Corruption

As with global governance generally, the governance of corruption in the global economy faces a number of significant challenges, three of which have to do with questions concerning compliance, effectiveness, and legitimacy. To begin with, what is the impact of this regime on the behaviour of actors in the international political economy? To what extent do states, firms, and other actors comply with the norms, rules, and principles of the international regime of anti-corruption? And, when there is evidence of non-compliance, what kind of enforcement do we see? The answers are not necessarily reassuring. When it comes to transnational business bribery, although OECD countries have implemented the OECD Convention's requirements in their domestic legislation and continue to participate in peer-review mechanisms to monitor compliance, the extent to which these countries enforce their national foreign bribery laws varies significantly. Even where there have been noteworthy prosecutions, such as in the US, Germany, and the UK, it remains extremely difficult to know the extent to which businesses continue to bribe abroad. Put differently, the compliance of *states* with their anti-corruption commitments under international law does not necessarily reflect the compliance of *individuals and firms* with anti-corruption rules. With regard to the UNCAC, even assessing state compliance is a real challenge, considering the much more heterogeneous character of the state parties and the broader anti-corruption requirements of the treaty. When it comes to private governance, compliance is purely voluntary and few, if any, mechanisms for enforcement exist.

A second set of questions concerns the *effectiveness* of the rules that are in place to curb global corruption. Even assuming robust compliance and enforcement of these norms, rules, and principles, would corruption be eradicated, or even significantly mitigated? Do the rules themselves offer an effective response? Take, for example, the ban in the OECD Convention on the bribery of foreign public officials in international business transactions. This rule is intentionally specific and narrowly construed so that compliance and enforcement might be feasible, at least in principle. Yet, insofar as this Convention is supposed to curtail corruption in the global economy, this narrow construal itself limits the effectiveness of the Convention as an instrument of anti-corruption by treating bribe transactions as isolated instances that occur within specific countries. Ignored are the *transnational corruption networks* in which specific transactions are embedded. The transactional corruption of business bribery exists within an international context that includes multinational companies, elites in both bribe-sending and bribe-receiving countries, offshore financial vehicles and conduits, middlemen and brokers, and financial institutions—which are not addressed by the OECD Convention nor in the international norm of anti-corruption, generally.[55]

In addition, the rules in place include some surprising loopholes. For example, under both the OECD Convention and the US Foreign Corrupt Practices Act, bribes characterized as "facilitation payments" are permitted. As well, only bribes paid to "foreign public officials" are forbidden; bribes within the private sector, or bribery of political party members are not covered. The UN Convention does have a broader application, however, broader rules are also more difficult to enforce, so there is a real trade-off in effectiveness.

The global governance of corruption is also challenged by questions of legitimacy. Are the norms, rules, and principles of international anti-corruption correct, and appropriate? Are the makers of these rules right and appropriate in doing so? Is it appropriate to rely on private governance to deliver results and expectations of the control of corruption? Questions of legitimacy raise complicated questions about power, democracy, ethics, and justice that are often glossed over in global governance, because the most powerful states—and the non-state actors of which powerful states approve—tend to be the ones who set the agenda and shape the rules.[56] Indeed, the emergence of the international regime of anti-corruption itself can be read as an exercise of American power, since the United States has sought to internationalize specifically American norms for the conduct of international business, which first took shape in the FCPA.[57]

What is Canada's Role?

What is Canada's role in the international regime of anti-corruption? What is Canada's position on domestic and international anti-corruption policy, and how does Canada fare in global rankings of corruption? The record is mixed. On the one hand, Canada ranks high on various corruption-related indices, including Transparency International's Corruption Perceptions Index and Bribe Payers Index, and on the World Bank's Control of Corruption index, which reflects perceptions of the extent to which public power is exercised for private gain. Canada also places highly on indicators of judicial independence, rule of law, and the Human Development Index.[58] Most Canadians would undoubtedly agree that encounters with public or private sector corruption are not a normal part of everyday life in Canada. On international anti-corruption, Canada was an early financial supporter of Transparency International, played a crucial role in bringing the OECD

Convention into force in 1999 by enacting anti-foreign bribery legislation in time, is a signatory of the UNCAC and the Inter-American Anti-Corruption Treaty, and is involved in anti-corruption policy formulation in the variety of international fora to which it contributes (including the G7, G20, the Commonwealth, the Organization for Security and Co-operation in Europe (OSCE), and various development banks).

On the other hand, Transparency International's 2013 Global Corruption Barometer survey reveals that 53 per cent of respondents in Canada felt that corruption has increased in recent years, and 62 per cent of respondents felt that political parties in Canada are corrupt/extremely corrupt, as well as Parliament (47 per cent), public officials (38 per cent), and business (48 per cent).[59] Corruption and scandal are increasingly perceived by Canadians to be problems in Canada's domestic governance arrangements, at the federal and local levels. Internationally, Canada's reputation on anti-corruption has also not been good. Citing long-standing inaction on transnational bribery, in 2011 international activists branded Canada an anti-corruption laggard.[60]

Compared with several of its OECD partners, Canada's efforts to control transnational bribery and corruption have indeed been poor. Both Transparency International and the OECD have identified Canada as failing to act against trans-national bribery. Whereas the United States, Germany, the United Kingdom, and others have pursued high-profile cases against prominent multinationals accused of transnational bribery, yielding hundreds of millions of dollars in criminal fines, disgorgements of profit, damages, and other penalties for violations of anti-bribery laws—including prison sentences for individual executives in 10 countries—by 2011 Canada had prosecuted just two cases, yielding relatively paltry fines.

Perhaps in response to this international criticism, Canada recently announced its intention to more vigorously enforce the Corruption of Foreign Public Officials Act (CFPOA), which implements the OECD Convention in Canadian law. In 2013 the government amended the CFPOA to close loopholes and increase sanctions.[61] Nonetheless, since its entry into force in 1999, there have been just four convictions under this Act, and three of them have been since international pressure increased in 2011: Hydro-Kleen Group Inc., ordered to pay a fine of $25,000 as a penalty for bribing a US immigration official at the Calgary International Airport (2005); Niko Resources Ltd., fined $9.5 million for offenses related to business dealings in Bangladesh (2011); Griffiths Energy International Inc., required to pay a total penalty of $10.35 million for offenses related to an oil and gas contract in Chad (2013); and, most recently, in August 2013, Canada's first foreign bribery trial resulted in the first conviction of an individual in Canada for bribery abroad, when the Ontario Superior Court of Justice convicted Nazir Karigar of offering bribes to Air India officials and the Indian Minister of Civil Aviation over the sale of passenger screening equipment for airport security, on behalf of an Alberta-based technology company.

That three of these cases involve Alberta-based firms in the energy sector reflects Canada's particular commercial strength in the mining and extractive industries, where the risk of corrupt expectations is notoriously high. As Canadian companies have invested over $60 billion in mining and extraction in developing countries where corrupt payments are likely to be expected, it is clear that Canadian companies are not immune to pressure nor incentives to pay bribes. Although the RCMP claims 34 active and ongoing CFPOA investigations, it remains to be seen to what extent the government will continue to investigate and prosecute them for doing so.

Conclusion: Taking a Critical View

Corruption is a principal issue of global governance. Most of the current scholarship agrees that in its many forms and manifestations corruption is costly to states, firms, individuals, and the global economy as a whole. At the same time, there is little agreement on how to define the problem, how to assess the costs, and how to respond. Thus, in addition to the challenges of compliance, effectiveness, and legitimacy raised above, the governance of corruption in the global economy raises a number of further problems and questions.

One problem involves the intense focus of global governance efforts on bribery, to the exclusion of other networked aspects of corruption and to the ways in which grand corruption in particular is integrally linked into the legitimate global economy. This selective focus can also be read as contributing to a "broadly neoliberal program of government" that is imposed especially on developing countries (and that includes the privatization of public institutions and the expansion of market-based mechanisms into spheres of public provision) suggesting a singularly western/Weberian institutional structure for the state—in which the distinction between the public and private sphere is clear and unproblematic.[62] In practice, in many states and societies, patrimonial systems blur these lines and such neoliberal anti-corruption programs make little sense. In addition, the focus on bribery, which is transactional and which is often modelled as a principal-agent problem, tends to single out specific actors for corrupt deeds and specific instances of corrupt transactions rather than tackling the embedded networks and practices in which opportunities for corruption are cultivated both locally and in the global economy writ large.

Another problem lies in the general practice of labelling actors as "corrupt," either in ranking systems such as TI's CPI and BPI or in development programs that focus on the priority of "good governance." The corruption label creates a powerful stigma for states and societies that do not conform to certain ideals set by outside powers, and some scholars question the value of this label in the context of anti-corruption struggles that cannot be won. Further, ranking and labelling itself is an exercise of power that serves to make "corrupt" actors responsible for their own governance challenges while obfuscating the contexts of both licit and illicit globalization, in which powerful actors are complicit, and in which those actors so labelled have very little control over the circumstances that lead them to be considered "corrupt."[63]

There are also problems with the basic research upon which anti-corruption efforts are based. Quantifying the extent of any activity in the illicit global economy is a perilous exercise and no truly reliable data actually exist.[64] When it comes to the costs of corruption in the realm of economic development and poverty alleviation, in particular, at least one scholar has identified anti-corruption as a "fetish" of development policy professionals.[65] Other scholars have shown that corruption in and of itself does not necessarily harm development; for example, corrupt countries such as Indonesia under the reign of Suharto experienced tremendous gains in development notwithstanding extensive grand corruption and kleptocratic practices.[66] Clearly, the impact of corruption on economic development depends on many factors.

In conclusion, when it comes to understanding the various and complex manifestations of corruption in the global economy—its main features, causes, effects, and solutions—explanations that overlook the role of networks, the socially and politically embedded nature of institutions, and expressions of global political and economic power, are both theoretically and pragmatically inadequate.

Notes

1   E. Gutterman, "¿Que Sabemos de La Corrupción En Canadá? (Corruption in Canada: What Do We Know?)," 343–71. The Sponsorship Scandal is the most significant Canadian corruption scandal in recent history. It originated in the federal government's response to the 1995 Quebec referendum and national unity crisis, following which the federal Liberals under Jean Chretien sought to "win the hearts and minds" of Quebecers—or at least raise the visibility of the federal government within the province of Quebec—through a federalism advertising campaign that sponsored various hunting, fishing, and other recreational and community events across the province. This sponsorship program disbursed approximately $40 million per year over seven years until it became mired in controversy and scandal when evidence of fraud, waste, negligence, and self-dealing revealed it to be little more than a corrupt boondoggle for the benefit of Liberal party supporters in Quebec.

2   S. P. Huntington, *Political order in changing societies*, 63.

3   F. Galtung, "A Global network to curb corruption: The experience of Transparency International," 17–47.

4   Ibid.

5   S-J. Wei, *How taxing is corruption on international investors?*; Paolo Mauro, *Why worry about corruption?*; K. A. Elliott (Ed.), *Corruption and the global economy*.

6   The World Bank, "Anticorruption home page," *The World Bank Group*; The World Bank, *Helping Countries Combat Corruption: Progress at the World Bank Since 1997*.

7   Transparency International, "What we do."

8   J. Burke, (2011), "Corruption in India: 'All your life you pay for things that should be free.'"

9   "Equatorial Guinea," *Global Witness*.

10 K. Silverstein, "Teodorin's world."

11 "IRAQ: Oil for food scandal"; United Nations News Service, "Oil-for-Food Probe"; "Corruption at the heart of the United Nations," *The Economist*.

12 D. Barstow, "Vast Mexico bribery case hushed up by Wal-Mart after top-level struggle."

13 Ibid.; D.Barstow and A. X.Von Bertrab, "The bribery aisle: How Wal-Mart got its way in Mexico."

14 S. Schubert, and T. C. Miller, "At Siemens, bribery was just a line item."

15 United Nations Office on Drugs and Crime, "Issue Paper: The role of corruption in trafficking persons," 11.

16 P. Andreas, (2011), "Illicit globalization: Myths, misconceptions, and historical lessons."

17 Elliott, *Corruption and the Global Economy*, 178.

18 Ibid.

19 M. Johnston, "Fighting systemic corruption: Social foundations for institutional reform."

20 Ibid., 89.

21 Ibid., 90.

22 "U4 Anti-corruption resource centre: Glossary," *U4 Anti-Corruption Resource Centre*.

23 World Economic Forum, "Global agenda council on anti-corruption & transparency 2013," *Global Agenda Council on Anti-Corruption & Transparency (2013) World Economic Forum*; The World Bank, "The costs of corruption," April 8, 2004, http://go.worldbank.org/LJA29GHA80. Others are skeptical of such estimates. See, for instance, Chris Blattman, "Corruption and development: Not what you think?."

24 D. Kaufmann, "Corruption and the global financial crisis."

25 W. Easterly, *The white man's burden*.

26 Transparency International, "What we do."

27 C. Weaver (2004), "The world's bank and the bank's world," 493–512; D. G. Hawkins, D. A. Lake, and D. L. Nielson (Eds), *Delegation and agency in international organizations*; M. N. Barnett and M. Finnemore, *Rules for the world: International organizations in global politics*.

28 D. L. Nielson, and M. J. Tierney, "Delegation to international organizations: agency theory and World Bank environmental reform"; D. L. Nielson and M. J. Tierney, (2005). "Theory, data, and hypothesis testing: World Bank environmental reform redux"; Hawkins, Lake, and Nielson, *Delegation and agency in international organizations*.

29 Hawkins, Lake, and Nielson, *Delegation and agency in international organizations*, 9.

30 N. Groenendijk, (1997), "A principal-agent model of corruption," 207–29.

31 R. Klitgaard, *Controlling corruption*, 181.

32 S. Rose-Ackerman, *Corruption and government: Causes, consequences, and reform*.

33 F. Khan, "Understanding the spread of systemic corruption in the third world," 16–39.

34 J. Zhan, (2012), "Filling the gap of formal institutions: The effects of guanxi network on corruption in reform-era China," 94.

35 J. R. Heilbrunn, "Oil and water? Elite politicians and corruption in France."

36 Ibid., 275.

37 Zhan, "Filling the gap of formal institutions," 94.

38 M. H. Khan, 1998 "Patron–client networks and the economic effects of corruption in Asia."

39 R. Holt, "Beyond the tribe: Patron-client relations, Neopatrimonialism in Afghanistan," 27–31; Morris Szeftel, "Corruption and the spolis system in Zambia,"163–89.

40 F. Huang, and J.Rice, (2012 "Firm networking and bribery in China: Assessing some potential negative consequences of firm openness," 533–45,

41 Zhan, "Filling the gap of formal institutions"; Huang and Rice, "Firm networking and bribery in China."

42 L. Garay-Salamanca, "Institutional impact of criminal networks in Colombia and Mexico," 177–94.

43 L. I. Shelley, "Transnational organized crime: The new authoritarianism."

44 M. P. Karns, and K. A. Mingst, *International organizations: The politics and processes of global governance*.

45 S. D. Krasner, *International regimes*.

46 Transparency International, "Bribe payers index: Overview."

47 Gutterman, E., "Easier done than said: Transnational Bribery, norm resonance, and the origins of the U.S. Foreign Corrupt Practices Act."

48 OECD, "OECD Working group on bribery elects new chair."

49 United Nations Office on Drugs and Crime, "Issue paper: The role of corruption in Trafficking Persons," 6.

50 G. Dell, "UNCAC coalition asks UN meeting to take action for transparency and accountability."

51 S. R. Weisman, "Wolfowitz corruption drive rattles world bank"; Sebastian Mallaby, "Wolfowitz's corruption agenda."

52 E. Gutterman, "The legitimacy of transnational NGOs: Lessons from the experience of Transparency International in Germany and France"; Hongying Wang and James N. Rosenau, "Transparency International and corruption as an issue of global governance," 25; Galtung, "A global network to curb corruption: The experience of Transparency International."

53 UN Global Compact, "Transparency and anti-corruption"; OECD, "Guidelines for multinational enterprises: Combating bribery, bribe solicitation and extortion."

54 World Economic Forum, "Partnering against corruption initiative."

55 A. Cooley and J. Sharman, "The price of access: Transnational corruption networks in Central Asia and beyond."

56 E. Gutterman, "The legitimacy of transnational NGOs: Lessons from the experience of Transparency International in Germany and France."

57 E. Gutterman, "Easier Done than said: Transnational bribery, norm resonance, and the origins of the U.S. Foreign Corrupt Practices Act."

58 Transparency International, "Corruption by country: Canada."

59 Transparency International, "Canada 2013—Global corruption barometer: World's largest opinion survey on corruption."

60 E. Gutterman, "Foreign bribery, homegrown inaction."

61 Foreign Affairs, Trade, and Development Canada, "Strengthening Canada's fight against foreign bribery."

62 B. Hindess, (2005) "Investigating international anti-corruption," 1389–98.

63 O. Löwenheim, (2008). "Examining the state: a Foucauldian perspective on international "governance indicators,'"

64 P. Andreas, and K. M. Greenhill, (Eds), *Sex, drugs, and body counts: The politics of numbers in global crime and conflict.* Cornell University Press.

65 Blattman, "Corruption and development."

66 R. Fisman and E. Miguel, (2008). *Economic gangsters.*

Key Terms

global governance of corruption
grand corruption
guanxi
kleptocracy

petty corruption
principal-agent (PA) model
transnational bribery

Questions for Review

1. What is corruption, and how does it manifest (what are some features and what are its costs) in the global economy?

2. How do the principal-agent model and the network model differ in their approaches to corruption, and what are the strengths and weaknesses of each approach?

3. What is the global governance of corruption, and what are some of its key challenges?

4. What is Canada's record on international anti-corruption efforts?

5. What problems are identified by the critical view of international anti-corruption efforts?

Further Resources

Andreas, P. "Illicit globalization: Myths, misconceptions, and historical lessons."

Fisman, R. and Miguel, E. *Economic gangsters: Corruption, violence, and the poverty of Nations.*

Gutterman, E. "Easier done than said: Transnational bribery, norm resonance, and the origins of the U.S. Foreign Corrupt Practices Act."

Hindess, B. "Investigating international anti-corruption."

Johnston, M. 2005. *Syndromes of corruption: Wealth, power, and democracy.* Cambridge: Cambridge University Press

Rose-Ackerman, S. *Corruption and government: Causes, consequences, and reform.*

Transparency International: www.transparency.org

Wang, H. and Rosenau, J. N. "Transparency International and corruption as an issue of global governance."

World Bank: Governance & anti-corruption. www.worldbank.org/wbi/governance

References

Andreas, P. (2011). "Illicit globalization: Myths, misconceptions, and historical lessons." *Political Science Quarterly 126*(3), 403–25.

Andreas, P. and Kelly M. Greenhill, K. M. (Eds). (2011). *Sex, drugs, and body counts: the politics of numbers in global crime and conflict.* Cornell University Press.

Barnett, M. N. and Finnemore, M. (2004). *Rules for the world: International organizations in global politics.* Cornell University Press.

Barstow, D. (2012). "Vast Mexico bribery case hushed up by Wal-Mart after top-level struggle." *The New York Times*, 21 April (sec. Business Day). www.nytimes.com/2012/04/22/business/at-wal-mart-in-mexico-a-bribe-inquiry-silenced.html.

Barstow, D. and Von Bertrab, A. X. (2012). "The bribery aisle: How Wal-Mart got its way in Mexico." *The New York Times*, 17 December, sec. Business Day. www.nytimes.com/2012/12/18/business/walmart-bribes-teotihuacan.html.

Blattman, C. (2012). "Corruption and development: Not what you think?" *Chris Blattman: International Development, Politics, Economics, and Policy*, 5 November. http://chrisblattman.com/2012/11/05/corruption-and-development-not-what-you-think/.

Burke, J. (2011). "Corruption in India: 'All your life you pay for things that should be free.'" *The Guardian*, 19 August, sec. World news. www.guardian.co.uk/world/2011/aug/19/corruption-india-anna-hazare.

Cooley, A. and Sharman, J. (2013). "The price of access: Transnational corruption networks in Central Asia and beyond." Paper presented to the annual meeting of the International Studies Association, San Francisco.

"Corruption at the heart of the United Nations." (2005). *The Economist*, 9 August. www.economist.com/node/4267109.

Dell, G. (2013). "UNCAC coalition Asks UN meeting to take action for transparency and accountability." *UNCAC Civil Society Coalition*, 21 May. http://uncaccoalition.org/learn-more/blog/248-uncac-coalition-asks-un-meeting-to-take-action-for-transparency-and-accountability.

Easterly, W. (2007). *The white man's burden.* London: Penguin Books,.

Elliott, K. A. (Ed). (1996). *Corruption and the global economy.* Washington, DC: Institute for International Economics.

"Equatorial Guinea." (2013). *Global witness.* Accessed 22 July (20. www.globalwitness.org/campaigns/corruption/oil-gas-and-mining/equatorial-guinea.

Fisman, R. and Miguel, E. (2008). *Economic gangsters: Corruption, violence, and the poverty of nations.* Princeton University Press.

Foreign Affairs, Trade, and Development Canada. (2013). "Strengthening Canada's fight against foreign bribery," 5 February. www.international.gc.ca/media/aff/news-communiques/2013/02/05b.aspx?lang=eng.

Galtung, F. (2000). "A global network to curb corruption: The experience of Transparency International." In *The Third Force: The Rise of Transnational Civil Society*, Ann Florini (Ed.), 17–47. Washington, D.C.: Carnegie Endowment for International Peace.

Garay-Salamanca, L. (2012). "Institutional impact of criminal networks in Colombia and Mexico." *Crime, Law and Social Change 57*(2) (1 March): 177–94.

Groenendijk, N. (1997). "A principal-agent model of corruption." *Crime, Law and Social Change 27* (3–4), 207–29. doi:http://dx.doi.org.ezproxy.library.yorku.ca/10.1023/A:1008267601329.

Gutterman, E. (2006). "¿Que Sabemos de La Corrupción En Canadá? (Corruption in Canada: What Do We Know?)." In *La corrupción En América: Un continente, muchos frentes*, Antonio Azuela (Ed.), 343–71. Mexcio City: Universidad Nacional Autónoma de México Instituto de Investigaciones Sociales. (20

———. (2011). "Foreign bribery, homegrown inaction." *The Mark News*, 13 October http://ca.news.yahoo.com/foreign-bribery-homegrown-inaction-130651225.html.

———. (2014). "The legitimacy of transnational NGOs: Lessons from the experience of Transparency International in Germany and France." *Review of International Studies 40*(2), 391–418.

———. (2015). "Easier done than said: Transnational bribery, norm resonance, and the origins of the U.S. Foreign Corrupt Practices Act." *Foreign Policy Analysis 11*(1), 109–28.

Hawkins, D. G., Lake, D. A., and Nielson, D. L. (Eds). (2006). *Delegation and agency in international organizations*. Political Economy of Institutions and Decisions. Cambridge, UK; New York: Cambridge University Press.

Heilbrunn, J. R. (2005). "Oil and water? Elite politicians and corruption in France." *Comparative Politics 37*(3) (1 April): 277–96. doi:10.2307/20072890.

Hindess, B. (2005). "Investigating international anti-corruption." *Third World Quarterly 26*(8) (1 January), 1389–98.

Holt, R. (2012). "Beyond the tribe: Patron-client relations, neopatrimonialism in Afghanistan." *Military Intelligence Professional Bulletin 38*(1) (March), 27–31.

Huang, F. and Rice, J. (2012). "Firm networking and bribery in China: Assessing some potential negative consequences of firm openness." *Journal of Business Ethics 107*(4), 533–45. doi:http://dx.doi.org.ezproxy.library.yorku.ca/10.1007/s10551-011-1062-z.

Huntington, S. P. (1968). *Political order in changing societies*. Yale University Press.

"IRAQ: Oil for Food Scandal." (2013). *Council on Foreign Relations*. Accessed 8 July www.cfr.org/iraq/iraq-oil-food-scandal/p7631.

Johnston, M. (1998). "Fighting systemic corruption: Social foundations for institutional reform." *The European Journal of Development Research 10*(1) : 85–104. doi:10.1080/09578819808426703.

Karns, M. P., and Mingst, K. A. (2010). *International organizations: The politics and processes of global governance*, 2nd ed. Lynne Rienner Publishers

Kaufmann, D. (2013). "Corruption and the global financial crisis." *Forbes*. Accessed 21 August, www.forbes.com/2009/01/27/corruption-financial-crisis-business-corruption09_0127corruption.html.

Khan, F. (2008). "Understanding the spread of systemic corruption in the third world." *American Review of Political Economy 6*(2) (December (20), 16–39.

Khan, M. H. (1998). "Patron–client networks and the economic effects of corruption in Asia." *The European Journal of Development Research 10*(1) (1 June), 15–39.

Klitgaard, R. (1988). *Controlling corruption*. University of California Press.

Krasner, S. D. (1983). *International regimes*. Cornell University Press.

Löwenheim, O. (2008). "Examining the state: A Foucauldian perspective on international "governance indicators."" *Third World Quarterly 29*(2).

Mallaby, S. (2006). "Wolfowitz's corruption agenda." *The Washington Post*, 20 February, sec. Opinions. www.washingtonpost.com/wp-dyn/content/article/2006/02/19/AR2006021901137.html.

Mauro, P. (1997). *Why worry about corruption?* Economic Issues. Washington, D.C.: International Monetary Fund. www.imf.org/EXTERNAL/PUBS/FT/ISSUES6/.

Nielson, D. L. and Tierney, M. J. (2003). "Delegation to international organizations: Agency theory and World Bank environmental reform." *International Organization 57*(2) (1 April), 241–76. doi:10.2307/3594852.

———. (2005). "Theory, data, and hypothesis testing: World Bank environmental reform redux." *International Organization 59*(3) (1 July), 785–800. doi:10.2307/3877816.

OECD. (2013). "Guidelines for multinational enterprises: Combating bribery, bribe solicitation and extortion." http://mneguidelines.oecd.org/themes/bribery.html.

———. (2013). "OECD Working group on bribery elects new chair." *OECD: Better Policies for Better Lives*, 7 August. www.oecd.org/daf/anti-bribery/oecd-working-group-on-bribery-elects-new-chair.htm.

Rose-Ackerman, S. (1999). *Corruption and government: Causes, consequences, and reform*. Cambridge University Press.

Schubert, S. and Miller, T. C. (2008). "At Siemens, bribery was just a line item." *The New York Times*, 21 December, sec. Business / World Business. www.nytimes.com/2008/12/21/business/worldbusiness/21siemens.html.

Shelley, L. I. (1999). "Transnational organized crime: The new authoritarianism." In *The Illicit global economy and state power*, H. Richard Friman and Peter Andreas, (Eds). Lanham, Md: Rowman & Littlefield Pub.

Silverstein, K. (2011). "Teodorin's world." *Foreign Policy*, April. www.foreignpolicy.com/articles/2011/02/22/teodorins_world?page=0,4&wp_login_redirect=0.

Szeftel, M. (1983). "Corruption and the spoils system in Zambia." In *Corruption: Causes, consequences, and control*, Michael Clarke (Ed.), 163–89. London: Frances Pinter.

Transparency International. (2013). "Bribe payers index: Overview." *Transparency International—The Global Coalition Against Corruption*. www.transparency.org/research/bpi/overview.

———. (2013). "Canada 2013—Global corruption barometer: World's largest opinion survey on corruption." *Transparency International: The Global Coalition Against Corruption*. Accessed 22 August. www.transparency.org/gcb2013/country/?country=canada.

———. (2013). "Corruption by country: Canada." *Transparency International: The Global Coalition Against Corruption*. www.transparency.org/country#CAN.

———. (2013). "What we do." *Transparency International—The Global Coalition Against Corruption* 20. www.transparency.org/whatwedo.

"U4 Anti-Corruption Resource Centre: Glossary." (2013). *U4 Anti-Corruption Resource Centre*. Accessed 24 July. www.u4.no/glossary/.

UN Global Compact. (2013). "Transparency and anti-corruption." www.unglobalcompact.org/AboutTheGC/TheTenPrinciples/anti-corruption.html.

United Nations News Service. (2013). "Oil-for-Food probe." *United Nations-DPI/NMD—UN News Service Section*. Accessed 8 July. www.un.org/apps/news/infocusRel.asp?infocusID=97&Body=Oil-for-Food&Body1=inquiry.

United Nations Office on Drugs and Crime. (2011). "Issue paper: The role of corruption in trafficking persons." UnitedNations.www.unodc.org/documents/human-trafficking/2011/Issue_Paper_-_The_Role_of_Corruption_in_Trafficking_in_Persons.pdf.

———. (2013). "United Nations convention against corruption." www.unodc.org/unodc/en/treaties/CAC/.

Wang, H. and Rosenau, J. N. (2001). "Transparency International and corruption as an issue of global governance." *Global Governance* 7, 25.

Weaver, C. (2007). "The World's bank and the bank's world." *Global Governance* 13(4), 493–512.

Wei, S-J. (1997). *How taxing is corruption on international investors?* Working Paper. National Bureau of Economic Research, May. www.nber.org/papers/w6030.

Weisman, S. R. (2006). "Wolfowitz corruption drive rattles World Bank." *The New York Times*, 14 September, sec. Business. www.nytimes.com/2006/09/14/business/14wolf.html.

World Bank. (2000). *Helping Countries combat corruption: Progress at the World Bank since 1997*. Washington, DC: The World Bank, 20 June. www1.worldbank.org/publicsector/anticorrupt/helping-countries.pdf.

———. (2001). "Anticorruption home page." *The World Bank Group*. www1.worldbank.org/publicsector/anticorrupt/index.cfm.

———. (2004). "The costs of corruption," 8 April. http://go.worldbank.org/LJA29GHA80.

World Economic Forum. (2013). "Global agenda council on anti-corruption & transparency." *Global Agenda Council on Anti-Corruption & Transparency World Economic Forum*. Accessed 15 August. www.weforum.org/content/global-agenda-council-anti-corruption-transparency-2013.

———. (2013). "Partnering against corruption initiative." *Partnering Against Corruption Initiative | World Economic Forum*. www.weforum.org/issues/partnering-against-corruption-initiative.

Zhan, J. (2012). "Filling the gap of formal institutions: The effects of guanxi network on corruption in reform-era China." *Crime, Law and Social Change* 58(2) (1 September), 93–109.

25 The Political Economy of International Migration and the Canadian Example

Yasmeen Abu-Laban

On New Year's Eve 2015, the United Nations International Children's Emergency Fund (UNICEF) released a world video version of John Lennon's classic song of hope and peace "Imagine," broadcast simultaneously in New York's Times Square and internationally. In the UNICEF world version the memorable lyrics "imagine there's no countries" are accompanied by images showing the name plaques of United Nations (UN) General Assembly members being replaced by the word "imagine" (UNICEF 2014). A free downloadable app allowing individuals to record themselves singing next to their favorite celebrity (with a star-studded cast including Katy Perry, Will-i-am, Idris Elba, and UN Secretary General Ban Ki-moon) made this the world's biggest sing-along. Yet despite this creative multimedia version of "Imagine," it still takes a good deal to envision a world without states, just as it did in John Lennon's time. States are a defining feature of the post-Westphalian world system, and state-controlled borders and barriers work to limit the free movement of people. How mobility is allowed or restricted by states thus makes migration a natural topic to consider from the perspective of international political economy.

Although today (as in the past) people do move and cross humanly created barriers, their experiences are very different: whereas a citizen from a country belonging to the wealthy states comprising the OECD typically enjoys visa-free travel, for the citizen belonging to a country of the global South, this is often not the case, especially when travelling to western countries. It is these sorts of highly differentiated experiences that can begin to attune us to the political economy of international migration—that is, the political, social, and economic factors that both cause and shape the experience and responses to international migration.

The purpose of this chapter is to expand on the relationship between IPE and migration. It does this by considering key dimensions of the political economy of international migration since the end of the Second World War, as well as recent developments in immigration in Canada. To facilitate a concurrent discussion of global and Canadian trends, this chapter uses the terms "migrant" and "immigrant" as well as "migration" and "immigration" interchangeably. As a country that until now has sought what the Canadian government calls "immigrants," and accepts relatively large numbers annually, the case of twenty-first-century Canada is highly pertinent for illuminating certain larger trends about who gets in, who gets to stay, and who gets citizenship. It is argued that northern states are placing a greater stress on regulating and controlling movement, as well as continued state control over the extension of citizenship. This is evident even in countries embracing new regional forms of citizenship (such as the 28 countries of the European Union) as well as countries like Canada that are still encouraging immigration.

To illustrate this argument, the chapter proceeds in a threefold manner. First, it advances a discussion of the international level, focusing attention on the relevance of rights and statistics for placing migration in relation to the international political economy. Second, it provides a discussion of two different regions—Europe and North America—to illustrate the complex ways in which regional trade blocs approach mobility. In the final section, it presents the case of Canada, with an emphasis on the period since 2000.

Rights, Statistics, and the Political Economy of International Migration

A starting point for understanding migration in relation to rights comes from considering the 1948 Universal Declaration on Human Rights (UDHR), which established a framework for universal human rights after the Second World War. Indeed, the **Universal Declaration of Human Rights**, now translated into over 400 languages, is widely seen to have ushered in what is sometimes referred to as the human rights revolution. Article 1 of the UDHR holds that "all human beings are born free and equal in dignity and rights" and that "everyone is entitled to all the rights and freedoms set forth in this Declaration, without distinction of any kind, such as race, colour, sex, language, religion,

political or other opinion, national or social origin, property, birth or other status." Most of the UDHR's 30 articles concentrate on civil and political rights (Articles 3–21) and, to a lesser extent economic, social, and cultural rights (Articles 22–27).

Because the rights laid out in the UDHR have not been achieved worldwide, it is frequently observed that human rights are aspirational in character. Equally significant however are the details of what the UDHR supports (and does not support). In particular, at the heart of the Universal Declaration of Human Rights lies a fundamental contradiction that exists in relation to human rights and migration as they have been articulated by the United Nations. This contradiction is that although there has been support for the idea that people can leave their country (i.e., the country where they hold nationality), they do not have a right to enter or stay in a different country. Consequently, Pierre Sané, former Assistant Director-General for Social and Human Services in UNESCO, has posited that a right of movement has not been fully potentiated. In his words:

> According to Article 13-2 of the Universal Declaration of Human Rights, "Everyone has the right to leave any country, including his own, and to return to his country." But the right to leave is not complemented by a right to enter: one may emigrate, but not immigrate. From a human rights point of view, we are faced with an incomplete situation that sees many people being deprived of their right to emigrate by an absence of possibilities to immigrate. It is therefore worth envisaging a right to mobility: in a world of flows, mobility is a resource to which everyone should have access (Sané 2007).

A seeming exception to the right to movement, and specifically a right to enter and stay in a state that is different than one's nationality, might be seen to pertain to a specific category of migration—namely, that of refugees. Legally, the United Nations has also played a critical role in defining who is entitled to asylum and the responsibility of states. Two important agreements, signed by many countries around the world, are the 1951 United Nations *Convention Relating to the Status of Refugees* and the 1967 *Protocol,* which define a refugee as someone who is outside his or her country and cannot return because of a "well-founded fear of being persecuted for reasons of race, religion, nationality, membership of a particular social group or political opinion." Many countries, including Canada and the United States, have incorporated this definition of refugee into their domestic laws, and by extension have agreed to the principle of **non-refoulement**, namely, that a refugee will not be returned to a country where his or her life or freedom is in danger (Macklin 2003, 1). However, it is equally important to note that an exception to the principle of non-refoulement might be made on grounds of national security. Moreover, non-refoulement only comes into play if and when a refugee is able to make a claim in a new state. The widespread and creative ways in which western states have worked in the twenty-first century to prevent refugees from even being able to make rights claims at all has led Gibney (2006) to refer to "a thousand little Guantanamos," a take-off on the infamous US-run Guantanamo Bay detention camp. This is because states have found ways to operate outside of international and domestic law (as well as the pressures of human rights groups) when it comes to refugees, through a variety of measures that prevent their arrival or claims (Gibney 2006). One example of a non-arrival measure that has allowed governments to operate outside of refugee law is seen in France declaring parts of a domestic airport an "international" zone and

therefore strictly off limits to an asylum claim by someone deplaning there (Gibney 2006).

Measures to prevent or deter the arrival of refugees, alongside the starkness of the incomplete situation of being able to emigrate but not immigrate, have given rise to a growing body of work in the past decade by political philosophers and social theorists addressing the relationship between migration and ethics, specifically the normative case for open or even no borders (Carens 1998; Carens 2013). Likewise, it is the reality of the incomplete nature of mobility that compels continued attention to states because it is individual states that still exert control over who may (or may not) enter their territory licitly. The relevance of state power is therefore important even in relation to refugees, even in this era of globalization where the flows of goods, capital, services, images, ideas, and people have created new and different patterns of international interaction, contributing to an erasure of the significance of territorial space. (One example may be the ways the Internet and social media allow for global communication across states).

The topic of international migration is particularly salient in our time because although people have always moved across humanly created borders and boundaries, today, in this era of globalization, the patterns of movement are much more complicated: all major world regions both send and receive migrants, and almost all states and regions import or export labour (Held, Mcgrew, Goldblatt and Perraton 1999, 297). Whereas economists studying migration have typically identified "push and pull factors" to account for the economic, social, or environmental factors that may propel people to move, political scientists have tended to look at issues of the role of the state in migration control, the impact of migration on citizenship and sovereignty, and issues of immigrant integration (or incorporation) in receiving states (Brettell and Hollifield 2014). Combining these disciplinary foci in economics and political science is a useful way of understanding the range of issues that might be addressed in an IPE approach to migration.

Consider, for example, how recent demographic statistics for migrants (i.e., foreign-born or foreign citizens) reveal the salience of global socio-economic inequality in accounting for emigration. Globally in 2013, there were approximately 232 million international migrants, with over half (59 per cent) living in countries of the global North (United Nations 2013, 1). Of the international migrants living in northern countries, the majority (60 per cent) came from developing countries. Likewise, 86 per cent of those international migrants living in southern countries also came from developing countries (United Nations 2013, 1). If there are "push" factors associated with global income and other inequalities, there are numerous "pull" factors that account for why countries of the North are magnets for migrants. For example, in the countries of Europe, and in the US and Canada, with their aging populations and costly welfare states, immigration may be seen as desirable. Northern countries have been competing with each other for migrants in certain business sectors, who are deemed highly skilled (Abu-Laban 2007, 10). Despite the possible flow of remittances from migrants coming from the developing world back to countries in the South, the competition in northern states for highly skilled labour has given rise once again to the long-standing concern about the possible negative consequences of the "brain drain" for the countries of the developing world. It has also generated new concerns about immigrants ending up in jobs for which they are overqualified (Abu-Laban 2007, 10).

The issues pertaining to refugees and displacement also reflect a North–South divide. Refugees and displacement are central to the agenda of migration in the twenty-first century, and, indeed, are increasing in importance. For example, when the US-based Migration Policy Institute identified the "top 10 migration issues for 2014," the world confronting "the largest humanitarian crisis" since the end of the Second World War took first place. In 2014, the total number of people forcibly displaced had reached a staggering 51.2 million (about 16.7 of these would be defined by the UN as refugees, and others would largely be internally displaced as a result of conflict within their countries of origin) (Migration Policy Institute 2014). The refugee experience and impact is uneven: in 2014 half of refugees worldwide came from just three countries (Syria, Iraq, and Somalia) and the bulk of the world's refugees were located in countries of the global South (Migration Policy Institute 2014). Indeed, when the United Nations High Commissioner for Refugees, António Guterres, referred to the increasing numbers of forcibly displaced people as a "mega crisis," he especially noted that the growing numbers from Iraq and Syria could destabilize neighbouring countries in the region (Morello 2014).

Understanding the growing and unrelenting refugee problem requires some attention to the specific contexts in which it arises: today, as noted, many refugees come from Somalia, Syria, and Iraq, which are conflict zones, that in turn have been shaped by regional and international dynamics as well as foreign or outside involvement. Likewise, the responses of states to refugees is also contextual, and variable. For example, the era of the Cold War (roughly 1946–91) drew a very different response from western states than the post-Cold War period. This is because the offering of asylum took on a different political meaning. The core of the international refugee regime, as represented by the 1951 UN Convention, emerged from the context of the 40 million Europeans displaced after the Second World War, as well as the Cold War; offering asylum to those fleeing Communist persecution enhanced the propaganda arsenal of the liberal-democratic West over the Soviet bloc (Castles 2002, 178). However, as refugees from the countries of the global South increased, and especially once the Cold War ended, western states altered their response. As Stephen Castles notes, since 1991 the refugee regime of the global North "shifted from a system designed to welcome Cold War refugees from the East and to resettle them as permanent exiles in new homes to a '**non-entrée regime**' designed to exclude and control asylum seekers from the South" (Castles 2002, 181).

The non-entry regime has also been justified through a discursive shift. Refugees came to be "securitized" (Buzan, Waever and de Wilde 1998) over the course of the 1980s and 1990s. Thus, as Sharryn Aiken suggests, "the refugee has been reconceived as the 'bogus asylum seeker,' illegal migrant, and even worse, criminal or terrorist" (Aiken 2001, 9). It should be noted that the discourse around "international terrorism" began to come to the fore in American policies as far back as the 1980s, and at the same time associated some countries and groups in the Middle East with both the Soviet bloc and terrorism (Abu-Laban and Bakan 2011). It was in this decade that terrorism also began to be a consideration in the responses to non-citizens in immigration and refugee discussions and policies (Abu-Laban and Bakan 2011). For example, Canadian politicians came to talk about refugees as a potential security threat in the 1980s, although the linkage between terrorism and migration, including the migration of refugees, was heightened much further after 11 September 2001. After 9/11, in the name of combating terrorism, even greater focus has been placed by

countries of the West on border controls and surveillance in relation to non-citizens, migrants, and refugees (Abu-Laban 2004; Abu-Laban and Bakan 2011; Bigo 2005; van Selm 2005). This is what makes for a strongly "securitized" discourse, in the face of alternatives (for example, given the language of the UN Convention on Refugees, connecting refugees to human rights, or even human security, would be another kind of discourse from that of national security).

A focus on immigration control has also been a feature in the responses of other sorts of migration flows—especially those deemed to be irregular. (As the term "illegal immigrant" has been critiqued on grounds that only an act, not a person, can be illegal, the term is not employed here, though it continues to be used widely in many popular and media circles). Since the 1980s in Europe, the emphasis on immigration control—whether in relation to irregular or wanted flows—has fed the rise of far-right parties and xenophobic as well as racist political discourse in and outside of elections (Betz 2002). All western states have become more (not less) restrictive over time because of flows coming from the developing world. For example, in an effort to control irregular migration from Mexico, from the 1980s the US government increasingly re-bordered and militarized this border zone, a pattern also replicated in the border areas of many European polities (Andreas and Snyder 2000; Andreas 2003). As well, some state level initiatives in the US reflect the backlash toward irregular immigrants as well as minorities who may be citizens. To give one example, in 2010 Arizona Senate Bill 1070 (or Arizona SB 1070) was passed, the first ever state-level law seeking to apprehend and deport undocumented immigrants by requiring state law enforcement personnel (like police) to determine a person's status in lawful stops or detentions. Since Mexico has been a large source of irregular migration, critics charge that the new law encourages racial profiling of Latinos, and a growing body of evidence illustrates the heavy toll this has taken on the normal human existence of undocumented workers (Plascencia 2013, 122). Not incidentally, undocumented workers may also have US-born children who hold American citizenship, and are thus difficult to differentiate from Latin-Americans holding US citizenship and living in Arizona (prior to 1848 the area now comprising Arizona was Mexican territory, so Americans with origins in Mexico might be considered an ancestry group with deep roots).

Notwithstanding the turn toward restrictiveness, as a result of post-Second World War migratory flows, one of the features that characterizes Canada, the United States, and countries of the European Union, particularly those that were members prior to 2004, is that they are demographically diverse, racially, culturally, and religiously. With some notable exceptions such as France, for most countries of Europe migration is really a post-Second World War feature. Specifically in the decades following the Second World War, there was a demand for workers, especially in the booming areas of manufacturing. Governments did not plan well for immigration, tending to favour "guest worker" schemas introduced in the prosperous years of the 1950s, 1960s, and early 1970s. Guest workers typically came from the developing world, were male, and filled subordinate roles in the labour market. It was envisioned, both by many migrants as well as policy-makers, that the situation was temporary. Migrants were not seen as new citizens. In fact however, by the 1980s it became clear that even if people had come in as "guest workers," they had developed roots as a result of work, family reunification, and the birth of children; effectively, they were there for good now.

In contrast to European countries, so-called "settler-colonies" like the United States and Canada historically pursued immigration policies that explicitly favoured the entry of white British-origin Protestants. In both countries these overtly racially discriminatory policies were abandoned in the 1960s, opening the door to more global flows. Both the US and Canada pursued a range of policies that reflected on the idea that newcomers were permanent, and, as such, needed to have access to citizenship as well as the other benefits of membership in a polity (Abu-Laban 2007). Put differently, although both Canada and the United States have made use of temporary labour and still do, such programs have traditionally been small. The difference in this tradition shows up in the fact that the term "migrant," which is used in many European countries, has next to no popular purchase in either Canada or the United States, where the term of choice is "immigrant." (As noted earlier, because of the salience of the term "migrant" in international policy and scholarly work, in this chapter the term *migrant* is employed interchangeably with *immigrant*).

Policies addressing integration cover a wide range of spheres, from the economic to the social to the political, which are designed to ensure that both newcomers and the host society make accommodations. One of the things scholars have learned as a result of a growing body of systematically comparative research on issues of immigration and integration, is that what receiving states do matters to outcomes for migrants, and that there are a range of choices. This is also reflected in the statements made by leading international figures, like UN Secretary General Ban Ki-moon. As Ban noted on the occasion of International Migrants' Day in 2011:

> When their rights are violated, when they are marginalized and excluded, migrants will be unable to contribute either economically or socially to the societies they have left behind

or those they enter. However, when supported by the right policies and human rights protections, migration can be a force for good for individuals as well as for countries of origin, transit and destination (United Nations, Meetings Coverage and Press Releases 2011).

In this regard it is also interesting to note that in relation to other western states, including the United States, Canada's contemporary policies on citizenship, multiculturalism, and settlement have been viewed as supporting successful immigrant integration (Abu-Laban 2014; Bloemraad 2006).

To sum up this first section then, it is clear that migration has been a "normal" feature of the contemporary world, sending to and receiving flows from all world regions. An IPE approach reveals that there are push/pull factors involved in migration, and in the context of an unequal division of wealth globally these factors can be expected to continue to compel movement. At the same time, it is also clear that migration is a political issue and states may find ways to exert sovereignty for and control on both migrants and refugees. These ways have included new methods of getting around the refugee convention—for example, as mentioned earlier, by declaring zones in airports international, so claims cannot be heard, as well as erecting innumerable barriers in far-flung airports worldwide. In more recent decades, migrants, and refugees in particular, have come under suspicion. Thus people fleeing the worst of state persecution can be cast as threats. Although the plight of statelessness prompted states to sign on to the United Nations Convention on the Status of Refugees in the aftermath of the Second World War, today signatory states may find ways around the guiding principle of non-refoulement. As it stands, however, the bulk of refugees are in the countries of the developing world.

Mobility and Regionalism: North America and Europe Compared

Contemporary IPE specialists, as this book establishes in the introductory chapter by Greg Anderson and Christopher Kukucha, are attuned not only to globalization, but also to regional economic integration. In particular, researchers interested in comparative regionalism have observed how North America, as defined through the 1994 **North American Free Trade Agreement** (NAFTA) between Canada, the United States, and Mexico, has produced a regime governing the mobility of people that is different from that of the European Union. This is because "the free movement of peoples" is not, in contrast to the European Union, a stated goal of the North American project.

The origins of today's European Union (EU), as noted in chapter 12 by Lori Thorlakson, date back to the 1951 Treaty of Paris, signed by France, Germany, Italy, and the Benelux countries (Belgium, the Netherlands, and Luxembourg), which established the European Coal and Steel Community (ECSC). Incorporating some principles and institutions reflecting supranationalism, the ECSC was an attempt to make war between France and Germany unthinkable by deepening economic ties and laying the foundation for greater political union. Although the project of European integration has not been steady (with the decade of the 1970s especially characterized by "Euro-pessimism") since the late 1980s and 1990 integration has deepened economically as well as politically, and the EU has more than doubled its size. The 1993 Maastricht Treaty introduced an EU citizenship that is held by virtue of being a citizen of a member state (with Croatia's entry in 2013, the EU today consists of 28 member countries). In other words, it is national citizenship that allows access to EU citizenship, and national citizenship is, notably, still completely determined by national states.

EU citizenship includes the right of free movement (i.e., the right to study, work, or move to another member state), the right to vote and stand for elections at the local level and at the European level when residing in any member state, and the right to obtain consular protection from the embassy of any member state when abroad. Although every citizen of an EU member state is considered to be an EU citizen, the rights of EU citizenship, and especially the right of free movement, were not fully implemented immediately for the nationals of countries that joined since 2004 (reflecting the fears that still attend the idea of large flows from former Soviet-bloc countries, these rights were delayed for a period of anywhere from two to seven years). Still, there are clear ways in which the EU arrangements offer a novel form of membership that is unparalleled in the world, and certainly exceeds what is offered to citizens of Canada, the US, and Mexico through NAFTA.

Although the 1994 NAFTA has led to the growing integration of the national economies of the three member countries, and correspondingly to more attention to both multilateral and bilateral (US–Canada and US–Mexico) mechanisms governing the flows of people, there is a marked difference between the NAFTA and the European Union (Abu-Laban 2004). The European Union accords the right of mobility and residence to all EU citizens, whereas the NAFTA arrangement simply allows for the expedited temporary entry of business people and professionals. There is nothing approaching a "North American citizenship." North America has instead been characterized by the paradoxical erasure of borders (for trade) and reinforcement of borders (for people) (Andreas 2003). This is particularly the case of the US–Mexico border, where irregular migration from Mexico has been a major American political issue

since the 1980s. Indeed, American officials held that trade would work to lessen irregular migration from Mexico into the United States, and, despite the wishes of Mexican officials, also explicitly prevented labour migration from being a point of discussion in the NAFTA negotiation (Abu-Laban 2004; 2005).

Although the idea of "Fortress Europe" has sometimes been used to refer to the way in which the EU countries would trade with each other to the exclusion of other (developing) countries, increasingly over the course of the 1990s the phrase came to be used in the idea of borders and border fortification in relation to refugees and migrants. This name captures how, as the internal borders between countries became less salient for European Union citizens, the external borders between Europe and the global South have hardened. Indeed, in addition to sending aid in hopes of stemming migration, the European Commission has actually funded Morocco to fortify its borders to prevent movement into Spain through walls and surveillance of air, ground, and sea (see also Adepoju, Van Norloos and Zoomers 2010). The growing Europeanization of immigration policy has been facilitated by two agreements: (1) the Schengen Convention, an agreement to drop controls on internal borders, endorsed by most member states, which required states to agree on how external borders were going to operate and (2) the Dublin Regulation, which encourages states to share information and holds that someone who makes an asylum claim in one EU country cannot do so in another).

In North America as well there is some evidence to suggest that immigration is becoming more regional than strictly national—at least in relation to bilateral (US–Canada) flows. In particular, in the aftermath of 11 September, Canada and the United States signed the "US–Canada Smart Border Declaration" in December 2001. This now landmark 30-point plan is trumpeted as the foundation that ensures that the US–Canada border facilitates some one million dollars in trade every minute (Canada 2014). This is because the Declaration set in motion joint management of the border through enhanced cooperation in areas such as the refugee determination process, visa policies, and the sharing of passenger information and the immigration database. Also, in 2004 the Canada–US Safe Third Country Agreement went into force. This agreement says that an asylum seeker must make a claim in the country where he or she first arrived (i.e., Canada or the US). This applies to land border ports of entry only, with certain specified exceptions (e.g., if a family member is present in the state where the claim is made, or if the claimant is an unaccompanied minor). The parallels with the Dublin Regulation, and the potential to make it more difficult for refugees to make claims, accounts for why some analysts speak to a "European turn in Canadian refugee policy" (Soennecken 2014).

Regionalism carries a different meaning in the North American as compared to the European context. It is evident that the NAFTA framework, with its emphasis on "free trade," is different from the European Union's emphasis on granting mobility and other rights to nationals of signatory countries, and the broader historically rooted goal of some kind of political union. Thus, not surprisingly, the movement of peoples is unfolding in different ways in each region. However, in both cases individual states still have a lot of power in determining who is granted citizenship and the rights associated with citizenship, and controls over state boundaries continue to etch out the lines upon which some groups are granted privilege and other groups are excluded from it.

Moreover, in both contexts, unfolding regional arrangements are characterized by an undemocratic, elitist, and exclusionary character when it comes to the flow of people (not to mention how these arrangements have been achieved in the first place). Thus, in both settings, the ability of people to "freely move," is differential. In the case of NAFTA, there is an overt class bias to its temporary-entry provisions. In the case of the European Union, residents in member countries not holding EU citizenship are denied mobility, and often other rights as well. In both North America and Europe, regional developments have been animated by the question of immigration control, particularly as it pertains to countries (and the nationals of countries) on the periphery of the global economy. In this context, national immigration debates may feed perceptions about the question of free movement in regional blocs. In the US, the focus on Mexicans and the discourse on the so-called "illegal problem" that has characterized debates since the 1980s fuels how both the NAFTA and post-NAFTA climate have been characterized, making it difficult to imagine a NAFTA that includes the free movement of people.

Given these points, does an easing up of control by states on the flow of capital, goods, and services in regional endeavours require an easing up of the control over people? The answer to this question clearly varies with locale. There is less evidence for this in North America than in Europe, although in both contexts states have ceded some power to facilitate the movement of some (but not all) people, as well as to share information.

In the final analysis, a full-blown "free movement of people" would likely serve to challenge the existing inequitable distribution of global resources and wealth. Indeed, the perception (or hope) of some American elites that third world immigration will lessen with trade, or of European elites that immigration from peripheralized countries will decrease with aid, poignantly underscores the extent to which immigration is implicitly recognized as a feature of an inequitable world system, in which western states have been advantaged. In consequence, both North American and European regional arrangements regarding the licit flow of people may also be read as attempts to protect the uneven global distribution of wealth. This suggests that citizenship connected to the territorial nation-state, and tied to illicitness, will likely remain central in the twenty-first century, just as it was in the twentieth century—despite contemporary globalization and regional processes.

The Case of Canada: A Study in Demand and Restrictions

Turning briefly to explore the case of Canada further is of interest because it becomes clear that recent developments reflect on broad themes covered in other sections of the chapter. Canada continues to seek more immigrants, and annually lets in somewhere in the order of 250,000 for permanent settlement, with an emphasis on attracting immigrants with high levels of skills and education, and, increasingly, extant offers of employment. Yet, although Canada continues to demand more immigrants, there are, at the same time, developments that reflect growing immigration restrictions, citizenship exclusions, and racialized socio-economic inequality in Canada. Two important legislative changes introduced by the Conservative government of Stephen Harper relate to refugees (in 2012) and to citizenship (in 2014). The discussion of these will be preceded by a discussion of three important trends that illuminate growing racialized socio-economic inequality over the twenty-first century (and prior to Stephen Harper coming to power in 2006).

First, one major development concerns the fact that the climate in the years following 11 September 2001 has led to renewed policy emphases (and justifications) for security, surveillance, and

even torture, that have especially been felt by those Canadians who are (or are perceived as) Muslim and/or Arab. This has dramatically exposed the fault lines of Canadian multiculturalism, human rights, and immigration (Abu-Laban 2014). Moreover, new and stronger legislation supporting surveillance has been introduced in the wake of the violence of ISIS—Islamic State—particularly individuals seen to be associated with ISIS, such as the 2014 Parliament Hill shooter. Debates over this legislation draw attention to the ongoing question of the balance between security and civil rights (especially free speech) as well as the question of whether it may be used disproportionately against some Canadians (Freeze 2015).

This post-9/11 securitized climate makes it possible, and indeed salable politically, to detain unwanted immigrants and refugee claimants in detention centres—which are really like medium-security prisons (Pratt 2005). Today, Canada is the only western country that has no limits on how long migrants can be detained. In fact, in 2014 the United Nations High Commissioner for Human Rights Working Group urged Canada to adopt a 90-day limit on detention. It is estimated that some 146 migrants have currently been detained for longer than six months in Canada (Katawazi 2014).

Second, in addition to the fallout from 11 September, which may be seen to especially target specific groups, even if growing forms of surveillance also carry implications for all citizens, there is also evidence of more generalized and growing racialized and gendered forms of inequality among immigrants and visible minorities (Galabuzi 2011; Sharma 2011). For example, it has been clear for some time that incoming immigrants (even if selected for their advanced skills) have not had the same success in the labour market since the 1990s as they once had in the 1970s and 1980s (Hiebert 2006). There are other ways to illustrate this. Statistics Canada reports that 14 per cent of university-educated immigrants who have come to Canada in the past five years are unemployed, and that immigrants earn about 67 cents to the dollar compared to those who are Canadian-born (Syed 2014).

Echoing concerns raised globally that highly skilled immigrants may end up in jobs they are overqualified for in northern states, there have long been anecdotal accounts about immigrants with PhDs or MDs driving taxis in Canada. Citizenship and Immigration Canada recently commissioned a report called *Who Drives a Taxi in Canada?*, corroborating these anecdotes, using 2006 Census data. The report shows that there are some 50,000 taxi drivers in Canada. In large- and medium-size cities like Montreal, Toronto, Vancouver, Ottawa, Edmonton, and Calgary, immigrants account for between 50 to 80 per cent of taxi drivers (Xu 2012, 1). Immigrant-born taxi drivers are four times more likely to have bachelors, masters, and PhD degrees than Canadian-born taxi drivers (about 20 per cent of immigrant taxi drivers are in this category compared with less than 5 per cent of the Canadian-born taxi drivers) (Xu 2012, 1). Notably, of the immigrant taxi drivers with postsecondary degrees, fully one third of them came from Canadian postsecondary institutions (Xu 2012, 1). Taxi driving is a very male-dominated occupation, and 97.5 per cent of immigrant taxi drivers are men (Xu 2012, 3). So where are immigrant women? Many immigrant women are tied into chains of care in which work is both demanding and poorly paid (such as nannies, daycare workers, and service industry workers) (Brodie 2008).

This broader and even deepening racialization of inequality may be seen to have been further aggravated by a third major trend: the increasing use of temporary migrant workers who are denied Canadian citizenship. Although the number of temporary entrants has grown steadily since the 1980s, it has been specifically under the Harper

Conservatives since 2006 that the number of all temporary residents admitted annually to Canada, including workers, students, and others, has exceeded the number of those who are selected for permanent residence (Rajkumar et al. 2012, 484). There has been a growing diversity and array of programs to facilitate temporary entry, which has led to a plethora of rules and practices governing issues relating to employment, employment for spouses, as well as social services, including settlement services. This policy turn toward temporary workers and residents produces all manner of distinctions not only between citizens versus non-citizens, but also among non-citizens, who experience very different treatment and rights when they live in Canada (Rajkumar et al. 2012). The announcement in June 2014 by Employment Minister Jason Kenney and Immigration Minister Chris Alexander that there would be an overhaul of the temporary foreign worker program was met with incredulity by the official opposition. NDP MP Pat Martin claimed, "They're not really . . . protecting Canadian jobs or raising wages for Canadians . . . nor are they taking active steps to protect foreign workers from abuse. They're just making it a little more uncomfortable for employers to use the program" (cited in Mas 2014).

Although these trends contributing to growing racialized inequality had already been happening before the Harper Conservatives came to power, this inequality may be seen to have been exacerbated by recent changes in federal policy on refugees, as well as Canadian citizenship for immigrants selected for permanent residency. The Canada–US Safe Third Country Agreement reduced the number of refugee claims heard in Canada. On average, 29,680 annual claims were accepted by Canada between 1989 and 2004 (Canadian Council for Refugees 2005, i). In contrast, in 2005, the annual figure was down to 19,935, and in 2010 it was 9,041 (Alboim and Cohl 2012, 30).

This trend to smaller refugee intake also needs to be placed in relation to the most recent refugee legislation came into effect in 2012. Two bills, *Protecting Canada's Immigration System Act/* Bill C-31 and the *Balanced Refugee Reform Act/* Bill C-11, have further transformed the refugee system in Canada, depending on the refugees' country of origin and how they arrived (e.g., alone versus in a group where someone got paid to assist travel to Canada). The ministerial discretion to determine whether a country produces refugees, and the fact that "irregular" arrivals face automatic detention are widely deemed to be problematic by many analysts (see Alboim and Cohl 2012, 30–40). The decision, in effect from June 2012, to deprive those arriving as refugee claimants of government-assisted health care has also been deemed by Canadian physicians to compromise the health care and safety of refugees and their Canadian-born children (Ubelacker 2012). In short, then, at the very moment when the numbers of refugees and displaced people worldwide has reached new heights, claims made in Canada have reached new lows, as have supports like health care. Moreover, in December 2014, the Harper government's seeming indication that minorities (i.e., Christians as opposed to Muslims) would be prioritized in any future intake of Syrian refugees has raised new concerns among international partners and refugee-aiding organizations because the UNHCR has a specific set of criteria to prioritize the most vulnerable (e.g., women, children at risk, survivors of torture etc.) (Khouri 2014; Lynch 2014).

Trends toward greater restrictiveness also characterize the extension of citizenship. To put it bluntly, even if one is selected to be a permanent resident (and potential citizen) it is harder to get Canadian citizenship and it is easier to lose it. This came out very clearly when **Bill C-24** was passed into law in June 2014. Bill C-24, the "Strengthening

Canadian Citizenship Act," was justified by Immigration Minister Chris Alexander as necessary to "protect and strengthen the great value of Canadian citizenship and to remind individuals that citizenship is not a right, it's a privilege" (cited in Black 2014). What this new law does is require permanent residents to wait four (as opposed to three) years to be eligible for citizenship; it opens the door to imposing higher fees to apply for citizenship; it requires permanent residents from 18 to 64 to take an official language test (or demonstrate official language knowledge) as well as the knowledge of Canada test, when this was previously only required of people from 18 to 55 years of age. None of this is neutral because fees are a burden, and the knowledge of Canada requirement already clearly favours certain groups over others. In particular, those coming from countries that are predominantly English-speaking have tended to fare dramatically better on such tests (Abu-Laban 2014).

Just as it has become harder to get Canadian citizenship, the Strengthening Canadian Citizenship Act has made it far easier to revoke it—at least for naturalized Canadians and dual citizens. This can be done if federal officials hold that a naturalized citizen did not intend to live in Canada, committed a crime or fraud, or acted "contrary to the national interest of Canada." Moreover, if citizenship is revoked, there are no grounds of appeal in federal court. These broad categories for revoking citizenship have raised concerns for many NGOs, including the Canadian Arab Institute, which notes in a policy brief that this may disproportionately and unfairly affect Canadians of Arab origin (Thompson 2014).

Conclusion

As this chapter has shown, a number of trends characterize Canada in the twenty-first century that reveal the ways in which incoming immigrants and minorities have been experiencing growing racialized inequality. But these trends—the securitization of immigrants and minorities, their labour market inequality, and the use of temporary foreign workers—have been further exacerbated with the new turn toward making citizenship acquisition more difficult, and the grounds for revoking citizenship even easier. This is creating new forms of inequality between the naturalized and the Canadian-born citizen. It is striking precisely because Canada has been seen as a world leader in the settlement and integration of immigrants.

As this chapter has also shown, Canada, as with other western countries, has been steadily receiving fewer refugee claims, a feature that may in part be tied to new forms of bilateral cooperation between the US and Canada (e.g., the Safe Third Country Agreement) as well as national legislation on refugees. A recent, and unusual development in relation to any global trend, concerns the possibility that the Conservative government of Stephen Harper would prioritize Syrians who are religious minorities (i.e., not Muslim). Since this deviates from UNHCR practice, it is something that deserves ongoing scrutiny.

Overall, as this chapter has shown, in relation to international migration rights and patterns, as well as regional developments in Europe and North America, states still carry considerable power in regulating and controlling movement, as well as the extension of citizenship. Moreover, the twenty-first century is one in which greater exclusions are in evidence, especially for migrants coming from peripheralized countries. In this way, although many elements of contemporary globalization and regionalism may indicate ways in which the world is borderless, it is indeed very hard to "imagine there's no countries" when it comes to the movement of people.

Key Terms

non-refoulement	non-entreé regime
Universal Declaration of Human Rights	North American Free Trade Agreement
Convention Relating to the Status of Refugees	Bill C-24/ Strengthening Canadian Citizenship Act

Questions for Review

1. Do you think responses to immigrants and refugees have been "securitized"? Provide examples.
2. Do you think northern countries can and should do more for refugees? Why or why not?
3. What criteria do you think should guide refugee intake in a country like Canada?
4. Do you think the Canadian government has struck an appropriate balance between "freedom" and "security" since 11 September 2001?
5. Do you think that North American regionalism can and should emulate the European Union (e.g., a common citizenship, currency, parliament etc.).

Further Resources

Ayres, J. and MacDonald, L. (Eds). 2013. *North America in question: Regional integration in an era of economic turbulence.* Toronto: University of Toronto Press.

Betts, A. and Loescher G. (Eds). 2011. *Refugees in international relations.* Oxford: Oxford University Press.

Bloemraad, I. *Becoming a citizen: Incorporating immigrants and refugees in the United States and Canada.*

Castles, S., Miller, M. J., and Ammendola, G. 2003. *The age of migration: International population movements in the modern world.* New York: The Guilford Press.

Walton-Roberts, M. and Hennebry, J. (Eds). 2014. *Territoriality and migration in the EU Neighbourhood: Spilling over the wall.* New York and London: Springer.

References

Abu-Laban, Y. (2014). "Reform by stealth: The Harper Conservatives and Canadian multiculturalism." In Jack Jedwab (ed.), *The multiculturalism question: Debating identity in 21st century Canada.* Montreal & Kingston: School of Policy Studies, Queen's University and McGill-Queen's University Press: 14972.

Abu-Laban, Y. (2007). "North American and European immigration policies: Divergence or convergence?" *European View* (European People's Party, EU Parliament) *5* (Spring 2007), 9–16.

Abu-Laban, Y. (2005). "Regionalism, migration and fortress (North) America." *Review of Constitutional Studies 10*(1 & 2), 135–62.

Abu-Laban, Y. (2004). "The new North America and the segmentation of Canadian citizenship. *The International Journal of Canadian Studies 29* (2004): 17-40.

Abu-Laban, Y and Bakan, A. B. (2011). "The 'Israelization' of social sorting and the 'Palestinianization' of the racial contract: Reframing Israel/Palestine and the war on terror" In Elia Zureik,David Lyon and Yasmeen Abu-Laban (eds.), *Surveillance and control in Israel/Palestine: Population, territory and power.* London and New York: Routledge, 276–94.

Adepoju, A., Van Norloos, F., and Zoomers, A. (2010). "Europe's migration agreements with migrant-sending countries in the global south." *International Migration 48*(3) (June), 42–75.

Aiken, S. (2001). "Of gods and monsters: National Security and Canadian refugee policy." *Revue québécoise du droit internatinal* 14(1), 7–36.

Alboim, N. and Cohl, K. (2012). Shaping the future: Canada's rapidly changing immigration policies." Toronto: Maytree Foundation.

Andreas, P. and Snyder, T. (Eds.) (2000). *The wall around the west: State borders and immigration controls in Europe and North America.* Roman and Littlefield.

Andreas, P. C. (2003). "A tale of two borders: The U.S.-Canada and U.S.-Mexico lines after 9-11." In Peter Andreas and Thomas J. Biersteker (eds), *The rebordering of North America.* New York and London: Routledge.

Betz, H-G. (2002). "Xenophobia, identity politics and exclusionary populism in Western Europe." In L. Panitch and C. Leys (Eds), *Fighting identities: Race, religion and ethno-nationalism (Socialist Register 2003).* London: Merlin Press, 193–210.

Bigo, D. (2005). "From foreigners to 'abnormal aliens': How the faces of the enemy have changed following September the 11th." In E. Guild and J. van Selm (Eds), *International migration and security: Opportunities and challenges.* London and New York: Routledge, 64–81.

Black, D. (2014). "Immigration experts Say Bill C-24 discriminatory and weakens citizenship. *TheStar.com* (27 June). Available: www.thestar.com/news/immi

gration/2014/06/27/immigration_experts_say_bill_c24_discriminatory_and_weakens_citizenship.html [Accessed 16 November 2014].

Bloemraad, I. (2006). *Becoming a citizen: Incorporating immigrants and refugees in the United States and Canada*. Berkeley and Los Angeles: University of California Press.

Brettell, C. B. and Hollifield, J. F. (2014). "Introduction: Migration theory talking across disciplines." In C. B. Brettell and J. F. Hollifield (Eds), *Migration theory: Talking across disciplines*, 3rd ed. London and New York: Routledge, 3–36.

Brodie, J. (2008). "Putting gender back in: Women and social policy reform in Canada." In Yasmeen Abu-Laban (Ed.), *Gendering the nation-state: Canadian and comparative perspectives.* Vancouver: UBC Press, 165–84.

Buzan, B., Waever, O., and de Wilde, J. (1998). *Security: A new framework for analysis*. Boulder and London: Lynne Reinner.

Canada (2014). "Perimeter security and economic cooperation." Available: http://actionplan.gc.ca/en/page/bbg-tpf/canada-us-border-cooperation [Accessed 15 May, 2014].

Canadian Council for Refugees. (2005). "Closing the front door on refugees: Report on safe third country agreement 6 months after implementation." Ottawa: August.

Carens, J. (2013). *The ethics of immigration*. Oxford: Oxford University Press.

Carens, J. (1998). "Aliens and citizens: The case for open borders." In D. Jacobson (Ed.), *The immigration reader: America in a multidisciplinary perspective.* Malden, MA: Blackwell, 365–87.

Castles, S. (2002). "The international politics of forced migration." In L. Panitich and C. Leys (Eds.). *Fighting identities: Race, religion and ethno-nationalism* (Socialist Register 2003). London: Merlin Press.

Freeze, C. (2015). "Harper's Anti-terror bill to criminalize the 'promotion of terrorism,'" *The Globe and Mail* (26 January). Available: www.theglobeandmail.com/news/politics/harpers-anti-terror-bill-to-criminalize-the-promotion-of-terrorism/article22633213/ [Accessed 26 January 2015].

Galabuzi, G-E. (2011). "Hegemonies, continuities, and discontinuities of multiculturalism and the Anglo-Franco conformity order." In M. Chazan, L. Helps, A. Stanley and S. Thakkar (Eds.), *Home and native land: Unsettling multiculturalism in Canada.* Toronto: Between the Lines, 58–82.

Gibney, M. J. (2006). "'A thousand little Guantanamos': Western states and measures to prevent the arrival of refugees." In K. E. Tunstall (Ed.) *Displacement, migration, asylum.* Oxford: Oxford University Press, 139–69.

Held, D., McGrew, A., Goldblatt, D., and Perraton, J. (1999). *Global transformations: Politics, economics and culture.* Stanford: Stanford University Press.

Hiebert, D. (2006). "Winning, losing and still playing the game: The political economy of immigration in Canada. " *Tijdschrift voor Economische en Sociale Geografie* 97(1), 38–48.

Katawazi, M. (2014). "UN human rights body slams Canada's immigration detention system." *Rabble.ca* (28 July). Available: http://rabble.ca [Accessed 15 November 2015].

Khouri, R. (2014). "What's the holdup on Syrian refugees?" *The Globe and Mail* (22 December). Available: www.theglobeandmail.com/globe-debate/whats-the-holdup-on-syrian-refugees/article22163219/ [Accessed 22 December, 2014].

Lynch, L. (2014). "Canada considers prioritizing religious minorities in Syria refugee resettlement." *CBCNews* (December 12). Available: www.cbc.ca/news/politics/canada-considers-prioritizing-religious-minorities-in-syria-refugee-resettlement-1.2870916 [Accessed 12 December, 2014].

Macklin, A. (2003). "The value(s) of the Canada-US safe third country agreement." Paper Prepared for the Caledon Institute of Social Policy, December.

Mas, S. (2014). "Temporary foreign worker overhaul imposes limits, hikes inspections." *CBCNews* (20 June). Available: www.cbc.ca/m/touch/news/story/1.2682209 [Accessed 15 November, 2015].

Migration Policy Institute. (2014). "Top 10 of 2014: Issue #1: World confronts largest humanitarian crisis since WW2." Available: http://migrationpolicy.org/article/top-10-2014-issue-1-world-confronts-largest-humanitarian-crisis-wwii [Accessed 1 January 2015].

Morello, C. (2014). "Refugee wave from Syria and Iraq now a 'mega crisis' UN official says." *The Washington Post* (17 November). Available: www.washingtonpost.com/world/national-security/refugee-wave-from-syria-and-iraq-now-a-mega-crisis-un-official-says/2014/11/17/ebc5ee50-6eab-11e4-893f-86bd390a3340_story.html [Accessed 12 January 2015].

Plascencia, L. F. B. (2013). "Attrition through enforcement and the elimination of a 'dangerous class.'" In Lisa Magana and Erik Lee (Eds), *Latino politics and Arizona's SB 1070*. New York, Springer, 93–127.

Pratt, A. (2005). *Securing borders: Dentention and deportation in Canada*. Vancouver: UBC Press.

Rajkumar, D., Berkowitize, L., Vosko, L. F., Preston, V., and Latham, R. (2012). "At the temporary-permanent divide: How Canada produces temporariness and makes citizens through its security, work and settlement policies." *Citizenship Studies* 16(3–4) (June), 483510.

Sané, P. (2007). "Foreword." In *Migration without borders: Essays on the free movement of people*. A. Pécoud and P. de Guchteneir (Eds). Paris and New York: UNESCO and Berghahn Books, ix–x.

Sharma, N. (2011). "Canadian multiculturalism and its nationalisms." In M. Chazan, L. Helps, A. Stanley and S. Thakkar (Eds)., *Home and native land: Unsettling multiculturalism in Canada*. Toronto: Between the Lines, 84–101.

Soennecken, D. (2014). "Shifting up and back: The European turn in Canadian refugee policy." *Comparative Migration Studies* 2(1), 101–22.

Syed, F. (2014). "Canada: The land of jobless immgrants." *Rabble.ca* (12 November). Available: http://rabble.ca [Accessed 15 November 2014].

Thompson, A S. (2014). "The need to protect rule of law: A response to Bill C-24." Canadian Arab Institute Policy Brief (May).

Ubelacker, S. (2012). "Doctors group calls on Ottawa to rethink cuts to refugee health program." *The Vancouver Sun* (28 September). Available: www.vancouversun.com/health/Doctors+group+calls+Ottawa+rethink+cuts+refugee+health+program/7310620/story.html [Accessed 4 October 2012].

UNICEF. (2014). "Press Release: UNICEF 'World Version' of John Lennon Classic Invites All to Imagine a Better World for Children" (31 December). Available: www.unicef.org/media/media_78348.html [Accessed 1 January 2015].

United Nations, Department of Economic and Social Affairs, Population Division. (2013). *International Migration Report 2013*.

United Nations, Meetings Coverage and Press Releases. (2011). "Migration supported by right policies, protections, can be a force for good, Secretary General Says in message for International Migrants' Day." *Press Release* (15 December). Available: www.un.org/press/en/2011/sgsm14022.doc.htm [Accessed 27 December 2014].

van Selm, J. (2005). "Immigration and regional security." In E. Guild and J. van Selm (Eds), *International migration and security: Opportunities and challenges*. London and New York: Routledge, 11–27.

Xu, L. (2012). *Who drives a taxi in Canada?* Citizenship and Immigration Canada (March).

Glossary

alternative development an approach distinguished from "mainstream" or neoliberal development by an emphasis on participatory and people-centred methods and objectives.

asset-backed securities (ABSs) the general term for securitized financial assets (see **securitization**).

assets a resource or property that an entity owns or controls in order to generate revenues. For example, a loan or mortgage is an asset for a bank.

balance sheet a financial report that indicates the value of assets, liabilities, and shareholders' equity (or capital) at a specific moment in time. The sum of **liabilities** and shareholders' equity must be equal to **assets**, because the former finance or fund the accumulation of the latter.

Bill C-24/ Strengthening Canadian Citizenship Act a 2014 law that makes it more difficult for permanent residents to obtain Canadian citizenship, and provides expanded grounds for revoking Canadian citizenship from citizens.

Canada Development Corporation (CDC) was not a crown corporation but was designed by the federal government to pursue projects through a mix of private and public investment. It is now known as the Canada Development Investment Corporation (CDEV).

capital corresponds to the shareholders' or owners' equity (i.e., investment) in a company. Owners' equity also includes retained earnings, which are the profits that have not been distributed to shareholders yet.

civil society the sphere of organized political action located between the market and the formal political institutions of the state. It is made up of groups seeking to represent the interests of their members or other members of society and to shape the rules that govern social life. The actions of these groups may be based on ethical, cultural, political, scientific, religious, or philanthropic considerations. Some definitions of the concept include business organizations while other definitions exclude these groups.

civil society organizations (CSOs) refer to a wide of array of organizations located in civil society including community groups, non-governmental organizations (NGOs), labour unions, indigenous groups, charitable organizations, faith-based organizations, professional associations, and foundations.

collateralized debt obligation (CDO) an investment vehicle whereby ABSs are split into tranches, which are sold off to different kinds of investors according to the latter's risk profiles. The most risk-averse investors, such as pension funds and insurance companies, would buy the top tranche of a package, which is the one to be paid before all the others and, as a result, would receive a AAA-rating from credit-rating agencies. The lower tranches, which would receive payments of principal and interest only once the top tranche was fully paid up, are sold to investment banks and hedge funds that sought higher returns in exchange for more risk. Obviously, these lower and riskier tranches would receive lower ratings from the agencies, with some having junk status because they would be paid last.

collectivization Collectivization in China occurred in three stages, with the first stage involving only five or six families in Mutual Aid Teams (MAT). Families in the MAT would work cooperatively during busy periods but each family would retain whatever their own land harvested. The second stage of collectivization moved into "elementary cooperatives" where a small village or a section of a village consisting of 20–30 households would amalgamate assets and resources and work the land together. The third stage was the "advanced co-operative," consisting of 150 to 200 households where all production was collectivized.

comparative advantage the ability to produce a good at lower cost, relative to other goods, compared to another country in terms of opportunity costs; how much production of one product do you need to give up to produce one more unit of another?

competitive liberalization the pursuit of multiple, overlapping market access agreements with varied national (or regional) trading partners to reduce barriers to trade and investment in pursuit of comparative advantage and opportunities to influence the broader global trade policy agenda.

complex multilateralism   the idea that a new era of global governance has emerged has replaced the old state-centric forms of cooperation and institution-building in the international community. In this new era, non-state actors like non-governmental organisations and multinational corporations are playing an important role in shaping and influencing the evolution of global governance.

constituent diplomacy   the foreign relations of constituent units (e.g., provinces, states, Länder) of federal countries, including their participation in national foreign policy-making and the actions directed at foreign public and private sector actors. *Bilateral constituent diplomacy* is constituent diplomacy between a constituent unit and a single foreign polity, be that another constituent or subnational unit or a country. *Regional constituent diplomacy* is a multilateral constituent diplomacy normally among proximate constituent and subnational units, but at times involving partners farther afield.

Convention Relating to the Status of Refugees   1951 UN agreement that defines a refugee and establishes state responses.

corporatist state   theories of corporatism explain patterns of organized interest. In a typical corporatist system, only one national organization is recognized by the state, and this system of interest coordination can be seen in all economic and social realms. A corporatist state often assists in organising and establishing sectoral associations.

cosmopolitan liberalism   (or liberal cosmopolitanism) is a variant of liberal theory that shares liberalism's support for individual rights and freedoms. While most liberal theorists tend to accept the principles of state sovereignty, cosmopolitan liberals (inspired in part by the work of philosopher Immanuel Kant) emphasize individuals' belonging within a global community, the equality of all world citizens and their interest in extending individual rights and freedoms across the globe in a new global public order.

creative destruction   a term used by Joseph Schumpeter that has persisted, referring to the effects of innovation in an economy and their tendency to overturn existing industries and companies and create new ones

credit default swap (CDS)   a type of insurance contract that pays the buyer a certain sum in case of non-payment on a security (e.g., a bond, an ABS, or a CDO) as a result of a default by a government, a company, or even an (or group of) individual(s). The buyer of the CDS does not have to own the underlying security; in such a case, this is referred to as a "naked" CDS.

critical juncture   a pivotal moment produced by transformations in economic, social, or political conditions that generates powerful pressures and incentives for government and industry to respond with major policy or business changes.

cycle of contention   a term taken from the work of Sidney Tarrow that refers to a historical phase of heightened political organizing by civil society organizations. According to Tarrow, civil society activism does not advance uniformly but tends to go through cycles of greater and lesser activism in response to factors internal to the organizations involved as well as to external factors. When a new cycle of contention occurs, there is an upsurge in participation in collective action, new forms of collection action emerge, and there is a rapid diffusion of protest techniques and frameworks throughout society.

deleveraging   cutting back on consumption/spending and selling assets in order to pay back debt.

derivatives   securities whose price is based on an underlying asset, such as an index.

developmental state   the concept of the developmental state was initially seen as a way to interpret and note the different paths to capitalist development. Two contrasting schools of thought emerged to explain the East Asian development: (1) East Asia's economic success can be largely attributed to the realms of free market forces, despite state intervention in certain areas and, (2) East Asia's development is a result of coordinated state action in the industrialization and modernization process that accorded the region with such high growth rates.

discourse   discourse analysis is a tool for examining social practices and political orders that are generally accepted as natural. The (re)telling of these practices, orders, or what are commonly perceived as truths serves to (re)construct them as so-called common sense. Embedded in all forms of language, cultural and ideological assumptions presented within these discourses often occur below the level of conscious awareness.

discursive approaches focus on the role of language, categories, ideas, and concepts, and how they shape our understanding of IR and IPE.

Doha Development Agenda A so-called "round" of multilateral trade negotiations launched in 2001.

dual bilateralism the development of separate processes for addressing bilateral issues between the United States and its two principal North American neighbours.

Economic and Monetary Union Economic and Monetary Union (EMU) was a policy objective of the European Community that was finally realized with the 1992 Treaty on European Union. EMU has at its core the creation of a single currency, the euro in 1999, with monetary policy controlled by the European Central Bank, as well as macroeconomic policy coordination among the member states of the EU.

economic liberalism an ideology favouring a market-oriented economy and free trade.

economic nationalism an ideology prioritizing nationalist values in economic policy.

economic regionalization processes of regional economic integration as major feature of economic activity; may take place at continental or subcontinental scale (e.g., cross-border regions).

embedded liberalism an ideology that supports a reconciliation of liberal multilateralism with the more interventionist state economic practices that became influential in the wake of the Great Depression.

epistemology the study of the nature of knowledge, how it is acquired, and to what extent a given subject or phenomenon can be known. Once the base objects of study are identified, questions arise as to the manner in which our knowledge about them is acquired and the extent to which the nature of those objects can be known.

European Central Bank (ECB) the central bank responsible for the euro, the single currency of the European Union. The ECB is one of the most independent central banks in the world. It is responsible for monetary policy in the 18 member countries of the Eurozone, guided by a treaty commitment of maintaining price stability.

financial capital any economic resource measured in terms of money used by entrepreneurs and businesses to buy what they need to make their products or to provide their services.

fiscal policy any macroeconomic policy involving the levels of government purchases, transfers, or taxes, usually implicitly focused on domestic goods, residents, or firms.

foreign direct investment (FDI) is direct foreign investment in a host country, usually in the form of facilities and infrastructure. It is the oldest and most common form of international investment.

foreign investment protection agreements (FIPAs) agreements signed by Canada as part of a larger international trend by states to pursue bilateral investment treaties (BITs). FIPAs and BITs are pursued in the hopes of expanding investment ties between signatories.

GATT (General Agreement on Tariffs and Trade) an agreement signed between 23 countries in 1947. Its main purpose was to reverse the protectionist trade policies of the 1930s through nondiscrimination and tariff liberalization. It successfully reduced tariffs via multilateral negotiations over the decades, growing in participants, and in the range of goods covered by the agreement. Until 1995, the GATT regime presided over international trade. Eventually it evolved into the WTO.

gender typically refers to socially constructed differences between boys and girls, men and women, which are acquired after birth. Gender differences might include cultural preferences and expectations that emphasize stereotypically masculine or feminine traits. It is important to note that gender differences do not simply catalogue equal but different preferences and expectations; they also refer to a hierarchical gender order that socially and politically values some forms of masculinity over femininity.

gender analysis vs. feminist analysis   closely related to discussions of gender as an empirical and/or analytical category, are debates concerning whether gender can be analyzed by conventional or non-feminist IPE/IR theoretical approaches. Not all scholars who examine gender as a category of analysis identify their research as necessarily feminist, nor do they aim to transform unequal gender relations. For feminist scholars, however, it is not possible to devise a non-feminist or "apolitical" analysis; all theory is political and designed to both explain and therefore maintain existing power relations or designed to transform them.

gender, analytical category   Feminist scholars may study gender and sometimes other social categories *analytically*, paying close attention to hierarchical constructions of socially valued forms of masculinity and unvalued femininities. For example, IPE/IR scholars privilege a masculine perspective when they define the field as the study of the high politics of global finance, international trade, and national survival—all masculinized sites of activity typically populated by powerful men. Other scholars may apply R.W. Connell's concept of *hegemonic masculinity* to the global political economy, considering how socially valued ideals of manhood, such as heterosexuality, rationality, objectivity, and physical strength legitimize the subordination of some men and of women.

gender, empirical category   Feminist and gender scholars may elect to study gender in the global political economy *empirically*, paying close attention to the lives of women and men, girls and boys. For example, researchers may collect quantitative data that capture the number of women and men employed in different economic sectors in the global political economy and measure differential gender education or employment patterns. Sometimes, such data are used to demonstrate gender inequalities to governments, employers, or other actors with the aim to transform unequal gender relations.

global governance of corruption   The collection of governance-related activities, rules, and mechanisms in place at a variety of levels in world politics, aimed at cooperative anti-corruption problem-solving and including sets of international rules or laws; norms; and formal and informal structures including intergovernmental organizations (IGOs), nongovernmental organizations (NGOs), transnational advocacy networks, and ad-hoc conferences and associations focused on anti-corruption efforts.

governance   processes of managing and governing not only by formal "governments" but also by various other public, private and non-profit actors.

grand corruption   Corruption at the highest levels of government, where political leaders, the bureaucracy, and the private sector all interact and typically including government decisions that cannot be made without high-level political involvement. Examples include the procurement of large budget items such as military equipment, civilian aircraft, or infrastructure, or broad policy decisions about the allocation of credit or industrial subsidies. Through grand corruption, political leaders and state agents use their authority to sustain their own power, status, and wealth.

Green Revolution in Africa   a notion popularized by an alliance (AGRA) of global foundations that the low-level status quo of African farming must be broken by applying science and technology (including biotechnology) to African agriculture.

guanxi   a type of social network "'corruption'" in China based on secondary relations such as professional and religious ties and drawing on underlying moral principles derived from the Confucian heritage including hierarchy, interdependence, and reciprocity—that is not captured by the PA model. In reform-era China, *guanxi* has served to fill in governance gaps during periods of uncertain transition, relative disorder, and social inequality and it often overrides the norms and desired outcomes of formal institutions.

Heckscher-Ohlin model   transforms the theory of comparative advantage into a concrete tool for understanding how countries will engage in international trade. It focuses on the relative distribution of the factors of production (or inputs) countries contain, to explain what they can produce efficiently, and what they cannot. The model's essential finding is that countries will export goods requiring inputs relatively abundant locally, but import the goods requiring inputs relatively scarce locally.

hegemony   a theoretical concept with both realist and critical meanings. As derived from the work of Italian Marxist Antonio Gramsci, and popularized by Canadian political economist Robert Cox, it is a form of dominance of one social group over another—that is, the ruling class over all other classes—featuring a high level of consent on the part of the ruled. The ideas of the ruling class come to be seen as the norm; they are seen as universal ideologies, or a common sense, perceived to benefit everyone while in reality principally benefiting the ruling class. Cox has extended this thinking to the transnational level, arguing that transnational "hegemonic orders" are pursued and sustained by transnational coalitions of elite groups.

hermeneutics   examines whether ideas are defined by meanings associated with specific periods of history, language, and culture.

heterogeneous firm models   The largest productivity gains come from new firms entering export and import markets and from incumbent exporters' introduction of new products into existing markets and diversification of their exports into new markets. This emerging theory provides an explanation for why relatively few firms export their output and why exports represent only a small portion of sales for firms that do trade.

immigration   moving to a new country, usually for the purposes of permanent settlement and citizenship.

industrial policy   refers in the general sense to any policy that affects an industry; however, it is more commonly used in the specific sense of policies directed towards the promotion of a particular industry.

industrialization   a process in which social and economic changes take place within a society, transforming from an agrarian society to an industrial one. Industrialization is part of a wider modernization process, whereby social change and economic development is closely linked with changes in technology. The economy during industrialization is reorganized to focus on manufacturing.

inflation targeting   a principle of monetary policy that the rate of inflation should be kept within a pre-specified range, using expansionary policy when the rate is below that range and contractionary policy above it.

intergovernmental relations   relations between two or more governments; in the case of this book, relations between federal governments and constituent units as well as constituent units among themselves, including policies, practices, and structures that affect these relations in the conduct of constituent diplomacy.

intergovernmental rule frameworks   This term refers to policy-making characterized by cooperation between governments. In the European Union, this occurs when member states want to retain some sovereignty over sensitive policy areas, but they still wish to cooperate to solve cross-border problems.

intermestic(ity)   the blurring of traditional distinctions between domestic and international policies as a result of growing international interdependence.

international regimes   a set of norms and ideas, sometimes encapsulated or incorporated into an institutional order, which enjoys support from a large number of countries in a particular area such as trade or finance and is able to dictate or influence the content of domestic policy-making in those areas.

international reserve currency   the currency against which all other currencies are valued.

intervention   when central banks try to influence an exchange rate by buying the currency they want to appreciate and selling the one they want to weaken.

joint service   production and infrastructure arrangements that jointly serve Canadian and American energy needs, usually in order to make a pipeline project economically viable (e.g., that pipelines built to transport energy produced in one part of Canada to another serve US markets along the way). Joint service has strengthened bilateral trade and north–south flows of energy between Canada and the United States, while helping to finance costly infrastructure projects.

kleptocracy   a political system dominated by elites who personally enrich themselves by direct theft from state coffers and who practise extortion as their modus operandi.

leverage   the use of debt to invest in assets in order to amplify potential gains for shareholders but often at the risk of greater losses. It is usually measured as total assets divided by capital (or shareholders' equity). The higher the multiple of assets over capital is, the higher leverage is.

liabilities   an entity's debts or obligations that are settled over time through the transfer of assets, provision of services or other yielding of economic benefits. Liabilities are used to finance an entity's operations and investments.

liberalism   focuses on the individual (unit of analysis); purpose is absolute gain (i.e., both parties gain more than they had before their economic exchange; takes the political environment as externally given.

liminality   a heightened sense of community arising from special events and public performances, including but not limited to sports mega-events.

liquidity   liquid assets; usually very short term in nature so that they easily be converted into cash, which is the ultimate liquid asset.

macroeconomic   referring to the variables or performance of an economy as a whole, or its major components, as opposed to that of individual industries, firms, or households.

market failure   failures that occur when the market does not allocate goods efficiently, often due to the absence of crucial institutions or information.

Marxism   emphasizes two materially opposed classes (bourgeoisie (factory owners) and the working class in a capitalist economy); no "national interest" independent of the dominant class; the lower class will ultimately overthrow the upper class in a violent revolution, leading to the next historical stage (socialism in this case).

Marxist theories of imperialism   theories that attribute the age of imperialism in the late nineteenth and early twentieth centuries to the dynamics of capitalism.

materialist   assumptions that highlight "material" inequality arising from the use of social, political, and economic power in a sovereign state system.

mega-events   "large-scale cultural (including commercial and sporting) events, which have a dramatic character, mass popular appeal, and international significance." (Maurice Roche 2000).

mercantilism   concentrates on the state (unit of analysis); theoretical basis is realism (international relations); anarchy of the international system means concern with

relative gain (i.e., state A gaining consistently more than state B); state B would cease economic exchange to avoid a worsening situation.

methodology   how one goes about the business of knowing; the procedures and principles for investigating a particular subject or issue. In other words, the processes by which we go about acquiring knowledge about the objects of study.

migration   the act of moving from one place to another (whether within a country or between countries)

monetary policy   the use of the money supply and/or the interest rate to influence the level of macroeconomic activity

mortgage   a loan to buy property whereby the property is used to guarantee the repayment of the loan. If the loan is not repaid on time and in full, then the creditor who made the loan can take over the property in order to sell it and repay itself.

mortgage-backed securities (MBSs)   The term used for securitized mortgages. MBSs are a subset of ABSs.

most-favoured-nation treatment   key principle of international trade whereby any trade advantage given by a state to another state must be extended to all other states, so as to avoid discrimination.

multi-level governance   the characteristic of many policy-making contexts in which multiple governments and non-governmental actors exist and interact with each other. Such contexts are more difficult ones for policy development due to the need for both horizontal and vertical coordination among policy actors.

neoliberalism   a view of the world that favours social justice while also emphasizing economic growth, efficiency, and the benefits of free markets.

new institutional economics   a liberal school of economics that emphasizes the importance of the institutions and norms that underlie markets and determines whether or not they operate efficiently.

NIS (national innovation systems)   a theory that innovation in an economy comes from the coordination of research, production of an industry, and government policy.

non-entreé regime   a regime designed to control and exclude asylum seekers.

non-refoulement   the agreement by which a refugee will not be returned to a country where his or her life or freedom is in danger.

non-tariff barrier (NTB)   Countries often use tariffs (a tax) to discourage imports. However, as GATT members lowered tariffs in the 1960s and 1970s, governments found new ways to impede or slow down inflows of foreign goods. By introducing complex regulations concerning product safety, environmental standards, and so forth, governments could protect their home producers from foreign competition. Technically, these did not violate GATT rules, even though they conflict with the spirit of GATT (and now WTO) principles. They are difficult to address through multilateral negotiations, since every state has legitimate responsibilities for regulating economic activity.

Olympism   "Olympism is a philosophy of life, exalting and combining in a balanced whole the qualities of body, will and mind. Blending sport with culture and education, Olympism seeks to create a way of life based on the joy of effort, the educational value of good example and respect for universal fundamental ethical principles." (From the International Olympic Committee Charter).

ontology   focuses on questions about what there is to know about particular objects of study. Specifically, what is important about the objects we study? What things exist, or can be said to exist? What elements are fundamental to our object of study? If the state, for example, is our subject matter, what are the base elements comprising the state?

pan-Africanism   a concept popularized by Kwame Nkrumah that stresses the need for African states to work together to achieve Africa's political and economic independence and autonomy. Before his death, Muammar Gaddafi promoted pan-Africanism through his rhetorical support for a United States of Africa.

partnership   a term often used by government officials and development policy-makers to describe the relationship between those that provide development finance and aid, and those that receive it. This term has replaced references to "donors" and "recipients" in many official government communications.

petty corruption   When low-level administrative bureaucrats extract personal benefits in transactions involving taxes, regulations, licensing requirements, and the discretionary allocation of government benefits such as subsidized housing, scholarships, and jobs. Where it is rife this type of corruption often permeates the everyday lives of ordinary people in myriad and obvious ways.

phenomenology   questions the possibility of any "objective" reality.

policy integration   the effort to coordinate policy-making to ensure that the various elements of policy, such as tools, objectives and goals, are coherent, consistent, and congruent with one another. This effort is made more complex in multi-level governance contexts.

policy legacy   a context in which past policy decisions inform the nature or constrain the scope of government policy responses in subsequent periods.

policy mixes   a characteristic feature of many policy areas in which multiple policy tools or instruments exist and are used in order to address policy problems. Tools in such mixes must be coordinated and planned in order to avoid conflicts and promote synergies.

policy parallelism   approach to policy development by different governments involving the pursuit of similar policy goals, but often using different "tools" and methods that reflect separate legal histories, institutional arrangements, and patterns of interest group competition or accommodation.

policy regimes   a set of actors, ideas, and institutions that develop and manage a policy area over a long period of time, usually acting as a stabilizing force in the area.

positivism   purpose of research is generalizing from particular events across a larger group of phenomena; using the latter for explaining and potentially predicting the likely outcome of similar occurrences; regards this endeavor as possible; thus, believes that social scientific advancement is not fundamentally different from the "hard" sciences.

post-positivism   draws from a wider range of non-science based philosophical traditions. It is also inspired by the debate within the philosophy of science that questions the reliability of positivism. One influence of post-positivist thought is *phenomenology*, which questions the possibility of any "objective" reality. *Hermeneutics* also shapes post-positivism with the assumption that all ideas are shaped by meanings associated with specific periods of history, language, and culture. Both phenomenology and hermeneutics are interpretive methods of analysis that inspire post-positivists to search for deeper and potentially hidden meanings behind observed realities.

poverty   a condition entailing multiple dimensions of deprivation, including income status below national and international poverty lines; a lack of basic needs; capability deprivation; disempowerment and low levels of happiness.

preferential trade agreements   an agreement that gives preferential access to the products from the participating countries. Most recent PTAs are bilateral and take the form of a free trade area, where tariffs and other trade barriers are removed for nearly all goods (and often services) traded between states parties.

price stability   the use of macroeconomic policies to reduce inflation.

principal-agent (PA) model   a model derived from economics in which *agents* are presumed to act on behalf of *principals* that have *delegated* authority to them and are empowered to monitor and enforce the extent to which agents carry out the principal's interests. Corruption enters the picture when a *third party* whose gains or losses depend on the principal or the agent interferes with the appropriate principal-agent relationship. In the P-A model, corruption is defined as any unauthorized transaction between an agent and a third party, usually *bribery*, and is an instance of institutional failure.

productive power   often associated with Michel Foucault, this concept of power does not treat it merely as coercive "power over" but also as a more productive "power to" do certain things, including the power to constitute particular kinds of identity.

regime complexes   a diffuse set of norms, rules and institutions, often partial, overlapping or incomplete, which can serve the function of an international regime in some areas of international activity, but without the compelling force often found behind an international regime.

regulatory capture   refers to the tendency for industries that are favoured by government policy to "lock in" those policies through lobbying, even when they no longer make sense for national or regional strategy.

securitization   pooling several financial assets together into a separate legal entity (often known as a special purpose vehicle) and then selling investors a security, or legal title (e.g., like a bond), giving them the right to a portion of the principal and interests to be paid by the borrowers underlying the financial assets. Financial assets that are often securitized include car loans, credit card loans, and mortgages.

sex   typically refers to observable or measurable anatomical, hormonal, and/or chromosomal differences between male and female bodies. It is frequently contrasted with the socially constructed category "gender." Such a division between sex as a fixed or stable category and gender as a constructed and therefore changeable social category is not so clear-cut, however. For example, according to biologist Anne Fausto-Sterling (2000), sexual characteristics vary among people, beyond just two categories. In this sense, sex is constructed along gendered lines we limit our definition of sex to "male" and "female" coded bodies based on our social and political recognition of only two genders, masculine and feminine.

shale oil and shale gas   oil and gas residing in sedimentary rock; although shale reserves are plentiful in North America, they have only recently been profitably produced through the twin technologies of hydraulic fracturing ("fracking") and horizontal drilling.

Single Undertaking   the regime norm that "The launching, the conduct and the implementation of the outcome of the negotiations shall be treated as parts of a single undertaking," meaning that nothing is agreed until everything and everybody is agreed, and all obligations apply to all members simultaneously.

social acceptance   an increasingly salient energy policy imperative referring to the need for energy policy to adequately address the variety of social concerns related to energy development (climate change, human health and safety, aboriginal rights and title, ecosystem health, water quantity and quality, etc.).

social protection   policies concerned with preventing poverty and enhancing people's ability to manage risks to their livelihood. Whereas earlier social welfare policies tended to respond to poverty after the fact, social protection policies take a more proactive approach.

social risk   an approach to poverty that focuses on the many risks poor people face that make them vulnerable to falling back into poverty even after they have moved out of it. The social risk approach takes a longer-term view of poverty and considers the various public and private mechanisms that can be used to reduce risks over time.

special and differential treatment   concept allowing "differential and more favourable" treatment for developing countries—that is, a derogation from other WTO norms—introduced with the "Enabling Clause" during the Tokyo Round, and found throughout the WTO agreements.

specialization   people producing a narrower range of goods and services than they consume.

stagflation   a term coined in the mid-1970s to describe a situation of high interest rates combined with high unemployment.

staples   refers to the theoretical perspective that the reliance on commodity production can retard economic development and therefore diversification including industrialization is necessary to improve standards of living.

Stolper-Samuelson theorem   Building off the Heckscher-Ohlin model, this theorem provides one way of understanding how the gains from trade are distributed domestically. The Heckscher-Ohlin model explains what each country is likely to import and export, based on the local supply of inputs (with scarce inputs being relatively more expensive than the locally abundant); countries export goods using the locally abundant inputs, and import goods requiring the locally scarce. The key insight from the Stolper-Samuelson theorem is that imports alleviate local shortage of a scarce input (therefore that input's earnings fall), while reducing the local supply of the abundant input (making its earnings rise).

structural adjustment   an approach to international development that became very influential in the 1980s and 1990s. International development organizations sought to obtain major structural changes to poor countries' economies, including privatization, financial and trade liberalization, in the belief that they were necessary for economic growth and poverty reduction.

subsidiarity   a principle stemming from practices in the middle ages in Europe and adapted to modern times, in which authority to act in multi-level governance contexts is pushed down to the lowest level possible that still allows effective policy-making to occur.

supranational policies   In the European Union (EU), these are policies that are carried out at the European Union level, "above" the national level. Member states have agreed in the EU treaties to pool their sovereignty in some policy areas and conduct policy-making in these areas at the European level because it allows them to achieve their policy goals more effectively than if these policies were handled at a national level. Member state interests are represented in policy-making by the Council of Ministers, but supranational institutions of the EU such as the European Commission, European Parliament and the European Court of Justice are highly influential.

tariff   a tax on goods or services traded across a border. By imposing a tax, a government can collect revenues, but also can shape the relative competitiveness of foreign versus domestic producers.

trade liberalization   the reduction in, or even removal of, states' measures that restrict the free flow of goods and services. Such measures include tariff (such as duties, import surcharges) as well as non-tariff barriers (such as quotas, licensing regulations, and arbitrary standards).

transnational bribery   the practice of sending corrupt payments from one national jurisdiction into another to secure influence in the recipient jurisdiction, which includes both supply-side and demand-side incentives embedded within a global context of transnational corruption networks involving multinational companies, elites in both bribe-sending and bribe-receiving countries, offshore financial vehicles and conduits, middlemen and brokers, and financial institutions.

transnational social movements (TSMs)   organizations with members in more than one country or social movements that have developed a relatively high level of cross-border cooperation with counterparts in other countries. This form of civil society activity has increased in response to the effects of globalization.

Universal Declaration of Human Rights   UN declaration that established a framework for universal human rights after the Second World War.

World Trade Organization (WTO)   international governmental organization established in 1995 to oversee the world trading regime, until then under the GATT, which comprised and managed various trade agreements but lacked the status of an IGO.

yield   the actual income return (or profit) that an asset will provide its owner (i.e., the investor), usually expressed as a percentage of the cost of acquiring the asset.

Index